CONTEMPORARY EUROPEAN THEATRE DIRECTORS

Second Edition

Edited by Maria M. Delgado and Dan Rebellato

LONDON AND NEW YORK

Second edition published 2020
by Routledge
2 Park Square, Milton Park, Abingdon, Oxon OX14 4RN

and by Routledge
52 Vanderbilt Avenue, New York, NY 10017

Routledge is an imprint of the Taylor & Francis Group, an informa business

© 2020 selection and editorial matter, Maria M. Delgado and Dan Rebellato; individual chapters, the contributors

The right of Maria M. Delgado and Dan Rebellato to be identified as the authors of the editorial material, and of the authors for their individual chapters, has been asserted in accordance with sections 77 and 78 of the Copyright, Designs and Patents Act 1988.

All rights reserved. No part of this book may be reprinted or reproduced or utilised in any form or by any electronic, mechanical, or other means, now known or hereafter invented, including photocopying and recording, or in any information storage or retrieval system, without permission in writing from the publishers.

Trademark notice: Product or corporate names may be trademarks or registered trademarks, and are used only for identification and explanation without intent to infringe.

First edition published by Routledge in 2010

British Library Cataloguing-in-Publication Data
A catalogue record for this book is available from the British Library

Library of Congress Cataloging-in-Publication Data
Names: Delgado, Maria M., editor. | Rebellato, Dan, 1968- editor.
Title: Contemporary European theatre directors / edited by Maria M. Delgado and Dan Rebellato.
Description: Abingdon, Oxon ; New York, NY : Routledge, 2020. | Includes bibliographical references and index.
Identifiers: LCCN 2019045384 (print) | LCCN 2019045385 (ebook) | ISBN 9780367023140 (hardback) | ISBN 9780367023164 (paperback) | ISBN 9780429400285 (ebook)
Subjects: LCSH: Theater–Production and direction–Europe–History–20th century. | Theater–Production and direction–Europe–History–21st century.
Classification: LCC PN2570 .C663 2020 (print) | LCC PN2570 (ebook) | DDC 792.02/330922–dc23
LC record available at https://lccn.loc.gov/2019045384
LC ebook record available at https://lccn.loc.gov/2019045385

ISBN: 978-0-367-02314-0 (hbk)
ISBN: 978-0-367-02316-4 (pbk)
ISBN: 978-0-429-40028-5 (ebk)

Typeset in Amasis and Scene
by Swales & Willis, Exeter, Devon, UK

For David Bradby (1942–2011) – a brilliant scholar, inspiring teacher, and great friend, without whose lifelong work on directors' theatre and the European stage this volume would not have been possible and to whom this volume is dedicated with love and respect

CONTENTS

x   List of plates
xii   Notes on contributors
xviii   Foreword by Mark Ravenhill
xxi   Acknowledgements

1   **Revised introduction to the first edition**
        Maria M. Delgado and Dan Rebellato

29   **Introduction to the second edition**
        Dan Rebellato and Maria M. Delgado

39   **1 Ariane Mnouchkine: Activism, formalism, cosmopolitanism**
        Brian Singleton

61   **2 Patrice Chéreau: Staging the European crisis**
        David Fancy

85   **3 Lev Dodin: The director and cultural memory**
        Peter Lichtenfels

103   **4 Silviu Purcărete: Contemporising classics**
        Aleksandar Saša Dundjerović

121   **5 Frank Castorf and the Volksbühne: Berlin's theatre of deconstruction**
        Marvin Carlson

CONTENTS

143   **6   Daniel Mesguich: 'Unsummarisable'** *mises en scène*
        Jim Carmody (with additional material by Dominic Glynn)

165   **7   Declan Donnellan and Cheek by Jowl: 'To protect the acting'**
        Aleks Sierz

185   **8   Piotr Borowski and Poland's Studium Teatralne: Where process becomes performance**
        Paul Allain

207   **9   Christoph Marthaler: The musicality, theatricality, and politics of postdramatic direction**
        David Barnett

229   **10   Jan Lauwers: Performance realities – memory, history, death**
        Janelle Reinelt

259   **11   Simon McBurney: Shifting under/soaring over the boundaries of Europe**
        Stephen Knapper
        (with additional material by Dan Rebellato)

275   **12   Ivo van Hove: Celebrity and reader**
        Denis Flannery

299   **13   Deborah Warner: Experiments of words, bodies, and place**
        Adam J. Ledger

325   **14   Romeo Castellucci: The director on this earth**
        Alan Read

341   **15   Kristian Frédric: Boxing with the 'gods'**
        Judith G. Miller

355   **16   Krzysztof Warlikowski: Rupturing taboos, curating publics**
        Bryce Lease

383 **17 Calixto Bieito: Staging excess in, across, and through Europe**
Maria M. Delgado

407 **18 Rodrigo García and La Carnicería Teatro/Boucherie Théâtre: From the collective to the director**
Lourdes Orozco

427 **19 Katie Mitchell: Learning from Europe**
Dan Rebellato

453 **20 Thomas Ostermeier: A 'sociological theatre' for the age of globalised precarity**
Peter M. Boenisch

475 **21 Peter Sellars: Identity, culture, and the politics of theatre in Europe**
Maria M. Delgado

493 **22 The director's new tasks**
Patrice Pavis
Translated by Joel Anderson

511 **Index**

PLATES

1. Hélène Cixous's *Tambours sur la digue* (*Drums on the Dam*), directed by Ariane Mnouchkine with the Théâtre de Soleil (1999)
2. Bernard-Marie Koltès's *Dans la solitude des champs de coton* (*In the Solitude of the Cottonfields*), directed by Patrice Chéreau (1995)
3. *Life and Fate* adapted from the novel by Vasily Grossman and directed by Lev Dodin (2007)
4. *Faust*, adapted (from the play by Johann Wolfgang von Goethe) and directed by Silviu Purcărete (2007)
5. Bulgakov's *The Master and Margarita*, directed by Frank Castorf (2002)
6. Molière's *Dom Juan*, directed by Daniel Mesguich (2003)
7. *Cymbeline*, directed by Declan Donnellan and designed by Nick Ormerod (2007)
8. *H.H.H.*, directed by Piotr Borowski in Studium Teatralne's space in Praga, Warsaw (2006)
9. Christoph Marthaler, Stefanie Carp, and Anna Viebrock's *Groundings*, directed by Christoph Marthaler and designed by Anna Viebrock (2003)
10. *Isabella's Room*, written and directed by Jan Lauwers (2004)
11. *Street of Crocodiles*, an adaptation by Simon McBurney and Mark Wheatley of the stories of Bruno Schulz, directed by Simon McBurney (1992)
12. *Scènes uit een Huwelijk* (*Scenes from a Marriage*) by Ingmar Bergman, directed by Ivo van Hove and designed by Jan Versweyveld (2005)

13 *The Testament of Mary*, with Fiona Shaw in the title role, an adaptation by Colm Tóibín of his 2012 book, directed by Deborah Warner (2012)
14 *Inferno*, part of the trilogy inspired by Dante Alighieri's *The Divine Comedy*, written, directed, and designed by Romeo Castellucci (2008)
15 Bernard-Marie Koltès's *La Nuit juste avant les forêts* (*Night Just before the Forests*), directed by Kristian Frédric (2004)
16 *Wyjeżdżamy* (*We Are Leaving*), directed by Krzysztof Warlikowski (2018)
17 *Macbeth*, directed by Calixto Bieito, designed by Alfons Flores (2002)
18 *After Sun*, written, directed, and designed by Rodrigo García (2001)
19 *Waves*, devised by Katie Mitchell and the company from *The Waves* by Virginia Woolf (2006)
20 Mark Ravenhill's *Shoppen & Ficken* (*Shopping and Fucking*), directed by Thomas Ostermeier (1998)

NOTES ON CONTRIBUTORS

Paul Allain is Professor of Theatre and Performance at the University of Kent. He has published extensively on Eastern European theatre including *Gardzienice: Polish Theatre in Transition* (1997) and *Grotowski's Empty Room* (2009). He also wrote *The Art of Stillness: The Theatre Practice of Tadashi Suzuki* (2002) and co-authored *The Routledge Companion to Theatre and Performance* (2006, second edition 2014). Edited collections include *Grotowski's Empty Room* (2009) and *Grotowski & Company* (2010).

David Barnett is Professor of Theatre at the University of York. He has published monographs of Heiner Müller (1998), Rainer Werner Fassbinder (2005), Bertolt Brecht (2014), and The Berliner Ensemble (2015). He has written articles and essays on German, English-language, political, and post-dramatic theatre.

Peter M. Boenisch is Professor of Dramaturgy at Aarhus University and Professor of European Theatre at The Royal Central School of Speech and Drama, University of London. His research specialisms are directing and dramaturgy in Continental European theatre, the politics of theatre aesthetics, and the institutional critique of theatre production. His publications include *Directing Scenes & Senses: The Thinking of Regie* (2015) and (co-authored with Thomas Ostermeier) *The Theatre of Thomas Ostermeier* (2016).

Marvin Carlson is the Sidney E. Cohn Professor of Theatre and Comparative Literature at the Graduate Center of the City University of New York. He is the founding editor of *Western European Stages*. His book, *The Haunted Stage* (2001), received the Joseph Calloway

Prize. In 2005 he was awarded an honorary doctorate by the University of Athens and in 2015 he was appointed to the faculty of the Shanghai Theatre Academy and head of the Marvin Carlson Theatre Center there. His most recent books are *10,000 Nights* (2017) and *Theatre and Islam* (2019).

Jim Carmody has written about *mise en scène*, translation, and theatre photography. He recently retired from the Department of Theatre and Dance at the University of California, San Diego. He now works as a professional dance and theatre photographer.

Maria M. Delgado is Professor and Director of Research at The Royal Central School of Speech and Drama, University of London, and is Co-editor of *Contemporary Theatre Review*. She has published widely in the area of Spanish- and Catalan-language theatres. Her books include *Federico García Lorca* (2008), *'Other' Spanish Theatres* (2003, revised Spanish-language edition 2017), and ten co-edited volumes.

Aleksandar Saša Dundjerović is Professor in Performing Arts at Birmingham City University and a practising director who has worked widely in Eastern Europe and Canada. He has published numerous books on the theatre of Robert Lepage, including *The Theatricality of Robert Lepage* (2007), *The Cinema of Robert Lepage* (2003), *Robert Lepage* (2009), as well as *In Process: Collaborative Theatre in Brazil* (2016).

David Fancy is Professor of Dramatic Arts at Brock University, Ontario, Canada, where he teaches performance studies at the Marilyn I. Walker School of Fine and Performing Arts. He has published on French playwright Bernard-Marie Koltès and extensively on the work of Gilles Deleuze, technology, and performance. He has recently published an edited volume of essays entitled *Art As Revolt: Thinking Politics Through Immanent Aesthetics* (2019).

Denis Flannery is Associate Professor of American and English Literature at the University of Leeds. Published works include *Henry James: A Certain Illusion* (2000), *On Sibling Love, Queer Attachment and American Writing* (2007) and, co-edited with Michèle Mendelssohn,

Alan Hollinghurst: Writing under the Influence (2016). Current projects include *The Chamber and World*, a new book about Ivo van Hove and ITA (International Theatre Amsterdam).

Dominic Glynn is Assistant Professor in Translation at the City University of Hong Kong. He is currently leading research projects on transnational theatre practices and on the translation of French plays to the UK stages. Previously, he was the principal investigator of an Arts and Humanities Research Network Grant entitled 'Literature under Constraint', which investigated how different factors (mindsets, political contexts, social environments, intermediaries) shape and constrain contemporary literary production. His publications include *(Re)Telling Old Stories* (Peter Lang, 2015) and *Lignes de fuite* (L'Harmattan, 2015), as well as the co-edited volumes *Littéraire. Pour Alain Viala*, volumes 1 & 2 (Artois Presses Université, 2018).

Stephen Knapper taught at Kingston University until his death in 2012. He published work on Complicite, Scaramouche, Molière, and clowning. He co-directed The Red Noses, a small-scale touring theatre company in the 1980s, studied at the École Jacques Lecoq, and worked in television and on the streets of Naples.

Bryce Lease is Reader in Theatre and Performance Studies at Royal Holloway, University of London and is Co-editor of *Contemporary Theatre Review*. His publications on Polish theatre include his monograph *After '89: Polish Theatre and the Political* (2016), the forthcoming co-edited volume *The History of Polish Theatre*, and numerous articles. Between 2018 and 2021 he is leading the AHRC-funded project 'Staging Difficult Pasts: Of Narratives, Objects and Public Memory'.

Adam J. Ledger is Reader in Theatre and Performance at the University of Birmingham, and is Co-artistic Director of The Bone Ensemble. He has published widely on performance practice, including the book *The Director and Directing: Craft, Process and Aesthetic in Contemporary Theatre* (2017).

Peter Lichtenfels was Artistic Director of Edinburgh's Traverse Theatre from 1981 to 1985 and Artistic and Executive Director of Leicester Haymarket Theatre from 1986 to 1990. He is now Professor of Theatre at the University of California, Davis. He continues to work as a professional director and writes about staging, directing, and Shakespeare in performance. His co-written book on *Romeo and Juliet, Negotiating Shakespeare's Language*, was published in 2009.

Judith G. Miller is Professor of French and Francophone theatre in the Department of French Literature, Thought and Culture at New York University. She has written widely on French and Francophone theatre and has translated some 25 plays from French. She has recently published a revised version of *Ariane Mnouchkine* (2018) with Routledge, as well as an anthology of plays by Koffi Kwahulé (2019); a translation of a novel by Gerty Dambury (*The Restless*, 2018); and will be bringing out with Routledge in 2020 a translation of Béatrice Picon-Vallin's comprehensive study, *The Théâtre du Soleil: The First Fifty Years*.

Lourdes Orozco is Associate Professor in Theatre Studies at the Workshop Theatre, University of Leeds. Her research interests are primarily in the area of animal studies and contemporary European theatre and performance. Her first monograph on theatre and politics in Barcelona was published in 2007. She is also the author of *Theatre & Animals* (2013), the co-editor of *Performing Animality: Animals in Performance Practices* (2015), and she is currently working on a monograph on animals in contemporary European theatre. She is also the Principal Editor of *Performing Ethos: International Journal of Ethics in Theatre and Performance*.

Patrice Pavis has been Professor at the Université de Paris 3 and Paris 8, as well as the University of Kent, different German universities, and the Korea National University of the Arts. He is an Honorary fellow of Queen Mary, University of London, Bratislava, and Sofia. His most recent publications include *Contemporary Mise en scène* (2013), *The Routledge Dictionary of Performance and Contemporary Theatre* (2016), *Performing Korea* (2016), and *Dictionnaire du théâtre* (fourth edition 2019).

Alan Read is the author of *Theatre & Law* (2015), *Theatre, Intimacy & Engagement: The Last Human Venue* (2007), and *Theatre & Everyday*

Life: An Ethics of Performance (1993). He is a Founding Consultant Editor of the journal *Performance Research* and is currently Professor of Theatre at King's College London, where he directs the Performance Foundation in the Anatomy Theatre and Museum on the Strand.

Dan Rebellato is Professor of Contemporary Theatre at the Royal Holloway University of London. He has published widely on postwar British theatre and his books include *1956 and All That* (1999), *Theatre and Globalization* (2009), *Modern British Playwriting: 2000–2009* (2013), *The Cambridge Companion to British Theatre 1945*, and *The Cambridge Companion to Contemporary British Plays and Playwriting* (2020). He is co-editor, with Jen Harvie, of the 'Theatre &' series, which contains around 50 titles and counting. He is also a playwright whose works have been performed on stage and radio in the UK, Europe, and the USA.

Janelle Reinelt, Emeritus Professor of Theatre and Performance at the University of Warwick, was President of the International Federation for Theatre Research (2004–7). She has published widely on politics and performance, receiving the 'Distinguished Scholar Award' for lifetime achievement from the American Society for Theatre Research (2010) and an honorary doctorate from the University of Helsinki in 2014. Her most recent publication is a collection of essays co-edited with Bishnupriya Dutt and Shrinkhla Sahai, *Gendered Citizenship: Manifestations and Performance* (2017).

Aleks Sierz FRSA is a journalist, lecturer, and theatre critic whose books include *In-Yer-Face Theatre* (2001), *Rewriting the Nation* (2011), *Modern British Playwriting: The 1990s* (2012), and *The Theatre of Martin Crimp* (2013). He has also written, with Lia Ghilardi, *The Time-Traveller's Guide to British Theatre* (2015).

Brian Singleton is Samuel Beckett Professor of Drama and Theatre at Trinity College Dublin and Academic Director of The Lir National Academy of Dramatic Art. He is Co-editor (with Elaine Aston) of the book series 'Contemporary Performance InterActions' for Palgrave, having co-edited the 40-volume series 'Studies in International

Performance' with Janelle Reinelt. Published work includes two books and many essays on the life and work of Antonin Artaud, André Antoine, Oscar Asche, Lily Brayton, and Ariane Mnouchkine, as well as two books on Irish theatre, *Masculinities and the Contemporary Irish Theatre* (2011, reprinted 2015) and *ANU Productions: The Monto Cycle* (2016).

FOREWORD

Mark Ravenhill

As I write this, the United Kingdom is in the throes of its Brexit crisis. It's an agonising struggle between a global and a national identity, between the centre and the periphery, and between the deliberative processes of representative democracy and the more irrational forces of a supposed 'popular' will. At the beginning of the Brexit process the British Prime Minister Theresa May, attacking the 'liberal elite', declared that 'if you believe you are a citizen of the world, you are a citizen of nowhere'.

A citizen of the world. Or nowhere. Or elsewhere, anywhere, everywhere, or somewhere. It's a question that each of the directors in this excellent book is working through in their own distinctive ways. And maybe in their work we might find some ways forward for our current impasse.

Much of the directing practice outlined in this book came about through twin impulses – complementary I believe and not, as Theresa May suggests, contradictory. An impulse both to develop a distinctive national or regional theatre in the director's place of origin but also to make work that is in dialogue with the best theatre from around the world.

Much of these directors' experience and work reflects the reality of exile, migration, and statelessness of our contemporary world. And a great deal of their work is widely seen in international festivals and tours. More than any previous generation of theatre directors they have spent their time at airports, travelling to show their work in other countries, and to experience the work of their international peers.

It will be fascinating to see how this international model develops in the next few years. Just this week I was discussing with colleagues the future of London's Royal Court Theatre's international work. In the light of the climate emergency, there is a rapidly increasing awareness that we need to limit the number of flights each of us takes. But is it possible to do this while at the same time continuing to work with our peers from around the world? Could cultural exchange be deepened when a quick flight there and back is no longer possible?

But alongside the global, each of these directors is also the product of a very particular city, region, and country in a particular moment in time. The pragmatic reality of theatre – that it is still largely made by a group of people in a room in real time – means that it always draws deeply on localised practices. Fundamental notions of language, psychology, beauty, and the social have very different nuances in each locale, however much they are now connected by global capital. The making of theatre draws deeply on the local, often in critical opposition to it, while at the same time looking towards the cosmopolitan and international.

For much of the second half of the twentieth century, international 'director's theatre' was founded on a shared canon of plays. The generation of Stein and Strehler were largely drawing on the 'masterpieces' of the European playwriting tradition, with their successors showing an increasing interest in deconstructing the individual plays without dispensing with the canon. The model of 'I'll show you my Hamlet, if you show me yours' was, for several decades, a common currency.

There is now an increased interest in making theatre that moves away from the Eurocentric and which draws on our multicultural reality. Inevitably the role and prominence of the director will change. In a theatre with a largely uncontested canon of great plays, the focus is clearly on a director's interpretation. With the canon diminished in prominence and the presence of the 'great writer' evaporating, will the director come even more to the fore? Or will he or she merge into a team of collaborators who create the work?

And in this post-Weinstein/#MeToo moment, does the role of director – which has been largely a role for the white male – need to be refreshed by diversity? Or is the favouring of the director's vision over his or her collaborators part of a patriarchal system which might be reaching the beginning of the end?

October 2019

ACKNOWLEDGEMENTS

We have accumulated numerous debts while preparing this volume. These include the directors who agreed to be interviewed and the writers who undertook the interviews and essays. We are grateful to them all for sharing their expertise with us. Our thanks go also to the photographers, theatres and archives who have granted us rights to reproduce images here.

Talia Rodgers has been an enthusiastic supporter of this project from its very inception. Ben Piggott, Niall Slater, Zoe Forbes, and Laura Soppelsa offered us practical guidance, and the production team at Routledge have seen the book expertly through to final publication. We owe them all a great debt of thanks.

Both the editors have been assisted by the support of staff and students at Queen Mary, The Royal Central School of Speech and Drama, and Royal Holloway, especially Joshua Abrams, Una Bauer, Peter M. Boenisch, the late David Bradby, Tom Cornford, Tony Fisher, Jen Harvie, Dan Hetherington, Paul Heritage, Bryce Lease, Chris Megson, Katie Mitchell, and Nick Ridout. The TaPRA working group on Directing and Dramaturgy provided a lively forum for discussion and debate on many of the issues that run through the book.

We would also like to acknowledge the support of producers, practitioners, and colleagues working in the field of European theatre who provided useful information during the conception and realisation of this volume, especially Anna Aurich, Michael Billington, Marina Brafa, Julia Carnahan, Ben Fowler, David George, Kevin Higa, Louise Jeffreys, Claire Macdonald, Virág Márkus, Bonnie Marranca, Joan Matabosch, the late Tom McGrath, Marcos Ordóñez, Winsome Pinnock, Annabel Poincheval, Josep Maria Pou,

ACKNOWLEDGEMENTS

Mark Ravenhill, John Rouse, Mercè Saumell, Kim Solga, Caridad Svich, David Whitton, Ella Wildridge, David Williams, and Simon Williams. Chris Baugh, Stephen Bottoms, and Maggie Gale offered advice and references at key stages of the project. Susan Letzler Cole and Joanne Tompkins provided concrete support in the early stages of development. Colleagues on the International Ibsen Award Committtee and the European Theatre Research Network provided a lively forum for discussion. James Rowson assisted us with the index. Joel Anderson's contribution to this volume goes beyond the translation of a chapter to valuable advice on photographs and image sourcing; his generosity deserves our special thanks.

This project was completed with support from the Spanish Embassy in London, Queen Mary University of London's sabbatical leave provision, the Arts and Humanities Research Council's Research Leave Scheme, and The Royal Central School of Speech and Drama's targeted completion fund.

Since the first edition we have learned of the sad deaths of one of our contributors and the subject of one of the chapters. Stephen Knapper, whose illuminating interview with Simon McBurney is published here, died two years after the first edition was published. We are grateful to Bridget and Rebecca, his sister and ex-partner, for their support for this new edition. In 2013, European theatre, cinema, and opera also lost Patrice Chéreau. We'd like here to pay special tribute to both of them.

Henry Little, Tom Delgado-Little, Lilla Rebellato, and Ethan Blue Rebellato were patient and supportive in the final stages of preparing this volume. This book could not have been completed without their support.

REVISED INTRODUCTION TO THE FIRST EDITION[1]

Maria M. Delgado and Dan Rebellato

David Bradby and David Williams's *Directors' Theatre*, published over 30 years ago, provided a ground-breaking guide to the new generation of directors that emerged from the tumult of the late 1960s to revolutionise the European stage.[2] Inspired by the cultural revolt of 1968 and the political visions it conjured, these directors worked to create new collective structures of theatrical production, took their work beyond the subsidised seats of European high culture to the streets and factories, warehouses and hangars, and disrupted the elitist divisions between art and popular culture so entrenched in European cultural traditions. They were culturally and politically eclectic, refusing the distinctions between art and entertainment, between the elite and the popular. Roger Planchon, oscillating between film and theatre, was typical of this wave, his politics less doctrinaire than Bertolt Brecht's, his method less formal than Vsevelod Meyerhold's, his results more successful than Antonin Artaud's. For directors such as Planchon, Ariane Mnouchkine, Peter Stein, and Joan Littlewood, theatre was a wholly collective activity in which people, meanings, and sensations would mingle and collide and find something none of them could have experienced apart.

The impact of the cultural renewals and exchanges of the 1960s generated models that moved beyond the significant scenic and directorial experiments of the early twentieth century. The new watchwords were openness and ambiguity, the old narrative theatre yielding to a dreamlike succession of images, technological and cultural forces conspiring to create arresting transformations of scale and speed. The work of Pina Bausch and Tadeusz Kantor created dizzying juxtapositions of image, text, and sensation. Jorge Lavelli and Víctor García brought excess, immediacy, and ecstasy to France with their sensory explorations of Arrabal, Gombrowicz, and Genet. For others, this was an opportunity to reinscribe art theatre in a network of political realities and responsibilities. Revelatory productions by Planchon, Mnouchkine, and Stein sought to rediscover the political dimensions of the European canon. In all cases the new directors played a role in overthrowing the pre-eminence of the text in the theatrical experience, and in its place offered a vision of what Planchon called *écriture scenique* (scenic writing):[3] the director marshalling all the resources of the stage in a wholly visual conception that was, perhaps for the first time, not dependent on the work of the playwright.

That generation of directors soon established a new chapter in contemporary theatre history and their work from that period is well covered by general books on the period, in some cases by monographs on particular directors, and even – in the case of Peter Brook – monographs on particular productions.[4] The widespread acceptance of their work has, however, tended to overshadow the generation of directors who have emerged since the time when Mnouchkine and Planchon were at their peak. There have been important articles on individual *auteurs*,[5] the work of directors like Thomas Ostermeier, Romeo Castellucci, and Calixto Bieito is seen and discussed across the world; they are interviewed and debated, championed and reviled. Alongside the significantly revised edition of *Directors' Theatre*, this book offers a selected overview of the range of work currently being undertaken in European directors' theatre, places that work in a broad artistic, cultural, and political context, and provides a guide to that whole generation whose careers were forged in the changing Europe of the 1980s and 1990s.

This volume brings together a series of 22 essays (both articles and interviews) that detail the aesthetics of a series of directors who crucially formulated their trajectories in the aftermath of 1968. These were figures shaped definitively (as with Mnouchkine and Chéreau) or tangentially by the events of 1968 and the political shifts in both Eastern and Western Europe that followed. A significant number (as with Frank Castorf, Chéreau, and Thomas Ostermeier) have emerged from a socialist tradition, shaping their trajectories within the structures of national or state-subsidised theatres whose remit included a sense of public and political accountability. Others have functioned ostensibly outside official structures (as with Declan Donnellan, Rodrigo García, Mnouchkine, and Simon McBurney), creating companies that have themselves become global brands, bartered, bought, and sold in the marketplace of the international festival. It is the festival circuit that offers the space of exchange where directors nurtured within both neoliberal and Marxist principles convene and converge.

The volume's organisation is broadly historical, beginning with an account of one of the great survivors from the 1960s, Mnouchkine, whose frequent reinventions act as a guide through the 1980s, through economic crises, changing patterns of migration, the fall of the Soviet bloc, the emergence of European integration, monetary union, and enlargement. Chapter 2 proffers an English-language overview of the directorial trajectory of Patrice Chéreau, an associate of Planchon's whose connection with Strehler – he spent time at the Piccolo during the early stages of his career – offered an engagement with Strehler's vision of theatre as a form of public service that might engage with the shifting boundaries of new European borders and policies (Strehler 1996: 268). Mnouchkine and Chéreau can be located as part of a group of practitioners who emerged in the 1960s and looked beyond their national frontiers for texts, collaborators, performance vocabularies, and commissions. One of Chéreau's defining productions, the 1976 *Ring Cycle* for Bayreuth, created with his Italian long-term scenographer, Richard Peduzzi, re-envisaged the *Cycle*'s mythical iconography in favour of a loose late-nineteenth-century setting witnessing the social upheaval of industrialisation.[6] Mnouchkine's array of performers and performatics imported from Asia and the Americas were part of a movement to internationalise the French theatre while simultaneously promoting a representation of the nation that stressed outward-looking credentials and social consciousness as fundamental to its sense of cultural legitimacy. That these ideals have served as foundations for directors both within and beyond the French state can be evidenced in the contributions to this volume on Lev Dodin, Silviu Purcărete and Ostermeier. The wave of directors who work within the theatre shaped so decisively by Planchon, Mnouchkine, Chéreau, Wilson, and Brook are also, in their turn, challenging that generation, finding new forms in which to make work, developing further styles of scenic writing, disconnecting and reconnecting the theatre with new political contexts, and providing practices of theatre where authorship itself is questioned and fragmented.

While it does not claim to be exhaustive, the coverage of the book is broad, taking in directors from Italy (Castellucci), Spain (García and Bieito), France (Chéreau, Kristian Frédric, Daniel Mesguich, Mnouchkine), Germany (Castorf and Ostermeier), Belgium (Jan Lauwers, Ivo van Hove), Poland (Borowoski, Krzysztof Warlikowski), Romania (Purcărete), Russia (Dodin), Switzerland (Christoph Marthaler), and the United Kingdom (Donnellan, McBurney, Katie Mitchell, and Deborah Warner).[7] It moves from the well known (Mnouchkine) to those working in more marginalised contexts (Borowski). It features directors who have worked primarily with the classics (as with Donnellan, Mitchell, and Purcărete), those who have worked extensively with new writing (as with Frédric and Ostermeier), and those who create new collaborative work (as with Castellucci, García, Lauwers, McBurney, and Mnouchkine). Recognising the intra-European currents that have shaped directorial practices in the latter half of the twentieth century, this volume seeks to provide an evaluation of directors whose work has circumvented political oppression (as with Castorf, Dodin, and Purcărete), demonstrated a continuing commitment to theatre as a medium for vigorous social debate (Bieito, Chéreau, Mnouchkine, Ostermeier, and Warlikowski), and probed new forms of working that question established roles by prising apart writer–director binaries (Borowski, Castellucci, García, and Mesguich). The choice of directors encompasses the generation that emerged during the 1960s (Mnouchkine and Chéreau); those whose work materialised in the aftermath of the 1960s (Dodin and Purcărete); those whose work built on the earlier examples of these figures (Donnellan, Castorf, and Bieito); and those who have questioned high-modernist ideals in ways that can be and have been considered 'postmodern' (Castellucci, McBurney, Lauwers, Marthaler, and Warlikowski). This range of choice also allows for the discussion of a cross-section of different stylistic vocabularies, from the corporeal theatres of Lauwers and McBurney to the theatricalised neo-realism of Bieito and Ostermeier, from the meticulous naturalism of Mitchell and Dodin to the minimalist bare landscapes of Donnellan, from the baroque theatricality of Purcărete to the exposed actors of Borowski's Studium Teatralne, from the Brook-inspired landscapes of Warner to the intense epics of Ivo van Hove, from the psychoanalytical paradigms of Mesguich to the experiential theatres of Castellucci and García.

While European directors have featured in recent volumes,[8] there has been no sustained examination of the phenomenon of directors' theatre in contemporary Europe, and this volume goes some way to finding new ways of discussing the theatre practices of a number of prominent directors working within this context.

The director, Europe, and national identity

What constitutes European identity is a subject of continuous debate through this volume, throughout the period covered by the first edition of this book, and with even greater intensity as we move into the second decade of the twenty-first century. At a colloquium on European identity held in 1990, in an address titled 'L'Autre Cap' (The Other Heading), Jacques Derrida asked what a new Europe might be; in the aftermath of Soviet Communism's vertiginous collapse in Eastern Europe a discourse had arisen of European 'reunification', which, Derrida observed, seemed to propose a mythologically whole European identity that was to be restored; he cites French President François Mitterrand's tremulous declaration that Europe 'is returning in its history and its geography like one who is returning home' (Derrida 1992: 8). At such a moment, more than ever, it was vital to insist that any identity is created within a structure of difference in which identity is never settled, never stable, and remains constituted by what it seems to exclude: 'what is proper to a culture is to not be identical to itself' (Derrida 1992: 9). Such questions have returned, in recent years, with even greater force as alternative visions of Europe – as a model of a borderless world or a nativist assertion of ethnic identity; as a landscape of cultural hybridity or a fortress to separate Europe from its others; as a celebration of human rights and collective action or an institute for neoliberal economic enforcement – and have generated new debates and conflicts across the continent.

Contributors to this book have, somewhat in the spirit of these debates, drawn and redrawn borders and boundaries that refuse to allow for a geographically fixed space that can authoritatively be defined as 'Europe'. The idea of Europe and the cultural ramifications and implications of such a political unit are discussed by a number of the contributors (pp. 54, 61, 64–5, 74, 75–6, 90–1, 169, 181, 234–8, 259–62, 399–401, 430–2, 481–4), as are the cultural policies and initiatives that such a geographical configuration offers (pp. 15–17, 64–5, 88, 106–7, 440–1, 484). For Sellars, Europe exists primarily through a shared high culture and intellectual heritage that generates further issues around representation and power (pp. 478–81). Indeed, Janelle Reinelt's 2001 speculations as to whether the development of a strong EU is primarily a 'financial strategy for competing with the United States and gaining a transnational presence in foreign, often developing countries' (2001: 366) find echoes in Sellars's comments on the wider social interventions that directors' theatre can make in the evolving landscape of Europe.

The director's relationship to national identity again features through the contributions to this volume. The roots of directors' theatre, as Bradby and Williams demonstrate (1988: 2–23), lie in the nineteenth century, and the director is a figure shaped in the forges of European nationalism and internationalism. Wagner's vision of the *Gesamtkunstwerk* was by sly analogy a vision of national renewal, of cultural identity, all the parts of the nation working together. More complex was the story of André Antoine's Théâtre Libre and its relation to national identity. Antoine started the Libre in 1887 in the hope of discovering new French playwrights. Instead he discovered the director, the naturalism that he became known for demanding a single figure capable of harnessing and organising all the multiple crafts and codes that make up the theatrical experience. But even as the playwright was displaced in the Théâtre Libre project by the director, the Frenchness of the enterprise, too, was dispersed as the plays whose productions made his company's name – Tolstoy's

The Power of Darkness, Ibsen's *Ghosts*, Strindberg's *Miss Julie*, Hauptmann's *The Weavers* – were all from abroad.

Between 1800 and 1900, Paris's population had grown from just over half a million to a number fast approaching 3 million, and the social impact of these changes was decisive and unsettling. In the second half of the nineteenth century, Paris's urban geography was dramatically reshaped, under the designs of Baron Haussmann, to enhance flows of commerce and capital. In doing so, successive French governments sought to enhance Paris's position as a pre-eminently world city, a nodal point for international finance, commerce, culture, and tourism, a rebranding exercise that also included the International Exhibitions held, somewhat obsessively, in the city in 1855, 1867, 1878, 1889, and 1900. Under Haussmann's reforms, the seedy theatres along the Boulevard du Temple (known as the 'Boulevard du Crime' because of those theatres' preference for lurid thrillers) were demolished to make way for the enlarged Place de la République, a crucial axis in the new organisation of the city space, a meeting point for no less than eight *grands boulevards*. In demolishing those boulevard theatres, Haussmann was laying the groundwork for a new internationalist urban flow that would permit unprecedented access between the wealthy financial districts of the west and the bohemian quarters of the north (where Antoine's theatre was initially located), and aided news of Antoine's work being disseminated to other urban centres such as Stockholm, Berlin, London, Dublin, Barcelona, Brussels, and Moscow, all of which had a theatre modelled closely on the Théâtre Libre, with a similarly international repertoire, within a decade. The emergence of the director in France at least was intimately entwined with the emergence of cosmopolitan, not nationalist, Europe.

The directors who emerged in the first three decades of the twentieth century, such as Stanislavski, Meyerhold, Brecht, and Reinhardt, can all be associated with the forces that were to solidify the director's role as a major cultural agent shaping and in turn being shaped by wider artistic and social practices. Over time, and sometimes despite themselves, they became national icons of cultural strength and achievement, while also manifestly exceeding any narrow identification with nation. ('All the legends about the national mentalities,' notes Lev Dodin with asperity, 'get destroyed when we go on stage' (p. 88).) They were associated with venues that came to embody something of the spirit of change of the age – as with the association of Stanislavski with the Moscow Arts Theatre, Meyerhold with its Theatre-Studio, Reinhardt with the Kleines Theater and the Neues Theater am Schiffbauerdamm, and Copeau's with the Théâtre du Vieux-Colombier. This laid the foundations for the roles that Gémier and then Vilar in France, Brecht and later Stein in Germany, and Strehler and subsequently Ronconi in Italy were to play in establishing organisational structures that were to contribute, as Fancy indicates in this volume, 'to the continued theatricalisation of the discourse of modern sovereignty, republican tradition and national prestige' and legitimation (p. 61).

Directors have been the figureheads of prominent national institutions. In these positions they have both endorsed the status quo and served to articulate potent critical responses to dominant trends in both their national and transnational cultures. Bradby and Delgado have seen this as, in part, due to the legacy of 1968 'as theatre activists digested the lessons of the momentous events in Paris and other parts of the old continent', with directors formulating a theory and practice of cultural opposition that promoted efficacy while 'avoiding the trap of naïve revolutionary activism' (Bradby and Delgado 2003a: 1). The director may have begun as *metteur en scène* but increasingly he – constructed predominantly as white and male – embodied particular bourgeois ideals of individual attainment, entrepreneurialism, and capitalist enterprise that saw a move towards cultural management: the *directeur* or *Intendant*.[9] It is perhaps no surprise then that Planchon and Jonathan Miller have both argued that directors are somewhat like museum curators (Bradby and Williams 1988: 6), and that the analogy of the museum and its relationship to the marketplace has increasingly come to feature in the discourses through which the work of directors across the festival circuit – suppressing 'the local in favour of the transportable', privileging 'the symbolic over the realistic, the metaphorical over the referential' (Carmody 2002: 251) – has been discussed and debated.[10]

Directors have become indelibly linked with the cultural institutions they lead and manage and these can be seen to function as national trademarks or 'showplaces', functioning as manifestations of a wider '"culture" of nations' (Knowles 2006: 181). Chéreau's association with the TNP (Théâtre National Populaire) haunted much of his later work – as has also been the case with Stein and the Schaubühne. Others' directorial identities are ineradicably bound up with the companies they founded (as with Mnouchkine's Soleil, Donnellan's Cheek by Jowl, García's La Carnicería Teatro, and McBurney's Complicite) or the theatres they now head (Dodin at the Maly, Ostermeier at the Schaubühne, van Hove at the International Theatre Amsterdam or ITA). All these companies tour regularly, aided with financial support from national governments and cultural agencies, foreign embassies and offices, displaying national cultural products 'in much the same way that other products are displayed and promoted at international trade fairs and through aggressive government/business trade delegations' (Knowles 2006: 181–2). Theatre proves part of the cultural economy that travels across the boundaries of Europe and beyond.

Nevertheless, we would argue that the identification between the director and the nation, which proved such a cornerstone of theatrical culture in the Europe of the post-war era, is no longer as solid as it might have been perceived to be in the 1970s. The Council of Europe was formed in 1949. In the 1950s, Europe was a continent feeling its way tentatively towards more unified structures – the European Coal and Steel Community (ECSC) was formed in 1952, the Treaty of Rome that established the European Economic Community (EEC) was signed in 1957 – whilst simultaneously protecting the interests of its particular nation-states in a climate shaped by polarisation between East and West. Reinelt has effectively mapped the gradual establishment of an infrastructure that has produced the 'common' working and trade environment that defines the new European Union of 28 member-states:[11]

> The European Union has gradually defined itself, not only through the EEC but also through a series of treaties on agriculture, environmental regulation, transportation, key industries, and also through the growth of a European Court, a European Parliament with directly elected members, and a Council of Ministers which decides issues on the basis of a majority vote. In addition to

> these juridical and regulatory matters, the EU has also established the discourse of 'nation,' albeit a unique notion of nation, through the adoption of a flag, an anthem, the introduction of a European passport (allowing open access throughout the EU on nation-member passports), and a single currency [...] all, of course, the classic symbolic means of national identification. In addition, the EU now has a common working environment (no immigration restrictions for EU members) and a common trade environment (no customs and limited trade tariffs).
>
> (Reinelt 2001: 368)[12]

In the aftermath of the Second World War, the need to rebuild a European heritage was crucially linked to key initiatives both political – as with the European Union – and cultural. Edinburgh and Avignon, the two most renowned post-war festivals, were

> launched on the wave of relief at the end of the war in Europe, and shaped by a modernist belief in the inestimable value of cultural activity as a means of allowing communities to reenvisage and reimagine themselves following epochs of profound trauma.
>
> (Bradby and Delgado 2003b: 2)[13]

Nation-building happened both through physical reconstruction and through the establishment of cultural infrastructures that would further promote the preoccupations of the new age. As the edifices of these political orders have collapsed – with the fall of the Berlin Wall in 1989 and the break-up of the Yugoslav Federation in 1991–2 – further redrawing the map of the continent, so directors have questioned and redefined their roles in relation to the cultural organisations that they work with and for. Although, as Marvin Carlson has suggested, the idea of a 'National Theatre' is a distinctively European one (2008a: 28), European directors associated with state-subsidised theatres, such as Ostermeier and van Hove, are increasingly reluctant to associate themselves with a nationalist agenda. Ostermeier strongly positions his work as a conscious move away from an idea of the national theatre that he views as connected with potentially discriminatory discourses of nation-building (see Woodall 2010: 363–4).

At a time when nationalist discourses have splintered the imagined whole of the continent with consequences that can be measured in painfully human terms – over 200,000 died in the Balkan conflicts of the 1990s – it is not surprising to see issues of nationhood running through the volume (and with perhaps greater intensity since the first edition was published). Language, territory, and political legitimacy emerge as dominant tropes through which the work of the directors covered here can be viewed. While this appears particularly marked in the work of Purcărete, Castorf, and Dodin, whose trajectories were shaped by the discourses of Communism during Ceauşescu's Romania, Honecke's East Germany, and Brezhnev, Andropov, Chernenko, and Gorbachev's Soviet Union, it can be traced even in the theatrical languages and concerns of those whose careers have been made in the climate of a post-dictatorial continent. The work of Marthaler and Ostermeier is indelibly contextualised within the debates and dilemmas that have marked the reunified German nation. Bieito lived and worked for many years in Catalonia which, in the years since Franco's death in 1975, has negotiated a move from being understood as a region within a centralised state to being recognised as a nation within a wider social and political body. Lauwers's *The Deer House* (2008) commemorates the brother of a regular member of Needcompany, killed in Kosovo during the Bosnian War (see p. 249). Katie Mitchell's *The Phoenician Women* (1995) found plangent echoes in Euripides' story of fraternal strife of the then current Bosnian conflict.

Theatre has been made and remade within a landscape shaped by exile, migration, and a shifting of the north–south, east–west binaries. As Castellucci states in Alan Read's chapter (see p. 329), the new 'enlarged' Europe 'means, and probably has meant, a rethinking of its own history, in the light of the conflicts that have accompanied its becoming'. On the one hand, the politics of the new directors has led them often to assert the *local* specificity of their work – most famously in the cases of Bieito's association with Barcelona's Teatre Romea and Borowski's with the Studium Teatralne. Meanwhile, however, these directors have found themselves increasingly involved in an *international* touring circuit, assisted by their frequently non-verbal scenic productions, which has created skeins of cross-fertilisation and

11

mutual influence such that directors' theatre may now be described as a truly pan-European phenomenon.

This reflects changes in the geo-political organisation of Europe. The European environment was a more hostile place in the late 1980s than it had been in the late 1960s. The political ideals of the counterculture gave way to retrenchment and disillusion. In 1989, a wave of revolutions brought down the old Soviet bloc and barriers between East and West. This accelerated a process that saw markets and capital flows dramatically changing the shape and power of the nation. Transnational corporations have the power virtually to erase national borders; in response, supranational forms of collective action (in the form of international trade union links, the European Union, international campaign groups, etc.) have developed, raising questions about the identity of the nation as such. Across Europe, nations are being compromised by new nationalisms, terrorism, regionalism, localism, and an axis of power that questions federal aspirations. Culture's role is shifting: the new utilitarian priorities of our increasingly corporate world are demanding new defences of art, new modes of working, a new internationalism. Europe's twenty-first-century 'state', to paraphrase the opinions of Bellamy and Castaglione, can be seen no longer as a collection of national entities but rather 'a complex mixture of the subnational, national and supranational' (2005: 293). As theatre moves in new directions, and the political ground shifts beneath it, this collection of essays probes where directors' theatre is in the new century and how it relates to the wider national and global movements that shape contemporary society.

Theatre, Europe, and globalisation

While the directors discussed in this volume are positioned within their nation-state and debates (both theatrical and social) that emerge from this contextualisation, there is also a focus on issues that transcend national boundaries. Mnouchkine's early productions with the Théâtre du Soleil seemed particularly embedded in the particularities of French historical narratives – whether those of the French Revolution and its aftermath in *1789* (1970) and *1793* (1972) or the Nazi occupation of France during the Second World War (through which Singleton reads *1789*). It is also possible to locate in her work a broader concern with the boundaries of exchanges of territory, peoples, and capital. *Le Dernier Caravansérail* (*The Last Halting Site*, 2003) draws on the untold stories of the refugees at the Red Cross Sangatte camp in northern France to examine both processes of narratology and their relationships to wider ideological frameworks. As with Lauwers's *The Lobster Shop* (2006), Stephen Frears's *Dirty Pretty Things* (2002), and Jean-Pierre and Luc Dardenne's *Le Silence de Lorna* (*Lorna's Silence*) (2008), the breakdown of boundaries in the new Europe sees the vulnerable caught in the lawlessness that marks the journey to securing European legitimacy in the form of an EU passport.

The global movement from east to west and south to north has rendered a generation of stateless migrants suspended in delegitimised territories. As such, there appears a direct link between Mnouchkine's *L'Âge d'Or* (*The Golden Age*, 1975) and Bieito's *Peer Gynt* (2006). Both probe the exploitation of migrant labour rendered by a shift in boundaries driven by economic gain for an elite class. Chéreau's *La Reine Margot* (1994) and Bieito's *Peer Gynt* similarly point to the dangers of nascent nationalism in a socio-political landscape where the power to buy and sell remains the ultimate marker of economic might. Marthaler's *Groundings* (2003) intersects the bankruptcy of Swissair in 2002 with the early termination of his contract at Zurich's Schauspielhaus that same year, offering a treatment of the intersections (and confrontations) between cultural and economic capital, 'something of a topos in German-language theatre since the fall of the Berlin Wall' (see Barnett, p. 209). Indeed, the trajectories of Castorf at the Volksbühne and Ostermeier at the Schaubühne similarly demonstrate a marked leaning both towards texts and – in the case of Castorf and his favoured invited directors at the Volksbühne[14] – an aesthetic concerned with the crumbling of a social order that both reflects and comments on the post-1989 tensions in a recently reunified Germany. Crucially, while it is possible, as Peter Boenisch does, to view Ostermeier's *Nora* (2002) and *Hedda Gabler* (2005) as a commentary on the frustration of thirty-something professionals in a crisis-ridden Germany grappling with a temporary affluence threatened by its own unstable edifice (pp. 460–2), the 'otherness' of the texts' trans-European roots serve to embed the discussion within wider discourses of global dissent and politics.

Globalisation, however, remains more than an economic phenomenon; here it is shown to cultivate the structures through which much of the work of the directors presented in this volume is produced – across international touring circuits that bring together capital from diverse national and transnational sources.[15] These debates move beyond the loose configuration now regarded as the 'new Europe' and touch on wider operations of cultural exchange and imperialist appropriation. For Ostermeier, 'as globalisation globalises economic interests and markets, it also globalises problems *coming* from globalisation' (see Woodall 2010: 364), and it is these problems that he has chosen to focus on in the playtexts from writers across Europe – including Mark Ravenhill, Sarah Kane, Jon Fosse, and Alexej Schipenko – that he has staged at the Schaubühne. Singleton's focus on Mnouchkine discusses particular indicators of Orientalism (from performance vocabularies to decor and scenography) as a way of indicating how it can be viewed as a process, a mode of exploring artistic and textual heritage (see pp. 47–58). Fancy argues that Chéreau's relationship with Koltès's writing was part of a process of probing encounters between Europe and the colonial Other also evident in his production of Genet's *Les Paravents* (*The Screens*, 1983) (see pp. 70–2). For García too, encounters with the post-colonial Other shape two of his most resonant pieces: *Borges* (1999) and *Goya* (2006). The vocabularies of torture, degradation, and intimidation – such a feature of the regime of terror unleashed by Argentina's military junta between 1976 and 1983[16] – are core terrain for the Argentine-born García, embodied in the aggressive, visceral aesthetic of *La historia de Ronald el payaso de McDonalds* (*The Story of Ronald, the Clown from McDonald's*, 2004). The language of corporate Western culture is shown by García to be indelibly bound up with the politics of globalisation. McDonald's and Ikea are, for García, more than just performance tools; they are the manifestations of a popular culture that binds north and south, east and west into an insidious imperialist web that eradicates difference and diversity. For Sellars, any discussion of a European tradition cannot help but acknowledge ties with African, South-East Asian, and American cultures; and a culture of segregation – played out in the geographical configuration of cities such as Paris, Barcelona, and Berlin – must be addressed through cultural encounters that try to envisage new communities and configurations (p. 483).

Many of the directors featured in this volume work across different languages and some – most conspicuously Bieito, Lauwers, and Marthaler – negotiate different linguistic registers in their productions as a way of commenting on both the structures of language and the modes through which language both controls and can itself be controlled. English emerges – broken, dismembered, reworked – as the language of global capitalism. It is also a language that can be re-envisaged and reworked through translation (as when Shakespeare is represented through the prisms of linguistic adaptation). Indeed, the challenges of handling the classic text, whether through the refractions of translation or in the source language, run through the volume. For many of the directors, including Bieito, Ostermeier, Chéreau, Mesguich, and Warner, directing is as much about archaeological exploration as it is about the construction of a reading. The shaping of the canon that inevitably comes through the prioritisation of certain plays in performance allows for issues, concerns, and tensions to emerge through the storytelling process that forms part of the public discourse of performance.

Intersecting genealogies of directing can also be traced through the volume: further testament to the pan-European currents discussed by many of the contributors. The Russian line from Stanislavski through to Meyerhold, Chekhov, Lyubimov and on to Dodin, Donnellan, Mitchell, and Ostermeier is commented on across various chapters (see pp. 90–1, 169, 181, 431–2, 469). There are, however, also routes from Italy to France – as with Chéreau and Warlikowki's debt to Strehler (pp. 63, 356) and Mnouchkine's to Ronconi (p. 46); from France to the UK through Brook; and then across Russia and into Eastern Europe (as with Dodin, Donnellan, and Warner's debt to Brook, pp. 91, 170, 172, 301). The legacy of Grotowski and Gardzienice can be sketched through to Borowksi and Mitchell. Borowski, however, also questions his relationship to such a Polish lineage through a marked focus on the urban underclass of a newly modernising Polish nation (pp. 197–8). Warlikowski's rejection of Polish romanticism remains a strong feature of his work. McBurney discusses his own encounters with Pina Bausch and a Parisian landscape that welcomed performers, artists, and intellectuals from across Europe and the Americas in the 1960s, 1970s, and 1980s (p. 264). Van Hove has acknowledged the influence of Ingmar Bergman, and Marina Abramović, while connections have also been made between his productions and the work of Chéreau (p. 287; see also Dickson 2014). García is positioned by Orozco within a European avant-garde that includes his acknowledged influences – Kantor, Fabre, Lauwers, and Castellucci (p. 409). Lease maps Warlikowski's 'training' as an assistant to Bergman, Brook, and Strehler (p. 356). Rebellato traces Mitchell's indebtedness to and her continuing investigation of a north-east European tradition of austerely powerful visual images and an implacably serious attitude to training (pp. 433–9). Dodin comments on a 'dialogue between nationalities through culture' that he traces from French theatre into Russian theatre, through Stanislavski and Meyerhold, across to Germany with Brecht, and then into England and France via Brook, and back to his own work (p. 89). Bieito may link his own work to the Spanish cultural landscape (pp. 392–3) but the influence of Donnellan and Cheek by Jowl is evident in his Shakespeare stagings (p. 388). The pan-European repertoire that directors negotiate further enforces this sense of a shared heritage that a number of the contributors to this volume comment on.

Directors are themselves migrants across different traditions and geographical landscapes. Purcărete articulates his own movement from East to West – Bucharest to Limoges in 1996 and then to Paris in 2002 – as that of 'a vagabond' (p. 108), evoking something of the wandering troubadour of the medieval cultural landscape. García left Argentina for Spain in 1986, shortly after the difficult years of the Argentine dictatorship that sought to eradicate dissent from both the political and cultural spheres. Swiss-born Marthaler now directs primarily within the structures of the German theatre. Van Hove is artistic director of ITA in the Netherlands but works regularly in London and New York. Since 1986, Donnellan has worked for extensive periods in Russia and France, and his contact with canonical texts from both nations has resulted in productions that move away from dominant ways of reading Corneille, Pushkin, and Racine. Directing is perceived as a negotiation of traditions, texts, materials, and processes. It is less about 'interpreting' than about collision and exchange. Marthaler is both musician and director; McBurney and Mesguich both actors and directors; Purcărete and Castellucci both designers and directors; García and Lauwers both writers and directors. Directors' theatre in Europe is haunted both by its own cultural memories and by the wider historical, social, and cultural structures in which it takes place.

Indeed, it is the directors themselves who initiate imaginative possibilities for cultural exchange and transnational theatre practices. Dragan Klaic laments the lack of European initiatives to encourage such work:

> Officials tend to think primarily in terms of exporting national prestige [...] The Brussels bureaucrats within the European Union's convoluted international structure [...] hopelessly circle around a few opaque and inefficient schemes, incapable of coming up with any plausible programs of cultural action that would further European integration in the eyes of the citizen.
> (Klaic 1999: 115)

It is perhaps the festival producers, the annual European Cultural Capital schemes, and directors of state-subsidised venues that now offer the most productive options for concrete pan-European collaboration, with cost-sharing possibilities for co-productions and long-term ventures. It is within these structures that many of the directors in this volume have consolidated their reputations. And indeed, as Klaic concludes,

> In Europe, where practically every large city contains a great diversity of religions, languages, ethnicities and countries of origin, international collaboration is not an elitist exercise but a way to catch up with urban reality, with its complex interactions between different groups and the emergence of a syncretic youth culture.
> (Klaic 1999: 127)

The director in Europe: from teacher to brand

The idea of the director as teacher or pedagogue features strongly in this volume. Mesguich began teaching at the Conservatoire National Supérieur d'Art Dramatique in 1983 and ran the institution between 2007 and 2013. Dodin, director of St Petersburg's Maly Theatre since 1983, links his own practice as a director to his work with the St Petersburg Academy where he continues to work with the actors who, in turn, join the Maly. Ostermeier is now a teacher at the Russian-influenced Ernst Busch Schule where he himself studied between 1992 and 1996. Donnellan (2003) and Mitchell (2008) have followed the example of Stanislavski in providing published volumes on the craft of directing that offer detailed guidelines on the process of constructing a production, and Donnellan talks, in his contribution to this volume, of 'a profound respect for teaching' that can be traced through his own careful work with actors (p. 172). For Dodin, teaching goes beyond the work in the conservatoire and is linked to a concept of theatre that probes the modes in which we process and engage with the courses of history (pp. 92–3). For Purcărete, working for 12 years in Communist Romania, theatre was a necessity, a way of speaking to a community about shared concerns and ideals (p. 107). Castorf's career, developed in Anklam under the watchful eye of the Stasi, challenged both the aesthetic and the political absolutes of Communist East Germany, offering openings that were simply not permitted under the ideological apparatus of the state (pp. 121–2). For Sellars, theatre is never 'a destination point; it's always the route towards something else' (p. 479).

For the directors discussed in this volume, the craft of directing is never simply a question of 'interpreting' but rather about shaping, representing, positioning, and creating. While there is a particular school of directors who see directing as something that should be rendered invisible, 'a demand that the production illuminate the play or the film rather than itself' (Eyre 2003: 111), there is also a clear reaction to this by those who perceive history as a construct rather than a given and who consequently position theatre as a means of commenting on the ideological structures of both theatre and society. Chéreau's work is thus positioned as an engagement with formative European discourses of political power played out in a choice of texts that moves between the *siècle des lumières* and the Balkan conflict (pp. 62–75). Dodin and Purcărete reflect on a choice of repertoire that allows for an exploration of the ways in which theatre creates and conceives our ideas of history and facilitates new discussions about the intersections between past and present (pp. 95–9, 116–17). Bieito envisages theatre as the space of moral debates, a place where norms can be rattled and certainty challenged and undermined (p. 401). Castellucci sees the director as a figure 'who *creates* problems instead of trying to solve them' (p. 329), and Mesguich too argues for a theatre that doesn't provide answers but rather offers a *mise en scène* that proves 'unsummarisable', a series of experiences that the spectator negotiates (p. 147). Sellars views 'text as a living being not as an object' (p. 480) and the definition of *how* one creates a theatrical text is at the forefront of many of the discussions conducted through the volume.

Crucially, the idea of the director as an embodiment of individual authority is also questioned through the volume in ways that testify to the influence of live art practices on directors' theatre. Text, when it exists, is there to be engaged with and reformulated, either directly through radical interventions (as with Bieito, Castorf, Castellucci, Marthaler, and Mesguich), or through performative and scenographic registers that themselves expose gaps and fissures in the dramaturgical play (as with Chéreau, Donnellan, McBurney, Mitchell, van Hove, and Warner). While some may prioritise narrative (as with Donnellan), for Castellucci, Lauwers, and García linearity and text are themselves constructs there to be questioned and challenged. It is a penchant for the episodic, for colliding micro-narratives, intersecting tales, and arresting images that dominate their theatrical work. The text is there to be negotiated, and its treatment and delivery become part of the process of making theatre in a contemporary era where directors no longer aim to provide answers through their work but rather ask questions with which to provoke, surprise, and disarm an audience. Often this comes, as Barnett observes, through eschewing mimeticism of speech and movement: 'in a theatre in which hierarchies have been undermined, the director is no longer the visionary interpreter but rather moderates his or her claim to authority' (pp. 207–8). Purcărete uses the term 'distortions' to discuss the ways in which his textual interventions have been read by UK critics (p. 111).

This volume presents no single understanding of what directing consists. For Singleton, Mnouchkine can be positioned within the model of the German *Probenleiter*, 'leading rehearsals' (p. 42); she has also referred to herself as a midwife (Mnouchkine 1996: 187). Bieito refuses to see himself as a patriarch in the sense of the earlier generation of *auteurs*, such as Bergmann and Strehler (Delgado 2003: 63). Warner defines herself through the term 'theatre maker' rather than director (p. 302). Frédric uses a sporting analogy when speaking of himself as a coach (p. 350) but later refers to his work as more sculptor than director (p. 352). García too positions himself within the visual arts, prioritising the visual in his exploration of the relationships between public and private spaces (p. 409). For van Hove, punk remains a seminal influence (Dickson 2014). For Warner, listening is a means to direct (p. 299). Stephen Knapper sees McBurney as an *imprimatur*, 'signing his work' like a cinematic *auteur* (p. 271). Katie Mitchell, with her connections to European dance theatre and mixed media performance forms, has been simultaneously acclaimed and denounced precisely for her *auteur* status, as Rebellato shows (pp. 427–8). While Kelleher and Ridout (2006: 1) have commenced from positions that signal the separation of UK directors from those working in Continental Europe, the UK artists and companies whose work is discussed in this volume are shown to be productively embedded in wider European structures of making theatre, treating issues of displacement, territoriality, and historical memory that are so pertinent to the wider discussions of the UK's position within the wider structures of Europe and the European Union.

Perhaps the most prominent of the shared reference points is the idea(l) of an ensemble company: a team, collective, or group that comes together for extended periods to develop a project, whether in the form of an individual production or a laboratory structure for generating work. For Bieito, Borowski, Castellucci, Castorf, Dodin, García, Lauwers, Marthaler, McBurney, Mitchell, Mnouchkine, Ostermeier, Purcărete, and Sellars, such organisational models offer a structure for both their methodologies and for a wider view of what it means to make and watch theatre across Europe. The relationship with wider company structures is evident not only in Mnouchkine's association with the Théâtre du Soleil but also in the modes through which McBurney discusses his own associations with Complicite (pp. 261–5), van Hove looks at his creative position within ITA (p. 281), and Bieito his function within the Romea which he led between 1999 and 2011 (pp. 386–7). And, while the idea of the ensemble may have evolved – as Orozco demonstrates in charting García's shift to a transient troupe that works intensively on a single project rather than across numerous ventures (pp. 417–18) – it serves as a powerful organisational model for theatre-making in Europe in the twenty-first century.

Indeed, the role of the director in an 'actor-centred creative process' (Singleton, p. 42) is the focus of a number of the contributions to this volume. Aleks Sierz writes of Cheek by Jowl as 'an unofficial acting academy' (p. 166), and Donnellan himself articulates a vision of directing founded on a consideration of acting and the actor as both individual and a member of an ensemble (pp. 178–9). This is not to say that Donnellan's decisions are entirely governed by a prioritisation of the actor; he admits that sometimes he chooses a play to suit particular actors, but at other times it is the play that comes first and the actors are cast subsequently (p. 172). Paul Allain notes the importance of the core group of performers working with Piotr Borowski at Studium Teatralne since 1995 (pp. 200–2). Bieito's reliance on a small team of regular actors at the Romea was crucial to his Catalan- and Spanish-language work for ten years (pp. 385–6). Ostermeier too has been able to work with regular performers – including Bruno Cathomas and Jule Böwe – at the Schaubühne and refers to his own job as that of letting 'actors grow' (Woodall 2010: 371). Van Hove's group of actors at ITA (formerly Toneelgroep Amsterdam) is a key part of the director's commitment to the idea of an ensemble; Katie Mitchell, who has maintained an informal company of actors over 30 years, remarks 'I think what I've been learning all the time is how to give the actors freedom rather than trying to control them' (Gardner 1998: 15).

But the process of making work marked by a signature aesthetic is repeatedly shown to go beyond the actor–director relationship.

Marthaler's trajectory since *Murx den Europäer! Murx ihn! Murx ihn! Murx ihn! Murx ihn ab! Ein patriotischer Abend* (*Kill the European! Kill Him! Kill Him! Kill Him! Kill Him Off! A Patriotic Evening*, 1993) is bound up with set designer Anna Viebrock and dramaturg Stefanie Carp. Donnellan's aesthetic is created with designer Nick Ormerod, Van Hove's is forged with his long-term design and life partner Jan Versweyveld; Frédric's visually opulent worlds are conceived with cartoonist-turned-scenographer Enki Bilal. Ostermeier's aesthetic is formulated with designer Jan Pappelbaum and dramaturgs Jens Hillje and Marius von Mayenburg. Mitchell's working relationship with designer Vicki Mortimer has passed the quarter-century mark, and her current work in multimedia rests heavily on her consistent collaboration with video artist Leo Warner. All these directors provide some indication through the essays collected here of how they work towards a production. The director may be the brand, but it is a brand cultivated by a team. This volume does not seek to see the director as a homogeneous individual but rather as a construct that itself articulates wider debates around the intersections between theatre, nation, state, and the broader structures through which geographical, political, and cultural spaces intersect or collide. Directing is shown to be both a function and a profession, a brand and a process, an encounter and a market force.

Journeys

The different chapters in this volume look at particular concerns that emerge in relation to European history in the productions discussed. With Chéreau, it is the 'investigation of the specifically European emergence of certain broad manifestations of institutionalised subjection' (p. 66); with McBurney, an internationalism that moves beyond the boundaries of Europe from which his early Lecoq- and Gaulier-trained collaborators came, to embrace collaborations with Japan's Setagaya Public Theatre, the Los Angeles Philharmonic, and the National Actors' Theatre New York; with Mesguich, an engagement with European Continental philosophy that has offered a mode of disarming established understandings of a text's dramaturgy. Van Hove has reflected on the fact that when his work was first seen in New York and viewed as controversial and provocative, he was referred to as 'Eurotrash' (Dickson 2014). Frédric's transatlantic journeys are crucial to the increasingly bilingual nature of his work. Ostermeier's work in establishing FIND (the Festival for New International Drama) allows for trans-European encounters that present alternatives to the formal network of Strehler's Union of Theatres of Europe.

Some contributors chose to focus primarily on a single production while others detail a wider body of work in constructing their argument. The emphasis is always on a treatment that allows for discussion of the particular characteristics of a director's aesthetic, working process, and directorial choices as well as the ways in which his or her work has been received by both critics and audiences. Some essays, as with those on Borowski and Purcărete, provide concrete examples of how loose ideas are converted into a performance. Others, as with those on García and Ostermeier, give close consideration to issues of space and place, examining the implications of the performance space and its location. McBurney addresses the ways in which theatre can serve to create and bind communities at a time when the concept of community is itself so fractured and fraught (pp. 268–9). For Pavis, the Europe of the past half-century is no longer the space 'where all contradictions are resolved'; in a globalised world *mise en scène* is now 'challenged and renewed' by the *performises* that lie beyond Europe's geographical, economic, and imagined boundaries (p. 508).

Indeed, while the realities of working in Europe shape this project, the volume also touches on the networks of associations that move beyond the parameters of the continent. Numerous contributions delineate working practices that draw on North American, Asian, and African practitioners and practices (pp. 40, 47–52, 91, 231, 254, 259, 341–2), and our final two chapters – an interview with Peter Sellars, a director who sees his own work in the USA only possible because of his trajectory of operatic and theatrical work in Europe, and an overview of directors' theatre by Patrice Pavis – return to the idea of exchanges that happen both within and beyond Europe. As the idea of Europe shifts to take in greater configurations and clusters, the boundaries of what the continent is and how it has been shaped are themselves called into question. Much of the work discussed in this volume is about 'testing the limits' (p. 483), examining the possibilities of how theatre can participate in the discussions about nationalism, migration, terrorism, capitalism's fault-lines, and excesses that now shape Europe's sense of self and 'other'. Sellars describes Europe as 'this place of the possible' (pp. 478–9); the contributions to this volume indicate the ways in which possibilities have been envisaged by directors across political, social, and cultural paradigms that make up the terrain, both imagined and real, of what is understood to be contemporary Europe.

Notes

1 We have lightly edited this introduction to update and add a few references, but have otherwise chosen to leave it as it was in 2010, with most of its Euro-optimism intact.
2 At the time of writing (2019), a new edition is in production, reflecting on developments in theatre directing since the late 1980s and drawing in some more recent major figures. See Boenisch, Bradby and Williams 2019.
3 See Bradby 1991: 101–28, 132–41; Bradby and Sparks 1997: 41–5; Bradby and Delgado 2002: 16.
4 See, for example, Bablet and Bablet 1979; Daoust 1981; Heilpern 1977; Hirst 1993; Hunt and Reeves 1996; Patterson 1981; Schumacher 1986; Todd and Lecat 2003; Whitton 1987; Williams 1999.
5 See the bibliography at the end of this introductory chapter for further details.
6 For further details on the production and Chéreau's other operatic work, see Sutcliffe 1996: 99–124.
7 In addition, the North American director Peter Sellars provides a commentary on the experiences of an 'outsider' working largely in Europe.
8 See, for example, the treatments of Bieito in Bieito, Delgado and Parker 2005; Castellucci and Societas Raffaello Sanzio in Ridout 2006, Giannachi and Kaye 2002: 137–69, Castellucci et al. 2007; García in Orozco 2010; Claus Peymann in Bradley 2008, Carlson 2008b; René Pollesch in Barnett 2006; Michael Thalheimer in Boenisch 2008; Olivier Py in Bradby 2005; as well as a range of contemporary German directors covered in Carlson 2009.
9 On the role of the *Intendant* as both artistic and executive director, see Barnett 2008. For further information on theatrical nationhood and cultural legitimation, see; Kruger 1992: 3–29.

10 See especially, Carmody 2002; Fricker 2003; Knowles 2006: 180–204; Zaiontz 2018.
11 The founder members of the ECSC were Belgium, France, Italy, Luxembourg, the Netherlands, and West Germany. The EEC was established in 1957 and in 1967 the ECSE, EEC, and the European Atomic Energy Committee merged into a single institution, the European Community. The six founder states were joined by Denmark, Ireland, and the UK in 1973 and Greece, Spain, and Portugal over a decade later. German reunification saw East Germany welcomed into the structure and, following the formal establishment of the EU with the 1993 Treaty of Maastricht, Austria, Sweden, and Finland joined in 1995. Ten further nations – Cyprus, the Czech Republic, Estonia, Hungary, Latvia, Lithuania, Malta, Poland, Slovakia, and Slovenia – joined in 2004. Romania and Bulgaria joined in 2007 and Croatia in 2013. For further details, see (Bickerton 2016; Usherwood and Pinder 2018).
12 On projects towards a unified Europe in the post-war era, see Duchêne 1996; Hallstein 1962; Kotlowski 2000.
13 At the turn of the twenty-first century, Klaic (1999: 116) estimated the number of European festivals at 350.
14 These include Andreas Kriegenburg and Marthaler.
15 On theatre and globalisation, see Rebellato 2009.
16 At least 30,000 civilians were 'eradicated' by the military dictatorship during these years.

Bibliography

Bablet, Marie-Louise and Denis Bablet (1979) *Le Théâtre du Soleil ou la quête du bonheur*, Paris: CNRS.

Barnett, David (2006) 'Political Theatre in a Shrinking World: René Pollesch's Postdramatic Practices on Paper and on Stage', *Contemporary Theatre Review*, 16 (1): 31–40.

——— (2008) 'The Problems and Pleasures of Running a Theatre in Berlin: The Changing Role of the *Intendant*', *Contemporary Theatre Review*, 18 (1): 80–3.

Bellamy, Richard and Dario Castiglione (2005) 'Building the Union: The Nature of Sovereignty in the Political Architecture of Europe', in Dimitrios Karmis and Wayne Norman (eds), *Theories of Federalism*, New York: Palgrave Macmillan, pp. 293–310.

Bickerton, Chris (2016) *The European Union: A Citizen's Guide*, Harmondsworth: Penguin.

Bieito, Calixto, Maria M. Delgado and Patricia Parker (2005) 'Resistant Readings, Multilingualism and Marginality', in Lynette Hunter and Peter Lichtenfels (eds), *Shakespeare, Language and the Stage: The Fifth Wall – Approaches to Shakespeare from Criticism, Performance and Theatre Studies*, London: The Arden Shakespeare and Thomson Learning, pp. 108–37.

Boenisch, Peter (2008) 'Exposing the Classics: Michael Thalheimer's *Regie* beyond the Text', *Contemporary Theatre Review*, 18 (1): 30–43.

Boenisch, Peter, David Bradby and David Williams (eds) (2019) *Directors' Theatre*, 2nd edn, London: Red Globe.

Bradby, David (1991) *Modern French Drama, 1940–1990*, Cambridge: Cambridge University Press.

—— (2005) 'Olivier Py: A Poet of the Stage: Analysis and Interview', *Contemporary Theatre Review*, 15 (2): 234–45.

Bradby, David and Maria M. Delgado (eds) (2002) *The Paris Jigsaw: Internationalism and the City's Stages*, Manchester: Manchester University Press.

—— (2003a) 'Editorial: The Director as Cultural Critic', *Contemporary Theatre Review*, 13 (3): 1–3.

—— (2003b) 'Editorial', *Contemporary Theatre Review*, 13 (4): 1–4.

Bradby, David and Annie Sparks (1997) *Mise en Scène: French Theatre Now*, London: Methuen.

Bradby, David and David Williams (1988) *Directors' Theatre*, Houndmills and London: Macmillan.

Bradley, Laura (2008) 'Contemporary Theatre? Brecht, Peymann & Co. at the Berliner Ensemble', *Contemporary Theatre Review*, 18 (1): 69–79.

Carlson, Marvin (2008a) 'National Theatres Then and Now', in Stephen Elliot Wilmer (ed.), *National Theatres in a Changing Europe*, Houndmills: Palgrave Macmillan, pp. 21–33.

—— (2008b) 'Claus Peymann and the Performance of Scandal', *Contemporary Theatre Review*, 18 (2): 193–207.

—— (2009) *Theatre Is More Beautiful than War: German Stage Directing in the Late Twentieth Century*, Iowa City, IA: University of Iowa Press.

Carmody, Jim (2002) 'Creating the Theatrical Museum: Theatrical Visions of an Alternative America; Cultural Politics and the Festival d'Automne, 1972–2000', in David Bradby and Maria M. Delgado (eds), *The Paris Jigsaw: Internationalism and the City's Stages*, Manchester: Manchester University Press, pp. 248–66.

Castellucci, Claudia, Romeo Castellucci, Chiara Guidi, Joe Kelleher and Nicholas Ridout (2007) *The Theatre of Societas Raffaello Sanzio*, Abingdon and New York: Routledge.

Daoust, Yvette (1981) *Roger Planchon: Director and Playwright*, Cambridge: Cambridge University Press.

Delgado, Maria M. (2003) 'Calixto Bieito: "Reimagining the Text for the Age in Which It Is Being Staged"', *Contemporary Theatre Review*, 13 (3): 59–66.

Delgado, Maria M. and Paul Heritage (eds) (1996) *In Contact with the Gods? Directors Talk Theatre*, Manchester: Manchester University Press.

Derrida, Jacques (1992) *The Other Heading: Reflections on Today's Europe*, Bloomington, IN: Indiana University Press.

Dickson, Andrew (2014) 'My Aim is the Ultimate Production: Ivo van Hove on Directing Arthur Miller', *Guardian*, 2 April, www.theguardian.com/stage/2014/apr/02/ultimate-production-ivo-van-hove-arthur-miller-theatre

Donnellan, Declan (2003) *The Actor and the Target*, London: Nick Hern Books.

Duchêne, François (1996) *Jean Monnet, the First Statesman of Interdependence*, New York: W. W. Norton & Co.

Eyre, Richard (2003) *Utopia and Other Places: Memoir of a Young Director*, London: Bloomsbury.

Fricker, Karen (2003) 'Tourism, the Festival Marketplace and Robert Lepage's *The Seven Streams of the River Ota*', *Contemporary Theatre Review*, 13 (4): 79–93.

Gardner, Lyn (1998) 'The Mitchell Principles', *Guardian*, 1 April, G2: 15.

Giannachi, Gabriella and Nick Kaye (2002) *Staging the Post-Avant-Garde: Italian Experimental Performance after 1970*, Oxford: Peter Lang.

Hallstein, Walter (1962) *United Europe: Challenge and Opportunity*, Cambridge, MA: Harvard University Press.

Heilpern, John (1977) *Conference of the Birds: The Story of Peter Brook in Africa*, London: Methuen.

Hirst, David (1993) *Giorgio Strehler*, Cambridge: Cambridge University Press.

Hunt, Albert and Geoffrey Reeves (1996) *Peter Brook*, Cambridge: Cambridge University Press.

Kelleher, Joe and Nicholas Ridout (eds) (2006) *Contemporary Theatres in Europe: A Critical Companion*, London and New York: Routledge.

Klaic, Dragan (1999) 'Close Encounters: European Internationalism', *Theater*, 19 (1): 115–27.

Knowles, Ric (2006) *Reading the Material Theatre*, Cambridge: Cambridge University Press.

Kotlowski, Dean J. (ed.) (2000) *The European Union: From Jean Monnet to the Euro*, Athens, GA: Ohio University Press.

Kruger, Loren (1992) *The National Stage: Theatre and Cultural Legitimation in England, France and America*, Chicago, IL: University of Chicago Press.

Miller, Judith G. (2007) *Ariane Mnouchkine*, London: Routledge.

Mitchell, Katie (2008) *The Director's Craft: A Handbook for the Theatre*, London: Routledge.

Mnouchkine, Ariane (1996) 'In Conversation with Maria M. Delgado at the Cartoucherie, Paris, 14 October 1995', in Maria M. Delgado and Paul Heritage (eds), *In Contact with the Gods? Directors Talk Theatre*, Manchester: Manchester University Press, pp. 179–90.

Orozco, Lourdes (2010) 'Approaching Mistrust: Rodrigo García Rehearses La Carnicería Teatro in *Une façon d'aborder l'idée de méfiance* (One Way to Approach the Idea of Mistrust)', in Jen Harvie and Andy Lavender (eds), *Making Contemporary Theatre: International Rehearsal Processes*, Manchester: Manchester University Press, pp. 121–39.

Patterson, Michael (1981) *Peter Stein, Germany's Leading Director*, Cambridge: Cambridge University Press.

Rebellato, Dan (2009) *Theatre and Globalization*, Houndmills: Palgrave Macmillan.

Reinelt, Janelle (2001) 'Performing Europe: Identity Formation for a "New Europe"', *Theatre Journal*, 53 (3): 365–87.

Ridout, Nicholas (2006) 'Make-believe: Societas Raffaello Sanzio do Theatre', in Joe Kelleher and Nicholas Ridout (eds), *Contemporary Theatres in Europe: A Critical Companion*, London and New York: Routledge, pp. 175–87.

Schumacher, Claude (ed.) (1986) *40 Years of Mise-en-Scène*, Dundee: Lochee.

Shevtsova, Maria and Christopher Innes (2009) *Directors/Directing: Conversations on Theatre*, Cambridge: Cambridge University Press.

Strehler, Giorgio (1996) 'In Response to Questions Put to Him by the Editors and Eli Malka', in Maria M. Delgado and Paul Heritage (eds), *In Contact with the Gods? Directors Talk Theatre*, Manchester: Manchester University Press, pp. 264–76.

Sutcliffe, Tom (1996) *Believing in Opera*, London: Faber and Faber.

Todd, Andrew and Jean-Guy Lecat (2003) *The Open Circle: Peter Brook's Theatrical Environments*, London: Faber and Faber.

Usherwood, Simon and John Pinder (2018) *The European Union: A Very Short Introduction*, 4th edn, Oxford: Oxford.

Whitton, David (1987) *Stage Directors in Modern France*, Manchester: Manchester University Press.

Williams, David (ed.) (1999) *Collaborative Theatre: The Théâtre du Soleil Sourcebook*, London and New York: Routledge.

Woodall, James (2010) 'Thomas Ostermeier: On Europe, Theatre, Communication and Exchange', in Maria M. Delgado and Dan Rebellato (eds), *Contemporary European Theatre Directors*, 1st edn, Abingdon: Routledge, pp. 363–76.

Zaiontz, Keren (2018) *Theatre & Festivals*, London: Red Globe.

INTRODUCTION TO THE SECOND EDITION

Dan Rebellato and Maria M. Delgado

The decade between the first and second editions of this book have been tumultuous for Europe. In 2010, as the book came out, the expanded European Union had a few months earlier succeeded in ratifying the Lisbon Treaty, perhaps the most large-scale and ambitious democratic exercise in international political cooperation ever seen on the continent. Two years later, in 2012, the EU would be awarded the Nobel Peace Prize for its six decades of contributions 'to the advancement of peace and reconciliation, democracy and human rights in Europe'.[1] The EU had expanded greatly in the previous decade, with ten (mostly) former Soviet-bloc countries acceding to it in 2004 and Bulgaria and Romania joining them in 2007 (Croatia would be the 28th country to join the Union in July 2013).

But things are changing. In June 2016, the United Kingdom voted by a wafer-thin majority to leave the EU. Doing this without devastating consequence to the British economy and our myriad ties to the European continent proved tricky, to put it mildly; but then, in December 2019, a minority of the British electorate managed to put in power a government determined to do Brexit at all costs and, at the end of January 2020, the United Kingdom technically became the first country to leave the EU since Greenland almost 40 years ago. We say 'technically' because, in this transition period, nothing much has changed, and there seems to be little sign that the new populist government is willing or able to reconcile a country divided between leavers and remainers, Europhiles and Eurosceptics, nationalists and internationalists, Somewheres and Anywheres,[2] nativists and globalists, between 'real, ordinary, decent people' and the metropolitan liberal elite, or between unicorns and reality.[3] While the UK's departure from the EU will inevitably have more serious consequences for the former than the latter, it does represent a blow to the vision of 'ever closer union' set out in the preamble to 1957's Treaty of Rome, a vision of nation-states overcoming their differences to forge a wider citizenship, founded on peace, solidarity, and freedom of trade and movement.

And this blow has also had repercussions here in the UK, unleashing and in some ways even legitimising a culture where it has been seen as permissible to attack those who either do not have English as a first language or whose otherness is perceived in racial or ethnic terms. Reports of hate crime increased by 57 per cent in the days following the Brexit vote (see Yeung 2016), with Poles in particular, the UK's largest community of foreign-born residents, subject to particular venom and vitriol (see Addley 2016; Bilefsky 2016; Press Association 2016); 76,000 EU workers were reported to have left the UK in 2018 (see Partington 2019). The idea of shared citizenry no longer appears an attractive proposition to those who have experienced hostility and xenophobia in a post-referendum Britain.

The figure of the theatre director was a shared European project. Its roots are complex, but in the modern era the director emerged as a key figure who could offer a global overview of a performance. As we wrote in the first edition, the director in the modern era starts in Germany (at the Meiningen Theatre) in the 1860s, is developed further in France in the 1880s, returns to Germany at the end of that decade, and spreads through northern Europe in the early 1890s, and Eastern Europe in the mid-1890s, before reaching beyond Europe to North America at the turn of the century, and to Asia and Africa later in the twentieth century (see pp. 6–8).

In each region, the figure of the director takes on a different character, a cultural combatant in France, overlapping and merging with the figure of the actor-manager in Spain and Italy, a fully professionalised figure of authority in Central and Eastern Europe, never entirely eclipsing the figure of the playwright in Britain and Ireland. Each form of the director continues to influence the others, with dialogue and mutual influence between north and south, east and west, enhanced after the war by the growth of the international theatre festivals in Edinburgh and Avignon (1947), Dublin (1957), Sarajevo (1960), Belgrade (1967), Zurich (1980), Madrid (1984), Taormina (1987), Poznań (1991), Sibiu (1994), and more. In the weave of languages across the European continent, the theatre festival encourages a more international outlook, a visual boldness over knotty text, a moment to think beyond the boundaries of the nation to a broader vision of who we might be, and it is the figure of the director that has offered Europe back to itself most consistently through these vital theatrical exchanges, dialogues, and confrontations.

The director has spent the first half of her life in a Europe deeply rent with division, rivalry, and conflict. It is tempting to think that the second half has been mostly spent in an era of relative calm. Certainly, central to the 'European Project' has been the maintenance of peace, mutual understanding and collaboration, the spread of democracy, and the protection of human rights. The theatre has been part of these post-war processes of European (and wider) integration: the International Theatre Institute (ITI) was set up in 1948 by Julian Huxley of UNESCO and the British playwright J. B. Priestley to promote theatre, education, and mutual understanding;[4] since 1987, the Premio Europa has marked outstanding achievement in theatre, but with a particular emphasis on advancing 'the development of cultural relationships' and strengthening 'the collective European consciousness';[5] The Union of the Theatres of Europe, a brainchild of Giorgio Strehler in 1990, seeks to use theatrical exchange and dialogue to promote collaboration, support young theatre artists, and encourage the theatre to reflect critically on the world.[6] The Lifetime Achievement Golden Lion Award of the Venice Biennale has been won by six directors featured in this volume: Ariane Mnouchkine (2007), Thomas Ostermeier (2011), Romeo Castellucci (2013), Jan Lauwers (2014), Christoph Marthaler (2015), and Declan Donnellan (2016). Donnellan's acceptance speech spoke overtly of the challenges posed by populism to understandings (and tolerance) of difference and the need for theatre to continue to provide a space for the development of empathy: 'to see that another human being is different to me is the first act of any political discussion'.[7]

These initiatives offer a benign image of European culture contributing to 70 years of calm and security. Yet for the first 40 years after the war, Europe was divided down the middle, locked in mutual, nuclear-armed stalemate, with flashes of tension and eruptions of violence illuminating the European night; parts of southern

Europe had not vanquished fascism, and in the early 1970s the governments of Spain, Portugal, and Greece were a scar on Europe. In the 1990s, atavistic, genocidal conflict erupted in the Balkans. Over the last decade, a brutal civil war on Europe's doorstep has left Europe looking hesitant at best, cruelly complicit at worst. Those of us who admire the project of European integration should not forget Walter Benjamin's famous warning: 'There is no document of culture which is not at the same time a document of barbarism' (1940: 392).

In truth, what Europe's culture and values might be are the subject of continued debate. The outcome of the EU referendum in 2016 was the culmination of around 25 years of political battles in Britain. Elsewhere in Europe, that period also saw the re-emergence of far right parties in East and West: the Freedom Party in Austria, the Danish People's Party in Denmark, the National Front (now the National Assembly) in France, the Golden Dawn in Greece, the Lega Nord (now just the Lega) in Italy, VOX in Spain, Law and Justice in Poland, Vlaams Blok and its successor Vlaams Belang in Belgium, and UKIP and the Brexit Party in the United Kingdom have all, in different ways, broken into mainstream politics, gaining sizeable votes and, in some instances, entering not just their respective parliaments, but governments too. Right-wing populists like Marine Le Pen, Pim Fortuyn, Viktor Orbán, Nigel Farage, and Matteo Salvini, who in an earlier generation would have been at the political margins, have come to national and international prominence, often expressing scepticism and hostility to the idea of European integration.

As these fault lines have deepened and the debates have raged, theatre directors have created interventionist theatre productions, asking searching questions about the state of the European *polis*. Thomas Ostermeier's production of Ibsen's *An Enemy of the People* (2012) replaces the speech Ibsen gives to his protagonist Doctor Stockmann with passages from a revolutionary anti-globalisation pamphlet, and then the microphone is passed to the audience to comment. When the production came to the Barbican, London, in 2014, what was most striking was how ill-prepared the audience was to participate and how, in some ways, Ostermeier seemed to be asking us if we were ready for democracy, if we were up to the job of fulfilling our role as citizens. (And the production, in exposing the fragility of civic democracy, anticipated the way Ibsen's title is used so often by far-right populists to denigrate their opponents.[8])

Calixto Bieito's *Die Soldaten* (*The Soldiers*), a staging of Bernd Alois Zimmermann's 1965 opera adapted from Jakob Lenz's 1776 play, similarly asks questions around the denigration of those who refuse to tow a particular populist line. A culture of surveillance is created within the theatre, with the sensation of the military taking over the auditorium: ushers, orchestra, and conductor are all in military fatigues. Rebecca Ringst's giant yellow metallic scaffolding structure creates the sense of a yellow inferno that traps the characters unable to escape the culture of surveillance promoted by an aggressive, masculine ideology. The audience is beaten both sonically and visually, witnesses to the abuses perpetrated on the two sisters, Marie and Charlotte, who fall victim to the predatory, populist masculinity that seduces them. As audience members we sit and watch; we do not act; we do not intervene. Shining spotlights on the audience puts us all under the scalpel. The production opened in Madrid in 2018 against the backdrop of the *manada* (wolf pack) case – five men from a group known as the 'wolf pack' who repeatedly raped an 18-year-old woman in 2015, then boasted about it and shared images among themselves. They received sentences in April 2018 – found guilty of sexual abuse but not rape – a move that generated widescale protests in Spain and two subsequent appeals (see Delgado 2019). One of the five men was a soldier and the second a member of Spain's rural police force, the Civil Guard. The timely quality of Bieito's production could not be more evident. Zimmermann's portrait of how institutions allow for the endorsement of criminality acquired a new relevance for twenty-first-century Spain as VOX's founder Santiago Abascal campaigned for 'the party that defends what Spaniards say on WhatsApp' (cited in Beatley 2019).

In *La Reprise* (2018), Milo Rau restages the murder of a 22-year-old gay man Ihsane Jarfi whose mutilated body was found two weeks after he was beaten to death in 2012. Rau's practice has put into operation a theatre which has explored the atrocities of the age – whether it's the horrors of paedophile murderer Marc Dutroux as performed by a cast of children in *Five Easy Pieces* (2016) or the excesses of communist dictatorships in *The Last Days of the Ceaușescus*

(2009). The first point of Rau's Ghent Manifesto, formulated as he took up the artistic directorship of NTGent in 2018, states that theatre 'is not just about portraying the world. It's about changing it' (www.ntgent.be/en/manifest). The current climate demands more than observation. It is about working out what intervention means and how it can be activated through the process of performance.

In *By Heart* (2013), actor-writer-director Tiago Rodrigues asks for ten audience members to join him in learning a Shakespeare sonnet by heart on stage as a way of thinking through how culture can be shared across difficult times. Language is here used as a way of binding rather than dividing individuals, as a way of considering how the personal and political intersect and how culture survives in times of political censorship. Memory becomes a way of forging community, a way of protecting the values of democracy and freedom, the power of the imagination, and the role of art in troubled times. Performed in Portuguese, French, English, or Spanish (and often indeed working across different languages), the production functions as a way of thinking through how works remain in our hearts and minds through the traces of the performances we share as audiences.

While these works deal overtly with the fissures of democracy and/or the rise of the right in Europe, other directors in this volume have engaged more broadly with issues around empathy and difference, migration and exile, participation, populism, and revolution, and the construction of history/ies as the political landscape of Europe shifts. Krzysztof Warlikowski's *Wyje d amy* (*We Are Leaving*, 2018), Deborah Warner's *The Testament of Mary* (2012), and Castorf's seven-hour adaptation of Hugo's *Les Miserables* (2018) are just some of the productions covered in this volume that engage with the politics of democracy in challenging times.

The inclusion of three new directors in this second edition – Ivo van Hove, Krzysztof Warlikowski, and Deborah Warner – also allows for different conversations to emerge.[9] Van Hove is positioned by Denis Flannery as a close reader of texts with a profound 'admiration for artists and art-works that alternate between intimate scales and vast scales' (p. 282). Warlikowski is described by Bryce Lease as 'grounded in a mode of resistance to a conservative public sphere that is increasingly marked by insularism, nostalgia, and xenophobia'

(p. 378). Warner is seen by Adam Ledger as 'governed only by a sense of discovery and the ultimately mutual event of performance', her directing 'deeply rooted in the trust placed in long rehearsal' (p. 318). 'To take the work abroad is to develop it hugely', Warner stated in 2009 (see p. 317); it is a comment that could apply to the work of any one of the directors included in this volume.

If Europe is to flourish and, most particularly, the aims of peace, community, and a shared open democratic culture are to succeed, we could do a lot worse than look to directors to show how we can think across boundaries, tear down the borders, reflect on who we are, and who we might be. The irony of British theatre's relationship to these debates is that in the decade since the first volume of this book, more and more British theatre directors have embraced a more 'European' style of direction and design. Ellen McDougall, Blanche McIntyre, Rupert Goold, Robert Icke, Ramin Gray, Carrie Cracknell, Michael Longhurst, and others have moved away from a British directorial tradition that places the play at the summit of theatrical production and ensures that acting, directing, and design's main role is not to distract from it. This generation engages in vigorous, rigorous dialogue with plays, intervening in them, testing them, tying them to strong design concepts, and offering a more genuine collaboration between writer, director, actor, and designer. Michael Longhurst's production of Simon Stephens's *Carmen Disruption* (Almeida Theatre, 2015) took a play that itself disrupted a European theatrical classic and opened it out, weaving the play's stories together on a bare stage that seemed to represent here and somewhere else, Europe and nowhere, both one European city and every European city. In its way, it anticipated the following year's debates over the meaning and value of Europe, while in the middle of the stage an astonishingly realistic gored bull slowly bled to death, obliquely foreshadowing the death agonies of British Europeanism.

But for now, in Britain, we wait, suspended in Schrödinger's Brexit: both leaving and remaining. But we hope in its multiplicity of voices and rich traces of numerous performances and cultural interventions from right across the continent, this expanded volume continues to celebrate the creativity and dialogue between European theatre cultures, between directors and audiences, and between the theatre and Europe.

35

Notes

1. 'The Nobel Peace Prize 2012', Nobel Prize Committee, www.nobelprize.org/prizes/peace/2012/summary
2. The terms come from David Goodhart's (2017) unconvincing book *The Road to Somewhere: The Populist Revolt and the Future of Politics* which gained some traction due to his influence on Prime Minister Theresa May's Chief of Staff, Nick Timothy, who seems to have inspired May's unlovely coining of the term 'Citizens of Nowhere' to describe Europhile remainers.
3. In his first speech after the referendum result was declared, Nigel Farage rhetorically claimed it 'a victory for real people, a victory for ordinary people, a victory for decent people' (see Withnail 2016). 'Metropolitan liberal elite' was an accusation frequently turned on voters in the big cities, who typically voted strongly to remain in the EU. Meanwhile remainers have often characterised Brexiter claims that forging a new trade deal with the EU would be 'one of the easiest in human history' (www.bbc.co.uk/news/av/uk-40667879/eu-trade-deal-easiest-in-human-history) as 'unicorns': mythical fictions that only the immature or delusional could believe in.
4. See the 'Mission, Vision & Goals' of the ITI on their website: www.iti-worldwide.org/goals.html
5. 'XIV Edition – Regulations', Premio Europa, www.premio-europa.org/open_page.php?id=1221
6. See the Union's description of itself on its website: www.union-theatres-europe.eu/ute
7. From the interview with Donnellan after receiving the Golden Lion at the Venice Biennale Teatro 2016. www.cheekbyjowl.com/resources/golden-lion-of-venice-declan-donnellan/
8. Donald Trump has repeatedly referred to the press and media as the enemy of the people ('The New York Times reporting is false. They are a true ENEMY OF THE PEOPLE!' https://twitter.com/realdonaldtrump/status/1098218016255414272). In November 2016, the High Court ruled that the Government could not take Britain out of the EU without the consent of Parliament and the British right-wing tabloid the *Daily Mail* splashed pictures of the three judges who made the ruling under the headline 'ENEMIES OF THE PEOPLE' ('Daily Mail's "Enemies of the People" front page receives more than 1000 complaints to the IPSO') (see Pells 2016).
9. These are just three directors out of many (including Milo Rau, Tiago Rodrigues, Susanne Kennedy, Vegard Vinge/Ida Müller, Oliver Frljić, and Angélica Liddell) who could have featured here for their work redefining and reshaping theatre in Europe in the twenty-first century.

Bibliography

Addley, Esther (2016) 'Polish man knocked unconscious in "serious and unprovoked attack"', *Guardian*, 8 October, www.theguardian.com/uk-news/2016/oct/07/polish-man-knocked-unconscious-serious-unprovoked-attack-near-lancaster

Beatley, Meaghan (2019) 'The shocking rape trial that galvanised Spain's feminists – And the far right', *The Guardian*, 23 April, www.theguardian.com/world/2019/apr/23/wolf-pack-case-spain-feminism-far-right-vox

Benjamin, Walter (1940) 'On the concept of history', trans. Harry Zohn, in Howard Eiland and Michael W. Jennings (eds), *Selected Writings Volume 4: 1938–1940*, Cambridge, MA: Belknap Press of Harvard University Press, 2003, pp. 389–400.

Bilefsky, Dan (2016) 'Fatal beating of Polish man fuels debate over xenophobia in Britain', *New York Times*, 1 September 2016, www.nytimes.com/2016/09/02/world/europe/britain-polish-man-killed-brexit.html

Delgado, Maria (2019) 'Misogyny on trial: Miguel del Arco's verbatim production offers a new trial for "la manada"', *The Theatre Times*, 7 April, https://thetheatretimes.com/misogyny-on-trial-miguel-del-arcos-verbatim-production-offers-a-new-trial-for-la-manada/

Donnellan, Declan (2016) 'Golden Lion Awards – Declan Donnellan July 2016', 17 August, www.youtube.com/watch?v=Sv-61MFhlys

Goodhart, David (2017) *The Road to Somewhere: The Populist Revolt and the Future of Politics*, London: Hurst.

National Theatre (2009) 'Fiona Shaw and Deborah Warner on *Mother Courage*', Platform Performance, 8 October.

Partington, Richard (2019) 'Poles will return east to higher wages and jobs, and UK will lose out', *theguardian.com*, 24 February, www.theguardian.com/business/2019/feb/24/poles-return-east-higher-wages-job-uk-lose-brexit

Pells, Rachael (2016) 'Daily Mail's "Enemies of the People" front page receives more than 1,000 complaints to IPSO', *Independent*, 10 November 2016, www.independent.co.uk/news/media/daily-mail-nazi-propaganda-front-page-ipso-complaints-brexit-eu-enemies-of-the-people-a7409836.html

Press Association (2016) 'Polish man attacked and beaten by gang of up to 20 teenagers in Leeds', *Guardian*, 13 September, www.theguardian.com/uk-news/2016/sep/12/polish-man-attacked-beaten-gang-20-teenagers-leeds-racially-aggravated-assault

Withnail, Adam (2016), 'EU referendum: Nigel Farage's 4am victory speech – The text in full', *Independent*, 24 June, www.independent.co.uk/news/uk/politics/eu-referendum-nigel-farage-4am-victory-speech-the-text-in-full-a7099156.html

Yeung, Peter (2016) 'EU referendum: Reports of hate crime increase 57% following Brexit vote', *Independent*, 28 June, www.independent.co.uk/news/uk/home-news/brexit-hate-crime-racism-reports-eu-referendum-latest-a7106116.html

Chapter 1

ARIANE MNOUCHKINE

Activism, formalism, cosmopolitanism

Brian Singleton

Most twentieth-century European theatre directors have been indissociable from the theatre companies they have founded; no closer relationship between director and company can be found than that between Ariane Mnouchkine (b. 1939) and the Théâtre du Soleil. This symbiosis is, in part, the result of the funding mechanism for theatre companies by the French state that subsidises the individual director rather than the company as an entity. But in Mnouchkine's case this symbiosis is furthered by several important factors including the theatre space the company occupies, the nature of the company as a collective, and the direct political action in which Mnouchkine, under the umbrella of her company, has been engaged. Mnouchkine's career has always been associated with her company. She has not directed outside its aegis, and the national and international accolades her productions have garnered have placed the Théâtre du Soleil at the very forefront of international theatre practice in the past 55 years.

Mnouchkine's practice has been engaged with the political from its earliest days and humble beginnings; she has exposed the myths and ironies of France's post-Revolution democracy, indicted the social inequities of contemporary European society in terms of race, class, and gender, and latterly has examined the trauma and suffering of those caught up in the global human movement of conflict migration. As her practice has evolved, so, too, has her company over four decades; the original, a group of student friends, has been replaced with a vast cross-section of performers from all over the world who have brought with them their indigenous performing traditions. And so, with an internationalised practice in terms of form and the subjects of representation, and her personnel increasingly transnational subjects, the global brand of the Soleil has attracted large-scale funding for the supranational festival touring circuit. Further, her direct political action in the student protests of 1968, 40 years later, has shifted to the contestation of tyranny and injustice on a global scale. Ariane Mnouchkine now is no longer simply a European director; she is a theatrical activist on the world stage.

Beginnings

Travels in the Far East after her student days (where she encountered the traditional theatre forms that were to inspire her for most of her career), as well as some embryonic attempts at directing while at Oxford University and most significantly at the Sorbonne, Université de Paris III, fostered a desire to pursue a career in theatre. Without ever subscribing to a particular political ideology, Mnouchkine, growing up in occupied and post-war France in the shadow of the Algerian War, and under the influence of major existentialist thinkers such as Jean-Paul Sartre and Simone de Beauvoir, has always been 'de gauche'. Sartre was invited to be the patron of her student company l'ATEP (L'Association Théâtrale des Étudiants de Paris) that later formed the embryonic template for her professional company in 1964. When that company was formed by ten student friends it was called a SCOOP (Société Coopérative Ouvrière de Production) – a workers' cooperative in which the original ten members invested equivalent sums and shared equal status in the running of the company, without an internal hierarchy. But its title, 'Theatre of the Sun', was Mnouchkine's homage to the treatment of light in contemporary cinema.

Unlike other profit-share theatre-company directors that had driven the historical avant-garde before her, Mnouchkine neither sought investors nor solicited subscribers for her enterprise. However, she did not rely solely and idealistically on the work to be the attraction in itself. Instead, she was actively engaged with the trade-union movement in the early days of the company, offering workshops and special concessionary tickets for union members, in an attempt to completely change the demographic of her audience. Her aim was to create a 'people's theatre' (see Bradby and McCormick 1978), and she had many antecedents within the historical avant-garde since the turn of the last century, through to the post-war projects of Jean Vilar (and his Théâtre National Populaire project) as well as Roger Planchon at Villeurbanne (Lyon). Her other source of inspiration was Jacques Copeau, whose work at the Théâtre du Vieux-Colombier from 1913 to 1924 aimed to strip the theatre of its commercial excesses and its attachment to realism. Copeau's subsequent company (known as Les Copiaus) served Mnouchkine as a model in terms of its being both a theatre and a school. The members of both companies needed to sign up to the principles of a cooperative working and social existence. Thus, Mnouchkine's place within the history of French theatre is determined as much by her political views as regards the nature and conditions for the production of art as by the quality and the representation of the world in the art itself.

It is impossible to chart the emergence of a directing style for Mnouchkine without acknowledging the influence of her company on it. But it is that very notion of the collective that was the cornerstone of her company that we must first look at in order to understand better how Mnouchkine's directing practice emerged and how it impacts on her theatrical creation. In the early days of the company, like many companies before the Théâtre du Soleil, the actors only met in the evening after long and arduous days working in menial jobs to earn a living. They would come together at night in order both to train and to rehearse. Mnouchkine was the exception in that she enrolled at the École Jacques Lecoq, training in corporeal mime and then, in the evenings, she would pass on the knowledge and skills learned during the day to her fellow company members. Of course, a hierarchy swiftly developed within the creative process, but this was as much out of expediency – as well as Mnouchkine's own wish not to be an actor – as from any other motivating factor. But that early training clearly set up from the outset an acting style as well as a directing practice. Lecoq training (see McBurney 2002) very much centres around the improvised creativity and corporeal awareness of the actor. It evokes in the actor a colourful imagination and builds up an idea of character as a mask that weaves a path through various 'states' starting from the neutral mask. What role then does the director have in such an actor-centred creative process?

In order to answer this question, it is important to establish the differing traditions of the concept of director that emerged with the historical avant-garde at the turn of the last century. The English word for the job was a development of the actor-manager idea of a corporate boss with an artistic vision. In French, the *metteur en scène* implies a functionality for the role in a predominantly author-centred theatre. But it is the German word, *Probenleiter*, that Mnouchkine herself chose to adopt in the 1960s to describe her function, with its sense of someone leading rehearsals. Given the embryonic Lecoq acting method that was emerging, Mnouchkine's self-fashioned role moved away from 'staging' to stimulating actors' creativity along the lines of various masked traditions, including Lecoq as well as *commedia dell'arte*. Very swiftly, Mnouchkine moved away from the psychological meaning of the text and its subtexts to a highly presentational style that evolved eclectically over the next five decades as it encountered various masked and other corporeal performance traditions from all over the world.

Collective creation: activism

It is within this semi-egalitarian business structure and improvised working methodology that emerged a theatre practice that was to be emulated throughout the world: *création collective*. 'Devising', in English, is an inappropriate translation of the idea in the sense that it does not take account fully of the political motivations that underpinned Mnouchkine's company work. The term used by David Williams, 'collaborative', is a much more accurate term for the process (Williams 1999). After much success with a production of Arnold Wesker's play *The Kitchen* (under the title of *La Cuisine*) in 1967, in which improvised scenes of manic kitchen activity brought accolades, and a highly sensual version of *Le Songe d'une nuit d'été* (*A Midsummer Night's Dream*) in 1968, inspired by Jan Kott's book *Shakespeare Our Contemporary* (1967), Mnouchkine turned her attention exclusively for the next ten years to productions that were created collectively. It would be wrong to state that the political events of the student protests and workers' strikes of May 1968 were solely responsible for this new development in the company's practice as the working method had already been established in the two previous productions, and Wesker's exposure of the conditions of labour clearly fitted in with the working method of improvisation in the political sense. Nevertheless, the idealism that accompanied the protests and strikes and Mnouchkine's direct involvement with the uprising, and her cultural contribution to it in the form of presentations, workshops, and debates with the striking workers, was a motivating factor for future work. It was also the source of complete disillusion since the whole protest was a failure. Coming to terms with that failure, Mnouchkine also had to come to terms with the fact that her earlier idealistic view that theatre could change society if not the world was a pipe dream. Theatre may not be able to change anything directly, Mnouchkine quickly discovered, given its elitist bourgeois form, its place in wider social practices, and its very narrow demographic attraction, but it still retained for her an agency in germinating and nurturing political consciousness.

This led to a complete rethink of her theatre's future. She dispensed with classical texts for the next decade and concentrated solely on collective creation that examined major political events and revolutions in France's history as well as the contemporary conditions of existence of the people who are never the subjects of historical representation. The focus thus for the collective was a desire to construct an alternative performative narratology that stood in opposition to the grand and hegemonic narratives of national history and to focus instead on the hidden histories that collectively make up much broader social struggles. Instead of 'being' characters from history, Mnouchkine's actors would self-consciously present them. Instead of keeping their audiences in the dark they would keep them active and offer them agency. Instead of waiting for the audiences to come to them they would go out and bus them into the theatre. And, most importantly of all, they would abandon theatre buildings for ever and perform in their new home, a disused ammunitions factory (Cartoucherie) in the middle of the Vincennes forest, far away from the bourgeois comforts of the boulevard theatres (see Cramesnil 2005). Acknowledging that theatre in itself could not change anything socially or politically, Mnouchkine was offering the possibility through the experience of a demystification of the art form of theatre, that spectators might emerge into social and political realities with a renewed desire for change and a new idealism that had been shattered by the events of May 1968.

From the late 1960s and through most of the 1970s, the Théâtre du Soleil produced four devised plays, *Les Clowns* (*The Clowns*, 1969), *1789* (1970), *1793* (1972), and *L'Age d'Or: première ébauche* (*The Golden Age: First Draft*, 1975). The first and last of these were productions in clowning and *commedia* forms that dealt with the conditions of contemporary life in France with an emphasis on the pursuit of happiness and escape for the marginalised in society (women and migrant workers). The middle two plays are now celebrated by historians for their theatrically innovative retelling of the story of the French Revolution. Mnouchkine now resists discussing these productions or even watching the film she herself made of *1789*, calling the style 'simplistic' and evoking certain 'interpretative imperfections' (Mnouchkine 2005: 130). Her retrospective unease with the work of that period is as much concerned with the form of the acting as it is with the dramaturgical choices made and the political naivety of her intentions.

A multi-focused spectacle, *1789* took place on and around five raised stages. Spectators had the option to either sit on a riser or to wander around the Cartoucherie choosing their viewpoint and, more often than not, bumping into the actors either in a scene or preparing for one. This element of choice given to the spectators was a deliberate simulation of a democratic ideal that was encouraged to be taken out of the auditorium after the production. Its aim also was to show more of a process, of how theatre was created as well as how histories are constructed, rather than a finished production. Although now a film version is extant, as is a script, the production evolved over a two-year period, and, as in all true popular theatre forms, the production differed night by night.

To prepare for the production, all of the company members immersed themselves in the political and social histories of the period, in various filmic representations, and, most notably, in collections of cartoons. The actors were divided into five groups, hence the ultimate five stages in the performance, and they all followed Mnouchkine's direction that they should represent fairground workers and entertainers of the period, telling their stories of the grand narrative of the Revolution from their own political perspective. And this is how the collective creation evolved, from a consensus on the subject matter, to a direction as to the form, and in a space that was to represent a sporting arena, which was a deliberate simulation of a reception area of an alternative form of popular culture. Given the heavy emphasis on visual representations of the Revolution, and particularly the lampooning of the central figures from press cuttings, as well as the choice of fairground workers as first-level characters, it is not surprising that the entire production was a series of parodies of seminal and iconic moments from the histories of the Revolution. Actors were able to explore and master various skills of popular entertainment ancillary to theatre, such as juggling, flute playing, acrobatics, and puppetry. The result was a cacophony of often simultaneous action that broke down the barriers between the watchers and the watched and exposed very clearly history as narratology, or 'the very difficulty of reconstructing history at all' (Bradby and Sparks 1997: 23).

The first part of the production was made up of a collection of improvised scenes, right up to the popular uprising that culminated in the storming of the Bastille prison in Paris. They were all designed to demonstrate the plight of the peasant classes in the face of an ignorant and carefree aristocracy. Illiteracy, poverty, and physical suffering were primary social ills on display, and the binaries of rich and poor were exacerbated by a haunting and romantic soundtrack. In the storming-of-the-Bastille scene, actors took up positions all over the playing area and gathered neighbouring spectators around them in order to tell them their own version of the time when the prison was taken. In this 30-minute improvisation, the actors began with a whisper and ended with a triumphant shout of victory. Spectators were free to wander from one actor to another and had the possibility of building up a collective version of the events of that day. As the actors were telling the stories from their own political positions, spectators were in the enviable position of listening to alternative histories and also of making choices in whose interpretation to believe.

This was a clear exposure of how meaning is constructed by the producers of theatre and how it is open to multiple interpretations by spectators. Further, the dismantling of a singular theatrical narrative clearly could be read against the totalitarian regime from which France had been liberated in 1945. The celebratory fairground scene that followed, and bled into the interval, was also a staged moment of idealistic celebration that captured the spirit of the students during their street protests in 1968. But just as the student revolution turned out to be a disappointment, the production resumed after the celebratory interlude with actors on patrol with guns and a very large banner with the word 'ORDRE' written on it that passed through the arena pushing the spectators aside and into 'obéisance'. Here came the bourgeoisie, the true victors of the Revolution, accompanied by the National Guard to fill the power vacuum and still leave the marginalised, disenfranchised and evicted from the stage space. And, like the Brecht-inspired sequel, *1793*, two years later, the remainder of the work evoked the failure of protest and the necessity for political change to be the true marker of any revolution outside the theatre.

Despite Mnouchkine's disinclination to celebrate this work as a major part of her canonical achievement over 40 years, contemporary spectators and critics acknowledge that they had never seen anything like it before. Mnouchkine also defers to her contemporary, Italian director Luca Ronconi (Mnouchkine 2005: 132), who had offered a similar environmental experience before this in *Orlando Furioso* at the Piccolo Teatro in Milan in 1969. Nevertheless, as historians, now we must acknowledge that this approach from improvisation based on collective research was a crucial template for much of the subsequent work of the company and would inspire many imitators. Although there was no consistently discernible acting form present yet in the work, there was a heavy emphasis on the power of popular entertainment as a vehicle for a political message, as well as a focus on the disjuncture between actor and character. For audiences to 'see' the construction of character in process (from behind the scenes) was a novelty at the time. Its exposure of the narratology of dramaturgical construction put paid to charges of the apolitical in postmodern theory that was emerging contemporaneously with similar recognisable cornerstones of form.

The subsequent production, *The Golden Age: First Draft*, in many ways replicated the dramaturgical structure of the history plays and also the environmental experience of the audience. Set in contemporary France and following the life of Abdullah, a North African migrant worker, the play exposed widespread corruption, social inequality, and racism. As they followed the story, spectators were taken on a journey up and down four craters covered with brush matting and again were left in no doubt as to the company's Marxist politics. Yet the most significant thing about the production was the very clear emergence of a distinctive acting form, rooted firmly in *commedia dell'arte* style with recognisable *commedia* masked characters. Thus, the contemporary had a formal appearance in a now-lost theatrical tradition that once was popular and improvised. Although Lecoq-inspired mask work drove the company in its early days, in many of the productions it simply was not visible in terms of an acting form, save perhaps for *The Clowns* in 1969. The choice of *commedia* was Mnouchkine's in the same way as was the fairground trope of *1789*. Mnouchkine explains the choice of *commedia* as a form: 'Only the most coded theatres like the commedia dell'arte, or the Chinese theatre, can really make visible and significant what the habitual prevents us from seeing' (Mnouchkine 2005: 131–2). This was the turning point for the company and for Mnouchkine as a director. That search for a form for the theatre was to reside for the next 30 years in the lost theatre of Europe (*commedia*) or the still extant traditional theatres of Asia. While retaining the collective approach to invention, despite the subsequent reintroduction of classical and contemporary dramatic texts, actors would then apply their own form of presentational acting starting from the masks of various traditions.

Oriental formalism

Much has been written about the subsequent 25 years of the company's creativity and Mnouchkine's directorial style in respect of her inspiration from oriental theatre forms. She herself has often been quoted as saying that the theatre is by definition 'oriental' because of the 'theatricality of form' (Féral 1998: 227) encountered in the Orient. Jean-François Dusigne clearly situates within the company itself the motivation for the work of that period. The Orient is cited as the cradle of European inspiration for the modern theatre (Dusigne 2003: 28), and a collection of examples of Mnouchkine's predecessors is assembled, from Max Reinhardt's use of pseudo-*hanamichi*, through to the philosophical musings of Antonin Artaud, inspired by Balinese and Cambodian dancing, the influence of Mei Lan Fang on Brecht, and the essays by playwright and diplomat Paul Claudel on the traditional theatres of Asia. Mnouchkine's borrowing, not only of the plastic surfaces scenographically in terms of settings and fabrics but, more importantly, her acquisition of some of the skills of various Asian acting traditions, firmly situate her within the European tradition of Orientalism in the theatre. Orientalism as a practice in literature and the theatre was a nineteenth-century trend, particularly prominent in art, fashion (costumes, interior design, architecture), and numerous cultural forms (most particularly in opera and musical comedy). However, it is also the name given to a body of scholarship at the height of the two European empires (Britain and France) that dominated world trade in the late nineteenth century. As a direct result of world economic and military domination, that scholarship, of course, was not only necessary for the perpetuation of domination but it also harboured personal fantasies and anxieties vis-à-vis the Orient. This anxiety/desire dialectic was always the motivating factor of the European popular theatre (in pantomime, melodrama, and musical comedy) with a safe distance being advocated between Us and Them. Further, the Orient figured as a Europe in oriental fancy dress onto which desires not permissible in rigid Western societies could be projected.

Mnouchkine's theatre obviously fits into that mould in terms of its plastic inspiration, but not politically, and certainly not in terms of the reformative mission that motivated the look to the Orient in the first place. Mnouchkine's obsession with the Orient comes very much from the same motivation that Dusigne lists (2003), namely the desire to rejuvenate theatre by searching for the very roots of theatrical traditions still extant. Those traditions, of course, had died out in Europe, or were resurrected, such as in *The Golden Age*, as a modernist invention. Far from keeping a distance from the Oriental sources, Mnouchkine visited many Asian countries from the end of her student days and all the way through her 'Orientalist' period, inviting master practitioners to give workshops and performances in her theatre and bringing her acting company on tour to see the conditions of creation at first hand.

The first of those Orientalist productions came in the form of a cycle of three Shakespeare plays performed in repertory and toured all over the world between 1981 and 1984. Two history plays, *Richard II* (1981) and *Henry IV (Part One)* (1984), were sandwiched together with one comedy *La Nuit des rois* (*Twelfth Night*, 1982). For the cycle, just one raised stage was used, but added to it were two long *hanamichi* runways as long as the stage itself which provided for spectacular entrances and exits. And, throughout the production, Jean-Jacques Lemêtre's live soundtrack from a collection of over 3,000 instruments from all over the world (not all used for the same production of course) followed the action, punctuated it, gave rhythm to it, and spoke in a musical and rhythmical dialogue with the actors, as he had followed the rehearsals and built up his score during them. This was all very much in keeping with the many theatre traditions of Asia. The actors wore a motley collection of costumes, some with Asian masks, others with whitened faces, and nearly all with brightly coloured fabrics draped around the body as kimonos and other Asian garments.

Apart from the plastic Orientalism thus described, it was in the acting form that the Orientalism was at its most potent and reformative. Following on from the *commedia* tradition of speaking lines directly to the audience rather than to another character on stage while the listening character looked directly at the speaking character, Mnouchkine built up a form of presentational acting which she called '*jouer frontal*': 'Every time in rehearsals the actors spoke to each other, it didn't work. I would say to them: Tell the audience!' (Déprats 1982: 10). This front-on mode of presentation of the text led to a very declamatory form of line delivery. This created a distance between the actor and the text and completely avoided all tendencies to 'become' the character in some act of psychological immersion (see Féral 1995). Through the scenes, the non-speaking actors reacted to the speaking actor in a series of improvised hand gestures or body movements. The result was a visual staging of sub-text and an exteriorisation of inner psychology. Actors were trained to visualise in the audience the people or objects they were talking about, and thus they were able to create a geography of the imagination in the audience and include us in the dramaturgical construction. The court scenes in the history plays were performed mostly in this manner with courtiers adopting, from the Beijing Opera, the characters of 'centaurs' (Miller 2007: 83) so that man and his mount were one and the same, and indeed the horse became the mask that dictated the behaviour and physicality of the character.

This form of *'jouer frontal'* came from a working method rooted firmly in masked traditions, from *commedia*, through Lecoq, to Beijing Opera, Kabuki, and Noh. The mask determined what Mnouchkine calls an *'état de base'*, a basic state that dictates all action and emotion (see Singleton 1993, 1994). As the play proceeds and the characters encounter others and new situations, the actors move through transitory emotional sub-states while never losing the primary basic state. All of these sub-states are exteriorised. Instead of the mask revealing emotion, it demands emotion to be exteriorised. It is not only a form of storytelling but also an example of stage formalism. As a working method it relies for the most part on the improvisatory abilities of the actors. And it is at this point of methodology where the form relates back to the creative impulses of collective creation. Mnouchkine's role was to establish a working form and then to harness the improvised scenes into a coherent set of visual images consistent with the overall aesthetic of that form. While the Shakespearian purists derided the absence of character psychology, many critics stood amazed at the creation of one of the most consistently spectacular forms ever witnessed on the European stage. Many of the subsequent productions continued the practice, such as in *Les Atrides* (1990–3), a tetralogy of plays by Aeschylus and Euripides on the House of Atreus, including *Iphigenia at Aulis*, *Agamemnon*, *The Libation Bearers*, and *The Eumenides*. Instead of the *hanamichi*, an entrance was created underneath the seats as a vomitorium. The Chorus was constituted by a dance troupe, forever present on stage, reacting to the principal action and dancing out their fury, inspired by numerous Asian traditions, including

Thai dancing. With the same motivation that drew Mnouchkine to Shakespeare, she went back to the source of Western drama to find a textual 'epic' in order to present a historically conscious staging of otherness that contextualised 'the *cultural production* of orientalism as a semiotic process in the way that epic theater has taught' (Bryant-Bertail 2000: 175). Sarah Bryant-Bertail's analysis situates Mnouchkine's use of otherness not as representation but as a means through which textual heritage might be uncovered. This is also similar to Françoise Quillet's idea of the link by Mnouchkine between the Orient and archaeology (Quillet 1999: 97).

One of Mnouchkine's greatest directorial triumphs and perhaps the pinnacle of achievement in terms of the creation of a new acting form was in the production of Hélène Cixous's play, written specifically for the company, *Tambours sur la digue* (*Drums on the Dam*, 1999). Prior to rehearsals proper, Mnouchkine led the whole company, including the technical staff, on a tour of the Far East. The result was a particular focus on the Japanese puppet tradition of *bunraku*. The story was a pseudo-mythical medieval tale, set in China, of political corruption and the deliberate sabotage of a dam that drowned an entire city. But it was the acting form that attracted most critical attention. Each principal character was the creation of two, and most times three, actors, one playing the character and two *jojuri* (acting assistants or puppeteers in black), who simulated at times, moving the actor's body as if it were a puppet (see Plate 1). The actor thus had to simulate the separation between the human form and its movement and the puppet's simulation of them. With two 'puppeteers', the actor was then also, like a puppet, able to perform extraordinary feats beyond the capability of the human, such as fly into the air, jump effortlessly onto a ramp, and glide backwards offstage. The result was a spectacular physicality that was more formalist than any of the previous Orientalist acting styles. As a final *coup de théâtre*, a central trapdoor was discreetly lowered to allow the stage to be flooded; and as the actors disappeared into the shadows, smaller puppet versions of their characters were drowned.

Between the Shakespeare cycle, the ancient Greek cycle, and the physical triumph of form in Cixous's *bunraku* play, there were many other Orientalist productions, most of them written by Cixous, rooted in historical fact, since the reason to return to the textual heritage of Europe was to find the tools necessary to tell stories of the grand passions and pains of the contemporary world. Such plays focused on the abdication of King Sihanouk and the subsequent destruction of the population of Cambodia by the Khmer Rouge (see Kiernander 1993), as well as the struggle for independence for India in 1947. One of the plays, *Et soudain les nuits d'éveil* (*And Suddenly Nights of Awakening*, 1997), even parodied the company's political activism, dealing with a theatre company harbouring Tibetan refugees under threat of deportation from France. Most of this work, while retaining a definite scenographic Orientalism, could never be truly formalist in its presentation for several reasons. First, the subjects represented were too recent and the living characters too mediatised to offer the possibility of being formalised. Second, it was felt too inappropriate to Orientalise an Orient that had been possible with the medieval and Greek mythological characters of the plays above. Instead, the acting style gave way to a reflective, almost Brechtian, approach that was reminiscent of the style and form of *1793* set against an exotic scenographic alterity.

Transnational cosmopolitanism

Summing up over 50 years of the journey undertaken by the Théâtre du Soleil in terms of theatrical practice, it is very easy to identify collective creation and an Orientalised acting form as the foundations of a working method. Of course, that method evolved over time. What remained constant throughout, however, has been Mnouchkine and her company's political activism that has motivated significantly the choice of material, the working method, and the dissemination of productions through touring. An interest in and engagement with Oriental theatre forms (and other popular acting traditions) has also been a constant throughout the working life of the company. The subjects of representation, one could argue, have shifted from largely French concerns to those of a transnational dimension. One such play, *Le Dernier Caravansérail* (*The Last Halting Site*, 2003), is perhaps the best example of the continuing international and cosmopolitan outlook of Mnouchkine's practice (Melrose 2006: 121). Featuring a collection of improvised scenes (of collective creation) over a period of seven hours of theatre time, the production told multiple stories of the refugees and asylum seekers of economic and conflict migration on a transnational basis.

In many respects, collective creation as a form of theatre might be read as an anachronism in a world of globalised culture where vestiges of traditional cultures are bought as local and sold as global. Neoliberal ideology maintains that all barriers and borders to the movement of goods, labour, and capital should be abolished; yet in practice economic globalisation thrives on exploiting statutory and regulatory differences between nation-states. The assembly of actors from all over the world, and the international touring policy of the Théâtre du Soleil, might also be read under the similar terms of globalisation as well as a form of cosmopolitan culture that is 'drawn from a variety of cultural repertoires [and from] traces and residues of many cultural systems, of many ethical systems' (Hall 2002: 26).

One of the last halting sites referred to by the play's title was the Red Cross refugee camp in Sangatte, near the Channel Tunnel, that had acted (from 1999 to 2002) as a waiting room for those crossing to England. Flitting back and forth geographically to the sites of conflict and the transit stops of the migrants, the collective political through-line was a huge indictment of neoliberalism and its endorsement of the nation-state as an enforcer of borders and controls on movements of people while goods and services are ensured free global passage. While the characters journeyed illegally (without passports) and were transnationally stateless, the destination countries devised Kafkaesque methods of thwarting entry. The scenes were devised from transcripts of interviews recorded by Mnouchkine herself, Hélène Cixous, and Jacques Derrida in various detention centres in France and Australia. A narrative voice-over and a symphonic soundtrack directed our sympathies against nationalism at its most totalitarian in religious terms (the Taliban in Afghanistan) to the most controlling in secular terms (Australia and France). This world on the move, representationally in terms of subject, met up with the formal dynamics of a theatre company well used to roaming ideationally across cultures. Much of the political driving force behind the production was idealistic, in the same way as *1789* several decades previously invited the social struggle to continue beyond the theatre. But in this instance, challenging the nation by transgressing its borders was portrayed as an affront to the state. The nation-state, therefore, and not the nation per se, was the object of the critique.

Many of the improvised scenes in *The Last Halting Site* were 'collected' while on tour with *Drums on the Dam* in Australia in 2002. And here lies the ironic double bind of transnational culture in a globalised economy. With actors performing reimagined versions of source cultures in a company funded by the global capital of the international touring circuit (most international festivals are funded by global companies), Mnouchkine and her company stand as an anomaly and an irony. While the Théâtre du Soleil is able to tour the world as ambassadors of a national culture to other national cultural forums funded by global capital, her subjects represented on that tour, in the case of *The Last Halting Site*, were those on whom global capital both depends and of whom it is fearful. Economic migration is the life blood of many European national economies, bringing in as it does cheap labour from Eastern Europe into the high-wage economies of Western Europe to drive down the cost of production and increase the profits for shareholders. But that other form of migration, that of illegal conflict migration, brings with it an expectancy of state subvention from the national economy and a 'state' classification of little economic 'use-value'. And it is a form of migration not favoured by global corporations that depend on population stability (and therefore border controls) because in the developing world it gives them a captive low-wage labour force. Mnouchkine's assembly of scenes ignores the legitimate forms of migration and focuses on the abuses inherent along the trade routes that link a largely prosperous West with an impoverished and embattled East. That journey exposes the migrants to the worst excesses of the transactions of capital in the form of bonded labour and prostitution to which state laws and borders have no answer. At the bottom of the ladder, like the 'actors' drowned in *Drums on the Dam*, the migrant workers living and working in atrocious conditions in *The Golden Age*, and the peasant classes after the French Revolution, the stateless in *The Last Halting Site* are the victims of economic and social inequity.

The exploration of globalism and modernity took a new turn in the company's 2010 production *Les Naufragés du Fol Espoir* (*Castaways of the Mad Hope*), a collective creation based loosely on a posthumous novel of Jules Verne (*Les Naufragés du Jonathan*). Here the practice of film-making in its earliest silent era was simulated on stage to create a new postmodern form as the process of making was in as much view as the subjects being filmed. The Cartoucherie was refashioned as a *guingette*, a turn-of-the-last-century restaurant/dance hall whose attic had been converted into a film studio. The audience enter the world of early cinema through the lens of a contemporary student who is researching popular entertainment before the First World War and her discoveries are played out in the attic where the first film being shot is of the Mayerling Incident of 1889 (the murder of Crown Prince Rudolf of Austria, heir to the Austro-Hungarian empire but who left no heir himself), a murder that destabilised Europe and ultimately led to the First World War. The political premise of the fledgling film company in the Mad Hope soon becomes clear through savage attacks on the conjoining of capitalism and nationalism. And so the production moved to the southern hemisphere on a ship containing both colonising industrialists and hardened criminals to the Tierra del Fuego. *Castaways of the Mad Hope* not only critiqued imperialism and colonialism from a political perspective, but also revealed through the folding of live theatre practice with simulated film-making, the political elision of postmodern interculturalism and its precursor, orientalism.

In the second decade of the twenty-first century, Mnouchkine revisited Shakespeare in a production of *Macbeth* in 2014 using the simulation of contemporary technologies to tell the stories, with a similar political impulse as in *Castaways of the Mad Hope*, of exposing how the contemporary frames of storytelling and newsmaking in relation to medieval history and early modern theatre expose the realities of corrupt political systems. Allegorical of the contemporary, in terms of the rise of the figures of the alt-right in Western societies stoking populist fears, the production also was a premonition of the ubiquitous bloodshed as a consequence of warped religio-political ideologies. And those ideologies framed Mnouchkine's next production. While researching in Pondicherry, India, in November 2015, news of a coordinated ISIS-sponsored terrorist attack in Paris, and the murder of spectators at the Bataclan theatre, profoundly affected Mnouchkine, and led to a crisis of confidence about what could be staged in light of such violence in a cultural venue. The resulting production in 2016, *Une Chambre en Inde* (*A Room in India*), staged that dilemma. The play opens with the director's assistant, Cornélia (played by Hélène Cinque), fast asleep when the telephone rings; it is a call that will change her life. The director of the company Lear, prompted by news from Paris, has run amok and defiled a statue of Ghandi, and it is up to Cornélia to lead the company to its next production. What follows is a series of staged dreams in which stories and characters from world cultures (from religious epics and the theatrical world canon – from Shakespeare to Chekhov) come to life all around the sleeping Cornélia. Interspersed among these are anxious visions about the contemporary world, from ecological disasters to terrorism and the Syrian war in particular. Emerging thematically from the loose episodic structure of the collected scenes is the disempowerment of women in multiple world contexts. And thus the theatre that Cornélia eventually decides upon comes in the staging of two scenes from the Hindu epic *The Mahabharata*, 'The Rape of Draupadi' and 'The Death of Karna', scenes that emphasise the agency of women. The assemblage of cultures on display in this production was the culmination of 55 years of exploring the classical traditions of world theatre and searching for universal truths about the human condition. And it is also symptomatic of the company's cosmopolitan make-up and its renown on the international touring circuit.

The international renown of the company certainly attracts a good deal of tourist spectators to the Cartoucherie but, I would argue, the company's work remains distinctively French. The period of collective creation in the 1970s was exclusively focused on French concerns, that exposed France's relationship with the rest of the world in terms of its empire, as a post-monarchical drive for the maintenance of class division mapped onto race (from *1789* to *The Golden Age*). The texts of Shakespeare in translation permitted the exploration of a working method, without the trappings of

English scholarly and production traditions, to explore more contemporary histories of the collapse of empire in the latter half of the twentieth century. And the entire project, since 1981, of exploring otherness in terms of an acting form, and the social and cultural conditions of those forms, was turned to analysing the restoration of new empires of global capitalism that use the border controls of nation-states selectively to fix rates, duties, and markets and that engineer conflicts to promote neoliberal concepts of 'democracy' in order to increase profit margins. In many respects, *The Last Halting Site* was the confluence of the multiple strands of the company's work (collective creation, formalism, cosmopolitanism). Throughout, Mnouchkine's work on masks from various traditions de-essentialised gender, exposing its constructedness and, once exposed, revealing the hegemonic forces of both traditional and secular societies, from the First to the Third World, and from East to West, as patriarchal. In *Les Éphémères* (2006), a collection of scenes tracing individual lives in the shadows of the concentration camps, the company presented its first trans-sexual character, an American from the Midwest seeking acceptance in 'liberal' Paris. But what he discovered was social isolation and bigotry that harked back to the experiences of Abdullah, the migrant worker in *The Golden Age*. Like the migrants in *The Last Halting Site*, Mnouchkine highlights otherness as difference that even the so-called liberal societies marginalise. And perhaps this is an indicator as to the whole political project of the Théâtre du Soleil in terms of theatrical presentation. While Mnouchkine formed an artists' defence association in 1979 (Association Internationale de Défense des Artistes (AIDA)) following a trip to Chile, gave refuge to Tibetan refugees under threat of deportation (in 1996), acting as the Church might have done in former times, signed protests and actively participated in demonstrations against injustice in many forms (see Mnouchkine 2005: 94–109), the focus of her theatrical creation has been on the acceptance of difference in terms of class, race, gender, and sexuality. While the company has toured under the aegis of global capital, its versions of revolutions, tyrannical regimes, and the great waves of history outside the control of the individual, it is the lives of the ordinary people, with all their aforementioned subjectivities, about which Mnouchkine has been concerned. The micro-politics inscribed in the micro-histories of the individual (sometimes without a name or a nation) have collectively made up the large canvases of the epic productions that Mnouchkine has toured all over the world. Playing otherness culturally and theatrically, thus, has been the working method for the ultimate portrayal of difference (in real social terms) that is affirmed and celebrated.

Five key productions

1789. Collective Creation. Set design by Roberto Moscoso. Perf. Philippe Caubère, Myrrha Donzenac, Gérard Hardy, Jean-Claude Penchenat. Cartoucherie, Paris. 12 November 1970.

Richard II. By William Shakespeare. Set design by Guy-Claude François. Perf. John Arnold, Georges Bigot, Cyrille Bosc, Philippe Hottier. Cartoucherie, Paris. 10 December 1981.

Les Atrides (*The House of Atreus*, Aeschylus' *Oresteia* prefaced by Euripides' *Iphigenia in Aulis*). Perf. Simon Abkarian, Georges Bigot, Juliana Carneiro de Cunha, Nirupama Nityanandan, Catherine Schaub. Cartoucherie, Paris. 16 November 1990.

Le Dernier Caravansérail (*The Last Halting Site*). Collective Creation. Set design by Guy-Claude François. Perf. Maurice Durozier, Sava Lolov, Serge Nicolaï, Ducio Bellugi Vannuccini. Cartoucherie, Paris. 3 April 2003.

Une Chambre en Inde (*A Room in India*). Collective creation. Perf. Ducio Bellugi-Vannuccini, Hélène Cinque, Maurice Durozier, Dominique Jambert, Nirupama Nityanandan. Cartoucherie, Paris. 5 November 2016.

Bibliography

Bradby, David and John McCormick (1978) *People's Theatre*, London: Croom Helm.

Bradby, David and Annie Sparks (1997) *Mise en Scène: French Theatre Now*, London: Methuen.

Bryant-Bertail, Sarah (2000) *Space and Time in Epic Theater: The Brechtian Legacy*, Rochester: Camden House.

Cramesnil, Joël (2005) *La Cartoucherie: une aventure théâtrale*, Paris: L'Amandier.

Déprats, Jean-Michel (1982) 'Le Besoin d'une forme: entretien avec Ariane Mnouchkine', *Théâtre/Public*, 46–7 (July–September): 8–11.

Dusigne, Jean-François (2003) *Le Théâtre du Soleil: des traditions orientales à la modernité occidentale*, Paris: Centre National de Documentation Pédagogique.

Féral, Josette (1995) *Dresser un monument à l'éphémère: rencontres avec Ariane Mnouchkine*, Paris: Théâtrales.

—— (1998) *Trajectoires du Soleil autour d'Ariane Mnouchkine*, Paris: Editions Théâtrales.

Hall, Stuart (2002) 'Political Belonging in a World of Multiple Identities', in Steven Vertovec and Robin Cohen (eds), *Conceiving Cosmopolitanism: Theory, Context, and Practice*, Oxford: Oxford University Press, pp. 25–31.

Kiernander, Adrian (1993) *Ariane Mnouchkine and the Théâtre du Soleil*, Cambridge: Cambridge University Press.

Kott, Jan (1967) *Shakespeare Our Contemporary*, London: Methuen.

McBurney, Simon (2002) 'Foreword', in Jacques Lecoq, Gabriel Carasso and Jean-Claude Lallias (eds), *The Moving Body: Teaching Creative Theatre*, trans. David Bradby, London: Methuen, pp. ix–x.

Melrose, Susan (2006) '"Constitutive Ambiguities": Writing Professional or Expert Performance Practices and the Théâtre du Soleil, Paris', in Joe Kelleher and Nicholas Ridout (eds), *Contemporary Theatres in Europe: A Critical Companion*, London and New York: Routledge, pp. 120–35.

Miller, Judith G. (2007) *Ariane Mnouchkine*, London: Routledge.

Mnouchkine, Ariane (2005) *L'Art du présent: entretiens avec Fabienne Pascaud*, Paris: Plon.

Picon-Vallin, Béatrice (2018) 'Review of *Une Chambre en Inde*', *Théâtre du Blog*, 18 March, http://theatredublog.unblog.fr/2018/03/18/une-chambre-en-inde-creation-collective-du-theatre-du-soleil-dirigee-par-ariane-mnouchkine/

Quillet, Françoise (1999) *L'Orient au Théâtre du Soleil*, Paris: L'Harmatton.

Singleton, Brian (1993) 'Mnouchkine's Shakespeare: A Textual Record of A Theatre's Practice', in Nicole Vigouroux-Frey (ed.), *Traduire le théâtre aujourd'hui*, Rennes: Presses Universitaires de Rennes, pp. 111–27.

—— (1994) 'Mnouchkine and Shakespeare: Intercultural Theatre Practice', in Holger Klein and Jean-Marie Maguin (eds), *Shakespeare and France*, Lewiston, NY, Queenston, Ontario and Lampeter: Edwin Mellen, pp. 307–26.

—— (2014) 'Performing Orientalist, Intercultural, and Globalist Identities: The Case of *Les Naufragés du Fol Espoir* by the Théâtre du Soleil', in

Erika Fischer-Lichte, Torsten Jost and Saskya Iris Jain (eds), *The Politics of Interweaving Performance Cultures: Beyond Postcolonialism*, New York and Abingdon, Oxon: Routledge, pp. 77–94.

Williams, David (ed.) (1999) *Collaborative Theatre: The Théâtre du Soleil Sourcebook*, London and New York: Routledge.

Chapter 2
PATRICE CHÉREAU

Staging the European crisis

David Fancy

The figure of the director has played a sustained role in the elaboration and investigation of the national imaginaries of Europe's constituent states, with 'first-wave' directors such as Firmin Gémier and later Jean Vilar in France contributing to the continued theatricalisation of the discourse of modern sovereignty, republican tradition, and national prestige with the founding and development of organisations such as the Théâtre National Populaire (Kruger 1992: 26–7). Directors' energies have not only been harnessed for the benefit of *national* prestige and legitimation, however. Indeed, the history of theatre in a country such as France is marked by an extensive array of festivals and organisations promoting the internationalisation of French theatre, such as the Théâtre des Nations and the Festival d'Automne, launched in the 1960s and 1970s respectively. These initiatives can be understood to serve as bridges to recent activity destined to reach a more focused international constituency. Highly visible European directors including Italian Giorgio Strehler have noted that in a climate of increasingly self-reflexive globalism directors can and must use theatre as a means of invoking important Europe-wide debates on the issue of European legitimation, what Strehler described as 'our common [European] humanistic culture which today is suffering a profound crisis' (Delgado and Heritage 1996: 268). The crisis observed by Strehler and others only intensified with the resurgence of populist nationalisms across the continent from the mid 2010s onwards. Theatrical explorations responding to such realities are complicated by the fact that contemporary Europe is in fact understood to be the 'New Europe', a slippery designation that Janelle Reinelt notes with Derridean flair can be considered to be 'an unfilled signifier, an almost-empty term capable of endless mutations and transformations' (Reinelt 2001: 365).

French theatre, film, and opera director Patrice Chéreau (1944–2013) is a particularly potent example of an artist who was always resolutely 'European' in various aspects of his creative practice, including the source and themes of many of the texts and libretti he staged and the films he made. The crisis of European humanistic culture Strehler referred to is, Chéreau might have argued, a rather long-standing one. From his early productions alongside director Jean-Pierre Vincent at the Lycée Louis Le Grand in Paris (1959–63), Chéreau's work embodied, with great dialectical energy, the major European theatrical as well as ideological questions and tensions of the times.[1] His first professional productions at the municipally subsidised Théâtre de Sartrouville (1966–9) were animated to a significant extent by the notion of theatre as *service public*, a vision articulated by the leaders of the post-war *décentralisation* movement in the French theatre. In addition to organising considerable para-theatrical programming such as conferences, expositions, and training/pedagogical opportunities, Chéreau's stagings at Sartrouville bore evidence of a desire to engage critically with plays such as Lenz's *Les Soldats* (*The Soldiers*, 1967) and Molière's *Dom Juan* (1969) in a way that shed light on the texts' own histories, as well as explored the relationship between theatricality and the complexion and arrangements of political power in European modernity. Attributed with having revived an interest in Marivaux, Chéreau also showed since those early years a fascination with the political and intellectual debates of the European *siècle des lumières*, the German high Romantic *Sturm und Drang*, and an attraction to Wedekind, Hoffman, and Wagner.

Chéreau was an artist who was notably reflexive about as well as haunted by the questions of legitimacy of his own practice:

> I've always had serious doubts about the usefulness of what I am and what I do. Not in the moment of doing, mind you: in the doing I rediscover my confidence. But in a general way, and this has never really changed, I've never really been able to answer questions like: is it useful? Can the theatre still be worthwhile?

> Is creating productions a necessary and essential activity? Isn't it useful just for those who do it and a few others?
>
> (Laurent 1991: 34)

These questions and the tensions they engender were evident in Chéreau's evolving approach to his stagings. The 1970s saw a peripatetic journey to Strehler's Piccolo Teatro in Milan, an invitation by Roger Planchon to co-direct the Théâtre de la Cité in Villeurbanne outside Lyon, a number of films, and a famous staging of Wagner's *Ring Cycle* (1976–80) at the Bayreuth opera festival, which engaged with themes around the emergence of the Industrial Revolution. During this period, Chéreau's earlier Brechtian-inflected stage practice – including extensive textual interventions and scenography filled with light – gave way to darker, more crepuscular designs, *mises en scène* flaunting theatre's full power of illusion, and flamboyant depictions of decadent societies on the verge of collapse. Chéreau's work was traditionally marked by a tremendous visual splendour achieved in conjunction with the collaboration of his long-term designer, Richard Peduzzi, a working relationship the director once likened to 'two painters working on the same tableau' (Benhamou 2001: 341). As a result, Chéreau found himself in the midst of the famous *querelle des images* during the 1970s – an ongoing discussion that raged for ten years in French theatre following the student and labour demonstrations of May 1968 – concerning the relative importance of the director's individual creative vision in relation to his or her socially critical impulses. During the *querelle*, left-leaning critics such as Bernard Dort of the Brechtian and Barthesian traditions found Chéreau's emphasis on the visual to be irresponsible and self-indulgent (Dort 1979: 342), although Dort points out that others in the popular press hailed Chéreau to be 'the best of our stage painters' (1979: 344). Indeed, a variety of Chéreau's French contemporaries, such as Ariane Mnouchkine or Armand Gatti, pursued with more vigour than Chéreau various political and politicised forms of film and theatre to respond to the critical social changes of the past 50 years – many of them Europe-wide in their manifestation – that coincided with the careers of the 'second wave' of major European directors. Nonetheless, Chéreau's work bore evidence of a desire to trace the tributary tensions at the heart of European modernity that flooded out into the alluvial plain of global violence, ecocide, and social unrest that characterised the twentieth, and now the twenty-first, centuries.

In the 1980s, during his tenure at the Théâtre Nanterre-Amandiers (1982–90) just outside of Paris, Chéreau's career was marked by a famous collaboration with playwright Bernard-Marie Koltès whose work, along with that of other playwrights of the time such as Michel Vinaver, in many ways further opened French dramatic writing to important questions around Europe's relationship with its former colonies and recent immigrants. So significant was this collaboration for Chéreau that when asked in 1995 about the state of contemporary French writing, he wondered 'What could there be after Koltès?' (Chéreau 1995: 62); and indeed much of his energy thereafter was directed towards film and less towards stagings of opera and theatre.

Charlotte Canning notes that traditional 'developmental reviews' (2005: 49) of the theatre-history narrative, such as Toby Cole and Helen Krich Chinoy's *Directors on Directing: A Source Book of the Modern Theatre*, focus on the director as a sole heroic individual (usually male). She writes that this 'historicization process has been (and continues to be) a disciplinary demonstration of power marked by the concomitant political operations of personal, geographical, and institutional identifications and affiliations' (Canning 2005: 49), with this chapter necessarily being a manifestation of both the maintenance and questioning of traditional underpinnings of the 'developmental review'. In the same way then that Canning asserts that a director is 'not a person but a disciplinary constellation of power' (2005: 57), the Europe in which directors such as Chéreau operate and address in their works is also heavily marked by a multitude of discursive and organisational investments. Indeed, what can be described as the current crisis of European legitimation began to emerge over the period of time leading up to and including Chéreau's career. The European Common Market that had been founded in 1957 was consolidated over subsequent decades by additional trade deals, as well as social, legal, and nascent representative political arrangements, reflecting the extent to which 'the forces driving market integration, in order to achieve hegemony, have necessarily promoted the introduction of new, compatible identities to achieve coherence within the emerging European social body' (Scott-Smith 2003: 261). Whereas Europe's constituent nation-states experienced a significant degree of popular participation in the late nineteenth and early twentieth centuries as universal suffrage, labour rights, and other democratic goals were pursued during the construction of the welfare state, no comparable development has occurred in Europe since 1945. As Cafruny and Ryner have noted of the European Commission's use of the term *democratic deficit*, 'during the [EU's] first thirty years, working class parties and trade unions either actively opposed the EU or were absent at its creation' (Cafruny and Ryner 2003: 3). Indeed, the 'personalised characters of traditional European nation-state sovereignty, associated with the idea of a *government*', were substituted 'by a more diffuse, and hence impersonal, idea of multi-layered *governance*' (Bellamy and Castiglione 2005: 309), resulting in an 'apparent inability of the political machinery to give expression to a common will' (2005: 300). This actuality is abetted by a problematic record on the delivery of goods and services (Reinelt 2001: 368), with Cafruny and Ryner concluding that 'if the EU is indeed a polity, it is, in Philippe Schmitter's words, a "novel form of domination"' (2002: 3).

With these broad contextual considerations of the director and of Europe in place, we might ask: in what ways does the figure of the director, itself potentially as much of an 'unfilled signifier' as the 'New Europe', contribute to the perpetuation of the broader social, cultural, political, and scholarly structures and discourses that permit its own continued existence in the European context? More specifically, to what extent does Chéreau, in the presentation of major tensions informing Europe's development in his stagings, representationally reaffirm a variety of European macro-political and cultural trends that he ostensibly sets out to critique, and in so doing thereby both facilitates the sustained development of those tendencies and the continuation of the particular 'disciplinary constellation of power' which is the director? Although there are many 'Chéreaus', I will discuss this question in relation to three influential stage productions and one film: Marivaux's *La Dispute* (1973, remounted in 1976), the production of Koltès's *Combat de nègre et de chiens* (*Black Battles with Dogs*, 1983), his film *La Reine Margot* (1994), and his production of Racine's *Phèdre* (2003).

La Dispute and the erosion of Enlightenment values

In a public address given in the spring of 1976, Michel Foucault traced a growing counter-reaction over the preceding ten to fifteen years in Europe and its former colonies to the consolidation of capital and its concomitant structures of discipline. He characterised the period as one marked by 'what one might term the efficacy of dispersed and discontinuous offensives' against capital's totalising effects in which he noted 'a sense of the increasing vulnerability to criticism of things, institutions, practices, discourses' (Foucault 1980: 80). It is precisely this context of criticism of contemporary domination, combined with a keen eye for European history, that fuelled Chéreau's pursuit, in a variety of productions, of an investigation of the specifically European emergence of certain broad manifestations of institutionalised subjection. Chéreau's cruelly precise exploration of certain forms of domination was in particular evidence in his production of Marivaux's *La Dispute*, first staged in Paris in 1973, a year after the opening of the renewed Théâtre National Populaire (TNP) in Villeurbanne, a theatre for which Chéreau was co-director along with Robert Gilbert and Roger Planchon. Following a number of years creating iconoclastic productions of classic texts for the Odéon-Théâtre de France (*Richard II*, 1970), the Spoleto Festival, the Piccolo Teatro in Milan (Wedekind's *Lulu*, 1972), and the Théâtre de la Cité in Lyon-Villeurbanne (Marlowe-Vauthier's *The Massacre at Paris*, 1972),[2] the Parisian press were, not surprisingly, interested to discover whether Chéreau, previously the Brecht-inspired 'breaker of the classics, the *enfant terrible*' of the popular theatre, had not suddenly become a theatrical 'prince charming' (Dort 1979: 154) with the new very spectacular 1973 Marivaux production.

Written in 1744, this play is the story of a rather extreme behaviouralist experiment pursued to determine whether or not men or women are the first to commit sexual and emotional infidelity. An older couple, the Prince and Hermione, have had an argument concerning this question, and the Prince unveils the results of an experiment devised 20 years earlier following a similar discussion: a previous generation of royals have had four adolescents, two of either sex, raised in isolation from each other (and the world). The youths are released into a simulated Garden of Eden while the older couple observe them from a distance. It is not long before self-interest, jealousy, and desire find their way into the garden, and the Prince concludes that neither sex can claim superiority over the other.

Despite other relatively recent productions of Marivaux texts in France by directors such as Vilar's *Le Triomphe de l'amour* (*The Triumph of Love*, 1956) and Planchon's *La Seconde Surprise de l'amour* (*The Second Surprise of Love*, 1959), the Parisian theatre-going public was not prepared for Chéreau's surprising vision of a text that had been considered by critics to be a minor work. Those attending Chéreau's production familiar with the staging conventions for Marivaux may have perhaps first noted a remarkable break from *marivaudage*, the lively back-and-forth élan of Marivaux's romantic comedy. Whereas traditionally Marivaux might have been presented with such a rhythm, Chéreau pursued a significant incursion into the play's metatext that resulted in all aspects of the production, including the delivery of the text, being presented with a much more sinister and lugubrious tone. Also, while Marivaux wrote a comedy about infidelity, Chéreau added a 40-minute prologue consisting of a montage mostly of texts from other Marivaux plays and reoriented the production towards an investigation of the dangerous character of an instrumentalist rationality run rampant, manifested in the type of thinking that motivates the potentially cruel and dehumanising experiment the Prince undertakes with the youths.

A clear metatheatrical design paradigm complemented the self-reflexive quality of the text and performance of the prologue. What would become, with the start of the play proper, the upstage world of the experiment on the youths was separated from the far downstage area of observation by an orchestra pit emitting thick multi-coloured smoke and light. Placed on this foregrounded area was a large comfortable leather chair, mirrors, and an orrery which began to revolve when light from the grid struck it indirectly through the mirrors. The overall picture generated was one of a world of reflection emphasising the increasing centrality of science set in counterpoint to the Eden-like paradise inhabited by the adolescents on the upstage area behind the orchestra pit where enormous walls moved seemingly on their own through the space, cutting and blocking perspective (Dort 1979: 154). Contrary to Chéreau's earlier productions, such as *Dom Juan* (1969), where the stage machinery, visibly operated by stage hands and extra characters, metaphorically suggesting the manipulation of the mechanism of power and sovereignty, was bathed in blinding light reminiscent of Brecht's lighting strategies, the stage for *La Dispute* was marked by ambiguity, an oneiric dark space, and an interiorisation and rendering-invisible of the control of the machine that critics noted shared elements of Robert Wilson's *Deafman Glance* (1970).

How had his turn away from elements of a Brechtian orthodoxy that had been a determining quality of left-oriented French theatre in the 1960s affected Chéreau's critique of the emergence of European rationalism at the heart of his production of *La Dispute*? Marivaux's somewhat whimsical comedy on the nature of infidelity became, in Chéreau's hands, an accusation laid against the *siècle des lumières*. The schism between the two worlds of the 'natural' environment of the adolescents and that of the variously cultured aristocrats, itself split along gender lines, would become the focus of the production, with the question of infidelity quickly ceding its place to broader philosophical investigations. Indeed, whereas a final encounter between these two worlds is part of Marivaux's text, Chéreau's version emphasised bifurcation by amplifying the difference and distance between them. Chéreau had the actors playing the characters of the youth released into their false Eden emphasise an 'improper' delivery of the Marivaudian language, suggesting that their 'education' in becoming a 'civilised' adult was actually an exercise in becoming feral. This effect of the degradation of nature through its contact with the detached reasoning and experimentation of the Prince was perhaps most manifest in the character of the Prince himself. He became increasingly savage and sadistic throughout the production, ultimately finding himself trapped in the cruel world he had helped engender, unable to escape back across the drawbridge over the orchestra to the place from which he could observe and judge with comfort and objectivity. Like Nietzsche, Chéreau recognised the anti-life force operating in the Enlightenment, with the character of the Prince acting out a hyperbolic response to this reality by means of a Sadeian *chronique scandaleuse*.

This exploration, staged as it was in the wake of the 1968 student riots and the general upheaval discussed by Foucault a number of years later, became an allegory for how the education system in France of the day, and the wider society in which it was couched, was failing youth by allowing the dominant bourgeois liberalism of the period to mask a significant will to power. Indeed, Chéreau explained around the time of *La Dispute* that:

> I'm thinking increasingly of qualifying, for my own usage, an aesthetic category that would be the allegory, in the way in which it was understood by certain sixteenth-century painters or authors (such as Lope de Vega, when he stages the heresy of Spain). I believe paradoxically, however, that the theatre is a location where you can see ideas and abstractions most clearly, where ideology becomes concrete.
> (Chéreau 1973: 11–12)

However, some notable slippages occurred in the course of the concretisation of the allegory: the extension, augmentation, and amplification of the metaphor of education in which the narrative embodied on stage was intended to be viewed symbolically.[3] With the world of the theatre become a snare, a '*lieu piège*' as Bernard Dort described it (1979: 154), a potent mix of the concrete and the abstract operated in the scenography: actual trees and vegetation functioned in a 'realistic' register existing alongside the split downstage and upstage worlds that invokes the symbolic divide between the natural and the cultural. Chéreau's concerns about the validity of theatre as an art form began to manifest themselves in this major post-Brechtian production with the suggestion that the reflexivity and inquiry of which the theatre is capable serves only as a means of falling prey to the theatre's many pitfalls and snares, that social and cultural prognosis is impossible via the theatre, and that the art form is constitutionally unable to function as a means of prying apart the complexity of social reality.

Black Battles with Dogs[4] and residual colonial desire

On the evening of 1 February 1983, a capacity crowd gathered at the government-subsidised Théâtre Nanterre-Amandiers in the Parisian suburbs to see Chéreau's staging of *Black Battles with Dogs* (1983) by Bernard-Marie Koltès, the first large-scale production in France of a text by a playwright whose work, in large part because of Chéreau's stagings, would become known throughout Europe over the course of the following decade. Koltès had witnessed the production of *La Dispute* as a young artist and felt very strongly that he wanted to write work for Chéreau to stage. A significant outcome of the aesthetic revolution Koltès experienced in response to Chéreau's work was what the playwright would describe as a 'realist hypothesis' (Koltès 1983: 37). Up until the writing of *Black Battles with Dogs*, Koltès's recurrent use of vaguely fantastical or undefinable settings for his plays – oneiric multi-spatial locations, a post-apocalyptic New York, a nondescript street corner – and his general avoidance of traditional plot lines resulted in plays which were decidedly unrealistic. This was all to change with *Black Battles with Dogs*, however. Written in part in response to Chéreau's use of stage allegory in *La Dispute*, Koltès was inspired to write the play by a brief trip to Africa in 1978 – a voyage which had left him overwhelmed at the imbalances of power between the so-called First and Third Worlds and disgusted by the behaviour of fellow French nationals living in Africa (see Koltès 1997). *Black Battles with Dogs*, like *La Dispute*, deals with the convergence of two worlds: in this case, those of the European petty bourgeois and the African 'Bush'. Central to this meeting is Koltès's depiction of whites as invaders and blacks as a source of noble resistance to such an incursion onto 'native' soil. The story involves a black man named Albury, unwise to the ways of white Europeans, who tries to reclaim the body of his dead brother killed under suspicious circumstances on a French-owned industrial site somewhere in post-independence West Africa. He is persistent in his demands for the body from the white characters – an engineer named Cal, the compound manager Horn, and his partner Leonie – in the face of their mendacity, cruelty, and racism. Alboury is honest, firm, and rooted in his people and place. He is unspoiled by the corrupt ways of the European characters and yet, when he is pushed too far, retributory violence soon follows. The play finishes when Alboury's black comrades guarding the industrial compound shoot and kill the white man responsible for the death of their brother. Like the fireworks that Horn ignites at the end of the play which briefly illuminate the sky before being smothered by the African night, the white characters flicker momentarily in this ageless landscape before fleeing from, or dying at the hands of, the blacks.

Chéreau was interested in *Black Battles with Dogs*, Dort has suggested, in part because the text permitted him to continue his search for the *théâtre allégorique* in which, as Chéreau had explained it, 'the ideas would ultimately release some emotion, as a result of the beauty of the production' (Dort 1988: 12). Additionally, Chéreau was attracted to the anti-Eurocentric valence in Koltès's writing, and was also taking up the encounter between Europeans and their colonial subjects in a production of Genet's *Les Paravents* (*The Screens*) – a text that deals with the French presence in Algeria – at Nanterre-Amandiers during the same season. If, as Chéreau suggested in his first ruminations about the use of allegory, 'the theatre is a location where you can see ideas and abstractions most clearly, where ideology becomes concrete' (1973: 11–12), then which ideological stances are embedded in the text of *Black Battles with Dogs* and in what ways were they in evidence in the production?

Clearly, the risks of exoticising 'otherness' – here, non-white ethnicity – are immense. In Koltès's text, Alboury's initial naive simplicity – the anchor of his resistance to the sophisticated and corrupt Western whites – incarnates a simplistic Rousseauian vision of the noble savage before giving way by the end of the piece to another role frequently given to the 'native' in colonialist discourse: that of the savage enabler of a primitive murderous retribution. Chéreau's production did little to challenge what is most likely the unintentional racism of the text and the director may have in fact been attracted to the text's exoticising elements. Indeed, Koltès's vision of the timelessly resistant and punitive role of the blacks in the face of the whites dovetails snugly with Chéreau's previous violent juxtapositions of the utopian and the dystopian in productions such as *La Dispute*. The production's complicity with Koltès's colonial representation of blackness occurred in a variety of ways, including the lack of any of Chéreau's famed textual interventions that could have served to historicise Koltès's misguided attempts to reposition blacks in a role of heightened 'authenticity', a hyper-realistic design, as well as Chéreau's rehearsal process that privileges a revelation of the actor's 'true self' to fuel the role he or she is playing. Again as with *La Dispute*, a less than subtle anti-historicism manifesting itself as a rhapsodic eschatology emerges from the ostensibly 'historical' allegorisation. As a result, Alboury remains a reductive projection, and the play's ostensible critique of ethnocentrism and colonialism is hoist with its own petard.

La Reine Margot and national nostalgia

La Reine Margot (1994) is a filmic adaptation, starring Isabelle Adjani, of Alexandre Dumas's novel (1845). It consists of the story of Marguerite de Valois, daughter of Henry II and Catherine de Medici, wedded in 1572 to the Protestant king of France, Henri de Navarre, in a marriage orchestrated to put an end to decades of religious war and rivalry. The religious wars were only to continue, however, after the St Bartholomew's Day Massacre of the Protestants, and Marguerite would become an object of suspicion because of her mixed allegiances to her Protestant husband and Catholic siblings. Her story has attracted significant popular, scholarly, and artistic attention in France, not least as a result of the misogynist and sexist myths of her alleged nymphomania, sorcery, and Machiavellian nature. Such myths emerged as part of the Protestant attack on the royal family, providing her with 'the dubious honour of being one of the most vilified women in history' (Sluhovsky 2000: 195). Historian Moseh

Sluhovsky provides a concise examination of Margot's representation as a sexualised caricature of a woman in Chéreau's award-winning film, despite the director's assertions that he was attempting to produce a 'Margot for the 90s', a 'liberated and modern woman' (Sluhovsky 2000: 201). Sexuality was no longer to be portrayed as a locus of shame but rather a source of emancipation. However, Margot's sexuality in the film is depicted solely as an acquisitive and objectifying drive, in which Margot rapaciously searches for fresh sexual encounters. Her fling with a nameless lover she finds while prowling the streets causes her immediately to be transformed into a woman in love, enacting male fantasies about being able to 'tame' and 'reform' a woman with one's advanced sexual prowess.

With respect to these questions of the affirmation of traditional gender roles in such a film, Brigitte Humbert explains that the way in which we tell stories of the past are frequently marked by gendered identity in relation to national discourse:

> Can Chéreau's homosexuality account for the ambiguities of the film when it comes to gender discourse, in spite of Thompson's collaboration? Or is it, as Geneviève Sellier contends [...], that his vision is in no way as personal as he seems to believe, but in great part influenced by a general cultural tendency in twentieth century France to depreciate the notion of emancipation as a reaction to the emergence of women in the political sphere?
> (Humbert 2002: 233)

She concludes by suggesting that, rather than attempting to demystify a tale that has become part of French collective memory and identity, 'Chéreau and [screenwriter] Thompson, on the contrary, have offered a beautifully acted and filmed, but very traditionally derogative vision of women in power' (Humbert 2002: 233). In a fashion similar to the xenophobia in *Black Battles with Dogs*, Chéreau's film is freighted with hesitancy in the face of the enfranchisement of politically under-represented women and the concomitant possibility of increased democratisation integral to the political potentials of the new Europe.

A second interest in the Margerite de Valois story for Chéreau was its potential for allegorisation. Once again, Chéreau compresses years of historical events into a shorter but indeterminate period of time over an unspecifiable series of locations in order to be able to mine the story for contemporary resonance, and thus, according to Adjani, 'reach the collective unconscious' (Humbert 2002: 226–7). The film shines a light on aspects of France's recent past, with the image of naked bodies evoking the experience of the Holocaust. CNN-style shooting and a soundtrack by Serbo-Croatian musician Goran Bregović allow the film to resonate with events contemporaneous to the film's release, such as the war in Yugoslavia.

What then are some of the implications of Chéreau's use of a story based on historical events in France as an allegorical anchor intended to resonate with pan-European events and struggles? Any discussion of Chéreau and Europe must take into account Chéreau's reality as a French citizen and the way in which 'Frenchness' manifests itself in his work. It is clear that, just like the concept of 'Europe', the French 'nation', Lawrence Kritzman writes, 'can no longer be observed from the perspective of a "horizontal gaze" that overdetermines the existence of an undifferentiated social conglomeration' (Kritzman 2000: 19). Rather than viewing French culture from the perspective of the Hegelian tradition, as a 'monolithic entity of synthesised contradictions' (Kritzman 2000: 19), we must understand it to be an 'ongoing series of agonistic relationships founded on the competition for symbolic values' (2000: 19). Kritzman explains that 'the distinctly French concept of *fraternité*' derived from the *Declaration of the Rights of Man*, had been used, following the French Revolution, 'to ensure the creation of the universal in terms of cultural and political issues; it established France's place in the community of nations as a country capable of realizing the legitimate representation of the "general will"' (2000: 19). Viewed through this lens, Chéreau's telling of the story of Margot and her family can be understood to represent a deployment of what many French citizens regard as a monument of national heritage (Humbert 2002: 224). Humbert informs us that François Mitterrand, determined to use 'the filming of France's historical and cultural past as a form of national education' (Humbert 2002: 224), subsidised through Jack Lang's Ministry of Culture what have come to be known as 'heritage films' (Humbert 2002: 224). Humbert discusses Chéreau's filmic style, suggesting it gives 'preponderance to character over setting, to the individual over society, to passion over politics, [...] highlighting the human condition and violence at its most extreme' (Humbert 2002: 223). *La Reine Margot*'s emphasis on intrigue among aristocrats leaves a contemporary French audience, one living in a liberal democracy, to understand themselves in the light of who they no longer are. Such an emphasis can be understood to deploy a nostalgia designed to comfort a public feeling somewhat concerned about a too-rapidly-evolving European context.

And neither does the film provide the audience with an opportunity to understand in any detail the historical moment in which the courtly machinations are occurring. Although Chéreau's allegorical model is ostensibly about drawing a relationship between past and present, *La Reine Margot* evacuates history in such a way that the film's emphasis then becomes about resituating and reinscribing arguably conservative national monuments into the present European landscape. Kritzman reminds us that 'the idea of nationhood is engendered by a nostalgic reflection, articulated through the disjunctive remembrance of things past. The quest for memory is therefore an attempt to master the perceived loss of one's history' (2000: 20).

La Reine Margot can be seen to reference a Europe whose future is uncertain, a vacuum into which various competing national myths are being inscribed with renewed vigour. Chéreau's role in playing a mediating function between constructions of a constituent nation and a new Europe reflects a range of theorisation about the continent's political future. Commentators such as Richard Bellamy and Dario Castiglione track and contest the many familiar arguments that would suggest that the 'processes of globalization and social differentiation have undermined the state's claim to sovereignty' or that the future lies with 'new forms of political and social order that take us below and beyond the sovereign nation-state, to regional blocs regulated by a cosmopolitan legal system based on individual human rights' (Bellamy and Castiglione 2005: 293). Such positions suggest that, as far as Europe is concerned, 'imperatives of both a functional and a normative nature impel the creation of an ever closer Union' (Bellamy and Castiglione 2005: 293). Auguring the current rise in populist nationalist sentiment throughout Europe, Bellamy and Castiglione 'believe these reports of the nation-state's demise to be exaggerated' (2005: 293), stressing that impacts of global forces have been far from uniform and that what have come to be the normative claims of national cultures actually show few signs of a reduction in their power of persuasion. They assert that 'the capacity of the nation-state to act as the primary locus of administrative, legal and political power and authority may have been weakened but not necessarily in ways that point in a cosmopolitan direction' (Bellamy and Castiglione 2005: 293). Rather than simply migrating to a *supranational* platform, Europe's 'state' is, in their view, rather one in which 'both the allegiances of citizens and their forms of economic, social and political interaction' have 'become a complex mixture of the subnational, national and supranational' (Bellamy and Castiglione 2005: 293).

Phèdre and French classicism at the heart of Europe

Evidence from Chéreau's case suggests that, given that the nation seems destined to continue to play an important role within the context of a federally arranged Europe, the figure of the director will continue to be necessary as a cultural legitimator, continuing to embody metonymically the relationship of sovereignty and nationhood. As we have seen in the historical emergence of contemporary Europe, legitimacy for the continental political arrangement has been 'top down' and induced primarily by bureaucratic and trade imperatives when viewed in comparison with the more populist desires for cultural cohesion and social justice that contributed to the emergence of the nation-state. As the shared culture across Europe has traditionally not been a popular but rather a high culture (Reinelt 2001: 368), mobilising cultural capital in a European context means appealing to that high culture. It follows that the artistic work of a director with European scope such as Chéreau's might then necessarily be involved in an antagonistic and 'top-down' inscription of national heritage into the space of European cultural legitimation. One then wonders whether Chéreau's textual choices in the twenty-first century, such as *Phèdre* (2003), unmarked by any of the textual intervention/contextualisation of the first phases of his career, contribute to a certain vision of European integration by positing the timeless quality of French, and by extension 'European', classics.

Chéreau's production of *Phèdre* ran through the winter and spring of 2003 in the cavernous Ateliers Bertiers as part of the Odéon Théâtre de l'Europe season. The austere warehouse setting, previously used only to build the decorations of the Odeon and the Opéra-Comique, was matched by Richard Peduzzi's minimalist scenography, with an alley performance consisting of two rows of audience facing one another. Annie Coppermann described the location as 'a kind of dark concrete runway similar to a highway pavement, where the actors, accompanied by the circles of the spotlights, get closer or move away in a very precise choreography' (Coppermann 2003). One end of the space featured a royal palace in the form of a stone wall complete with a large triangular classical Greek pediment, the only semiotic anchor into the reality of the place and time of the text's source. At the other end: broken down and mismatched contemporary chairs. In this large and oppressive location Chéreau pursued a resolutely contemporary approach to the delivery of the language of the rhyming alexandrines.

What would have led Chéreau, who when he was 30 famously swore off ever staging rhyming alexandrins – a staple of French classical dramatic texts – to return to this persistent of forms so late in his career? Indeed, *Phèdre* was the first full theatre production he had undertaken since his remount of Koltès's *Dans la solitude des champs de coton* (*In the Solitude of the Cotton Fields*) in 1995 (see Plate 2). In the time between the productions, he explained that he had come to the realisation that 'if I've been able to have Koltès' language heard and understood, his particularly complex language that hides the truth, maybe there's a way I can have Racine heard and understood' (Chéreau 2003). Chéreau's way forward ultimately involved having the text delivered in a fashion unconstrained by what he felt were limiting theatrical conventions:

> I respond well to a few alexandrins, like everyone. I don't respond well to this false, scary music that I hear every time

I hear a tragedy. I mean the 'music' that you are used to from high school, which goes 'tatata, tatata, tatata, tatata.' And then it starts again, 1,600 times over. The problem is that you cannot *hear* anything through this music. [...] With *Phèdre*, I tried to tell myself, naively, 'What do I hear? What do I understand? What do I not understand?'

(Ibid.)

In order to 'hear' the text, Chéreau pruned it in parts with a view to intensifying and accelerating the action of the story that involves the disastrous consequences of Phèdre's love of her stepson Hippolytus. Chéreau also discovered that the 1677 edition of the text was much clearer than later versions from the eighteenth and nineteenth centuries that had introduced colons and semi-colons to help actors know when to breathe. 'The difference only plays on punctuation,' Chéreau explained, 'but it is essential. It breaks the false musicality, and it allows us to better understand each line's meaning' (ibid.). A highly physical performance from Dominique Blanc as Phèdre, operating in tandem with the less constrained delivery of the text, resulted in a character 'tortured, in pain, and shaking' (Lafargue 2003) with her forbidden love. Similarly, other characters such as Hippolytus (played by Eric Ruf) and his father Theseus (Pascal Greggory) were generated via untraditional and highly physical performances, ones accentuated by contemporary costumes that revealed much of the bodies of the actors playing them. These factors, combined with the actors' choreography in proximity with the audience, all contributed to a high level of intimacy in the otherwise cavernous space.

As with much of his previous work, productions that railed against insidious social mores and conservatism that would suppress and minoritise those outside the social majority, Chéreau explained that the main exploratory impulses informing his production of *Phèdre* was a wish to unmask 'repression of desire and guilt in the face of pleasure':

Phèdre says there is a crime. But there is no crime. Phèdre is bursting with an unfulfilled desire and a life of horror. For years, she has thought about Hippolyte continuously. She adored him on the altars instead of worshipping the gods, she feigned hatred to drive him away, she was exiled [...]. During all this time, she led a double life, raising the children Theseus fathered with her, always hiding her true desire. She thinks that desire is a crime. But she did not kill anyone.

(Chéreau 2003)

For Chéreau, betraying one's own desire is the ultimate crime. It is notable that he further explored this theme in his final staging of opera, Strauss's *Elektra*, in the summer of 2013 at the Aix-en-Provence festival. Deeply attracted to Strauss's modernist revisioning of the classical Greek story of a woman seeking revenge for her father's murder by her mother, Chéreau once again generates a simultaneously spectacular and intimate context in which to explore Elektra's estrangement from the mother she seeks to kill. As in *Phèdre*, a powerful emotion born of complex sources in this case drives the character to an unyielding desire for some form of justice in an unbearably cruel world, a desire with which Chéreau signals he sympathises via Evelyn Herlitzius's sympathetic portrayal of the character (Bofill 2016). The extent to which pursuing an ethical vision of desire as the final arbiter of social truth in *Phèdre* and *Elektra* manifests an acquiescence to an apolitical and subjectivist order on one hand, or a destabilising and revolutionary libidinal release on the other, remains a pivotal question in the ongoing evaluation of Chéreau's body of work.

Central to this engagement will necessarily be the fact that a yearning for a simpler, less explosive connection between people marked Chereau's final theatre production, Norwegian Jon Fosse's *I Am the Wind*. With echoes of Beckett, the text – featuring two characters named The One and The Other at sea on a raft – recedes from the discursive proliferation of a text like Koltès's *In the Solitude of the Cotton Fields* in favour of a bleak Bergmanesque encounter replete with silences, sounds, and laconic exchanges. Staged at the Young Vic in the spring of 2011 and transferred to the Avignon Festival in the summer, Chereau desired to work with the text in English in part to avoid comparisons: he noted that it was his wish 'that my shows do not bear too much resemblance to one another'

(Festival D'Avignon 2011). Additionally however, Chéreau observed that 'with British actors who can propose a different way of listening to Jon Fosse's language, a language, the author often points out, consists more in rhythm than in meaning' (ibid.). The sight of two men, bereft of all prospect of survival, floating at sea in the middle of Richard Peduzzi's water-filled set, using simple language and visceral effect to bring attention to their loneliness and to the potentials of love was not only the vision of a body politic in its rawest form, but a passionate expression of the essence of some of Chéreau's longest lasting affections and collaborations: with Richard Peduzzi, with Pascal Greggory, with Bernard-Marie Koltès ...

Chéreau, Europe, the future

Loren Kruger may well be right when she suggests that theatrical nationhood of the type seen in nineteenth-century Europe, alongside the growth of mass political parties and the rise of national politics deployed in the project of shaping and containing energies of a recently mobilised 'lower class' population (Kruger 1992: 3), will most likely not arise in the context of *le tout Europe* for a variety of reasons – not the least among these the more variegated, fractured, and diffuse notions of identity and class affiliation amongst contemporary European populations. Directors, however, are nonetheless well positioned to continue their forays into reflexive interventions around notions of a 'European' identity, however marked by national concerns these propositions may be. Additionally, if ongoing calls for the recognition of theatre's relevance as an influential site for counter-hegemonic formulations of identity and social formation in Europe (see Reinelt 2001) sound somewhat unconvincing on account of the increasing prevalence of other popular and more cost-effective media, it would appear to be quite likely that the director function – in the Foucauldian sense of 'author function' (Rouse 1992: 147) – will endure. It may be that the day has not yet passed for this notion of a representative individual who stands in for the work of a creative team as the apex of authorial intentionality and anchor of bourgeois humanist subjectivity. The director function, perhaps because of its media-ready and profoundly identitarian nature, will continue to be fetishised by a cultural and critical industry fuelled and subtended by festival marketplaces and cultural tourist industries thirsty for acts and individuals of distinction. Neither can we forget that sub-state, state, supra-state, or post-state structures seek, as part of a tradition as old as the first manifestations of the state itself, to deploy cultural products as a means of increased legitimation of their founding principles and visions of future prosperity.

Viewed in this context, Chéreau's elegant and paroxysmic theatre could perhaps ultimately be read as a decadent 'answer-in-kind' to the turbulent aesthetic and political circumstances in which he found himself creating over the course of his career. It is entirely possible that this director's excoriating pessimism will, with the benefit of further retrospect in some (not so?) distant future, be taken to have been a particularly prescient necrology, a kind of wry and visceral gallows humour destined for an unwitting Europe rushing headlong towards the global cliff top of an ecological, political, and cultural implosion of its own.

Five key productions

Dom Juan. By Molière. Stage design by Patrice Chéreau. Perf. Marcel Maréchal, Gérard Guillaumat, Roséliane Goldstein, Jacques David, Alexis Nitzer, Jacques Debary, Michèle Oppenot. Théâtre du Huitième, Lyon. January 1969.

La Dispute. By Pierre de Marivaux. Stage design by Richard Peduzzi. Perf. Roland Bertin, Norma Bengell, Véronique Silver, Micheline Kahn, Elizabeth Kaza, Madeliene Marie, Lubov Nusser, Mabel King, Theresa Merrit. First version, Théâtre de la Musique, Paris (Festival d'Automne) 24 October 1973 (second version TNP, Villeurbanne, 24 April 1976; third version, National Theatre, Belgrade, 18 September 1976).

The Ring Cycle. By Richard Wagner. Stage design by Richard Peduzzi. Perf. Donald MacIntyre, Jerker Arvidson, Heribert Steinbach, Heinz Zednik, Eva Randova, Rachel Yakar, Ortrun Wenkel, Zoltan Kelemen, Wolf Appel. Bayreuth Festival. 1976–80.

> *Combat de nègre et de chiens*. By Bernard-Marie Koltès. Stage design by Richard Peduzzi. Perf. Michel Piccoli, Philippe Léotard, Sidiki Bakaba, Myriam Boyer. Théâtre Nanterre-Amandiers, Nanterre. 22 February 1983.
>
> *Phèdre*. By Racine. Set design by Richard Peduzzi. Perf. Nathalie Bécue, Dominique Blanc, Christiane Cohendy, Michel Duchaussoy, Pascal Greggory, Marina Hands, Eric Ruf. Odéon-Théâtre de l'Europe aux Ateliers Berthier, Paris. 15 January 2003.

Notes

1 See Bradby (1997: 75) for a list of productions by Chéreau.
2 The TNP reopened in May 1972, after a number of years being closed for renovations, with this production.
3 I have kept the French title for the sake of consistency. Both *La Dispute* and *La Reine Margot* are often referred to in the English-speaking world by their French titles.
4 Roger Fowler notes that 'allegory's distinctive feature is that it is a structural, rather than textual, symbolism; it is a large-scale exploration in which problems are conceptualised and analysed into their constituent parts in order to be stated, if not shown' (Fowler 1987: 6).

Bibliography

Bellamy, Richard and Dario Castiglione (2005) 'Building the Union: The Nature of Sovereignty in the Political Architecture of Europe', in Dimitrios Karmis and Wayne Norman (eds), *Theories of Federalism*, New York: Palgrave Macmillan, pp. 293–310.

Benhamou, Anne-Françoise (2001) 'Patrice Chéreau: la chair du visible', in Béatrice Picon-Vallin (ed.), *La Scène et les images: les voies de la création théâtrale*, 21, Paris: CNRS, pp. 341–61.

Bofill, Antoni (2016) '*Elektra*: Patrice Chéreau's Testament,' *Opera Online*, www.opera-online.com/en/columns/xavierpujol/elektra-patrice-chereaus-testament

Bradby, David (1997) 'Bernard-Marie Koltès: Chronology, Contexts, Connections', *New Theatre Quarterly*, 13 (49): 69–90.

Cafruny, Alan and Magnus Ryner (eds) (2003) *A Ruined Fortress? Neoliberal Hegemony and Transformation in Europe*, Oxford: Rowman & Littlefield.

Canning, Charlotte (2005) 'Directing History: Women, Performance and Scholarship', *Theatre Research International*, 30 (1): 49–59.

Chéreau, Patrice (1973) 'La Mousse, l'écume', *Travail théâtral*, 11 (April–June): 3–26.

—— (1995) 'L'Entretien de Inrocks: Patrice Chéreau', *Les Inrockuptibles*, 8–14: 60–5.

—— (2003) 'Pourquoi et comment monter *Phèdre* de Racine,' interview with Brigitte Salino, *Le Monde*, 14 January.

Coppermann, Annie (2003) 'Des Purs moments de théâtre,' *Les Echos*, 27 January.

Delgado, Maria M. and Paul Heritage (eds) (1996) *In Contact with the Gods? Directors Talk Theatre*, Manchester: Manchester University Press.

Dort, Bernard (1979) *Théâtre en jeu: essays de critique 1970–78*, Paris: Editions du Seuil.

—— (1988) 'A double tranchant: Patrice Chéreau', *Théâtre en Europe*, 17: 4–13.

Festival D'Avigon, Archives (2011) www.festival-avignon.com/en/shows/2011/i-am-the-wind

Foucault, Michel (1980) *Power/Knowledge: Selected Interviews and Other Writings*, New York: Pantheon.

Fowler, Roger (ed.) (1987) *A Dictionary of Modern Critical Terms*, London: Routledge.

Godard, Colette (1977) 'Patrice Chéreau: Poets Invent the Future', *TDR: The Drama Review*, 21 (2): 22–44.

Humbert, Brigitte (2002) 'Emotion, Modernization, and Female Emancipation in Patrice Chéreau's *Queen Margot*', *Quarterly Review of Film and Video*, 19 (3): 223–35.

Koltès, Bernard-Marie (1983) '"Des lieux privilégiés", Interview with Jean-Pierre Han', *Europe*, 648: 34–7.

—— (1997) 'Lettre d'Afrique', *Europe*, 823–4: 13–22.

Kritzman, Lawrence D. (2000) 'Identity Crises: France, Culture, and the Idea of a Nation', in Marie Le Hir and Dana Strand (eds), *French Cultural Studies: Criticism at the Crossroads*, Albany, NY: State University of New York Press, pp. 11–28.

Kruger, Loren (1992) *The National Stage: Theatre and Cultural Legitimation in England, France and America*, Chicago, IL: University of Chicago Press.

Lafargue, André (2003) '*Phèdre*: la passion, enfin!', *Le Parisien*, 28 January.

Laurent, Anne (1991) 'Rencontres avec Patrice Chéreau', *Théâtre/Public*, 101–2: 33–41.

Pavis, Patrice (1983) 'Pour une *Dispute*: analyses émiologique de la mise en scène de Patrice Chéreau', *Australian Journal of French Studies*, 20 (3): 361–89.

Reinelt, Janelle (2001) 'Performing Europe: Identity Formation for a "New" Europe', *Theatre Journal*, 53 (3): 365–87.

Rouse, John (1992) 'Textuality in Theater and Drama: Some Contemporary Possibilities', in Janelle Reinelt and Joseph Roach (eds), *Critical Theory and Performance*, Ann Arbor, MI: University of Michigan Press, pp. 146–57.

Scott-Smith, Giles (2003) 'Cultural Policy and Citizenship in the European Union: An Answer to the Legitimation Problem?', in Alan Cafruny and Magnus Ryner (eds), *A Ruined Fortress? Neoliberal Hegemony and Transformation in Europe*, Oxford: Rowman & Littlefield, pp. 261–83.

Sluhovsky, Moshe (2000) 'History as Voyeurism: from Marguerite De Valois to *La Reine Margot*', *Rethinking History*, 4 (2): 192–210.

Chapter 3

LEV DODIN

The director and cultural memory

Peter Lichtenfels

The Maly Drama Theatre, based in St Petersburg, has for more than 35 years had a major impact on theatre within the old Soviet Union and the new Russia. Today, wherever the Maly Drama Theatre visits, audiences are eager to see them. The company is celebrated for the kinds of play it has developed from the classical prose and dramatic literary repertoire, magnificent detail in the acting, high production values, and an exceptional ensemble structure. This recognition revolves around the artistic director, Lev Dodin, who was born in Siberia in 1944 and became director in 1983. Dodin trained at what is now the St Petersburg Academy and went on to train most of the actors within the Maly Drama Theatre, a family that he has created.

In many ways, the Maly Drama Theatre could be considered the first new theatre of post-Soviet Russia. The first internationally toured production, to Toronto in 1987, was *Stars in the Morning Sky* by Alexander Galin, which has gone on to play all around the world and has established a pattern for Dodin's theatre direction. Plays remain in the repertoire for many years and continue the same values from production to production. Audiences know the high quality of the acting and staging, and the exploration in depth of themes and interpretation. *Stars in the Morning Sky* deals with the removal of sex workers from Moscow's streets just prior to the 1980 Olympics and their temporary relocation within a rural community.

Brothers and Sisters by Fyodor Abramov (1984) is possibly the Maly Drama Theatre's best-known production in the international theatre community and continues to tour. The play has an ensemble of 40 actors and looks at a community in Siberia during the Second World War. It follows the lives of characters as tensions rise in their community between those who believe in the Soviet ideal and others who do not. There is a primal level in the play about how you cope with deprivation. Soviet audiences recognised this as central to their existence, and, after the Soviet Union's collapse, with the great poverty and mismanagement of the economy in the new Russia, the production took on a new energy. At the same time, for audiences around the world, the question of how to survive on a personal level against a background where so many people live in deprivation has proved pertinent and meaningful.

Lev Dodin has sometimes been compared to his erstwhile contemporary Yuri Lyubimov in terms of their detailed attention to acting and their eye for design and ensemble environments, yet there is a significant difference. Unlike Lyubimov, whose energy was predicated on being anti-Communist, and whose fate was therefore closely entwined with the Communist Party, Dodin's production of *Brothers and Sisters* (1985) was celebrated as the first post-Soviet production, anticipating perestroika, by openly examining Russia's history during Soviet rule. In that sense, Dodin and the Maly Drama Theatre had already gone beyond reacting to Communist rule. While Dodin eschews the political, he is certainly politically engaged, becoming a strong critic of Soviet Union involvement in Afghanistan and, later, Russian involvement in Chechnya. He is also concerned that Russians never openly examine their history and are therefore in danger of repeating its mistakes. Hence, alongside productions such as *Stars in the Morning Sky* and *Brothers and Sisters*, there are examinations of Russian history during Soviet times with Fyodor Abramov's *The House* (1980), *Gaudeamus* (1993, based on Sergei Kaladin's 1988 novel *Construction Battalion*), and Vasily Grossman's *Life and Fate* (2007) (see Plate 3). Dodin wouldn't claim he was doing political plays but that he is looking at the imperfections, fears, cruelties, and hopes of people, and getting at Russian history through communities, via their 'soul', sex, food, and arguments. He looks at the characters from the cradle to the grave and then places them in a cultural situation, rather than using character to exemplify cultural issues. Although one critic argues that Dodin takes tough subjects but stages them beautifully and makes them seductive (Smeliansky 1999: 393–4), this can be politically powerful just as much as it may work against any concept of agency or change.

Dodin's productions often find a central metaphor or image to tell the story, such as the pool of water in Anton Chekhov's *Play Without a Title*, better known in English as *Platonov* (1997). The visual clarity in both his direction and the sets he uses may be another reason why Dodin's productions are readily accessible to non-Russian audiences. Audiences also understand the primary structure of nineteenth-century realism that inhabits many of his productions, although there are striking exceptions, such as his celebrated *Gaudeamus*, which looks at the life of Soviet army conscripts who are required to build, clean, and tear down latrines, in a series of non-linear segments and scenes.

Dodin works on productions until he thinks they are ready. This can be just a few months or years. He tells a story of directing Chekhov's *Three Sisters* in the early 1990s and after many months having a run through and deciding they needed to begin again (Cavendish 2005). On the other hand, Chekhov's *Uncle Vanya* (2003) was produced in under 50 rehearsals. In most of Dodin's productions there is a unity of time and place in a stage picture. This insisted-upon and hard-earned way of working enables the depth and qualities of the acting and other production values to develop. Theatre critics invariably comment on the freshness and the memorable qualities of the acting, whether in a new or early production from their repertoire. Audiences feel that the actors are capable of portraying many different things in one moment, enacting the conflicts and complexity of life, of reaching the heights and depths of human reaction. This creates a sense of place and situation that helps audiences understand that the portrayed characters' lives are as complex and difficult as their own.

The Maly Drama Theatre is now one of the oldest established theatres within the new Europe. This interview took place in Lev Dodin's office at the Maly Drama Theatre on 18 November 2007 with Dina Dodina translating.

PETER LICHTENFELS: I would like to talk about four areas related to your work at the Maly Drama Theatre. The first is about Europe and the Maly Drama Theatre's membership of the Union of Theatres of Europe. What does it mean for the Maly Drama Theatre to be a theatre in Europe?

LEV DODIN: Théâtre de l'Europe is just status. We didn't give it to ourselves; we were given it. But it is quite important for us because we view it as a responsibility. It's important for several reasons. First and foremost, I'm firmly convinced that Russian theatre is really closely linked with European theatre, and Russian theatre is a part of European theatre. I think that despite all our differences, a common theatre history is still there for Europe and Russia. Russian theatre is carrying on naturally many traditions generated by European theatre. I'm firmly convinced that the last century of European theatre has been heavily nourished by what has happened in Russian theatre.

Secondly, it's very important for me to prove by deed what I've just claimed – that we are part of a European theatre tradition. So our international world touring and, in particular, our European touring is very important to me. We have been all over the world. The main attraction for European touring for me is always the moment when both the actors and the audience realise that theatre language, in essence, is the most cross-cultural language for people all over the world to understand each other.

No matter how often we go abroad, to Britain or to Japan, the locals would say at first that the difference of mentality was overwhelming: 'Our audience is much more taciturn than your audience. We might applaud as loudly or we might not applaud at all. Our audience is not used to reacting, or our audience won't laugh in the same places where your audience is laughing.'

In Italy they always say 'Our audience is way too impatient, please be prepared. They might not be tickled to watch your ten-hour *The Possessed*, Dostoevsky's saga, so they might leave in the interval, please don't be offended'.

But every time we perform in another new place, we are convinced yet again that people cry in the same places and people laugh in mostly the same places all over the world. It never happens that in one country they laugh and in the other country watching the same scene they cry. All the legends about the national mentalities get destroyed when we go on stage. When it pertains not to the form, but the essence, we're all alike. Maybe the British laugh louder than the Japanese, or the Germans laugh louder than the British, but we're not measuring decibels here. Americans laugh the loudest, of course, but even that differs inside a particular nation.

Also I am convinced that whenever an audience laughs or cries sitting in a theatre, they always laugh and cry only in connection with their own lives. They cry about themselves and they laugh about themselves. Nobody in any country is going to watch ten hours of *The Possessed* if that performance is about the life of others, about the life of people who are completely unlike yourself. Nobody would be up to watching seven hours of *Brothers and Sisters* out of educational interest to see how in a Soviet collective four members lived and died. Nobody would watch *Uncle Vanya* for three hours only because people would be theoretically interested in the everyday life of Russian gentry.

When I watch theatre on stage I am only interested in something that pertains to me and to every single spectator sitting in the auditorium. So when people at opposite points of the world map laugh and cry in the same places, in the very same bits of our performances, it means that we are the same. I know that I'm saying a banality now, but the horror and the tragedy of our life is that this banality has to be repeated.

Unfortunately, people keep underestimating themselves, their nations, and their audiences. So we constantly seem to ourselves to be more different than we are in reality. My realisation of our common nature happens both on a personal scale and when I sit in the theatre. On a national scale and nowadays with national layers, the underestimation of our alikeness is still one of the main tragedies of the epoch. There's dialogue between nationalities through culture, and that dialogue has become increasingly important. So to finish my answer to your question, for us it's very important to be the Russian Theatre of Europe in Europe, but it might even be more important for us to be the Russian Theatre of Europe in Russia.

PETER LICHTENFELS: I remember a time when I was running theatres and Mrs Thatcher said 'You can take somebody from Poland, even after the Jaruzelski putsch, but nobody from Russia'. As a guest director we could bring them in, but we would never get government money again. This was specifically coming from her views of Russia in Afghanistan. I remember how difficult and delicate it was for cultures to keep speaking to each other. The reason why I asked about the Theatre of Europe is whether it helps guarantee that Europe can keep speaking to Russia and Russia can keep speaking to Europe, whatever the political ups and downs.

LEV DODIN: The Soviet aggression in Afghanistan was much more upsetting and much more tragic for the people of Russia than for Madam Thatcher. When the troops were taken out of Afghanistan, partially as a result of perestroika, it had a lot to do with how Russian culture tried to oppose the aggression, as well as Russian writers and Russian theatre directors. So I think nothing should interfere with the connections that cultures of different nations have with each other. I think politicians will always go on being the ones who try to disunite us. I think anyway this is what they are for and this is why they exist. If nations united, politicians would be completely out of work.

I think culture should be spinning its own barely noticeable thread, and this is the thread of human unity. I don't really like it when they talk about the dialogue of cultures because I think there's only one culture at the end of the day. The dialogue of cultures is a political cliché that has been invented, because culture is singular.

For Turgenev, French literature was native literature. He was raised a francophone. And I know for the French intelligentsia he is, in a way, one of their native writers. I think also that for Faulkner and Eugene O'Neill, Dostoevsky – judging by what they wrote about Dostoevsky and by what they wrote themselves – was part of their world outlook. Go find me a nation in Europe that would call Chekhov a Russian playwright. Yes, of course he's originally Russian by birth, but for such a long time now he's been part of the European cultural legacy.

The same goes for theatre. Russian theatre originated with its roots being firmly planted in the French theatre, then it drew from the German theatre. And then Russian theatre gave birth to Stanislavski, who impregnated world theatre for the whole of the twentieth century. And then came Meyerhold, but for whom there would have been, I think, no Brecht. A lot of the things I've been doing and I've done in my directing career I would never have done if I'd never seen the shows done by Peter Brook. And I don't think you can say that Peter Brook is a representative of British culture. He's been working in France for years now and yet nobody would say that he's a representative of French culture. Peter Brook, in a way, is the essence of everything that's best about European culture, including some roots of African and Japanese culture.

It's very important to keep all those things in mind. I think the best moments in world theatre happen when a person has roots firmly grounded in this geographic national location, but his branches reach out across the world in a way. I would say that today the problems the European theatre is suffering and the problems that the Russian theatre is suffering are very much alike. Modern theatre very often tries to cut off its roots, so that being modern becomes more important than being eternal. I'm firmly convinced that development in culture means carrying on something that was always there.

PETER LICHTENFELS: I was going to ask about the responsibility of a company or ensemble. Could you talk about the difficulties of ensemble work?

LEV DODIN: The issue of ensemble, though, is much wider and one of the biggest crises for modern theatre. Of course a lot of things in this universe are a matter of great coincidence but everything is relative. Most of my company, most of my actors, I didn't just bump into in the street. These are students of mine from different years, so we got to know each other – some of them I got to know more than 30 years ago. I think the issue of an ensemble being formed is the issue of the soul. When a writer's writing a book, if he's a real writer with a capital W, and not just a novelist, he's writing a book mostly with his soul, not with his hand, or sense of language, but mostly with his soul. This is why we talk about the spiritual world of Dostoevsky, of Tolstoy, of Chekhov. If theatre wants to be an artistic equal with writing, with literature, then theatre has to have a soul, as a writer does, as a painter does, as a composer does. Theatre is not created by one person alone; on stage mostly there is always more than one person.

Here we come to the issue of a company, of an ensemble, of a team, and I am yet again going to use a term that is hopelessly out of date: collective. The word leads us to the issue that it's important for this team to have a collective soul. Both love and hate are carried out firstly by our soul. The birth of this collective soul is the main problem of theatre and the main miracle of theatre. While developing we make new discoveries in ourselves and in each other. And we finally realise, or gradually realise, that the process of knowledge about each other and about yourself is never ending. The process of getting to know the material we're studying and working on is never ending.

It's one thing to do a play in three months and then close it down and forget about it, but with *Brothers and Sisters* we've been living with it for twenty years already and we don't only keep it in repertoire because we earn money. We only stick with a show for so many years because we keep discovering new things about our characters, about the plot, and about each other in this work.

In every theatre generation when you grow up and become adult professionals, suddenly you feel that horrible generation gap behind your back when you don't have enough young blood in your company. We are fortunate; in our company we have three or four generations. Between those four generations there is a certain competition, but also the inner connections between those four generations develop and strengthen from year to year. When I see the youngest leading actor in our company on stage with the oldest leading actor in our company trying to out-act him, it firstly comes out of the fact that the youngster adores the older one so much he wants to be better. I think it's very important for the younger generation to have idols, to have those they revere, those they respect, and for that link to go on.

What I'm driving at is that live theatre is a lengthy process. Stanislavski had a title of genius for his best book, *My Life in Art*. Not 'my work in art', not 'my activity in art', not 'my job in art', but 'my life'. The theatre is much more than a profession; it's a way of life. It doesn't mean at all that such a theatre's development is a process of continuous and utter harmony and happiness. It's a process full of conflict, full of difficulties, and every day you seem to feel as if the very essence is collapsing under your feet, and everyone is letting everyone down. But as long as you have this feeling that every day everything is falling apart, at least you know what you're trying to preserve. Something living and breathing in art would never develop without drama, tragedy, and conflict.

Even in Russian theatre it gets increasingly more fashionable to get together for a very short period because of a project. You hire a director who in a short period of time will deliver their known and reliable product. You take a group of actors, each of whom is bound to produce his part in a reliable way because he's done these parts brilliantly 100 times, and you give that group a precise amount of time – five weeks, six weeks, eight weeks – and when the clock strikes, the performance is opened like a tin off the conveyor belt.

When you speak about conveyor belts, only mass products come off them. But we do jewellery, which is a complete one-off. If we don't call ourselves artists these days because it's now an unfashionable word, at least we should be good craftsmen in the medieval sense of the word. A good medieval craftsman would never have been able to answer when exactly he would finish doing his thing, because when starting on a piece he would not know what he's actually trying to create until he had created it. In this respect, I think theatre has to be able to resist very many aspects of today's life and work. I would even go so far as to risk offending the sacred cows of today, such as trade-union norms and schedules. If a break in rehearsal has to happen at 3 p.m. and not when it naturally comes to the participants, and if a rehearsal is bound to finish at 8 p.m. on half a feeling and on half a word being pronounced, no life would ever emerge. These people could go on endlessly saying that they work in the arts; they work in mass production.

We so easily bow to the conditions that are imposed on us. I think theatre gains, as any artist gains, only when the most important aspects of its art are dissident – when theatre is breaking rules as opposed to following rules. I remember when I came into the Maly Drama Theatre for the first time in my life: it used to be a small theatre that worked mostly not in the city or for city audiences, but would go out into the Leningrad region and work and perform for the workers. Every Soviet theatre would be given a plan of work, and the Maly Drama Theatre in Soviet times was obliged to open five or six shows a year. When I came to work at the Maly Drama Theatre as a young guest director, it was obliged by its Soviet plan to do 540 performances a year. Only if the theatre complied with all those impossible tasks would the theatre people get their meagre salaries. Yes, you would get the state sponsorship, but this sponsorship would be only enough for producing those five or six plays. If you invested a little bit more in the set for the first play you produced, it meant the rest would be produced for less money.

Now, there is a tendency to nicely reminisce about the conditions of theatres under Soviet rule, as if everything was possible, as if the state supported every luxury theatre wanted – no way. Under these horrible conditions you had to produce a show serious enough to ignite respect for your theatre. And when you would succeed in igniting this respect in the party officials, you would try and aggressively get something more from them, more freedom in manoeuvring. I spent years of my life trying to prove to the party officials that one new performance, that had been rehearsed for a year and opened at the end of the season, is as worthy as or even more worthy than the five or six we were scheduled to open over the season.

Today, when we're living under a different economic regime, in a sort of free-market economy, the money that the state gives us – and I'm grateful for the fact they still give us the money – is still never enough for the work we do and for the way we do that work. So we have to look for sponsorship, and if you want to find sponsors you have to make them believe that this is the way theatre should be developing. When we were working on the Grossman novel *Life and Fate*, we needed first to go to the country of the former gulags in Siberia. The aeroplane ticket to the country of Stalin's gulag costs more now than an airfare to

Paris or London. We also knew the whole company needed to go to Auschwitz in Poland. We needed to find a sponsor who would be able to believe that this was something honourable and fascinating to be done on his money. On the other hand, one has to keep in mind that such a lengthy life of performance is economically profitable. We could afford to work months and years on a new show, because our old shows which are in the repertoire are still bringing us a profit. A minimum of 50 per cent of what we spend on developing new work comes from our ticket sales, something we earn ourselves.

PETER LICHTENFELS: Does the theatre have a responsibility to history?

LEV DODIN: I think the theatre's link with history is very linear and direct. From my point of view, the main thing about history that stays on through the centuries is culture. One might treat the memoirs of Talleyrand or the memoirs of Churchill as history, but the things Tolstoy wrote about Napoleon and Tsar Alexander, or Hemingway about the First World War, are much more pertinent to how we see history.

With all due respect to Darwin, our idea of Genesis still comes firstly from the Bible. The Bible for me is both a sacred book and a complete work of art. I think that telling the difference between what is sacred and what is art is very hard; they usually go together.

No matter how alluring the World Wide Web is and no matter how easy it now is to go on the Internet and find any actual historical fact and the date, still when I open writing by Abramov, Solzhenitzyn, or Faulkner, or Grossman, I feel immediate breathing, living history in connection to us. Art doesn't only interpret history; it conceives and creates history. In this respect, art is responsible for history to come.

This for me is the responsibility of art to history and the responsibility of art for the coming history of human beings. If, as an artist, you misdescribe or misinterpret what has happened centuries ago, you are impregnating the centuries to come with errors and shortcomings. Of course, not everyone knows how to read the historic testimonial of art correctly. In this respect humans are amazingly apt at not hearing the foreboding incorporated in works of art. Sooner or later, however, people go back to the works of art and see that there was a message that everyone ignored. At a certain historical point, Chekhov was accused of being completely apolitical, of not being interested enough in public life. Today we've realised that maybe Chekhov has given the most apt analysis of what was happening with Russian society at his time.

In this respect, if you use your brain and your intellect when you read Chekhov, I think it gives you a lot of clues about what's happening in the contemporary society of this or that country. So when they do Chekhov in modern costume nowadays it looks a little bit amusing to me. What amuses me is narrowing the problematics consciously, because what Chekhov writes is the incredible complexity of human relationships and the great interconnectedness of humans who feel hopeful in humanity's essence because, though we make each other miserable, we're still connected. When a theatre director uses Chekhov to say everything is shit and everyone is shit, it's not using Chekhov at all – it's driving in nails with a diamond necklace. In such a moment, the so-called art of a so-called theatre loses all responsibility for history, or to history, and starts creating the fool's pretended new history.

The fool's new history is not only being created by politics or politicians. The fool's new history is also being created by those so-called artists who always know the answers without asking the questions, who present us with a dogma, or who present us with an immediate diagnosis without any analysis. This is how being radical could be as bad as being excessively formal. Those two things might seem to be completely opposite, but sometimes they work the same way because both camps seem to be telling us 'I know what happened'. I think a real artist is in no way capable of saying 'I know how it was'. The only thing a real artist could say is 'I don't know how it happened because I'm trying to analyse a thing which nearly defies knowledge, but I'm trying to make my input into this not-understandable thing; try and follow me, maybe together we could find out how it was.'

Only in such a way can great discoveries and great surprises come. This is how Chekhov – who always proclaimed himself an atheist – managed to write I think the most Christian work of literature: his short story called *The Student*, where you suddenly feel how things that Christ tried to communicate to all of us are connected to our daily life and to each one of us. I'm sure Chekhov didn't know himself how he managed to achieve this result.

I think that if we could always feel and believe history is an eternal number of questions, we would have been way more careful about past history and future history.

PETER LICHTENFELS: When I think of *Brothers and Sisters*, the whole of *Life and Fate*, and other productions of yours, I think of this company also writing about the history of people alive now and inscribing into history new stories. I wonder if that's part of the responsibility of a theatre?

LEV DODIN: The history that art tries to write, as opposed to the history that historians try to write, is first and foremost the fates and lives of private, particular people. History as a subject – especially as the favourite subject of politicians – operates through huge figures, but these huge figures never touch anyone's heart. Initially humans as a breed started off being horrified by the fact that hundreds died in battle. Then a few centuries afterwards, humans were horrified by the fact that thousands died in battle. Then tens of thousands and then with the atomic bomb it was hundreds of thousands, and in the Second World War millions and millions of people were annihilated. In a way we stopped being horrified by those big figures. We just think that it's a kind of proof of the quality of the historical event that took place. It's official that a large number of people were killed. But the only way we could try and feel the horror of what has taken place, and the pain of what has taken place, and the overwhelming suffering that has taken place, is for us to feel for one particular person who's suffered, who's striven, and who's died. I as a reader or I as a spectator am capable of identifying myself only with this particular character. I can't identify myself with the millions lost in the battle of Stalingrad. When we try to tell the story of a particular person on stage we destroy all the idealistic historical mess of totalitarianism.

PETER LICHTENFELS: We go from the abstract to the human.

LEV DODIN: Yes. You know the story of Electra could be a hymn to unforgiving heroic loyalty. Or, it could be a story of a girl whose father has been killed, herself killing her mother, which means a story about one crime generating another crime. And those crimes, in my eyes, are equal. In this respect, when we tell the story of a particular character, we try to show how he's been a victim of history.

PETER LICHTENFELS: I wanted to ask about the role of memory in theatre. It seems to me that when you do plays like *Brothers and Sisters* or *Life and Fate*, in a way we're giving voice to the dead. It seems to me incredibly important that we hear the dead speak.

LEV DODIN: I think an attempt to do art, even if it's art speaking about very modern things, nonetheless always speaks in the context of eternity – I'm not afraid of the word. So, take the relatively modern performance called *The House*, which is the third instalment of the *Brothers and Sisters* epic by Abramov: when Abramov published it, it was a book about the same years we were living through. But it's impossible to say anything about today's human beings without the connection of these beings to yesterday's people, the day before yesterday's people, and people who were always there; it's not possible to avoid the eternal topics.

Art is most importantly the instrument of the interconnection between today and yesterday, and an instrument to strengthen this interconnection. So we, as a company, not only give memories due to those who were dispossessed or shot by Stalin, but we're also speaking about us today and us tomorrow. When we perform and when we rehearse *Uncle Vanya*, we speak first and foremost about us, ourselves – about us who carry on the plight of yesterday's people, who carry on certain traditions. The circle of tragedies and problems today isn't that much different from the circle of problems and tragedies of Chekhov's characters or Chekhov's contemporaries. Otherwise Chekhov would have turned out never to be the most modern of playwrights. When we performed *King Lear*, we spoke mostly about ourselves, about us as fathers, and about us as children, about our fathers with whom we might have had conflicts, and about our fathers who I'm sure had conflicts with their fathers. In a way, we just keep looking for the way out of the vicious circle of human nature, human psyche, and human essence. I think this is the most important and the most interesting thing you do theatre for, looking into yourself on the scale of eternity. When we negate this amazing possibility, this outlandish joy, when we say we're different or we're 'other', we have no roots, we come from nowhere and are heading to nowhere, in essence we're negating the possibility of art and we destroy the culture we're all striving for.

Five key productions

Brothers and Sisters. Adapted for the stage by Lev Dodin, Sergei Bekhterev, and Arkady Katsman, based on the trilogy of novels by Fyodor Abramov. Set design by Eduard Kochergin. Costume design by Inna Gabai. Perf. Natalya Akimova, Misha Arakcheyev, Vladimir Artyomov, Sergei Bekhterev, Galina Filimonova, Natalya Fomenko, Svetlana Gaitan, Lidiya Goryainova, Marina Gridasova, Svetlana Grigoryeva, Igor Ivanov, Anatoly Kolibyanov, Arkady Koval, Sergei Kozyrev, Ilya Kudriavtsev, Liya Kuzmina, Nikolai Lavrov, Sergei Muchenikov, Kseniya Naumova, Irina Nikulina, Bronislava Proskurnina, Nadia Radionycheva, Tanya Radionycheva, Tatyana Rasskazova, Mikhail Samochko, Pyotr Semak, Alla Semenishina, Nina Semyonova, Tatyana Shestakova, Vasili Skliar, Igor Sklyar, Nikita Slabodyanyuk, Yelena Vasilyeva, Sergei Vlasov, Vladimir Zakharyev, and Aleksandr Zavialov. Maly Drama Theatre, St Petersburg. 9–10 March 1985.

Stars in the Morning Sky. By Aleksandr Galin. Co-directed by Tatyana Shestakova. Set design by Aleksei Porai-Koshits. Perf. Galina Filimonova, Sergei Kozyrev, Natalya Akimova, Irina Seleznyova, Marina Gridasova, Tatyana Shestakova, Vladimir Osipchuk. Maly Drama Theatre, St Petersburg. 17 July 1987.

Gaudeamus. Based on the story *Construction Battalion* by Sergei Kaledin. Adapted by Lev Dodin. Conceived and performed by students of Lev Dodin at the Academy of Theater Arts in St

Petersburg and actors of the Maly Drama Theatre. Set design by Aleksei Porai-Koshits. Perf. Igor Chernevich, Oleg Dmitriyev, Sergei Kargin, Yuri Kordonsky, Natalya Kromina, Igor Koniayev, Igor Nikolayev, Tatyana Olear, Irina Tychinina. Maly Drama Theatre, St Petersburg. 11 July 1990.

Play Without a Title. By Anton Chekhov. Adapted by Lev Dodin. Set design by Aleksei Porai-Koshits. Costume design by Irina Tsvetkova. Perf. Tatyana Shestakova, Oleg Dmitriyev, Irina Tychinina, Sergei Kuryshev, Maria Nikiforova, Natalia Kalinina, Igor Ivanov, Arkady Koval. Weimer. 4 July 1997.

Life and Fate. Based on the novel by Vasily Grossman. Written by Lev Dodin. Set design by Aleksei Porai-Koshits. Costume design by Irina Zvetkova. Lighting design by Gleb Filshtinskiy. Perf. Tatyana Shestakova, Segey Kuryshev, Elena Solomonova, Daria Rumyansteva, Elizaveta Boyarskaya, Alena Starostina, Vladimir Seleznev, Alexey Zubarev, Georgy Tsnobiladze, Igor Chernevich, Pavel Gryaznov, Anatoly Kolibyanov, Adrian Rostovskiy, Alexander Koshkarev, Oleg Ryazantsev, Alexey Morozov, Sergei Kozyrev, Oleg Dmitriyev, Vladimir Zakharyev, Danila Kozlovskiy, Stanislav Tkachenko, Stanislav Nikolskiy, Valery Lappo, Urzula Malka, Anastasia Chernova, Alexander Pulinets. Bobigny MC93 Theatre, Paris. 4 February 2007.

Bibliography

Beumers, Birgit (2001) 'Post-Revolutionary Russian Theatre', in Neil Cornwall (ed.), *Companion to Russian Theatre*, London: Routledge, pp. 209–22.

Cavendish, Dominic (2005) 'The Big Drama Is in the Tiny Detail', *Daily Telegraph*, 21 May, www.telegraph.co.uk/culture/theatre/drama/3642402/The-big-drama-is-in-the-tiny-detail.html

Dodin, Lev and Anna Karabinska (2005) *Journey without End, Reflections and Memoirs, Platanov Observed, Rehearsal Notes*, trans. Oksana Mamyrin and Anna Karabinska, London: Tantalus Books.

Shevtsova, Maria (2004) *Dodin and the Maly Drama Theatre: Process to Performance*, London: Routledge.
—— and Christopher Innes (2009) *Directors/Directing: Conversations on Theatre*, Cambridge: Cambridge University Press.
Smeliansky, Anatoly (1999) 'Russian Theatre in the Post-Communist Era', in Robert Leach and Victor Borovsky (eds), *A History of Russian Theatre*, Cambridge: Cambridge University Press, pp. 382–406.
Thornber, Robin (1996) 'Lev Dodin', in Maria M. Delgado and Paul Heritage (eds), *In Contact with the Gods? Directors Talk Theatre*, Manchester: Manchester University Press, pp. 67–78.

Chapter 4
SILVIU PURCĂRETE

Contemporising classics
Aleksandar Saša Dundjerović

Silviu Purcărete (b. 1950) is a Romanian director-*auteur* who has, since the mid-1990s, forged an international reputation for working in European theatre through theatrically new adaptations of classical texts. He uses the dramatic text as a starting point for a theatricality that is founded on adaptation through collaboratively created performances that combine expressive acting, visually compelling images, grotesque physicality, masks, intense colours, and rhythmical sounds to communicate human experiences of foolishness, violence, suffering, and pain. Purcărete's theatricality exemplifies what Roland Barthes describes as 'theatre-minus-text, it is a density of signs and sensations built up on stage starting from the written argument' (1972: 26). In 2012, at the Edinburgh Festival, in his dark monumental version of *Gulliver's Travels*, Purcărete turned Swift's childish fantasy into visually shocking series of macabre, powerful, visceral tableaux. In doing so, he reinforced his directorial signature, like a visual artist 'painting' in theatre space to offer a political critique of the contemporary world. In 1996 he toured Europe and the USA with his reconstruction of *Les Danaïdes* (*The Suppliants*) – a part of Aeschylus' trilogy that survives only in fragments. This devised production inspired by the Balkan wars of the 1990s presented the violence and savagery of humanity, founded on powerful visualisation and with a cast of over 100 performers.

In 2007, Purcărete directed Eugene Ionesco's *Macbett* for the Royal Shakespeare Company (RSC). As re-envisioned by Ionesco, Shakespeare's *Macbeth* becomes a surrealist take on political dictatorship conceived in relation to the Cold War era. The production is emblematic of a director who has, like Ionesco, continued to personalise classical texts in search of new meanings. Purcărete staged *Macbett* as a grotesque carnival, giving the actors masks to play on the idea that all political systems and human interactions are prone to corruption with tyranny hidden behind the most festive of celebrations. As a director-author he goes beyond the present moment and into history to create experiences that elucidate the contemporary human condition.

Purcărete's director-*auteur* approach was built on a rich European tradition of what David Bradby calls 'directors' theatre' (Bradby and Williams 1988: 4–7). French director Roger Planchon referred to theatricality as *écriture scénique* (scenic writing), a concept derived from discussions in the early 1960s about how to adapt and modernise a classical text for contemporary theatre.[1] Purcărete's *écriture scénique* uses text as a personal stimulus in the devising of a highly subjective performance. This approach follows a practice in Romanian theatre where the director is the author of the performance and the *mise en scène* remains independent of the written text.

During the 1960s, a new generation of Romanian directors and stage designers (Liviu Ciulei, Radu Penciulescu, Lucian Giurchescu, Ion Popescu-Udriste, and Lucian Pintilie among others) connected to the tradition of director-author of *écriture scénique*, challenging politics and the official cultural policy of Romanian state art. In the 1970s, when Purcărete was a student of theatre directing at the Academy of Theatre and Film in Bucharest, he entered a cultural space dominated by directors' theatre, but it was a directors' theatre conceived through the particular circumstances of Romania's political situation and a culture of censorship that watched over all cultural activities.

The powerful expressiveness of Purcărete's theatrical images is founded in his visual arts background. When he was a student he wanted to be a painter and trained as a puppeteer before moving into directing. His theatricality is dominated by strong images and the disorder created by grotesque and carnivalesque expressions. He maintains that his work is eclectic and that there is no method to his directing process, but he is always drawn to canonical texts that allow him historical distance and ideological criticism (as with his adaptations of Aeschylus, Shakespeare, Molière, Goldoni, Chekhov, Jarry, and Rabelais). This approach was partly conditioned by the social and cultural circumstances of Eastern Europe. In pre-democratic

Romania, classical texts provided a space where one could create social and cultural interventions by offering the types of commentary that were not allowed within the rigid political discourse enforced by state censorship. More than that, Purcărete was particularly drawn to the rich aesthetic and ideological signification of Aeschylus and Shakespeare, to what he sees as their 'timeless' thematic relevance to humanity and the possibilities they offer for theatrical experimentation. Purcărete is also aware (somewhat nostalgically) that in the new European post-capitalist mass-media societies, theatre no longer has the political relevance and danger that it enjoyed in the climate of Communist Eastern Europe. It is tourist entertainment, a cultural and intellectual extravaganza for festival audiences, or an almost completely ignored form of experimental art. Since theatre now, in Purcărete's view, lacks real political significance, it is free to say whatever it wants.

For Purcărete, theatre remains a personal art, a coded subjective experience collectively shared with the audience. He rejects institutional culture and the ideal of an all-embracing European theatre. He is sceptical towards new theatre that illustrates present-day circumstances in a very realistic way. For Purcărete, theatre is a metaphor. He is a painter and puppeteer who uses the stage as a canvas and performers as expressive, and often grotesque, puppet-like figures for his intuitive and visual responses to historical texts in which the audience can recognise their experiences.

From 1989 to 1996 Purcărete worked extensively as a director at the National Theatre, Craiova, and at the Bulandra Theatre, Bucharest. After Romania's opening to the West in 1990, Purcărete gained international recognition at the Edinburgh International Festival with his version of Jarry's *Ubu Roi*, mixing it with sections from Shakespeare's *Macbeth* and his own experience of Ceaușescu's dictatorship and its chaotic aftermath. In 1996, Purcărete was invited by the French Minister of Culture to be the artistic director of Théâtre de l'Union, at the Centre Dramatique National de Limoges, where, in 1997, he established the Union Theatre Academy, a training centre for young actors. Since 2002 he has lived in Paris, using the city as a central European base from which he directs theatre and opera in different European locations (Romania, Britain, Germany,

France, Austria, Portugal, and Norway). From 2003, Purcărete has been a personal member of the Union des Théâtres de l'Europe (UTE), an association that has forged theatrical exchanges between different European partners since 1990. In fact, most of his productions result from collaborations between Romanian and other European theatres and festivals. A number of his stagings have been co-produced by companies in the UK. These include *Decameron 646* (Tramway Theatre, Glasgow, 1994), *Phaedra* (LIFT, Riverside Studies, 1995), *Titus Andronicus* (Lyric Hammersmith, London, and Nottingham Playhouse, 1997), *A Romanian Oresteia* (Barbican Theatre, London, 1998), *Scapino; or, the Trickster* (Chichester Festival Theatre, 2005), and *Twelfth Night* (Bath Shakespeare International Festival, 2006). In 2008, he directed the premiere of Peter Eötvös's opera of Gabriel García Márquez's novel, *Of Love and Other Demons*, for the Glyndebourne Festival and in 2009 his staging of *Faust* was presented at the Edinburgh International Festival. Since the 2010s, his work has been predominantly on a grand scale, such as his adaptation of *Gulliver's Travels* (2012) and the operas *L'Artaserse* by Leonardo Vinci for the Opéra National de Lorraine, Nancy (2014), the world premiere of Anton Lubchenko's *Doctor Zhivago*, for Theater Regensburg (2015), and *Le malade imaginaire* (*The Imaginary Invalid*) by Molière, for the opening of the 96th season of the Vakhtangov Theatre, Russia (2016).

This interview took place at the Centre Georges Pompidou in Paris on 10 March 2008. Silviu Purcărete was 'home' in Paris and between two directing projects in Romania. He had just returned from directing Shakespeare's *Measure for Measure* at the National Theatre in Craiova for the 2008 Shakespeare Festival and was preparing to start work on his adaptation of Wedekind's *Spring Awakening* and *Lulu* as a collage for the Radu Stanca National Theatre, in Sibiu, Romania.

ALEKSANDAR SAŠA DUNDJEROVIĆ: What do you see as 'European theatre' and do you perceive yourself as part of it?

SILVIU PURCĂRETE: I do not know. When I was in Britain I discovered that they talk about European theatre. I was surprised by a wonderful expression used by a critic, I do not remember who, somehow concerning my theatre: it was 'lugubrious, high concept European theatre'. I adore this expression because I have worked several times in Britain and I have discovered that when they refer to 'the European' they are thinking about a Continental theatre which they perceive as extremely bizarre and somehow to be rejected.

We in Romania started to speak about European theatre when Europe started to open up for us and for others from the East. There was a time when Romania and Eastern Europe were not connected to Europe; then at some point we started to work outside of the country in Europe, and then we said this is European theatre. I'm part of this Union of the Theatres of Europe, which was created by Giorgio Strehler. This organisation still exists in order to bring together different artistic institutions. The aim is to find a way for art theatre to survive in a commercial and quite hostile context.[2]

ALEKSANDAR SAŠA DUNDJEROVIĆ: Romania has a strong culture of directors' theatre. What kind of cultural influences produced a generation of world-class directors?

SILVIU PURCĂRETE: I really don't know why that happened, but since the 1960s there was an explosion of high-quality directors like Lucian Giurchescu and Lucian Pintilie. There was an interesting combination between a somehow imposed Russian school of theatre – through the academy of theatre in Bucharest, a wonderful and very academic institution based on realist principles – and some kind of frivolity mixed with dreams of Western values and a certain sense of humour.

There are certain common experiences in all Balkan and East European countries due to Communism. This was the connection that all these countries had in common. Theatre was also an intellectual weapon, an intellectual means of political resistance or ideological-intellectual resistance. To be that, it had to develop a kind of metaphorical language, very subtle and very complex. Probably this is another reason why theatrical events became so developed and more focused on intellectual problems and very important existential problems and less focused on amusement and entertainment. Theatre was necessary. It happened in Russia, it happened in a very drastic way in Poland, it happened everywhere else [in the former Eastern bloc] and also in Romania, but in a more 'Balkanic' way.

ALEKSANDAR SAŠA DUNDJEROVIĆ: Your production of *Ubu Rex with Scenes from Macbeth* in 1990 came at a shifting political point in Romania. Can you tell me about pre-democratic Romania? Was this production a response to your vision of humanity at that time?

SILVIU PURCĂRETE: It was much simpler than that. I consider myself to be a craftsman, an artisan, not a visionary; I am not a philosopher. I do not have a message that I feel I have to transmit to humanity through theatre. *Ubu Rex* was a project I started when I was a student. Of course it was not possible to do it at the time for political reasons, so when the opportunity came, because of the democratic change, it offered the chance to do something new. It was a play very near to my personal, social, and political experience. The subject imposed itself; I didn't have to reflect too much because the play was very good for what we were all living through at the time, this grotesque part of history. That was why I created *Ubu*.

In pre-democratic Romania, I worked in Bucharest's theatres for 12 years in a classic way negotiating the dictatorship and censorship. The productions were extremely complicated but you didn't feel like you could express yourself freely. It was quite a sick way of doing things. After the shift to democracy I started to work with some kind of pleasure. Before there was no pleasure, it was more like an effort, a slalom, to hide things [from the censors], to make compromises without making compromises. It was extremely complicated and lugubrious.

ALEKSANDAR SAŠA DUNDJEROVIĆ: Did emigrating to France in 1996 influence your work thematically?

SILVIU PURCĂRETE: I don't think so. Of course, when I started to work in France new things happened because it was in a different culture. It was not exactly emigrating because I was called to direct in Limoges and I accepted the opportunity. I did not emigrate, I moved. Emigration would have happened earlier. Now I started to be a vagabond, which is very different. There was no real change of perspective. I continued to do the same kind of theatre that I always wanted to do, maybe in better personal conditions, with lesser or greater success.

I do not believe in giving messages to the audience. I do not like theatre that is programmatic and wants to change humanity. I think that any kind of art that has the purpose of changing human beings is dangerous. This must not happen; the purpose of art is to preserve humanity, not to change it. When you want to change it you fall into ideology and demagogy. I have very reactionary concepts against what I call programmatic art and I know that my way of thinking is politically incorrect.

ALEKSANDAR SAŠA DUNDJEROVIĆ: How is theatre in Romania responding to the new Europe?

SILVIU PURCĂRETE: I don't know if theatre has a response to this. For instance, international touring theatre is almost a new invention, at least for East European theatre. The idea of presenting a play in an unknown language in a different country, which is, of course, for a very strange audience, turns it into a kind of exotic merchandise. There are other inventions and responses, as with the mixing of different languages and cultures in the same performance. I did it myself, but it's a little bit artificial and a bit of a touristy approach.

ALEKSANDAR SAŠA DUNDJEROVIĆ: Has the role of the director-author changed in Eastern and Central European theatre?

SILVIU PURCĂRETE: No, I think it's more or less the same, but there is a new generation that is more rebellious. They hate us (the older generation) which was not the case in my generation. But this is not only in Romania; it is everywhere. There is a new generation of dramatists/directors, playwrights/directors, underground rebels, young protesters, violent in their aesthetic – what I call the Sarah Kane family – who are very connected to today's problems and they very programmatically cut the links with our generation.

ALEKSANDAR SAŠA DUNDJEROVIĆ: What is the function of classical text in European theatre directing?

SILVIU PURCĂRETE: Probably classic texts are best for a very theatrically new piece of art. Performance is always something different from a play [text]. Sometimes performance can discover a new meaning in the text. The director is an author, or at least the director should be the author of the performance, but of course theatre is not a pure art. There is a great mixture of things so you cannot see the percentage of creativity of each element.

In Britain, I think, theatre is much more direct. The expression is more connected to the text than to the director's interpretation or his artistic expression. That is why the British think about 'lugubrious' high-concept 'Eurotheatre', and sometimes they may be right. In my opinion the best theatre now in Europe is in Germany, or at least it has been for the past few decades. This is because there is a form of directors' theatre here combined with very good professional acting and an audience that is very interested in what this combination offers. There are many good directors working in Germany on quality artistic theatre. Russia is also very interesting, but there it is more isolated to a few individual cases. I cannot say the same thing about other countries; although you can have exceptional experiences they are less widespread.

I was in Limoges for seven years as artistic director of the Théâtre de l'Union. Now, I live in Paris but I have not worked in France for the past five years. If we think about how French theatre enters into dialogue with classical texts then we cannot avoid talking about clichés. French theatre is – speaking about classical texts especially – very deferential to the written text. In France they even say that the actor is *porteur du texte*; so the actor should be like a waiter who should serve you the text on the tray as an elegantly presented dish, but often offering nothing more than that. This is a problem. This is a cliché in French theatre. In the same way as the cliché for British theatre is 100 per cent efficiency. Shakespeare is played as a gospel in Britain. What is interesting is that Shakespeare is not a playwright any more for the English; it is just a sacred text. You don't need to understand it. You just need to tell it. I exaggerate of course, but when I worked on Shakespeare's *The Tempest* at the Nottingham Playhouse many years ago, I wanted to cut a few lines, but it was like asking to cut off the arms of the actors, they almost fainted. Interestingly, I also directed French plays in Britain, and in French plays you can make cuts. I just wanted to cut a fragment [from *The Tempest*] that made a reference that nobody understands any more, to ropes and ships in the navy in the seventeenth century. When I asked them to explain what it meant nobody understood it but still you could not cut it because it is Shakespeare.

ALEKSANDAR SAŠA DUNDJEROVIĆ: Do theatre directors have more freedom with classical texts in Romanian theatre?

SILVIU PURCĂRETE: There is a lot of freedom. The director can change the text, and we are blamed for that very often. I am almost always blamed for all the distortions that I do on a classic text, like cuttings or inversions of things, but I think it is necessary to keep the text alive. Trying to be very respectful with classic texts is hypocritical. The most respectful way of treating a classic text is just to dive into it, to try to dig inside it, and to open up and try to discover new things. This means a respect for classic texts: you open them up and consider them to be alive. Even if we talk about classic texts my choices are very eclectic. I did not only stage Shakespeare and Aeschylus, I have also handled Labiche and light comedies, Molière and Goldoni.

ALEKSANDAR SAŠA DUNDJEROVIĆ: You still direct in Romania?

SILVIU PURCĂRETE: Yes, in the past year I did a few productions there: *Faust* in Sibiu [see Plate 4], opera in Cluj, Shakespeare's *Measure for Measure* in Craiova, and now I am going to do Wedekind's *Lulu* in Sibiu.

ALEKSANDAR SAŠA DUNDJEROVIĆ: When the audience and critics talk about Wedekind's *Lulu* they are going to say Purcărete's *Lulu*. How do you work on the dramatic text?

SILVIU PURCĂRETE: I am a very instinctive director. I do not have a method of working. My way of thinking is more visual; it's also about space and sound. It is not theoretical. The theoretical things come after the analysis. With actors I work very much on rough improvisations and in rehearsals I provoke some kind of chaos. Then from this chaos we start to articulate, to build something.

ALEKSANDAR SAŠA DUNDJEROVIĆ: How do you choose a text you want to work on?

SILVIU PURCĂRETE: It is usually a commission. For example, my last play, Shakespeare's *Measure for Measure*, will be part of the Shakespeare Festival in Craiova that takes place every two years. Four years ago, the director of the festival insisted that I should direct a Shakespeare play for the festival that year, and he asked me to propose a text. I read several plays and I was thinking about how the actors in the company matched what is in the plays. I was also interested because *Measure for Measure* was not often done in Romania. It's a very enigmatic play, and it is a play that I didn't understand at all, and this was more exciting for me to do. It is not that I understand it now, on the contrary, but at least I know why I don't understand it.

ALEKSANDAR SAŠA DUNDJEROVIĆ: What is the situation with collective creation in the climate of individualism and consumerism? As a freelance director, do you have a group you work with?

SILVIU PURCĂRETE: No, I don't have a company any more. It is difficult to work in a very short and compact rehearsal period. I have companies that I have known for many years, for example Craiova or Sibiu have permanent ensembles, so there is continuity there. I prefer to work with companies that I know, if I can. I even have a little group of French actors that I take with me when I have an international project because it is more like a family.

Before 1989, I used to rehearse for a period of between eight and twelve months, and you opened the production when it was ready. Now I have to do it in four or five weeks so you don't have time to explore. When you work with actors that you know, it is easier to put the piece together, but still there is the pressure of time.

ALEKSANDAR SAŠA DUNDJEROVIĆ: Can you compare your directing experience with a permanent ensemble that you know well, for example the National Theatre Craiova, with a more recent experience as a guest director, working in July 2007 on Ionesco's *Macbett* for the RSC?

SILVIU PURCĂRETE: It is different. For example, in 2005 I directed a performance for the Chichester Festival, *Scapino*, with actors that I chose in auditions. It all went very well. I didn't have miraculous expectations, but we communicated well and a few days into rehearsals we all became friends, and it worked. However, working in Stratford, it was not me who chose the actors. When you choose the actors they all adore you because you have chosen them. In Stratford, we worked for about four or five weeks. The company was there, and they had a further project, Shakespeare's *Macbeth*, so they completely ignored Ionesco's *Macbett*. They hated it, but they had to swallow that frog because it was part of the package with Shakespeare's *Macbeth*. It was a difficult experience, and I don't think it worked.

All this systematisation of rehearsal time is very problematic because you have to be perfectly clever between 10.30 and 13.30 with a break of ten minutes, and then you have to start being very clever again from 14.30. I think when you have these permanent companies you should accept there are moments of failure, moments when nothing works, and then you go and have a drink. You cannot do that in Britain. If you have a bad day and nothing is coming out you should abandon the rehearsal. In Craiova for instance there were times when I was cancelling rehearsals day after day because nothing came out. Then we would go to the pub, and then abruptly on the fourth day everything would come out, and we would do everything in one day. This is some kind of freedom that you can afford with permanent ensembles, but you should also control this because it is not only in pubs that you can get good ideas.

ALEKSANDAR SAŠA DUNDJEROVIĆ: When I directed in the Hungarian Theatre of Cluj-Napoca in 2005, actors frequently talked about working with you on a project they had just finished which was very visual and physical. Can you take me through your rehearsal process on this?

SILVIU PURCĂRETE: The project I did in Cluj was not a written play but something from François Rabelais, from *La vie de Gargantua et de Pantagruel* (*The Life of Gargantua and Pantagruel*). The actors were from mixed companies. Some were from the permanent company in Cluj, some came from Sibiu, and some were French actors I had brought with me. They had never worked together before as group. The artistic director, Gábor Tompa, asked me to write a play, but of course I didn't do it because I didn't know what to do. I decided we should do a performance without any words: 100 per cent visual without text. I had some themes in my mind and some images that I started from, taken from Rabelais's poetry. I started by giving the actors themes to improvise on, little poetic verses from Rabelais, compositions of three or four words, but completely enigmatic, that could inspire various interpretations. I told them to think about them and make whatever they wanted to. I gave them one week to prepare that. They did it like children playing: half-afraid, half-excited. After a week I told them: 'We have an opening tonight and you'll show us everything you have done.' They performed five or six hours of improvisations. From these improvisations I just took a few elements (physical movements, images) that were interesting and then connected them with what else I had in my mind and tried to compose them into a whole. I left the actors to be very free during the improvisation sessions but after that I was extremely selective, shaping the work and creating the architecture of the performance.

My approach is very visual. If I see something that I like I try to capture it, and then I build on it. Often actors can improvise well but they don't know what they are doing or even worse they believe that they did something different. When you use improvisations with actors, you have to be extremely clear about what you want to take out of them.

ALEKSANDAR SAŠA DUNDJEROVIĆ: Is the visual image the main inspiration for you?

SILVIU PURCĂRETE: I came to theatre from the fine arts. When I was a student I first wanted to be an artist so I was doing a lot of painting and drawing. I went into theatre more because of the visual attraction, to look at the aspects of visual performance. My first impressions, even of a written text, are more visual. When I am working with my designer on an opera we look at the visual arts for inspiration: paintings, sculpture, movies, and installations. I am very eclectic in my taste so there are various styles that influence me.

ALEKSANDAR SAŠA DUNDJEROVIĆ: What holds your performance together? Since the text is very volatile, what can actors hold on to in your performances? Is it your vision? Your concept?

SILVIU PURCĂRETE: Yes, absolutely, but the concept is always hidden and it's not clear. The concept is like a puzzle that is in your brain, but you don't know it's there. You find the little pieces and at some moment everything becomes clear. I am not one to explain the concept. I don't call actors to go towards the concept. Even for me it is blurred. This is why I work with intuition, with actors that know me, can accept me and act instinctively on what I suggest. Sometimes I say very little and at other times I direct specific details. English and German actors must first understand very well why they are doing something and only then will they try to do it. My actors, those that I appreciate, if you say jump they just jump without asking why. The actor will eventually ask why, and they would understand and then they would ask 'What if I jump this way or that way?', and step by step we come together to a certain architecture, to the idea that is behind all that. But you do not start to build or to put bricks on a theory. The most difficult thing is to explain first and then try to get them to do it. It never works for me.

ALEKSANDAR SAŠA DUNDJEROVIĆ: Do you do dramaturgical work on the text or do you have a dramaturg that adapts texts?

SILVIU PURCĂRETE: No, I do it myself. I always do my dramaturgical work with actors in the rehearsals, with actors and a pencil, just that. Lots of things will come out of rehearsals. Of course, I have a general architecture of the performance because we have to build the set, we have to do the costumes and other technical requirements. For the past ten years I have worked a lot with the same group of collaborators. They include my designer Helmut Stürmer and Vasile Sirli who lives in Paris and who does the music. I also do my own design. For the last production, *Measure for Measure*, I was also the stage designer. When it's clear to me how it is supposed to look, I don't need a designer. Sometimes the space is very clear from the beginning, as it was for *Ubu Rex*, and sometimes the space comes before the performance; it depends on the project.

ALEKSANDAR SAŠA DUNDJEROVIĆ: What was your rehearsal methodology for your adaptation of Aeschylus's *Oresteia* [titled *A Romanian Oresteia* when it came to the Barbican Centre, London]?

SILVIU PURCĂRETE: It is a big play. It was a big production. I did it first in Limoges with French actors focusing on the first part of the *Oresteia*, *Agamemnon*. This was the part of the performance where text matters the most, although of course it was edited and cut. In the second part, *The Choephori*, the text was very difficult to understand, it was so lyrical. So our solution was to intentionally take the text completely out of the performance. *Choephori* did not have one word and everything was staged as a nightmare. The whole story from *Choephori* was there, but without any words.

I have always been attracted to old texts, classic texts. I was never inspired by new and freshly written plays. I don't know why. Maybe because I think theatre needs a distance. Theatre that I like is not meant to show the everyday pressures but to cool them and to put them far away in different contexts as a way of trying to understand them. Part of the theatrical process involves detachment; it's not reality on stage, there are filters and deflections. This is what I always look for, instinctively. I am attracted by old literature like Chekhov, Aeschylus, or Ionesco, not only by the text but the history around the text, as in Shakespeare's texts.

Shakespeare's plays work. Some people think that they should be done from cover to cover; they have layers and layers of references, history, and themes, and that is interesting. I have staged 11 or so Shakespearian texts, more than that of any other playwright, because he is the most enigmatic and the most surprising playwright.

ALEKSANDAR SAŠA DUNDJEROVIĆ: How do you bring the historicity within the classical texts to the present moment?

SILVIU PURCĂRETE: It's like looking at a big painting. You have to push it far away and sit in an armchair to have a wider and more distant perspective. This is how I try to dig into the text, to discover new meetings between the present and the historical. The basic discovery is that, through history, human beings never change. Their problems are exactly the same. The lesson you learn is that what happens to us is what happened to our ancestors years ago. The difference is in the experience, that's why

I like to go into classic texts because it's comforting to believe that thousands of generations lived exactly the same way without computers and without media, but absolutely the same way.

ALEKSANDAR SAŠA DUNDJEROVIĆ: What is the role of theatre in contemporary Europe?

SILVIU PURCĂRETE: I am not the right person to answer that question. This is more for those who observe theatre from the outside, or for an audience. I make theatre. That is the only thing that I can do. I am a craftsman; I am just a worker in the field of theatre. I do not ask myself what a human being is and then try to give answers. I started to do theatre when I was very young. I don't know why I do it; I just do it.

Very often and especially in past years I am very sceptical and more pessimistic about the role of theatre. More and more I think that theatre in Europe does not have much to do with our lives and is becoming mere entertainment and mundane. It's paradoxical, but during the Communist era, theatre and theatre artists were 'high' caste. They belonged to some kind of aristocratic tribe in all East European countries. It was felt that theatre was something extremely necessary and extremely valued by people. Moreover, there was no cinema or television in the present-day sense, no other things to see. And now, I don't know why people go to the theatre.

Five key productions

Ubu Rex with Scenes from Macbeth. Adapted from Alfred Jarry and William Shakespeare by Silviu Purcărete. Design by Silviu Purcărete. Perf. Lucian Albanezu, Constantin Cicort, Mirela Cioaba, Ion Colan, Valer Dellakeza, Leni Pintea-Homeag, Gheorghe Ilie, Remus Mărgineanu, Theodor Marinescu, Marian Negrescu, Roxana Pera, Tudorel Petrescu, Gheorghe Tudor, Minela Zamfir. National Theatre of Craiova, Romania. December 1990.

Titus Andronicus. By William Shakespeare. Set design by Stefania Cenean. Perf. Lucian Albanezu, Constantin Cicort, Mirela

Cioaba, Valer Dellakeza, Tudorel Filimon, Ilie Gheorghe, Tudor Gheorghe, Stefan Iordache, Valentine Mihali, Marian Negrescu, Ozana Oancea, Tudorel Petrescu, Angel Rababoc. National Theatre of Craiova, Romania. March 1992.

A Romanian Oresteia after Aeschylus. Adapted, directed, and designed by Silviu Purcărete. Perf. Lucian Albanezu, Constantin Cicort, Mirela Cioaba, Eugen Titu. National Theatre of Craiova, Romania. October 1998.

Pantagruel's Cousin (also known as *Pantagruel's Sister-in-Law*). Conceived by Silviu Purcărete. Set and costume design by Helmut Stürmer. Perf. Miklós Bács, József Bíró, Zsolt Bogdán, Áron Dimény, Molnar Lebente, Jacques Bourgaux, Ofelia Popii, Cristian Stanca. National Theatre Radu Stanca Sibiu, Romania, Hungarian Theatre of Cluj, Romania, and Compagnie Silviu Purcărete France. June 2003.

Faust after Goethe. Adapted and directed by Silviu Purcărete. Design by Helmut Stürmer. Perf. Miklós Bács, Eliza Blănaru, Eveline Buta, Cezara Crețu, Iunis Minculete, Simona Negrilă, Francesca Pop, Andreea Preda, Alexandra Spătărelu, Oana Vlad. National Theatre Radu Stanca Sibiu, Romania, 2007 and Edinburgh International Festival 2009.

Notes

1 For further details on *écriture scénique* and its impact across Europe, see Introduction to the first edition, pp. 1–5.
2 On the Union of Theatres of Europe, see Lichtenfels's interview with Lev Dodin, pp. 87–8.

Bibliography

Barthes, Roland (1972) *Critical Essays*, trans. Richard Howard, Evanston, IL: North Western University Press.

Bradby, David and Annie Sparks (1997) *Mise en Scène: French Theatre Now*, London: Methuen.

Bradby, David and David Williams (1988) *Directors' Theatre*, Houndmills and London: Macmillan.

Bristol, Michael, Kathleen McLuskie and Christopher Holmes (eds) (2001) *Shakespeare and Modern Theatre: The Performance of Modernity*, London: Routledge.

Christine, Dymkowski (ed.) (2000) *The Tempest*, Cambridge: Cambridge University Press.

Lehmann, Hans-Thies (2006) *Postdramatic Theatre*, trans. Karen Jürs-Munby, London and New York: Routledge.

Remshardt, Ralf (2004) *Staging the Savage God: The Grotesque in Performance*, Carbondale, IL: Southern Illinois University Press.

Stevanova, Kalina (ed.) (2000) *Eastern European Theatre after the Iron Curtain*, London: Routledge.

Tompa, Andrea (2009) 'Silviu Purcărete's World', *Theater*, 39 (2): 33–41.

Wiles, David (2000) *Greek Theatre Performance: An Introduction*, Cambridge: Cambridge University Press.

Chapter 5

FRANK CASTORF AND THE VOLKSBÜHNE

Berlin's theatre of deconstruction

Marvin Carlson

During the final decade of the twentieth century, the Berlin and indeed the German stage was dominated by the figure of Frank Castorf (b. 1951), who, at the helm of the Berlin Volksbühne, not only assumed a leading position among the German stage directors of this period but also presented at his theatre a very large proportion of the most praised and influential directors, authors, and designers of this period.

The twentieth-century German theatre produced many of the outstanding actors, designers, and dramatists of the period, but its most highly visible theatre artists were the directors, from Max Reinhardt onward, through Erwin Piscator, Leopold Jessner, and Bertolt Brecht, then Peters Stein and Zadek, and finally to Castorf and the directors his age and younger whom he encouraged.[1] In a culture where the theatre holds a position of great importance and visibility and in which young artists traditionally establish their reputation by challenging accepted political, social, and cultural norms, Castorf was soon recognised as a director with a love of provocation but whose artistic vision made him much more than a briefly controversial and stimulating provocateur.

He first gained attention as managing director of the small East German theatre at Anklam, where he served from 1981 to 1985. In Anklam his unconventional productions troubled the East German police, the Stasi, from the beginning. His first production, *Othello*, was played in semi-darkness, with the dialogue reduced to scattered half-heard mutterings in English. The production attracted the close attention and the condemnation of the Stasi, whose secret reports complained that it was equally offensive 'to Shakespeare and to the public', that it 'deprived the play of all human values', and, most damning, that it 'undermined socialist cultural politics' by emphasising 'the impossibility of communication along with a blighted view of humanity' (quoted in Detje 2002: 84–5).

In an interview 13 years later, Castorf wittily characterised the production as the '*Verwurstung* of a Soviet problem-play [...] instead of the old familiar material using buckets of water, the Rolling Stones, shrieking women, idiotic jokes' (Castorf 1994: 38).[2] That Castorf should launch his directing career with a calculatedly outrageous production of a standard classic was highly appropriate, and the police report was by no means unperceptive in suggesting a subversive political dimension as well. From the beginning, Castorf's work challenged both the aesthetic and political establishment. That he saw a relationship between the two, and to the difficulty of communication, may be seen in the formidable but highly suggestive title of his highly praised doctoral dissertation at Berlin's Humboldt University in 1976: 'Grundlinien der "Entwicklung" der Weltanschaulich-Ideologischen und Künstlerisch-Ästhetischen Positionen Ionescos zur Wirlichkeit' (The Foundations of the 'Evolving' of the Philosophical-Ideological and the Aesthetic-Artistic Positions of Ionesco Concerning Reality). One dramatic image from the Anklam years has become legendary in the modern German theatre. Near the end of Castorf's 1984 production of Heiner Müller's *Der Auftrag* (*The Mission*), his designer Hartmut Meyer provided at the rear of a starkly minimalist setting a practical door that opened onto the actual outside of the theatre. The protagonist's departure through this door, an escape not provided by the Müller text itself, was widely interpreted as the expression of a desire for a kind of political as well as artistic opening not easily achieved in the current theatre of East Germany.

Castorf's 1984 production of Ibsen's *A Doll's House* (called *Nora* in German) was widely considered the pinnacle of his Anklam years. It had less clear political implications than most of his early works and so was less directly offensive to the authorities, even though it was anything but a traditional reading. The production began quietly, but Castorf's Nora, Silvia Rieger, soon descended into delusions and hysteria, singing snatches of music from The Rolling Stones (a favourite Castorf source). Her confessed desire (to Mrs Linde and Rank) to shock Torvald with a forbidden word became a hysterical several minutes of shouting the favoured shocking word of the German stage, *Scheiße!* (*Shit!*) directly out into the audience. Henry Hübchen, who would become one of Castorf's favoured actors, worked with him here for the first time as Helmer, displaying a disturbing blend of slapstick, neurosis, elegance, and instability that precisely suited Castorf's serio-comic approach.

The success of *Nora* opened other East German theatres to Castorf. In 1986 he presented Heiner Müller's *Der Bau* (*The Construction Site*) in Karl-Marx-Stadt (now Chemnitz) in a production that ran counter to established conventional, even reverential, stagings of this depiction of the founders of Communism. Castorf, as usual, broke up the action with musical interludes, slapstick routines, dance sequences (inspired in part by the work of Pina Bausch in the West), and long sequences of silence and inaction (it lasted some three and a half hours, the extended evening becoming also a characteristic of Castorf's work). This iconoclasm attracted some and infuriated others, but his reputation as a young director of unusual energy and imagination continued to grow. The freedom to experiment opened by Gorbachev made this sort of work not only acceptable but also fashionable. A national theatre festival established in Berlin in 1988 distinctly favoured work that moved away from the hitherto mandated socialist realism, and no fewer than three Castorf productions were featured in the second such festival, in 1989. One of these, Castorf's iconoclastic production (audience members entered the theatre through a toilet and were entertained by music by The Beatles) of Ibsen's already iconoclastic *An Enemy of the People*, was hailed by one Berlin critic as 'a classic play for *Glasnost*' (Wengeriek 1989). In the final days before the fall of the Berlin Wall, in November 1989, Castorf was seen, particularly by West German theatre reviewers, as a leading figure in the East's struggle for artistic and political freedom.

Earlier that same year, the West had experienced its first direct contact with the controversial young director when he was granted permission from the DDR authorities (doubtless not unhappy to be rid of him for a time) to direct productions during 1989 in Cologne, Basel, and Munich of *Hamlet*, *Ajax*, and *Miss Sara Sampson*. The reviews of these iconoclastic productions were generally negative, calling Castorf's work simply sensationalistic and irreverent, suitable perhaps for the East but too crude and naive for Western taste. In Lessing's familiar classic, *Miss Sara Sampson*, actors cut themselves out of cardboard boxes, Mellefont masturbated into a Kleenex, and The Beatles' 'Why Don't We Do It in the Road?' served as a musical leitmotif. The premiere resulted in a near riot. Many critics were outraged, but others, led by Peter Iden, praised the production's freewheeling theatricality and insisted that it in fact revivified Lessing's critique of bourgeois culture for contemporary times (Iden 1989). *Miss Sara Sampson* put Castorf firmly, if surrounded by controversy, on the German theatrical map and gained him his first invitation to the prestigious annual Berlin theatre festival, the spring Theatertreffen. It was also taken on tour to South America.

An extended interview with Castorf was published in West Germany's leading theatre journal, *Theater Heute*, in December 1989, the month after the Wall fell and two months after the premiere of *Miss Sara Sampson*. Clearly the tone of the interview reflected a certain concern on the part of the interviewing critics that freedom for this new *enfant terrible* from the East might not be entirely to their own taste. 'Theatre is not simply self-expression or private therapy,' they warned, expressing concern that 'if the train is called Lessing or Shakespeare, you open the throttle and take control of the locomotive.' Castorf's reply was both clear and typical: 'I would like to clean out the traditional state theatre apparatus with my productions and work with the actors to change it from within' (von Becker and Merschmeier 1989: 18). Freed from the constraints of the East German establishment, Castorf found a whole new set of challenges in the West, its self-styled theatre authorities in the academy and among the press, its reactionary conceptions of the staging of classic texts, and Western capitalism itself, which Castorf soon viewed as a system as repressive and reactionary in its own way as the now discredited East. As always, aesthetic provocation was inextricably tied in his work to political concerns and especially to the Marxist concern with the subjugation of the working class under capitalism.

The post-Wall Castorf was clearly displayed in his first production at the theatre with which he would soon be primarily associated, the Berlin Volksbühne. Here in 1990 he presented another shocking reworking of a German classic, Schiller's *Die Räuber* (*The Robbers*). In Castorf's reading, this youthful play of rebellion became a requiem for the departed DDR and a cry of outrage and frustration at the failed promise of both East and West, the former sinking into depression and the latter devoted to soulless materialism. Other major reinterpretations followed, all mixing slapstick and violent physical action, improvised and inserted material, direct addresses and other confrontations with the audience, music by such Western icons as Led Zeppelin and The Beatles, and violent, even hysterical, outbursts from the actors. Castorf's growing reputation as among the most provocative of a new generation of German directors was solidified by his invitation to participate in the Berlin Theatertreffen both in 1991 (with a production of Ibsen's *John Gabriel Borkman* from the Deutsches Theater) and in 1992 with *King Lear* from the Volksbühne.

In the years immediately following the unification of Berlin, the city's cultural world faced a major problem of adjustment. Before the division of the city, most of its major theatres were located in what became East Berlin, and so West Berlin was forced to build up its own equivalents of these institutions. After unification, the city found itself with many more theatres than could be supported in the lavish manner traditional in Germany, even with the massive funding allocated for the re-establishment of Berlin as the nation's political and cultural capital. A number of major houses were threatened with closure, among them the Volksbühne, despite its position as a leading house through much of the twentieth century under the direction of such figures as Max Reinhardt and Erwin Piscator. During the 1970s, under the leadership of Bruno Besson, with Manfred Karge and Matthias Langhoff as directors and Heiner Müller as playwright, the theatre was among the most important in Germany, East or West. With Besson's departure, however, the theatre went into decline, drifting along under continued interim directorships.

The ailing Volksbühne was therefore a prime candidate for closure when the new, post-Wall administration began looking for ways to address the surplus of Berlin theatres. In January 1991, Minister Ulrich Roloff-Momin was made responsible for this difficult task, and one of his first reports (in June) found the Volksbühne in an 'unsupportable situation', that renewal with its present leadership and ageing company was 'unthinkable and unachievable' (Nagel 2001: 134–5). Roloff-Momin's theatre adviser from the German Senate, Ivan Nagel, called the Volksbühne ensemble the worst in the city. Instead of what might be expected, an outright closure (which in fact befell the major Schiller Theater two years later), Nagel and Roloff-Momin suggested a radical alternative, a forced attempt at renewal under the leadership of Berlin's most controversial young director, Castorf. The task put before Castorf was perfectly suited to his reputation for confrontation and change – to put together 'a young ensemble with a thirst for artistic innovation and the courage to create contemporary, politically relevant theatre' (Nagel 2001: 134–5). His time to achieve this formidable undertaking was severely limited, however. If he did not achieve a major renewal of the theatre within two years, it would be permanently closed.

This mandate precisely suited Castorf's own interests, and he proceeded to embrace with astonishing success the original goal of the Volksbühne, seeking out not only a younger audience but also a populist audience uninterested in the more conventional fare of other Berlin theatres. The location of the Volksbühne was ideal for this project, in the heart of former East Berlin in a neighbourhood, the Prenzlauer Berg, that had long been associated with the marginalised, struggling students, would-be artists, the homeless, and the unemployed. Castorf reached out to this population, providing production support to impoverished theatre workers in the neighbourhood, offering reduced price or even free tickets to workers and students, running trailers in local cinemas and street performances to broaden acquaintance with the theatre's new approach. In enthusiasm, commitment, and indeed in rhetoric, the new venture took on the feeling of a military campaign. Castorf spoke of 'radicalising' the 'endangered' people (Castorf 1991a) and claimed that the physical and historical situation of the Volksbühne made it ideal for such a crusade, situated 'in the most conflict-ridden city of Germany, where one can snipe at today's reality with a cockiness and radicalism unlike the theatres in the West' (Castorf 1991b).

Like many former East Germans, Castorf was deeply troubled by the ruthless and soulless materialism of the new West-dominated Germany and sought, by stressing his Eastern roots and those of his theatre, to uphold the values of classic Marxism, however much these had been tarnished by the actual historical experience of the DDR. He placed giant letters OST (East) proudly above the massive facade of the Volksbühne and even kept the portrait of Stalin left from DDR days hanging in the theatre lobby.

All of these leftist and populist activities might have brought Castorf a temporary renown in his Prenzlauer Berg neighbourhood, but he could hardly have maintained this audience, or attracted a more general one, had he not offered them theatre that would keep them coming back, and this he did in a series of productions that, like his previous works, were innovative, confrontational, and enormously theatrical – in short the most exciting theatre in Berlin, indeed in Germany. Conservative theatregoers were appalled at his antics, his politics, and his outrageous reworkings of the classics (at a time when 'deconstruction' was a prominent, if not particularly understood, critical term, he was often styled as Germany's leading 'deconstructionist' director), but the Volksbühne rapidly became the essential theatre to attend for anyone with any pretensions to being up to date in the German theatre, whether one loved the productions or hated them. There was a unique energy and excitement in the lobbies of the Volksbühne, where the most elegant Berlin theatregoers rubbed shoulders with unemployed students and workers from the neighbourhood amid tables laden with free publications and boxes of matches and condoms bearing the now-famous logo of the theatre, a crude line drawing of a cartwheel with two stick legs (taken from a secret symbol from the medieval underworld exchanged between such marginal travellers as robbers and actors).

The Volksbühne was by no means a socialist or artistic utopia, however, where all classes mingled in a common appreciation of an artistic event. On the contrary, the audiences were much like those Brecht desired but never really attained: active, engaged, often shouting out their approval and disapproval, and, not infrequently, when skinheads and members of the conservative bourgeoisie held sharply differing opinions, erupting into scuffles and violence. All of this, however, only added to the theatre's reputation and fascination.

Eight productions were mounted on the main stage of the Volksbühne this first year, four of them directed by Castorf: *King Lear*, Arnold Bronnen's expressionist *Rheinische Rebellen*, a stage version of Anthony Burgess's *A Clockwork Orange*, and Euripides' *Alcestis*. Despite the formidable range of dramatic literature these choices represent, all concerned the breakdown of order in society, and the post-Wall tensions in the East were clearly reflected not only in the violent and shocking visual images but in the pounding rock accompaniments, the almost obsessive repetition of key words and phrases, and the adding of supplementary filmic and verbal material from a wide variety of contemporary and historical sources. *A Clockwork Orange*, for example, supplemented its extreme onstage violence with films from the concentration camps, spraying the audience with liquids and the suspending of an actor drenched with blood far above the orchestra pit. Castorf's reputation and following continued to grow. His opening production of *King Lear* gained him his second invitation to the Berlin Theatertreffen, and for the second, *Rheinische Rebellion*, he was the first director awarded the Friedrich Luft Prize, which had been established the previous year by the Berlin *Morgenpost* to honour 'the best Berlin theatre production of the year'.

Both of these productions clearly showed not only Castorf's famous radical reworkings of texts but equally significantly were deeply involved in the contemporary cultural and political imaginary of East Berlin, a world betrayed by its leaders, fallen into ruins, and with little prospect of redemption. Typical was the play's opening, which began with lines from Gloucester screamed out by an accordion-playing woman who wandered through the production rather like a Brechtian ballad singer: 'These late eclipses of the sun and moon portend no good to us [. . .] Love cools, friendship falls off, brothers divide: in cities, mutinies, in counties, discord' (*King Lear*, Act I, Scene 2). The bumbling senile Lear evoked the memory of the deposed DDR leader Erich Honecker, and he and his failed fellow politician Gloucester were left alone on stage while first the other actors, then the audience, departed into the lobby where a dance band was performing.

Although the Volksbühne has since 1992 been thought of, rightly, as Castorf's theatre, rivalling his own work has been his presenting of many of the other leading experimental directors of contemporary Germany. This function was also quite clear from the opening season. Four other directors, extremely different in approach but all sharing Castorf's daring, imagination, and political commitment, directed the season's other four productions, each in large part an occasional piece on the current situation in the former East Berlin. First came Andreas Kriegenburg's *Stadt der Gerechtigkeit* (*City of Justice*). Kriegenburg was 12 years Castorf's junior and came to be widely considered his protégé, although he in fact had arrived at the Volksbühne in 1991, the year before Castorf, and caused a Castorf-like sensation with his 'deconstructed' version of *Woyzeck*, which was the only production from the East invited to that year's Theatertreffen. Like Castorf, Kriegenburg was fascinated by clowning and slapstick. Buster Keaton was his stated role model, and wildly physical comic action fills his spirited productions, even when, or perhaps especially when, the subject is deadly serious (in his 2002 production of Aeschylus' *Oresteia*, George Bush and Donald Rumsfeld, finding Cassandra in an oil can in a kind of satyr-play interlude, killed her with baseball bats).

Next, after Castorf's *Rhenische Rebellen*, came the only non-German director, Jeremy Weller from Scotland, the founder in 1990 of the Grassmarket project in Edinburgh, devoted to what Weller called 'reality theatre', which encouraged people on the margins of society to enact their own stories. His new 'reality' piece at the Volksbühne drew upon the homeless population of the Prenzlauer Berg. After this one production, Weller returned to Scotland, but Castorf's other three German directors went on to become major figures in the German theatre of the 1990s.

Christoph Marthaler from Basel followed Weller. His first Volksbühne production, *Murx den Europäer! Murx ihn! Murx ihn! Murx ihn! Murx ihn ab! Ein patriotischer Abend* (*Kill the European! Kill Him! Kill Him! Kill Him Off! A Patriotic Evening*), established his reputation, was invited to the Theatertreffen, and became one of the best-known productions of the period. The title strongly suggests Castorf's iconoclasm, although it is typical of Marthaler's early work (a previous

Swiss production's title might be translated as 'When the Alpine Mind Overheats, Kill, Free Swiss, Kill'). Castorf invited Marthaler to create a new piece on the theme of German national identity, and, after considerable research in East Berlin, Marthaler created a work typical of his approach, an evening of songs reflecting German history, sung by his regular company in their own distinctive style, interspersed with moments of frantic, often meaningless activity and long passages of total or almost total stillness. The many visual and vocal references to local events delighted Berlin audiences, but the musical and theatrical elements of the piece were sufficiently exciting and original to make the work a great success also at the London International Festival of Theatre in 1995.[3]

After Castorf's *Clockwork Orange* came *100 Jahre CDU: Spiel ohne Grenzen* (*100 Years of the CDU: Games without Borders*) by Christoph Schlingensief. Before this season, Schlingensief had done only film work, but of a highly political and provocative nature (*100 Jahre CDU* echoes his first film, the 1989 *100 Jahre Adolf Hitler*, his focus now the ruling Christian Democratic Union party headed by Helmut Kohl). The live theatre opened to him the possibility, which became central to his work, of direct, personal intervention in both artistic and political spaces, erasing the boundaries between performers, directors, and the public both inside and outside the theatre (Roselt 2000: 159–60). During the performance of this, his first staged work, the director appeared, announcing 'Here is the druggist's son from Oberhausen. Now you know who I am. What I am showing you is all true' (quoted in Bierbichler et al. 1998: 52). Subsequently he mounted Volksbühne productions dealing with past and current political icons such as Helmut Kohl and Rosa Luxemburg and street actions dealing with the homeless, the unemployed, and the disabled, arousing perhaps the most enduring controversy of all the Volksbühne's radical directors.

Following this miraculous first season, Castorf's Volksbühne was named 'Theatre of the Year' by a panel of critics assembled by *Theater Heute*. Castorf had more than fulfilled Nagel's challenge. He had not only assured continued support for this venture but had established the Volksbühne as Berlin's most exciting and innovative theatre, a position it retained into the new century. Subsequent seasons continued to build on the base Castorf laid in this opening year, and he soon became the director against whom all others were compared (Detje 2002: 216). He continued to direct generally four of the main stage productions, with others directed most often by Marthaler, Schlingensief, and, for the first three seasons, Kriegenburg. In 1995, Kriegenburg, much in the iconoclastic mould of his mentor Castor, denounced the Volksbühne 'deconstructive' theatre as 'famous and dead', and left to direct the Hanover theatre and to develop there a different approach to aesthetic and social issues. However, that same year, Angelika Czekay characterised the achievement of the Volksbühne in these words: 'Within today's theatrical landscape in Germany, the Volksbühne stands alone as a theatre that combines a political agenda with an experimental aesthetics which links Brechtian elements with contemporary styles, taken, for example, from *Tanztheater*' (Czekay 1995: 44). The most striking evidence of this latter influence was the replacement of Kriegenburg as a Volksbühne regular by choreographer Johann Kresnik. Kresnik, born in 1939, was a full generation older than Castorf and his colleagues, but his work in dance closely paralleled theirs in theatre. One of the founders of the German *Tanztheater*, he specialised in violent works with strong political overtones such as his 1988 *Macbeth* and 1990 *Ulrike Meinhof*. The horrific effects of both capitalism and a corrupt socialism on prominent historical artists and political figures was his favoured subject matter, and he began his tenure at the Volksbühne with a revival of *Ulrike Meinhof* and a new work, *Rosa Luxemburg: Rote Rosen für Dich* (*Rosa Luxemburg: Red Roses for You*). He contributed three works to the next season, including *Gründgens*, on the noted actor of the Hitler era, the last play in a dance trilogy on the founders, fellow travellers, and supporters of National Socialism in Germany.

Another major event of 1995 was the opening of an alternative stage in the Prater, Berlin's oldest beer garden, located not far from the Volksbühne. From the beginning of his directorship, Castorf had utilised a small alternative space on the third floor of the theatre for more intimate productions, but the Prater provided a larger and more flexible alternative. The first productions there were outdoors, but a building in the grounds was soon fitted up to provide a large black box space, and this provided an important extension of the Volksbühne activity. Kresnik, Marthaler, Schlingensief, and Castorf all directed there between 1995 and 1999 in addition to their work on the main stage, most ambitiously with an eight-part 'War of the Roses' cycle created by Castorf in 1999; but the Prater more often exhibited the work of younger directors still establishing their reputation.

For the remainder of the 1990s it was these four directors who dominated the Volksbühne seasons and indeed the Berlin theatre in general. Fittingly, a joint interview with them was held in the fall of 1999 in *Theater Heute* entitled 'Die Vier von der Volksbühne' (The Four from the Volksbühne). Moderator Franz Wille began the interview by remarking that in view of the contributions of these four men 'the Volksbühne is among the few indisputably major theatres of the 1990s' (Wille 1999: 13). Still, it was Castorf whose presence and work dominated the theatre. In 1994 he was awarded the Fritz Kortner Prize, named in honour of the leading German experimental director of the post-war period.[4] Ivan Nagel composed the Laudatio, which compared the two directors in their commitment to a truth that went far beyond conventional theatre realism. Nagel hailed his work as the fullest expression of contemporary German, and especially Berlin, consciousness, where his 'fragmented plays and characters' reflected the essence of a city 'filled with the experiences of its past and the uncertainties of its future' (Nagel 1995: 10). During the following decade, Castorf was chosen director of the year by *Theater Heute* another four times, and his productions became a yearly feature of the Theatertreffen.

Although these award-winning productions represent only a part of Castorf's work, they show a clear evolution in both his material and his technique. Having achieved major artistic and financial success for himself and the Volksbühne, primarily through his brilliant deconstructive interpretations of the standard classics – Ibsen, Shakespeare, and Schiller – Castorf turned towards more contemporary and more discursive considerations of the spiritual hollowness of the new freedom of the West, under the rubric: 'The freezing cold of freedom'. In a 1995 interview he spoke with nostalgia of his lost East German identity: 'I need a strong foundation to which I can place myself in opposition. Democracy makes me unhappy' (Schütt 1996: 126). The sense of emptiness Castorf felt in the post-Cold War era seemed to him parallel to the feeling of the absurd in the post-war literature of France, especially in the work of Sartre and Camus. His 1998 production of Sartre's *Les mains sales* (*Dirty Hands*) wove contemporary speeches and other material from the Bosnian War into Sartre's text, giving it powerful current resonance, making it even darker than Sartre's original and undermining the easy optimism that had swept over most of Europe, East and West, at the end of the Cold War.

This year proved transitional in Castorf's career. The 1999/2000 season was given the title 'Life without Hope', and for the central work, Castorf turned from Sartre to Camus, suggesting in the nihilistic theatricalism of Camus's *Caligula* something of a parallel to his own desperate search for meaning through transgression in the new post-socialist, late-capitalist world order. The review in the *Berliner Zeitung* began: 'Caligula is Castorf and Caligula's work of destruction is Castorf's work of destruction' (Koburg 2000). This highly theatrical but deeply pessimistic tragedy of a life without hope was thought by some to be Castorf's most personal and also darkest expression. In any case it marked the end of the productions reworking post-war material. Later productions would go in a related but quite different direction, and with a radical departure in staging. This new phase of work was introduced in the spring of 1999 with Camus in a sense providing the bridge, since the first work of this new series was based on his dramatic reworking of Dostoevsky's *The Possessed*, titled *Demons* in line with the German title of the novel, *Die Dämonen*.

In a round table of four leading directors in 1998, Castorf suggested how the theatre had changed during the 1990s and what adjustments must now be made. The explosion of communication technologies has radically altered the way in which works are received, he argued, diluting the provocative power of the fragmentary, deconstructive approach that he found so congenial and so effective earlier in the decade. The new political theatre, he suggested, will work more directly, if not more simplistically, telling stories and presenting political reality. He cited the use of contemporary Bosnian material in *Dirty Hands* and Schlingensief's public events outside the theatre (Castorf 1998: 31).

Demons indeed inaugurated a distinctly new phase of Castorf's work, not philosophically, perhaps, because he remained deeply committed to an examination and critique of contemporary social, political, and economic realities, but certainly in terms of both subject matter and presentational technique. Previous Castorf productions had primarily been radical reworkings of theatre classics, and occasionally of films. Now he turned to the novel, and particularly the modern Russian novel. Four of his next five major productions were such dramatisations, three of them from Dostoevsky. Even more striking, however, was his shift in approach, both in a steadily increasing use of film and video and in a new kind of physical stage space. Central to both of these was his chief designer Bert Neumann. Neumann had begun working with Castorf in 1988 and came with him to the Volksbühne as chief designer in 1992. After 1999, however, he became almost as important as Castorf in creating the new performance image of the Volksbühne. Two features of this work were particularly important from *Demons* onward. For this production Neumann built a complete small brick bungalow on stage, mounted on a turntable so that various sides could be turned toward the audience. No side was open, however, so the audience could see interior action only in two ways, through open windows or doors or by means of video cameras placed within the bungalow and producing images on a huge screen mounted above the house. A programme note situated this dwelling not only geographically but also culturally and temporally: 'one of the last houses just beyond the Western border of Russia, somewhere between *Paris, Texas*, Cindy Sherman, Dogmé 95 and Duma 2000'. The conversations and conflicts of the disillusioned intellectuals gathered in this symbolic locale are similarly shot through with contemporary references, and in the ironic ending most of them flee what they see as a doomed Russia for Germany, which they see as a utopian alternative.

These various features – the bungalow, the enclosed spaces, and the live video – became, in various combinations, the hallmarks of the post-1999 Castorf/Neumann style. Indeed, his 2001 adaptation of Dostoevsky's *Insulted and Injured* was both visually and thematically almost a sequel to *Demons*. Castorf himself called these the first and third elements in a trilogy on the putative End of

History, collectively designated as 'Enjoying Humiliation: Capitalism and Depression'. These Russian works framed his adaptation of the American *Streetcar Named Desire* (under its usual German title, *Endstation Sehnsucht*), in which Stanley Kowalski was shown as a Polish immigrant to America, a former champion of the Solidarity movement, who finds this capitalist state anything but utopian. *Insulted and Injured*, as if to emphasise the growing loss of hope, is set in the dead of winter, the walls tarpapered against the cold, the swimming pool frozen over (in one striking sequence the actors ice skate on it). The production, typically for these novelistic adaptations by Castorf, was lengthy (nearly five hours), sprawling, and filled with a phantasmagoria of characters, whose multiple interactions provided no coherent plot but rather a collage of impressions, political and psychological, shot through with moments of striking theatricality. Ralf Remshardt noted, 'I can name no other ensemble in the German-speaking theatre that possesses this peculiar histrionic sensibility', an energy which suggested to him 'nothing so much as a small troupe of circus artists bonded by their cool exercise of death-defying stunts' (Remshardt 2002: 27).

Sharing the honours of the 2002 Theatertreffen with *Insulted and Injured* was a remarkable new venture from the Volksbühne Prater, the Prater Trilogy of René Pollesch. Although the Volksbühne continued to offer the work of most of the leading young experimental directors of the 1990s – Leander Haußmann and Stefan Bachmann in 1996, Stefan Pucher and Armin Petras in 1998 – the director most closely associated with this theatre was Pollesch, who, after gaining a reputation for his innovative productions at Frankfurt's experimental Theater am Turm, made his Berlin premiere at the Prater and was invited by Castorf to become the artistic director of that theatre in 2001. His first project there was a trilogy that occupied the entire season and established him as one of the leading new dramatist/directors at the new century's opening. Typical of the Volksbühne in theme and general approach (the stresses of global capitalism, extensive contemporary pop-cultural and mass-media references, violent and demanding non-realistic physical action), Pollesch productions nevertheless, like those of Castorf, Marthaler, Kresnik, and Schlingensief, had their own unique style, which others attempted in vain to imitate.

Pollesch's hysterical performances combined the style of television entertainment and academic debates on such subjects as outsourcing, marketing, globalisation, or networking, creating textual and visual satirical montages, with actors often breaking up their lines with acrobatics or screamed delivery. The very titles of the trilogy suggest something of the approach – *Der Stadt als Beute* (*The City as Booty*), *Insourcing des Zuhause: Menschen in Scheiss-Hotels* (*Insourcing at Home: People in Shit-Hotels*), and *Sex* (based on Mae West's comedy of that name). Equally important to the distinctive effect of the trilogy was its stage arrangement, one of Bert Neumann's most distinctive designs – in a sense an expansion of his now-famous Castorf bungalows. The playing space was the same for all three productions, a series of domestic rooms surrounding the audience on three sides, with performers hurtling from one room to another (and sometimes out into the audience as well).

Spatial and visual experimentation continued to expand as Castorf and Neumann presented adaptations of Dostoevsky's *The Idiot* in 2002, Bulgakov's *The Master and Margarita* the same year, and O'Neill's *Mourning Becomes Electra* in 2003 (both invited to the Theatertreffen that year). For *The Idiot*, the audience was placed on various levels of an open tower built on the theatre's huge stage turntable, surrounded by several-story-high buildings in front of and inside which the action took place, sometimes directly visible, other times seen only on video. *The Master and Margarita*, although it returned the audience to the auditorium, created an even more complex visual and phenomenological world on stage, befitting the phantasmagoric world of the Bulgakov novel. Neumann displayed a series of rooms on two levels partly open to the audience, but backstage were a variety of other spaces – a lunatic asylum, a film set, a model of Moscow – through which actors wandered, their movements revealed by live videos, which sometimes followed them out onto the stage (see Plate 5). Film clips were also used, creating a fluid visual world where the lines between reality and image were continually blurred. In these works from the opening years of the twentieth century at both the Volksbühne and the Prater, video designer Jan Speckenbach became a critical additional member of the Castorf–Neumann creative team.

All of these Volksbühne-based projects did not diminish Castorf's interest in taking theatre to the disadvantaged. With Neumann he designed a travelling production, the Rollende Road Show, part theatre, part carnival, with material ranging from Pollesch's *Sex* to fast-food and cheap souvenir stands, that performed in marginal industrial and workers' suburbs. From this, in turn, came the 'Neustadt' (New City) projects of 2003, which used the set design for *The Idiot*, converting the entire interior of the Volksbühne, auditorium, and stage alike into a kind of modern indoor mall, with the sort of cheap commercial outlets familiar to those who inhabit the fringes of today's urban sprawl. Both Pollesch and Castorf created productions within this setting in 2004, among them Castorf's adaptation of Frank Norris's *Greed* and Pollesch's *Das Revolutionäre Unternehmen* (*The Revolutionary Enterprise*).

Not long after the dazzling first season of Castorf at the Volksbühne, Christopher Salter concluded one of the first English-language reports on the new venture, in *American Theatre*, by remarking that 'Castorf has more than once expressed his adoration for the Berlin Dadaism of the 1920s, and he is well aware of that movement's short life. How long the Volksbühne's Dada moment lasts will remain to be seen' (1995: 71).

By the end of the first decade of the new century, the ominous undertone of Salter's appraisal 30 years before seemed well justified. Castorf's star had distinctly faded. No longer was he among the directors that were invariably mentioned whenever Germans discussed the current theatre, and not one of his productions had been selected for the Theatertreffen since 2003, while he had been represented in eight of the nine previous festivals. To understand fully the significance of this, one must realise that the rise of the modern 'directors' theatre' (*Regietheater*) in Germany was accompanied by and in certain measure shaped by the critical establishment that grew up alongside it. During the mid- to late 1960s, when the foundations of the modern *Regietheater* were being laid by Peter Stein in Munich, Peter Zadek in Bremen, and Claus Peymann in Frankfurt, the foundations of the modern German theatrical criticism establishment were also being laid by the founding of the Berlin Theatertreffen in 1964 and of Germany's leading theatre journal,

Theater Heute, in 1962. The later establishment of such awards as the Kortner Prize and *Theater Heute*'s Director of the Year award increased the authority of the relatively small group of critics who were regular contributors to this journal and judges of these committees. By the end of the century there had developed a clear pattern to the directors most reviewed and interviewed in *Theater Heute*, most invited to the Theatertreffen, and most honoured with other prizes. They were overwhelmingly younger directors and particularly those who brought highly innovative insights and approaches to the standard classics. Peter Stein and Claus Peymann, both highly favoured by this system and later almost totally rejected by it, have both been highly critical of what they consider its cultural faddism.

Whether one agrees with their criticism or not, however, there seems a clear ongoing pattern to the directors favoured by this establishment, which may be traced either by viewing the Theatertreffen selections over the years or the directors most interviewed and whose productions are most featured in *Theater Heute*. During the 1970s and 1980s, Stein, Zadek, and Peymann dominated the field, although by the later 1980s other names were replacing them in popularity – Andrea Breth, Thomas Langhoff, Hans Neuenfels, Jürgen Flimm. In the 1990s, a whole new generation dominated, headed by Castorf but including Schlingensief, Marthaler, and Kriegenburg. At the turn of the century this generation was in turn replaced by new names – Thomas Ostermeier, Luk Perceval, Michael Thalheimer, Stephan Kimmig, Sebastian Nübling.

This might seem a natural process if there were in fact a generation change, with older directors dying or retiring as young ones appeared, but Stein, Zadek, and Peymann remained highly active; they were simply outside the circle. The critical invisibility of Stein is perhaps understandable, since he now works almost entirely outside Germany, but Peymann was located in the heart of Berlin, directing what is still for many the best-known German theatre, the Berliner Ensemble, and yet he remained almost invisible to the critical establishment. On the other hand, age does not automatically mean critical rejection. Among the most fashionable current directors in German is Jürgen Gosch, who gained modest critical attention in the early 1980s, fell totally out of favour, and re-emerged in the new millennium. Although the sort of revival Gosch enjoyed has been rare, an even more striking example of such a return to prominence has recently been enjoyed by Castorf as well.

A kind of prologue to Castorf's return to official prominence was his highly controversial production of Wagner's *Ring Cycle* in Bayreuth in 2013. For the past several decades, some of Europe's most radical postmodern directors have been invited to Bayreuth and have as a rule predictably scandalised the operatic world, as did Castorf, with their attacks on Wagner's plots, characters, and music. Some such scandalous productions, like Patrice Chéreau's 1974 *Ring*, have come to be accepted as important contributions; others, like Christoph Schlingensief's 2004 *Parsifal*, have not survived. It is still too early to appraise the eventual fate of Castorf's highly contemporary, non-Wagnerian, and even non-musical *Ring*, but it heralded his clear return to prominence in the German theatre world. The visual world of this *Ring* was the creation not of Bert Neumann, now in declining health, but of a young Serbian designer, Aleksander Denić, who would replace Neumann as Castorf's leading collaborator after this time. Neumann designed only one more significant Castorf production, the 2015 *Brothers Karamazov*, before his death that year.

Denić's designs resembled Neumann's in their complexity, piling up of fragmentary spaces, and frequent use of spaces observable to the audience only by live video projections, but the Serbian designs were even more monumental and complex and often utilised ironic or parodic icons or signs, which fitted well with Castorf's montage approach. In 2014, Castorf and Denić applied this distinctive style of multiple settings, perspectives, and sources to an elaborate interpretation in Munich of Céline's epic novel of the sufferings of the twentieth century, *Reise ans Ender der Nacht* (*Journey to the End of the Night*). With this production, Denić was named 'stage designer of the year' by *Theater Heute*, and Castorf returned to the Theatertreffen for the first time in a decade. This was followed at the beginning of January 2015 by another notable Munich production, a radical reinterpretation of one of the most radical plays in the modern German repertoire, Brecht's quasi-expressionist *Baal*. The staging, drawing heavily upon physical and filmic references to the Vietnam War, so offended Brecht's heirs that the Residenztheater had to curtail the run.

These events were soon overtaken by a much larger scandal. In March the Berlin city authorities abruptly announced their decision to end Castorf's virtually unprecedented quarter-of-a-century directorship of a major Berlin theatre. Even more surprising, and to many highly disturbing, was the decision to replace him with an international figure who was not a theatre director, but an artistic curator – Chris Dercon, the former director of London's Tate Modern art gallery. Both liberals and conservatives protested at this new orientation, which seemed based on a contemporary interest in global market culture rather than traditional artistic concerns, and in fact the besieged Dercon administration never managed to find a successful artistic direction. After six turbulent months, Dercon resigned from the post. This major controversy put Castorf again into the artistic spotlight and many of the critics who had dismissed his work a few years before as outdated and predictable now hailed him as a central example of Germany's ongoing dedication to radical and politically involved staging. He returned again in triumph to the Theatertreffen in 2018, with special arrangements made with the Brecht heirs to allow two presentations there of the banned Munich production of *Baal*.

During his final two seasons at the Volksbühne, Castorf continued his mission with little diminishment of spirit or imagination. His final production, in the Spring of 2017, was, suitably, a monumental adaptation of *Faust*, one of his most ambitious undertakings, which, hardly surprisingly, was selected to open the 2018 Theatertreffen. Far less noted this year was the departure of another pillar of the modern German stage, Claus Peymann, who, despite his high visibility in the late twentieth century, never won over the German critical establishment in his almost 20 years as head of the Berliner Ensemble. His successor, Oliver Reese, not sharing Peymann's intense dislike of Castorf's approach, shrewdly invited Castorf to create his first post-Volksbühne production there. This was a seven-hour adaptation of the Hugo classic, *Les Miserables*, which Castorf and Denić read through the lens of a meditation on modern revolution, with a particularly Cuban flavour. The critical response generally considered Castorf to be back at the peak of his form and once again established as a central star in the Berlin firmament.

> **Five key productions**
>
> *Miss Sara Sampson*. By Gotthold Lessing. Design by Hartmut Meyer. Perf. Karlheinz Vietsch, Silvia Rieger. Bayerisches Staatsschauspiel Munich. 18 April 1989.
>
> *Die Räuber*. By Friedrich Schiller. Design by Bert Neumann. Berlin Volksbühne. 22 September 1990.
>
> *Dämonen*. By Frank Castorf, after Dostoevsky. Design by Bert Neumann. Berlin Volksbühne. 19 May 1999.
>
> *Endstation Sehnsucht*. By Tennessee Williams. Design by Bert Neumann. Berlin Volksbühne. 13 October 2000.
>
> *Faust*. By Johann von Goethe. Design by Alexsander Denić. Berlin Volksbühne. 4 May 2017.

Acknowledgement

A version of this chapter was first published in Carlson 2009: 95–115, expanded in the first edition of the current collection, and updated for this second edition.

Notes

1 On German directors in the second half of the century, see Carlson 2009.
2 *Verwurstung* is an untranslatable pun combining the word for 'destruction' with the traditional figure of Misrule, the farce figure Hans Wurst.
3 On Marthaler, see Barnett's essay in this collection, pp. 207–27.
4 Kortner was the leading actor in Germany in the pre-Second World War period defining a whole new acting style. Only after his return to Germany from exile in America did he turn to directing.

Bibliography

Bierbichler, Josef, Harold Martenstein and Christoph Schlingensief (1998) *Engagement und Skandal*, Berlin: Alexander Verlag.

Carlson, Marvin (2009) *Theatre Is More Beautiful than War: German Stage Directing in the Late Twentieth Century*, Iowa City, IA: University of Iowa Press.

Castorf, Frank (1991a) 'Man muß kämpfen um sein Daseinsrecht', *Junge Welt*, 16/17 March.

―――― (1991b) 'Im Gespräch', *Süddeutsche Zeitung*, 23 June.

―――― (1994) 'Held Hübchen', *Theater Heute* (Yearbook): 37–40.

―――― (1998) 'Auf der Suche nach dem Trojanischen Pferd', *Theater Heute* (Yearbook): 24–39.

Czekay, Angelika (1995) 'New Directions in (East) Berlin', *Western European Stages*, 7 (1): 37–49.

Detje, Robin (2002) *Castorf: Provokation aus Prinzip*, Berlin: Henschel Verlag.

Iden, Peter (1989) 'Review of *Miss Sara Sampson*', *Süddeutsche Zeitung*, 24 October.

Koburg, Roland (2000) 'Bevölkerungs-vernichtung', *Berliner Zeitung*, 7 January.

Nagel, Ivan (1995) 'Radikalität und Wahrheit: Laudatio auf Frank Castorf', *Theater Heute*, 1: 7–10.

―――― (2001) *Streitschriften*, Berlin: Siedler Verlag.

Remshardt, Ralf (2002) 'Touring *The Insulted and the Injured*: Theater der Welt in Koln, Bonn, Dusseldorf, and Duisburg, 2002', *Western European Stages*, 14 (3): 25–32.

Roselt, Jens (2000) 'Postmodernes Theater: Subjekt in Rotation', in Paul Michael Lützeler (ed.), *Räume der literarischen Postmoderne*, Tubingen: Stauffenburg Verlag, pp. 147–66.

Salter, Christopher (1995) 'Castorf's Rebellion at the Volksbühne', *American Theater*, 12 (10): 71.

Schütt, Hans-Dieter (1996) *Die Erotik des Verrats: Gespräche mit Frank Castorf*, Berlin: Dietz Verlag.

von Becker, Peter and Michael Merschmeier (1989) 'Ich möchte nicht in den Untergrund! Theater Heute-Gespräch mit dem Ostberliner Regisseur Frank Castorf', *Theater Heute*, 12: 18–27.

Wengeriek, Reinhard (1989) 'Review of *Nora*', *Die Union*, 26 April.

Wille, Franz (1999) 'Die Vier von der Volksbühne', *Theater Heute*, 8/9: 12.

Woolf, Brandon (2018) 'Frank Castorf's Art of Institutional Dis/avowal: A Volksbühne Elegy', *Theatre Survey*, 59 (2): 249–64.

Chapter 6

DANIEL MESGUICH

'Unsummarisable' *mises en scène*

Jim Carmody (with additional material by Dominic Glynn)

In the concluding remarks to his *Stage Directors in Modern France*, David Whitton expresses some reservations about the emerging trend of 'uncompromising intellectualism' in French theatre of the 1970s and early 1980s that 'invites the reflection that its ideal audience would be composed entirely of Ph.D.s in performance theory' (1987: 279–80). One of the directors Whitton identifies with the most extreme aspects of this trend is Daniel Mesguich. At the time, Mesguich was in the early years of his career, an iconoclastic provocateur, either lauded or reviled for his extravagantly poetic, aggressively theatricalist work with classic texts, especially those of Racine (*Andromaque*, 1975) and Shakespeare (*Hamlet*, 1977). Despite enjoying high visibility in the first decade of his career – his *King Lear* appeared on the main stage at the Avignon Festival in 1981 – he was still on the experimental margins of the French theatre when Whitton was writing his book in the mid-1980s. Today, however, more than 47 years after his first *mise en scène* (Kafka's *The Castle*, 1972), Mesguich, a former Director of the Conservatoire National Supérieur d'Art Dramatique (2007–13), is very much a respected figure in French theatre. Resistance to his 'intellectualism' has abated over the years, though it has not entirely disappeared, as a major crisis at the end of his term in charge of the Conservatoire proved.[1] This intellectualism remains, along with his often extravagantly overt theatricality, a signature feature of his work.

Born in Algiers in 1952, Daniel Mesguich has been working as an actor and director for nearly 50 years. He founded his first company, Le Théâtre du Miroir, in 1974; his current company, Miroir et Métaphore, dates from 1998. Twice, he has been named director of a state-sponsored theatre, first at the Théâtre Gérard Philipe in the Paris suburb of Saint-Denis (1986–8), and later at the Théâtre National de Lille (1991–8). For much of his career, Mesguich has devoted a considerable portion of his energies to teaching. He was the youngest professor of acting ever appointed when he began teaching at the Conservatoire National in 1983, an institution he ran from 2007 to 2013. In 2017, a theatre school bearing his name, the 'Cours Mesguich', opened its doors to the public, providing actor training in a 'utopic space for research and pleasure'. Further evidence for Mesguich's interest in teaching can be found in the number of masterclasses that he gives all over the world, as well as in his collaborations with theatre historian Alain Viala, which include joint authorship of a book on theatre (Viala and Mesguich 2011), and audio recordings of poems and extracts of novels for a series on French literature from the Middle Ages to the present day (Viala and Mesguich 2012).

From the beginning of his career, critics and scholars have focused on the degree to which his work has been, and remains, intellectually challenging. At times, the challenge has emerged from a treatment of the classic text (the majority of his energies have been devoted to staging classic texts) that breaks with the prevailing understanding of its dramaturgy. Mesguich has argued that staging a classic involves an interpretative reading of both a visible and an invisible text, the second being composed of the memory of the visible text, 'its *history*, its *dust*' (2011: 7). This explains the second challenge that has emerged from what was often seen as a semiotically overcharged *mise en scène*, a scenography replete with imagery whose function was far from obvious. As the ideas that nourished Mesguich's work became more and more widely understood, as his audiences and critics (some of them, at least) absorbed the ideas of Barthes, Borges, Derrida, Lacan, and so many others, Mesguich's *mises en scène* became less puzzling, less enigmatic, although a substantial degree of puzzle and enigma always remains.[2]

However familiar Mesguich's poetics might be to today's audiences, the 'intellectualist' aspect of his cultural identity continues to be foregrounded. Armelle Héliot's review of his 2006 play *Boulevard du boulevard du boulevard*, for example, invokes this identity in its opening sentence: 'Daniel Mesguich is a rigorous intellectual who is good, very good, at reading texts [...] and decoding their analytical, philosophical, and ideological ramifications' (Héliot 2006).[3] Scholars, too, invariably identify Mesguich's work with his philosophical and theoretical interests. Marvin Carlson, for instance, introduces Mesguich's Shakespeare productions as being 'heavily influenced by contemporary French literary and psychoanalytic theory' (1993: 213), while Nicole Fayard locates Mesguich's place in French theatre history as being 'one of the first French directors to apply the teachings of Jacques Derrida and Jacques Lacan on the stage' (2007: 42).

Rather than present himself as an artist who espouses a particular theory – a pupil of either Cixous or Derrida or Freud or Lacan, to name the theorists most frequently associated with his work – he presents himself as the sum of all his readings and re-readings without prejudice with respect to culture, genre, language, or period:

> All of my work in the theatre [...] has been underpinned by the 'idea' that texts are not beautifully self-contained entities with definitive, stable, and assigned beginnings and endings; that each text [...] is always open, linked to other texts [...]; and that faced with a text, we are never alone, that we are able to read it only with the help of another, a thousand others.
>
> No doubt that's why I turn more readily toward the writers who always seem 'to say the same thing' [...] [whose] names are to be understood less as the names of individuals than as the titles of enormous books; they are: *Shakespeare*, the book; *Borges*, the book; *Claudel, Blanchot, Chekhov, Aragon, Marivaux, Derrida, Racine, Cixous, Proust*, etc.
>
> (Mesguich 2004a)

In short, he presents himself as first and foremost an intertextualist. In recent years, Mesguich's intertextual practice has extended beyond directing to the creation of plays, such as *Boulevard du boulevard du boulevard* (2006), an exploration of late nineteenth-century comic and melodramatic dramaturgy, and *Phasmes* (2008), a one-man show that invites the audience into Mesguich's own 'library', an event he characterises in the press dossier as 'a *spectacle* about intertextuality'.

While Carlson and Fayard provide excellent descriptions of the specific ways in which Mesguich's intertextualism manifests itself in his work on Shakespeare, all the strategies of textual intervention (with the obvious exception of translation in the case of plays written in French) and *mise en scène* they mention are readily identifiable in his work on other authors. Textual strategies include the radical cutting of the original and/or the interpolation of text(s) selected from a variety of time periods, genres, and cultures; and the creation of a new translation, either by Mesguich himself or in collaboration with others, that usually foregrounds the relative linguistic inaccessibility of the source text. Mesguich's interest in translation is both testament to his training at the hands of the director and translator Antoine Vitez, and evidence of how closely he reads texts, to the extent of quibbling with other translators' choices. Such textual strategies often resulted, especially in the first decade of his career or so, in the creation of a text that many of his spectators found quite impenetrable, so far was it from their experience and expectations. Unfamiliar as spectators were with the extraordinary range and depth of Mesguich's reading, initial exposures to his ebullient intertextuality can only have been intensely frustrating.

Strategies of *mise en scène* enumerated by Carlson and Fayard include the introduction of additional characters or additional actors playing aspects of the same character; the use of mirrors and mirror images, especially presenting actors and/or characters as mirror images of each other (this strategy often appears in an attenuated form in which actors/characters merely look alike and mirror each other); the frequent use of books and images of books, libraries, and archives; the use of images of fire, decay, and destruction; and the extensive use of music and complex sound effects. In a talk after the screening of a documentary that followed the rehearsals of a production of *Hamlet* he directed in Chinese with students of the Shanghai Academy of the Performing Arts, Mesguich explained that the double is at the heart of his conception of representing characters.[4] The real Hamlet is neither big nor small, young nor old, but all of these at once. Having two actors portray the same character forces audiences to read the character as the synergy of the two bodies. Generally, these strategies have encountered far less resistance from spectators and critics than Mesguich's textual strategies, perhaps because the beauty of his scenography and his overt theatricality could readily be enjoyed for their own sakes.

Over time, audiences have become increasingly familiar and comfortable with Mesguich's style – the techniques that he was among the first to introduce in France are now in every director's toolkit – and yet some discontent remains. Some spectators and critics continue to expect something from Mesguich that he has never been able to offer: a legible reading or interpretation of the classic text being performed. Mesguich is, of course, well aware of this expectation and often addresses it head on. In the programme notes for his 2002 production of Molière's *Dom Juan*, for example, he explains that it is not his intent to offer an interpretation that can be reduced to a thesis statement: 'I'm not going to tell you what "my" reading of *Dom Juan* is, you'll have to read, in the present, all of the present of the performance. The theatre is, precisely, the Art of the Unsummarisable' (Mesguich 2002).

When Mesguich makes a claim for the 'unsummarisability' of his *mises en scène*, he is not suggesting that his *mises en scène* cannot be read at all, but that they can best be read as an evolving experience during the performance. That is, they can best be understood by individual spectators as an accumulation of their own impressions, reflections, and hypotheses, some of which are retained and some discarded as the *mise en scène* unfolds, while meaning remains speculative, provisional, fragmentary, deferred. What he would like his spectators to accept, in short, is the opportunity to enjoy their own intertextual adventures.

What follows is an account of my own response to one of Mesguich's recent invitations to intertextual adventure, his 2002 production of Molière's *Dom Juan*, which I saw during its initial run at the Athénée Théâtre Louis-Jouvet. The descriptions of elements of the *mise en scène* and their effect on the spectators are based on both my memories and the published video documentation (*Dom Juan*, 2004). I have chosen to focus on the strategies Mesguich employs to guide the spectators towards an understanding of his compositional methods, his extensive augmentation of female presence in the play, and the difficulty of arriving at an understanding of the *mise en scène* as a whole.

Mesguich and *Dom Juan*

Dom Juan (1665) was Molière's most incendiary play, quickly suppressed after only a few performances and never revived during his lifetime. Indeed, the play was so incendiary that scholars continue to add to the catalogue of its provocations.[5] After the playwright's death, the play was known only in Thomas Corneille's radically rewritten and utterly unprovocative version well into the nineteenth century. Even when interest in Molière's original play began to develop in the late nineteenth century, the play was almost universally considered weak, if not severely flawed. Theatre artists and scholars alike found its episodic, fragmented structure impossible to reconcile with their own understanding of neoclassical dramaturgy. Equally puzzling to them were Molière's numerous departures from Tirso de Molina's well-known story of Don Juan Tenorio, the great seducer. Reservations about the quality of the play changed abruptly, however, when Louis Jouvet staged it in 1947 at the Théâtre de l'Athénée. Since then, virtually every prominent French director has staged the play (see Whitton 1995 for a detailed stage history). Invited to direct a play from Jouvet's repertoire as part of the 2001–2 season at the Athénée, a season dedicated to honouring the 50th anniversary of Jouvet's death, Mesguich chose *Dom Juan*, and so France's most aggressively intertextual director for the second time approached Molière's most overtly intertextual play.

It has been a feature of Mesguich's career that he has returned to direct the same classic texts several times – *Hamlet*, for instance in 1977, 1987, 1996, 2011, and 2016. Mesguich's first *Dom Juan* was staged at La Métaphore in Lille in 1995–6 and abounded with the director's signature elements. Mesguich intertextually embraced other directors (recorded quotes from directors such as Jouvet and Vilar discussing *Dom Juan* preceded the raising of the curtain) and other playwrights (offstage voices spoke lines from Corneille, Racine, and Shakespeare during the third act). Like many of his productions, *Dom Juan* featured a complex soundscape of music and other sounds; there was a grand piano onstage, sometimes played by the actors, and Don Juan occasionally played a saxophone (Carlson 1996: 24–5). The setting for the third act presented a signature Mesguich image, an archive – in this case, a storage room filled with leftover bits and pieces from productions of other plays. Mesguich created the most remarkable visual effects of the production in this quintessentially theatricalised space:

> The beggar emerges like a troll from a prop hillock. Sganarelle [...] finds a huge book that tells of a man ambushed and killed by robbers. Don Juan seizes a pen, rewriting the text to save the traveler, who then literally bursts up out of the pages of the open book, to reveal himself as Elvira's brother. No statue is seen, but his lines are spoken in whispers from all sides of the stage. As mysterious (double) spotlights cast their beams like the eyes of hidden creatures across the fantastic landscape [...], globes float in the air, windlasses whirl about, puppets creakingly wave their arms, baskets and hampers slam open and shut, all without apparent human agency.
>
> (Carlson 1996: 25)

With respect to his treatment of Molière's characters, Mesguich introduced two radical departures from the traditional manner of staging the play: he cast a young woman (Luce Mouchel) in the role of Sganarelle and presented M. Dimanche as 'an Armenian merchant' who was accompanied on stage by his entire family, creating the impression of being 'refugees' (Carlson 1996: 25).

Although the 2002 *mise en scène* develops some of the ideas initially explored in 1996, the two productions are quite dissimilar; indeed, some of Mesguich's most frequently employed techniques are either absent or significantly diminished in scale. Explicitly theatrical intertextual references of the kind employed in Lille are completely absent: there are no quotes from other directors and no lines from plays by other writers. Molière's text is performed with only a few cuts.[6] The production incorporates a single, repeated (brief) citation of another work: in Acts I, IV, and V, Don Juan listens to the 'Là ci darem la mano' duet from Mozart's *Don Giovanni* on an antique gramophone that appears to be of museum quality, almost untarnished by the passage of time. Absent also is the elaborate display of scenographic magic in the scenery and prop-filled space of 1996's

Act III. Now the stage is relatively bare for Act III; the Poor Man and Elvire's brothers simply walk on from the wings.

Some elements of the 1996 production remain, notably the idea of having M. Dimanche come onstage with his entire family; only in 2002, M. Dimanche is no longer an Armenian merchant but a red-haired French Jew, whose orthodoxy is signalled by his long locks. While Sganarelle is now played by a man (Christian Hecq), the additional female presence introduced by Luce Mouchel in the first *mise en scène* is now replaced by a set of ten female nude statues: seven of these statues define the contours of the playing area in three different configurations presented of Don Juan's living space (Acts I, IV, and V); three are played by actresses who provide a gasp-provoking *coup de théâtre* in Act III.[7]

Principles of composition

Mesguich seats Sganarelle, incognito, in the auditorium as the spectators take their seats. Suddenly (in response to no perceptible cue), the actor puts on a hat, jumps to his feet, and begins to speak Sganarelle's opening lines. As he speaks, he climbs onto the stage and stands before the elaborately painted facsimile of a baroque curtain. In his unmistakably modern clown costume (high-waisted baggy black pants too short in the leg, a red-and-white striped shirt, tight-fitting black cap), Sganarelle appears visually out of place when juxtaposed with the sumptuous baroque image that provides his backdrop. Immediately prior to the first mention of 'tobacco', his speech is interrupted by the banging of the stage manager's baton signalling the imminent start of the performance. Sganarelle's speech is similarly interrupted on two further occasions, each time immediately before he pronounces the word 'tobacco'. After the third of the traditional *'trois coups'*, Sganarelle announces 'that's enough on that subject'. His next words, 'Let's get back to our conversation', cues the raising of the curtain, after which he steps into the world of the play already waiting, brightly lit, in suspended animation, behind the curtain. At that moment, the auditorium lights dim.

Gusman stands as if asleep on his feet, his arms and head succumbing to the pull of gravity; several stagehands either stand like Gusman or lie on the floor. Gusman is dressed identically to Sganarelle, lacking only the hat. The scenic elements – a bed draped in red, seven alabaster-white statues of nude women, an S-shaped love seat upholstered in red – remain shrouded for now in white dust cloths. A shout from Sganarelle quickly reanimates Gusman and the stagehands, who scramble to get back to work. Sganarelle and Gusman initiate a *commedia*-inspired sequence in which Sganarelle asks Gusman for his assistance in removing his hat, which is apparently 'glued' to his head. Having successfully removed Sganarelle's hat, Gusman discovers – much to his volubly expressed delight – that Sganarelle's head is bald just like his own. Both turn to the audience to babble their pleasure at discovering the astonishing extent to which they resemble each other. Both Sganarelle and Gusman vocalise frequently throughout this sequence, but without using a word of Molière's text; their language consists entirely of apparently improvised nonsense syllables, a staple of the *commedia dell'arte* traditions that this scene – and much of Hecq's Sganarelle – draws on.

The addition of the nonsense dialogue inevitably breaks the flow of Molière's text, just as the noises from behind the curtain interrupted the flow of Sganarelle's opening monologue. The nonsense dialogue, it soon becomes apparent, is itself subject to interruption when, sensing the presence of a stagehand, Sganarelle and Gusman abruptly fall silent. As the scene progresses, repeated entries of the stagehands bring Sganarelle and Gusman's conversation, verbal or non-verbal, to a halt. These stagehand entries – removing the dustcovers, carrying Don Juan's paintings and books across the stage, changing the placement of the statues – are invariably accompanied by the same loud, repetitive music cue, a cue that calls to mind circus animals on parade. The music and the two clowns belong, apparently, in the same theatrical universe.

Mesguich's extended version of the scene introduces the audience to the compositional principle of the *mise en scène*, providing them with a guide to processing the even more complex stream of words, images, and events to come. This compositional principle is succinctly expressed in Mesguich's 'Note d'Intention' (Note About Intentions) in the programme handed to the spectators as they take their seats: 'First we make theatre, then we perform *Dom Juan*' (2002). While the principle as stated seems to be a simple one, its realisation on stage is quite the opposite, for Mesguich has composed a multi-layered theatrical narrative in which the *mise en scène* and Molière's text are continually juxtaposed – intertextualised – in a manner that reveals, even accentuates, the difference and the distance between them.

During one of these stagehand interruptions, Gusman's attention is drawn to the brightly spot-lit statue placed just upstage of centre, which represents a young woman leaning forward, facing partially upstage right, her hands resting on a truncated column. While Sganarelle is busy dealing with a stagehand, Gusman approaches the statue, his hands outstretched to fondle the statue's buttocks. Sganarelle returns, catching Gusman in the act before he manages to touch the nude figure. Embarrassed, Gusman explains his reaction to the statue with a series of facial expressions, eloquent hand gestures, and a squirming torso, which in turn leads to a conversation made of grunts and grimaces in which both agree that the representation of the young woman's buttocks is indeed sexually exciting. The audience responds with laughter, amused by Gusman's comic inability to differentiate between real women and art objects. By the end of the scene between Gusman and Sganarelle, Mesguich has prepared his audience for his own entry as Don Juan – he often plays the lead in the productions he directs – and the rest of the play.

With respect to the relationship between the *mise en scène* and Molière's play, Mesguich has alerted the audience to two potential possibilities – 'potential' because he never definitively opts for one possibility or the other, and he constantly, at times simultaneously, plays on both. The first of these possibilities is exemplified by the line Sganarelle speaks to cue the raising of the curtain: 'Let's get back to our conversation.' Here the staging appears to coincide with great precision with the literal meaning of the words in their dramatic context – this is indeed the line that Molière uses to segue from the tobacco monologue to the opening dialogue between the two servants. And since the raising of the curtain is such a large-scale event, and the words employed to trigger that event relatively unambiguous, it is virtually impossible for a spectator to miss this blatantly obvious framing of an almost 'perfect' scenic realisation – almost an illustration, even – of a line from the play. The second possibility, of course, is the absence of any obvious connection, causative or otherwise, between Molière's dialogue and the events on stage. The opening sequence offers a whole catalogue of examples that draw attention to the nature of the relationship between Molière's text and Mesguich's *mise en scène*: Sganarelle and Gusman's extensive non-verbal dialogue, their identical costumes and hairstyling, the stagehands, the statues, the music, none of which can be connected with specific lines in Molière's text, and many of which function as interruptions of the flow of Molière's dialogue.

Bit by bit, the combination of identical costuming, *commedia*-inspired gesture, elaborate non-verbal dialogue, and music create a relationship between Sganarelle and Gusman that exists almost, but not quite, separately from Molière's text. Watching the performance thus demands a triply split focus on the part of the spectator: the spectator is asked to follow the unfolding of Molière's text and construct on the basis of the spoken dialogue (both the words themselves and the manner in which they are spoken) a developing narrative; the spectator is also asked to follow the unfolding relationship between the actors as expressed in gesture and expression and construct a developing narrative on that basis; finally, the spectator is asked to follow a complex scenic text – a combination of visual and sound images – and construct a developing narrative on that basis, too. These three narratives unfold without pause throughout the performance, forcing the spectator to recalibrate on an ongoing basis his or her understanding of the relationship between them. In effect, Mesguich invites his spectators to read all of these narratives intertextually, without privileging one over another.

I have chosen to focus on how these narratives develop in the opening sequence because that sequence presents Mesguich's contrapuntal narratives at their least complex and provides an accessible introduction to the director's poetics. Other complex examples of this technique employed later in the play would require the kind of extended description and analysis that is beyond the scope of this essay. Particularly effective examples of this triple-focus technique include Mesguich's treatment of the relationship between Don Juan and Elvire, which involves a startling amount of physical contact (several times, in both Act I and Act V, Don Juan embraces Elvire with affection without indicating in any way to the audience that he is being hypocritical), and the first scene between Don Juan and Don Carlos, in which a strong emotional connection develops between the two characters that seems unrelated to the scripted scene itself. To some extent, these sequences provoke us to imagine alternative outcomes for these characters quite different from those scripted by Molière. Another outstanding example occurs in the first scene of Act II, in which Pierrot appears as a kind of reincarnation of Jean-Louis Barrault's clown character in Marcel Carné's 1945 film, *Les Enfants du Paradis*, performing slow-motion magic tricks with a rose before ending the scene by climbing on to a moon from which he observes the second scene of the act, suspended high above the stage (one of the most appealing images in a visually beautiful production). Another and perhaps related example arrives in the M. Dimanche sequence in Act IV, which Mesguich stages as an escalating series of threats and taunts directed at M. Dimanche that culminates in a terrified family leaving the stage to the sound of barking dogs, air-raid sirens, marching boots, and an over-amplified voice shouting in German. These sequences from Act II and Act IV call to mind French collaboration with the Nazis (Arletty, the object of Barrault's desire in the film, was a collaborator) and in particular the effects of that collaboration on the Jews, a painful and shameful history that continues to resonate in France.

The statue narrative

Mesguich has already focused our attention on the statues at the beginning of the play during the comic scene between Sganarelle and Gusman. Throughout the play, Mesguich develops what might be called a 'statue narrative'. Throughout the first act Mesguich uses the statues as points of reference for the placement and movement of the actors. Two statues stand downstage, one stage left, the other stage right almost on the plane of the proscenium arch. A third statue stands upstage right, a group of three statues stands upstage left; both groups are placed about three metres from the edge of the stage. These six statues form an almost perfect virtual trapezoid that defines the boundary of the playing area. A seventh statue – the object of Gusman's desire – stands slightly upstage of centre. In Act I, Elvire's movements appear to be anchored by the upstage-right and centre-stage statues. At one moment, she adopts an emotionally agonised pose that almost mirrors that of the upstage-right statue, which she is standing beside at the time; the audience is clearly expected to notice the similarities between the two female figures, but it is too early in the performance to do anything more than simply notice. At another moment, Don Juan moves into the middle of the upstage-left group, a movement that attracts attention because it appears to break through the invisible boundaries of the trapezoid delineated by the statues without the character making an exit (when Elvire breaks this boundary, she does so only to make entrances and exits).

In addition to anchoring the actors' movements, the statues have an almost overpowering visual presence in a very high contrast environment (black, white, and red are the dominant colours). They are the brightest objects on a stage with a black floor treated so as to function like a mirror (under certain lighting conditions, and depending on where the spectator sits in the auditorium, the actors appear doubled by their own reflections); even Elvire's white dress does not reflect as much light. In subsequent acts, the statues are never quite as brightly lit, although they always function as boundary markers for the principal acting area (see Plate 6).

The seven white statues are absent from Act II, although some of the characters do stand in statue-like poses on plinths made of piles of extremely oversized books to be painted by Pierrot (in this production, Pierrot is both a clown and a painter). While the seven white statues are also absent from Act III, the statue motif takes on new degrees of complexity in Mesguich's treatment of the Commander's tomb.

At the beginning of Act III, a pedestal holding four statues stands in deep shadow upstage left. On the downstage edge of the pedestal, a man lies, his body stretched out in agony. Only his feet and hands make contact with the ground. His face is invisible, his head thrown far backward, his neck fully exposed, his abdomen and ribs stretched to their physical limits. His genitals are prominent, although covered by an abstract modesty panel. Surrounding this male in agony are three young female figures, all nude. One sits on a small rock, another kneels on one knee, a third sits on what may be a cloth. The tips of their swords penetrate the man's torso. The image itself constitutes something of a visual puzzle. While the women are clearly represented in the act of stabbing the man, the man is clearly represented as being still alive – his body remains suspended above the ground by his hands and feet. The women seem to be at ease, exerting no physical energy whatsoever, apparently completely uninvolved either emotionally or physically. It's as if the sculpture presents two time frames simultaneously: the women exist in a time after the killing while the man exists in the moment of being killed.

Throughout the act, the pedestal with its puzzling statuary remains in shadow until the moment when Don Juan invites the Commander to supper. At that moment, the light on the statues fades up and the three female statues begin to move. Mesguich thus creates the most startling effect of the entire production using live actors. The 'coming to life' of the female statues is so effective because Mesguich has dared to place them in full view of the audience, requiring the performers to remain immobile for nearly 30 minutes, during which time they are frequently in the spectator's direct line of vision as the earlier scenes of Act III unfold in front of or beside them.

This 'coming to life' of the female statues introduces another level of complexity to the sculpture, for it emphasises the extent to which the sculpture on stage represents something quite different from what is presented in Molière's script. Molière's dialogue explicitly identifies the tomb as the Commander's and Don Juan as both the agent of the Commander's death and the character who invites him to supper; it also identifies the Commander's statue as the one that moves. In Mesguich's *mise en scène*, the Commander's statue does not move – if, in fact, the male figure on the pedestal represents the Commander – and indicates no acceptance of Don

Juan's invitation. On the contrary, the female figures not only move, they also issue an invitation of their own, beckoning Don Juan with flirtatious smiles and 'come to me' gestures with their fingers.

In this sequence, Mesguich performs Molière's script as written: Mesguich's Sganarelle, like Molière's, praises the 'beautiful marble' and the 'beautiful columns' and his Don Juan, like Molière's, is bemused by the apparent disconnect between the Commander's restrained behaviour in life and the extravagance of his memorial. The spectator, on the other hand, is invited to contemplate quite a different disconnect, the disconnect between the tomb suggested by Molière's text and the tomb presented by Mesguich's *mise en scène*. Molière's characters are not talking about Mesguich's tomb.

The seven statues from Act I return in Act IV, where they are arranged around the periphery of the acting area. The setting for this act adds a number of columns to the statues to define the space, as well as a number of chairs and tables. The seven statues are again featured in Act V, although here they are arranged in a straight line running from just left of upstage centre to downstage right, effectively reducing the playing area by as much as 25 per cent. Towards the end of Act V, the three actor-statues from Act III return to join Don Juan in his bed where, under cover of an oversized sheet, they 'burn' him to death, after which they take their places in the line of statues. The fact that the Commander plays no part in Don Juan's death in this production comes as no surprise, given Mesguich's staging of Act III. As in Act III, Mesguich introduces a counter-narrative to that presented in Molière's text.

As the three actor-statues take their places, each adopts a pose similar to those displayed in the seven statues. The actor-statue closest to the audience, for example, crosses her arms over her breasts in a manner that mimics without perfectly replicating the arms of the statue immediately downstage of her; further upstage, another actor-statue stands with her head thrown back and her forearm braced against her forehead, echoing the statue immediately upstage of her. The already complex statue narrative thus acquires yet another dimension as the three actor-statues take on the same function as the seven statues that come into view when the curtain is raised in Act I.

Mesguich introduces additional elements that further complicate the ending of *Dom Juan*: he reintroduces all of the characters encountered in the four earlier acts of the play with the exception of the added characters, such as M. Dimanche's family and Don Juan's mother. Don Carlos and his brother play an especially active role, pushing the bed closer to centre stage. As they move the bed, flames burst forth from the downstage bedposts. Don Juan climbs onto the bed by stepping over the bed rail, literally walking between the flames. All of the characters are, it seems, participating in a familiar ritual. In addition, Mesguich employs recorded dialogue throughout the final two scenes of the play, with the exception of Sganarelle's final speech, which is delivered with intense, realistically 'genuine' emotion. The live emotion of Sganarelle's concluding speech contrasts sharply with the languid, almost weary voice employed by Mesguich in Don Juan's final moments, a vocal technique that makes Don Juan's final 'Ah!' sound more orgasmic than terrified.

In its final moments, Mesguich's contrapuntal narrative technique reaches a climax of complexity that defies unravelling: the sheer theatricality of Mesguich's *mise en scène* appears to loom ever larger in the foreground as Molière's narrative recedes bit by bit from view while the dialogue – with the important exception noted – is subsumed into the soundscape. It almost seems as if the theatre is appropriating Molière's play, incorporating it into the very fabric of its technology. Here, perhaps more than at any earlier moment, Mesguich remains true to his intention of making theatre his first priority, of privileging the activity of theatricalising over that of performing *Dom Juan*.

Conclusion

Mesguich's approach to *mise en scène* is unquestionably 'theatricalist', rather than 'humanist' or 'historical or ideological' (Whitton 1995: 177–8), and therefore resistant to summarising with a set of thematic statements about character morality or psychology or the socio-politico-historical realities of the world of the play as represented on stage. On the other hand, it is quite easy for a spectator to come to some speculative conclusions about what Mesguich might think about certain aspects of the play, Molière's world, or Mesguich's own. For example, it is difficult not to read Mesguich's references in the Monsieur Dimanche sequence to the status and treatment of Jews in France, both historically and in the present, as a pointed commentary on how little has changed in three centuries.[8] On the other hand, his allusion to the Nazi occupation of France and its effects on French cultural production in the Pierrot figure of Act II is quite opaque, relying on the spectator to recall Carné's film, the circumstance of its production and the pertinent details of its star actress's personal life. In both the Dimanche and Pierrot episodes, Mesguich may also be relying on the audience's knowledge of the fact that he himself is a Jew, an aspect of his personal identity more visible in his professional life in recent years.[9]

Regardless of the degree of legibility of Mesguich's allusion, via Pierrot, to the Nazi occupation, the relationship between this Pierrot and the Pierrot of Molière's play remains indiscernible. Similarly, it is difficult to reconcile with anything in Molière's text Mesguich's decision to represent Charlotte, Mathurine, and the other inhabitants of their community as members of an amateur painting group. Many other elements of Mesguich's *mise en scène* remain just as puzzling, and none more so than his decision to create statuary on the Commander's tomb that offers a narrative very different from Molière's. Mesguich offers an explanation in an interview published with the video documentation of the production:

> Commander [is] the metaphoric name, the code name [...] for [...] the memory of women [...] the bodies of women from his past and from his future. [...] He turns them into statues, he kills them; that's what he does with women.
> (Mesguich 2004b)

But that explanation was not available to his audiences, and while the idea of women turning into statues is clearly presented in the closing moments of the performance, an event that connects the actor-statues from the tomb with the other statues, the Commander's physical absence from the stage remains inscrutable – not only 'unsummarisable' but incomprehensible – perhaps because it has more to do with the Don Juan of Mesguich's own intertexts – his own 'dust' or 'history' – than with the Don Juan of *Dom Juan*.

A *mise en scène* that I found thrilling in performance has, under repeated scrutiny and questioning, turned gradually into a source of many frustrations, each of which is provoked by an element of the *mise en scène* that resists comprehension, whether approached as a separate entity or as part of a larger whole. Although critics and scholars have developed a detailed understanding of Mesguich's scenic language, no understanding of his poetics can situate the spectator at Mesguich's precise location in intertextual space. Ultimately, comprehending Mesguich's *mises en scène* will entail comprehending Daniel Mesguich himself.

Five key productions

Dom Juan. By Molière. Costumes by Dominique Louis. Lighting by Patrick Méeüs. Perf. Daniel Mesguich, Christian Hecq, Anne Cressent, Laurent Montel. Athénée Théâtre Louis-Jouvet, Paris. March 2002.

Antoine et Cléopâtre. By William Shakespeare. Translated by Daniel Mesguich. Set design by Jean-François Gobert. Perf. Mathieu Marie, Sarah Mesguich, William Mesguich. Athénée Théâtre Louis-Jouvet, Paris. February 2003.

Le Prince de Hombourg. By Heinrich von Kleist translated by Daniel Mesguich. Set design by Jean-François Gobert. Perf. William Mesguich, Catherine Berriane, Xavier Gallais, Jean-Louis Grinfeld, Claudie Guillot, Elsa Mollien. Athénée Théâtre Louis-Jouvet, Paris. March 2005.

Boulevard du boulevard du boulevard. By Daniel Mesguich. Costumes by Dominique Louis. Lighting by Patrick Méeüs. Perf. Christian Hecq, Sarah Mesguich, Florence Muller, Laurent Montel, Eric Verdin. Théâtre du Rond-Point, Paris. March 2006.

Phasmes. By Daniel Mesguich. Perf. Daniel Mesguich (solo). Théâtre du Rond-Point, Paris. March 2008.

Notes

1 In 2013, the students of the Conservatoire wrote a letter to the Minister for Culture calling for Daniel Mesguich not to be reappointed at the end of his term in charge of the institution. The reasons given included the fact that the Conservatoire was, under his direction, progressively isolating itself from the rest of the profession as a result of the director's intellectualism. Mesguich responded by a furious and snide lengthy letter in which he stated his professed aim was to school his students.

2 In addition to acting, directing, and teaching, Mesguich has published a number of articles and books about the art of theatre that address questions of aesthetics, poetics, and politics (see especially, 1991, 2004a).

3 All translations are by Jim Carmody and Dominic Glynn.

4 The talk took place on 19 April 2018 at the University of London, following the screening of *Il était une fois Ophélie et Hamlet à Shanghai*, directed by Ellénore Loehr (2016).

5 Joan DeJean (2002) gives an excellent account of both the play's many transgressions and the history of its suppression.

6 Virtually all of Mesguich's cuts occur in Act III, Scene 4. Mesguich reduces the number of lines spoken by Don Carlos by almost half, radically simplifying the conversation between Elvire's brothers by removing Don Carlos's justifications for delaying taking their revenge.

7 Mesguich adds other female figures to the play. In Act II, he adds Fat Thomasse (played by a man in drag); in Act III, he adds a nurse, dressed identically to Sganarelle (played by the same actor as Thomasse); in Act IV, he adds Madame Dimanche and her daughter, Claudine. Fat Thomasse, Madame Dimanche, and Claudine are mentioned by name in Molière's text. In Act V, he adds a character Molière does not name, who I assume is meant to be identified as Don Juan's mother; although she is in tears throughout the scene, neither Don Juan nor his father pay any attention to her.

8 Cournot gently challenges the historical accuracy of Mesguich's choice by reminding his readers that although there were indeed Jews, then called 'New Christians', in Molière's France, they had been expelled in 1656, almost ten years before the first performance of the play (Cournot 2002).

9 In 2001, Mesguich staged a production of Racine's *Esther* at the Espace Rachi commissioned by the United Jewish Social Front (Front Social Juif Unifié). That was followed by *The Dybbuk* in 2004 at the same space. In

2008 he directed Jacques Attali's *Du cristal à la fumée* (*From Kristallnacht to Smoke Plumes*) (Théâtre du Rond-Point), a documentary play dealing with early Nazi planning for their treatment of Jews.

Bibliography

Carlson, Marvin (1993) 'Daniel Mesguich and Intertextual Shakespeare', in Dennis Kennedy (ed.), *Foreign Shakespeare*, Cambridge: Cambridge University Press, pp. 213–31.

———— (1996) 'Doubled Myths', *Western European Stages*, 8 (3): 21–5.

Cournot, Michel (2002) 'Le Dom Juan en liberté de Daniel Mesguich', *Le Monde*, 16 March, www.lexisnexis.com/us/lnacademic

DeJean, Joan (2002) 'The Work of Forgetting: Commerce, Sexuality, Censorship, and Molière's *Le Festin de Pierre*', *Critical Inquiry*, 29 (1): 53–80.

Dom Juan (2004) Paris: SOPAT. Set of 2 DVDs. DVD 1: Digital video recording of Daniel Mesguich's *mise en scène* of Molière's *Dom Juan* made during performances at the Théâtre du Gymnase, Marseilles in 2003. DVD 2: Additional material.

Fayard, Nicole (2007) 'Daniel Mesguich's Shakespeare Plays: Performing the Shakespeare Myth', *Theatre Journal*, 59 (1): 39–55.

Héliot, Armelle (2006) 'Un pitre céleste', *Le Figaro*, 31 March, www.lexisnexis.com/us/lnacademic

———— (2013) 'Conservatoire: la lettre des élèves contre Mesguich', *Le Figaro*, 14 February, www.lefigaro.fr/theatre/2013/02/14/03003-20130214ARTFIG00504-conservatoire-la-lettre-des-eleves-retrouvee.php

Mesguich, Daniel (1991) *L'Éternel Éphémère*, Paris: Editions du Seuil.

———— (2002) '*Note d'Intention*'. Unpublished theatre programme. Reproduced in press dossier for Théâtre de Saint-Quentin-en-Yvelines, www.theatresqy.org/2003/spectacles/dom_juan.html

———— (2004a) 'C'est ma bibliothèque: le livre de chevet de Daniel Mesguich', *Le Figaro*, 12 August, www.lexisnexis.com/us/lnacademic

———— (2004b) Interview with Philippe Jousserand, *Dom Juan*, DVD 2.

———— (2006) *Boulevard du boulevard du boulevard*, Paris: L'Avant-Scène.

———— (2008) 'Entretien', press dossier for *Phasmes*, http://2007–8.theatredurondpoint.fr/saison/fiche_spectacle.cfm/42596-phasmes

———— (2013) 'La Lettre de Daniel Mesguich à ses élèves', www.madinin-art.net/la-lettre-de-daniel-mesguich-a-ses-eleves/

Viala, Alain and Mesguich, Daniel (2011) *Le Théâtre*, Paris: Presses universitaires de France.

—— (2012) *Histoire de la littérature française, Vol 1*, Paris: Presses universitaires de France.
Whitton, David (1987) *Stage Directors in Modern France*, Manchester: Manchester University Press.
—— (1995) *Molière: Don Juan*, Cambridge: Cambridge University Press.
—— (2012) *Histoire de la littérature française Vol 1. Le Moyen âge*, Paris: PUF-Frémeaux.

Chapter 7

DECLAN DONNELLAN AND CHEEK BY JOWL

'To protect the acting'

Aleks Sierz

'In Britain, as in many other countries, audiences will now be drawn to the theatre as much for the person who directs a play as for the story, the author who wrote it or the actors who perform it' (Delgado and Heritage 1996a: 1). While this is true, I would argue that, although there are many good British theatre directors, there are only a handful of truly great ones. At present, I can think of very few whose work is so distinctive as to be immediately recognisable, so thought-provoking as to vigorously divide opinion, and so exciting that you could risk inviting friends from Continental Europe to come and see their work. For although it is arguable that in Britain, as in the rest of Europe, 'the cult of the director dominates theatre practice' (Giannachi and Luckhurst 1999a: xiii), most plays are presented in a naturalistic and social-realist style which tends to flatten out the differences between individual directors. Exceptions that spring to mind include Katie Mitchell, Simon McBurney, Deborah Warner, Robert Icke, Rupert Goold, Emma Rice, and Declan Donnellan. So who is Declan Donnellan and what is distinctive about his work?

Michael Declan Martin Donnellan was born on 4 August 1953, in Manchester, of Irish parents, who came from Roscommon. The family moved back to Ireland when he was four or five, then to London, where he attended St Benedict's School in Ealing. Donnellan enjoyed performing in school plays and wrote his first play at the age of nine. He spent his summers in Ireland and remembers 'winning second prize for the Irish jig at Roscommon Fair' (Sierz 2002). In 1972–5, he studied English and Law at Queens College, Cambridge, where he met Nick Ormerod,[1] his partner, in 1972, and both men were involved in theatre as well as studying law. Donnellan was called to the Bar at the Middle Temple, but 'even when I was at the Bar, I was in the Bar Theatrical Society, appearing in *School for Scandal*. So I never stopped acting as an amateur' (Sierz 2002). In the late 1970s, Donnellan and Ormerod worked both separately and together at various fringe theatres, and formed Cheek by Jowl in 1981.

From the beginning, Donnellan's trademark has been his work with actors. Indeed, he is an example of the kind of director whose aim is 'liberating the actor to achieve the closest possible relationship with the audience' (Delgado and Heritage 1996a: 11). The company name, which comes from *A Midsummer Night's Dream*,[2] refers to the closeness of emotional contact both between the actors and between the actors and audience. Since the 1980s, Cheek by Jowl has been an unofficial acting academy, numbering Daniel Craig, Sally Dexter, Anastasia Hille, Paterson Joseph, Adrian Lester, Matthew Macfadyen, Stephen Mangan, David Morrissey, Lloyd Owen, Saskia Reeves, and Michael Sheen 'among the more famous alumni' (Cavendish 2006). Added to this, Donnellan has also played an important, and occasionally controversial, role by casting 'local black actors in major roles' (Shevtsova 2005: 232). In 1989, for example, his *Fuente Ovejuna* at the National Theatre was a milestone in the advance of colour-blind casting for classics of the European repertoire.

The director's mission, Donnellan said in 2004, is 'to protect the acting, and to look after the acting, and very specifically to look after the health of the ensemble playing' (Cavendish 2004). Three aspects of his work have been identified as characteristic: first, 'care for the text'; second, 'uncluttered space' on stage, with Ormerod's minimalist design; and finally 'concentration on the actor' (Shevtsova 2005: 233). Other commentators have enumerated stylistic devices such as the use of overlapping scenes, formal stage groupings, spatially geometric oppositions, simplicity of gesture, austere costumes, and colourful but simple designs. In the early years, the effect was described as a 'mannered exuberance', which 'burst afresh upon their audiences' (Trussler 1994: 370), and Donnellan's distinctive style (at the time of *Angels in America* in 1992) was evocatively described as 'a highly refined theatricality; a choreographic respect for stage movement; crystalline renderings of the text' (Geis and Kruger 1997: 245). More particularly, Donnellan has used imaginative, non-naturalistic devices to emphasise aspects of the story. In *Measure for Measure* (1994), Claudio stays on stage, imprisoned, so the audience can never forget that his life is at stake; in *As You Like It* (1991), the Duke rushes in while Rosalind and Celia are talking about the Forest of Arden, thus aiding the transition to that enchanted place; in *Le Cid* (1998), Chimene is dressed by the ghost of her father, a reminder of who it is she must avenge; in *Angels in America* (1992–3), two men have sex but are separate and facing the audience, implicating spectators in their relationship; in *Cymbeline* (2007), a tableau – the father and his three children – shows the family before its members become separated. In general, Cheek by Jowl productions often begin with all the actors on stage, gazing at the audience, and thus emphasising their role as storytellers, 'the makers of the tale' (Delgado and Heritage 1996b: 80).

For almost 40 years, Cheek by Jowl has toured its versions of classical and canonical plays to audiences at home and abroad. As well as providing international exposure, this has also meant that the actors were able to develop their craft over long periods of time and on widely different stages with different audiences.

> This is more than just theatrical tourism, it also reveals the distinctive art of both director and designer. Extended tours, sometimes of over a year, allow for the organic growth of the actors within the classic texts that have been the company's hallmark, and make essential the bare simplicity of the designs that allow the plays to appear so fresh and uncluttered [...] it is on the international stage, where the actor has nothing easy or false to rely on, that Donnellan and Ormerod have developed their skill.
> (Delgado and Heritage 1996b: 80)

Early productions included *The Country Wife* (1981), *Vanity Fair* (1982), and Donnellan's own play *Lady Betty* (1989), about an eighteenth-century Irish hangwoman. The company also introduced British audiences to foreign classics, some of which had never previously been seen in the UK: Racine's *Andromaque* (1985), Corneille's *Le Cid* (1986), and Ostrovsky's *A Family Affair* (1988). To date, Cheek by Jowl has staged the British premieres of at least ten European classics. The company grew rapidly throughout the 1980s – creating 18 productions over the decade and touring across the globe. But the core of the repertoire has been Shakespeare: by 2010, with *Macbeth*, Cheek by Jowl had presented 14 Shakespeare plays, including an innovative all-male *As You Like It* (1991). And this core preoccupation has continued. As associates of the National Theatre, Donnellan and Ormerod's productions included Lope de Vega's *Fuente Ovejuna* and Tony Kushner's *Angels in America*, one of the landmark new plays of the early 1990s. Other highpoints would number *Measure for Measure* (1994), *The Duchess of Malfi* (1995), *Much Ado about Nothing* (1998), *Othello* (2004), and *Andromaque* (2007). Donnellan has also directed musicals and opera: very successfully with Sondheim's *Sweeney Todd* (National Theatre, 1993) and Verdi's *Falstaff* (Salzburg Festival, 2001); much less so with Boublil and Schönberg's *Martin Guerre* (Prince Edward Theatre, 1996).[3]

Donnellan is 'neither militant nor didactic' (Shevtsova 2005: 232), but that doesn't mean that he is unpolitical. His politics are implicit, for example, in the colour-blind casting of classics, from *Fuente Ovejuna* to *As You Like It* to *Le Cid*. His all-male *As You Like It* was a revelation: it was enormously refreshing to see both a revitalisation of the Elizabethan convention of men playing women and, at the same time, the location of a contemporary sense of the visibility of a gay subtext. In 1994, his *Measure for Measure* felt politically topical because it seemed to comment on the sex scandals that were affecting the Conservative government of John Major. Yet, as he pointed out, 'theatre doesn't answer political questions, though it asks them' (quoted in Shevtsova 2005: 232). An example of this might be his version of Pushkin's *Boris Godunov* (2000), in which Godunov was dressed like Russian President Vladimir Putin, implying a comparison between two different autocracies. By contrast, with Kushner's *Angels in America*, Donnellan presented an epic play whose themes, especially its account of AIDS, had a direct emotional and political impact on audiences (see Croft 1993: 26). In 2002, Cheek by Jowl's premiere of Kushner's *Homebody/Kabul* at the New York Theater Workshop was a controversial production in the wake of the 9/11 terrorist attacks. Donnellan has spoken of the strange juxtaposition of rehearsing a scene with the Muslim call to prayer while the smell of the burnt Twin Towers still hung in the air (Donnellan 2007b).

Donnellan's politics are also evident in his international perspective, especially in his implicit questioning of the Englishness of English theatre. His preference for overtly theatrical devices is a quiet but firm rejection of the confines of strict naturalism and social realism. Although his focus on the acting and on the unadorned simplicity of staging feels like an English understatement, a conscious refraining from the excesses of some European *auteurs*, Donnellan is also clearly a European director: he has staged plays in Russian, French, and English and obviously works across the European repertoire. His work has been affected by the fall of the Berlin Wall to the extent that few British directors now have had such 'an intense relationship with the Russian theatre' (Shevtsova 2005: 236). Since 1986, Donnellan and Ormerod have had a close relationship with Lev Dodin's Maly Drama Theatre (see Shevtsova 2004: 30–3). In 1997, they directed and designed *The Winter's Tale* for the Maly, the first Shakespeare production performed by that company. Meanwhile, the Russian Theatre Confederation invited Cheek by Jowl to Moscow, and, in 1999, asked Donnellan and Ormerod to form their own company of Russian actors in Moscow (for many years its repertoire included Pushkin's *Boris Godunov*). In 2003, the Bolshoi invited Donnellan and Ormerod to stage a new version of Prokofiev's ballet of *Romeo and Juliet*. In 2005, they formed a partnership with the Barbican Theatre in London to produce an annual season consisting of a play in English and a play in Russian. The first season in 2006 featured Middleton and Rowley's *The Changeling* and *Twelfth Night* (Donnellan's Russian version has been revived annually between 2003 and 2014), the second season Chekhov's *Three Sisters* and *Cymbeline*, and the third *Boris Godunov* and *Troilus and Cressida*. Of these, *Three Sisters* – like *Twelfth Night* – has had, by British standards, a particularly long production life. First staged in France in 2005, it was restaged by the company with Russian actors every year until 2013. Reviews of its international tours praised its revelatory immediacy, clarity, delicacy, and freshness, with the relationship between the three sisters being seen as completely convincing and moving. More recent Cheek by Jowl productions include John Ford's *'Tis Pity She's a Whore* (2011–14) and *The Tempest* (2011–14), plus French versions of Alfred Jarry's *Ubu Roi* (2013–15) and *Périclès, Prince de Tyr* by Shakespeare and George Wilkins (2018–19). In the West End, their crowd-pleasing production of Lee Hall's adaptation of *Shakespeare in Love* (2014) was commercially successful. Donnellan's first feature film, *Bel Ami*, co-directed with Nick Ormerod, and starring Uma Thurman, Christina Ricci, and Robert Pattinson, was released in 2012.

The company's international tours have also helped influence other European directors, such as Calixto Bieito and Àlex Rigola. Looking at Donnellan's book, *The Actor and the Target* (which first appeared in Russian), the European perspective of his work is clear. Apart from Shakespeare and Beckett, no other English-language dramatist is mentioned, although there are dozens of references to Chekhov, Corneille, Mozart, and the ancient Greeks, as well as other cultural figures from Homer to Freud. The most important influence on his directing style was Stanislavski, and *The Actor and the Target* can be seen as an implicit questioning of the tradition, derived from a simplified notion of Stanislavski-inspired acting, that the actor discovers a universe from within. Instead of finding everything inside yourself, Donnellan argues that you discover everything outside yourself by aiming at specific targets: an object to be seen, a question to be asked, a decision to be taken. His other influences range from that most European of British directors, Peter Brook, to Spanish and Dutch Old Master painters (Giannachi and Luckhurst 1999b: 22–3). But as well as being European, Donnellan is also associated with Tony Kushner, one of the most robustly American writers of the past three decades. Moreover, the very fact of touring extensively with English-language plays means that he has been an ambassador for British theatre and the English language. In Donnellan's work, then, there is a creative tension between his 'Britishness' (focus on acting rather than on elaborate design or intellectual high-concept auteurship) and his 'Continental' qualities (focus on a pan-European repertoire, questioning British naturalism and social realism, and working across several languages). The result is a theatrically thrilling mix.

The following interview was conducted at Keats House, Hampstead, London, in October 2007 especially for this book.

ALEKS SIERZ: When did Cheek by Jowl start and what was your artistic vision for the company?

DECLAN DONNELLAN: Nick and I had been trying to scrape together projects on the London fringe. It was a hand-to-mouth life and, like many young people, we fed ourselves off odd jobs. For me it was taking around American tourists. We set up Cheek by Jowl simply as a means of working because it was extremely difficult for a young director and designer to work in the theatre – and I am told it is still the same, but find it hard to believe it could possibly have got any worse! When we began we had no manifesto as such; we just wanted to work and to work together. But now looking back it seems as if we did actually have some sort of vision to re-examine classical texts in a fresh and unsentimental way, avoiding directorial and design concepts, and to focus on the actor's art. We just weren't very conscious of it at the time. It has always struck me as good advice always to take your work seriously but never your career.

The director has many roles, but a primary one is to release the actor's confidence in their ability to act. It is not a teacher–pupil relationship. If anything, it is like the relationship between the coach and the athlete. Our first production to tour, supported by a small Arts Council grant, was *The Country Wife*, which opened at the Edinburgh Festival Fringe in August 1981.

ALEKS SIERZ: What were your influences as a director?

DECLAN DONNELLAN: Well, my family is Irish and respect for language, particularly spoken language, runs very deep. Colourful language, metaphor, poetry, never seemed artificial. I do still remember being fascinated as a tiny child by storytellers calling round at night to sit at the hearth of my grandfather's remote Galway farm. Although home was a book-free zone, it was never considered an accomplishment to be bashful. Talking well was prized, and boring visitors was just rude. I guess there were advantages and disadvantages ... But there were plenty of books and less chat. At school I had several excellent teachers – Frank Hanley, Dennis Johnson, Sean Moore – and it is no exaggeration to say that they not only shaped my life, they actually gave me one. In particular they gave me a profound respect for teaching.

A very important influence was my English teacher at St Benedict's, Philip Lawrence.[4] Philip introduced me to Shakespeare and pushed open the intimidating arts door. These teachers gave me an enormous gift, and, like many great gifts, it involved not a giving but a taking away. They removed any self-consciousness I might have had about reading classic plays. They never let me be intimidated by the seventeenth-century engravings that often adorned the covers. They lifted the lid on the language. I recognise that I was very, very lucky to be given this. Or, rather, I am very grateful to have had this intimidation surgically removed. Philip was also Irish, a great theatre enthusiast, and he brought me to [see Peter Brook's] *A Midsummer Night's Dream* [Royal Shakespeare Company, 1970] when I was 16 and I have never forgotten it. I was so happy and I felt like I had in some way come home. Then, and later on, I was profoundly affected by Peter Brook's work, by his qualities of simplicity and showmanship, and by his humanity. I loved the way that he managed to encompass both the spiritual and the vulgar. I also used to take the Tube up from Ealing Broadway to Sloane Square and learned how to buy cheap tickets for matinees at the Royal Court, so I saw a lot of new writing in the 1970s. Other strong influences were dance and the visual arts. In those days, I sat in the audience and longed to be part of the performance; now, I'm part of the performance in a different way. But this sense of participating is a vital part of my understanding of live performance: it is a shared experience.

ALEKS SIERZ: Tell me about your work process.

DECLAN DONNELLAN: It varies. Sometimes, the play comes first; sometimes the actor. In Russia, where we have a stable ensemble, we normally choose the play to suit the actors we have, so we decided on *Three Sisters* [2005] because we knew Alexander Feklistov would make a wonderful Vershinin. It's always good to have actors you know and then build the cast around them. Occasionally that happens in the West. When we worked with Nonso [Anozie] on a student *King Lear*, we thought, 'Yes, we would do *Othello* for him.' Normally, however, in the West, we choose the play and then scout around for suitable actors. At the start of the 1980s, it was very much a question of what we could do with a young company. So we chose *A Midsummer Night's Dream* [1985] because we were doing very long intercontinental tours, which are particularly tough on older actors with families.

ALEKS SIERZ: When you started, how long did you have for rehearsals?

DECLAN DONNELLAN: I've spent my working life doing basically the same thing in the rehearsal room, but the conditions have improved. At the beginning, the cast size was six or seven and now it's about fourteen. At first we had three weeks' rehearsal and now it's about seven. But most of the actors' work on the play takes place on tour after it opens. The seven weeks of rehearsal are enough for the actors to begin the process. It gives them a good skeleton.

With any production, you have to distinguish between what cannot be changed and what must be changed. Some things must be the same every night, but many things must change. You have to be clear which is which. To begin with, in a three-week rehearsal period, I would take lots of short cuts. If you only have three weeks, you have to make major decisions early on, well before you can know what the actors are capable of. So in a very short rehearsal period it is harder to help the actors to challenge themselves or to explore new terrain. And the director and designer have to make so many decisions before the rehearsals begin, even before you meet the actors, that it is difficult for the work to grow organically. It is possible to avoid being glib during a short rehearsal, but it is not easy. However, even in the early days, we would open and then on tour would start re-rehearsing. So the actors would rehearse every afternoon and then perform in the evening too. It was quite intensive. But I was always struck by how much the actors, particularly actors in the West, love to work hard.

It always helps to choose a really great play that you know will repay your interest, with the performances gaining in vitality as the tour progresses. That's why we perform Shakespeare's work, and why we chose *Angels in America* – unusually, it was a complex and imaginative new play that we knew would more than repay long-term exploration. In order to support the level of work that we do, you have to have a big, rich text, robust, surprising, and richly felt and experienced by the author.

ALEKS SIERZ: Could you describe your rehearsal process?

DECLAN DONNELLAN: Perhaps the best way to start is to say what we don't do: there are no discussions with actors hunched around a table chewing pencils; there are no lectures on history and ideas: there is no imposed concept on the play. Nick does not present a model box on the first day and show costume drawings to a bemused circle of actors who have only just met each other.

Instead, we set about trying to discover how to do the play, and then Nick decides what design would work best. The actors are rehearsed by getting them on their feet and moving around the space. Normally the acting starts off rather dull, then after a while it gets more interesting, and I spend my time waiting and watching for the actors' inventiveness. Their inventiveness is what matters, their capacity to see. The audience, after all, goes to the theatre to watch something happen in the spontaneous present. But there is plenty of discipline too. A lot of work, for example, has to be done on the verse if appropriate, for example the Alexandrine in French or blank verse in English or Russian. We have to explore and learn. But we normally find ways of doing even verse work on our feet. We have devised plenty of exercises that connect the different verse forms to pacing and running for example.

Last week, to give you one instance of how we work at the Bouffes du Nord in Paris, we opened *Andromaque* by Racine, and we would rehearse every afternoon. By the fourth week, we might rehearse every second day, and thereafter maybe one rehearsal a week. More rehearsal time means you can keep things fluid for longer, and I am more confident now and better at keeping my nerve and helping the company keep theirs!

With *Boris Godunov*, we did an enormous amount of work on free movement, and – at the same time – an enormous amount of incredibly disciplined work on the Russian blank verse, finding the feet, finding the beats, finding the rhythms. Once the first breath is taken on stage, the verse has to keep pumping through the whole performance. Of course, there are a million variations, but there's also a baton of energy that is passed between the characters and is carried right through to the end.

ALEKS SIERZ: When you rehearse, do you want your actors to know their lines before you start?

DECLAN DONNELLAN: Yes, actually I do. I can't do anything with the actors if they have their noses buried in the script.

We don't sit around and read the play: we start by doing movement and then quickly try out scenes. Often we start with a dance so, for example, in *As You Like It*, we thought the tango would work well. And it expressed a lot, and was useful and alive so it stayed in the show. But it's very unusual that a movement idea lasts to the very end of the process. Normally, it gets discarded. With *Cymbeline*, we started out with some step dancing which we thought might be useful because the play does have a strong Celtic basis, and we were also thinking about James I and the creation of a new Britain. So we worked on an Irish dance called 'The Siege of Ennis', but, after a while, we discarded it. You nearly always have to discard. 'The Siege of Ennis' strengthened backs, brought the company together, focused us, and was not wasted. But it was never actually seen.

With all this movement, the play does get read of course! And many times. But actors tend to be so nervous on first days that physical work is more useful – and more human.

One aspect of the design is the exact positioning of the few elements that we use. And also the shapes that the actors make across the stage, whether in diagonals or at right angles, their entrances and exits, are all part of the design. In *The Duchess of Malfi*, for example, the actors would cross the stage obliquely to the audience, which was unsettling. And that was part of the design. When you are touring, you have to adapt and change these ideas to suit the size and configuration of the stage and the auditorium. When we take *Andromaque* from Paris to Marseilles we will have a different *mise en scène*. I really like that kind of change because the connections between the actors can become more acute if the *mise en scène* is adapted with care. With the French company we have sometimes fantasised: 'Wouldn't it be great to do *Andromaque* as a promenade performance in a palace?' Moving from door to door, from room to room, up and down staircases, the text would really be tested, as would the links between the characters.

ALEKS SIERZ: You've been quoted as saying, 'The job of the director is simple. You're in a room with actors, then on the stage – you can find that it's a bit dead and you're trying to get rid of the dead thing and find ways of making it alive' (Hallett 2004). Could you expand?

DECLAN DONNELLAN: Somebody once said to a rabbi, 'Why can't anybody see God anymore?' And the rabbi replied, 'Because nobody can stoop low enough.' One thing that I am still in the process of learning is that the work of a director is all about very humble increments. The living experience is what matters. Acting needs to be spontaneous, true, and in the moment, in other words, genuinely experienced [see Tom Hiddleston as Posthumus and Jodie McNee as Imogen in *Cymbeline*, Plate 7]. So, for example, rehearsing *Cymbeline*, there's no point in me saying to Jodie [McNee], playing Imogen, at the beginning of rehearsals, 'This is how we are going to do the headless body scene.' The point of rehearsal is to help her experience what that event would actually be like. It's as simple as that. And it has absolutely nothing to do with having ideas. Instead we tend to collect fragmentary experiences.

For a director, it's about not controlling the experience. A rehearsal is a journey and the journey continues through the performances as well. No voyage of discovery can know for sure where it will end. (But we may well start with some idea of where we are headed, an idea that will probably have to be jettisoned.) But we have to be open to the fact that the destination may well not be what we had anticipated. It is curious that faulty research often occurs because the scientists had started from their conclusions. Similarly, in the theatre, we have to start at the beginning, and the beginning is experience, experience that is felt and seen in the living moment. So, we go through the scene step by step: Imogen must touch the feet of the body. When does she realise this is a body? When does she realise it's cold? When does she realise it's her husband? These are only some of the small increments. We do not start with the global and grandiose idea of 'How would a woman feel if she woke up next to the headless corpse of her husband?' How could we know? And just as importantly, how could Imogen possibly know either? Imogen is no expert on her bizarre situation. Here ignorance is our friend. Or rather, admitting ignorance is wisdom. We need to use our ignorance to help us experience. Ignorance can be really useful as long as we admit it.

The job is not to imagine how we could stage the emotionally powerful scenes that are written: the job is how to put the actors through the living experience of what might spontaneously happen in the moment. You look at the story of the play, say *Cymbeline*, and ask, 'What would it really be like if two children got kidnapped – what would that actually be like? What would it really be like to find them again?'

In our *Twelfth Night* [in Moscow 2003], our Malvolio breaks into floods of tears when he reads and believes that Olivia loves him. And audience members have sometimes asked, 'How did you have that idea?' I always had to answer, 'I didn't have an idea – I only worked with the actor in rehearsal, exploring what it would actually be like if the woman you loved most wrote you a letter saying that she was madly in love with you. And then what would it be like when you found out that it was all a joke?' It is important to discover the experience without preconceptions, to discard what we think we know. It is important not to start like the bad scientist from our imagined conclusion. It is important to rehearse this scene without being distracted by the thought that, 'Oh, in the end, this scene should be funny.' As it happens, in the end our letter scene is often very funny, funny in a horrible way, and upsetting in a funny way. But we cannot control its effect on the audience. We do something and let the audience react as they will. The audience is free to laugh or not to laugh; to be moved, or not to be moved. But Dima [Dmitry Scherbina] would not have achieved that if he had started out in rehearsals trying to be funny. Nor would it have helped if he thought I was there saying: 'Let's really see what it would be like to read the letter?' but secretly thinking: 'Experiment as much as you like Dima, but I know where we have to end up. You've gotta make 'em laugh!' You cannot start with your conclusions. You have to start with felt experience and be open to any journey and graciously accept the destination you discover.

Some time ago, I used to think that there were two registers: the top register is the text and the bottom register is the story. In everyday life, we listen to what people say, but if what they do contradicts what they say, we soon learn that we should ignore what they are saying and look instead at what they are doing. What we do is invariably more significant than what we say. Whatever Hamlet says, he spends four acts not killing Claudius. However, now it seems to me that there is yet another, a third register, and this is the most fundamental. This exists underneath the level of the story, it underpins the narrative itself; it is the spring of what we do; it is the moment of living experience. Rehearsal for me is nothing more nor less than the chase for the living moment. We cannot actually create life, but we can try to minimise the effects of death.

It is, however, very difficult to describe death. Death is an absence, and absence is by its very nature impossible to describe. For example, it is notoriously hard to stage. So also it is hard to describe what death in the rehearsal room looks like. All we can say is that death always looks the same. It is the absence of life, so when you are watching Malvolio in rehearsal, there may be a feeling that the scene is fine, but … but … but what? But, well, not really alive. So bit by bit you help the actor to experience exactly what is happening. You have to be aware of self-deception: we so easily put up with the inauthentic. Although the imagination liberates us, it also enables us to deceive ourselves.

Normally, the way out of deadness is to make sure that the connections are working. Sometimes the problem with the faulty television set is that it hasn't been plugged in. What exactly is the actor seeing? It is important to be tough on the clichés that come so easily to hand. For example, the actor playing Malvolio needs to explore the event as concretely as possible: what happens to his skin? Does he get sweaty? Does he need to undo his clothes? Is he ashamed of what the audience is thinking? These are not so much ideas, as experiences. Then, bit by bit, something that was dead starts to crackle into life. Then you can start directing in a more traditional sense, 'Move down stage a bit' or 'Can we light this bit?' but that is way down the line for me. The pace of the production comes from the detail of the work the actors do: I rarely have to say, 'Let's do a quick bit here, or a slow bit there.'

Kierkegaard has a marvellous image of a man who is starving because his mouth is so full of food that he can't swallow. Sometimes we are pushing and striving so much that we need to take something away to go free.

I usually work with the whole company, but sometimes we do split up and the actors also work in parallel on their own or with an assistant. The Russians are trained to work away from the director in small groups. They have no problem with being sent off in pairs and then bringing back what they have discovered or developed.

ALEKS SIERZ: Why can't the ensemble playing be left to look after itself?
DECLAN DONNELLAN: Through the ages there has always been somebody directing the actors. Sometimes the role is taken by the most powerful actor in the company. It's not true to say that once in history there were no directors – everyone in the company (writer, producer, manager) can become a director. People adore directing: I had a driver once in Moscow who sat in on rehearsals and loved giving his opinion on every moment. There is a fairly rigid principle, however, and that is that, on the whole, actors really don't like being given notes by someone they are on stage with. When you're on stage with somebody you've got to be absolutely alive with them. You have to be completely in the moment, to react spontaneously. So the actor simply cannot be in the scene and watching it at the same time. All of the actor's attention is needed by the situation – if the actor has enough spare mental power to monitor the acting of other actors

then something is seriously wrong. So actors need someone outside to witness, someone who can shoulder that responsibility. That outside eye frees them. The actor's biggest responsibility is to be alive in the moment. It's always bad discipline for one actor to comment on another's performance.

ALEKS SIERZ: Has your rehearsal method changed much?

DECLAN DONNELLAN: No, I just hope I've got better at it! Quite early on I realised that acting was about seeing something 'outside' yourself rather than trying create something 'inside'. Trying to show an emotion is not good. Emoting is always horrible. For me it is crucial that there is a difference between acting and pretending. I cannot exactly describe the difference in words. On the whole we intuit this difference. But just because the difference is hard to put into words, it does not mean that it is vague or unimportant. It is important to remember that a large part of the art of directing is knowing when to leave well alone.

ALEKS SIERZ: How do shows change during a tour?

DECLAN DONNELLAN: I can't answer that because often I don't really remember what they were like in the beginning. In order to do what I do there's a permanent discarding, so while I do remember the early stages of certain rehearsals, I don't really remember the dozens of intermediate phases. I do remember how hard it sometimes is in early stages of rehearsal trying to help the actors see how high the stakes are for their characters, and how far they may be from experiencing that. Sometimes actors unconsciously resist this because it is quite uncomfortable to keep the stakes high. After all, most of our everyday life is about increasing comfort, trying to lower the stakes. 'Stress is bad', the advert says, 'buy this car/shampoo/drink to relax yourself and lower the stakes!' So, basically, raising the stakes is contrary to most of our culture.

As a result of both rehearsal and touring, the performances develop. Consequently, the *mise en scène* might change, and we might have to change some or all of the movement, so Nick and I and our lighting designer Judith [Greenwood] might change the shape of the *mise en scène* and the lighting during the course of the life of the play. It's like a domino effect: change one thing and you have to change the rest. For this reason, yes, the final performances of a tour will be quite different from the first ones.

ALEKS SIERZ: How has your work been affected by recent political changes in Europe?

DECLAN DONNELLAN: Since the collapse of the Soviet Union we have been able to work much more closely in Russia. Before then, we first visited Russia in 1986, when Lev Dodin invited us to Leningrad to see his company perform at the Maly. Then we directed and designed *The Winter's Tale* for them. And, meanwhile, the Russian Theatre Confederation invited us to Moscow, and we performed *Measure for Measure*, *As You Like It*, *The Duchess of Malfi*, and *Le Cid* in Moscow. Later the Chekhov Festival invited us to form our own company of Russian actors. So Cheek by Jowl now has a sister company of Russian actors, and its current repertoire includes *Boris Godunov*, *Twelfth Night*, and *Three Sisters*. The key to the Russian system is the stability of the companies, which allows us to work with the same ensemble over several years – so I have a longer-term commitment with Russian actors than with actors in the West. All in all, these massive political changes have enabled us to enjoy this enriched contact with Russian theatre that would have been impossible under the Soviet regime. We are very lucky. But to the question of how these changes have affected my actual work? Well the answer is clearly a lot, but it would be too hard to describe in words.

Five key productions

Fuente Ovejuna. By Lope de Vega. Set design by Nick Ormerod. Perf. Wilbert Johnson, Rachel Joyce, James Laurenson, Helen McCrory, Joy Richardson, Clive Rowe, Mark Strong. National Theatre, Cottesloe, London. 10 January 1989 and 14 May 1992.

As You Like It. By William Shakespeare. Set design by Nick Ormerod. Perf. Richard Cant, Simon Coates, Michael Gardiner, Scott Handy, David Hobbs, Tom Hollander, Adrian Lester, Peter Needham. Lyric Hammersmith, London. 2 December 1991. Albery Theatre, London. 25 January 1995.

Angels in America. By Tony Kushner. Set design by Nick Ormerod. Perf. Daniel Craig, Nancy Crane, Marcus D'Amico, Stephen Dillane, Susan Engel, Henry Goodman, Clare Holman, Jason Isaacs, Rosemary Martin, Felicity Montagu, Joseph Mydell, Nick Reding. National Theatre, Cottesloe, London. Part One: 17 January 1992 and Part Two: 12 November 1993.

Le Cid. By Pierre Corneille. Set design by Philippe Marioge. Perf. Michel Baumann, Philippe Blancher, Sarah Karbasnikoff, William Nadylam, Patrick Rameau, and Sandrine Attard. Municipal Theatre, Festival d'Avignon, France. 11 July 1998.

Three Sisters. By Anton Chekhov. Set design by Nick Ormerod. Perf. Evgenia Dmitrieva, Irina Grineva, Nelly Uvarova, Alexander Feklistov, Vitaly Egorov, Valery Pankov, Viktoria Tolstoganova, Andrei Kuzichev, Andrei Merzlikin, Mikhail Zhigalov, Yury Makeev, Galina Morachyova. Les Gemeaux, Sceaux, France. 6 April 2005.

Acknowledgements

I would like to thank Declan Donnellan, Jacqui Honess-Martin, and Anna Schmitz of Cheek by Jowl, and Maria M. Delgado and Dan Rebellato.

Notes

1. Nick Ormerod was born in London on 9 December 1951.
2. Demetrius's exit line from *A Midsummer Night's Dream*, Act III, Scene 2 is: 'Follow! Nay, I'll go with thee, cheek by jowl.'
3. Donnellan has won awards in London, Paris, New York, and Moscow, including Laurence Olivier Awards for Best Director for *The Cid*, *Twelfth Night*, and *Macbeth* (1987); Best Director of a Musical for *Sweeney Todd* (1994); Best Director of a Play for *As You Like It* (1995). In 1989–90 he won the Observer Award for Outstanding Achievement for *Fuente Ovejuna*. In 1992 he was awarded an honorary degree by the University

of Warwick and in 2004 he was made a Chevalier de l'Ordre des Arts et des Lettres for his work in France. He is President of the Russian Theatre Confederation Foundation and in 2008 won the Charlemagne Award. A year later he was awarded the Carlemany Prize by the Principality of Andorra, alongside Craig Venter and Archbishop Desmond Tutu. In 2016 he was awarded the Golden Lion Lifetime Achievement Award at the Venice Biennale.

4   Philip Lawrence later became headmaster of St George's School, Maida Vale in North London, where he was murdered by 15-year-old Learco Chindamo on 8 December 1995. Subsequently, the Philip Lawrence Trust was set up to recognise young people who have made outstanding achievements.

Bibliography

Cavendish, Dominic (2004) 'Interview: Declan Donnellan', *TheatreVoice Website*, 27 May, www.theatrevoice.com/listen_now/player/?audioID = 189 and www.theatrevoice.com/listen_now/player/?audioID = 188.

––––––– (2006) 'From Kitchen Table to Global Stage', *Daily Telegraph*, 8 May.

Cheek by Jowl (2007) *Cheek by Jowl Theatre Company Website*, www.cheekbyjowl.com.

Coveney, Michael (2006) 'As He Likes It', *Guardian*, 4 February.

Croft, Giles (ed.) (1993) *On Angels in America*, London: National Theatre Platform Papers.

Delgado, Maria M. and Paul Heritage (1996a) 'Introduction', in Maria M. Delgado and Paul Heritage (eds), *In Contact with the Gods? Directors Talk Theatre*, Manchester: Manchester University Press, pp. 1–13.

––––––– (1996b) 'Declan Donnellan and Nick Ormerod', in Maria M. Delgado and Paul Heritage (eds), *In Contact with the Gods? Directors Talk Theatre*, Manchester: Manchester University Press, pp. 79–92.

Donnellan, Declan (2005) *The Actor and the Target*, rev. edn, London: Nick Hern Books.

––––––– (2007a) *Cymbeline: Interview with Heather Neill* ((podcast)), London: Cheek by Jowl.

––––––– (2007b) 'Declan Donnellan in Conversation with Professor Maria Shevtsova', Conversations Series, Goldsmiths College, University of London, 22 October.

––––––– (2008) 'Introduction to Konstantin Stanislavski', in *An Actor's Work*, trans. Jean Benedetti, London: Routledge, pp. ix–xiv.

Edwardes, Jane (1994) 'Directors: The New Generation', in Theodore Shank (ed.), *Contemporary British Theatre*, London: Macmillan, pp. 205–22.

Gardner, Lyn (2002) 'Home Again', *Guardian*, 22 May.

Geis, Deborah R. and Steven F. Kruger (eds) (1997) *Approaching the Millennium: Essays on Angels in America*, Ann Arbor, MI: University of Michigan Press.

Giannachi, Gabriella and Mary Luckhurst (1999a) 'Introduction', in Gabriella Giannachi and Mary Luckhurst (eds), *On Directing*, London: Faber & Faber, pp. xiii–xvi.

—— (1999b) 'Declan Donnellan', in Gabriella Giannachi and Mary Luckhurst (eds), *On Directing*, London: Faber & Faber, pp. 19–23.

Hallett, Bryce (2004) 'Duo Takes the Stage by Storm', *Sydney Morning Herald*, 5 August, www.smh.com.au/articles/2004/08/04/1091557907765.html?from = storylhs.

Practitioners on Practice ... Cheek by Jowl: An Interview with Declan Donnellan, Digital Theatre (2016) www.digitaltheatre.com

Reade, Simon (1991) *Cheek by Jowl: Ten Years of Celebration*, London: Oberon Books.

Shevtsova, Maria (2004) *Dodin and the Maly Drama Theatre: Process to Performance*, London: Routledge.

—— (2005) 'Declan Donnellan (1953–)', in Shomit Mitter and Maria Shevtsova (eds), *Fifty Key Theatre Directors*, London: Routledge, pp. 231–36.

—— and Christopher Innes (2009) *Directors/Directing: Conversations on Theatre*, Cambridge: Cambridge University Press.

Sierz, Aleks (2002) 'An Actor's Director', *Plays International*, 18 (2) (November/December): 15, 46.

Trussler, Simon (1994) *The Cambridge Illustrated History of British Theatre*, Cambridge: Cambridge University Press.

Chapter 8

PIOTR BOROWSKI AND POLAND'S STUDIUM TEATRALNE

Where process becomes performance

Paul Allain

Directing is not just about making shows, and academics need to keep exploring how to write about theatre as a process as much as an event. Rehearsals may be the new frontier for theatre studies, but we can't analyse them as we would a performance. Much Polish theatre reinforces this notion, as does the work of director Piotr Borowski (b. 1953), who is as focused on developing a process and working on the performer as a human being as on the regular production of performances. Borowski collaborated with the Gardzienice Theatre Association from 1977 to 1983 and with Jerzy Grotowski from 1985 to 1992. Both these acclaimed Polish theatre names have eschewed production-line theatre-making: Grotowski over decades of relatively closed research and Gardzienice with only 11 productions in over 40 years. Such a practice as Borowski's needs different evaluative criteria from the more usual frames of value and recognition linked to critical or public acclaim, reception theory, and performance reviews. I will therefore analyse his process and his performances to trace how he uses the theatre for continual self-investigation and questioning for both his performers and audiences.

Borowski's background

Borowski could be considered the consummate Polish experimental theatre director, one who physically connects Grotowski and Gardzienice in that he worked long-term with both. This connection began with his involvement in paratheatre in the 1970s. As was the case for many Poles interested in alternative culture at that time, he participated in several paratheatrical activities. This came about through his friend Tomasz Rodowicz, founder and artistic director of Teatr Chorea, who had been in the year above Borowski at music college and who already had contact with Grotowski's Laboratory Theatre. As well as attending the University of Research as part of the Theatre of Nations Festival in 1975, Borowski took part in the 'Special Project' earlier that year in Brzezinka in the countryside outside Wrocław in a group led by Włodzimierz Staniewski, a key paratheatrical collaborator with Grotowski from 1970 to 1976. Staniewski's Special Project was one of many such open process-based sessions exploring 'a cycle of meetings between people who do not know one another at first [...] causing themselves to release in themselves the simplest most elementary inter-human expression' (Leszek Kołodziejczyk, quoted in Kolankiewicz 1978: 8). None of these 'meetings' were theatre as such, for they had no audience.

When in 1976 Staniewski left the Laboratory Theatre to set up his own company, the Gardzienice Theatre Association (Gardzienice for short), Borowski joined him, again following Rodowicz who was to become one of the group's core long-term members. Based in the tiny village of Gardzienice, south-east of Lublin, Borowski collaborated on their early performances, *Spektakl Wieczorny* (*Evening Performance*, 1977) and *Gusła* (*Sorcery*, 1981), as performer, cultural animator, and musician, reflecting his earlier college studies. In interview, Borowski has reiterated how the Gardzienice group members did not see themselves as actors at this time, preoccupied instead with an inspiring sense of closeness to nature and to each other (Kornaś 2002: 75). This was the period of most intense activity for Gardzienice's 'Expeditions and Gatherings' in the remote, ethnically diverse, and marginalised communities along the border of eastern Poland. Gardzienice's early performances were forged partly from materials (including songs and gestures) gathered in this rural context. Staniewski defined such areas as a 'new natural environment for the theatre', where they could use theatre to achieve simple, direct communication with local people. Borowski took particular responsibility for a three-month rural project, the Winter Expedition, near the north-eastern city of Białystok, once home to many Jews, and culturally heterogeneous with its small communities of Tatars, Old Believers, and Belorussians. He spent almost three years on and off in the area, an experience he returned to in 2007 to make the film *Koniec Pieśni* (*The Song is Over*), which I will discuss later in the chapter. Expeditions had to stop, though, when travel was restricted from December 1981 by martial law, imposed by the Communists under General Jaruzelski in order to prevent a Russian invasion, as had previously occurred in two former countries of the Soviet Union, Hungary (1956) and Czechoslovakia (1968). The group therefore pursued intensive rehearsals on *Avvakum* (1983), the piece that sealed Gardzienice's acclaim overseas with their movement away from a rural context of touring to international festival presentations (see Allain 1997: 92). Borowski left the group before this critical stage in Gardzienice's evolution began and in 1985 went from one extreme to the other in his move to the Workcenter of Jerzy Grotowski: from intense public artistic activity in the 'new natural environment' of eastern Poland to reflective isolation in a tiny group of researchers, though once more in a small village, this time outside the industrial town of Pontedera, Italy.

In light of their acquaintance established through paratheatre, it is no surprise that he returned to work further with Grotowski, a relationship Borowski later described as a kind of 'spiritual brotherhood' (Kornaś 2002: 76). Little has been articulated about his seven years in Italy, though he evidently ensured a connection with Grotowski's native Poland – we learn about him writing a letter in Polish dictated by Grotowski (see Osiński 2001). As a key 'doer'[1] and researcher involved in daily activities linked to what Grotowski called Art as Vehicle,[2] a phrase coined by Peter Brook, Borowski helped develop the structure of *Downstairs Action*.[3] He has explained his role thus: 'Grotowski knew that I wasn't an actor at all, that I was looking for something else. I was only involved in those things that weren't theatrical. For example, in the exercise sequences, which Grotowski called the Motions and Watching' (Kornaś 2002: 76).[4] In Mercedes Gregory's film of *Downstairs Action*, made as part of the documentation of this research, we see Borowski working alongside Richards and his associate Mario Biagini and two other 'doers'. At one point he holds absolutely steady a long metal bar that emits a resonating chime when struck by Biagini. Borowski's quiet concentration and intense focus is made even more evident in the repeated practising of this moment, seen in short 'Preparation' extracts, as they are titled, that are shown before the whole film sequence of *Downstairs Action*. Later we see him dance wearing a woolly hat, as he spins and whirls to a vibratory song. Key aspects of the ethos of this work and some of its actual practices – daily training, demanding physical work such as the Motions, rigour and precision, rhythm and musicality – have remained a constant for Borowski, even though he utilises them extensively though by no means exclusively for the creation of performances, which Grotowski post-1970 never did. Continuity is further demonstrated by the fact that Studium Teatralne offer regular Motions as well as other body-based workshop sessions for the public in their Warsaw space.

After leaving Italy, the combination of predominantly closed research (Grotowski's Art as Vehicle) and open group-centred activities (Gardzienice and paratheatre) began to coalesce. Borowski's formative experiences had happened away from any metropolitan audience's gaze. Counter to this, and typical of Borowski's continual search for challenges, his first artistic impulse back in Poland was in 1995 to lead a month-long 'Theatre Workshop' at what is now called the Centrum Sztuki Współczesnej Zamek Ujazdowski (Centre of Contemporary Art at the Ujazdowski Castle) in the heart of Warsaw. In September 1996, seven years after the Berlin Wall fell, the Studium Teatralne Association was formally registered in Warsaw, incorporating several young actor/students from this workshop, in what was fast becoming an increasingly capitalist free-market Poland.

Bodywork and self-exploration

All Studium Teatralne's performances are richly complex. They recall the self-reflexive exploration of Grotowski's research, which in all periods used the craft of acting to 'penetrate' the self, even if latterly Grotowski did not do this through performance. *Hamlet*, the core text behind *Henryk Hamlet Hospital H.H.H.* (2006), is similarly metatheatrical in going beyond the form to analyse what it is to be human. *Północ* (*Midnight*, or alternatively *The North*, 1998) was a response to Romantic writer Adam Mickiewicz's classic poetic drama *Dziady* (*Forefathers' Eve*) and thematically explored creativity and youth, suggesting how performance can provide a space in which to reimagine things and to reawaken the dead. Even when not overtly metatheatrical, their work turns inwards to ask questions of the company members in a way that is probing and developmental. An explanatory text about *H.H.H.* (for short) describes how it asks 'Who am I? What do we want? What do I want to be?' Such questions recur at the core of this piece and several others: 'work, or our sustenance, is something we can measure ourselves against, something known, something unknown'.[5]

The company's young members are not concerned so much with what kind of actor they might be, but rather how they want to live, what it is today to be human (*człowiek* in Polish, the title of their 2001 performance). Paratheatre, in which everyone was a participant, with no observers or audience, had posited similar questions in the 1970s. Post-1989, Poles were asking themselves the same things but with particular urgency, as choices became possible after decades of constraints and relative isolation behind the iron curtain: only now these issues touched every aspect of life rather than being confined to aesthetic activities. Like their other performances, *H.H.H.* provided a framework within which to face such challenges. By asking this of themselves, the company hoped then to turn these questions out towards the audience, getting them also to reflect. Given such an aspiration, we can understand why Studium Teatralne do a lot more than create performances, involving themselves in a range of social and cultural activities.

Borowski is looking for 'real contact between people', which on paper sounds bland in the extreme but which in practice in their performances is qualified by a precise process and physical effect. Rather than being an abstract notion, though, this contact becomes almost tangible in the performers' intense interactions, their openness on stage that manifests itself as a ready availability and constant preparedness, and their heightened, very specialised movement vocabulary. The exploratory nature of their work shares some affinities not just with paratheatre but also with Grotowski's later research into the human condition in Art as Vehicle, with the actor as 'doer', working on their craft but somehow outside aesthetics and therefore doing rather than acting. Yet they are not seeking the transformative upward progression of energy from the base to the subtle that Grotowski referred to with the term 'verticality' (quoted in Richards 1995: 125). Rather, they are digging deep. And their primary aim is to deliver public performances, even if these are based on extensive personal exploration in an almost laboratory process. Borowski's vision for Studium Teatralne draws from both paratheatre and theatre, as active culture[6] meets physical action.

How do these theatrical and metatheatrical values manifest themselves in Studium Teatralne's performances? Their works draw eclectically on world and especially European literature, but arise as much from these textual starting points as from rigorous training and development of the actor's body. Their physical expertise was helped by the fact that a core group from that opening 1995 workshop initially stayed with the company, including Borowski's partner Gianna Benvenuto from Uruguay, a key collaborator and constant driving force in the group. The spectator is perhaps struck first by the performers' technical skill, particularly in the early days when the discrepancy between their abilities and their young age was all the more striking. Borowski demands extreme precision and craft yet with the shared understanding that nevertheless they all can and should still improve and grow. They work hard, often for five to six hours a day, every day – a lot for the very demanding physical practice this comprises.

Studium Teatralne's work has a spatial density and complexity with extreme movement that borders on dance (as nearly all commentators have observed). Each *mise en scène* is built on rhythm as much as textual dramaturgy, reflecting Borowski's early education in a music college. A further cornerstone of their technique is absolute attention to and lightness on the feet, as the performers must make no noise as they move. This is practised in a way of moving referred to as 'silent dance' (see Allain 1999: 20; Slowiak and Cuesta 2007: 134). In performance, in preparation and in workshops, the feet are rarely flat, providing great mobility, with the legs consequently operating as an ever-ready spring. This difficult positioning is compounded by high leaps and jumps that end in silent landings (see Plate 8). Such lightness is enabled by absolute control and attentiveness – qualities shared by traditional hunters (Richards 1995: 52–7; Slowiak and Cuesta 2007: 127). The hunter needs alertness and dexterity for his or her livelihood; for the performer, such positioning is instead a matter of choice rather than necessity, but the same physical benefits appear, without question, in the economy of movement and conservation of energy it promotes, the ability to respond quickly, and the readiness this hangs on. The performers exhibit an alert openness to each other, seeking each other out, looking for connections, contact with their 'prey'. This lightness also affects the whole body, for it is only possible with a specific way of holding the spine.[7] The simple demand of 'silent stepping', as it is also called, changes everything in the way the performer moves and thinks.

The performers' silent dance is visually compelling. Spatially, this dance, which is one cornerstone of their training, manifests itself in their performances as a carefully structured and controlled use of space, balanced and harmonious but somehow also ever-shifting and rarely at rest. The idea of balancing the space is an exercise familiar to many training approaches. But in this work the idea becomes actualised, as much as is possible, for such balance is never attainable or achieved and the performers have to keep striving. With this imperative, their work always has an extraordinary flow of movement based on the interweaving of actors. When looking for performance spaces for their first overseas tour with *Miasto* (*The City*, 1996) that I organised at British universities in 1998, the company demanded only two things: a flat (not necessarily wooden or sprung) floor and a large space, preferably 12 metres by 12 metres. The performers then covered this ground with a driving momentum, energetic leaps, twists and turns, and expansive strides, with the flat floor surface giving them secure footing and a solid grounding. This flow is made more precise without being choreographed by the fact that in rehearsal and training Borowski urges the actors to work with the space between them, as though they are operating within a field of 'compressed air', which is pushed tighter rather than displaced through proximity. Of course, with the exception of breath, air lies outside the body and beyond individual control, but the performer's hypersensitivity to it creates what seems almost like an electrical charge amongst them. Moments of physical contact involve cutting through the kinesphere, which in itself takes on a kind of material visibility. Kinaesthetically, this feeling is enhanced for the spectator by the performers passing each other by at speed with centimetres to spare. Even the air, so it seems, has to be under their control and becomes, since they use few props and limited scenography, an absolutely vital part of the *mise en scène* of all their works.

As well as this extreme physical responsiveness, the actors also have muscularity and flexibility, which they link to a very emotional and expressive inner motivation and acting process. Their virtuosity is never for show but is always centred upon the development of their roles and to a lesser extent the narrative. Whereas Gardzienice eschew psychological aspects of performing to emphasise the musicality and expressivity of rhythm in their songs (Hulton 1993: 25; Staniewski with Hodge 2004: 99), Studium Teatralne's actors work with scores that appear emotionally rich, with emotions connected to a precise physical structure of actions. This feeling is clearly tangible, for example, in Żakowski's anguished and suffering line of actions in *H.H.H.* In this he plays murderer Henryk M. who has been institutionalised in an asylum. He cites Hamlet's own introspective questioning with frequent direct addresses to God and other texts taken from dancer Vaslav Nijinsky's diaries and Sarah Kane's *Crave* (1998). These ideas of 'associations' and physical actions recurred throughout Grotowski's work. Studium Teatralne's pieces share with Gardzienice's performances such as *Metamorphoses* (1998) and *Elektra* (2004) a lightness of touch and a gentle, open, playful musicality and movement vocabulary, but linked to an acting style located in the Stanislavski–Grotowski tradition. In such conjunctions we can perceive Borowski's formation as a director.

Textual practices

Like Grotowski and countless other Polish directors from the mainstream as much as the avant-garde, Borowski has directed and drawn from several Polish and European classical dramas, including *Hamlet* and *Forefathers' Eve*. While the performers' footsteps may be silent in their physical dancing, their voices are not. As well as desemanticised sighs, groans, and cries that emerge almost inseparably from the movement and its effort, the textual layers of their performances are based on the quick utterance of text spoken in flight more than in stillness, their heightened speech supported by the flow of the body. The actors' way of speaking is not sing-song, but varies little in pitch and tone and is spoken mostly very fast. This does not always ensure totally clear diction, but the text emerges forcefully, with full breath support, and is usually intensely impassioned. As much as he wants the voice and body to 'meld together' (Borowski, quoted in Allain 1999: 22), Borowski is looking also for a merging between the material for performance and his actors' own lives, linking the body's movement and physical actions with something to say, related intimately to their world views and experience. His approach to directing is clear, controlled, precise, and demanding, but his choices are always closely negotiated with the rest of the company. The group's repertoire seems to be driven by personal interests and desires, emerging slowly from and drawing on collaborative consultation, rather than any sense of individual will or imposition. In this process, there is no overt textual hierarchy of classics over contemporary literature, of drama over daily speech. The company actors pull on diverse sources: from Mickiewicz's verse drama in *Midnight* through an Old Testament genealogy and transcripts of *milicja* (the state police) conversations during riots in Gdańsk in 1970, both in *Człowiek* (*The Man/Human*, 2001). There is a recurring fascination with Jewish culture and literature, most explicitly seen in *Król Kier Znów na Wylocie* (2008), based on Hanna Krall's 2006 book about the Holocaust *Chasing the King of Hearts*. The rehearsal process for *Parsifal* (2004) began with Celtic myths, but in the act of preparing and elaborating the performance, *Hamlet* became the dominant text. So evolved the next performance, titled and based more directly on *Hamlet* (2005). The material of *Midnight* only turned to *Forefathers' Eve* after extensive work on propositions based on the stimulus of what the family signifies for the actors (*Dziady* also means ancestors in Polish). Borowski has stated that 'our dramas are written on stage, that is, not before but in the course of rehearsals the dramatic skeleton forms' (Kornaś 2002: 78). Their working methodology is unpredictable, open, and continually evolves, and performances are not preplanned or prestructured. One piece leads to another, each performance's needs and questions giving birth to the next.

In this way, a loose idea gradually becomes a structure for the performance. In *Midnight*, a young suicide (it is explained at the start that this is based on Marek Chaber, a friend of former actor Dawid Żakowski) comes back from the dead to conduct a dialogue with Romantic writer Mickiewicz and his text *Forefathers' Eve*. This opening gave the piece a painful personal immediacy for the company actors. Any sentimentality was held in check by the formal ritualistic structure that progressed through an exorcism, prison, a crucifixion, and a pilgrimage, amongst other scenes, in sections modelled on the Stations of the Cross and the ritual pattern of *Forefathers' Eve*. Just as All Souls, when *Forefathers' Eve* is set, has for centuries been a night when the living 'speak' to the departed, so in this performance was a lost friend 'summoned' on stage. Mickiewicz's text was reformulated so that it was

> imagined as a dream that Mickiewicz has on his deathbed. Following the logic of a dream, the ritual of Forefathers' Eve becomes very condensed with things that couldn't take place in the original drama happening in our performance. And so we've prepared a wedding for our hero and liberated him from torments in the world beyond penitent souls.
>
> (Programme notes)

The theatrical ritual resurrected the dead, his fate altered even if only for the brief lifetime of the performance.

A performance's structure usually takes shape quickly but is then filled out through painstaking and always long rehearsal processes, to which the actors make fundamental contributions. The material is as much theirs as it is Borowski's. He has not overtly articulated his dramaturgical principles, but many of his pieces follow a simple story as in these following two examples. Three people (the 'instigators') desperately want to improve the world; anticipating a Second Coming they challenge God and force the arrival of a supposed Messiah by adopting a fatherless newborn infant, who grows up to become a violent general; mass destruction and death follow in a battle which he loses, resulting in his execution and the subsequent restoration of peace by the very same instigators (this is the narrative of *The Man*, based on an idea from Martin Buber's novel *Gog and Magog*, a further indicator of the group's strong interest in Jewish culture).[8] A young man arrives in the city from an outlying Polish village; after awakening to its violence, threats, and vicissitudes, he adjusts to survival in this harsh environment (*The City*). Their pieces then add on layers of music, live and recorded (such as that specially composed by Arek Waś for *Midnight*), with sound effects – like automatic gunfire in *The Man*. They mix colloquial text, oaths, street slang, and verbatim texts with high literature. Polish texts combine with Celtic myths and French contemporary literature, such as that by Bernard-Marie Koltès (*Roberto Zucco* for *The City*). They find what they need for the mix, a collage process familiar to much Polish experimental theatre.

How do these elements knit together? Their productions tell simple stories, but this is not what drives them. Borowski believes that narrative is important but emphasises that their pieces rely more on a central 'core' of actions. Their textual eclecticism could create a mess, but the group has a precise shared physical and gestural vocabulary, and material is always carefully distilled on the studio floor. Theirs is ensemble work of the highest order, with all actors on stage nearly all the time. The setting up of a wedding feast in *The Man* demands strict complicity and split-second timing. Every object is placed with delicate care. Later in the performance rows of helmets are laid out on stage to depict soldiers' graves. Pictures melt as fast as they appear. The actors all move with synchronicity, building the aural and spatial kinaesthetics of the piece, not a step out of line. Out of such set group pieces individual propositions and lines of physical action emerge with monologues and dialogue layered over song. Everything has its place, but the work rarely feels fixed or mechanical. Occasionally it overwhelms, the layers too dense and intense, the noise levels pitched too high, but such moments soon give way to calm and concentration. This work is dynamic and alive, always developing and in flux.

A social project?

Beyond such artistic experimentation, there is clearly a significant social aspect to the company's overarching project. In terms of sense and dramaturgy their pieces demand multiple viewings – Borowski wants his audiences to work, and to come back repeatedly. This outward-facing aspect of their practice is crucial for contemporary Poland as artists struggle in the difficult cultural climate of politically sanctioned neo-nationalism, homophobia, and anti-Semitism, conditions in which the arts are being increasingly co-opted for political and social ends by PiS (Prawo i Sprawiedliwość/Law and Justice), who are, at the time of writing in 2019, the ruling party. Although Borowski in the company's mission statement on their website states that theirs is not a 'political theatre', he believes it has to 'breathe with the contemporary times' (Borowski 2005). This perhaps says more about Borowski's dislike of labels, compartmentalisation, and his avoidance of sloganeering than it does about any desire to be politically disengaged. Yet one has to wonder, given the fast-declining situation for all arts in Poland, how long such a view is tenable.

Studium Teatralne have always asked big questions: about the vulnerability of young people in an increasingly tough and competitive urban environment in *The City*; about people's desire for leadership and guidance, even if this manifests itself in a dictator and war in *The Man*, a piece which in many ways caught the temper of the times surrounding 9/11 in its exploration of mass slaughter in the name of belief; about homosexuality, sanity, and identity in *H.H.H.*; or about contemporary Jewish relations and the holocaust through *Chasing the King of Hearts*. One might define their work as social rather than political, though Borowski would be equally sceptical about any such labelling, however general or benign this might seem. These questions all turn to the city, the company's and the actors' home, the place in which their performances begin and are made. In their early years they were one of the few experimental theatre companies in the country's capital, a precarious and difficult position with Warsaw's exorbitant costs and overheads, but the social interaction and dialogue this necessitated has now become central to their work. As you sit on benches in the quiet of their small studio space with its four pillars and mirror-like parquet floor, you hear trains rumbling past. Audiences turn out into dusty courtyards, heading home past Warsaw's once notoriously rough east station. Praga is a long way from the forests of Brzezinka, the Tuscan slopes of Pontedera, and the open fields of Gardzienice. Yet it is at the heart of Warsaw and Poland's ongoing and rapid transformation. The violent protests against Oliver Frljić's *Klątwa* (*Curse*) in 2017 outside Teatr Powszechny took place just minutes away from the group's base.

The company's city context opens up extensive possibilities and helps the group to stay in touch with urban sensibilities and progress, which are now driving the Polish economy forward. It also allows a wider economic base. The company members have often had to do other work to survive, often for money rather than for other theatres. For the first few years they had a collective agreement to clean the offices of the tabloid newspaper *Superexpress*, which they would take it in turns to do in the early mornings. Their Romanticism, a notion so intrinsic to pre-1989 Polish theatre, is not founded on Polish soil so much as on city pavements. Borowski manages to explore a familiar canon of classical texts, some of them Romantic, such as *Forefathers' Eve*, while elaborating unusual but extremely pertinent interpretations of them. This 'realistic Romanticism', coupled with a very practical methodology, enables their work to break out of over-familiar or closed circles of reference. When the newly formed group started to plan their first performance in 1996, the young actors, many of whom were also drama students immersed in Polish theatre history, lamented that they wanted to escape to the countryside to work in peace in a barn. Based as they were in what was then a notoriously rough part of Warsaw full of drunks and scruffy pre-war tenements, one can understand this impulse. But Borowski turned their desire on its head and asked them instead to deal with the urban experience of a rapidly modernising new Poland – facing their urban fears in their first show, *The City*. With this choice, he moved away from long-standing historical precedents: away from Juliusz Osterwa[9] and his Reduta's rural tours in far-flung eastern Poland (now Ukraine), from Grotowski in Brzezinka where he

197

conducted paratheatrical work, and from Gardzienice village and the Polish borderland where they travelled.

It is ironic that the area of Studium Teatralne's karate-club-turned-studio-space is now highly sought after, with trendy apartments and restaurants for Warsaw's new 'hip' elite. As their website shows, they have hosted and co-organised several projects across contemporary and traditional music, graphics, and art, involving numerous local and Warsaw-based artists, activities, and communities. One indicative example was the Historia Jednego Obrazu/The History of a Single Painting project, which exhibitions have presented several privately owned and thus rarely seen paintings with a particularly strong autobiographical context, in a process of visual storytelling. Studium Teatralne have helped Praga become a hub of artistic and cultural activity, again proving culture's power to regenerate deprived urban areas. In some things Studium Teatralne are very much ahead of the game.

The troubling generational divides in Polish society today are made worse by the differences in how the older generations lived and the relative ease of most things for young people today, such as the ready availability of goods and overseas travel. Studium Teatralne focus purposefully on young people. Their workshops and collaborations have often targeted secondary-school-age children. The role of Konrad in *Forefathers' Eve* is usually given to older actors deemed capable of tackling this substantial role. Borowski wanted to find connections between his actors and the fact that Mickiewicz wrote much of this largely autobiographical verse drama in his early to mid-20s. He cast the young Dawid Żakowski as the Konrad-like figure in *Midnight*, a departure critics observed appreciatively. The huge post-2004 EU accession exodus of young Poles to work overseas and especially in Britain[10] is only now beginning to reverse following the Brexit referendum. Young people are also returning home to mobilise themselves against the increasing slide to the right, as evidenced by the large street protests against the government's tightening of anti-abortion legislation in 2017 and higher education reforms in 2018. The importance of engaging young people is beyond question in Poland's current challenging political and social climate.

Another way in which Borowski appears to stand outside familiar models in the Polish lineage is the fact that so far in the group's history he has not constructed a discursive frame around the work. His is a kind of research theatre, as the practice demonstrates and the name implies (a loose translation of Studium Teatralne is 'theatrical study', though the word *studium* derives from Latin rather than Polish), but Borowski is focused much more on nurturing group members artistically, rather than presenting a theorised vision of his theatre. This is not to say that he doesn't have a clear directorial view but that he does not seem to prioritise its articulation outside the spaces where it is pragmatically necessary – the rehearsal room and training/workshop studio. He rarely gives conference presentations or public talks. But while he appears almost sceptical about overstating the theories behind the company's work, he is never anti-intellectual. Many of his actors were initially also university drama students who had outlets and a structure for their curiosity and enquiries, which did not need to be fixed on the company and their development of a single manifesto or world view. This emphasis on the pragmatics rather than the language of performance is refreshing in these times of oversaturation of documentation, marketing, and justification. That such an approach is even possible with the demands of the marketplace of European theatre is a real tribute to Borowski, even if at the same time it limits and circumscribes the public reception of his work and more widespread 'success'.

Although he is keen to avoid compartmentalisation and categorisation, Borowski does not deny his forebears. In fact, he makes great efforts to recognise those who have supported him. In 2015, for Studium Teatralne's 20th anniversary he dedicated the whole year to the memory of the late artistic director of acclaimed Polish alternative group Akademia Ruchu, Wojciech Krukowski, who had subsequently led the Centre of Contemporary Art and thus been Borowski's first host when he arrived back in Poland. Accordingly, Borowski created the performance *Party: take (a)part* with a scenography and concept that referred back to Akademia Ruchu's 1979 piece *Polski Stół* (*The Polish Table*). At the same time, they hosted and supported a new performance *Raz* (*Once*) by Akademia Ruchu's former members, created as a homage to Krukowski.

In my 2005 interview, he stated that he is not really a director but works *with* the actors as an equal, relying always on their propositions and contributions in all areas of the process (Borowski 2005). He prefers the term 'outside eye' to 'director'. While this sentiment is admirable for its permissiveness and for the freedom it gives the performers, in practice the experience is very different and the term misleading. Borowski does not just watch his performers, but, as I have observed in rehearsal and workshop, he moves with them, urging them on under his breath, almost as though he himself is physically engaged in the event or the actions. It is as though he is directing from the inside, almost feeling whether the connections and contact they talk about are really there. This carries over even into performance, where I have sat next to him and noticed his tensed body subtly moving, have heard his almost silent whisperings, as he somehow directs or at least communicates with the performers even in the very moment of performing. The process does not stop.

Conclusion

Studium Teatralne's first performance *Miasto* won the *Gazeta Wyborcza* jury's prize at the Lublin International Confrontations festival in 1997, and many more accolades have followed. They have frequently received positive critical and press feedback, including in Poland's national dailies such as *Gazeta Wyborcza*. They have been invited to several important festivals in Europe and Latin America, including in their early years the Third Theatre Olympics in Moscow (2001), Fabbrica Europa in Florence (2003), and Caracas, Venezuela (2002). They have been hosted worldwide, including by Teatro Varasanta in Bogota, Columbia in 2009 and La MaMa in New York in 2014, as well as by numerous European companies. They have collaborated with the Grotowski Institute in Wrocław and Roberto Bacci's Pontedera Theatre as well as the Workcenter of Jerzy Grotowski and Thomas Richards. Yet their profile in Polish theatre circles and amongst Polish academics and students is remarkably low level given their longevity and such international appearances. What might seem a lack of ambition could be considered a strength. It certainly allows them to remain rooted and quietly active in Praga amongst their local communities and to look after their members with great care. In interviews, Borowski is always measured, circumspect, and hesitant to make definitive statements. His artistic ambitions focus on the need to allow time for the next performance to germinate, protecting the delicate work of his company.

As the group has developed, members have found ways to gain more autonomy both inside and outside the company structure. Former Studium Teatralne actor, Zbigniew Kowalski, developed a solo performance in 2006: *Solo na Pradze* (*Solo in Praga*). Most of the founders from the 1995 workshop have now moved on to create independent work. Dawid Żakowski left in 2007 and set up his own group, Sztuka Nowa (New Art), based in the same building, which also houses other cultural bodies with whom collective events are organised. As I understand it, his departure was an amicable, mutually considered next step for him to develop personally and artistically. After several years working in the UK, Studium Teatralne actor of ten years Magda Tuka premiered her *1923.Webcam* performance with her company TukaWach in the Praga space in December 2017. Given Borowski's focus on the person as much as the performer, such changes seem inevitable, even desirable. This freedom also benefits Borowski. In 2006, he worked on a version of *King Lear* at the Pontedera Theatre in Italy. The following year, guest director Paweł Passini directed the Studium Teatralne actors in a piece called *Brama Raju. Krucjata Dziecięcia* (*The Gates of Paradise: The Children's Crusade*). This was while Borowski was filming his return after 27 years to the dying villages around Białystok, where he had led the Winter Expedition with Gardzienice. This moving and extraordinary film[11] of great anthropological and cultural interest documents him playing back his own recordings of traditional songs to the children of the now-dead singers. It has been shown at the University of Kent in Canterbury, UK, in 2009 as well as in London in 2017 at the Polish Hearth Club. The film shows how much Studium Teatralne is more than a theatre group that only makes performances, and Borowski is more than just a theatre-making director, following in the mould of Staniewski and Grotowski before him, both of whom operated as cultural animators. *The Song Is Over* is just part of their wide range of activities that happen both beyond but, more importantly, in their Praga base.

Polish theatre has moved on a long way from its norm during Communism of having well-established fixed ensembles of actors; Studium Teatralne reflect such organisational changes. Today, performers in Warsaw migrate across artistic platforms and work internationally. In terms of international acclaim and recognition, Studium Teatralne might be considered to have been held back by their self-fashioning as a research and community-based theatre group. Yet if we cast such usual criteria aside – of volume of output, scale of audience attendance, academic recognition, and public renown as signs of success, to name but a few – and instead focus on quality of intention and process and local engagement, we have to admire Borowski's ability to meld advanced physical training methods and movement with original interpretations of Polish and world drama, all supported by a strong social mission. They present a singular but vital model of practice, especially in their address to a highly mobile youth in a new Poland where villagers no longer sing and where experimentation risks being drowned beneath market values and a renewed political control, all too reminiscent of former Communist times, though now in a quite different guise.

Postscript. Regrettably, in April 2020 Studium Teatralne along with other community artists and organisations lost their space in Praga due to reasons beyond their control.

Five key productions

Note: year dates rather than months are given for the following pieces as these tend to appear and then evolve without there being what could be called a premiere as such. This reflects the processual and exploratory nature of the company's performances and their presentation.

Miasto (*The City*). By Piotr Borowski. Perf. Gianna Benvenuto, Jolanta Denejko, Zbigniew Kowalski, Agnieszka Kruszewska, Anna Olejnik, Piotr Piszczatowski, Anna Skorupa. Praga, Warsaw. 1996.

Człowiek (The Man/Human). By Piotr Borowski. Assistant Director Gianna Benvenuto. Perf. Marcin Cecko, Monika Dąbrowska, Jolanta Denejko, Zbigniew Kowalski, Anna Olejnik, Piotr Piszczatowski, Marcin Szymański, Magdalena Tuka, Dawid Żakowski. Praga, Warsaw. 2001.

Henryk Hamlet Hospital H.H.H. By Piotr Borowski. Co-directed with Dawid Żakowski. Perf. Gianna Benvenuto, Monika Dąbrowska, Dominika Jarosz, Zbigniew Kowalski, Anna Olejnik, Piotr Piszczatowski, Martina Rampulla, Monika Sadkowska, Magdalena Tuka, Dawid Żakowski. Praga, Warsaw. 2006.

Król Kier Znów na Wylocie (Chasing the King of Hearts). By Piotr Borowski. Perf. Gianna Benvenuto, Waldemar Chachólski, Magda Czarny, Danny Kearns (from the premiere until 2013: Piotr Aleksandrowicz, Gianna Benvenuto, Waldemar Chachólski, Martina Rampulla). Praga, Warsaw. 2008.

Party: take (a)part. By Piotr Borowski. Perf. Gianna Benvenuto, Danny Kearns, Rafał Kocemba, Paulina Masiak, Małgorzata Zielińska. Praga, Warsaw. 2015.

Acknowledgements

With thanks to Studium Teatralne (especially Piotr Borowski and Gianna Benvenuto and former member Dawid Żakowski), Giuliano Campo, Joanna Labon. All translations are by the author.

Notes

1 Grotowski had abandoned the term 'performer' as the group were not making performances as such but structures or 'opuses' as they called them that could be and later were shared with 'witnesses'.
2 See Wolford and Schechner 1997: 367–71.
3 Borowski has made the distinction that for much of his time there he was primarily working with Richards rather than Grotowski (Kornaś 2002: 77), for Richards was the 'creator, the motor, and the heart of the

work on *Action'* – though he also asserts that Grotowski always had the final say. The notion of transmission of course complicates the matter. For the sake of this piece I conflate Grotowski with Richards, not least because Borowski worked in what was then still the Workcenter of Jerzy Grotowski (before it became the Workcenter of Jerzy Grotowski and Thomas Richards in 1996), and Richards was very much Grotowski's apprentice at that time. I am grateful to Kornaś for his piece whence several facts stated here are derived.

4 The Motions are a core set of movement sequences, originally developed by Teo Spychalski as part of Theatre of Sources. See https://opere.org/works/On-the-Long-and-Winding-Road

5 This is taken from www.studiumteatralne.pl/onas.html accessed 8 October 2007 though the web page has since disappeared.

6 This is another term for paratheatre. See Kolankiewicz 1978.

7 Richards refers to Grotowski's key text from the Theatre of Sources period, 'Tu es le fils de quelqu'un', where he elaborates on the 'primal' (Richards) or 'primary' (Grotowski) position. Grotowski has written about such postures in various traditions, including a Haitian dance, the *yanvalou* (in Wolford and Schechner 1997: 297–8).

8 Interestingly, Buber's writings on Hasidism were a crucial inspiration to Grotowski throughout his working life. See, for example, Buber 1999, 2002.

9 See Osiński 2009.

10 By 2015, according to the Migration Observatory, Poles had become the largest foreign-born population in the UK with over 800,000 residents. Poles are part of the new exodus from the UK sparked by the Brexit referendum vote on 23 June 2016.

11 The film is titled *Koniec Pieśni* (*The Song is Over*, 2008). A substantial section is viewable here, www.youtube.com/watch?reload=9&v=Xc2U4g_-ihU

Bibliography

Allain, Paul (1997) *Gardzienice: Polish Theatre in Transtion*, Amsterdam: Harwood, OPA.

—— (1999) 'Interview with Piotr Borowski: Artistic Director of Studium Teatralne, Warsaw', *Slavic and East European Performance*, 19 (3): 15–23.

—— (2005) 'Grotowski's Ghosts', *Contemporary Theatre Review*, 15 (1): 46–56.

Borowski, Piotr (2005) Unpublished private interview with Paul Allain, Canterbury, England, April.

Buber, Martin (1999) *Gog and Magog*, Syracuse, NY: Syracuse University Press.
—— (2002) *Between Man and Man*, 2nd, trans. Ronald Gregor Smith, London: Routledge.
Gregory, Mercedes (1989) *Art as Vehicle (Film)*, New York: Atlas Productions.
Hulton, Dorinda (ed.) (1993) *Gardzienice, Poland: Włodzimierz Staniewski*, Interview with Włodzimierz Staniewski, Exeter: Arts Archives, Arts Documentation Unit.
Kolankiewicz, Leszek (1978) *On the Road to Active Culture: The Activities of Grotowski's Theatre Laboratory Institute in the Years 1970–1977*, trans. Boleslaw Taborski, Wrocław: Instytut Aktora-Teatr Laboratorium.
Kornaś, Tadeusz (2002) "Oś: z Piotrem Borowskim rozmawia Tadeusz Kornaś' ('The Axis': Tadeusz Kornaś talks to Piotr Borowski)', *Didaskalia*, 48 (April): 72–79.
Kornaś, Tadeusz (2009) "Strategia przetrwania' (Survival Strategy)', *Didaskalia*, 90 (April): 110–12.
Osiński, Zbigniew (2001) "*Grotowski o 'parach teatralnych' (Osterwa – limanowski, Stanisławski – niemirowicz-Danczenko, Grotowski – flaszen) i swoim Centro di Lavoro – workcenter w Pontederze* [Grotowski on 'Theatre Pairs' (Osterwa – Limanowski, Stanislavski – Nemirovich-Danchenko, Grotowski – Flaszen) and his Workcenter in Pontedera]", *Pamiętnik Teatralny*, 1–2 (197–8): 5–13.
—— (2009) 'Grotowski and the Reduta Tradition', in Paul Allain (ed.), *Grotowski's Empty Room*, London, New York and Calcutta: Seagull Books, pp. 19–54.
Richards, Thomas (1995) *At Work with Grotowski on Physical Actions*, London and New York: Routledge.
—— (1997) *The Edge-Point of Performance*, an interview with Lisa Wolford, Pontedera: Documentation Series of the Workcenter of Jerzy Grotowski.
Slowiak, Jim and Jairo Cuesta (2007) *Jerzy Grotowski*, London and New York: Routledge.
Staniewski, Włodzimierz with Alison Hodge (2004) *Hidden Territories: The Theatre of Gardzienice*, London and New York: Routledge. http://studiumteatralne.pl
Wolford, Lisa and Richard Schechner (eds) (1997) *The Grotowski Sourcebook*, London and New York: Routledge.

Chapter 9

CHRISTOPH MARTHALER

The musicality, theatricality, and politics of postdramatic direction

David Barnett

Postdramatic theatre, a phenomenon identified and theorised by Hans-Thies Lehmann, comes in many forms. A theatre that attempts to go beyond representation has a range of means at its disposal for either calling representation into question or banishing it from the stage altogether. The postdramatic seeks to convey something akin to the contemporary experience of 'ambiguity, polyvalence and simultaneity' (Lehmann 1999: 141, 2006: 83).[1] As a result, a postdramatic aesthetic articulates a new modality of using signs in the theatre in that the relationship between signifier and signified no longer requires clarification and thus poses an audience a set of questions that the stage refuses to answer. In turn, master signifying systems in the theatre, such as those associated with the actor and speech, give way to an all-encompassing event defined by a thoroughgoing relativisation of definitive signification, in which the actor is as important as the gestures, the set, or the lighting.

The dramatic director's role in the twentieth century was primarily to interpret text through the medium of the actor. The flow of time was structured, and the set tended to serve the interpretative strategies of the particular reading. The bracketing of representation, on the other hand, asks directors to reconsider the fundamentals of their craft – how theatre treats actors, text, time, and space – but offers no concrete pointers. In the advent of a postdramatic sensibility, the role of the director itself has undergone a shift; in a theatre in which hierarchies have been undermined, the director is no longer the visionary interpreter but rather moderates his or her claim to authority. The new paradigm dethrones the director to an extent by reinstating the co-workers on the production team who previously had to defer to a unifying idea. Yet this palace revolution is more about shifting emphases than necessarily robbing the director of an erstwhile omnipotence. The director still plays a considerable part in the creative process.

Postdramatic direction takes many forms, and German-language theatre, in which a variety of practices has been developing for the past decades, has presented a wealth of approaches and stances. Frank Castorf, for example, directs a theatre of disruption and aggression, while Einar Schleef preferred the radical redefinition of the chorus as a site of collective trauma. Heiner Müller, partly under the sign of Robert Wilson, offered a slowed-down dialectical theatre, while René Pollesch assaults his audience with a stream of words delivered at breakneck speed, suggesting the compression of time and space in the context of globalisation.[2] In this chapter, I shall be discussing the Swiss director Christoph Marthaler (b. 1951), who combines a peculiar take on the contemporary chorus, musicality as a structuring principle, and the confrontation of actors with amorphous sets and (found) text. Nicholas Till argues that 'Marthaler [has] found a distinctive theatrical format', and I will thus be investigating the director by focusing on typical features found in a single production (while briefly referring to other projects) in order to interrogate Marthaler's approaches to direction beyond representation as a whole (Till 2005: 219). It is difficult to discuss Marthaler's development as such, as his work in the theatre, from its beginnings to the present day, is far more a series of refinements and reconfigurations.

Marthaler started life in the theatre as a musician and directed critical, ironic evenings of song and performance in the late 1980s and early 1990s. His productions brought him to the attention of the Berlin Volksbühne where his *Murx den Europäer! Murx ihn! Murx ihn! Murx ihn! Murx ihn ab! Ein patriotischer Abend* (*Kill the European! Kill Him! Kill Him! Kill Him! Kill Him Off! A Patriotic Evening*, 1993) became a hit and led to prominent commissions at major theatres in Germany and Switzerland. Such was Marthaler's reputation that he was appointed *Intendant* ('artistic and general manager') of Zurich's premier venue, the Schauspielhaus, for the period 2000–5. However, the Management Board of the theatre decided in autumn 2002 to terminate Marthaler's contract early, due to the large cost of his productions. A popular campaign ensued to keep the *Intendant* in post, and the Board allowed him to remain on a provisional basis. The theatrical upshot of the affair was the project *Groundings*, which will provide the focus for this chapter.[3] Its subtitle, *Eine Hoffnungsvariante* (literally 'a hopeful variant' but perhaps more accurately translated as 'a best-case scenario'), is a quotation from the Board itself and euphemistically describes their decision temporarily to retain Marthaler.

Groundings, like much of the work Marthaler has made since *Murx*, involved set designer Anna Viebrock and dramaturg Stefanie Carp, and, indeed, all three were credited as the project's leaders. Carp described the working process of the triumvirate in 2001 when she said that the team proceeded from a theme or a 'world' suggested by Marthaler. Scenes would then follow and only later would text be incorporated, in relation to actions or images developed in rehearsal (quoted in Schwerfel 2001). The stimulus for *Groundings* was clearly the uneasy relationship between economic pressure and theatrical production, and minutes from the Management Board's sittings were used as raw material in places. Yet the idea of performing the internal tussles of a theatre was not exactly the stuff of sell-out stage runs. The lens was thus widened to include another instance of a 'grounding', the bankruptcy of Swissair in 2002, though as one review put it, the combination of Swissair and the Schauspielhaus was 'less analytical than associative' (Müller 2002). The unifying motif was the confrontation of human beings and the market, something of a topos in German-language theatre since the fall of the Berlin Wall; its theatrical form actively avoided representational detail. *Groundings* was a production with little in the way of plot. Rather, it moved through a series of episodes and routines, the order of which had no tangible sense of cause or effect. As Lehmann puts it, the postdramatic is not concerned with 'action but *circumstances*' (1999: 113, 2006: 68). This principle of treating themes in a depersonalised fashion is characteristic of Marthaler's and postdramatic theatre's approach to signification and the actor.

Material for *Groundings* was gathered from a series of documentary sources that charted the demise of the airline and the ructions in the theatre. More specifically, Carp collected 'speeches of thanks and farewell held at official occasions of the same companies', which emphasises an interest in ritual, in the speaking patterns demanded on such occasions, independent of their speakers, yet generated by social sanction (Carp 2003: 46). Extra stimulus was taken from the novel *Doktor Billig am Ende* (*The Demise of Doctor Shoddy*) of 1920 by the Dadaist Richard Huelsenbeck and books by management gurus such as Tom Peters. Arno Paul describes Carp as a person 'who arranges polyvalent texts for performance from the verbal garbage [*Wortabfall*] of everyday communication' (2000: 106). The diverse sources demonstrate the function of text in postdramatic theatre: it is no longer the locus of coherent meaning, and it does not structure narrative. Rather, it provides a series of discrete thematic nodes whose points of contact are established by the audience and not by the cast. Text in Marthaler's theatre is also alive with word play and humour, and the generation of comic inconsistency is allied to the ways in which actors deliver their lines, as we shall see below.

The treatment of text is one example of the way in which clear, coherent meaning is frustrated on the postdramatic stage. The dispersal of words, and indeed other material, such as gesture and song, within the production, is closely connected to the ways in which linear time schemes are actively frustrated in postdramatic performance. Lehmann locates the structuring of time in dramatic theatre as a defining quality when he writes 'drama is the flow of time that is controlled and made manageable' (1999: 61, 2006: 40). Dramatic action is the representation of events, and when these are ordered, tensions, developments, and climaxes arise. The postdramatic, on the other hand, looks to the paradigm of the dream as a formal means of suspending the flow of time from the beginning to middle to end of a narrative. Dreams are episodic and non-linear: meaning is diffused throughout their structures, so that, say, knowledge of a dream's conclusion may not necessarily shed light on the dream's possible significance. The lack of sequential logic in dreams led Freud to wonder whether individual elements should be interpreted literally, ironically, historically, or symbolically (1991: 344). The epistemological uncertainty of the dream is used to infect the theatrical event in postdramatic theatre and rob the stage of its ability to make material meaningful in itself. Instead, language and images are presented and passed over to the audience to experience; interpretation, either on stage or in the auditorium, is no longer a given. Clearly *we* do not experience theatre outside of time, but the postdramatic aims to suspend linearity or at least to make it highly problematic in performance so as to mediate a rich and unprivileged flow of material.

Groundings, in the light of the above, presents a series of actions and repetitions, each connected in some way to the central themes of the production without telegraphing those relations or offering narrative cohesion as a way of supporting an argument or reading. The production featured eight male actors and one female.[4] The company, as in other projects, modulated between moments of communality, solos, duets, and other smaller scale arrangements. One of the recurring motifs in which the ensemble was involved was, for example, the announcement of a delay to the putative flight on which the cast may have been travelling. The length of the delay moved from a ridiculously short thirty-five seconds to eight to ten days, to a retrospective delay, calculated from 4 January 1984, of nineteen years. Each announcement was met by a ritualised response from the actors. Elsewhere, at other moments, the eight men would report a set of niggling bodily dysfunctions to each other and ask for the nearest chemist. More ritual would follow a particular solo performance. Take, for example, the lecture delivered by Sebastian Rudolph. His comical presentation on marketing concluded with the idea that the firm's product, whatever it might actually be, would be best advertised using the device of a large grey rectangle. He was then invited to take a seat on a comfy chair that, as had been previously seen in the evening, careered off stage on an unseen rail into a wall made of styrofoam. Rudolph sat without resistance and was greeted by the rest of the cast offering the same clichéd lines of regret, condolence, and encouragement, also heard earlier in the production. And as soon as Rudolph had disappeared into the managerial afterlife, he, like others before him, returned to the stage as if nothing had happened. Rudolph's solo was distinctive, yet it echoed those that preceded it despite its individuality, and conformed to structures found in the speeches that were to follow. The individual, even during a solo, exposed his insinuation within a social discursive system. Such a positioning relates closely to the precarious status of the subject in contemporary European capitalism – the illusion of individual specificity coexists with the acknowledgement that the market pays little attention to this.

Rudolph, like many of the other actors, was visually identified (through his hairstyle and make-up) with a real-life counterpart, in this case the Canadian-born founder of the interior-design 'bible' *Wallpaper**, Tyler Brûlé. Others actors were made up to resemble the head of the Schauspielhaus's management board, Peter Nobel, for example, or the brains behind the Swiss investment group BZ, Martin Ebner. Clearly, such a satirical move can site meaning in the realm of allegory, where one set of signs stands in a definite, mappable relation to another. However, Stefan Zweifel argues that the speaking figures should be understood more ambivalently: 'whoever sees only Ebner and Nobel in the figures have themselves to blame, as the masterful art of the actors avoids any hint of denunciatory caricature' (2003). Marthaler's approach to his actors makes simple satirical critique problematic, in that representation, in whatever form, is never the end that is sought, or indeed achieved. The same is true of Marthaler's approach to dramatic character in productions such as Chekhov's *Drei Schwestern* (*Three Sisters*) (1997) or Horváth's *Geschichten aus dem Wiener Wald* (*Tales from the Vienna Woods*) (2006). The actors' models were little more than ciphers or visual indices as there was no attempt to mimic mannerisms or speech. Such a refusal is located in the very different understanding of the actor in this kind of theatre.

Marthaler's rehearsal process is remarkable for its relaxed nature. Erstwhile dramaturg Matthias Lilienthal observed: 'Marthaler uses almost two-thirds of the rehearsal period to make a bed for the actors to tuck themselves into. The actors find the freedom to create through a feeling of comfort' (2000: 120). The actress Olivia Grigolli, who has appeared in several of Marthaler's productions, elucidates: 'Christoph continually tries to take the acting away. One has to trust oneself just to be there [on stage]. [...] He's always reassuring you' (quoted in Anon 2000b: 148). Marthaler's calm and calming rehearsal processes are concerned with allowing his actors to present text without too much colour or character-based pretence entering into the deliveries or movement. One critic summed up the performance of a particular actor in *Groundings* as follows: 'Kienberger embodies the essence of Marthaler's theatre insofar as he never appears to be acting. He *plays* – like a child (but never childishly); he remains himself and he never pretends before us' (Müller 2002). The actors do not seek to repress their own personalities, and they are encouraged to perform without adopting a character. They play with their lines and their gestures without offering concrete or sustained points of reference in terms of a unified creation. One watches how the 'character-less' actors negotiate the tasks set by the director. A sense of helplessness and resignation thus also emerges because the actors are never in control of what they are executing but are always subject to the will of others. In a concrete sense, they are part of the creative team's design, and in performance they also convey the impression of having to submit to speech patterns and rituals that are not of their own making. The tension between such impositions and the playfulness of the actors' struggle generates comic inconsistency.

The speeches themselves are actively drained of interpreted meaning in rehearsal. Grigolli continues: 'the text is a given for Christoph, he is more concerned with the atmosphere and the environment. [...] It's an atmosphere in which one can create space for associations and imagination' (quoted in Anon 2000b: 152). The transformation of referential text into something that can detach itself from denotation is highlighted in *Stunde Null* (*Zero Hour*) of 1995. This production, concerned with the recuperation of political discourse in the wake of the linguistic abuses of the Third Reich, drew, like *Groundings*, on documentary material. It also ran the risk of presenting little more than a parody of politicians seeking security in cliché. Graham F. Valentine, another of Marthaler's regular actors who played the role of 'The Ally without a Homeland', created his monologue from decrees made in post-war Berlin (delivered in German, Russian, English, and French), speeches by Churchill, and Dada poetry by Kurt Schwitters. He notes: 'I [made] an aria out of the proclamations, which [wasn't] only intended to be satirical' (Valentine 2000: 80). Valentine suggests that the speech produced a materiality of its own, turning language into a thing in itself, removed from his sources' obvious points of reference and his own delivery as an actor. The multilingual textures combined with Schwitters's vowel-dominated verse to produce a relationship between speaker and spoken that called the agency of the speaker into question: was he speaking language or was language speaking him?

The potential for humour in this style of performance is increased because of the uncoloured presentation of language. In *Groundings*, the English-influenced business-speak and the economic 'logic' that produces it allowed the actors to articulate some rather peculiar formulations. However, rather than parodying the lines or offering ironic commentary through facial gesture or tone of voice, the actors presented the language 'as is' and consequently as if it were being imposed upon them. They were quite literally the victims of what they were saying, as in their extensive babble of meaningless but 'necessary' business-speak; the cleavage between the rhetorical force of the texts and their unsuitable speakers opened up comic discrepancies. This approach to text informs Marthaler's theatre as a whole and calls much of what is said on stage into question by offering incongruity to the spectators and leaving them to evaluate it. The strategy is closely linked to Brecht's attempts to criticise language by divorcing actor from character, although it deliberately rejects Brecht's ideologically derived interpretative strategies.

The cleavage between sense and reference in the spoken texts is something that is carried over into the way songs are sung in Marthaler's productions. One of Marthaler's early rehearsal gambits is simply to get his cast to sing together, usually in several-part harmonies, without colour, delivering words and music in such a way that their meaning remains suspended on stage. As Till finds, Marthaler

> has developed a highly distinctive style for his singing actors that precludes outward performative 'putting over' of the songs, so that they seem to become internalised, and yet also give the impression that the performers are being passively ventriloquised by the songs.
>
> (2005: 227)

In *Groundings*, the cast sang the folk song, 'Wenn ich ein Vöglein wär' ('If I Were a Little Bird'), as they peered into the hole in the styrofoam wall after every departure. The song is one of longing, that if the singer were a bird, he or she would fly to his or her beloved. On first hearing the song, one could understand it as an ironic lament for the recently ejected colleague, suggesting that the last thing the group would do would be to follow the hapless executive. Yet, as the song was repeated after each of the other departures, one might start to wonder just why the song was being sung. Was it a ritual, a compulsion, was it a joke whose staleness its singers could not appreciate, was it a moment of harmonious beauty in the face of corporate brutality done to one of their number? The melody, the lyrics, and the delivery failed to vouchsafe any of these interpretations yet were suggestive of the perverse sense of community that runs through Marthaler's productions.

The harmony of the songs employed in *Groundings* (which are found across Marthaler's directing *oeuvre* as a whole) contrasted with the often pathetic attempts at individuation witnessed elsewhere in the production. At one stage, the men formed a queue in front of the woman, bemoaning their fate that, for example, they had not received as many millions in compensation after the failure of their firm as others. The men failed to realise that they were all implicated in the same system and could not hear the reverberation of their own laments in the words of the others. Here we view a disunified collective, that is, they are all subject to the same pressures, yet they only come together, and with no little beauty, in song. The actors are not, as we have seen, given psychological characters, and so this sense of disjunction becomes a critique of a system rather than an indictment of a universal 'human condition'.

It is, as previously acknowledged, something of a misnomer to speak of 'characters' in *Groundings*, and the nominal titles given to them are generic, for the most part, and elusive. We find 'a casino capitalist', 'a hugely disappointed man', and 'a nationalist globalist', for example. Suffice to say, none of these descriptions informed the acting, as characterisation had been eschewed. Even where names were used – we find 'Doktor Billig' in the programme – there was little to anchor the actor to a character, as he had also been made up to resemble Peter Nobel and played a variety of mutually contradictory roles, just like the rest of the cast. Individuation and self-definition simply did not take place in *Groundings*, and they are conspicuously absent in most of Marthaler's work. The men, whose epithets had little meaning in any specific sense, resembled each other in their business suits and their mannerisms, which seemed to be drawn from a common store as opposed to a discrete and individual source. The effect was highlighted through the tactical use of props. Each of the actors carried a suitcase, which tallied with the themes of travel and flight. It was only later that we learned precisely what was being carried. Each suitcase contained the torso and head of a dummy, of the type used by medical organisations for training in mouth-to-mouth resuscitation. While vain attempts were made to resuscitate the dummies at one stage, the men later exchanged clothes with their inanimate counterparts, donning in turn the dummies' uniform blue vests, and wandered around the stage with their arms in the dummies' empty sleeves. They caressed and mounted the dummies, and engaged in a series of mimes that descended into violence. By the end of the production, the dummies sat around the only actress, nominally 'Margot', who read them a story from a children's book, while the men sat together upstage. The crisis of individuality that began with the interchangeability of the actors and their disconnection from their own texts found its endpoint in the actors' replacement by identical models. Such a motif runs through Marthaler's theatre, and is presented in *20th Century Blues* (2000) in a variation in which the stage was finally occupied by several sets of identical twins.

Yet, although Marthaler is interested in erasing individuality, gender differences are most definitely maintained. Carp stresses that the men 'never function on their own, but in a group, dependent on each other, even though [...] they're also alone. [...] The men-machine is infantile. Its modest needs are poorly serviced' (Carp 2000b: 110). The men on stage presented the contradiction between the potential of wielding economic power and being a part of a hierarchy at whose apex was capital itself. As each tried to climb that little bit higher up the corporate ladder, each was potentially the next to exit through the ever-repaired styrofoam wall. The single actress, on the other hand, was hardly a contrastive figure of embodied power either. One of her first tasks was to sing a solo whose score and lyrics were provided by the production's pianist. Later she led a seminar in which the men pretended to be aircraft with arms outstretched as she tried to fly them back into profit (see Plate 9). She certainly helped to administer the 'men-machine', as she was the person who invited the various actors to sit on the ejector seat, and she became an erotic fetish to Doktor Billig, who confessed his corporate sins to her from a position of sexual submission. So, a distinction was made between the men and the woman, yet its nature, like so much of the production, was ambivalent and shifting. Margot was, for the most part, differently marked on stage, although she occasionally sat with the men and participated in their collective routines and songs. The gendered binary was, however, too unstable to posit a fixed opposition, and thus continued to beg questions about its nature as the production progressed.

Marthaler is also concerned throughout his work with the onstage condition of '*Erschöpfung*', which is usually translated as 'exhaustion' but which attains more metaphysical qualities here. '*Schöpfen*' is the German verb 'to create', although it also means 'to scoop out'. The 'er' prefix once denoted the perfective aspect of a verb, and '*erschöpfen*' is therefore to scoop something out completely, to exhaust further activity. So, Marthaler's actors do not traverse the stage in states of physical exhaustion as such (although sleeping often occurs in the productions and they almost all have a characteristic slowness), but are rather caught in states in which novelty and invention are no longer possible. This mode of performance coincides with a sense of problematic temporality as articulated in the term '*Zwischenzeit*'. This translates as 'meantime', yet it too requires qualification: the word may be contrasted with '*Endzeit*', an 'end of history', associated with Samuel Beckett's *Endspiel* (*Endgame*), and so becomes literally a 'between time' (Carp 2000b: 109). The figures on stage are thus discovered in situations that they cannot necessarily affect and repeat actions, speeches, songs, and gestures in the hope that they might break the cycle after sufficient attempts. This was certainly one of the central structural motifs of *Murx*, set as it was in a giant waiting room.

The organising principles that underlie Marthaler's work cannot be accounted for in terms of linearity and are informed by the sense of a *Zwischenzeit* which finds form in concepts taken from music.[5] Michael Kunitzsch notes, with respect to *Stunde Null*: 'the whole thing is like listening to a piece of modern jazz in which a solo follows a chorus, in which breaks are reacted to, and in which every musician is of equal rank in an all-star line-up' (quoted in Reiter 1996: 98). Marthaler, with a wealth of musical knowledge and experience, organises his work in terms of tempo and rhythm, repeating and varying motifs without resorting to any sort of narrative explication. Not only does this approach help to create the dream state discussed earlier, it also engages the audience's less conscious perceptive facets so as to engender the sense of an experience, just as when one listens to music. The physical routines that structure the productions resemble musical themes in that they are not attached to definite referents; they may suggest moods or associations but are little more concrete than that. Their repetition corresponds to concepts of musical variation.

Marthaler's work in the theatre is also intimately associated with the spaces within which it takes place, and it is no surprise that when Marthaler won the Berliner Theaterpreis in 2004, it was awarded jointly to him and his set and costume designer, Anna Viebrock. Viebrock's sets are epic creations, almost always extremely large and full of associative detail. They are also sealed; nature remains without and we are left with spaces in which only human beings operate, albeit defectively. Viebrock makes a connection here: 'closed off rooms have always occupied me and for Christoph the state of being cut off is a basic theme' (quoted in Anon 2000a: 54). Indeed, one critic asserted that 'Marthaler's theatre takes place within a monumental coffin' (Henrichs 1995). The sheer size of Viebrock's designs overwhelms, and when *Murx* was brought over to the London International Festival of Theatre in 1995, an alternative venue had to be found which could accommodate the giant structure.

Viebrock's spaces are always difficult to penetrate cognitively, although this impression may only emerge over time, as the designer notes: 'at first sight, the space should preferably appear concrete, but when one then views a certain element in relation to another, one has to conclude that the space can't work and that there's a contradiction in there somewhere' (Viebrock and Masuch 2000). The contradictory relations, which reveal themselves upon closer inspection, call the whole space into question, as Klaus Zehelein notes: 'the artificiality does not admit the commensurable' (2000). The sense of location is thus thrown open and neither spectators nor actors can settle because of the impossibility of applying a meaningful yardstick. The sets are also repositories for a meditation on the flow of history, as Carp notes: 'it's difficult to find a contemporary image for today on the stage. Anna Viebrock's spaces show the present as something that has just passed, always with the traces of yesterday, always being shifted into yesterday' (Carp 2000a). Design components, as we shall see below, opened up a dialogue in *Groundings* between the comfortable past and its less pleasant present. And there is also a metatheatrical feature, identified by Lehmann: 'more or less, [the sets] stay close to the reality of the theatre building itself. That confers on them something mysteriously real' (2000).[6] Thus, what we find in general terms for a Marthaler production is a stage that actively makes itself problematic on a variety of fronts: it does not cohere to representational models, it announces its debt to the past, and it acknowledges that it is a part of the theatre through its recognition of the theatre's own dimensions and form.

The set for *Groundings* corresponded to these features and foregrounded the materiality of the theatre from the outset. As the pianist arrived, the metal safety curtain remained shut. His opening chords were to provide a musical cue to open the portal yet there were still 'teething problems' with the 'new' two-year-old computer system, as he told the audience. The pianist also acknowledged the reality of the theatre in that he divided his time between the orchestra pit and the stage, a communication made possible by a trampette in the pit. Once the curtain was eventually raised, a second set of fabric curtains also failed to part and only later revealed a slightly raised platform on which two rows of chairs stood, with a small aisle in between them. The main space was rather empty and large, with, for Viebrock, a low ceiling, used to accommodate a safe that sat above the actors for the duration of the performance. The floor covering was an aerial view of Zurich. The sense of claustrophobia was thus augmented by a strangely vertiginous perspective. The second, smaller room with the chairs was more associative and was based on Lynne Cohen's photo, 'Halt'.[7] It could have been a seminar room, a departure lounge, a particularly wide aeroplane, or an auditorium. Two blackboards were fixed to the back wall and displayed the complementary legends 'Compensation Dispensary' on the left and 'Responsibility Disposal' on the right. The kitschy curtain that separated the two rooms evoked the time when Swissair was indeed flying high, its pattern suggestive of the 1970s.

The collision of the machinations of business with the directorial approaches of Marthaler's theatre functioned as textbook Brechtian *Verfremdung* in that besuited managers were presented in circumstances and attitudes very different from the norm. Yet while Brecht sought a level of commentary on stage, Marthaler deferred the act of making judgements to the audience. The actor Josef Bierbichler notes: '[Marthaler] would never admit it, but all the same his work is always highly political' (quoted in Anon 2000c: 137). Yet we have to understand the political in terms that go beyond the obvious politico-economic themes of the production.

In an interview, Carp said that a possible subtitle for *Groundings* could have been 'forlorn attempts at survival by the Western world and contemporary culture' (quoted in Landolt and Wälchli 2003). Clearly her ambit is very broad and not a little ironically overblown, but the crux of her position is that a postdramatic approach to such integral aspects of our society as presented in *Groundings* will connect with far wider contexts. Peter Kümmel asserts that 'the business of the executives can't be represented', due to the abstract nature of its mechanisms and its rationales (2003). A purely character-based dramaturgy would thus reduce the problems addressed by the production to the individual whims of the psychologies on stage. The refusal to represent character leaves the spectator with a set of attitudes and relationships that exist beyond individual motivation or volition and reveal broader connections with forces that interpellate the figures. The audience is invited to look beyond the actors to identify arrangements of human beings, texts, and actions and to ask what has brought them about and what is perpetuating them. As we have already seen, the problems of human agency are traced back to systems and structures that are social and economic. While Marthaler does not arraign anyone on stage, he is clearly pointing to a constellation of forces that are in need of closer interrogation and alteration.

It is tempting to see Marthaler as a maverick outsider – a Swiss who has a certain distance from the Germans, for whom *Murx* and *Stunde Null* were made. The former was a meditation on former citizens of the German Democratic Republic and their place in a recently reunified Germany; the latter, as already mentioned, considered post-war political discourse on the 40th anniversary of European liberation. Yet my discussion of *Groundings* suggests that Marthaler is just as comfortable with critiques of his own national traditions and values. It is far more Marthaler's ironic and distanced relationship to his subject matter, as presented in his postdramatic stagings, that allows a simultaneous tenderness for and critique of his actors and their situations than his nationality. His mode of direction, with its outright refusal to offer interpretation, grants a licence to approach the grandest of themes without reducing them through the restrictions of representation.

In 2018, Marthaler was awarded only the seventh International Ibsen Award by the Norwegian government (although the award has no direct connection to the work of the playwright after whom it is named). At 2.5 million Norwegian Krone (roughly £250,000), it is one of the most generous (and prestigious) theatre prizes in the world. The list of the six previous recipients reads like a 'who's who' of contemporary theatre's most important innovators. The jury's commendation concluded that the award 'honours this inimitable theatrical language, its capacity for formal abstraction and experimental arrangement, its humanistic receptivity but at the same time also the challenge that it continues to be for the audience' (Anon, n.d.: n.p). The citation echoes the analyses above in its richness and expanse. What it also reflects is how Marthaler's theatre continues to work in a way reminiscent of DJ John Peel's appraisal of his favourite band, The Fall: 'they are always different; they are always the same' (Peel quoted in Smith and Middles 2003: back cover). That is, what is remarkable about Marthaler and his directorial practices is that he applies a similar process to the most diverse of materials, be they plays, operas, or found material, and creates productions that are both recognisable as his work, yet particular in their treatment of themes. They continue to fascinate and open radically new vistas.

These qualities can be seen clearly in Marthaler's production of Alban Berg's unfinished opera, *Lulu* (Staatsoper Hamburg, 2017). The reviewer from *The Financial Times* noted:

> Tenderness, humour, humanity and loneliness are all things that Christoph Marthaler expresses superbly on the stage. None of them are core themes of Alban Berg's *Lulu*, making the Hamburg State Opera's decision to allocate this work to this director a curious one from the start.
>
> (Apthorp 2017)

Such a contradictory point of departure set up Marthaler's treatment of this classic tale of passion, betrayal, murder, and self-centredness. One reviewer observed that the production 'relativizes the emotional performances [that] never drift off into a dominant life of their own' (Theurich 2017). Once again, the director was able to move the focus away from the remarkable personalities on stage in order to consider the environment in which Lulu makes her way through a string of lovers and ultimately finds herself the victim of Jack the Ripper. Her rise and fall, potentially the tragic core of the opera, became a more distanced experience of social mechanisms and their fatal outcomes, without forsaking the personal suffering of those involved. However, the comic and humorous possibilities of the piece were not ignored, and the richness of texture, typical of Marthaler's work, was also evident in this dark opera.

One element that the team resolved with great originality was the fragmentary status of the opera's final act. Marthaler, musical director Kent Nagano, assistant conductor Johannes Harneit, and dramaturg Malte Ubenauf decided to include Berg's *Violin Concerto* as Lulu lay dead. This piece had been composed in honour of a friend, whose death interrupted Berg's work on *Lulu* and thus prevented the completion of the music. Once again, one sees the integration of real contexts into the fictional world, a way of shifting perspective and challenging the audience further. Marthaler won the

Faust, the German theatre's equivalent to the British Olivier or the American Tony Award, for Best Director of Musical Theatre for the production.

The theatre of Christoph Marthaler is the result of a collaborative process which extends from the key members of the production team to the actors, who are given the space to play with their linguistic and gestural material rather than being asked to surrender to the interpretations of the director. The texts, the rituals, and the set are never permitted to create a sense of timelessness or ahistoricity and are thus always connected to a range of material contexts. Marthaler's political theatre does not rely on political themes as such but more on the ways in which human subjects encounter manifestations of the social. In many ways, the actors on stage resemble the audience in that both are subject to circumstances that are increasingly beyond their control. (This was particularly evident in *Groundings*, where the direct importation of English management-speak subjected the actors not only to a foreign language but also to one marked as the language of the global economy.) Yet the recognition is only partial, as the artifice of the productions creates its own experience of time, space, and language. Marthaler's is a theatre of disruption, yet it is one that does not rely on violent shocks but a slow and sustained challenge to the audience's traditional modes of perception.

Five key productions

Murx den Europäer! Murx ihn! Murx ihn! Murx ihn! Murx ihn ab! Ein Patriotischer Abend (*Kill the European! Kill Him! Kill Him! Kill Him! Kill Him Off! A Patriotic Evening*). By Christoph Marthaler. Design by Anna Viebrock. Perf. Wilfried Ortmann, Klaus Mertens. Volksbühne, Berlin. 16 January 1993.

Die Stunde Null oder die Kunst des Servierens (*Zero Hour; or, The Art of Serving*). By Christoph Marthaler and Stefanie Carp. Design by Anna Viebrock. Perf. Eva Brumby, Graham F. Valentine. Deutsches Schauspielhaus, Hamburg. 20 October 1995.

Drei Schwestern (*Three Sisters*). By Anton Chekhov. Design by Anna Viebrock. Perf. Olivia Grigolli, Heide Kipp. Volksbühne, Berlin. 11 September 1997.

Groundings. By Christoph Marthaler, Stefanie Carp, and Anna Viebrock. Design by Anna Viebrock. Perf. Ueli Jäggi, Josef Ostendorf. Schauspielhaus, Zurich. 22 February 2003.

Lulu. By Alban Berg. Design by Anna Viebrock. Musical direction by Kent Nagano. Perf. Barbara Hannigan, Jochen Schmeckenbecher. 12 February 2017.

Acknowledgements

I should like to thank the Humboldt Foundation of Germany for funding which supported the research for this chapter.

Notes

1. All translations from the German are mine unless otherwise stated.
2. Further material on these directors: Castorf – Detje 2005 and Carlson's chapter in this volume, pp. 121–42; Schleef – Gerecke et al. 2002; Müller – Linzer and Ullrich 1993 and Barnett 1998: 66–9 and 105–9; Pollesch – Irmer 2004; Barnett 2006.
3. I am indebted to Sabine Zolchow of the Akademie der Künste, Berlin, for the loan of the tape of this production.
4. Here I deliberately avoid the usual epithet of 'performer' as, for the most part, the bodies on stage in German-language postdramatic productions are (trained) actors. Jens Roselt (2004) makes the argument for the term 'actors'.
5. Marthaler also has extensive experience of opera and other music-related pieces. For example, he directed Debussy's *Pelléas et Mélisande* in 1994, and Beethoven's *Fidelio* and a project based on Ives's *The Unanswered Question* in 1997, all in Frankfurt. He moved further afield in the twenty-first century, staging Verdi's *La Traviata* in 2007 and Berg's *Wozzeck* in 2008, both at the Opéra National de Paris.

6 The actors also occupy a liminal space between the 'constructedness' of the theatrical event and their detachment from acting.
7 Reprinted in *Programme for 'Groundings. Eine Hoffnungsvariante'*, Pfauenbühne, Schauspielhaus Zürich, premiere 22 February 2003, pp. 16–17.

Bibliography

Anon (n.d.) 'Jury Decision 2018: Christoph Marthaler', www.internationalibsenaward.com/jury-decision-2018

Anon (2000a) 'Die Kunst der Einkerkerung. Gespräch mit Anna Viebrock', in Klaus Dermutz (ed.) *Christoph Marthaler*, Salzburg and Vienna: Residenz, pp. 53–66.

—— (2000b) '"Man hat gesagt, er ist ein Spinner": Gespräch mit der Schauspielerin Olivia Grigolli', in Klaus Dermutz (ed.), *Christoph Marthaler*, Salzburg and Vienna: Residenz, pp. 147–60.

—— (2000c) '"Marthaler ist viel zu schlau, um Grenzen zu überschreiten": Gespräch mit dem Schauspieler Josef Bierbichler', in Klaus Dermutz (ed.), *Christoph Marthaler*, Salzburg and Vienna: Residenz, pp. 135–46.

Apthorp, Shirley (2017) 'A loveable but strange Lulu at the Staatsoper Hamburg', *The Financial Times*, 15 February.

Barnett, David (1998) *Literature versus Theatre: Textual Problems and Theatrical Realization in the Later Plays of Heiner Müller*, Frankfurt: Peter Lang.

—— (2006) 'Political Theatre in a Shrinking World: René Pollesch's Postdramatic Practices on Paper and on Stage', *Contemporary Theatre Review*, 16 (1): 31–40.

Carlson, Marvin (2009) *Theatre Is More Beautiful than War: German Stage Directing in the Late Twentieth Century*, Iowa City, IA: Iowa University Press.

Carp, Stefanie (2000a) 'Geträumte Realräume', in Bettina Masuch (ed.), *Anna Viebrock*, Berlin: Theater der Zeit, n.p.

—— (2000b) 'In der Waagerechten auf die Fresse fallen', in Klaus Dermutz (ed.), *Christoph Marthaler*, Salzburg and Vienna: Residenz, pp. 99–112.

—— (2003) 'Zum Stück', in *Programme for 'Groundings: Eine Hoffnungsvariante'*, Pfauenbühne, Schauspielhaus Zürich, premiere 22 February 2003, pp. 44–6.

Dermutz, Klaus (ed.) (2000) *Christoph Marthaler*, Salzburg and Vienna: Residenz.

Detje, Robin (2005) 'Remembering Never-Ever Land: How Frank Castorf Reconjured Berlin's Volksbühne', *Theater*, 32 (2): 4–17.

Freud, Sigmund (1991) *Die Traumdeutung*, Frankfurt: Fischer.

Gerecke, Gabriele, Harald Müller, and Hans-Ulrich Müller-Schwefe (eds) (2002) *Einar Schleef Arbeitsbuch*, Berlin: Theater der Zeit.

Henrichs, Benjamin (1995) 'Deutschlandschlaflied oder sieben im Bunker', *Die Zeit*, 27 October.

Irmer, Thomas (2004) 'A New Vision of Theatre: The Timely Introduction of Video and Film in the Work of Frank Castorf, René Pollesch, and Olaf Nicola', *Western European Stages*, 16 (1): 23–28.

Kümmel, Peter (2003) 'Aus Swissair wird Ich-Air', *Die Zeit*, 27 February.

Landolt, Patrik and Tan Wälchli (2003) 'Wenn am Theater die Luft brennt', *Die Wochenzeitung*, 20 February, www.woz.ch/archiv/old/03/08/6229.html

Lehmann, Hans-Thies (1999) *Postdramatisches Theater*, Frankfurt: Verlag der Autoren.

—— (2000) 'Spiel mit Rahmungen', in Bettina Masuch (ed.), *Anna Viebrock*, Berlin: Theater der Zeit, n.p.

—— (2006) *Postdramatic Theatre*, trans. Karen Jürs Munby, London and New York: Routledge.

Lilienthal, Matthias (2000) 'Eine untergegangene Welt ein letztes Mal imaginieren', in Klaus Dermutz (ed.), *Christoph Marthaler*, Salzburg and Vienna: Residenz, pp. 113–24.

Linzer, Martin and Peter Ullrich (eds) (1993) *Regie: Heiner Müller*, Berlin: Zentrum für Theaterdokumentation und–information.

Masuch, Bettina (ed.) (2000) *Anna Viebrock*, Berlin: Theater der Zeit.

Müller, Peter (2002) 'Auch Uriella ist zum Grounding gekommen', *Tagesanzeiger*, 24 February.

Paul, Arno (2000) 'Vom Krebsgang des Stadttheaters: Trotz der nationalen Wiedervereinigung blieb das deutsche Schauspiel im Schatten der siebziger und achtziger Jahre', *Forum Modernes Theater*, 15 (2): 99–112.

Reiter, Wolfgang (1996) 'Der lustige Theaterkönig', *Profil*, 20 April, pp. 98–100.

Roselt, Jens (2004) 'In Ausnahmezuständen: Schauspieler im postdramatischen Theater', in Heinz Ludwig Arnold (ed.), *Theater fürs 21: Jahrhundert*, Munich: Edition Text und Kritik, pp. 166–76.

Schwerfel, Heinz Peter (2001) *Rasender Stillstand: Das Theater des Christoph Marthaler*, WDR and ARTE, originally broadcast 29 August.

Smith, Mark E. and Mick Middles (2003) *The Fall*, London: Omnibus.

Theurich, Werner (2017) 'Intim bis zum Exzess', *Spiegel Online*, 13 February, www.spiegel.de/kultur/musik/lulu-von-christoph-marthaler-kritik-zur-hamburger-inszenierung-a-1134300.html

Till, Nicholas (2005) 'On the Difficulty of Saying "We": The *Unheimliche Heimat* in the Music Theatre of Christoph Marthaler', *Contemporary Theatre Review*, 15 (2): 219–33.

Valentine, Graham F. (2000) 'Ich bin ein heimatloser Alliierter', in Klaus Dermutz (ed.), *Christoph Marthaler*, Salzburg and Vienna: Residenz, pp. 67–82.

Viebrock, Anna and Bettina Masuch (2000) 'Damit die Zeit nicht stillsteht', in Bettina Masuch (ed.), *Anna Viebrock*, Berlin: Theater der Zeit, n.p.

Zehelein, Klaus (2000) 'Bereits erfahrene Räume', in Bettina Masuch (ed.), *Anna Viebrock*, Berlin: Theater der Zeit, n.p.

Zweifel, Stefan (2003) 'Das Gewinsel nackter Seelen', *Die Weltwoche*, 21 February.

1

Hélène Cixous's *Tambours sur la digue* (*Drums on the Dam*), directed by Ariane Mnouchkine with the Théâtre de Soleil (1999).
Photograph © Martine Franck/Magnum Photographs.

2

Bernard-Marie Koltès's *Dans la solitude des champs de coton* (*In the Solitude of the Cottonfields*), directed by Patrice Chéreau (1995).
Photograph © Ros Ribas.

3

Life and Fate adapted from the novel by Vasily Grossman and directed by Lev Dodin (2007).
Photograph © Viktor Vasiliev.

4

Faust, adapted (from the play by Johann Wolfgang von Goethe) and directed by Silviu Purcărete (2007).
Photograph © Scott Eastman.

5

Bulgakov's *The Master and Margarita*, directed by Frank Castorf (2002).
Photograph © Thomas Aurin.

6

Molière's *Dom Juan*, directed by Daniel Mesguich (2003). The production opened at the Athénée Théâtre Louis-Jouvet in Paris on 14 March 2002. Still by Jim Carmody, from La Gestion des Spectacles's DVD recording of the production.

7

Cymbeline, directed by Declan Donnellan and designed by Nick Ormerod (2007).
Photograph © Keith Pattison.

H.H.H., directed by Piotr Borowski in Studium Teatralne's space in Praga, Warsaw (2006). Photograph © Marin Cecko.

9

Christoph Marthaler, Stefanie Carp, and Anna Viebrock's *Groundings*, directed by Christoph Marthaler and designed by Anna Viebrock (2003).
Photograph © Leonard Zubler.

10

Isabella's Room, written and directed by Jan Lauwers (2004).
Photograph © Maarten Vanden Abeele.

11

Street of Crocodiles, an adaptation by Simon McBurney and Mark Wheatley of the stories of Bruno Schulz, directed by Simon McBurney (1992).
Photograph © Nobby Clark.

12

Scènes uit een Huwelijk (*Scenes from a Marriage*) by Ingmar Bergman, directed by Ivo van Hove and designed by Jan Versweyveld (2005).
Photograph © Jan Versweyveld.

13

The Testament of Mary, with Fiona Shaw in the title role, an adaptation by Colm Tóibín of his 2012 book, directed by Deborah Warner (2012).
Photograph © Hugo Glendinning.

14

Inferno, part of the trilogy inspired by Dante Alighieri's *The Divine Comedy*, written, directed, and designed by Romeo Castellucci (2008).
Photograph © Luca del Pia.

15

Bernard-Marie Koltès's *La Nuit juste avant les forêts* (*Night Just before the Forests*), directed by Kristian Frédric (2004).
Photograph © Guy Delahaye.

16

Wyjeżdżamy (*We Are Leaving*), directed by Krzysztof Warlikowski (2018).
Photograph © Magda Hueckel.

17

Macbeth, directed by Calixto Bieito, designed by Alfons Flores (2002).
Photograph Ros Ribas © Ros Ribas / Teatre Romea.

18

After Sun, written, directed, and designed by Rodrigo García (2001).
Photograph: Daniel Alonso, from the collection of the Centro de Documentación de las Artes Escénicas y de la Música, del Gobierno de España.

19

Waves, devised by Katie Mitchell and the company from *The Waves* by Virginia Woolf (2006). Photograph © Tristram Kenton.

Mark Ravenhill's *Shoppen & Ficken* (*Shopping and Fucking*), directed by Thomas Ostermeier (1998). Photograph © Gerlind Klemens.

Chapter 10

JAN LAUWERS

Performance realities – memory, history, death

Janelle Reinelt

To imagine is not to remember.
Henri Bergson

But the being of the past can be said in many ways.
Paul Ricoeur

On an open stage, mostly white – white back wall, floor, side panels – a curious collection of objects is arranged. These objects/artefacts are displayed on tables, some on small bureaus, some on special pedestals; some are arranged on what might be altars. Panels with photos provide 'close-ups' of a few images in colour. One is predominantly in reds; another displays an icon against a partially green and earth-tone background. One photo hangs from the flies. The objects are puzzling: many of them are too small to be seen well from the auditorium, but African and Egyptian icons seem to predominate. The large space, although open, also seems eerie, claustrophobic, over-packed with significance. This territory comprises *Isabella's Room*. It is good to have some time before the actors come on to observe the 'room' and its objects, for the room is the focus of the fable about to be spun here: the 'room' is the play's *raison d'être*, and the performance transforms its already multiple meanings.

Jan Lauwers (b. 1957), the Belgian artistic leader of the Needcompany, created this piece in 2004 and continued to produce it through 2019; it can be considered his signature piece. Lauwers combines his personal family history with the fictional life of Isabella Morandi, a blind old woman who has 'seen' all the horrible events of the twentieth century. Now in her 90s, blind Isabella is nevertheless unrelenting in her pursuit of happiness and her passion for life. 'What a waste of time is pain,' she proclaims in a key scene/song. The performance Lauwers has created combines a commemoration of the life of his father with a meditation on the tensions between memory, history, and imagination. Felix Lauwers, who died in 2002, had collected 3,800 objects and artefacts, mostly from Egypt and Africa, and displayed many of them in the family home. Growing up among these objects, Lauwers simply saw them as his father's obsession, but when he died and left them all to his wife and children, the question of what to do with them and what they might mean became urgent. A history of colonialism, mementoes of a past time sealed off from the present – Lauwers felt they had no useful purpose. 'And when such a collection is just handed to you, you also have to decide what you're going to do with it,' he said. 'It's an ethical question too, because many of these objects were probably stolen from their original creators and ended up in a setting where they don't belong' (quoted in T'Jonk 2004).

In deciding to make a piece of theatre around the objects, however, Lauwers did not want to put his father at the centre of the piece, so he created Isabella instead. Although some of the actual objects are used on stage, mixed in among them are several fakes, thus blurring any claims to 'authenticity' or inherent value. Since we are told that some are not genuine, and not shown which ones are which, spectators also confront their own practices of discrimination, often called 'taste'. One of the central actions of the performance consists of revaluing the objects, or alternatively stripping them of value. However, it is too early for this part of the discussion.

The relationships between history, memory, and imagination become the dramaturgical pillars of the narrative. While the passing years are announced with a deliberate formal and epic character, the events portrayed mix memory and imagination as well as archival facts. The narrator announces, '1910: The Desert Princess'. The first section of the performance, about Isabella's childhood, is told through her reminiscences, corrected and enhanced by the comments of Arthur and Anna, her foster parents. All the cast is on stage for the entire performance, including Lauwers himself, who watches and reacts to the action, and sings along in some of the choruses (see Plate 10).

Isabella was abandoned as a baby on the side porch of a Carmelite convent; her first 'real memory is of the nuns in the cellar washing their hair in the icy cold water with a bar of hard soap'.[1] She is entrusted to Arthur and Anna, and grows up in a lighthouse on an island. They explain to her that her real father was a desert prince who mysteriously disappeared one day. 'I called myself Isabella,' she tells us, 'the Desert Princess.' Already at the beginning, the mix of memory, imagination, and historical event structures the performance, simultaneously blending and separating the elements. The fable-like elements of the lighthouse on an island (mythical? symbolic of the border between two worlds? merely coincidental?), the mysterious desert prince, and the sense of enchantment carried through music and dance create a chimerical experience, while the specificity of Isabella's memories and the tie-in to 'real' history pull in the opposite direction. (Lauwers has associated this piece with the magical realism of Gabriel García Márquez in opposition to an aesthetics in the style of James Joyce, a previous model for some of his work, a contrast perhaps between fabulation and figuration.)[2] The artefacts that litter the stage also pull in two directions – the archival facticity of historical objects against the artistic and sensuous qualities of their undecidable signifying potential. And, of course, there's the dead father, signifying in many registers from biographical to fantastic.

The story of Isabella's life proceeds not only through her own reminiscences but also through the corrections and additions of the other characters, who include Arthur and Anna, her long-time lover Alexander, and her young lover and grandson, Frank. Two sprightly dancer/actor/singers called Sister Bad and Sister Joy represent the left and right sides of her brain. In addition to the Narrator, the Desert Prince is also present, and, while he is mostly silent, his dancing and participation in the physical action and choruses of the performance make him a full contributor. He is never exactly portrayed as 'the Desert Prince'; it would be more accurate to say he represents the idea of, the spectre of, the trace of the non-existent father. For we learn that Arthur and Anna are actually Isabella's parents after all as she reads a letter Arthur left her after his death. He also gives her a key to a room in Paris, which holds all the artefacts. She lives in the room for the rest of her life.

These themes of history, memory, and imagination, along with death and the relation between the living and the dead, have long marked Lauwers's *oeuvre*. The fable form, half history, half dream/nightmare or myth, is tempered in his work by a preference for metonymy over metaphor, visual effects, music, and dance that contribute as much as the text to a surreal landscape of desire or dread. Over 35 years and as many productions, Lauwers has built a unique and compelling dramatic universe. *Isabella's Room*, the focus of this chapter, is part of a trilogy of plays under the title *Sad Face/Happy Face*. In choosing it as exemplary of Lauwers's work and indicative of his ventures since, I also call attention to this extraordinary sum-up of twentieth-century Europe.

Lauwers needs company

Jan Lauwers originally studied painting and sculpture and continues to practise as a visual artist in addition to his theatre work. In 2016 his exhibition Silent Stories was shown at McaM, the new museum of contemporary art in Singapore, and his art work and installations under the title The House of Our Fathers has been seen in museums in Brussels, Munich, Leuven, and Hanover. He also frequently designs his own sets. He formed the Needcompany in 1986 after several years as part of an artists' collective working in a mode of visual arts-based performances. From the beginning, he worked with performers who were dancers, actors, and musicians. This blending of performing arts in performance is central to his work:

> the use of all other media in theater is very dangerous and most of the time disrespectful toward these media. By changing the idea that theater has only one center into the idea that there isn't a center, but a series of off-centers, I discovered freedom in the theater.
>
> (quoted in Melillo 2004: 12)

Thus there are times when music, dance, and text construct parallel but separate 'centres' and the audience chooses which part of the performance to privilege. The dancing and music does not merely enhance the narrative; sometimes it does things the narrative cannot itself do – such as creating a hypnotic affect in a repeating melody played against a comic or otherwise dissonant physical expression or piece of text. The richness of the performances lies in no small part in the multi-layered artistic expressions which combine yet remain distinct and robust in their execution.

In his early shows with the collective Epigonentheater zlv, the emphasis was on physical movement vocabularies and experiments with the limits of their possibilities for human expression, with little or no narrative and a deliberately uncoordinated *mise en scène*, as with *Already Hurt and Not Yet War* (1981). When he formed the Needcompany with choreographer Grace Ellen Barkey, Lauwers embarked on a new period of artistic design and control that formed his personal signature as both a writer and director. Lauwers is a collaborative *auteur*, leading a company of artists who work with him over substantial periods of time. For example, Viviane De Muynck, who plays Isabella, has worked with the company since *Orfeo* (1993). Tijen Lawton first performed with Needcompany in *Caligula* (1998). Hans Petter Dahl and Anneke Bonnema took part in Lauwers's production of *King Lear* (2000) and have been a part of the company since. A series of Shakespeare productions Lauwers undertook during the 1990s featured repeated performances from both Tom Jansen as Lear and as Mark Antony in *Julius Caesar* (1990) and from Dirk Roofthooft who played Kent and the Fool in *Lear* and Cassius in *Julius Caesar*. Lauwers writes with these specific artists in mind and in turn they are major contributors to the final *mise en scène*.

According to Lauwers, he named the company Needcompany because he literally needs company. Artists join him because 'they want to think about things and make conclusions ... It's like a think tank' (quoted in Rundle 2003: 66). Although this could indicate a cerebral process, it is rather a matter of 'thinking' corporeally and sensuously as well as through language. He also thinks about the company as a family, drawing strength from their long associations. Lauwers and Barkey are married, as are Dahl and Bonnema, and

Maarten Seghers is his nephew. But it is more than literal family bonds; it is a unique coalescence of the talents and skills of long association and deep reservoirs of shared imagination. In *The Blind Poet: on the lies of history* (2015) the family trees of seven members of the company become the raw source material for the production. Lauwers took the personal pasts of the performers to fashion seven monologues that delve into the past as far as the Crusades, combining fact and fantasy to give voice to their identities, personas, and characters.

Lauwers's collaborations have also included other major artists. In *No Comment* (2003) he envisioned four solo performances (including one dance) and invited American playwright Charles Mee and Belgian playwright Josse De Pauw to write monologues for two of the pieces and six composers to collaborate on music for choreographer Tijen Lawton's solo. His Joyce-inflected piece, *DeaDDogsDon'tDance/ DJamesDJoyceDeaD* (2000), was created at the request of William Forsythe for a Needcompany collaboration with the Ballett Frankfurt. In 2018 he directed his first opera, Monteverdi's *L'incoronazione di Poppea*, in collaboration with musical conductor and baroque specialist William Christie.

Another key characteristic of Lauwers's company is its Europeanness. Of course, first of all, the company is international: members have come from Sweden, France, Turkey, the UK, Indonesia, Japan, Tunisia, Norway, Holland, Austria, and of course Belgium. The productions tour internationally, appearing in venues as far apart as Montreal, New York, Rio de Janeiro, São Paulo, Tokyo, Perth, Bogota, Taiwan, and Seoul. Lauwers explicitly seeks a 'universal' level as well as a specific milieu appropriate to the particular piece he is creating (see his comments on tragedy below). At the same time, however, the company is also decidedly European, both in terms of its languages and its style and dramaturgy. The company's productions are played in multiple European languages (e.g. *Isabella's Room* and *The Lobster Shop* (2006) in English and French; *King Lear* was played in Dutch and German with bits in French and English). Dutch is a principal language alongside French and English, but not all the performers speak Dutch. The multiple languages used in performance are developed organically to ensure communication not just between the stage and its audience but also among the performers themselves. Surtitles present some of the text in an alternative language – for example, in Slovenian when *Isabella's Room* toured Ljubljana. Marvin Carlson has argued this opens up an independent communication channel, especially since the surtitles do not simply duplicate the spoken text (Carlson 2007: 188–200).

Multiple effects follow from these choices. As Janine Hauthal has argued, this multiplicity of nationalities means that the text is spoken with various accents that

> situate the speaker between body and language [...] It renders a speaker's connection with his/her mother tongue audible, because of its contrast to the habitual pronunciation and intonation of a particular language [...] The accent implies 'a coded memory, the repository of community and national knowledge' and can thus never be personal or original, but individual only.
>
> (Hauthal 2007: 169)

The perception of an accent, then, alerts an audience to an individual's membership in an alternative language community. This is a general indication (thus not personal or original), but it does keep the multiplicity of subject positions on stage and before the spectators. The accents mark not only the diversity of the group but also its explicit Europeanness as opposed to one dominant national identity (of course Belgium is itself multilingual). In other words, Europe becomes the umbrella term, and this is a stronger signifier than the company's home country – the polyphonic characteristics and the deliberate multilingualism of the performances pre-empt a strong identification with Belgium, even though the company resides there, and instead put forward a more broadly European signature. When they are playing to European audiences, they seem to address a common cultural memory, history, and Continental identity through their terms of address.[3]

In fact, it is especially in performances such as *Isabella's Room* and *The Lobster Shop* (2006) that Europeans are evoked and addressed. Both stories refer to a shared colonial past, a shared experience of twentieth-century horror, and to a recognisable contemporary reality.[4] While the Belgian Congo may be the most direct referent for colonialism in *Isabella's Room*, the narrative takes place in France, and the main character has an Italian name: Morandi. The English colonial context is also referenced in the mocking quotation, 'Dr Livingstone I presume.' In *The Lobster Shop*, a Russian called Vladimir who might actually be French transports immigrants across borders as his day job, while Mo does not know whether his name is Mohammed or Moses, and the first clone of a bear has an unmistakably British name: Sir John Ernest Saint James.

Life and death and the question of beauty

This representation of a larger European identity is inextricably linked to the critique of contemporary life embedded in these works. Even the Shakespeare productions were contemporary, costumed in low-key neutral dress, on more or less bare stages. (He describes these productions as exercises or studies – he used the Shakespeare texts to develop new theatrical techniques [Reinelt 2007].) The trajectory of Lauwers's work is always to probe the nature of humans' efforts to live in relation to each other and to the impending inevitable fact of death. Although he writes with universal terms of address in mind, he also acknowledges the specific and local in his work:

> You are who you are, you speak the language of that specific country. I'm from Flanders, and the influence is there, rue de Flanders [the key location in *The Lobster Shop*], it's about Flanders metaphorically speaking, but at the same time I try to have the world as big as possible.
>
> (quoted in Reinelt 2007)

Lauwers rejects overtly political theatre of the explicit or topical type but his work confronts the concrete situations of reality in a deep meditation on how we are to live (and die) together.

I try to write contemporary tragedy. I read somewhere that it may be cowardly to use humour to survive, but I think it is a necessity to use it to survive. I think it makes the tragedies I'm writing bearable. My aim these last years has been to use a form of tragedy, Greek tragedy even, with its time and place, to use tragedy because it's a solid heavy form and I use it to make theatre that is as human as possible. I think this 'humanness' is the future of theatre – the here and now as human as possible.

(quoted in Reinelt 2007)

In the dramaturgical notes for *Isabella's Room*, Erwin Jans references Tzvetan Todorov's concept of dealing with extremes and Jean Baudrillard's notion that our era 'is not characterized by the end of history but by the impossibility of bringing history to an end' (Jans 2004).[5] As the events of the twentieth century pile up, how are we to avoid sinking into a numbness, a defeat? Lauwers answers this dilemma in *Isabella's Room* by creating a character whose strength, generosity, and humour seem to lead the company and the audience in a kind of aesthetic reaffirmation of life, in the face of death and madness. In *The Lobster Shop*, he stages an apocalyptic vision of a future gone wrong from which death is at least a partial release.

Death is figured as intimately connected to daily life in almost all of Lauwers's productions. For him, it is the reality that awaits us, haunting the present and anticipated by those who are conscious of it and face it. In *Julius Caesar*, the dead remain in the *mise en scène*, sitting on painted hobby horses at the side of the stage. In *Isabella's Room*, Arthur and Anna continue to interact with the living characters long after their death – in the final scene, Anna advises Isabella to sell the artefacts so she can pay the heating bill. In *The Lobster Shop*, Jef tries to explain to his parents, 'I am not dead. I'm here.' It is possible although not certain that Axel and Theresa are dead from the beginning of the play and act from another plane of existence. Asked about this seeming obsession with death, Lauwers says, 'the necessity of life is death, and longing is inevitably connected to that' (Rundle 2003: 67).

At the ethico-political edge

In a long interlude that takes place as Isabella moves into her new room and registers at the Sorbonne to study anthropology, specialising in Africa, the company shows the audience the artefacts. Each actor declaims something about an object: Anna begins with a small bronze figure, then Alexander shows a walking stick reputed to belong to Stanley's companion on the campaign in which he met Livingstone. Following the inevitable laugh, Alexander reminds us that the Belgian Congo is almost as big as the whole of Western Europe. Sister Joy speaks for the first time to describe a bronze libation vase in which slaves were said to keep their master's tears, and even the Desert Prince speaks to describe a small statuette. But gradually the music grows louder and the characters begin to shout. The shouting seems to represent the increasing outrageousness of the artefacts or their responses to them. Sister Bad shows us the 'stuffed head of a tortoise' and says that Isabella 'absolutely hated it'. A petrified whale penis is funny, but Anna showing us slave shackles she believes were only collected by cutting off the hands of the slaves is shocking. The Egyptian mummified falcon is perhaps intriguing, but there is also a small tattoo knife with an ivory handle used to 'make women unattractive'. Anna models the chainmail mask used to prevent strangers from gazing on women. Finally, all the company stands very still; the music comes to a crescendo and ends the inventory. Isabella has mostly listened to the recitation of her colleagues but now she tells us about some of the uses she makes of the objects, including hanging her keys on an African fetish, using a libation vase as a salt shaker, and keeping the whale penis behind the door in case of burglars. (Anna says Isabella only liked beauty when it was useful.) The multi-vocal and multi-tonal range of expression concerning these objects creates an affect which will be received differently by each audience member, but at the very least, the complicated relationship between humour, outrage, appreciation, and dismay that accompanies such a collection is evoked and triggered by the *mise en scène*. These possessions are the detritus of colonialism, left-over testaments to brutality, and evidence of the ransacking and appropriation of cultures.

This scene captures the dangerous quality in much of Lauwers's work as it deliberately provokes confrontation at the borderline between disturbance and offence. The performances put audiences in the position of questioning their own reactions to such scenes. *Snakesong Trilogy* (1994–8) investigated the relationships between voyeurism, eroticism, pain, desire, and cruelty, loosely based on texts by Moravia, Bataille, Huysmans, and Wilde; in a number of Lauwers's shows rape or sexual violation are significant events or themes (although never represented graphically).[6] The racial material in *Isabella's Room* provoked an outraged American dance critic to call it 'racist, nihilistic garbage' (Ben-Itzak 2005).

Before addressing directly this matter of race, it is necessary to develop some perspective on Lauwers's gender politics. Women are agents in his dramas: often strong, sometimes violent, insightful commentators, but sometimes victims too. This range of representations means that sometimes gender seems essential and at other times totally constructed. In *King Lear*, Cordelia (Grace Ellen Barkey) serves as a moral compass, largely through her silent presence and dance sequences, external to the main action. In *Julius Caesar*, Portia (Grace Ellen Barkey) is more than a passive reactor to the action – she intervenes with her clear insight, but she also commits suicide because of her powerlessness to make anything better. In *Macbeth* (1996), Viviane De Muynck plays the title role with a strength and power normally perceived as masculine. As played by De Muynck, Macbeth is absolutely the centre of the play. He/she watches his own perfidy, since this production emphasises the watching and longing of Macbeth for death.

These aspects of Needcompany's productions form the backdrop for De Muynck's portrayal of Isabella and Lauwers's characterisation of his protagonist. Viviane De Muynck is well known throughout Europe for her work with Needcompany. This accomplished and much-loved actress brings to Isabella the historicity of her own long career and the embodiment of the purposive will power and passion necessary for this story to ring true. Lauwers wanted to 'create a female counterpart to such mythical characters as Zorba the Greek and Mark Antony of Shakespeare' (quoted in T'Jonk 2004). He had previously cast De Muynck as Molly Bloom, and her combination of exuberant sensuality and intelligence anchors Isabella as a no-nonsense powerful woman who likes and enjoys sex (we are told she had 76 lovers by 1975). Reviews of De Muynck's performance are replete with comments on her affect:

> all around the wonderful Isabella, played by Viviane de Muynck, we feel the breath of life in a way we seldom do, when bodies and voices unite beyond death, to say simply and with a smile; 'We just go on, go on and on'.
>
> (Salino 2004)

In part, her overflowing corporeality makes Isabella materially present; in part, it is her strong and sonorous voice that commands attention and respect, and can modulate commanding as well as comforting tones; in part, the textual role combines an ethical commitment to loyalty and love with a genuine enjoyment of life in spite of suffering. All the people Isabella loves actually die or go mad, but unlike Alexander, who cannot accept loss and tragedy, Isabella finds a way to continue and to be reconciled to the facts of the past. And as these figures remain with her on stage, interacting with her from beyond the grave, the fable stages an ability to maintain connections, defeating death. This is perhaps the utopian promise of the performance.

However, Isabella is also the source of the major 'offensive' behaviour of the piece. She treats the objects in a purely instrumental fashion and finally sells them off without a second thought. She has an incestuous relationship with her grandson, who is purported to be the son of the child Isabella bore after paying a black man named Vendredi for sex after watching him performing in a sex club. She is, after all, blind – culturally blind; shut up in her Paris apartment, she can be criticised as the European epicurean she obviously is. However, to do so is to focus on only one aspect of her character. Isabella is portrayed as a sexually greedy and yet self-contained woman. She is content to be Alexander's mistress, and never asks him to leave his wife – in fact, 'it suits her very well since she was very fond of her freedom', the Narrator tells us. In a humorous scene, Alexander pouts because Isabella is not jealous and accuses her of having a lover:

ISABELLA: Well, you see, sometimes I'm alone a long time and I like sex. Especially with you. But with others, too. You have sex with your wife don't you?
ALEXANDER: Yes, but that's different! I was having sex with her before I met you!
ISABELLA: And it doesn't bother me at all.

Isabella tells Alexander she is pregnant, but that she does not think it is his baby. She tells him the father was 'Vendredi/Friday'.[7] It is never clear how much of this, or if any of it, is true. It repeats the mythical infatuation of Europeans with black sexuality but reverses the usual gender positions. Lauwers thus achieves a comic effect with an ironic critical undercurrent and also makes Alexander the butt of the joke because of his traditional jealousies, egoism, and racism. Thus the performance repeats but also criticises a typical white European racial trope. This does not seem to be racist but instead problematises racial constructs at the intersection of race and gender. From this point of view, Itzak's pronouncements seem excessive and misguided.

Isabella's relationship with Frank is deliberately provocative, but less because he is her grandson than because Lauwers stages their mutual sexual desire in a long kiss. Isabella is an old woman and Frank is 19 – old enough to be responsible for his own sexual involvement with her but young enough to create a dissonance in representation because while older men are often seen kissing much younger women, the opposite is seldom true. It creates quite a jolt as an image of desire.[8]

Experiences of tragedy and loss pile up in this story. The secret of Isabella's own birth is finally revealed in Arthur's letter: he actually raped Anna without her knowledge (she was unconscious), then married her, and together they maintained the fiction that Isabella was adopted. Anna's sadness eventually kills her (perhaps a suicide), and Arthur drowns himself inconsolably in the sea. Alexander, who lives through Hiroshima and kills a woman who calls him 'White Devil', is broken and driven mad by what he has seen and done. Frank, Isabella's young half-grandson lover, is wounded in her beloved Africa by a stray bullet, working in Africa in 1983, and dies on the way home of a heart attack. The company responds with a mad dance, led by the Desert Prince, to David Bowie's 'Rock 'n' Roll Suicide'. The choreography combines postures and movement, suggesting rage, with ones that suggest great exertion and effort. While many significations are possible, it seems that the response combines mourning and anger for his young senseless death with feats of endurance, or training routines to develop endurance. This section comes to an end – Isabella has been watching it – when the Narrator announces '1995' (over ten years later). Isabella takes the microphone, and in the style of a jazz singer, begins the most important 'solo' of the performance. As she sings it, the other company members accompany her on guitars, keyboard, violin, and percussion, and some of them come in on the chorus while others dance.

> When Anna died, I
> I felt no sorrow
> When Arthur died, I
> I felt no pain.
> When Alex went mad
> I wasn't lost
> When Frankie died
> I didn't feel sad
> And I simply understood there's no other way
> Maybe I know there's always a tomorrow
> Maybe I know it's all in vain
> Maybe I know today is full of sorrow
> Maybe I know ...
> What a waste of time is pain
> What a waste of time is pain
> What a waste of time is pain
> What a waste of time is pain
> What a waste!

With each of the repetitions of 'What a waste of time is pain', Isabella seems to get stronger, marching around the stage, supported by the others, growing louder and more forceful in her delivery: the song becomes the means by which she is not defeated by her experiences, and also the means of going on without bitterness – perhaps it is a kind of exorcism, but she stays aware and self-reflexive throughout. Nothing has changed. But she has triumphed over bitterness and regret. It is a theatrical epiphany.

You will see that I have interpreted Isabella's performance in a positive ethical light. Yet the very equivocation between memory and imagination can also underpin a less celebratory reading of the piece. While German performance scholar Katrin Sieg, for example, found Isabella's characterisation as a feminist heroine appealing, this did not blot out the negative side of her behaviours:

> As an allegorical figure resonating with a long tradition of colonial and now global fantasies, I came to see Isabella's sexual voraciousness as a sign of the promiscuity of European capitalism, which had to let go of its African objects, and now entertains fleeting and multiple relations to other parts of Europe and the formerly colonial world. I see her femininity as a mask for the benign-ness and harmlessness of Europe, its inability to confront its history of violent domination (which would have to be gendered masculine).
>
> (Sieg 2007)[9]

It is this Janus-faced representation of Isabella that forces its audiences to the ethico-political edge. Lauwers stages the wilfulness of Isabella's choices not only to celebrate them but also to explore their liabilities and failures, in which (white, European) audiences are implicated. While Lauwers intended *Isabella's Room* to be more light-hearted than his frequently dark visions allow, the fundamental facts of the situation and of history remain strongly in the frame. He says, 'I still play on the same themes "eroticism, power, death" but this time the actors keep it friendly for the audience' (quoted in T'Jonk 2004). Of course, audience perceptions will vary depending on which elements they find most dominant in their own experience of the performance. This possibility of multiple interpretation is one of the reasons Lauwers's work has been deemed 'postdramatic' by Hans-Thies Lehmann, who, like Lauwers, rejects information-oriented political theatre in favour of a

> *politics of perception*, which could at the same time be called an *aesthetic of responsibility (or response-ability)*. Instead of the deceptively comforting duality of here and there, inside and outside, it can move the *mutual implication of actors and spectators in the theatrical production of images* into the centre and thus make visible the broken thread between personal experience and perception. Such an experience would be not only aesthetic but therein at the same time ethico-political.
> (original italics; Lehmann 2006: 185–6)[10]

Conceptually, Lauwers is trying to conceive and represent a mode of being in the contemporary world, a consciousness cognisant of the terrible past and of still living through an impossible time, yet without lapsing into a tortured circle of sin and guilt or, alternatively, blind indifference.[11] He calls this 'Budhanton', a mixture of Buddha and Antony. Isabella admires and incorporates this philosophy, pointing out that Arthur was defeated by his guilt and sorrow and Alexander became an embittered old man. Nevertheless, we might argue that Isabella pays a price for her perseverance – cultural blindness and a certain callousness to suffering accompany the ability to reject pain. The theatrical epiphany is, perhaps, only partial.

Memory and forgetting

In *Memory, History, Forgetting*, Paul Ricoeur explains the relationship between memory and imagination. He believes memory can only return through becoming an image. The experience leaves an impression or mark on a subject who then searches for its recollection. This comes up as an image but has at least two aspects – that of the trace of the original event and the representation of the affect-impression through the image. When recollection takes place, the memory-image corresponds 'to an intermediary form of imagination, half-way between fiction and hallucination, namely, the "image" component of the memory-image' (Ricoeur 2004: 54). This instability in the truth-claim of the process of remembering might otherwise be described as the creative principle in history, for it allows a figuration of images in modes that bear a direct relation to the archival trace of the past while simultaneously manifesting a subjective signification.

Put negatively, this function of imagination in the heart of memory might be responsible for a 'faulty' or even 'delusional' memory, but Ricoeur cautions his readers against this interpretation:

> It is important, in my opinion, to approach the description of mnemonic phenomena from the standpoint of the *capacities*, of which they are the 'happy' realization. [...] We have no other resource, concerning our reference to the past, except memory itself. To memory is tied an ambition, a claim – that of being faithful to the past. In this respect, the deficiencies stemming from forgetting [...] should not be treated straight away as pathological forms, as dysfunctions, but as the shadowy underside of the bright region of memory, which binds us to what has passed before we remember it [...] Testimony constitutes the fundamental transitional structure between memory and history.
> (Ricoeur 2004: 21)

Within the theatrical apparatus, Lauwers has constructed a memory machine. Isabella's blindness is the subject of study by an institute that has hooked up her brain to a camera and projected images from it. Although not a strong point of focus during the performance, images are projected through a computer onto a television screen, visible to the audience as the painted panels are visible. Its screen is about 32 inches, and its placement is below waist level downstage right, close to where Lauwers and Assistant Director Elke Janssens sit watching the show and manipulating the camera. The projected images are representations of the icons, which are themselves representations of cultural practices and symbol systems from the past – their original meanings all but lost. Isabella thus has technology-driven sight, but its images are products of history, memory, and imagination (and, of course, Lauwers's father is implicated in all three of these aspects as well as Isabella). In insisting on the reality of her picture of the Desert Prince, Isabella is remembering and reconstituting the story of her birth. The Desert Prince operates as a kind of condensation of her past with her desires; it is the way she chooses to remember her life. Her blindness seems to suggest that there is no sight without art, the camera apparatus or the stage apparatus standing in for the function of the imagination in this equation. Nor is this solipsism – the traces of the archival past remain, the events of the past – two world wars, Hiroshima, fascism – are all there, the memories are present through the characters and the images they produce – but the images are themselves constructed through the interaction between the experiences of events and their manifestation through the imagination. This 'memory-apparatus' works through choreography and music as well as visual media, since these are also modes of creative re-presentation.

Lauwers has evoked the memory-apparatus in several of his other productions – exploiting images as condensations of experience, often trauma, and imagination. In *The Lobster Shop*, the key events concern the death of a child, but, surrounded with mystery, it is not certain what exactly has happened. In *Images of Affection* (2002), a traumatic moment bringing devastating loss to its protagonist is refigured 'in the form of a kaleidoscopic sequence of remembered images' (Le Roy 2007: 242). In describing this production, Frederik Le Roy characterises the memory threshold of many of the performances:

> Jan Lauwers points out to us the profoundly human dream of being able to rewrite one's own past. Counter to this illusory desire to be able to exercise power over the past is the uncontrollable influence the past continues to have on us (the demands for satisfaction on promises pledged, the guilt about lapses or missed opportunities that continue to haunt us).
>
> (Le Roy 2007: 246)

In the second and third parts of the trilogy, *The Lobster Shop* (2006) and *The Deer House* (2008), Lauwers returns to questions of guilt and responsibility and their relationship to memory and imagination. Lauwers designates *Isabella's Room* as being about the past while *The Lobster Shop* is about the future, and *The Deer House* confronts the present (Reinelt 2007).

The Lobster Shop, a much less linear narrative than *Isabella's Room*, with its contradictory central events unable to be verified, is best described by its organising topoi rather than a central narrative. *Kindermord* (*Child Killings*) is the central motif, and three young people are linked in the play through a series of equivalences.[12] Jef, the son of Axel and Theresa, mysteriously dies at the beach on an outing with his father. The sexual abuse of a young Eastern European girl called Nasty results in her social exclusion when her abuser tries to make amends for his deed but only makes her situation worse, and the first cloned human, Salman – also a child of Axel's since he is a professor of genetics responsible for cloning Salman – becomes a destructive street marauder, setting fires and committing other violent acts. The three make up a trio whose future has been ruined by the older generation. At the domestic level, we are talking about bad parenting; at the metaphorical level, about creating a world with no positive possibilities for the future generation because we have abdicated or destroyed their patrimony.

In a moment of scathing self-criticism, Axel describes the contemporary triumph of science:

> We don't want to get cancer. That is much too old-fashioned. We, the scientists, have evolved much further. We are no longer interested in cancer. We are interested in clones and bodiless entities. So that we no longer have to scratch where it itches.[13]

This indictment of technology furthers the critique in *Isabella's Room*, where in addition to the technology of the atom bomb, we were shown the personal technology of Isabella's sight machine which addressed only one limited aspect of her larger cultural blindness.

In addition, Lauwers makes allusion to Belgium's political crisis through the fires and riots that are figured on the Rue de Flanders in *The Lobster Shop* and the stark portrayal of violence against immigrants. This engagement with the present, while not exactly issue-based politics, is unmistakably topical. The image of conflagration gives an apocalyptic edge to the stories that are being told. Lauwers figures a postmodern tragedy in which the 'sins of the fathers are visited on the sons' in an almost literal sense. As part of the performance, we see a film showing Jef on the beach with Axel, a friend, and his father: two fathers, two sons. The sons play while the fathers stand and watch with little expression. The boys are doing martial arts – karate. The play gradually turns more and more rough, even violent, and suddenly Jef goes down. The camera gives only glimpses and partial views of what happened, but the dream-like images condense many symbolic aspects of masculine identity formation: the highly formalised warrior poses, the paternal role-modelling and approval, the sudden and senseless violence when something unseen 'happened'. By showing this only on a screen, Lauwers evokes both a powerful realism and a distanced and remote quality – is this a 'document' or is it the film that Axel, in his guilt and confusion, sees in his mind?

The status of life in *The Lobster Shop* is always in doubt. A chance accident in the Rue de Flanders links a group of men: Axel, the geneticist and father of Jef; Mo, the waiter in the restaurant who is also a boat refugee; Vladimir, the driver of the truck that hits them; and Salman, the junkie living on the street, whom Axel has cloned. These four men end up on the beach. They watch the lobster slowly crawl back into the water. But what is their status: are they dead or alive? Theresa, Catherine, Nasty, and Jef are telling us the story – Catherine says 'they all drown' and no one contradicts her. We have been told that Vladimir has been sentenced to death for child rape and that Salman was cloned because he was terminally ill. The image on stage of four men lying on the beach can be interpreted as the threshold of death, but on the other hand, none of them may actually be dead. Theresa describes and evokes this chimerical effect:

> It's a beautiful scene. The moon, the wind and the rocks. The sea in the distance. The men lying there, immobile. Everything becomes one. The moon and the water, the sand and the rocks, the men and the darkness. Connected by the lobster. Can you imagine? Connected in time and space for all eternity.

In a practice Lauwers developed for his Shakespeare productions, the dead remain active on stage, so Jef talks to his parents and denies that he is dead, further blurring his status. Theresa, Axel's wife, may have walked into the sea and drowned because of her grief over Jef. If so, she is a phantom character as much as Jef or the other men. The phantasmatic quality of these stories is created in music, dance, image, and text. Needcompany performances invite audiences to enter into an intense relationship with the artists, the characters, and the dramaturgy; it is a self-reflexive relationship, but also, in every sense, an imaginary one. This paradox features most strongly in the third part of the trilogy.

The Deer House

Scholars and critics who write about contemporary theatre directly experience the fleeting temporal order of performance, sometimes quite literally. I followed the Needcompany to the Salzburg Festival for the first full production of the trilogy, *Sad Face/Happy Face*. I saw the second performance of *The Deer House* on 3 August 2008. When I returned to the UK I learned I had missed an important aspect of the events in Salzburg. Let me explain.

The Deer House, as with *Isabella's Room*, commemorates an actual human loss of someone implicated in the company – in this case, Tijen Lawton's brother Kerem Lawton, a war photographer who was killed in Kosovo during the Bosnian War, and the news of whose death came to the company while they were on tour in France. Lauwers explains, 'His tragic death provided the starting point for a play about a group of theatre-makers who are increasingly faced with the harsh reality of the world they travel around in' (Needcompany website). Thus, the new play opens on a quasi-documentary scene: the company, in their dressing room, re-enact some of their responses to the news of the death. Yet already the play is a fiction, because, apart from anything else, while the actors may call each other by their own names, they are seen 'acting'. They behave like actors, playing pranks on each other, dressing up in nothing but their bath towels, getting ready for a next hypothetical show. The scene also features a bit of self-criticism: some members of the company bicker or are self-centred; others are casually racist about Yumiko, a young girl who is found in the wings (all Asians look alike; is she there to steal from them?). Those in the audience like me, who have seen this company and perhaps followed it and who have forged relationships (even if imaginary) with the 'real' people behind the actors and their characters, will wonder, 'Are they really like that when they are alone backstage?' The shape of the fable reasserts itself and moves away from this scene. The last line in Kerem Lawton's diary, we are told, is 'I must find the Deer House'.[14] Is this true or a fiction? Before there is time to ponder, the actors, who have dressed up as gnomes with fake pointed ears and strange skin-like costumes, have taken us to the Deer House.

In the second part of the play, Lauwers and his company imagine what might have happened to Lawton and how he lost his life. The fable involves a community of people who have tried to avoid the war raging around them by keeping their clan close together. They make their living from selling the antlers of deer they tend, and the stage is littered with rubber effigies of the deer, that bounce when moved in disturbing grotesque and comic ways. The mentally disabled daughter of this family, played by Grace Ellen Barkey, takes special care of the deer and massages their hearts before the antlers are harvested, so they will not be afraid. Benoît Gob, playing Kerem Lawton, comes to the Deer House to tell the family that he has killed a member of their family, Inge, because he was told he must choose between shooting the mother or her young daughter. He decides to save the seven-year-old and kills Inga, bringing her back to her family for burial. In turn, he is killed by Inga's husband, Julien, in grief and rage. In turn, Julien is killed by Maarten since Gob had been forgiven and taken into the community. The three bodies are laid out on a platform, resembling the *ekkyklema* of Greek tragedy, and on one level the performance is a funeral rite or ceremony for all the war dead, and especially for Lawton. Tijen Lawton arrives looking for the truth about what happened to her brother, and with her she brings a bag/coffin: the young girl he tried to save when he killed her mother eventually committed suicide and so is also dead. As in many of Lauwers's works (see above), the dead continue to converse with the living, so Tijen is able to say to Kerem/Gob:

> I would like to believe that what you did was necessary, but your sorrow will never be mine. I was angry with you. My heart is hurting. But I understand you won't give me any more explanations. The world was bigger for you than for me. I still have to forgive you for it. But time was too fast for us. I had feared this sort of farewell, yet it is still unexpected. No one knows what comes next. What has to happen now? My dear brother, can you forgive my self-pity?

Are the tears Tijen's rather than 'Tijen's'? Which one is bidding farewell to her brother? Can we grieve with the company – is there a role for us, the audience? The fiction has an ambiguous ending, and the company unites in a last song:

> Oh we are small people with a big heart
> We are not looking good but we are smart
> We love each other and it's a real art
> To build the deer house so strong
> That it doesn't fall apart.

Who is singing? Is it the characters? Is it the company? Are we part of the 'we'? Am I?

When I left Salzburg to return to England, I learned with a shock from reading the reviews of the premiere of *The Deer House* that company member Anneke Bonnema had injured her back shortly before the premiere on 28 July and had performed her (considerable) role lying on a stretcher on the stage, taking her curtain call in a wheelchair (Andres Müry). The jolt I felt was in part because I did not know, and in part because I did not notice anything wrong when I saw her perform just a few nights later. The real and imaginary intimacy I have experienced in relation to the company over several years of closely following their work suddenly provoked concern for the person of Bonnema but also less rational concerns for her 'characters'; and finally, I confess, a feeling of having been caught off guard by something traumatic impinging on (my) 'real life'. As a line originally from the Velvet Underground, modified and ironised in the performance, has it, 'Watch out, the world is not behind you.' In all its ambiguity, the line now had new meaning for me.

At the Festival, the critical reactions to the play and to the whole trilogy were very positive, describing Lauwers as 'an old hand of the international avant-garde, whose productions remain so refreshingly unconventional' (Dössel 2008), or, celebrating the company: 'this touring theatre lives from the radiance of its actors' (Klinger 2008), or, in terms of the production, finding 'light effects, dialogues, music, theatre and dance all fuse together to become a coherent whole; texts referring to current-day politics become universally comprehensible through their multilingualism and topical clarity' (Anon. 2008).

This company which purports to be family can leave its spectators deeply implicated in its actual and imaginary biographies. When I saw *The Blind Poet* at the Southbank Centre, London, in 2018, I was immediately transported back to the liminal feelings I had in Salzburg. Not only were the personal stories and histories of many familiar company members the very subject matter of the drama, the creations evoked and embodied other works in their repertoire. Grace Ellen Barkey's spectacular appearance, dressed in Indonesian costume and clown face, begins the evening. She announces 'I am Grace Ellen Barkey', and then builds through repetition, rhythm, and sound on this affirmation and creation of her identity until she is yelling 'I am Grace Ellen Barkey'. She is assisted by the company who chant with her, applaud her, support her (including of course Jan Lauwers, who is on the set for the entire performance, as he was in *Isabella's Room*). Besides a virtuoso display of her dance and vocal skills, Barkey also provides a discussion of her multicultural past and present, and shares her struggle with Lynch Syndrome. Her assertion of identity (I am Grace Ellen Barkey) takes on the quality of determination to will oneself into existence, while her prodigious creativity and skill recall many of her previous performances. Benoît Gob's monologue follows his violent and abusive childhood, family alcoholism, and neglect, a tale so dark it seems the actor's talent and skills are a kind of miracle. But his physical comedy, dexterity, and finesse also grow out of his personal experiences, contributing to the portrait he created of Arthur's drunkenness and despair in *Isabella's Room* as well as his personification of a large robust bear in *The Lobster Shop*. Spectators are watching the combinations of talent and fate that these performers have fashioned into identities, personas, and characters with grace and wit, pathos and passion. As for me, I felt again, as I had at *The Deer House*, overcome with emotions which were suspect for they failed to discriminate between roles, artists, people. Once again, I was bewitched and humbled by this company.

In 2007 Lauwers and the company began to receive the critical attention in English they richly deserve with the publication of *No Beauty for Me There Where Human Life Is Rare: On Jan Lauwers' Theatre Work with Needcompany*, an edited collection of in-depth essays about the company and its work (Stalpaert, Le Roy, and Bousset 2007). The productions have received many awards across the world, and in 2014 Jan Lauwers was awarded the Golden Lion Lifetime Achievement Award at the Venice Biennale.

Five key productions

Isabella's Room. Written and directed by Jan Lauwers. Set design by Jan Lauwers. Costumes by Lemm and Barkey. Music by Hans Petter Dahl and Maarten Seghers. Assistant Director, Elke Janssens. Perf. Viviane De Muynck, Anneke Bonnema, Hans Petter Dahl, Julien Faure, Benoît Gob, Ludde Hagberg, Elke Janssens, Tijen Lawton, Louise Peterhoff, Maarten Seghers. Cloître des Carmes, Festival d'Avignon. 9 July 2004.

The Lobster Shop. Written and directed by Jan Lauwers. Set design by Jan Lauwers. Costumes by Lot Lemm. Music by Hans Petter Dahl and Maarten Seghers. Assistant Director, Elke Janssens. Perf. Hans Petter Dahl, Grace Ellen Barkey, Tijen Lawton, Anneka Bomnema, Benoît Gob, Inge Van Bruystegem, Julien Faure, Maarten Seghers. Cloître des Célestins, Festival d'Avignon. 10 July 2006.

The Deer House. Written and directed by Jan Lauwers. Set design by Jan Lauwers. Costumes by Lot Lemm. Music by Hans Petter Dahl, Maarten Seghers, and 'Song for the Deerhouse' by Jan Lauwers. Assistant Director, Elke Janssens. Perf. Grace Ellen Barkey, Anneke Bonnema, Hans Petter Dahl, Viviane De Muynck, Misha Sowney, Julien Faure, Yumiko Funaya, Benoît Gob, Tijen Lawton, Maarten Seghers, Inge Van Bruystegem. Perner Insel, Hallein, Strasburger Festspiele. 28 July 2008.

Needcompany's King Lear. By William Shakespeare; adaptation by Jan Lauwers. Set design by Jan Lauwers. Costumes by Lot Lemm. Choreography by Carlotta Sagna. Perf. Tom Jansen, Dirk Roofthooft, Mil Seghers, Grace Ellen Barkey, Anneke Bonnema, Muriel Hérault, Hans Petter Dahl, Misha Downey, Simon Versnel, Tijen Lawton, Eduardo Torroja. Lunatheater, Brussels. 11 January 2000.

The Blind Poet: on the lies of history. Written and directed by Jan Lauwers. Set design by Jan Lauwers. Costumes by Lot Lemm. Assistant direction and dramaturgy by Elke Janssens. Perf. Grace Ellen Barkey, Jules Beckman, Anna Sophie Bonnema, Hans Petter Melø Dahl, Benoît Gob, Maarten Seghers, Mohamed Toukabri, Elke Janssens, Jan Lauwers. Kunstenfestivaldesarts, Brussels. 12 May 2015.

Notes

1 All quotations taken from the unpublished manuscript in English of the performance, provided to me courtesy of the company.
2 These associations to Joyce and García Márquez are mentioned in a number of interviews and on the company website material. For example, 'Now when I think about communication with the audience, I think more of Marquez [sic], whereas in the past Joyce was the model' (Lauwers, quoted in Jans 2004).
3 Of course, there are also some company members from outside the EU, such as Yumiko Funaya, and Grace Ellen Barkey is Indonesian by birth, but the preponderance are Europeans.

4 *The Deer House*, the third play in the trilogy, does not refer to the colonial past, but is directly linked to the Bosnian War (see pp. 249–51).
5 Erwin Jans is a cultural critic, dramaturg, and lecturer at the University of Leuven whose commentaries on Needcompany's work appear on their website and also published with the programmes for the productions.
6 For a discussion of *Snakesong Trilogy* and its specific textual references, see Pieters 2007: 218–31.
7 This reference to Robinson Crusoe's native companion is deliberate. The mythical island connection seems obvious. This is also an example of Lauwers being playful – the references to Vendredi and Alexander's jealousy elicited delighted laughter on every occasion I witnessed the production (four times between 2004 and 2008).
8 A similar moment occurs in *Snakesong Trilogy* when De Muynck stands naked on stage. 'Some people were offended,' Lauwers comments. 'They don't want to be reminded of aging and death, but to me it's beautiful. It's life' (quoted in Rundle 2003: 67).
9 Katrin Sieg is the author of *Ethnic Drag: Performing Race, Nation, Sexuality in West Germany*, which deals specifically with questions about the ambivalence of representations in post-Holocaust performances (Sieg 2002).
10 Lehmann was an early enthusiast of Jan Lauwers's work. His description of the company's acting style as *détachement* is particularly useful in connection with the quotation above. See Lehmann 2007: 70–80.
11 I am grateful to Elke Janssens, Assistant Director and one of the company dramaturgs, for her discussion of Lauwers's thinking about the contemporary situation in relation to the play (Reinelt 2005).
12 I spoke to Lauwers about the strong connection between his narrative and Ibsen's *Kindermord* plays such as *The Wild Duck* and *Little Eyolf*, but Lauwers professed little interest in Ibsen. Yet Ibsen's symbolic uses of *Kindermord* are very close to Lauwers's own vision (Reinelt 2007).
13 Unpublished English manuscript of *The Lobster Shop*, courtesy of the Needcompany.
14 All quotations taken from the unpublished manuscript in English of the performance, provided to me courtesy of the company.

Bibliography

Anon. (2008) Unsigned Review, *Salzburger Nachrichten*, 4 August, www.needcompany.org/cgi-bin/www_edit/projects/nc/scripts/nc.cgi?session=656&a=r&id=11018&t=FR&r=1058.txt

Ben-Itzak, Paul (2005) 'Skin Games Dunham at the Source; Lauwers's Racist Titillation; Valeska Storms the Pompidou', *Flash Review Journal*, 2 (10), www.danceinsider.com/f2005/f0210_2.html

Carlson, Marvin (2007) 'Needcompany's *King Lear* and the Semiotics of Supertitles', in Christel Stalpaert, Frederik Le Roy, and Sigrid Bousset (eds), *No Beauty for Me There Where Human Life is Rare*, Ghent: Academic Press and International Theatre and Film Books, pp. 188–200.

Dössel, Christine (2008) 'The Unbearable Lightness of Being', *Suddeutsche Zeitung*, 4 August, www.needcompany.org/cgi-bin/www_edit/projects/nc/scripts/nc.cgi?session=656&a=r&id=11018&t=FR&r=1057.txt

Hauthal, Janine (2007) 'On Speaking and Being Spoken: Reading on Stage and Speaking with Accents in Needcompany's *Caligula*', in Christel Stalpaert, Frederik Le Roy, and Sigrid Bousset (eds), *No Beauty for Me There Where Human Life is Rare*, Ghent: Academic Press and International Theatre and Film Books, pp. 169–86.

Jans, Erwin (2004) 'Laugh and Be Gentle to the Unknown', www.needscompany.org/html/engels/voorstellingen/txt/eng_txt_room.html

Klinger, Eva Maria (2008) 'Needcompany Give a Convincing Performance with Their Trilogy about Life and Death', *Nachtkritik*, 1 August, www.needcompany.org/cgi-bin/www_edit/projects/nc/scripts/nc.cgi?session=656&a=r&id=11018&t=FR&r=1056.txt

Le Roy, Frederik (2007) 'When Pop Meets Trauma: Needcompany's *Images of Affection*', in Christel Stalpaert, Frederik Le Roy, and Sigrid Bousset (eds), *No Beauty for Me There Where Human Life is Rare*, Ghent: Academic Press and International Theatre and Film Books, pp. 233–48.

Lehmann, Hans-Thies (2006) *Postdramatic Theatre*, trans. Karen Jürs-Munby, London and New York: Routledge.

—— (2007) 'Détachment: On Acting in Jan Lauwers' Work', in Cristel Stalpaert, Frederik LeRoy, and Sigrid Bousset (eds), *No Beauty for Me There Where Human Life is Rare*, Ghent: Academic Press and International Theatre and Film Books, pp. 70–80.

Melillo, Joseph V. (2004) 'Interview with Jan Lauwers', Programme for the BAM Performances of *Isabella's Room*, December, p. 12.

Müry, Andres (2008) 'Tijen Must Wear Mourning', *Tagesspiegel Berlin*, 31 July, www.needcompany.org/cgi-bin/www_edit/projects/nc/scripts/nc.cgi?session=8284&a=r&id=11017&t=EN &r= 1054.txt

Pieters, Jürgen (2007) 'Rough Play at the Limits of Thought: *The Snakesong Trilogy* by Jan Lauwers', in Christel Stalpaert, Frederik Le Roy, and Sigrid Bousset (eds), *No Beauty for Me There Where Human Life is Rare*, Ghent: Academic Press and International Theatre and Film Books, pp. 218–31.

Reinelt, Janelle (2005) Interview with Elke Janssens, Montreal, Canada, 3 June.
—— (2007) Interview with Jan Lauwers, Frankfurt, Germany, 29 September.
Ricoeur, Paul (2004) *Memory, History, Forgetting*, trans. Kathleen Blamey and David Pellauer, Chicago, Ill: University of Chicago Press.
Rundle, Erika (2003) 'Images of Freedom', *Performing Arts Journal*, 33(1): 59–71.
Salino, Brigette (2004) *Le Monde*, 13 July, www.needcompany.org/cgi-bin/www_edit/projects/nc/scripts/nc.cgi?session=5916&a=r&id=ISABE&t=EN&r=1012.txt
Sieg, Katrin (2002) *Ethnic Drag: Performing Race, Nation, Sexuality in West Germany*, Ann Arbor, Mich.: University of Michigan Press.
—— (2007) Personal email, 1 August.
Stalpaert, Christel, Frederik Le Roy, and Sigrid Bousset (eds) (2007) *No Beauty for Me There Where Human Life is Rare*, Ghent: Academic Press and International Theatre and Film Books.
T'Jonk, Pieter (2004) 'Because Women Are Tremendously Important', *De Tijd*, 21 September, www.needcompany.org/cgi-bin/www_edit/projects/nc/scripts/nc.cgi?a=r&t=EN&id=ISABE

Chapter 11

SIMON McBURNEY

Shifting under/soaring over the boundaries of Europe

Stephen Knapper

(with additional material by Dan Rebellato)

With his 2015 piece of technological storytelling, *The Encounter*, Simon McBurney (b. 1957) follows *National Geographic* photographer Loren McIntyre into the Brazilian rainforest and a spiritual-hallucinatory encounter with the people of the Javari Valley, the story told almost entirely through sound. In so doing he provides further evidence of Complicite's internationalist shifts in the twenty-first century. The shifts were eastward, with the company's work building, with *Shun-Kin* (2008), on a previous partnership with the Japanese Setagaya Public Theatre in the highly acclaimed *The Elephant Vanishes* (2003) and the technologically dazzling *A Disappearing Number* (2007), which traced the odyssey, life, work, and death of the Indian mathematician, Srinivasa Ramanujan. And they were westward too, in collaboration with the Los Angeles Philharmonic in *Strange Poetry* (2004); the National Actors' Theatre, New York, with Brecht's *The Resistible Rise of Arturo Ui* (2002) starring Al Pacino and satirising George Bush. The political drive of this production was complemented by one on Broadway of Arthur Miller's *All My Sons* (2008) that coincided with Barack Obama's historical presidential victory. Though Gorbachev dreamed of a new Europe stretching to the Urals, Complicite's shape-shifting internationalism, as evidenced in the work after the Soviet-set *The Noise of Time* (2000) and *The Master and Margarita* (2012), has now spread its artistic wings to soar far beyond that terrain.

The linguistic diversity of the transcontinental *Mnemonic* (1999) was evident in the scene where scientists argue over the national identity of the newly discovered 5,000-year-old Iceman and reflects the European roots of Complicite, the collective of international performers that McBurney has led since the early 1990s. It also recalls the centrality of the Alps in their history. Their teacher, Jacques Lecoq, had a retreat there, as did McBurney's collaborator John Berger, whose short stories *Pig Earth* were adapted by Complicite under McBurney's direction to form the exploration of central European peasant culture that was *The Three Lives of Lucie Cabrol* (1994). Further cooperations between the two delved into the history of cave painting, in the site-specific installation *The Vertical Line* (1999) presented in the disused Aldwych tube station, and into the themes of deportation, immigration, and conflict in *Vanishing Points* (2005), seen at the German gymnasium at London's King's Cross station. Berger helped McBurney articulate a profound reverence for the power of community, place, storytelling, and imagination, all of which intersect in acts of theatre. After Berger's death, McBurney would call him 'Listener, grinder of lenses, poet, painter, seer. My Guide. Philosopher. Friend' (McBurney 2017). The association with Berger began after the Marxist critic and writer had seen McBurney's production of *The Street of Crocodiles* (1992), commissioned by Richard Eyre for the National Theatre. Here, in one of its flagship productions, inspired by the short stories of the executed Jewish Pole Bruno Schulz, the company's inimitable style of visual and devised theatre with an emphasis on strong, corporeal, poetic, and surrealist image-supporting text was consolidated by the invitation to create for the National Theatre (see Plate 11).

McBurney's artistic direction of the company was confirmed at the same time. In common with many other European companies – Théâtre du Soleil and Els Joglars, for example – the initial emphasis on collective creation and decision-making gave way to a more director-led operation in such ground-breaking productions as Dürrenmatt's *The Visit* (1989), where McBurney directed alongside his fellow company co-founder Annabel Arden, and the inspired satire on bureaucracy and corporate life (containing spirited acting from Arden, co-founder Marcello Magni, and Kathryn Hunter), *Anything for a Quiet Life* (1987). Earlier devised work and their creation in the years of high Thatcherism – *Put It on Your Head* (1983) with the fourth co-founder of the troupe, the Canadian Fiona Gordon; *A Minute Too Late* (1984) with long-term collaborator Jos Houben; and *More Bigger Snacks Now* (1985) – are considered in this interview together with the importance of his Parisian sojourn in the early 1980s at the Jacques Lecoq School of International Theatre and working with Compagnie Jérôme Deschamps.

The interview took place in the rehearsal rooms of the English Touring Company in Waterloo on 3 February 2006 (although it was subsequently revised through email correspondence in 2007–8). McBurney had been rehearsing his Complicite cast of *Measure for Measure* all day in preparation for their return to the National Theatre the following week. In the autumn of 2005 the company had been on tour in Europe and India, and McBurney had taken over the role of the Duke from David Troughton, who had opened *Measure for Measure* at the Olivier auditorium of the National Theatre in 2004. Here McBurney reflects upon his experiences of rock concerts and punk in the 1970s, his forays onto the comedy circuit at the beginnings of the alternative comedy scene with his Cambridge peers, and the opening up of theatrical horizons in Paris at the end of that decade. Although many of his productions have dealt with specifically European themes – as with *The Visit, The Street of Crocodiles, The Three Lives of Lucie Cabrol, Mnemonic, Light* (2000) – in the interview he aligns himself more particularly with an international search for the roots, meaning, and vitality of the theatrical event in the world of late modern consumer capitalism. By staging Fausto Paravidino's *Genoa 01* at the Royal Court's International Playwrights' season in 2002 he signified an overt commitment to the cause of anti-globalisation and makes a plea for recognition of the crucial role theatre plays in the establishment of a collective human community. His acting, particularly now in cinema,[1] informs his directing to the extent that he has difficulty being defined as solely a director.

STEVE KNAPPER: Do you consider yourself a European director?
SIMON MCBURNEY: I don't really know what that means. Britain is part of Europe and I live in Britain, so, in location, yes, I'm a European

director. But, if being a European director means that there is a specific identity for European theatre which I recognise and align myself to, I would say no, I don't think of myself as a European director. I would go further and say that an awful lot of the time I don't think of myself as a director, simply a director. I think simply about the way that I have come to do what I do. I began making theatre with a small group of people in the 1980s and the intention was simply to make the kind of theatre that I didn't see: a theatre which was largely a place that combined several different disciplines. So you weren't just being an actor but also a writer and an explorer, a maker of things, and you just felt free to do whatever the fuck you wanted to do. My opinion at that time was that if I wanted to be in theatre, if I wanted to act in theatre, if I wanted to make theatre, then I should simply do it. I had no time to hang around and say I would like to do this and wait until it happens. I simply started making it and doing it and telling the stories that I wanted to tell, which were often very simple and frequently they were stories about the minutiae of life around me as I saw it. Very often they were based on tiny moments which were then exploded into scenes which were then put together and then suddenly there was a piece of theatre.

For example, the very first piece [*Put It on Your Head*] we did was a kind of desire to make something about nothing, about what happens if you do nothing. The second piece [*A Minute Too Late*] was partly about my relationship with my father's death, but a very small aspect of it, just blowing up a tiny moment of what my relationship with my father was into a fantasy surrounding death.

The third piece, *More Bigger Snacks Now*, was about the situation that we found ourselves in when you have nothing. It was the height of Thatcherism: we felt powerless; we felt kind of assaulted as young people. But looking back I suppose the subject matter of those three shows was rooted in a search for understanding simply where we were.

It was also hugely motivated by the fact that we liked to make people laugh. That in itself gave meaning to the piece because people have always said that the tragic is somehow more serious:

comedy is light, artificial, and escapist. But of course, it always seems to most comics that the opposite is true: that the tragic very often preserves an illusion of human dignity whereas if you look at the world around us there is very often no dignity in humanity (certainly in the way that the Western world is going about its business currently). So glorifying it with great and serious tragic intent seemed to me at the time extraordinarily pretentious, and laughter seemed to cut through and expose all that – which was why I hated being laughed at in real life because it exposes the truth and it's not always palatable to see ourselves for what we truly are. So, necessarily, humour was part of it.

What I see now, in all the shows, is the constant question: what the fuck are we doing? Who are we and what does it mean to be who we are? On one level everything about being British or whoever we were was completely clear. It was assumed to be a certain set of values, a certain way of life, and yet it was quite clear that there was something about the past which was not what people said it was. There was a vast nostalgia in the 1980s propagated by Thatcher particularly.

STEVE KNAPPER: In terms of nationhood?

SIMON MCBURNEY: In terms of nationhood. What it means to be British. The reinvigoration of 'Rule Britannia'. A fake identity while at the same time they were selling off all forms of social justice which had been put in place since the Second World War. For young people at that time growing out of the punk era and the notion that there was [*sings*] 'no future', we didn't really know what our identity was; we felt we were starting from nothing. It was the beginning of another form, something that had been building since the beginning of the Industrial Revolution, the development of mass consumer capitalism. We couldn't see the point of things very often. What interested me were the tiny gestures that people lived out in their everyday lives behind which were oceans of despair and unhappiness. So *More Bigger Snacks Now* was just four men in a flat on a sofa; four men who were unemployed, and nothing happened and yet people roared with laughter. It won the Perrier Award[2] and then people also wept at the end. They didn't quite know why they wept.

We wanted, consciously or unconsciously, to create what I would see whenever I used to go to rock concerts in the 1970s: an event which people lived through. It seemed to me that very often there was more theatre in a rock concert, or more theatre in contemporary dance. It seemed that dance had stolen the language of theatre, when you looked at what Pina Bausch was doing, when you looked at what those crazy guys from Belgium, a group called Radaeus was doing. If you went to any rock concert at that time: Tangerine Dream, David Bowie, the whole punk movement, the Rolling Stones for that matter, they took the language of theatre and they exploited it; whereas of course theatre itself was kind of retreating into its shell.

So I had no particular truck with theatre; I thought I was just doing a gig, making people alive to stories as an event. The action was very important; what people did was as important as what they said – not that what they said was not important: on the contrary. We wrote our pieces of dialogue and text very carefully, we tried to make them funny, place the jokes just right, and so on. But because we were living in an era without any particular beginning, middle, or end, where there was no great story to tell, the stories became tiny stories, which were then explored vertically rather than horizontally. Rather than saying this thing happened and then that thing happened, we said this thing happened and that thing happened *simultaneously*.

We didn't really think of it as theatre in the way that other people were thinking about theatre at that time. As a result we appeared on *Wogan* and on *The Tube* with Jools Holland and Paula Yates.[3] We appeared as a support act to rock bands. We played in the streets. So then when suddenly we did take over a legitimate piece of theatre like *The Visit* we just did whatever the fuck we wanted to do with it.

Then, of course, there was the influence of what I had seen in Paris. I saw Pina Bausch, a lot of German theatre, a lot of South American theatre – but it wasn't just the theatre, really. It was everything. It was an engagement in other parts of life. I had no particular ambitions in theatre. I knew that I loved acting. I knew that I wanted to be an actor. I knew I wanted to do whatever the fuck I wanted to do and that I didn't want to be bound by the idea of conventional social structures as regards that form.

STEVE KNAPPER: So the Parisian experience was an international experience more than it was a European experience, you would say? A liberating experience?

SIMON MCBURNEY: Yeah. And it was being aware that our life and times were changing very fast. The culture of the people I met in France was exactly the same as my culture. The shops were all beginning to be exactly the same. The things that we'd watched on TV were the same. We were all making the same references. Where my grandfather would have found it almost impossible to communicate with Japanese people of the same generation in the mid-nineteenth century, suddenly you all have exactly the same reference points. They listen and talk about Blondie in the same way that you listen and talk about Blondie. They might regard their own past – the Kabuki theatre, say – as we might regard Shakespeare, as something inaccessible.

Because, since the arrival of television, theatre had become more and more an upper-middle-class activity, there was that tradition of theatre – very class-dominated, literary, intellectual – and we didn't feel part of that. I think it was very different for some of my colleagues in other countries: for example, my friends Robert Lepage and Marie Brassard and many others at the Théâtre Repère or Josef Nadj, who was really a dancer. For them, it was very different because in Canada and sometimes in America there was a kind of liberation from tradition, which had started in the 1960s. In the American theatre in the 1950s you were required to have an English accent and suddenly, a decade or two later, you got people like Pacino and Cassavetes. All these people suddenly go, 'Fuck it, we speak in our own language.' Indeed, in the British theatre, you are still expected to speak in RP – Received Pronunciation – even in drama schools, even now. People are having their regional accent flattened and taken away from them because you have to speak in RP.

STEVE KNAPPER: Did you consciously reject that by deciding to go to Jacques Lecoq's International Theatre School in Paris?

SIMON MCBURNEY: I didn't know what Lecoq was then. I knew that I wanted to train even though I was very heavily involved in comedy before I went.

STEVE KNAPPER: You did the Comedy Store on its first night, didn't you?[4]

SIMON MCBURNEY: Yes, that's right. Well I was very young then, 19 or 20 or something. You know I was asked by an unknown radio producer, Griff Rhys Jones, if I would do something. I had a whole thing opening out in front of me. I could go on into TV comedy which many of my contemporaries did, Hugh Laurie, Stephen Fry, Emma Thompson.

STEVE KNAPPER: Did you act with them when you were at Cambridge? Was it a Footlights scene there?[5]

SIMON MCBURNEY: Yeah, God, yeah. I was in Footlights but I looked at all of that and I thought actually I want to run away from here. My father died and all sorts of things happened in my life and I thought I want to be somewhere else. So I went to Paris and lived there for four years and, after training, worked with a company called Compagnie Jérôme Deschamps. Jérôme Deschamps was a Comédie-Française actor who had set out on his own to make pieces: almost like pieces of Beckett[6] but without words and they were very fascinating to me and he went on to have huge success in all sorts of different things.

STEVE KNAPPER: So you obviously had first-hand experience of French theatre.

SIMON MCBURNEY: Yeah, I went to see Peter Brook and the Bouffes du Nord, that was *de rigueur* and I admired what Ariane Mnouchkine was doing. You saw everything – dance, theatre, movement theatre, bits of weird mime, sort of séances and performance art, and I even saw the Living Theatre after they were, by that stage, completely fossilised. But I had no intention to become a director, ever. I was much too irresponsible but I loved improvisation. That was very important to me as it was to all those people who grew up at that time. That's the way all the theatre-makers I know who grew up at that time worked. We worked through improvisation.

I think there is a fundamental difference in the way one culture looks and another culture looks, in the way one culture listens and another culture listens. It wasn't lost on me the fact that we call the people who go to the theatre 'the audience', the people who listen, and the French call them *les spectateurs*, the people who watch. I enormously responded to that aspect.

STEVE KNAPPER: The visual aspect?

SIMON MCBURNEY: To the visual aspect. Simply because as an actor I was used to playing from a very young age. I liked to play, so I liked doing things. On a stage I wanted to do something, fiddle with this or that and have people watch what you do. Not just declaim to people.

STEVE KNAPPER: I remember seeing Giorgio Strehler giving a lecture at the Centre National de Recherche Scientifique when I was in Paris in 1989–90, and he said that he was very struck by how we have in English the verb 'to play' and the noun 'a play'. We have the same word which is both verb and noun and that this was something quintessentially Anglo-Saxon, if you like, and he seemed almost envious of this from a central European perspective. Do you think there's anything in that?

SIMON MCBURNEY: Yes, of course there is. Of course there is. I had a teacher who said that if an actor has forgotten what it is to play as a child they should not be an actor. The amusement of developing an action and what occurs within that action; what is involved in playing is living out imaginative acts constantly. Constantly involving your imagination to take you ... constantly involving stories which rise and fall and change. The notion of playing as opposed to acting has always been incredibly important.

STEVE KNAPPER: Would being a player better describe your process than being a director?

SIMON MCBURNEY: I don't know really. It's very important to have a good time. It's very important to amuse yourself, I think. I don't quite know what my process is sometimes; I mean, you know you tend to do things the same way, you tend to bring the same things into the rehearsal room and you tend to more or less start your day at ten and finish it at six ...

One of the hardest things in this particular production [*Measure for Measure*] is how you bind people together. What is the nature of social interaction? What is it that binds a group together? Whether I'm a European director is much less important to me than the question, what is it that motivates theatre at all? What's behind it? Do we need it in any context, in any place, at any time, in the human environment, the human world, wherever we are? We live in the generation that can go to Heathrow tomorrow, get on a plane, and go anywhere in the world. We can be within a matter of days anywhere and, of course, we can now be in touch within a matter of seconds with anybody in the world.

So we have access to each other and, at the same time, we have destroyed enormous quantities of things which actually root us physically and psychologically to where we are and give us meaning in our lives. We are constantly going, what does this actually mean? In reaction, people become ever more obsessed with the exterior of things and become ever more confused, have ever more encounters with their darker sides. One of the things I suppose that has constantly interested me when you are working in the theatre is: what is a piece of theatre? Why do it? Why is it there?

I think that it is quite clear that everybody acts things out. It's how our brains work; we are constantly acting. We are constantly producing events and – it seems to me – in the same way as we produce music. Similarly, we can ask, is music essential to life? Is it on every level essential? Well, one of the interesting aspects of music is that part of the brain is dedicated to the understanding or the decoding of music and as we know every part of the human body is there for a reason. So this necessity within us to play and act things out seems to be a necessary part of what it is to be human.

So why the theatre? Well, the image of the theatre is the image of the human community. You perform to a group of people. My father was an archaeologist and so I know something about the scale of prehistoric communities. You perform to people of a size which is pretty much of a scale of the human community. You get as many people together as can see that thing. Anywhere between 200 and 2,000. It is the basic human community. I don't know how many people you know or who are friends with but it could be anywhere between 50 and 2,500 which is about the same number as you find within an audience in the theatre. One of the aspects of music or dance or an event within the human community is that it binds the community together. It has an essential function because if we are only at each other's throats we can't survive. So some sort of social coherence is necessary for us not simply to go crazy like lemmings and throw ourselves all over the cliff (though possibly something like that is happening to us now …). So the theatre now, in a sort of distant echo, reflects the event of making and remaking the human community.

We make funny little pieces of theatre, we have dinner parties which are actually in many ways theatrical events. People applaud when somebody has actually made a dish. 'Oh!' we applaud. We have birthday parties. We have marriages. We have weddings. We have funerals. We have celebrations when you are 21, when you are 30, when you are 40, when you are 50, when you are 60, when you are 70, when you are 75. We are making and remaking theatrical events all the time. People have always signalled theatre is coming to an end, 'People don't go to the theatre any more.' There's more people going to the theatre now than 50 years ago in terms of theatrical events.

STEVE KNAPPER: Is that including these social events that you were saying – birthdays, funerals, etc.?

SIMON MCBURNEY: Yeah. But even just the theatre itself. New theatres have opened all over the place. At one point there was just the West End and the music hall but now there are theatres coming out of our ears. You look at the Edinburgh Fringe in the 1970s and it was one sheet of paper. It's now a book the size of the Bible to see all the different shows.

People need theatre. So what is going on when they go and see it? What they need is not just actors or a good play but that the audience is full. Without the audience theatre does not exist. It doesn't exist like a film as an object on its own. It can only exist with an audience. Further than that, in fact, it only exists in the minds of the audience. It doesn't exist on stage because if you go up on the stage there's nothing there. It's a complete illusion. You see very quickly people changing and pretending and you come up close to them and there isn't anything. It is only with the distance and in the minds of the audience that the theatre exists.

What happens when the audience watches a piece of theatre is that they imagine and they imagine almost the same thing at the same instant. They recognise this when they laugh together and they also recognise it when they weep. They recognise it when there is that moment of holy silence and when they recognise – perhaps unconsciously – the lie: the modern lie that we are all individuals who are not connected with other people, whose internal lives are entirely their own. Because at the moment when you all imagine together your imagination, your consciousness is joined as a whole and you know at that moment that you are not alone. This is absolutely fundamental because we believe more than anything else that only we can think the things that we think. Only I – me – only I think like that. Nonsense. We all think and we think together and our internal lives are as much a part of the collectivity as our external lives. The collective experience.

That is where theatre is important. It tells us who we are, which is not one person but many.

STEVE KNAPPER: Can you see the possibilities of a single story, a single production, a single company of actors – thinking of Brook's experiments – that you could take anywhere in the world and have that effect? Or is what you're saying culturally specific?

SIMON MCBURNEY: I'm just talking about the act of theatre. In terms of specific theatres, specific buildings, there are massive variations. It's the same as if you go, for example, to different restaurants across this city, across London, the experience is going to be enormously varied. Sometimes you'll get a great meal, sometimes you'll get a terrible meal. Sometimes you'll get an incredibly simple meal, but it's absolutely the best meal. Sometimes you'll get a very expensive and complicated one which is completely meaningless, and so on. So what I say is not true of all theatre but it is true of theatre.

And the act of theatre can take many different forms; so that, for example, theatre in another culture doesn't necessarily have the form that we have developed since the Renaissance. When I was in Uganda in 2005, I saw specifically African theatre which is being developed by this man at a place called the Ndere Theatre Centre by Stephen Rwangyzei, a wonderful, wonderful actor and director. Every Friday, Saturday, and Sunday there is theatre at the Ndere Theatre Centre but it is African theatre. It begins at six o'clock and it is still going at one o'clock the next morning. It includes stories and then people stop and they dance and the whole audience come up and there are people who are eating and it just goes on continuously but it is one piece of theatre. It is not a piece of theatre as we would understand it.

STEVE KNAPPER: As one event we could say?

SIMON MCBURNEY: Yes, but that is the form of the event. It is very different to the form that we would employ, even though most people when they go to theatre will make an event of it. The event of theatre begins before the theatre. They say, we will meet here. They meet whoever they're meeting, then they go to the theatre; then they have their drink; then they go into the theatre; then they come out and then they discuss it and then they go to a meal. So the event of theatre is always something other than the theatre, which is why of course there's an enormous problem with theatre criticism. Because you have these people rushing in to see a piece of theatre and rushing home and writing.

STEVE KNAPPER: They're not engaged in the whole social event. The normal social event.

SIMON MCBURNEY: I think they are rarely capable of seeing what is in front of them. Very often because they are simply thinking of something else while they are watching it. They are already thinking of what they are going to write rather than engaging with what is in front of them. Mind you, my God, it must be a frightful life being a theatre critic. Imagine seeing all that theatre. It must be absolutely ghastly. It must be appalling because you can't pick and choose what you want to go and see.

STEVE KNAPPER: There's a really strong sense of you collaborating with everybody but then *shaping*. Is that what you'd say your role is?

SIMON MCBURNEY: I don't really know. Everybody collaborates. It's a collaborative art form. Even a playwright might write the play, then you have to have a director and some actors. Theatre will always be collaborative and some of the least successful plays that I have ever seen have been those which have been wholly – and in a holy way – reverent to every word of the writer. All theatre is like life. Forever changing, surprising, and the moment it doesn't change, it's not alive and there isn't any point. Inevitably, if you work in the way that I do, everyone has their own opinion as to how it comes together or about what happens. That's the way they see it.

STEVE KNAPPER: But you are conscious of your *imprimatur*, of your signing of a piece, almost like an *auteur* in a cinematic sense?

SIMON MCBURNEY: Well, you know, there were all sorts of things which came together to make *Mnemonic*. I couldn't have done it without the relationship with my father who was an archaeologist. I couldn't have done it without the fact that my emotional life had fallen apart, you know, and so on. *Voilà*.

Five key productions

Anything for a Quiet Life. Devised by the company. Set design by Jan Pienkowski. Perf. Annabel Arden, Celia Gore Booth, Kathryn Hunter, Marcello Magni, Myra McFadyen, Stefan Metz, Boris Ostan. Eden Court, Inverness. 29 January 1988.

The Street of Crocodiles. Based on the writings of Bruno Schulz, devised by the company from an adaptation by Simon McBurney and Mark Wheatley. Set design by Rae Smith. Perf. Annabel Arden, Lilo Baur, Hayley Carmichael, Antonio Gil Martínez, Joyce Henderson, Eric Mallett, Clive Mendus, Cesar Sarachu, Matthew Scurfield. National Theatre, Cottesloe, London. 13 August 1992.

The Three Lives of Lucie Cabrol. Adapted from John Berger's short story by Simon McBurney and Mark Wheatley. Devised by the company. Set design by Tim Hatley. Perf. Lilo Baur, Mick Barnfather, Hannes Flaschberger, Simon McBurney, Tim McMullan, Stefan Metz, Hélène Patarôt. Dance House, Manchester. 4 January 1994.

> *Mnemonic.* Conceived by Simon McBurney. Devised by the company. Set design by Michael Levine. Perf. Katrin Cartlidge, Richard Katz, Simon McBurney, Tim McMullan, Stefan Metz, Kostas Philippoglou, Catherine Schaub Abkarian, Daniel Wahl. Stadtkino, Salzburg. 21 August 1999.
>
> *The Encounter.* Directed by Simon McBurney. Co-directed by Kirsty Housley. Design by Michael Levine. Sound by Gareth Fry with Pete Malkin. Lighting by Paul Anderson. Projection by Will Duke. Perf. Simon McBurney. Edinburgh International Festival: Edinburgh International Conference Centre. 8 August 2015.

Notes

1. There have been roles in popular UK television series, such as *Absolutely Fabulous* (1996), *The Vicar of Dibley* (1994–2004), and *Rev* (2010–14), as well as film roles in *The Last King of Scotland* (dir. Kevin Macdonald, 2006), *The Manchurian Candidate* (dir. Jonathan Demme, 2004), *Eisenstein* (dir. Renny Bartlett, 2000) in which he played the title role, *Harry Potter and the Deathly Hallows Part 1* (dir. David Yates, 2010), and *The Theory of Everything* (dir. James Marsh, 2014).
2. This is an annual comedy award given at the Edinburgh Festival. It was awarded to Complicite in 1985.
3. *Wogan* was a chat show for the BBC, *The Tube* a ground-breaking popular music programme for Channel 4, UK.
4. The Comedy Store first opened above a strip club in Soho in May 1979 and is now off Leicester Square and one of the principal venues in the UK for stand-up comedy. See www.thecomedystore.co.uk.
5. The University of Cambridge Drama Society which has gestated the talents of, amongst others, Peter Hall, *Beyond the Fringe*, and McBurney's contemporaries Emma Thompson and Stephen Fry. See http://footlights.org/history.html
6. McBurney directed Beckett's *Endgame* as a Complicite production at the Duchess Theatre, London, in 2009. He played Clov alongside Mark Rylance as Hamm.

Bibliography

Ainslie, Sarah [photographer] (2010) *Complicite Rehearsal Notes: A Visual Essay of the Unique Working Methods of the Company*, London: Complicite.

Alexander, Catherine (2010) 'Complicite *The Elephant Vanishes* (2003/04): "The Elephant and Keeper Have Vanished Completely … They Will Never Be Coming Back"', in Jen Harvie and Andy Lavender (eds), *Making Contemporary Theatre: International Rehearsal Processes*, Manchester: Manchester University Press, pp. 59–80.

Knapper, Stephen (2000) 'The Theatre of Memory: Théătre de Complicite's *Mnemonic*', *Theatre Forum*, 17 (summer/fall): 28–32.

―――― (2004) 'Complicite's Comintern: Internationalism and *The Noise of Time*', *Contemporary Theatre Review*, 14 (1): 61–74.

―――― (2005) 'Measure for Measure', *Western European Stages*, 17 (1): 209–10.

McBurney, Simon (2017) 'Listener, Grinder of Lenses, Poet, Painter, Seer. My Guide. Philosopher. Friend. John Berger left Us This Morning. Now You Are Everywhere.' *Twitter*, 2 January, 6.58pm, twitter.com/SimonMcBurney/status/815980569586757632

Shevtsova, Maria and Christopher Innes (2009) *Directors/Directing: Conversations on Theatre*, Cambridge: Cambridge University Press.

Williams, David (2005) 'Simon McBurney (1957–)', in Shomit Mitter and Maria Shevtsova (eds), *Fifty Key Theatre Directors*, London: Routledge, pp. 247–52.

Wiśniewski, Tomasz (2016) *Complicite, Theatre and Aesthetics: From Scraps of Leather*, Basingstoke: Palgrave-Macmillan.

Chapter 12

IVO VAN HOVE

Celebrity and reader

Denis Flannery

To write about the work of Ivo van Hove (b. 1958) is, in part, to write about the output of a celebrity. This is due in no small part to the super-visible recognition his achievements have received – two Obie awards in 1999, the French government making him *Chevalier de l'Ordre des Arts et des Lettres* in 2004, a Best Director Laurence Olivier Award in 2015, among many others. This celebrity status is also in part due to the name, number, and extent of the very famous artists and performers with whom, especially in recent years, he has worked. These include: Gillian Anderson, Juliette Binoche, David Bowie, Bryan Cranston, P. J. Harvey, Jude Law, and Saoirse Ronan.

When, on 11 January 2016, David Bowie's death was announced, van Hove had, for the previous 18 months, been collaborating with the singer on the musical *Lazarus*. Co-written by Bowie and Enda Walsh, it had premiered at the New York Theatre Workshop the previous month.[1] On that day, in TV interview after TV interview, van Hove was asked about the last months, works, and final illness of his collaborator and friend, becoming a kind of conduit to the public about the hitherto unknown 'truth' of the circumstances in which Bowie left the world.

In one of those interviews, on Sky News, van Hove joined celebrity, the initial focus of this chapter, with a display of his seriousness and sensitivity as a reader, my second, and major, focus. Asked about the reasons Bowie had for keeping his final illness and his approaching death secret, van Hove engaged in the following reading of the final song on *Blackstar*, Bowie's then-new album:

> The last line of *Blackstar*, it's the last line of the last song, it's something (I am very bad at quoting) but something like

'I couldn't give it all'. That means like I gave everything possible but I had to keep something to myself. And I must say, as a human being, I totally respect that somebody keeps his suffering and his death to himself, to a secret for him and his family. I totally can understand that and respect that.

(Van Hove 2016)

Van Hove does, it's true, misquote (the song in question is called 'I Can't Give Everything Away'; these words constitute the last line he sets out to read in recollection). But he goes on to confidently assert that the line has a meaning: 'That means ... I gave everything possible but I had to keep something to myself'. Misquoted or not, van Hove's reading takes a very emotionally focused approach to a specific situation. No matter how focused the approach or how specific the situation, though, this reading has a very broad, near-universal, emotional resonance. In this interview van Hove repeatedly emphasises that 'I must say, as a human being, I totally respect that somebody keeps his suffering and his death to himself, to a secret for him and his family'.

In the process of recollection (and translation from English to Dutch and then to English again), senses of the phrase 'I Can't Give Everything Away' may get slightly lost. To 'give everything away' can colloquially mean to give away a secret that one is holding or a game that, unbeknownst to others, one is playing. Giving 'everything away' also entails renunciation and/or abandonment.

But the song is read with an intense, thoughtful attention to its emotional specifics. Even if 'I Can't Give Everything Away' is read in terms of a meaning, message, or code, the intensity, the thought, and the affect are all in play; the song is not read reductively. For all the assertive force of purpose in this reading, van Hove manages to broaden out the song's terms of reference along with those of Bowie's death and of the interview itself: 'as a human being, I totally respect that somebody keeps his suffering and his death to himself.' Yet this broadening out leaves a certain mystery intact – the mystery, the privacy of Bowie's final months in this case – and the mystery of 'I Can't Give Everything Away'. The reading is also set in the context of *Lazarus*, the musical. Van Hove claims that both the play and *Blackstar* were 'like two testaments' by Bowie, adding that they were 'full of signals' (Van Hove 2016).

Reading the song in this way, van Hove quietly insists on a certain decency in collective life. This insistence echoes comments he made about Sophocles' *Antigone* in 2015 when ITA (International Theatre Amsterdam, of which he is General Director, formerly Toneelgroep Amsterdam) made a co-production of that play with London's Barbican and Luxembourg's Théâtre de la Ville:

> The dilemma of dealing with Polyneike's body became a terrifying reality recently when Malaysia airlines Flight 17 was shot down over a Ukranian war zone. The dead were left in an open field, rotting in the burning sun for over a week. The whole world saw this as an act of barbarity. Once the bodies were recovered and brought to the Netherlands for identification, the Dutch government arranged a convoy of hearses in a 100km burial procession. This was a civilized and humane response, a mark of respect to the victims.
> (Van Hove 2015: 4–6)

If his reading of the final line in Bowie's song is premised on a confident assertion ('That means,' he says of the line) then, with equal confidence, van Hove takes the cultural dynamics of Sophocles' play from 442 BC into a very brutally conceived 'now'. And, again, his reading broadens out the text's terms of reference, this time moving from one unburied body in the ancient world to nearly 300 (the bodies of the airline passengers and crew) in the very recent past. And if van Hove uses the verb 'to respect' as he speaks of somebody (in this case David Bowie) keeping their suffering and death a 'secret for him and his family', then he also draws on 'respect' as a noun when he describes the 'civilized and humane' response of the Dutch government when they arranged for the recovery and processional return of the victims' bodies as a 'mark of respect'. This word cuts across both readings and indicates the extent to which van Hove's practice as a reader is ethically driven and intensely related to urgent senses of reality. His use of the word 'respect' in these two contexts is also indicative of the centrality, for him, of theatre as a means for members of his audiences to encounter and contemplate some of the most raw and difficult issues in their lives. 'I want reality to really gnaw on theatre,' he once said, going on to claim that:

> In my plays, violence is ritual. People come to watch theatre in order to cry, not to cry about the play or its characters, but about themselves. At the end of it they walk out and carry on as if nothing has happened. Yet something has happened. You have to allow yourself to be emotional, to learn how to love, that's what theatre is meant for. If you don't learn that, life is horrible.
> (Veraart 2018: 79)[2]

The quotation above comes from Karin Veraart's *Ivo van Hove: Regisseur, mentor, manager*, a book which bears on its front a black and white headshot of its subject with his first name, IVO, printed in thick white type on a scale that dwarfs the smaller, darker printing of his surname and the thinner printing of the three key terms (director, mentor, manager) of Veraart's subtitle. For a director, even a well-known one, this is an intense level of public recognition. For a theatre director it's even more rare.

Veraart thinks of van Hove as a director (*regisseur*), as a mentor, and as a business-man or manager, whether as running the Café Illusie in Antwerp in the 1980s, directing Het Zuidelijk Toneel in Eindhoven in the 1990s, or, finally, as General Director since 2001 of what is now ITA. What underlies all these three strands of activity is a fourth – van Hove's readerly passion(s), his practice as a reader. This practice is emotionally focused, highly responsive to the specifics of the situations and texts it encounters, ethically driven, and motivated by an urgent wish to connect with the realities of its present moment.

Celebrity and extremity

'Celebrities,' Sharon Marcus has noted, 'are people known *during their lifetimes* to more people than could possibly know one another' (Marcus 2019: 9). In this basic sense Ivo van Hove is emphatically a celebrity. But different aspects of the history of celebrity, as recounted by Marcus, have resonance for his work and career. Locating the origins of contemporary celebrity culture in a powerfully visible, and international, nineteenth-century theatrical world, Marcus points out that theatre has, since the 1800s, become a more minoritised, 'niche form of entertainment, albeit one still able to generate blockbusters such as *Hamilton*' (Marcus 2019: 12). Van Hove's celebrity status and the mutual push and pull of his work with celebrity culture would begin to suggest, if not a return to the heady nineteenth-century days of an automatic equation between celebrity and theatre, then a certain removal of the theatrical from the 'niche'.

Marcus claims that 'intellectuals have been decrying the ills of celebrity culture' since the early 1940s at least (Marcus 2019: 14). She also points out that 'media producers' (among whom she includes photographers and gossip columnists as well as directors) 'can become celebrities themselves' (Marcus 2019: 7). Van Hove might well be considered an instance of this. But he has always taken into his work his own status as a fan, be that of music (David Bowie, Neil Young), of cinema (his admiration and adaptations of Ingmar Bergman or Pier Paolo Pasolini), or other forms of cultural work.

Celebrity culture has, for Marcus, a triangular structure with celebrities, media, and publics each having 'partial, contested but real agency', with each using that agency 'to collaborate and tussle with the others' (Marcus 2019: 217). Van Hove is certainly not an intellectual decrying celebrity or solely a media producer who has become a celebrity. Rather he is a vivid instance of celebrity culture's uneven (and unpredictable) distribution of real agency. His 'fandom' in part motivates the making of work that re-imagines and re-energises celebrities. This process expands (if it doesn't consolidate) his celebrity status, frequently drawing celebrities into working with him. He is dedicated to a field (theatre) that Marcus reads as the original creator of celebrity culture. And at the heart of all this is his practice and passion as a reader.

Such, was the almost 'Woodstock' impact of *Romeinse tragedies* (*Roman Tragedies*), van Hove's six-hour, multi-media take on William

Shakespeare's *Coriolanus, Julius Caesar,* and *Antony and Cleopatra* that, according to Toni Racklin, 'some people lie, to this day, about being at the show (at London's Barbican Centre) in 2009 because Ivo's debut on the Barbican stage has acquired the aura of a cornerstone in British drama' (Massai and Racklin 2018: 53). Of that famous show van Hove claimed:

> The idea is originating from the texts. I did not come up with something out of the blue and then search for texts to match it, that's not my way of working. Obviously, from out of the Shakespearean jungle, I have to chop and make a forest. But I am someone who needs the original material to create something of importance today.
>
> (Veraart 2018: 108)

'When I do a play,' van Hove once said, 'I want to do it in the most extreme way possible' (Dickson 2014: 1). And few would deny that to encounter one of his shows, either with his 'home' company ITA or with, say, the Comédie Française or the New York Theatre Workshop, is to have an experience of visceral, sometimes coarsely energising, extremity, and an experience with a massive, intense, complex, affective reach.

It takes a lot to put me into a stunned silence, but it was in precisely such a state that I found myself by the end of *Angels in America* (the first van Hove show I ever saw in Eindhoven, May 2008). And it was in an equally stunned state that I drifted out of the Barbican's auditorium with the rest of the audience after six hours of watching/participating in *Roman Tragedies* in London in 2009. In his description of that performance Christopher Billing ranked it as 'one of the most intense vicarious experiences of my life' (Billing 2010: 439). I agree. *Kreten en gefluister* (*Cries and Whispers*), after the film by Ingmar Bergman, in Amsterdam reduced me to a more tearful version of this state in 2011. Seeing *Na de repetitie/Persona (After the Rehearsal/Persona* – again after films by Bergman) in Paris in 2013, brought home to me the fact that there exist powerful emotions for which we have yet to find names. *Les Damnés* (*The Damned*, produced with the Comédie Française from the screenplay for the 1969 film by Luchino Visconti, written in collaboration with Nicola Badalucco and Enrico Medioli) took intensity to new levels, laced, this time, with a more timely political terror when I saw it at London's Barbican in 2019.

'Van Hove' is also shorthand for the name of a team. The shift in name/brand from Toneelgroep Amsterdam to International Theatre Amsterdam downplays, inevitably, the word 'group', but that collaborative energy is powerfully, inevitably there in work under the new (ITA) name. When van Hove has directed productions for other companies, this has inevitably meant that other members of the team work with him on those projects. Actors from Toneelgroep Amsterdam/ITA might not perform in shows like *Lazarus* or *All About Eve*, but such shows will feature set design and lighting by Jan Versweyveld, van Hove's artistic and life partner. Like the ITA actors, performers such as Michael C. Hall (in *Lazarus*) or Gillian Anderson (in *All About Eve*) will be costumed with sleek and searching intelligence by An D'Huys. The composer Erich Sleichim works with van Hove on many of his productions, both with ITA and with other international companies. And Tal Yarden's video work, combining the use of 'found' archive footage, pre-recorded footage of actors and action, and live onstage filming (and sometimes combinations of all three), has been vital to van Hove's impact worldwide.

Joseph V. Melillo has claimed of van Hove and Versweyveld that 'when a creative partnership is as long and fruitful as that of these two men, a kind of alchemy of assurance occurs'. For Melillo, this produces a 'confidence that the audience can sense', making us 'willing to follow these artists everywhere' (Melillo 2018: 49). That alchemy of assurance extends to the other members of the creative team I have mentioned (as well as to a bigger network of creative, administrative, technical, and managerial labour) and it is, as van Hove has acknowledged many, many times, central to the formation of his directorial approaches.

But at the heart of those approaches is reading. Interviewed in October 2014, when his production of *Angels in America* was about to open at BAM in New York, van Hove said: 'People talk about me as if I rip apart texts. I don't do that I always start with the text.' He then went on to emphasise the importance of textual fidelity and intimate reading to the approach(es) taken by Jan Versweyveld. 'He's a designer,' van Hove said, 'that really reads the text ... he knows the text better than me' (Van Hove 2014). This is one of van Hove's most vocal articulations of the centrality of texts and of 'really' reading, and knowing, texts. He is also keen to emphasise that he is not alone in this – that his closest collaborator (and perhaps, by implication, everyone with whom he collaborates) shares with him a belief in the centrality of (re-) reading as a foundation of theatre-making.

Scale and reading

Speaking once about *Amour* (2012) by Michael Haneke, a film van Hove has not (at least not yet) adapted for the stage, he said 'Nothing is smaller and more intimate than that film but at the same time nothing is more larger than life. Phenomenal' (Veraart 2018: 189). The terms of van Hove's fan-like praise reflect the intensity of his own admiration for artists and art works that alternate between intimate scales and vast scales. His praise for Haneke also reflects the importance of this alternation to his own artistic practice.

Movement between the intimate and the vast can happen between different productions: the intense, sparse intimacy of a one-man show like *Song from Far Away* (2015) by Simon Stephens as opposed to the vast, densely peopled technical amplitude of *The Antonioni Project* (2009). The latter, based on three films by Michaelangelo Antonioni, combined live performance with live filming of actors, their faces often displayed in intense close-up on large screens. This demonstrated a tendency to move between the intimate and the vast in one performance. Given, too, that in most instances, actors are close-miked, their enunciation can range from the whispered to the declamatory with no loss of verbal comprehension on the parts of the audience.

Scènes uit een huwelijk (*Scenes from a Marriage*), based on the 1973 film/TV series by Ingmar Bergman, a show that has been in ITA's repertoire since 2005, provides a vivid instance of this aspiration. The *mise en scène* of Part One of *Scenes* consisted of a vast, almost-tent-like structure, divided into three parts by canvas walls separating each part. The audience sat inside this structure on tiny metal seats, one-third of us (each with wristbands of one of three different colours) in each section. Three different pairs of actors played simultaneously in each section a scene of 40 minutes or so, each pair portraying Johan and Marianne, Bergman's couple, at three different life stages: youth (Alwin Pulincx and Suzanne Grotenhuis), early middle-age (Roeland Fernhout and Hadewych Minis), and later life (Hugo Koolschijn and Janni Goslinga – see Plate 12). The audience sat through the scene very close to the action with the actors, and the other audience members visible in a sickly off-gold light. Throughout, sounds (laughter, beer bottles clinked in celebration, sudden movement, sharp questions, shouts of rage) could be heard coming from the other sections (and the other times of the marriage). In the middle of this structure there was what P. A. Skantze describes as 'a small central room with plastic windows through which one could see the actors at rest' (Skantze 2018: 183).

Every 40 minutes or so the 'scene' came to an end and an actor would lift the canvas wall and invite the audience to take their places for the next scene, and so on for a total of three times. By the end of Part One, each audience member had encountered the couple at all three stages of their relationship, though not necessarily in chronological order (the first time I saw the production at London's Barbican in November 2013, I went from middle aged, to late middle aged, to young). This all sounds intense, claustrophobic, initially confusing, alarming on a very primal level – and it was. There was very little music, no video. The other members of the audience, visible in the sickly light, became almost like visual accompaniments to the action: a tear running down the face of a woman sitting nearby became an almost charged physical event. At one stage early in the 'young' section, two young men sitting in the row in front of me who had been holding hands from the minute they sat down suddenly ceased to do so. Again, this shift in their physical relationship resonated in a very theatrical way. I was reading other members of the audience and on some level aware that I too could be read.

But the show moved on to other elements of spatial grandeur that, if they compensated for some of the more distressing and almost gothic elements of the first part, lost none of their power to create powerful collective emotion. When you entered the late middle aged section (in a sense the 'final' scene of the show's first part), you fully realised that you were sitting on the Barbican's stage and that you were visible to what Skantze describes as 'the huge cavernous space of empty theatre seats' as the empty (and cold) auditorium opened up to you. The vacant rows described by Skantze constituted, for her, 'a perfect evocation of the afterlife waiting, of passing beyond relationship towards the swirling atoms of our next stage of being' (Skantze 2018: 184). I remember it differently, feeling that I could sense the presence of audiences from the past (and from the future) responding to performances from times past, passing, and to come, watching us and being part of what felt, by now, like 'our' show.

That was Part One of *Scenes from a Marriage*. Part Two worked on a virtually empty stage with the audience sitting on bleachers and with, at times, all six actors playing Johan and Marianne combining, recombining (and sometimes speaking all at once) as they took us through the next stages, and the next, of the relationship between Bergman's couple.

All this amounted clearly to a reading, to a 'smart' adaptation, especially given that Bergman made his *Scenes from a Marriage* not just for the cinema but as a TV series. Seriality was both denied and given a more theatrically plausible form. This was extremity that provoked a form of attention in the audience that required occupying what Skantze calls the 'in-between of recognition and interpretation' (Skantze 2018: 185). Something, in short, that sounds a lot like reading.

Elsewhere I've written about how van Hove's work can demand from the audience the activity of reading in more literal ways. His shows sometimes compel audiences to *read* onscreen and onstage text as an integral part of their experience (Flannery 2018: 191). His *Scenes from a Marriage* is a reading of Bergman's original, and one, furthermore, that sounds a lot like the practice of close reading as described by Elizabeth Freeman who writes that 'to close read is to linger, to dally, to take pleasure in tarrying' (Freeman 2010: xvi–xvii). Even if, in Part One, an audience member only sees the scene covering each period of the marriage once, the fact that at all times each section of the audience can hear the sounds of the other scenes (and can know thereby that the scene is being performed three times over a two-hour period) creates a sense of lingering. Even though an audience member in Part One sees each scene only once, the other scenes can be heard playing in the next 'rooms', creating a lingering effect, where each scene is accompanied by a simultaneous re-reading of the others. It has also been noted that close reading pays attention to 'elements in the text which ought to be quietly subordinate to the main idea, but which textually call attention to themselves' (Gallop 2000: 8). There is rich thematic ore in *Scenes from a Marriage*; it's an exploration of what time can do to love, of ambiguity in love, and of compromise. But in the intimacy, the closeness of this production, that is not where the audience's attention is taken. Small details – an overcoat dropped on the floor, a tiny photograph the elder Johann shows the elder Marianne of Paula, his new lover – are given calm, forceful prominence. Like the tears and the (non-)handholding of one's fellow audience members, these details invite close reading.

Ideas on stage

If many of van Hove's shows traffic in emotional, scenographic extremity that is driven by (and in turn invites) close reading, they also debate and probe *ideas*. And they often do so by, quite literally, asking questions: 'How far can one go in the love of one's country?', 'Can politics change people's minds?', 'Is it always praiseworthy to fight to the death for a belief?' These are questions posed, in written form, onscreen, at the end of *Roman Tragedies*. Of his 2015 *Antigone* van Hove claimed that it was 'ambivalent and dark, modern and mythical, leaving one with more questions than answers' (Van Hove 2015: 6).

His 2008 production of Tony Kushner's *Angels in America* cut, especially in the second of that play's two parts, large swathes of Kushner's text, taking its near seven hours down to a more compact four while – perhaps unexpectedly – leaving the moments of theory and debate untouched. 'The Great Question before us is: Are we doomed? The Great Question before us is: Will the Past release us?'; 'Why has democracy succeeded in America?' – these are all questions posed very vocally by different characters in Kushner's plays and van Hove was sure to give space and time to the articulation of these moments of anxiety, speculation, and wonder (Kushner 2017: 137, 93). 'We gave our country a vile democracy,' says one of the characters in *The Damned* early in that play, evoking the collusion between democratic process and authoritarian government, a question that speaks sharply to European and North American politics at the time of writing (August 2019).

In July 2019, as part of the Manchester International Festival, the entire cast of ITA's adaptation of Ayn Rand's *The Fountainhead*, along with British actors such as Adjoa Andoh, Juliet Stevenson, and Lemn Sissay, performed *Re:Creating Europe*, a staged reading, but with lighting and video projection, of an assembly of texts that comprised poems (John Donne's Meditation XVII, 'No Man is an Island'), extracts from political speeches (by Helmut Schmidt, Margaret Thatcher, Ann Widdecombe, and others), essays (e.g. Susan Sontag's 'The Idea of Europe'), songs (e.g. 'Stop the Cavalry' by Jona Lewie), and plays (extracts from Shakespeare's *Richard II* and *Henry V*) read in English, Dutch, French, and German. For van Hove, this was 'a mix of visions for Europe that are often diametrically opposed' (Van Hove 2019a: 3). For the cultural-media organisation Balie (who collaborated with ITA on the project), the show explored 'the ambivalent idea of Europe through many different voices' (Albrecht and Geurts 2019: 5).

Although *Re:Creating Europe* was not a play in any conventional sense, the experience of sitting through it was not far removed from some of the van Hove shows I've mentioned so far. The need to present questions even (or especially) if they are untimely, awkward (or even unanswerable), was, indeed is, of paramount importance. If *Scenes from a Marriage*, free as it was of any necessity for the audience to read onstage or onscreen text, invited a response that worked and felt like reading, then *Re:Creating Europe* made a visual, theatrical virtue of the spectacle of its actors and performers reading aloud from copies of scripts they held in their hands.

And even when questions are not explicitly posed, or projected in written form, onstage, van Hove's sense of the texts on which he bases his plays remains sharply focused on the specific questions they pose. With ITA, van Hove made a 2018 stage adaptation of *A Little Life*, based on the 2015 novel by Hanya Yanagihara. 'Reading *A Little Life*,' he claimed, 'is much more than just reading a book. It's a destructive descent into areas of pure pain, pure loneliness, pure helplessness, friendship' (Van Hove 2018: 1). The experience of encountering Yanagihara's novel was intensely affective for him and so too were the questions it posed. These are 'questions about good and evil, about how to deal with losing whom [*sic*] you really love. But also about the contemporary tyranny of being happy, about the connection we automatically make between love and sexuality' (Van Hove 2018: 1). Unlike the civic, political questions posed in and through *Roman Tragedies* and *Re:Creating Europe*, these are broader questions about ethics and affect – which are, in turn, two driving forces in his practices of reading.

Reading 'the director and his library'

Veraart's book has a 12-page chapter entitled 'De Regiseeur & zijn bibliotheek' (The Director and His Library). This begins with an account of van Hove's attachment, from the age of 20, to plays by Arthur Miller and Tennessee Williams. And it very promptly links van Hove's responsiveness to those figures with the artistic and intellectual debts he has to his teachers and exemplars: Alex van Royen, Robert Wilson, Peter Stein, Patrice Chéreau. A link exists, therefore, between reading and a heritage of theatrical inspiration and pedagogy. The chapter also broadens out one's expectations of what might be in a '*bilbiotheek*' and the sometimes surprising routes by which a director can choose texts he wishes to adapt. The library contains Miller and Williams but also the French writer (and film maker) Marguerite Duras and a number of auteur-directors/writers: John Cassavetes, Michaelangelo Antonioni, Pier Paolo Pasolini, Luchino Visconti. Over the years, van Hove's name has become powerfully linked to these figures and that linkage has been driven by his often-avowed fan-relationship to them.

There is an intensely reciprocal and unboundaried relationship between reading, cinema, and the making of theatre in this account of the director's library. Repeatedly, for van Hove, what he was reading or seeing when he was 20 years old is a frequent point of return – 'When I was about 20 years old, I saw all the films by Visconti', van Hove claimed in an interview. 'These films', he goes on, 'stir up emotion and broach controversial topics' (van Hove: 2019: 8). He then goes on to emphasise that he re-read the screenplay as part of the process of developing the show.

Such re-reading is integral to van Hove's directorial approaches. 'I re-read the plays and I thought they could be stronger now,' he said when I asked him why, in 2008, he had decided to stage both parts of Tony Kushner's *Angels in America* (Flannery 2014: 172).

'Those who fail to reread', Roland Barthes once noted, 'are obliged to read the same story everywhere' (Barthes 1974: 16). Van Hove's commitment to re-reading chimes with his practice of reading texts with openness and alertness. It is perhaps a certain failure to take into account the importance and impact of this commitment to re-reading that makes van Hove's work easy to mimic and, perhaps, easy to parody. At the very same time, the visceral impact of that work is very difficult to reproduce. This may because at the heart of van Hove's work is not just reading, but *re*-reading. Barthes goes on to claim that if re-reading has a goal it is to 'obtain, as though under the influence of a drug not the *real* text, but a plural text: the same and new' (Barthes 1974: 16). Re-reading, for Barthes (and, I suspect, for van Hove), constitutes an affective, potentially mind-altering process aimed in part at accessing the sameness of a text. Hence van Hove's (often overlooked) scrupulous fidelity – to Shakespeare, to Kushner, to Visconti, and to others. But re-reading also drives a will to access a newness in the texts he chooses, often one that is historically resonant for the audience in very immediate ways – something that is, as he puts it, 'of importance today'.

Van Hove's approach to reading is distinguished by great emotional precision, and by a very alert ear for the resonances across time and cultures of the texts he considers and adapts. His reading as preparation for the making of theatre is marked by a combination of fidelity, respect, and motivation to use fresh encounters with texts to make work that is, in his words, 'of importance today'. Veraart's account of van Hove's library sheds light on what we might call the archive of his practice: the importance of 'classic' texts, especially (though not exclusively) American ones, his engagement with writers who made films in the 1960s and 1970s, as well as directors many of whom (such as Visconti) felt a close connection to a literary, often canonical, tradition. This is accompanied by van Hove's readiness to allow theory (especially sociological theory) to influence his work. Veraart quotes his claim that he is greatly influenced by the sociologists Richard Sennett and Zygmunt Bauman (Veraart 2018: 193). All of this indicates high levels of engagement and action, affective response, courage, and critical acumen. Yet very recently, van Hove's work has been read as either potentially or excessively distanced from texts or else open to a naïve susceptibility to those texts' more wily ways – and it is to this kind of response that I will now turn.

Reading van Hove in 2019

A rather lukewarm, response to van Hove's *The Damned* (Comédie Française, 2016; also performed at London's Barbican in 2019) provides an instance of this. 'Roll up', Dominic Cavendish writes 'for male and female nudity, a man being tactile with a girl in a way that signals paedophile intent, the simulated sexual assault of a barmaid – and Hitler salutes' (Cavendish 2019). Cavendish goes on to claim that 'the immediate explanation for what's on stage and its ready acceptance can be laid at the door of the venerated Visconti' (Cavendish 2019). As he trivialises the play, Cavendish rhetorically attributes trivialising motivation (and rhetoric) to van Hove and the company (hence the use of the phrase 'Roll up'). The onstage presence of nudity and representations of intergenerational sexual intent and sexual assault is attributed by Cavendish, in a confusedly causal way, to the power and status that appear to emanate from the 'venerated Visconti'; that is either from Visconti himself or from some – implicitly unworthy – veneration of Visconti on van Hove's part.

What is not entertained (or acknowledged) is that these things are there in the screenplay that, van Hove emphasises, he re-read. Their onstage presence is part of an almost doggedly literal process of adaptation. It also emerges from, again, a re-reading process, this time of Visconti's screenplay: 'I did not watch the film again,' van Hove claimed, 'since it is vital to me that the stage performance not be an adaptation of the film.' Cavendish particularly takes issue with a moment at the show's end when the character of Martin von Essenbeck (Christophe Montenez) 'strips off, covering himself in an urn-full of family ashes' (Cavendish 2019). Those ashes with which Montenez covers his naked body are ceremonial objects and their presence is consistent with van Hove's claim 'in my plays, violence is ritual' (Veraart 2018: 79). Each time, in this production, a character dies or is killed, that character is ceremonially led to one of six coffins placed on a slightly raised platform, stage left, and guided by blackshirted attendants therein. After each of these deaths and entombments, an attendant takes a small urn of ashes from behind each coffin and ceremonially empties its contents into a larger, wider urn, centre stage front. By the play's end, when the Essenbeck family's collusion with the Nazis and the SS is total and young Martin has eliminated all of his enemies (and all of his loved ones), he does indeed strip naked, removing his black SS uniform, and then covers himself in ashes as Cavendish describes. More than this, he takes a machine gun and mounts a table at the back of the stage in front of a large video screen which, at this final climactic moment, goes blindingly white. This change in colour and lighting is swiftly followed by the amplified rat-tat-tat of machine gun fire. The show's searing final image is Montenenez's now-silhouetted Martin firing into the audience in his naked, raging, ash-covered triumph.

Cavendish describes some of these aspects of the performance as van Hove's 'own striking choices', and in some ways he is right, especially about the coffins, the repeated recourse to which is utterly consistent with the director's emphasis on violence as ritual. But the coffins, and many other aspects of the show to which Cavendish takes exception, are van Hove taking Visconti's screenplay absolutely to the letter.

Various characters in the film – the Baron Joachim von Essenbeck (Didier Sandre in this production), Elizabeth Thallman (Adeline d'Hermy), and, by the end, Martin's mother Baroness Sophie von Essenbeck (Elsa Lepoivre) and her lover Friedrich Bruckmann (Guillaume Gallienne) encounter off-screen deaths or there are, in the film, significant gaps and silences around their killings. The ritual with the coffins 'literalises' these deaths and makes them physical in a vividly theatrical way. This ritual, ceremonial aspect also echoes what David Willinger has claimed is the influence of Antonin Artaud on van Hove's work (Willinger 2018: 13–17). Experientially, this repeated ritual, wherein the audience is filmed by onstage cameras and our image projected onto the large screen at the back of the stage, makes each death part of one narrative chain and, it feels, an inexorable politico-cultural force (or nightmare) in which it is all too easy to feel agonisingly involved.

The preference van Hove exhibits for the act of re-reading, the vitality of the re-reading of a text (as opposed to watching a film again), is yet another indication of how engagement with a text, on a verbal, material level, is at the heart of his work.

When it comes to nudity and ashes, the name 'Essenbeck' is a near-homophone of the name Von Aschenbach. This evokes Gustave von Aschenbach, the central character of Thomas Mann's novella *Death in Venice* (1912), famously adapted for screen by Visconti two years after *The Damned*, and also adapted by van Hove's ITA in 2019. More fundamentally still, this surname evokes, indeed is, the German word for 'ashtray'. Cavendish, wrongly, believes (or needs to be seen to believe) that some of the most doggedly faithful and textually attentive aspects of van Hove's Visconti adaptation are exercises in perversity, caprice, or European directorial *droit du seigneur*. And there is a vocally anti-European thread in Cavendish's comments. For him *The Damned* is 'hard to follow' because it is in French (hardly surprising since it is a production for the Comédie Française). Not to react to it with 'uproar' is, for him, to 'bow low before shock European "regietheater"' – another unsupported assertion (Cavendish 2019).

Cavendish's response to this production of *The Damned* finds a perhaps surprising partner-in-approach in the work of queer theorist

Lisa Duggan as she responds to another production. 'Prominent Belgian director and self-identified gay social democrat Ivo van Hove', Duggan writes in *Mean Girl*, her book on Ayn Rand, 'fell in love with *The Fountainhead* when he received it as a gift in 2007' (Duggan 2019: 11). That falling-in-love culminated in one of van Hove's and ITA's most visually stunning, technically complex, vast and politically controversial plays – a four-hour adaptation of Rand's 1943 novel that was first performed in 2014 and has toured internationally ever since. This production is in four parts, each with a different title, and each title displayed on a video screen. Part Four is, for example, entitled 'War of Ideas'. Duggan claims that the particular focus of ITA's and van Hove's adaption of *The Fountainhead* is an emphasis 'on the struggle of a creative architect, Howard Roark, against the forces of conventionality and mediocrity' (Duggan 2019: 11). Cavendish casts van Hove's inherent sense of theatre as a ritual event and his textual fidelities as manipulations of his material, partly motivated by a suspect veneration of Visconti. Duggan, though, sees van Hove as all-too-susceptible to Rand's mean-girl manipulations. Duggan claims that 'this kind of focused, selective emphasis' is something that Rand's novels all too commonly and insidiously invite. 'Even the readers most loyal to Rand's overall political vision', Duggan goes on to write, 'often fiercely advocate some of her views while ignoring others – especially her atheism' (Duggan 2019: 12).

But, again, there is more involved in van Hove's adaptation of Rand than either political naivety or susceptibility to the novelist's wily ways. The first is fidelity, a certain respect. Elsewhere, I've argued that two different aspects of the novel get very faithfully treated in van Hove's production. The first is the characters' huge erotic and personal investments in each other or, for want of a better term, love. Dominant rhetoric about (and produced by) Rand does not encourage seeing love as a force in her writing. Love is, though, a very real force in *The Fountainhead* – and in readers' responses to it. Second, the novel's poetic emphasis on light – the light of the sun, light on waterfalls, cityscapes – is paid massive tribute by Versweyveld's sometimes searing, often hazy, and subtle lighting (Flannery 2018: 192–94). Of course, *The Fountainhead* is also about the world of architecture, something that provides abundant visual opportunities at which Verswyveld's design gracefully leaps.

There are also tensions within the production that indicate a relation between van Hove and Rand's novel that goes beyond the susceptibility of which Duggan accuses him. 'Man's first duty is to himself,' Howard Roark (Ramsey Nasr) says in the course of his final speech in the show. 'No man can live for another.' As he says this (and much more) in *The Fountainhead*'s final moments, the other members of the cast stand behind him in silhouette. 'They make haunting, beautiful sounds (based on samples of their own voices) by slowly passing their hands over infra-red-sensitive electronic instruments' (Veraart, 2018, 154). Peter van Kraaj, who worked as a dramaturg on the show, said the following about this moment:

> While in the foreground, Ramsey is making a speech about ego-centricity and the need to make yourself *the* starting point, you see a collective of actors who, *together*, provide the soundtrack to his speech: direct evidence of how a *group* can generate beauty. Those are two theatrical signals and a fundamental statement.
> (Veraart 2018: 154–55)

In van Kraaj's reading – and this was certainly my experience when I saw the show – Rand's right-wing individualism is being implicitly critiqued by a vision of theatrical and social collectivity. Just as the audience of *Scenes from a Marriage* is invited to engage with an in-between state of recognition and interpretation, so the audience of *The Fountainhead* is invited to ask the kinds of questions which are so important to van Hove's sense of theatre, and never more so than in these last minutes. These questions are not only responses to Roark's/Nasr's discourse on individual agency but they are also questions about what is in front of them. If Roark the character eschews collaboration and radical dependence then how can that be squared with the fact that not only the specific theatrical event of *The Fountainhead*'s conclusion but theatre itself is utterly driven by both collaboration and radical dependence? The audience might wonder if Erich Sleichim's stunning music played by the other cast members (and based on their voices) is music that emphasises or celebrates what Roark proclaims. Does this music excavate the weakness of his argument or reinstate the disavowed affect of belonging and attachment that drives those arguments into being in the first place? Central to the audience's attachment to the performance is a process of recognition, questioning, interpretation – reading.

Cavendish and Duggan are both keen to emphasise the extent to which aspects of both shows emerge from a political stance that is either naïve or just undesirable. For Cavendish, *The Damned* is a liberal parable; for Duggan, van Hove's decision not to stage *The Fountainhead* in a way that chimes with her own total hostility to Rand emerges in part from his status as a 'self-identified gay social democrat' (Duggan 2019). For both commentators, van Hove is suckered in by entities cast in paranoid terms: 'the venerated Visconti' for Cavendish; the insidious invitations Rand's fiction issues, in Duggan's view, to 'focused, selective emphasis', as if adaptation were even possible without focused, selective emphasis.

Conclusion

Van Hove's fame and personal celebrity status, his spectacularly intense directorial practice, and the readiness of his work to ask and explore (sometimes with a slowness that can appear to risk verging on the foolhardy) theoretical and philosophical questions can, wrongly, create an impression of remove, rootlessness, a distance from the 'ordinary'. It is sometimes assumed that this can entail a distance from texts and a near-delegation of the process of reading. In this chapter, I have set out to question these assumptions.

The overlap of celebrity and reading with which I began is far from common in the early twenty-first century. Barthes, in his reflections on re-reading, describes it as 'an operation contrary to the commercial and ideological habits of our society' and goes on to claim that it is 'tolerated in certain marginal categories of people (children, old people and professors)' (Barthes 1974: 16). Neither 'celebrities' nor 'directors' make it onto Barthes's list of tolerated 'marginal' (re-)readers. The case of van Hove would suggest that perhaps one or both of these categories should, or at least could, have been included. 'As a theatre-maker you need to have cultural baggage, and you need to be able to select from that, whenever necessary,' he once remarked. 'I want participate in evolutions ... in processes' (Veraart 2018: 188). What happens when van Hove selects from his 'cultural baggage' appears to be an activation of his habits and skills as a reader – his emotional focus, his alertness to the specifics of the text/situation he reads. There is also, of course, the ethical drive of his reading habits and his insistence that the theatre he makes from them speaks to some of the most raw and difficult areas of present realities. This is accompanied by a rich and necessary history of collaboration and a recognition of the necessity to re-read, not only to avoid the trap of reading 'the same story everywhere' but also to be open to the opportunities that occur when theatre occupies, as it always needs to, a space between the same and the new.

Five key productions

Scenes from a Marriage. By Ingmar Bergman. Set design and costumes by Jan Verswyeveld. Perf. Roeland Fernhout, Bart Slegers, Celia Nufaar, Hugo Koolschijn, Janni Goslinga, Alwin Pulinckx, Benjamin de Wit, Camilla Siegertsz, Charlie-Chan Dagelet, Claire Bender, Eva Heijnen Maartje van de Wetering. Staddschowburg, Amsterdam. 1 February 2005.

Roman Tragedies. By William Shakespeare. Set Design by Jan Versweyveld. Costume Design by Lies van Assche. Perf. Bart Slegers, Chris Nietvelt, Fred Goessens, Frieda Pittoors, Gijs Scholten van Aschat, Hans Kesting, Hélène Devos, Hugo Koolschijn, Janni Goslinga, Maria Kraakman, Marieke Heebink, Alwin Pulinckx, Eelco Smits, Harm Duco Schut. Staddschowburg Amsterdam. 17 June 2007.

The Fountainhead. By Ayn Rand. Set design by Jan Versweyveld. Costume design by An D'Huys. Perf. Aus Greidanus jr., Bart Slegers, Frieda Pittoors, Halina Reijn, Hans Kesting, Hélène Devos, Hugo Koolschijn, Janni Goslinga, Maarten Heijmans, Ramsey Nasr. Staddschowburg, Amsterdam. 15 June 2014.

Lazarus. By David Bowie and Enda Walsh. Set design by Jan Versweyveld. Costume design by An D'Huys. Perf. Krystina Alabado, Sophia Anne Caruso, Nicholas Christopher, Lynn Craig, Michael Esper, Michael C. Hall, Cristin Milioti, Bobby Moreno, Krista Pioppi, Charlie Pollock, Brynn Williams. New York Theatre Workshop, New York. 7 December 2015.

The Damned. By Luchino Visconti, Nicola Baddaluco, Enrico Medioli. Set design by Jan Versweyveld. Costume design by An D'Huys. Perf. Syvlia Bergé, Éric Génovèse, Denis Podalydès, Guillaume Gallienne, Elsa Lepoivre, Loïc Corbery, Pierre Louis-Calixte, Adeline d'Hermy, Clément Hervieu-Leger, Jennifer Decker, Didier Sandre, Christophe Montenez, Sebastien Baulain. Cour d'Honneur, Avignon for the Avignon Festival. 7 July 2016.

Notes

1 Such is van Hove's celebrity status that not only would his name appear on the credits for the *Lazarus* original cast recording a few months later as the play's director, but he would also appear in no fewer than five photographs (mostly shots taken in rehearsal) included in the booklet that accompanied the recording's CD and vinyl release. Bowie himself, who wrote all of the songs in the show but did not appear in it, has two photographs on the recording's sleeve and in its booklet.

2 I am very grateful to Adriaan van Klinken for his helping me with the translation of this passage – and others – from Veraart's book.

Bibliography

Albrecht, Yeuri and Merlijn Geurts (2019) 'What is Europe?', *Re:Creating Europe*, Manchester International Festival Programme, pp. 4–5.

Barthes, Roland (1974) *S/Z: An Essay*, trans. Richard Miller, New York: Farrar, Straus and Giroux.

Bennett, Susan and Sonia Massai (eds) (2018) *Ivo van Hove: From Shakespeare to David Bowie*, London: Methuen Drama.

Billing, Christian (2010) 'The Roman Tragedies', *Shakespeare Quarterly*, 61 (3) (fall): 415–39.

Cavendish, Dominic (2019) '*The Damned*, Barbican, review: With nudity, Sexual Assault and Paedophilia, Ivo van Hove Tests the Boundaries of Acceptability', *The Telegraph*, 22 June, www.telegraph.co.uk/theatre/what-to-see/damned-barbican-review-nudity-sexual-assault-paedophilia-ivo/

Dickson, Andrew (2014) '"My Aim is the Ultimate Production": Ivo van Hove on Directing Arthur Miller', *The Guardian*, 24 April, www.theguardian.com/stage/2014/apr/02/ultimate-production-ivo-van-hove-arthur-miller-theatre

Duggan, Lisa (2019) *Mean Girl: Ayn Rand and the Culture of Greed*, Oakland: University of California Press.

Flannery, Denis (2014) 'Floating in a Most Peculiar Way: *Angels in America*, David Bowie, Toneelgroep Amsterdam', *Contemporary Theatre Review*, 24(2): 156–76.

—— (2018) 'The Intensification of the Novel: Ayn Rand's and Ivo van Hove's *The Fountainhead*', in Susan Bennett and Sonia Massai (eds), *Ivo van Hove: From Shakespeare to David Bowie*, London: Methuen Drama, pp. 187–94.

Freeman, Elizabeth (2010) *Time Binds: Queer Temporalities, Queer Histories*, Durham and London: Duke University Press.

Gallop, Jane. (2000) 'The Ethics of Reading: Close Encounters', *Journal of Curriculum Theorising*, 16 (3) (fall): 7–17.

Kushner, Tony (2017) *Angels in America: A Gay Fantasia on National Themes: Part One: Millennium Approaches, Part Two: Perestroika*, London: Nick Hern Books.

Marcus, Sharon (2019) *The Drama of Celebrity*, Princeton and Woodstock: Princeton University Press.

Massai, Sonia and Toni Racklin (2018) 'Staging Ivo van Hove at the Barbican', in Susan Bennett and Sonia Massai (eds), *Ivo van Hove: From Shakespeare to David Bowie*, London: Methuen Drama, pp. 52–55.

Melillo, Joseph (2018) 'Staging Ivo van Hove at BAM', in Susan Bennett and Sonia Massai (eds), *Ivo van Hove: From Shakespeare to David Bowie*, London: Methuen Drama, pp. 49–51.

Skantze, P. A. (2018) 'Archaeological Adventures in Spectating: *Obsession* and *Scenes from a Marriage*', in Susan Bennett and Sonia Massai (eds), *Ivo van Hove: From Shakespeare to David Bowie*, London: Methuen Drama, pp. 178–86.

Van Hove, Ivo (2014) 'Artist Talk: Ivo van Hove and Tony Kushner', www.youtube.com/watch?v=stvpFanEU30

—— (2015) 'The Unanswered Question: How to Get to the Dark Soul of Antigone', *Antigone*, Barbican programme, pp. 4–6.

────── (2016) '*Lazarus* Director Ivo van Hove on David Bowie's Death', www.youtube.com/watch?v=RDq2LfeBxnc

────── (2018) '*A Little Life*', *A Little Life* ITA Programme: 1.

────── (2019a), 'Europe', *Re:Creating Europe*, Manchester International Festival Programme, 2–3.

────── (2019b) 'Interview with Ivo van Hove, Jan Verswyeveld, Tal Yarden and Erich Sleichim', *The Damned*, Barbican programme, 8-9.

Veraart, Karin (2018) *Ivo van Hove: Regisseur, mentor, manager*, Amsterdam and Antwerp: Querido.

Willinger, David (ed.) (2018) *Ivo van Hove Onstage*, London and New York: Routledge.

Chapter 13

DEBORAH WARNER

Experiments of words, bodies, and place

Adam J. Ledger

Speaking during rehearsal for *The Testament of Mary* (2012), an adaptation by Colm Tóibín of his book of the same year, the actor Fiona Shaw assesses her long-term collaboration with Deborah Warner.[1] Shaw concludes that

> she listens, really, like a sort of well. You just feel that everything you say is heard very deep down. So the more that Deborah helps root what is being said ... the sound has more depth for me, or more 'hold'.
>
> (Shaw and Warner 2014)

As well as a reminder of one of the most enduring director–actor relationships in contemporary theatre, Shaw's comments reveal Warner's fundamental prioritisation of the text, how it is 'heard', and, in turn, experienced by actor and audience.[2] In an early interview, Warner adds 'I tend towards texts which, through their own ambition, depth and complexity, might be difficult to direct' (Giannachi and Luckhurst 1999: 136). If Warner is fundamentally interested in those texts that offer implicit challenges to how their dramatic fabrics might be performed, this reinforces her focus on the actor, who, as Shaw puts it, must 'hold' meaning through textual expression.

But the centralisation of 'listening' as a means to direct also suggests the lack of any fixed rehearsal method. Warner goes on to say 'I can't accurately describe what takes place in the rehearsal room because it depends on what happens in front of me. This determines how I react and how I channel what I witness' (Giannachi and

Luckhurst 1999: 137). Warner places her responsive directorial eye and ear as the determinants of rehearsal progress. It also renders Warner curiously elusive in terms of theatre scholarship; beyond the extensive press coverage of her work, academic publication tends to appear in the form of interviews (Warner 1996) or commentary on her productions.[3] The latter is often grouped together in terms of genre, such as her work on Shakespeare (Rutter 2006, 2008), or her site-specific projects (McEvoy 2006), or issues such as gender (Klett 2006; Silverstone 2007).[4] The need either to individuate productions or to group them as a typology (the 'what' of Warner's directing) suggests too that it is not easy to identify a consistent directorial 'signature' across an *oeuvre*, such as the prolific output of Ivo van Hove (Chapter 12).

In contrast to the extensive academic interest in Katie Mitchell (Chapter 19), who claims a more or less step-by-step process in play rehearsal, it is this lack of definitive approach (the 'how' of her directing) that, in part, resists a scholarly determination of Warner's practice. And unlike some directors, Warner has not published her own writings. Yet she features regularly in the press, in video interviews, and has appeared in several 'Platform' performances at the National Theatre, often with Shaw; Warner's 'voice' has thus been foregrounded in this chapter. And in contrast to many international directors who guard their privacy, Warner has her own website and online archive. Three aspects characterise her comments on her active Twitter account: the work at hand, an evident fondness for her fellow artists, and her political views.[5]

Alongside the text, the actor, and the gendered body, a consideration of space and scenography can start more clearly to illuminate Warner's practice, even if she might appear curiously invisible; and as I suggest here, Warner does employ regular approaches or techniques in rehearsal. Her work is also fundamentally international; as well as a significant presence in New York, her productions are typically conceived as co-productions with European partners, enabling them to continue to develop through tours and revivals as they reach new spaces and audiences. Indeed, Warner's first production for the Royal Shakespeare Company (RSC), *Titus Andronicus* (1987), toured to Madrid, two cities in Denmark, and – significantly given her acknowledgement of Peter Brook as an influence – the Théâtre des Bouffes du Nord, Paris.[6]

Warner's burgeoning presence in France (where she was made a Chevalier, and then L'Officier de l'Ordre des Arts et des Lettres; 1992, 2000) and in Madrid led to a burgeoning Continental European career after leaving the RSC and, later, the National Theatre (NT, where she was an associate director from 1989 to 1997).[7] Although she admitted that initially she 'actively did not want to do opera' (Taylor 2006), Warner's major Shakespearean productions, including *Julius Caesar* (2005), which also transferred to Paris, Madrid, and Luxembourg, also led to increased invitations to direct opera, in which she now largely works.[8] While Warner mainly circulates in Europe through opera, the focus of this chapter is on how these are punctuated by quite particularly chosen theatre projects, as well as, latterly, site-based performance and installation work.

Eye

In his book *Directing Scenes and Senses*, Peter Boenisch rightly identifies the discursive shift from 'directing' to the term 'theatre direction' to denote the shaping of a cultural-political artistic intervention (Boenisch 2015: 3). Yet Warner seems to eschew the discourse of the director as a determining individual. In Schneider and Cody's terms, such an artist embodies the 'mark of the individual eye, the signature of an individual visual guide' (Schneider and Cody 2003: 4) as the distinguishing, authorial feature of the modernist director. Catherine Alexander similarly describes Complicité's Simon McBurney (Chapter 11) as one who, after an extended rehearsal exploration, 'rips and trashes through the mounds of material and crafts the show. He wrestles with subject, form, space, sound and actor to make something new' (Alexander 2010: 72). While she similarly insists upon long rehearsal periods for what she explicitly refers to as 'experiments', Warner contrasts with the apparently directorial force of nature that is McBurney; her later honing of a production centres on clarifying her actors' work as it has emerged in rehearsal, rather than the authorship of a dramaturgy. Long before the term became widely popular, Warner thus referred to herself as a 'theatre "maker"' (Rutter 2008: 475), and does not consider her work ever 'finished', continuing to work on productions over international tours.

A further understanding of Warner's identity lies in her appreciation of Brook. She suggests his *The Empty Space* is 'the best book written about the nature of theatre' (Giannachi and Luckhurst 1999: 139). To return to Brook's classic text (first published in 1968) is quite instructive: *The Empty Space* distinguishes between the 'Deadly', the 'Holy', the 'Rough', and the 'Immediate' theatre. But Brook warns of too-easy categorisations, since 'sometimes they are metaphoric: two of them mixing together within one evening, within one act. Sometimes within one single moment' (Brook 1988: 11). Like Brook, Warner appears keen to get out of the way of the material she directs, to resist a personalised stamp upon it, to watch and, as above, to listen for essentials. Even if some can find her work cool or 'intellectual and risky' (Klett 2006: 180), Warner explains, 'Peter inspired me to trust in the form and illuminated the way brilliantly. In his writings, he has been able to articulate the invisible and the indefinable: to write about the essence of theatre' (Giannachi and Luckhurst 1999: 139). Here, again, is the trust in the text and the way it suggests theatrical expression as a revelation of its 'essence'.

Event

Following her training at the Central School of Speech and Drama in stage-management, Warner founded Kick Theatre Company (1980) when she directed Bertolt Brecht's *The Good Person of Szechwan*. From the beginning of her work, Warner's focus has been the classic repertoire. Warner also garnered several awards, including two Laurence Olivier Awards (1988, 1992). She moved to the RSC, first to direct *Titus Andronicus* in the Swan Theatre, thus becoming the first female director to lead a production on a main RSC stage; her *King John* (1988) appeared in the RSC's smaller The Other Place. Her productions at the NT included *The Good Person of Sichuan* (1989), *King Lear* (1990), and *Richard II* (1995), with Shaw in the title role.[9]

Certain responses in the British press to Warner's perceived directorial interventions have sometimes been rather personal and unpleasant; but in New York, it was pressure from a sector of the public that eventually closed *The Testament of Mary*.[10] During previews, the production attracted sustained protest from elements of the Catholic community; Warner has commented ruefully that very few protesters had actually seen it. Rather than religious iconoclasm, the piece, which explores Mary's account of the death of Jesus, is, for Shaw, about the 'human experience of family' (Shaw and Warner 2014).

Notwithstanding the events in New York, Shaw and Warner regularly comment on the presence of an audience as an intrinsic part of each performance (Shaw and Warner 2014; Giannachi and Luckhurst 1999: 138). I therefore also assess Warner's work following Erika Fischer-Lichte's suggestion that 'the artistic and aesthetic nature of performance would instead be derived solely from its nature as an event' (Fischer-Lichte 2008: 162). Fischer-Lichte suggests meaning is not just *in* the performance content, but produced *of* the work at the moment of its enactment.[11] So for Rhys Ifans, who played the Fool in Warner's 2016 production of *King Lear* (Old Vic, London), with Glenda Jackson as Lear,

> it wasn't always very clear what she was looking for and probably wasn't for her either, but there was a quiet confidence throughout, never a moment of panic, and then as soon as we hit the stage, with an audience, it went to another level.
> (BBC Radio 4 2016)

Brook himself concludes, 'this is more than a truism: in the theatre the audience completes the steps of creation' (Brook 1988: 142). Warner thus animates the live event through her prioritisation of the actor as both character and performative figure, inside an ensemble, and explicitly sharing a performance. As I go on to explore in relation to design, Warner's work should further be understood as the making of 'eventful' space or, to follow Fischer-Lichte, the material production of 'spatiality' of theatre (Fischer-Lichte 2008: 162).

Actor(s)

Warner is quite open about the fact that when the Old Vic approached her to consider directing *King Lear*, she was not looking again to direct a play she had already staged twice (at the National Theatre and with Kick Theatre in 1985). What persuaded her was meeting Glenda Jackson, who had not performed on stage for some 23 years following her move into politics (BBC Radio 4 2016).[12] It is from Jackson that the idea for this ambitious theatrical comeback stemmed, and at the age of 80.[13] Age aside, Warner also cuts through issues of gender in relation to Jackson, to insist 'she's speaking as Glenda. There's no question as to who's there' (BBC Radio 4 2016). Even with the iconic figure of Lear, Warner places the exposure of Jackson's own persona, identity, and indeed body centrally in the production.

Indeed, a fundamental, consistent directorial approach across Warner's work is the casting of actors on the basis of not only their ability to work in an ensemble, but what they offer as creative personalities; Carol Chillington Rutter draws on an older interview (1989) in her assessment, where Warner confirms, 'I don't direct plays [...] I direct actors' ideas' (Rutter 2008: 475).[14] Attested to by her long-standing collaboration with Shaw, this insistence also explains the length of Warner's rehearsals, in which mutually acceptable ideas need time to emerge and be proven.[15] If Warner requires actors who collaboratively contribute something to the creative process beyond sheer skill, her stance also maintains what Fischer-Lichte elaborates as the

> tension between the phenomenal body of the actor, or their bodily being-in-the-world, and their representation of the dramatic character. [...] Humans have bodies, which they can manipulate and instrumentalize just like any other object. At the same time, they are their bodies, they are body-subjects.
>
> (Fischer-Lichte 2008: 76)

Despite choices in characterisation, for Fischer-Lichte, actors cannot erase their individuated, corporeal beings, and how they are perceived by spectators. Notwithstanding the general critical admiration for Jackson's stage technique, it is thus Warner's attraction to Jackson as someone 'being wholly oneself and flowing into the role' (BBC Radio 4 2016) that enforced her decision to direct this major play for the third time.

Most importantly, Warner's promotion of not only an ensemble ethos, but also a set of consciously individual personalities, intends in some way to confront and revitalise a text. In her conversation with Simon Russell-Beale, Rutter reports how Warner actively used Russell-Beale's own uncertainty when playing Cassius in *Julius Caesar* (Barbican Theatre, London, 2005). Russell-Beale felt he was not a 'typical' casting for the role, not athletic or 'cool' enough. But Warner urged Russell-Beale to continue, 'to strip away his preconceptions [...] to find "needy"' (Rutter 2008: 480) and an interpretation where Cassius would be 'the lone grammar school boy amongst a load of Etonians' (Rutter 2008: 480). And for *King Lear*, Warner brought together, as she puts it,

> not your usual Shakespearean crowd and that was [...] pointed. I wanted to do that, I wanted to bring in new sounds, new noises, if you will. And sitting on top of that was not an old sound at all, because Glenda could never do that. Glenda new-mints in the moment.
>
> (BBC Radio 4 2016)

Here, Warner again suggests her listening to and 'sounding' of a text; her description suggests almost a pre-emptive acoustic event (to recall Fischer-Lichte's term). Nevertheless, Jackson's status or, perhaps, reputation as 'body-subject' was inescapable; as Morfydd Clark (playing Cordelia) reports, 'we all had to see what Glenda was offering really, and then we've created a play around that' (BBC Radio 4 2016). Yet Warner seems to be a director unlikely to seek out some sort of leading actor, though, in this case, she productively harnesses the inescapable presence of the conjoined body-subject of, so to speak, the hybridised Jackson-Lear.

Warner conjoins an ensemble ethos and mutual 'sounding' of the text through her regular technique of shared reading in rehearsal. For *King Lear*, the text was read repeatedly for the first two weeks of the eight-week rehearsal period, but with no actor reading her or his own part. In the iterative readings, actors thus perform those characters they will eventually play opposite in a scene. The strategy serves initially to expose the text outside of any interpretation filtered through an individual's personality and as an ensemble tactic predicated on the text.

If Warner clearly intended to promote a mutual understanding of the play, Jackson's 'phenomenal body' emerged as an initial interpretative position for both Lear and the play itself. Warner reports how she was

> struck by the possibility of having an eighty-year-old Lear and what that did to the play. And in the mind the possibility of casting somersaults, and you think, ah, but this is really interesting because of course this lifts the ages of the daughters.
>
> (BBC Radio 4 2016)

To foreground the issue of particularly middle-aged children dealing with elderly parents was not an initial decision, but one where, for Warner, 'suddenly that part of the play shot into the fore', offering, to recall Brook, a different sort of essence (BBC Radio 4 2016). Yet set against this apparently frail Jackson-Lear body-subject was the sizeable bodily presence of Ifans. Warner reveals how she not only had to convince Ifans to take part, but that casting him deliberately upended the iconic image of Lear, at whose feet the Fool crouches (BBC Radio 4 2016). In Warner's production, it is the actually aged figure of Lear that follows the comparatively statuesque Ifans.

The body emerges as a key site of meaning in Warner's other productions; she cast David Threlfall as Bolingbroke in *Richard II*, who physically resembled Shaw. Describing the inherently complex, sexualised behaviour between the two, Elizabeth Klett reinforces how 'the mirroring of the two characters through the physical resemblance of the actors [...] indicated that Richard was losing half of himself' (Klett 2006: 192). Like the example of Russell-Beale, casting is, here, Warner's tactic to create the preconditions not only to undo received production traditions, but also to create an ecology of possibility.

Rehearsal

Speaking of rehearsing *Happy Days* (National Theatre 2007), Warner describes her rehearsal room as 'a place of colossal experimentation', in which 'something different happens every day and every second' (National Theatre 2007). Warner's rehearsals are defined by their intense sense of enquiry, a refusal to impose staging possibilities unless they emerge out of the collision of space, objects, actor, and text, all of which is constantly evaluated by her. Rehearsals for *The Power Book* (National Theatre 2002) appear most like an early devising phase in other companies' or directors' work (National Theatre 2002).[16] The author of the source novel, Jeanette Winterson, had agreed to produce a shortened version as the basis for rehearsal. Around a quarter of the text was used, but, in the early workshop period, Warner had not determined the final cast numbers.

While Warner's rehearsals demonstrate a fundamental respect for the text, they are always the basis for an investigation of clear physical action, discovered by the actor, up on her or his feet. Describing Shaw, Warner observes that 'bravery characterises Fiona. She will, in rehearsal, do and try anything. When she's with a group, what is fantastic is that she'll lead [...]. People will absolutely follow and get better because of her' (Shaw and Warner 2014). Again, Warner's concern is what her actors are *like*, what they offer, but, as Rutter suggests, where they must also 'remember physically' (Rutter 2008: 479). Mitchell typically starts with analysis of the text 'around the table' as the basis for imaginative speculation, decision, and improvisation; Warner, however, is closer to the actor-centric intent of Ivo van Hove, though without the contemporary 'cool' of his aesthetic, in which bodies collide in works closer to performance than introverted drama.

Reflecting on preparing *Happy Days*, Warner sees her role in rehearsal as creating 'a situation where that [experiment] can occur, and help people towards that place' (National Theatre 2007). *Happy Days* continued its experimentation in relation to an audience as it toured extensively in Europe, including an outdoor performance in Epidaurus, Greece.[17] And despite her previous problems with the Beckett estate – which insisted Warner close her production of *Footfalls* (1994) after she made minor textual changes (see Warner 1996: 230–31) – part of the 'situation' for *Happy Days* involved erasing the stage directions, with which the text is peppered, including gestural and delivery instructions.[18] As Shaw explains, she did not want to feel 'choreographed', both physically and in terms of delivery, clearly anathema to how the pair prefer to work in rehearsal (National Theatre 2007). In terms of pauses, Shaw is adamant that, as an actor, 'you have to find what that space is' (Shaw and Warner 2014); despite the dictates of the text, it is only in rehearsal that such space can be discovered. Further, Shaw and Warner wished to 'experiment' and find 'a new Winnie' in the play, one of glamour and charm, and based, they reveal, on someone they knew (National Theatre 2007).

For Warner, it is the slow *doing* of rehearsal that allows actors to 'grip', actually, amid the evolving, material environment. Objects populate the space: in rehearsal for *The Testament of Mary*, for example, a bird cage, a ladder, a vase, and dice appear in the room; some items support characterisation, such as a roll-up cigarette, a bottle of booze; some are emblematic: nails, a wound rope, a sponge, a coil of barbed wire. Like her work when approaching *Mother Courage* (National Theatre 2009), when Shaw added objects to a belt and tied other items of clothing around her waist, she experimented with costume here too, wrapping herself in a blanket; finally, she moves forward slowly, holding a hammer sideways (Shaw and Warner 2014). Here, there is a taxonomy of objects: to be used instrumentally; to enhance characterisation; as costume; and emergent from the world of the play (see Plate 13). These objects were largely maintained in the French production, though explored with and performed by another long-term collaborator, Dominique Blanc.[19] In Warner's directing, props are carefully selected 'ordinary objects, their simplicity charged with unstagey truthfulness' (Rutter 2008: 476). These are things of haptic possibility: objects to be grasped, thrown, used as weapons; or given place because of their power of memorialisation. Thus, Warner allows the materiality – the graspability – of objects to link the organising scenography of the space with the precise materiality of the actor's work.

Gender

One of the most hostile critical responses to Warner's work has been to her production of *Richard II*. Some of the most vitriolic (and ill-considered) criticism accused the pair of wishing slowly to deprive male actors of 'their' canon of Shakespearean roles.[20] Warner simply claims Shaw was for her 'the most exciting and suitable Richard I could think of' (quoted in Klett 2006: 176) and has subsequently formed a 'remarkably low opinion' of the critics since the debacle (Warner 1996: 234).

Notwithstanding the irony of the typically effusive press response around Declan Donnellan's all-male productions of Shakespeare, press criticism also seems to miss Warner's fundamental respect for the text, from which, in this case, the Warner–Shaw decision arose.[21] Rather than a politicised attempt to stimulate discussion about societal construction of gender, and certainly not deliberately to provoke critical ire, Warner's view of *Richard II* is that the play is 'not about the nature of gender, it's about the nature of being' (Klett 2006: 176; see also Silverstone 2007). And despite what the press might assume as her directorial machinations with canonical text, when Warner directs Shakespeare she asks that her contract states it should be played uncut.[22] This apparently purist stance is not to avoid directorial intent and interpretation, but rather not to shirk 'knotty text' (Rutter 2008: 479). Warner makes her task harder through her textual integrity, here illuminated by her apparent political avoidance yet materially visible staging of gender. Thus, critic Paul Taylor sprung to Shaw and Warner's defence, writing

> the invidiousness rampant in the critical reaction was well-nigh illogical. Fiona Shaw's dazzlingly discomforting impersonation of Richard is so integral to the thinking behind Deborah Warner's gripping, lucidly felt production that it would only make sense to like neither or both.
>
> (Taylor 1995)

Here, Warner's direction and Shaw's performance are critically indivisible; this is no wilful 'experiment', but a production in which

Warner's insistence on Shaw's suitability for the role needs to be understood in the context of a pre-emptive directorial vision.

The overt *performance* of Richard as a gender-based construction exploits in the extreme what Fischer-Lichte determines as the 'oscillation between phenomenal body and character' (Fischer-Lichte 2008: 86). To clash Shaw's female physiology with Richard was, for Klett, further to create the theatrical androgynous; this Richard should not be understood as stable, since it 'confounds the spectator's interpretations through her indecipherability, and alienates gender identity, showing it is a spectrum rather than static binary' (Klett 2006: 182). Shaw remains Shaw, but in this case is not just doubled as the character, but sets up a tripartite, and in fact overlapping, 'oscillation' between her identities as, simultaneously, actor, intersecting bodies of man and king, and her own female body.

As Klett discusses, Warner's material staging choices magnified the constructed complication of 'Richard'. Shaw had a kind of base costume, which tightly bound her body, and in which she could be seen being dressed behind a screen at the outset of the performance, along with the additional trappings of kingship.[23] In fact, something of a feature in Warner's direction is the staging of this kind of preparation as a kind of prologue. As in *Mother Courage*, *The Power Book* (National Theatre 2002) presented the space as functionally theatrical too: the ensemble appeared before the performance, and fly bars and television screens were flown in.[24] Such tightly choreographed prologues are deliberate presentations; in *Richard II*, Shaw shattered the staging of constriction behind the screen and entered the playing space at a run. But Richard's clothing further complicated the androgynous presentation by incorporating tunic or skirt-like apparel, underneath which the staged binding of Shaw's body cannot somehow erase her female corporeality, merely render it performatively constrained. Her body is not 'just' an actor's body, but remains resolutely female; even in staged moments of its erasure, she is *made ready* to display the kingly, 'other' body of Richard. In the evidently staged eventfulness of this performance, Warner draws attention to a Richard that both performs and is already quite obviously performed by a woman.

Typical of Warner's work, the central relationship between Richard and Bolingbroke was explored as intensely complex and personal. Alongside the pluralising of roles through dress and, as explored by Klett, the various regal objects handled by Richard, Shaw's performance was replete with the consciously chosen physical behaviour of touches, embraces, kisses, and submission. For Klett, such physicality was neither 'heterosexual or homosexual because the kiss was performed by two androgynous actors who resembled each other [...] and thus presented a queer take on Shakespeare's play' (Klett 2006: 193). As Warner entirely intended, her production troubled the received homosexual readings of the play. Klett makes the point that critics may well have been responding to such deliberate unsettling (Klett 2006: 187–8); this Richard was just not as apparently stable as a woman in male drag. In contrast, Jackson regularly refers to Lear as 'he' (BBC Radio 4 2016); if questions of gender seemed always deferred in that case, for Warner, age was of most concern as a thematic exploration. In both productions, it is however bold casting which necessarily draws attention to the eventfulness of the act of performance, which in *Richard II* radically undid the 'baggage' of the play through theatrical conditions, not a political investigation. Indeed, when *Richard II* travelled to France, Warner's vision, and the British critical reaction to it, made the front page of a bemused *Le Monde*.[25]

Audience

In contrast to her overall ethos of rehearsal, Warner admits she will take a more proactive, decisive role as first performances approach. She observes, 'this often surprises actors I haven't worked with before, because up until that point they have felt very free, and then, suddenly, I urge them to follow one path [...] they have to trust me completely' (Giannachi and Luckhurst 1999: 138). While not evidencing a domineering stance, Warner clearly *makes* things occur, yet still places the actor as the material basis of the performance event and its first encounter with an audience, after which the 'experiment' continues. Yet there is not *an* audience; as Shaw, speaking of *Happy*

Days, puts it, 'the audience doesn't laugh as a group' (National Theatre 2007). Each performance causes a particular plurality of reaction both within its 'eventfulness' and in comparison to previous performances, through, as Fischer-Lichte puts it, a circumstantial 'circulation of energy' (Fischer-Lichte 2008: 162).

The exploration of emotion as a particular 'circulation of energy' can especially be traced in Warner's work. Warner finds *Richard II* 'Shakespeare's most emotional play', since 'its theme is intimacy, and that's a very emotional thing' (Warner 1996: 231), a kind of Brookian 'essential' that prefaces, too, Shaw's view of *A Testament of Mary*, above. Much earlier, work on *Electra* (RSC, 1991) explicitly foregrounded emotion in a production where, for Warner, 'grief could be almost a character' (Almeida Theatre 2015). As Warner recounts, to construct credible 'backstories' in rehearsal provided a secure basis for the emotional territory of the play, a strategy Jackson also recounts in relation to *King Lear* (BBC Radio 4 2016). Again, Warner's work centralises the profundity, fragility, and (as in *Medea*, 2000), the treachery of relationships.

Space(s)

For Warner, 'the question of space lies at the heart of theatre' (Giannachi and Luckhurst 1999: 139). She has had a particularly enduring partnership with the designer Hildegard Bechtler, and latterly others including Jean Kalman and Tom Pye, sustained relationships that suggest that, alongside her primary interest in the actor, she centralises design in the collaborative, aesthetic realisation of the chosen play.[26] Yet some commentators have found her 'minimalist' staging austere; as Rutter puts it, 'emptiness appeals to her' (Rutter 2008: 475). Warner's spaces are not empty though, but much like Donnellan and Nick Ormerod's approach in Cheek by Jowl's work (another long-term director–designer partnership), they are rather uncluttered spaces, where decor is often displaced to the actor's bodies.

Perhaps it is not emptiness (to recall Brook) that Warner desires, but the potentiality of space, or what Fischer-Lichte calls 'performative space', which offers the preconditions for the 'kinaesthetic and perceptual opportunities granted to actor and spectators' (Fischer-Lichte 2008: 107). Warner's sets are thus environments that open up a conception of the play, an approach linked also to her exploration of site-based performance (see below). If, as van Hove puts it, 'if you look [the set] already tells a story' (Thielemans 2010: 458), then Warner's sets should be understood as productive spatialities (Fischer-Lichte), with only carefully selected elements of material power. Rutter observes of the early *King John*, featuring a set comprised of metal ladders, that Warner's 'collision of (modern) ladder with (antique) armour was a materially precise visual proxy for the collision of ideas located at the heart of her production' (Rutter 2008: 484). This is no reductive minimalism, but rather a form of expressive essentialism.

Understandably, at one point in her career, Warner wanted radically to reject her studio-based early experience; reflecting on *Richard II*, she declares

> I'm sick to death of small studio spaces. I find them the death of theatre. I was brought up on them and they nurtured me, but they're so boring now. I find them dull, and I wanted the Cottesloe to excite me.
>
> (Warner 1996: 232)

She has bemoaned the lack of flexible spaces encountered in her early work at the RSC and the fact that the National's Cottesloe Theatre (latterly modified and renamed the Dorfman) is relatively small. These venues appear restrictive, uniformly tight spaces that in their black boxes oppress Warner's preferred aesthetics of space, especially width. For *Richard II*, Warner eventually challenged the space restriction of the Cottesloe, explaining 'we made it as big as we could. We made it worthy of the design' (Warner 1996: 232) and used traverse staging.[27] Bechtler's design offered a figurative expression of the play; as Warner puts it, 'it happens in a corridor [...]. Your focus is not on the rooms either side of the corridor, but on the corridor itself and the people passing through it' (Warner 1996: 232). The audience thus might be at 'a tennis match. Or on the benches in the House of Commons. Or behind barriers at a joust. Heads had to swivel left, right; to take in this, then that; there was no consensus viewpoint' (Rutter 2008: 488).

In a play that explores the double nature of Richard and Bolingbroke, the audience too is doubled in its 'reflected' self in the parallel seating bank across the 'corridor', a staging configuration most common in the work of Eugenio Barba (see Kuhlmann and Ledger 2018). Rather than passive spectators, the seating banks support, in effect, witnesses who somehow have a viewpoint not on the machinations of the corridors of power, but on a lack of power and its negotiation in transitional places amid a kingless state. This production is hardly austere, but a deliberate design construction, implicating the audience in a space that offers the possibility of multiple voyeurism. As with Barba's work, here the traverse staging is a political scenography of the spectator.

Spatiality

Speaking of *The Power Book*, Warner states she wished to 'provoke a new form' (National Theatre 2002) and that she knew from the beginning video would be part of the means to convey the content drawn from Winterson's novel, which shifts around in terms of place and time. It was further developed on tour (2003) at Warner's regular venue, the Théâtre de Chaillot, Paris, and as part of the RomaEuropa Festival, Rome. *The Power Book* was, for its time, ambitious, making full use of available video technology and projection. For Fischer-Lichte, such 'spatiality [...] does not exist before, beyond, or after the performance but emerges in and through it' (Fischer-Lichte 2008: 107); here space is made, it is an active expression of theatrical content, and performance becomes the material arena of its occasion. Like the self-conscious Brechtian tactics of *Mother Courage*, *The Power Book* also demonstrated the means of its theatrical production.

In Warner's work, space is not bounded by a passive set, which encompasses the play, but rather the platform upon which the ensemble continues its exploration of the material. At the outset of *King Lear* stage hands appear, setting out chairs as if at a rehearsal. Co-designed with Warner by French designer and artist Jean Kalman, the production slowly evolved into scenographic life and characters emerged out of the gloom, traversing the length of the large Old Vic stage. As one review noted, Warner's tactic was one of 'continually bringing the action from its depths: it is as if the audience sees tragedy coming towards it through the mists of time' (Clapp 2016). Such figurative spatiality – here, a theatrical phenomenon of the foreboding of tragedy – was reinforced when the iconic storm scene was realised through the resolutely practical billowing of black plastic. To recall van Hove's link between set and story, Warner finds the form to tell her story, but her story is also the means – the spatiality – of its making.

Site

Warner's site-based projects may seem distinct from her theatre work, but nevertheless demonstrate a continued experimentation around the materiality of space and the (sometimes solo) experience of the audience. Warner resists the term 'site-specific', and suggests that *Footfalls*, which was staged using the auditorium of the Garrick Theatre, London, and site-responsive iterations of *The Waste Land* (1995), constitute, for her, a beginning to this area of work (Giannachi and Luckhurst 1999: 139–40). A more obvious starting point comprised her taking over of the Midland Grand Hotel (London) to create the *St Pancras Project* (1995), in which individual spectators followed a line through the dilapidated building to encounter half-glimpsed figures and objects.[28] Similarly, *The Tower Project* (1999) explored an empty office block in central London, prefiguring the several iterations of *The Angel Project* (2003) (London, New York, Perth); in this latter work, Warner's tactic was to 'set images, symbols, artifacts and people, then inviting the viewer to traverse them, looking inward and outward to the landscape we call home' (The Angel Project). *The Waste Land*, based on T. S. Eliot's poem of the same name and performed by Shaw, was also enhanced by each 'found' site it was revived in, and is Warner's most worldwide production.[29] A further multi-site project for the 2012 Cultural

Olympics, *Peace Camp*, which celebrated love poetry, created simultaneous installations of illuminated tents around the UK coastline, to be visited at night. Taken together, this is a remarkable *oeuvre* of work, demonstrating not only Warner's focus on the specifically and poetically poignant, but her insistence on securing European and international venues to continue her innovations.

While William McEvoy rightly explores Warner's site-based projects as a kind of textuality, to be 'read' intertextually (McEvoy 2006), to call her explorations of place 'site-specific' is not quite correct (McEvoy 2006: 591). In the instances where actual text is used (most notably *The Waste Land*), the performance is not made in order to explore and articulate a site, but to resonate against it, and where the core of the performance remains the same. Following McEvoy's reference to Mike Pearson, and his survey of writings on site-based work, *The Waste Land* is better understood as 'site-referenced', 'site conscious', 'site-responsive', or '*site-generic*' (Pearson 2010: 8, original emphasis); that is, regardless of the terminology, it was reworked according to its many different performance locations, but did not rely on them. It appears also to work in *kinds* of space; those abandoned, damaged, bereft, or awaiting restoration.

If, for Fischer-Lichte, spatiality is produced, these productions do so via 'special possibilities for the relationship between actors and spectators and for movement and perception' (Fischer-Lichte 2008: 107). In the various versions of *The Angel Project*, for example, spectators journeyed between a sequence of installations, constituting the site-specific piece. In *The Tower Project* too, installation elements were thus both a response to and imposition on, an intervention in, or a 'haunting' of the site, such as the fax machine in one room printing pages from Milton's *Paradise Lost*, at once an isolated, dehumanised action, yet curiously thematically appropriate. And in *The St Pancras Project*, the solitary, walking spectator glimpsed staff, objects such as half-finished meals left abandoned, and perceived fragments of sound and movement. Echoing Pearson and others on the 'host' and 'ghost' in site-based work, Kate Kellaway reflects, 'the remarkable effect of the walk was that it turned the walker into a ghost haunting the building, upsetting its occupants with the heavy tread of another time' (Kellaway, in McEvoy 2006: 595).

Warner's site-based 'experiments' concern not only place, but also its storification, in order to offer an experience built of carefully selected interventions inspired by the space. These found and installed material elements oscillate against the location in moments that are (to use another term) site-sympathetic, albeit with, as McEvoy puts it, 'a self-consciousness about intertexts, their artfulness, cultural capital, and symbolic power' (McEvoy 2006: 601). The relationship between solo spectator and site creates the 'text' through Warner's fabricated revelation of possible buried narratives, whereas with *The Waste Land*, this relationship is that between an audience and the content of the material, yet which is influenced by the space of the 'host'. Warner's work is, then, not completely about the site per se, but affords an experience *of* a site; the solo spectator or, in the case of *The Waste Land* in particular, the text and its delivery, become visiting ghosts, each housed (hosted) and affected by a site.

Director

For Warner to suggest that she has no particular approach to directing is not to say that she neglects process. Quite the contrary; her approach is one of enquiry based over considerable time. Given her sense of exploration, she is unusual as a director in that she will see a production as often as she can, regularly giving notes. But, as she clarifies, 'giving lots of notes is not about trying to keep the thing in one place' (National Theatre 2009). For Warner, a production cannot remain a homogeneous, methodically repeatable whole: as she confirms in terms of her European presence, 'to take the work abroad is to develop it hugely' (National Theatre 2009); even once a production has opened, the experiment continues.

If Warner begins directing inside the Brookian 'empty space', this is conceived as an already imaginative invocation; in collaboration with her designers, the place of performance invites her eventual vision of the theatrically eventful. Some may find Warner austere, but this is not to say that her designs are bleak. To look at her online archive hardly gives the impression of a scenographic austerity (deborahwarner.com), nor do designs repeat themselves as a particular directorial 'signature', as in some of her European contemporaries' work. Next, textual formalities must be both respected and penetrated in order to expose the magnitude of relationships and the complexity of situations. Especially given her interest in the bodily presence, action, and reaction of actors, Warner's work is resolutely material; and, in some of her work, the politics of a gendered theatrical telling come too from an interest in such essentials made particular.

In her site-based work, Warner opens up a locale in the same way as a play is 'opened'. Like the theatre work, an audience – even if an audience of one – is always acknowledged as part of the unfolding event; as Taylor puts it of *The St Pancras Project*, 'the building in this case constituted the experience, as vestigial ghosts of its former existence stirred, flitted, and half-materialised at the corner of your eye, making you feel like Alice alone in a serially haunting dream' (Taylor 2006). Here, and across her work, Warner constructs the possibility of experience; as a director, her role is to shift the articulation of the dramaturgy of space and spectatorship, to *make* the spatiality of a perceptual, mental, or imaginative landscape. To return to Brook, Warner takes the 'empty space' and carefully populates it, such that her theatre is (again to follow Brook) a mixture of the rough and the holy, but intends, primarily, always to be the immediate.

Governed only by a sense of discovery and the ultimately mutual event of performance, Warner releases ideas through the actuality of objects and shared space, and the 'sounding' of text through the body of the actor. Her directing is deeply rooted in the trust placed in long rehearsal; it may not demonstrate an objective methodology, but certainly a confidence in the risk of process.

Five key productions

The Waste Land. By T. S. Eliot. Lighting by Jean Kalman. Perf. Fiona Shaw. Théâtre du Vaudeville, Kunsten Festival, Brussels. 13 May 1995.

Richard II. By William Shakespeare. Set design by Hildegard Bechtler. Perf. Fiona Shaw, David Threlfall, Graham Crowden. Cottesloe Theatre, National Theatre, London. 26 May 1995.

The St Pancras Project: A Fantastical Walk. Devised. Designed by Hildegard Bechtler. Midland Grand Hotel, London. 18 June 1995.

Medea. By Euripides, trans. Kenneth McLeish. Set design by Tom Pye. Costume design by Tom Rand. Perf. Fiona Shaw, Patrick O'Kane, Barry McGovern. Abbey Theatre, Dublin. 1 June 2000.

King Lear. By William Shakespeare. Set design by Jean Kalman. Costume design by Zeb Lalljee. Perf. Glenda Jackson, Rhys Ifans, Jane Horrocks. Old Vic Theatre, London. 25 October 2016.

Notes

1 *The Testament of Mary*, with Fiona Shaw, was staged at the Walter Kerr Theatre, New York, in May 2012; it was revived at the Barbican Theatre, London, in May 2014.
2 Warner and Shaw began working together in 1982 when Shaw appeared in *Woyzeck* for Warner's Kick Theatre Company.
3 See too the discussion of Warner in Helen Manfull's *Taking Stage: Women Directors on Directing* (Manfull 1999).
4 See also my earlier account of Warner in Ledger (2013).
5 See www.deborahwarner.com and @deborahwarner59.
6 Brook established the theatre in 1971. *Titus Andronicus* was supported by the British Council and toured to the Sala Olimpia, Madrid, 9–19 March 1989; Théâtre des Bouffes du Nord, Paris, 22 March–1 April 1989; Ostre Gasvaerk Teater, Copenhagen, 4–9 April 1989; and the Ridehuset, Aarhus, 12–14 April 1989.
7 Warner received an Honorary Fellowship from Central in 2017; she has been the Cameron Mackintosh Visiting Professor of Contemporary Theatre at the University of Oxford; she is an associate artist of the Barbican Theatre. In January 2020, Warner was named artistic director of the Theatre Royal Bath's Ustinov Studio.
8 Warner's website documents the major opera productions that developed through the early part of the millennium. See also Warner's quite different reaction to opera in *Le Monde* (Roux 2008).

9 The title of Brecht's play *Der gute Mensch von Sezuan* is variously translated, hence the different spellings employed in this chapter. The ensemble cast of *King Lear* also performed *Richard III*, directed by Richard Eyre.
10 One of the most self-regarding British responses being Spencer (2011). See also n. 20.
11 Fischer-Lichte acknowledges that she builds upon, and departs from, the work of Heidegger, Derrida, and Lyotard.
12 Jackson was Member of Parliament for Hampstead and Highgate, London (latterly Hampstead and Kilburn) from 1992 to 2015. She was Parliamentary Under-Secretary (Department of Environment) from 1997 to 1999 and Shadow Spokesperson (Transport) from 1996 to 1997, and served on the Work and Pensions Committee from 2010 to 2015.
13 The idea appears to stem from Jackson seeing Núria Espert, who had directed her in *The House of Bernarda Alba* (1986), play Lear at 80 in Lluís Pasqual's production (see Teatre Barcelona). Jackson subsequently played Lear in a new production on Broadway (2019), directed by Sam Gold; see Sehgal (2019). It is also worth noting that Brian Cox, who played the title role in *Titus Andronicus*, encouraged the RSC's then artistic director, Terry Hands, to consider inviting Warner to direct it; see Dupont (1989).
14 Rutter quotes from an interview in *The Observer*, 30 April 1989.
15 Warner reports that *Mother Courage* was not even run through before technical rehearsals began (National Theatre 2009).
16 *The Power Book* also toured to Paris and Rome in 2003.
17 The production opened in the Lyttelton Theatre (NT, 2007) and that year toured to: the Epidaurus Festival, Greece (where it returned in 2008); the Théâtre de Chaillot, Paris; the Matadero, Madrid; and the Kennedy Center, Washington. In 2008, it toured to: BAM, New York; the Stadsschouwburg, Amsterdam as part of the Holland Festival; and the Abbey Theatre, Dublin.
18 The Beckett Estate also banned Warner from staging Beckett plays for a while.
19 At L'Odéon, Théâtre de l'Europe, Paris (2017), translated by Anne Gibson and co-produced by the Comédie-Française.
20 See Klett (2006) for a summary.
21 See, for example, the British Council's gloss of 'enraptured audiences' for Donnellan's Russian all-male production of *Twelfth Night* (which toured extensively internationally from 2003) (British Council) and his own reflection on the global success of Cheek By Jowl's *As You Like It* (1991, 1994) (Donnellan 2014).
22 Rutter (2008) also mentions this stipulation.

23 The tactic of 'costuming' the king has appeared in other productions, though here takes on a further meaning, of course.
24 This flying was cued in the prompt script to make it part of the performance, rather than pre-show rigging; it, and others, are available in the National Theatre Archive. I remember that before the second half of *Mother Courage* began, Shaw was quite visible offstage chatting 'on cans'.
25 Paul Taylor also mentions this in his useful overview of Warner (Taylor 1996).
26 Similar, international points of comparison might be Ivo van Hove's work with Jan Versweyveld, Katie Mitchell's with Vicky Mortimer and Alex Eales, and Thomas Ostermeier with Jan Pappelbaum.
27 Traverse staging is sometimes known as alley staging in the USA.
28 The hotel was later refurbished and is now known as the St Pancras Renaissance Hotel.
29 *The Waste Land* was performed internationally from 1995 to 2010; see www.deborahwarner.com/2010-the-waste-land-madrid.

Bibliography

Alexander, Catherine (2010) 'Complicité - *The Elephant Vanishes*', in Jen Harvie and Andy Lavender (eds), *Making Contemporary Theatre: International Rehearsal Processes*, Manchester: Manchester University Press, pp. 59–80.

Almeida Theatre (2015) 'Why Greeks Matter – Rupert Goold, Ivo van Hove and Deborah Warner', 12 June, www.youtube.com/watch?v=i6kYz-wx2rg

'The Angel Project', www.deborahwarner.com/2003-the-angel-project-new-york

BBC Radio 4 (2016) 'Glenda Jackson and the Making of King Lear', 27 December, www.bbc.co.uk/programmes/b085t2wd

Boenisch, Peter (2015) *Directing Scenes and Senses: The Thinking of Regie*, Manchester: Manchester University Press.

British Council, "Twelfth Night" by the Chekhov Festival, www.britishcouncil.ru/en/en/events/chekhov-international-theatre-festival

Brook, Peter (1988) *The Empty Space*, London: Penguin.

Clapp, Susannah (2016) 'King Lear Review – Glenda Jackson is Magnificent', *Observer*, 13 November, www.theguardian.com/stage/2016/nov/13/king-lear-review-glenda-jackson-old-vicDeborahwarner.com

Donnellan, Declan (2014) 'All You Need is Love: Adrian Lester and the Miraculous All-Male *As You Like It*', *The Guardian*, 12 November, www.theguardian.com/stage/2014/nov/12/all-male-as-you-like-it-cheek-by-jowl-declan-donnellan-adrian-lester

Dupont, Joan (1989) 'Life and Death Are the Actors On Her Stage', *New York Times*, 23 April, www.nytimes.com/1989/04/23/theater/theater-life-and-death-are-the-actors-on-her-stage.html

Fischer-Lichte, Erika (2008) *The Transformative Power of Performance: A New Aesthetics*, trans. Saskya Iris Jain, Abingdon: Routledge.

Giannachi, Gabriella and Mary Luckhurst (1999) 'Deborah Warner', in Gabriella Giannachi and Mary Luckhurst (eds), *On Directing: Interviews with Directors*, London: Faber and Faber, pp. 136–42.

Klett, Elizabeth (2006) 'Many Bodies, Many Voices: Performing Androgyny in Fiona Shaw and Deborah Warner's *Richard II*', *Theatre Journal*, 58: 175–94.

Kuhlmann, Annelis and Adam J. Ledger (2018) 'Eugenio Barba', in Paul Allain (ed.), *The Great European Stage Directors, Vol. 5*, London: Methuen Drama, pp. 145–202.

Ledger, Adam J. (2013) 'Great Britain', in Anne Fliotsos and Wendy Vierow (eds), *International Women Stage Directors*, Urbana, Chicago, and Springfield: University of Illinois Press, pp. 148–60.

Manfull, Helen (1999) *Taking Stage: Women Directors on Directing*, London: Methuen.

McEvoy, William (2006) 'Writing, Texts and Site-Specific Performance in the Recent Work of Deborah Warner', *Textual Practice*, 20(4): 591–614.

National Theatre (2002) 'Transformation Platform: On *The Power Book*', Platform Performance, 30 May.

—— (2007) 'Deborah Warner and Fiona Shaw on *Happy Days*', Platform Performance, 27 February.

—— (2009) 'Fiona Shaw and Deborah Warner on *Mother Courage*', Platform Performance, 8 October.

Pearson, Mike (2010) *Site-Specific Performance*, Basingstoke: Palgrave.

Roux, Marie-Aude (2008) '"Je suis convertie à l'opéra": Deborah Warner, issue du théâtre, met en scène "Didon et Enée", de Purcell, à Paris', *Le Monde*, 4 December, www.lemonde.fr/culture/article/2008/12/04/deborah-warner-je-suis-convertie-a-l-opera_1126822_3246.html

Rutter, Carol Chillington (2006) 'Facing History, Facing Now: Deborah Warner's *Julius Caesar* at the Barbican Theatre', *Shakespeare Quarterly*, 57(1): 71–85.

—— (2008) 'Deborah Warner', in John Russell Brown (ed.), *The Routledge Companion to Directors' Shakespeare*, Abingdon: Routledge, pp. 474–92.

Schneider, Rebecca and Gabrielle Cody (eds) (2003) *Re: Direction: A Theoretical and Practical Guide*, London and New York: Routledge.

Sehgal, Parul (2019) 'At 82, Glenda Jackson Commands the Most Powerful Role in Theatre', *New York Times*, March 27, www.nytimes.com/2019/03/27/magazine/glenda-jackson-king-lear.html

Shaw, Fiona and Deborah Warner (2014) 'Fiona Shaw and Deborah Warner', *Financial Times*, 9 April, www.ft.com/video/4b996f07-7246-363d-ae37-97e8ed440954

Silverstone, Catherine (2007) 'It's Not About Gender': Cross-Gendered Casting in Deborah Warner's *Richard II*', *Women: A Cultural Review*, 18(2): 199–212.

Spencer, Charles (2011) 'Did I Really Deserve to be called a Toad', *The Telegraph*, 6 June, www.telegraph.co.uk/culture/8560356/Did-I-really-deserve-to-be-called-a-toad.html

Taylor, Paul (1995) 'Second Opinion/Paul Taylor Defends Fiona Shaw's *Richard II* from the Baying Critics', *Independent*, 14 June, www.independent.co.uk/arts-entertainment/second-opinion-paul-taylor-defends-fiona-shaws-richard-ii-from-the-baying-critics-1586371.html

―――― (1996) 'Deborah Warner – Space, the Final Frontier' *Independent*, 13 April, www.independent.co.uk/life-style/interview-deborah-warner-space-the-final-frontier-1304528.html

―――― (2006) 'Deborah Warner – how I Learnt to Love Opera', *Independent*, 2 July, www.independent.co.uk/arts-entertainment/music/features/deborah-warner-how-i-learnt-to-love-opera-6096443.html

Teatre Barcelona (2015) 'Lluís Pasqual dirigeix Núria Espert a "El Rei Lear", 20 January, www.youtube.com/watch?v=YiqFBYGbz6g

Thielemans, Johan (2010) 'Ivo van Hove's Passionate Quest for a Necessary Theatre. An Interview', *Contemporary Theatre Review*, 20(4): 455–60.

Warner, Deborah interviewed by Geraldine Cousin (1996) 'Exploring Space at Play: The Making of the Theatrical Event', *New Theatre Quarterly*, 12(47): 229–36.

Chapter 14

ROMEO CASTELLUCCI

The director on this earth

Alan Read

Inferno

'Je m'appelle Romeo Castellucci.' 'My name is Romeo Castellucci' introduces the *Inferno*, from Dante's *The Divine Comedy*, in Avignon in 2008[1] and plunges this audience in the vast Cour d'Honneur of the Palais des Papes into a vertiginous aesthetic adventure. The man who has entered centre stage rear and walked to the apex of the playing space dons a padded suit and tenses himself. Downstage, seven Alsatian dogs from Les Cavaliers Voltigeurs de France are led on howling by their handlers and chained close to the customers, while Balkan, Bonzai, and Robin are unleashed to set about the Director of Socìetas Raffaello Sanzio (SRS) (see Plate 14). Self-scapegoating on behalf of us, the spectators, the director on this earth would appear to be guilty of something, but heaven knows what.

The faux-theatricality of the scene – the dogs are manifestly trained to within an inch of their canine senses and are possibly the best paid living organisms we will see in the next 24 hours – mixes humility with the grand gesture. Humility in the announcement: 'Je m'appelle Romeo Castellucci', a fact not doubted by a well-informed, festival-going, theatre-expert public in Avignon who in annual succession have witnessed his direction of *Giulio Cesare* (1998), *Journey to the End of the Night* (1999), *Genesi* (2000), *Tragedia Endogonidia Episode A2* (2002), *Tragedia B3 Berlin* and *Tragedia BR4 Brussells* (2005), and *Hey Girl!* (2007).[2] The definition of a grand gesture might as well be this centre stage introduction in the Cour d'Honneur with the founding text of Italian culture in the founding seat of Papal peripateticism.

Between this miniature announcement and this inconceivable architectural magnitude, another man emerges to take the skin of the director (an animal pelt passed on like so many other identities in this quixotic show). As unassuming as the earth-bound director, this figure begins to scale the windowed, sheer face wall of the Palais des Papes. Without apparent effort and little ceremony (a quality shared by Romeo Castellucci's work over more than a quarter of a century) this climber, who I guess from the programme to *Inferno* is Jeff Stein, works his way at an acute angle diagonally traversing the seams in the fourteenth-century masonry.

Obviously secure destinations such as window sills and the rose are passed without a second thought for us who from our seats offer concern, who will project care through the night towards the diminishing figure, but who accept the inevitable. On the way he swaggers in a manner that suggests Romeo Castellucci has bartered a strict allowance of showmanship in return for the climber tempering his excessive ease with this phenomenally daring act. It is not that his director on earth would ever remind this sure-footed ascendant above the earth that to be able to fall is a prerequisite for our affections; rather, it is so that his rate and manner of ascent might more literally play with our expectation of what it means to scale the largest domestic architectural structure we are ever likely to inhabit.

On the acutely angled porcelain roof 150 feet above us, unhooked from his safety wire (this is theatre, it is not about the suspension of disbelief in unlikely lines but the suspending of our belief on a line),[3] the climber holds a bright orange standard-issue basketball above his head and calls to a boy in spectacles way below who has wandered onto the stage. We are still recovering our stomachs from a reverse vertigo that, as the climber has climbed unfeasibly high towards the night sky, pitches us, the audience, somehow upwards to the building itself which in homeopathic symmetry comes falling down to meet us halfway. There has been some talk of theatrical effects but the direction of this particular manoeuvre, in this infernal place on earth, introduces us to the deepest, most interior sense of being fixed to our seats while being propelled from them.

The ball, meanwhile, familiar from *Tragedia Endogonidia R07 Rome*, in which a group of seminarians play a miraculous game of hoops, is pitched towards the earth and, following a line of flight that can be counted in one thousand heads, one, two, three, four terminates with an authentic-sounding thud and bounces to the second-storey window, to the first-storey lintel, and, this being a well-directed ball, on a third bounce into the hands of Jean. We know the boy in spectacles is Jean because, like other entrants to this *Inferno* who have introduced themselves, he has helpfully graffitied his name on the wall facing us (the one the climber has just climbed). This is the last time we hear the authentic bounce of the ball, because from this bounce on, each time Jean propels the ball to the stage, the stage and the ball unleash an amplified version of what a bouncing ball in this place (now not Earth but palpably some unearthly place) must sound like. This in turn unleashes a terrifying spectral presence in the building itself as though to remind us there will be no shelter there. That this is more *Exorcist* than naturalist introduces us to the first of many cinematic directions essential to this director's work.

By this time, perhaps 20 minutes into Romeo Castellucci's trilogy from Dante's *The Divine Comedy*, we have been introduced to the director, the edifice, and the *Inferno*.[4] There is little summative imperative, as this bare description attests, but rather a sequence of realised spectacles, gestures, and sounds that begin to hint at a job description for a director on this earth. The director's role would apparently be to remind us in hell that before we reach the inevitable stars (*étoiles*) of Dante's final stanzas, stars that in this version sit high above us on television monitors that crash to earth with their flickering linguistic sign of the heavens blacked out, that before that fall *we* have some accounting to do for our human life on this earth.

What follows is steady in its successive beats: a population of gaily dressed Avignonnaises falling backwards and downwards in front of a back projection naming those in this company who have died before this night; a limbo-like chamber of sealed, lit, and apparently audience-unaware playing children who are monitored by an officious-looking outsize soft toy sitting in the corner of this one-way mirrored kindergarten from hell; a billowing black crepuscular material growth from a wall the size of a house; a white horse who is rewarded for making one of theatre's longest and most anticipated entrances by being sprayed with blood red paint; and a Lucifer in a burnt-out auto wreck played by the girl from *Hey Girl!* in an Andy Warhol mask. This coda-like arrival of the most literal-minded of artists suggests that the director meant it all literally. As in Romeo Castellucci's other shows there is no metaphor or allegory to be hermeneutically plundered here (hence my straight description of what I saw the climber *do*): everything is on show and everything is in the show. And in the end, after two hours of congress on this honourable stage, we are left with only three small television screens of illumination, everything else is dark. We are left with 'T' 'O' 'I' from 'ÉTOILES', and Romeo means *us*. We are Romeo's YOU; he has constructed *Homo Spectator* again.

The figure of the director as artist, in this case Romeo Castellucci, is thus here fashioned in reverse vertigo to the Spectator as Witness on whose presence he depends. And never more so than in the topsy-turvy of (the) festival. What is it for us to be spectators of him and his spectacle, here in Avignon, in a festival that precisely purports to show showing? What does it mean for us as civic citizens to go in and out of theatres to journey between Romeo Castellucci's *Inferno* at night, Alvis Hermanis's *Sonia* the following day, Romeo Castellucci's *Purgatorio* that evening? We do fulfil our own spectatorial version of Aristotle's unities of time and place, 24 hours in Avignon, in this back and forth of looking. But we also in this epileptic, flickering encounter alternate our attentions like the alternating current that strobes the naturalistic, wallpapered back wall of Romeo Castellucci's *Purgatory*.

We will go there in a moment, there is no hurry, it is not about to go anywhere, that is its defining feature, but in the meantime to account for the interminable time between *Inferno* and *Purgatorio* I ask Romeo Castellucci some questions that have been given to me by the editors of this book. All directors should answer these questions, and Romeo Castellucci is no exception. He graciously accepts the rules of the game while hinting that conversation would be preferable. This is no idle chat, there is never a hint of dilettantism in his dialogues, and he is perhaps the most conversant director currently working on this earth as myriad conversations he has engaged in emerge from the past 25 years of his practice. Here are his answers, translated for me in the afternoon between *Inferno* and *Purgatorio* in the Cloître Saint-Louis by one of his trusted conversants, Joe Kelleher.

ALAN READ: How is theatre responding to the new Europe?

ROMEO CASTELLUCCI: Contemporary theatre is neither a critical reaction nor a comment on these times. No, contemporary theatre acts on the future and on that which is going to happen; indeed, even more: it holds past, present, and future in the same channel. Contemporary theatre has always been an operation on time and on the ineffability of time's fleeting capacity to run in all directions. 'New Europe' is now the political and communitarian dimension of this past of the West. To be 'enlarged' means, and probably has meant, a rethinking of its own history, in the light of the conflicts that have accompanied its becoming. It signifies, perhaps, rethinking its irreducible 'heart of darkness'; it signifies rethinking the collapse of representation that here, on these new European lands, took place during the epoch of the death camps, beyond any reservation that 'poetry was no longer possible'. This aesthetic tension of crisis, which derives from the ethical, has, it seems to me, been rethought. Contemporary theatre can continue to be the laboratory in which is rehearsed, *in vitro*, language and our sense of belonging to the species.

ALAN READ: How has the director's role changed?

ROMEO CASTELLUCCI: The director is a figure who has completely invaded the field of theatrical aesthetics. Their invention is total and their terrain is a radical emptiness from which to depart. I believe that the repertory theatre is destined to be a 'minor art' and to have other functions and tasks. The director of contemporary theatre has become an *artist* in the more complex and difficult sense of the term and his language can be compared to the visual arts. The director has become a figure who *creates* problems instead of trying to solve them. The repertory theatre director delivers a message, a sense, an evident meaning or a pedagogy which is derived from the interpretation of the great texts of the past, which are, as we know well, invincible, untouchable, marvellous.

ALAN READ: Can collective creation survive in an individualised, consumerist world?

ROMEO CASTELLUCCI: I don't believe that collective creation can still have the propulsive and generative force that it had in the 1970s. But that is not for a political reason. The reasons are, above all, the rediscovery of a language of investigation that draws nearer to the experience of the artist as a singular figure. I'm not talking about a reflection of the individualist world. I would rather speak of the solitude of the artist. And solitude is the other face of individualism, the more human and sincere face of a human condition common to us all, as in a sort of great city.

ALAN READ: Is theatre complicit in, or resistant to, these changes?

ROMEO CASTELLUCCI: I believe complicit, yes. By necessity theatre cannot but be favourable to these changes.

ALAN READ: How do directors engage with the global hegemony of the English language?

ROMEO CASTELLUCCI: Obviously this is a question that can have as many different responses as there are directors on this earth. In my personal experience the English language has no influence. I read and often document myself through the language (though I have never studied it), but I think and express myself in Italian. But also Italian is not a problem for me. First of all, there are images and sounds, which don't have a country nor a place of belonging nor a language.

ALAN READ: What is the function of the (classic) text in European directors' theatre?

ROMEO CASTELLUCCI: Very often an easy choice, a certain rhetoric as I said before. But obviously there are extraordinary exceptions. The problem is, however, that of escaping the illustrative or the mere 'reactualisation' of classic texts. Too many times Richard III is seen as a 'hunchback' or leather waistcoat and the invention is all in that. The great texts of the past will get exploded, will be absorbed epidermically, will be interiorised until their disappearance. A body of work emerges only to be overcome in the struggle.

ALAN READ: What is the future of the director in European theatre?

ROMEO CASTELLUCCI: I don't know the future of the director in European theatre. Everything can happen; and this possibility, this absolute opening, this possibility of the disappearing of everything, is the most exciting and vital thing in this work.

P u r g a t o r i o

In Purgatory we are decidedly 'at home'. Or at least what the director Romeo Castellucci has decided 'home' might stand for. You know you are in Purgatory because there is a sign outside that says *Purgatorio*. The inferno is now outside, 40 degrees in the shade as you wait with 600 hot souls to enter the Parc des Expositions in Chateaublanc on the outskirts of Avignon. Here we are apart from the historical traces of the city, beyond the city limits of the night before and the archaeology of vertical differences that site contains. Here it is all similar, not similar to anything, just similar. There is another Salle next door, and another and another. Horizontal existence. For all you know in this heat this is an endless suburb of exposition and exposure, playing an infinite loop of human abuse night after night. It is the perfect setting for the repetitions and uncanny similarities of naturalism with its violences in the world we think we know, the quiet betrayals of the really real.

As you enter *Purgatorio* from the inferno outside you first notice, on your skin and then in your head, that it is cool. It must be air-conditioned in here. The first and perhaps only prerequisite for Purgatory is that it should maintain conditions appropriate to its continuation. A limbo has to offer a condition of lasting – never last as in an end, just lasting. We are in the waiting room with nothing to read except something which is offered to us that we are not sure we want.

We have then gone indoors, and 'her indoors' (La Première Étoile played exquisitely by Irena Radmanovic, and this being naturalism one might respect an unusual admission of acting here) is washing up dishes in an acoustically enhanced sink. The clatter of porcelain is keyed up by Scott Gibbons and the SRS technical crew to a register just one notch above nature's true ordination of scale. It is instantly recognisable as such and confirms we are still sentient beings whose sense of being alive is precisely calibrated through the registration of such niceties. This is the first of a series of plays with scale and proportion that domesticate and naturalise the vertiginous shifts of perspective that characterised Hell. But this Purgatory is a lower-case hell we can all have and already do. Being Purgatory, this is much, much worse. Yesterday they knew they were in Hell and played out their solaces there. The '*je t'aime*' passed choreographically through 100 occupants on that stage the night before would be inexplicable in the truer isolation felt here.

The first and only word in this wallpapered chamber is '*chérie*' spoken by the woman at the sink to another room in which we are to assume there is a loved one. But the call hangs unanswered in this house. Our previous experience of an enlarged domestic interior in *Inferno* at the Palais des Papes was a demonically occupied interior that vomited objects through its epidermal skin. Here the ghosts are closer to domestic-scale Ibsen; by the end of this play, if not purgatory, an abusing father of that object of love, *chérie*, is rendered as the reduced spastic progenitor of a St Vitus dance that is now what a distended child would appear to have inherited. Or maybe just, like father like son, the primordial power of mimetic contagion is shown to be in good working order?

If this is premature and risks spoiling the surprise, Romeo Castellucci himself finds a way through projective surtitles of telling us what will happen at each stage without telling us what does happen. What does happen, what is fated to take place, is the abuse of a child (La Deuxième Étoile played exquisitely by Pier Paolo Zimmerman) in an upstairs, offstage room, where the deep-throated imperative 'Open your mouth!' punctuates screams, cries, and paternal groans. The father (La Troisième Étoile played exquisitely by Sergio Scarlatella) has arrived 'home' from work and sets about toying with a reheated supper. He appears to be intimate in his exhaustion with his wife but when he asks for '*le chapeau*' the way she responds suggests she knows he means his rancher's hat and not a condom. Both would be possible at this point in the action if we were anywhere else. But we are not. For at this point the surtitles rest on *la musique* (the hands not playing the notes) which is only fulfilled as a promise (unless one is willing to accept anguish as a certain form of human melody) when the father returns downstairs and, with the back of his hands resting on the keyboard of a grand piano we last saw the evening before burning in Hell, gives rise to Arvo Pärt's elegaic *Für Alina*.[5]

At this accompanied moment the boy does something predictable, logical, and, for the liberal seeking a quick prosecution of the unspeakable, terrible. He sits on his father's knee and embraces him. He can do this because while the act was unspeakable, he has spoken it, voiced it over from offstage, and while we are left dumbstruck he can fill the ensuing bars not with forgiveness – this is Purgatory – but with tenderness. The man behind us who, at the reappearance of the father on the landing after the abuse, bellowed out 'Was that good, was it?' has already left Purgatory for the inferno outside. But meanwhile, and unusually this far into a Romeo Castellucci show, almost everyone in this ever-waiting audience is present and correct, unified in a scattered way in a willingness or necessity to stay. This distended naturalism, sort of David Lynch circa *Mullholland Drive* (2001) but much better than that film's moral paucity, would appear to have absolved the witnesses from recognising this as Romeo Castellucci's cruellest drama.

Purgatory is cruel because it is not exceptional. The extreme world of catastrophic politics borne by the *Tragedia* episodes that have toured Europe over the previous four years (with the exception of the final bed-bound episode) is gone: there is no Mussolini or Charles de Gaulle here to vent anger upon. This is the limbo of Inferno, that had a day before been characterised as a glass room, a viewing chamber, lead-rimmed, sealed equally from gamma rays or infernal sounds, transparent yet mirrored to the incarcerated three-year-olds. Here in the Parc des Expositions the room with no view has become the house that demands *to be viewed*. As we do that viewing the boy does his own from within a tower of optical devices. His father emerges from a sugar-beet forest, to the incessant beat of one of Scott Gibbons's most persuasive tracks, and is scrutinised through a magnifying lens, a robot amplified from the boy's hands to gigantic proportions in a cupboard illuminated by the boy's pocket torch.

This repertoire of shifting scales is destined to continue because, despite the Vatican Council's cancellation of Limbo as a topography of soulful excursion, we know now that this is all we have to look forward to. Indeed, not only are we directed by this director on earth to look forward to it, the surtitles deny us the excuse of ignorance before the act, but we are also directed to see what is taking place. A vast lens descends at right angles between us and the stage action through which we are compelled to watch a final, awful, and beautiful choreography. A cerebral-palsy dance by a man who would appear to be a reduced version of the abusing father is inherited, restored, and amplified by a shaking fit from an enlarged version of the boy who was once, and again, abused. The lens has become an eye, a dark eye through which we now see what we have been seeing *as seeing*. These are the same people, played by different people (Juri Roverato and Davide Savorani, exquisitely), but the director plays havoc with our expectation, by directing our looking as much as that object of attention requires our embarrassed witness. Indeed, this director would appear to invest everything in *our* care while crediting those on stage with an absolute freedom born of trust. A man with cerebral palsy with a hat will be trusted to be perfect, which he is, while we as spectators are utterly incomplete, we, YOU, are as yet unfinished.[6] They are stars, in a galaxy, far, far away, *les étoiles*, numbered but stars nonetheless, we are a black hole called audience whose gravity folds in upon itself. It is all we can do to leave.

Paradiso

As for the narrative, and Romeo Castellucci is never without a good story, even if that story often simply brings perfect acting to the stage rather than troubling us with reiterating why the action is perfect in the circumstances, the potentially distressing lack of a terminus here ought to be resolvable after a fashion. *The Divine Comedy* is a trilogy after all, and if Dante is to be any kind of guide we could expect Paradise to follow. Dante might offer *Paradiso*, but there is no *Paradiso* in Avignon (well at least not until Sunday).

Paradiso is cancelled because paradise is still, according to the sign outside the venue, 'under construction' by the director, the director who is busy on this earth. And while the earth was made in six days, Hell, Purgatory, and Paradise will take this director a couple more.

So what to do in the absence of redemption? Well, rather literally as invited by another utopian some years ago, I imagined Heaven, it was easy when I tried, Hell was below me and above me only sky. *Paradiso* is after all *an installation* at Église des Célestins. In the absence of paradise, which was ticketed strictly for a 13.00 entry (we were to be the first to enter Paradise perhaps on the presumption that Hell is other people), we gather to eat nearby. A director called Romeo Castellucci walks up and greets us individually in a familiar, warm, generous way that respects our own solitude. A breath, an open vowel that sounds like a soft aaah, and then the name by way of embrace: Joe, Nick, Becky, Piersandra, Celine, Alan. He is with Scott Gibbons who tells us, quite straight-faced, that Romeo is taking him away to be decapitated. Given that I know that Scott's score for *Inferno* was partly made up of the sounds of an autopsy, this seems like too much information on this good Friday lunchtime. As the director who is Romeo Castellucci walks away from the Église des Célestins, in the opposite direction to Paradise, I am left wondering what Scott could have meant by this. It is not a problem of translation: Scott Gibbons is from Chicago, and he would appear to know what he means by decapitation – he smiles and as he goes gestures a florid, suicidal version of the cut-throat action that punctuated the latter half of *Inferno* with the residents of this city falling to the floor one after the other, despatched there by a civil war of thumb strokes administered by one citizen advancing behind another cutting across their windpipe between their Adam's apple and their chin.

On reflection, when others have left for home and I am left looking through the fourteenth-century keyhole of Paradise to see what its construction looks like, like everything else in Romeo Castellucci's universe, which includes this earth but would also appear to transcend it, it is perhaps sensible to take this departing comment quite literally. If Scott does expect to be decapitated by his director it would suggest that he at least believes the director to be sovereign. Or at least he expects to experience the sovereignty of the director. The sovereign makes the law and is above the law, he is the exception to the rule that requires those who kill to be killed. To be set upon by dogs and to walk away to join us on the audience side, yet above us in a glass box from which his word is heard by all who wish to participate in his theatrical anti-republic, would therefore appear to be a demonstration of that sovereignty. There is no doubt now, in the shadow of this suspended Paradise, on this late afternoon in Avignon that Romeo Castellucci is absolutely exceptional. He *is* the director on this earth.

That is not to say there are not other directors on this earth, and have not been others – in the middle of all this unforgiving afternoon glare I have seen a production by the Latvian director Alvis Hermanis called *Sonia* that in its transcendence of exquisite naturalism throws the harshest comparative light on everything about it, including Romeo Castellucci and what on earth he is doing with all that freight. But this one, Castellucci that is, in one subtractive sense, is the true heir to that other director who on this European earth set the pace for everything that followed. Carl Weber, a member of Bertolt Brecht's Berliner Ensemble in the late 1940s and early 1950s is able, on this day, to remind those of us who have experienced fewer directors on this earth, quietly and wisely, that history has a habit of repeating itself – I would just add, as divine comedy. Weber tells us that on the eve of the premiere of *The Caucasian Chalk Circle*, Brecht abandoned most of the scenery that had been designed and built for that first production. In this willingness to change (almost) everything Romeo Castellucci at least follows an honourable directorial precedent.

And change everything he does. There will never be another reduced premiere of *The Divine Comedy* in Avignon in the summer of 2008 but many more divine comedies in which nothing here will be recognisable and in which all will be amplified. That is as it should be. The musical notes by Scott Gibbons in the programme for *Paradiso* (and in our case the programme is all we have) gives us a modest sense of what we have missed: 'The deafening roar of angels' wings, of incomprehensible speech and song. Such saturation of the senses as to be at the edge of comprehension and beyond the limits of human description or poetry. Exclusion.' Well, that is at least accurate and again quite literal. Scott concludes: 'The music for Paradiso is created from [...] cicadas (in swarm and singularly).'

I am, then, writing this in Paradise, with just the sound of cicadas, loving and lonely, for company. Above us? Only stars.

Five key productions

Note: between 1980 and 2008 SRS under the shared direction of Romeo Castellucci, Chiara Guidi, and Claudia Castellucci made 54 productions. From 2006 the artists began to take separate paths in their subsequent work though often collaborating according to curatorial demands. The work of Romeo Castellucci since 2008 and the Dante trilogy discussed here has increasingly responded to invitations from Europe's leading opera houses to open up the operatic repertoire to the kinds of question expressed in the interview that forms an interlude in this essay. Significant among these productions would be *Orpheus and Eurydice* (after Gluck) 2014, and *The Magic Flute* (after Mozart) 2018, both for the Brussels Opera House, La Monnaie.

The following selection of five examples is random. Any other five would merit attention.

Cenno. SRS, Private Apartment, Rome. November 1980.

Giulio Cesare. SRS, Teatro Fabbricone, Prato. March 1997.

Tragedia Endogonidia, C.01-C.11. SRS, Teatro Commandini, Cesena. January 2002–December 2004.

Inferno, Purgatorio, Paradiso. SRS, Cour D'Honneur du Palais des Papes, Chateaublanc, Église des Célestins, Festival d'Avignon. July 2008.

Orphée et Eurydice. Dir. Romeo Castellucci. Music Dir: Hervé Niquet. La Monnaie, Brussels. June/July 2014.

Acknowledgements

With thanks to Gilda Biasini, Romeo Castellucci, Maria M. Delgado, Rebecca Groves, Joe Kelleher, Cosetta Nicolini, Nicholas Ridout, Dan Rebellato, and Suzie Thorpe-Woods.

Notes

1. The interview took place between 8 July and 11 July 2008 during the run of *The Divine Comedy* at the Avignon Festival.
2. This decade of festival appearances, less than half of the two-decade repertoire of the company, marks a sequence of preoccupations that could be described as indicative of the work of SRS and Romeo Castellucci as director: radical adaptation of Shakespeare involving professional and non-professional performers at the extremes of physical range and versatility; literary transformation from the canon of European literature from chamber scale to great magnitude; biblical and Catholic liturgical interest; long-term research exploration involving peripatetic, Europe-wide co-production, and the centrality of Castellucci family members in performance; installation and site-sensitive sculptural manifestations indexing concerns evident in the theatrical repertoire.
3. Directors for stages on this earth have more commonly concerned themselves with finessing our disbelief in a character's lines that try as they might do not quite add up to the person named in the dramatis personae.
4. Castellucci announces himself within the drama as director prefiguring Dante's own self-reflexive identification at the outset of *The Divine Comedy*.
5. There is also a longish period where the 'stage directions' in the surtitles diverge from what we see on stage. Castellucci would appear in this commentary to be less concerned with glossing an action that has the inevitability of tragic fate about it than interrupting each stage of a reading (our witness) that might presume to collapse sounds, spoken words, and writing to a consistency that conceals multiple abuses elsewhere.
6. The actor who 'has' cerebral palsy might be described by some as having 'disabilities' away from this stage. The 'dis' here I would take to refer to strategies of locomotion, presumptions as to the momentum and direction 'we' as 'able' humans might consider standard. But on this stage on this earth (Avignon, the Barbican where the production was

seen in the UK in April 2009) these actions are exposed as perfect: they are beautiful, strange, revealing, obsessive, clear, funny, flowing, in other words all the things that dance has tried to work on over a few years but finished up rather missing the point, which is what this performer shows us.

Bibliography

Castellucci, Claudia, Romeo Castellucci, Chiara Guidi, Joe Kelleher and Nicholas Ridout (2007) *The Theatre of Societas Raffaello Sanzio*, Abingdon and New York: Routledge.
Castellucci, Romeo (2004) *Epitaph*, Milan: Ubulibri.
Mondzain, Marie Jose (2007) *Homo Spectator*, Paris: Bayard.
Read, Alan (2007) *Theatre, Intimacy & Engagement: The Last Human Venue*, Houndmills: Palgrave Macmillan.
—— '*Orfeo e Euridice* di Romeo Castellucci: Scene dall'ultimo spazio umano', in Francesca Bortoletti and Annalisa Sacchi (eds), *La Performance Della Memoria*, Bologna: Baskerville, pp. 453–88.
—— (2020) *The Dark Theatre: A Book About Loss*, Abingdon: Routledge.

Chapter 15

KRISTIAN FRÉDRIC

Boxing with the 'gods'

Judith G. Miller

Kristian Frédric (b. 1962 in Champagne of 'a landlocked sailor and a housewife') is one of France's most passionate and non-conformist theatre directors destined, as he says, 'to look farther than the wheat fields of my home' (Frédric 2009). He is drawn to contemporary works marked by extreme lyricism and exceptional emotional violence: Bernard-Marie Koltès's *Dans la solitude des champs de coton* (*In the Solitude of the Cotton Fields*, 1994–5) and *La Nuit juste avant les forêts* (*Night Just Before the Forests*, 2000–4); Jean-Pierre Siméon's *Stabat Mater Furioso* (2003–5) and *Ya Basta* (2004); Koffi Kwahulé's *Big Shoot* (2005–7) and *Jaz* (2010); and Daniel Keene's *Moitié, Moitié* (*Half and Half*, 2007–8). Since 2010, he has added operas to his repertory: Gluck's *Orphée et Eurydice* (2010), Mascagni's *Cavalleria Rusticana*, and Léoncavallo's *Pagliacci* (2017) – crafting his own librettos for some of his more recent creations: *Quai Ouest*, after Koltès, with music by Régis Campo (2014–15) and *Fando et Lis*, after Fernando Arrabal, with music by Benoit Menut (2018). His *mises en scène* are stunningly physical, sculptural, anguished, and increasingly technologically bold, all the more so since he began designing many of his own sets in 2010. His varied career in the arts has taken him from technical work (lighting, stage managing, stage crew), notably at Paris's Les Folies Bergères in the early 1980s, to assisting directors such as Jean-Louis Thamin, François Nocher, Pierre Romans, Yves Gourvil, and Patrice Chéreau (a central influence on him) in the late 1980s and 1990s, to running his own company. Of working with Chéreau on *Hamlet* for the 1986 Avignon Festival, Frédric readily offers that the experience showed him how sacred theatre is: 'Chéreau taught me that we must push our dreams as far as

341

possible, and that it takes supreme energy, like Chéreau's own, to confront the abyss [that precedes creation]' (Frédric 2006).

Frédric has held together the theatrical company, Lézards Qui Bougent, out of Bayonne since 1989, hosting annually a festival of new plays and performance art which allows him to bring dramatic readings to schools, prisons, psychiatric hospitals, and retirement homes throughout the French south-west. His outspokenness has garnered some enemies within the local politicised subvention system. On the whole, however, he continues to receive support for his work from the regional governments of Aquitaine and the Atlantic Pyrenees. His inspiration for continuing theatrical experimentation comes especially from the community of European and Québecois theatre professionals who frequently co-produce his work. He appreciates the stimulation of working to bridge the methodological chasm that seemingly separates him from his Swiss, German, and Québecois collaborators. He has even found in the Québecois lighting designer Nicolas Descôteaux an ideal partner for his disquieting and graphic stagings and in the Italian opera conductor Daniele Callegari a perfect interlocutor in his ongoing quest for artistic sublimity. His work has been recognised by a prestigious fellowship to the Villa Medici in Italy (2005), and he has been knighted by the French government for his commitment to theatre arts (2007).[1]

The following interview took place in phases: between Montreal and New York on 10 August 2006, with a further conversation between Bayonne and New York on 15 January 2009, and a follow-up in Paris on 5 July 2018. Judith G. Miller translated these meanderings into English.

JUDITH G. MILLER: Your theatre company has a bizarre reptilian name, 'Lézards Qui Bougent' (Moving Lizards). Where does this come from?

KRISTIAN FRÉDRIC: I wanted a non-theatre name, a name that connotes something that moves and regenerates in the event of attack. When you cut a lizard's tale, the tail grows back. Lizards even resist radiation. Besides, the name made a banker laugh, and when you make a banker laugh, you feel like The Little Prince: a miracle's about to happen.

The verb '*bouger*' describes my profession as well as my life. I think this profession should keep you moving and constantly questioning yourself. Artists who hang onto their territory for fear of losing everything frighten me. They often reach their goal via political manoeuvrings, becoming characters in a version of Alfred Jarry's *King Ubu*. But someone who's constantly moving rubs elbows with the void and is prepared to lose his balance. Everything becomes possible on the edge, where the sacred finds its way back, where you question the deepest parts of yourself.

The Dealer's lines in Koltès's *In the Solitude of the Cotton Fields* come to mind here:

> And after – when we'll have filled up the hollows and flattened the hills within us – we'll take our distance, finding our balance on the thin flat rope of our latitude, satisfied in the midst of men and animals unsatisfied to be men and animals.[2]

During a brief encounter, we can discover the whole new universe of the other. Movement allows this, not stagnation.

Or take 'The Square', the Giacometti sculpture I visit regularly at the Guggenheim Museum in Venice. The work depicts bodies in motion and states of loneliness, as well as the sense of lack of movement in movement itself that takes you far within yourself and allows you to empathise with the other. This is the kind of movement that helps you 'screw' death, as Shakespeare's Mercutio might say.

JUDITH G. MILLER: You've built a career that has you travelling back and forth between Europe and Canada. What's been the impact on your art?

KRISTIAN FRÉDRIC: I've not really 'built' a career, but rather ended up spending time with various writings or people who made me want to stop and be with them. None of what I've done has been part of a career plan. My collaboration with Québec, for example, started in 2000 when I first met Claude Poissant of the Théâtre Petit à Petit in Montreal in order to speak about contemporary authors. At that time, I was struggling to defend living artists in a festival called Paroles à Ma Tribu in my home base in Aquitaine. Paroles à Ma Tribu came to include Québecois authors, and for two consecutive years this festival took place in both Aquitaine and Montreal. This led me in 2002 to do a staged reading of *Big Shoot*, Koffi Kwahulé's play, with two North American actors, Sébastian Ricard and Daniel Parent, to whom Claude had introduced me. Rehearsing with these actors taught me another way to think about process as well as texts. I felt as though I'd landed on another planet. I had to re-examine everything, especially unlearn things, in order to better understand the way these actors addressed stagework. They had a much quicker take on their characters. They were so efficient. This was a true shock, the discovery of a mind-blowing text and two captivating actors who forced me to really think, to know what I wanted from the outset.

I again experienced the necessity of knowing from the beginning what you want in a performance when I started staging operas after 2010. No one works harder than opera professionals. In opera you have to plunge into an interpretation. There's no time for process. For my development as an artist my physical and artistic nomadism has been salutary and energising. Working with a Québecois engineer, for example, got me into robotics. So I used a kind of robotic transformer to create the torture chamber that enfolded the character Jaz in Kwahulé's *Jaz* (2010). My interest in new technologies stems from my work in Québec.

JUDITH G. MILLER: How exactly has this nomadism translated into your work in opera?

KRISTIAN FRÉDRIC: Well, again, it seemed like fate decided to land opera in my lap. In 2011, Peter Taylor, directing the Gluck Festival in Nuremberg, Germany, asked me to stage, with two other directors, one-third of the opera *Orphée et Eurydice*. It was then I began to understand that opera really is the supreme art; nothing matches it. But it was really in taking on Koltès's play *Quai Ouest* and turning it into a libretto with Florence Doublet in 2015 that I discovered the extraordinary organicity of working with a conductor, who is, after all, the real visionary in an opera production, the *maestro* who holds everything in his hands. You might say I moved internally in terms of seeing I could produce a text that would adjust itself as Régis Campo's music developed, just as the music evolved with the text when it was performed.

JUDITH G. MILLER: What about working with singers rather than actors?

KRISTIAN FRÉDRIC: I can't begin to tell you how impressive I find singers. Their bodies are their instruments. They work constantly to stay in top form. And the ones I've worked with have been ready for anything. When I staged *Cavalleria Rusticana* and *Pagliacci* in 2017 in Strasbourg for the Opéra du Rhin, I imagined a two-part movement taking place at a 20-year remove in an Italian slum. I asked some of the singers in *Cavalleria Rusticana* to act in *Pagliacci*. They were superb, not at all stuck in some notion of what singers can't do. You might remember that I wanted to have Kwahulé's *Big Shoot* performed by the same actors in both English and French but, unfortunately, as I was staging the play in French, I learned that the rights for the USA had been bought by another producer. So I put on hold the bilingual project. That old dream of mine to direct actors in a language I don't really know has come true in my opera work. I have to rely on other senses and other ways to engage with the singers.

JUDITH G. MILLER: It seems that you're attracted, even in the operas that you do, to the hallucinatory, destabilising, and also ritualistic theatrical world of French and francophone contemporary authors such as Arrabal, Koltès, Siméon, and Kwahulé. In choosing these authors, do you see the possibility of inscribing your own aesthetic on stage?

KRISTIAN FRÉDRIC: Today's authors don't talk about love, life, and everything around us in the same way authors did 100 or 200 years ago. Times change, so do ways of life. Our *mots/maux* (in the double sense of 'words' and 'troubles') are no longer the same and no longer translate the same preoccupations.

The authors that move me are the ones who – often outside of the story they're telling (if there is one) – allow me to better understand my contemporaries and where I live in society. To work in theatre means to question our soul and our world. I often feel that if I'd not been doing this, I would probably have taken up arms. What perhaps saves me is that I believe, maybe naively, that theatre and more generally art offer the means to struggle against adversity and general amnesia. That's what is prompting the production I'm working on now that will be performed in the fall of 2018. *Camille*, scripted by François Douan, is a multi-media project, a combination arts installation and play production that tells us that art is the way humans respond to the craziness of our world. I was in Nuremberg working on the Koltès opera when two madmen shot up the offices of *Charlie Hebdo* in Paris and killed 12 journalists. Ordinary people left poems, cartoons, and sketches to commemorate the dead. They used art to confront sordid killing, fanaticism, and horror.

I'm more and more afraid of this world, of its frenzied neoliberalism and schizophrenia. I feel obliged to dissect the violence in it, to show this violence as it really is in order to question our state of being and to think about our future. Media and notably television feed us information in a way that desensitises us. We eat daily horrors like a happy child drinking his mother's milk. My aesthetic derives from anger about this as well as dreams for a new world. Even though I remain convinced that the reason for today's mess is the loss of the sacred (and I don't mean religion) in our daily lives, I remain certain that (may Malraux forgive me) the twenty-first century will be angry or it will perish. I want to show that anger and provoke a reaction to it.

JUDITH G. MILLER: What does this mean in terms of how you depict the world on stage? What about collaboration with the cartoonist-turned-scenographer Enki Bilal, as you did for *Big Shoot*, in the creation of a Kwahulean world I find to be situated somewhere between a nightmare and expressionist dance?

KRISTIAN FRÉDRIC: In order to make violent theatre, you have to find partners or playmates who also have their own reading of the world, who are capable, with you, of entering into nightmares and bringing out a kind of beauty in them. Sometimes artists are criticised for this. Take Coppola and *Apocalypse Now* (1979). He was scolded for depicting an aesthetically pleasing evil. But we don't say the same of Picasso's painting, *Guernica*, do we?

That's why, whatever the topic at hand, I've always wanted my works to be perceived as paintings, where beauty has a place. I developed my pictorial sense while collaborating with Enki Bilal and working with lighting designers Yannick Anché (*Night Just Before the Forests*) and Nicolas Descôteaux (*Big Shoot*). With Bilal and Descôteaux, we managed to create a show entirely in black and white, with line definitions you find in graphic novels, and with lighting which recalled *film noir* cinema. I learned about the centrality of lighting when I worked as a technician at Les Folies Bergères. These different designers all helped me isolate gestures, highlight facial features, create a dream space where emotion is exteriorised.

I can't conceive of directing a play that doesn't refer to the universes of artists I admire (artists who resurface in my mind throughout the process of directing). Giacometti haunted my nights and days while working on *Night Just Before the Forests*, and cinema artists like David Cronenberg, Quentin Tarantino, Marco Ferreri, and Murneau accompanied me during *Big Shoot*. For the operas I staged, especially *Fando et Lis*, in 2018, Pasolini and Buñuel lived in me. That imminent danger, that murky and ironic spirituality that are theirs, spoke to me of Arrabal's own post-apocalyptic mindscape. With each new show, new artistic guests knock at my door and I can't help but let them in. Max Ernst is always just around the corner.

I think my aesthetic has been shaped the way a tree grows, made up of multiple layers that keep rejuvenating. For example, the shock I experienced 20 years ago when I saw Van Gogh's *Tower of Perdition* stays with me and somehow informs my choices today, as does Archie Shepp's rendition of 'Sometimes I Feel like a Motherless Child', music I heard on an ordinary evening but which, thanks to him, has become unforgettable to me.

JUDITH G. MILLER: Considering your aesthetic sensibilities, what made you take on Racine's *Andromaque*, which is for many people the prime example of neoclassical theatre?

KRISTIAN FRÉDRIC: For one thing, creating *Andromaque 10–43* in 2013 was the chance to work with Denis Lavant again. He brings to the stage everything I believe in as a director, a kind of fierce intelligence that doesn't shrink from taking tremendous risks. But I also wanted to explore the kind of control dictators thrive on through promoting espionage. So I showed Pyrrhus, played by Denis, benefitting from a huge technological spy machine. We often forget that in his works Racine also denounced a closed society that crushes men and their dreams. There are many echoes of today's world in Racine. It's a terrifying play, really, because there's no more room for love.

I tried to tease Racine's alexandrines and imagine a performed diplomatic language that's not 'the mother tongue' of Orestes and Pyrrhus. I wanted the alexandrines to be heard as if they were an actual but clearly hypocritical language, a language of untruth.

JUDITH G. MILLER: You're currently contemplating creating another opera based on Koltès's work, going back to his best known play *In the Solitude of the Cotton Fields*.

KRISTIAN FRÉDRIC: Koltès never completely leaves me. When it comes down to it, as Koltès tells us, the individual is truly alone. It's this solitude that propels him in life. When I meet someone I like, I always feel our respective solitudes recognise each other. Our solitudes feel and smell each other; they say something like: 'I recognise you with your burden. It belongs to you but I'm not unfamiliar with it.' I believe in this brotherhood, these crossings where we recognise each other, where we don't resolve anything but where we name each other. This is what eternity is for me: living in someone's memory by inscribing oneself in the multitude of layers that constitute another person. I believe that all great and long-lived theatrical writings explore – and ask the audience to explore – this brotherhood. It's obvious when we read Shakespeare, Koltès, Pinter, and many others.

Unfortunately, too many theatre managers and owners do all they can to transform the stage into a profane place where only entertainment, at its most obscene, is allowed. How many times have I heard, 'This project is not for my public. This is too complicated for them.' The Romans put this into action when they created their mindless circus games. Reality TV has also bought into it: entertainment as ridicule, exclusion, and voyeurism. Now politics has picked up the theme.

JUDITH G. MILLER: Do you think that psychological destabilisation, exile, and violence are the lot of today's 'world citizens'?

KRISTIAN FRÉDRIC: I think that true violence is in indifference, to be blasé, and to think there's nothing you can do to change all this. It's what our neoliberal rulers would have us believe. It's a way to take away our responsibility in order to better rule over us and impose destructive economic policies. What matters is to profit through manipulation at the expense of what is essential, the human soul. The ensuing chaos can only destabilise feelings of identity and promote violence. That's why I remain convinced that contemporary creation must be insolent and provocative. I'm always very surprised to discover that an 'educated' person can be xenophobic or intolerant. For me, it means that pages have remained stuck together, unread, that the person has not seen or has forgotten what really matters. Unfortunately, readers of such sealed-up pages fill our world. Our theatres can work to unstick the pages.

JUDITH G. MILLER: I was able to see two of your productions: Koffi Kwahulé's *Big Shoot* in Montreal in 2005 and Bernard-Marie Koltès's *Night Just Before the Forests* in Paris in 2001; and I've just watched an excellent recording of your 2010 staging of Kwahulé's *Jaz*. I was particularly affected by the actors' physicality [see Denis Lavant in *Night Just Before the Forests*, Plate 15]. It was downright frightening because I felt the comedians were playing on a borderline where their own psyche was perilously engaged.

KRISTIAN FRÉDRIC: When we want to access layers of humanity, layers I mentioned earlier, we need to call upon the body, its ancestral memory. We have to struggle not to call only on the intellect. That's why I'm fascinated with boxing, a sport I practised for a few years. In a ring, there's absolute awareness of the other and at the same time total submission to combat, to a form of sacrifice. In order to get in a ring, a boxer must train heavily and challenge his limits. The ultimate reward is the right he wins to bring everything into play, maybe even his life, for at least two minutes. Similar to the boxing ring, theatrical engagement must be absolute and you must walk near death and challenge it to better understand and affect life. Too many actors go on stage as if climbing onto the couch of a psychoanalyst or buying drugs at the corner dealer's. They don't realise the 'gods' are watching.

The stage is a dangerous place: being on stage means facing the abyss. You have to be ready to be generous and willing to get hurt. For example, to work with a language like that of Bernard-Marie Koltès is not without danger. It leads you to a universe that directly shakes your inner self. You have to confront the ugliness in yourself. It would be a serious mistake not to see that. 'Boxing' with Koltès's language requires the actor's full engagement – physical and psychical.

I often think about Miles Davis with whom I was lucky enough to work as a technician during two of his concerts in France. One day, at a rare moment when he was accessible, someone asked why he always played with his trumpet pointing towards the ground. He answered, 'in order to bounce the notes back and send them to the farthest point upwards . . . maybe verging on a wrong note, but striving for the highest note possible'. In his own way, he was also challenging the 'gods'. Any artistic endeavour is like this musical note, which though anchored in the ground also travels near the stars. Actors must negotiate this anchor and this elevation if they want to outperform themselves.

JUDITH G. MILLER: Do you always choose to work with actors who are capable of such commitment?

KRISTIAN FRÉDRIC: I like to work with 'Stradivarius' or 'Muhammad Ali' types; but they might at first ignore their potential. A director works like a coach. He has to love his actors, help them get closer to their selves, and learn to speak to the 'gods'. When an actor faces difficulties or falls down, we fall too. That's why, starting several years ago, I decided to go to each performance of my shows, not to judge but rather to be there with my actors in case of a bad kick. When I see one of the actors reach a state of grace, I think about Muhammad Ali's 'float like a butterfly/sting like a bee' and I'm happy. Actors give me the gift of serenity. I don't really think the idea of 'character' exists on the stage – at least the stage that interests me – in the same way it used to. What matters most in my eyes is to let oneself be guided by the forces embedded in the language, to abandon oneself to the actions, to flow with them and slowly drift in a universe that will open up other doors to the imagination. I'm not denigrating the intellect or the analytical. But for me, the actor must entirely inhabit his gestures and speech. Gestures and speeches should, in turn, be like the paint that lodges itself under the nails of a painter.

JUDITH G. MILLER: What kind of actor training would you like to see?

KRISTIAN FRÉDRIC: I don't think you can think about stage work by reducing it to a particular form of training. It's true that everything the Russian school brought, Stanislavski and later the Actors Studio, has been central for twentieth-century theatre and the way to address the question of 'character'. But as I mentioned, the theatre of the twenty-first century is really more about the force of language.

JUDITH G. MILLER: I quote from your words from the Montreal programme of *Big Shoot*:

> In Koffi Kwahulé's play, the executioner's interrogation makes me think about a prayer spoken by the Polish director, Tadeusz Kantor: 'O Lord, grant me that admirable and rare moment, blurry like a breath, invisible like a black hole, which in its limitlessness would permit the creation of something finite, like death – a work of art.'

Can you comment more on this?

KRISTIAN FRÉDRIC: The act of being just right, the perfect moment, which succeeds in being everything and being complete, a full success, a 'work of art', is what every artist, whatever his medium, strives for. In a show, it can be a one-second instant, a gesture, a glance, yet it will belong to all of the audience and move them, just as a birth or a death does. It's a paradox because it is inscribed in time yet it's timeless. In this sense, we use the stage to pay off the debt we owe to the life running through our veins.

JUDITH G. MILLER: I'd like to go back to the issue of words because while we've spoken of the ambiance and themes of your favourite authors, we haven't yet talked about what attracts you about their language – so lyrically full, impulsive, and very surprising in terms of images and references.

Kristian Frédric: I have a strange relation to theatrical texts. First, I find that reading theatre is very difficult work. If I can, I try to have several people read aloud. I'm fond of these 'reading' sessions because they make it possible to grasp the text's musicality. Sometimes, I even hire actors to decipher the text with me. I often have a carnal connection to the text. If I feel that it's come my way, I don't necessarily try to know why. I let it get inside me little by little. I let it kick me and watch it box. If intrinsically I feel like fighting with it, I get in the ring. Then, I let it be, taking time to move around it. I don't re-read it. I turn and observe its indelible traces. That's what attracts me about a text, the feeling I have of communicating with the universe it offers me.

Judith G. Miller: Then how about music?

Kristian Frédric: Music transports me directly to the gods and even beyond.

Judith G. Miller: How, in the end, should we define you as a director?

Kristian Frédric: How difficult your questions have become! I don't even know how to define myself as a man! Is there such a big difference between the two? I'm looking for a way to bridge the void or probe the abyss. The theatre, and especially operas, allow me to question the 'gods'. In the past, onstage during a rehearsal, I've even felt a physical force sucking me upwards, then winding itself up deep within. I had this same feeling when I saw the ultrasound of my first daughter in her mother's belly. I even had the taste of earth in my mouth.

Maybe this is what I'm looking for, the different earth we're made of. I'm convinced we all know the same dance, and that we've forgotten it, erased it, but that this dance stays within us all as a guarantor of our brotherhood. Maybe that's what I am in the end, an earth digger, searching for the dance of our 'selves'. Or, maybe I'm a sculptor or a painter rather than a director. I don't really know.

Five key productions

Dans la solitude des champs de coton (*In the Solitude of the Cotton Fields*). By Bernard-Marie Koltès. Set design by the collective. Perf. Jean-Marie Broucaret, Alain Simon. La Scène Nationale de Bayonne Sud Aquitain, Bayonne. 20 October 1994.

La Nuit juste avant les forêts (*Night Just Before the Forests*). By Bernard-Marie Koltès. Set design by Enki Bilal. Perf. Denis Lavant. La Scène Nationale Bayonne-Sud-Aquitain, Bayonne. 15 October 2000.

Big Shoot. By Koffi Kwahulé. Set design by Enki Bilal. Perf. Sébastien Ricard, Daniel Parent. Théâtre Denise-Pelletier, Montreal. 6 September 2005.

Cavalleria Rusticana and Pagliacci. By Mascagni and Léoncavallo. Set design by Bruno de Lavenère. Musical direction by Daniele Callegari. Opéra National du Rhin, Strasbourg. 15 May 2017.

Fando et Lis. After a work by Fernando Arrabal. Libretto by Kristian Frédric. Music by Benoît Menut. Set design by Fabien Teigné. Musical direction by Daniel Kwaka. Opéra de Saint Etienne, Saint Etienne. 2 May 2018.

Notes

1 The Villa Medicis Hors les Murs prize is given annually by the French Cultural Ministry to finance French artists who wish to do research outside of France.
2 This translation of Koltès is by Judith Miller, for a production staged by Roland Auzet at the Skirball Center of New York University in October 2017.

Bibliography

Frédric, Kristian (2006) 'Interview with Judith G. Miller', August.
—— (2007) *A feu et à sang ou le désir brûlant*, Québec: Editions de la Pleine Lune.

—— (2009) 'Interview with Judith G. Miller', January.
—— (2018) 'Interview with Judith G. Miller', July.
Gagnon, Lise (2008) 'L'Homme qui danse: Entretien avec Kristian Frédric', *Cahiers du théâtre Jeu*, 128 (October): 165–70.
Website: www.Kristianfredric.com

Chapter 16

KRZYSZTOF WARLIKOWSKI

Rupturing taboos, curating publics

Bryce Lease

Krzysztof Warlikowski (b. 1962) is a member of the first generation to work exclusively in postcommunist Poland as a theatre director. No longer concerned with the same political struggles as his predecessors, Warlikowski has confronted the apathy and disappointment in the political and social spheres that dominated Polish life after 1989 while making visible emerging concerns and identities in the aftermath of communism. Krystian Lupa, one of his most significant mentors, introduced Warlikowski to subjects that informed his work, such as cultural dispossession, spiritual atrophy, and the breakdown of collective identity. However, early in his career, Warlikowski quickly moved on to shape previously taboo discourses in the Polish public sphere. Eschewing texts and directing styles that rely on assimilationist or exclusionary cultural strategies, attempts to essentialise Polish history or embody the essence of the Polish nation, Warlikowski's theatre has disrupted accepted historiography, broken down traditional gender roles, embraced Jewish memory, frustrated dominant cultural discourses, and produced alternative sexual identities. I will argue that he has shaped new audiences and made one of the most significant cultural impacts of any Polish artist working in the early decades of the twenty-first century.

Generational divides

Warlikowski studied at the prestigious Jagiellonian University before joining the Directing Faculty at the National Academy of Theatre Arts (PWST) in Krakow in the early 1990s. From the outset, he rejected the philosophy and aesthetics of Polish Romanticism, which had dominated the political theatre practice of preceding generations. He was drawn more to the German *Regietheater* of Peter Stein than to compatriots like Andrzej Wajda, Jerzy Jarocki, or Jerzy Grzegorzewski. After completing his training, he went on to shape his unique directorial style by assisting a number of Europe's most eminent theatre directors, including Peter Brook, Ingmar Bergman, and Giorgio Strehler.

As well as shunning the valourised Romantic national canon, Warlikowski also rejected modern Polish writers such as Sławomir Mrożek and Tadeusz Różewicz, choosing instead to stage Western contemporary playwrights like Bernard-Marie Koltès and Sarah Kane, whose writing expanded formal strategies while flouting social mores so as to diagnose the new social reality under neoliberal capitalism that was constituting Poland's nascent Third Republic.[1] By the end of the 1990s, Warlikowski had embraced Shakespeare, leading one critic to announce that a new style of staging was emerging with his production of *Winter's Tale* at the Teatr Nowy in Poznań in 1997 (Schiller 1999). After a number of successful international productions in Germany, Italy, and Israel, Warlikowski firmly established his reputation in Poland with his feminist retelling of *Taming of the Shrew* in Warsaw's Teatr Dramatyczny in 1998, claiming that Shakespeare provided the necessary form for expressions and contestations of human rights (cited in Wyżyńska 1999b). The production was widely reviewed and the depiction of graphic profanity, pornographic images, and homosexuality made it the focus of public debate. Trading on this publicity, Grzegorz Jarzyna, the youngest artistic director in Poland at the time, invited Warlikowski to direct at the Teatr Rozmaitości in Warsaw. This began a new artistic cooperation that would last through much turbulence over the subsequent eight years. Fearing that Warsaw had become a cultural desert, Jarzyna wished to open a venue for the production of avant-garde theatre similar to those in neighbouring Germany, such as the Kulturbrauerei in Berlin or Hamburg's Kampnagel. Fuelled by substantial media attention, it quickly became fashionable for young artists and progressive intellectuals to be seen in the Teatr Rozmaitości on Warsaw's Marszałkowska Street, and many critics remarked on the immense enthusiasm, even impatience, mounting in audiences that matched the energy of the productions.

After joining forces in 1999, Warlikowski and Jarzyna established themselves as the most vibrant, daring, and perspicacious directors of their generation. Their relationship was far from simple, but the rumours of their large riffs over creative control that determined much of their artistic cooperation only served to increase their popularity and notoriety. Young audiences that had abandoned theatres at the demise of communism for television and cinema came crowding back, and many performances sold out at the Teatr Rozmaitości, which soon underwent a name change. If Teatr Rozmaitości was too difficult to pronounce for foreigners, the stylishly rebranded TR Warszawa could circulate more easily on international stages. As provocateurs, Warlikowski and Jarzyna appeared in tabloids, celebrity magazines, and gossip columns, and their openings were the most widely publicised events on the theatrical calendar. Their work toured to major theatre festivals around the world, including Edinburgh, Avignon, New York, Hong Kong, and Moscow's Golden Mask, which marked them as ambassadors for contemporary Polish theatre on a global scale. While their choice of texts for theatre did not rely on plays or novels from Poland, the foreign press – particularly in Italy, France, and the UK – frequently labelled their approach to acting and scenography as uniquely Polish.

Warlikowski's institutional collaboration at the TR Warszawa provided him with the resources, the space, and the ensemble of highly skilled actors to create many of the artistic processes that have formed his career. *Hamlet*, his inaugural production, is still considered iconic and highly emblematic of a new mode of directing after the political transition of 1989. Historically, stagings of *Hamlet* in Poland have functioned as a commentary on sociopolitical and historical impasses. In his 1904 *A Study of Hamlet*, Stanisław Wyspiański argued that the puzzle of Hamlet encapsulates the locus of the Polish revolutionary and melancholic spirit, engendering a crucial visible confrontation between the actor and the assumption of a dramatic character. The character Hamlet has stood as the archetypal Pole fighting for the national cause and as a meditation on the Polish national character. The play is overdetermined and charged with political meanings that reflect both its performance history and Poland's struggles from the partitions of the country in the late eighteenth century through communism and political transition. Warlikowski's production in the final year of the twentieth century reflected these historical associations while offering a daring new mode of determining Polish culture. A number of his directorial signatures were in evidence, including male nudity, androgyny, sexual ambivalence, haunting soundscapes, polychronicity, and an overlaying of multiple narratives. Privileging the personal family narrative over the state affairs of the court, Warlikowski revealed how political autonomy leads to new forms of theatre production, both in material and thematic terms. Małgorzata Szcześniak's hyperminimalist scenic design consisted of a narrow podium surrounded on three sides by the audience, the background panel taken from a Jewish synagogue. Elsinore became a highly theatricalised, open-ended space in which characters often performed on the sidelines in almost total darkness. Burnished mirrors, a stage sign that would reappear in many of Warlikowski's future works, produced a lively interplay of surfaces. In all of his productions, these reflective interiors produce an aesthetic dynamism that eschews easy interpretation. In *Hamlet*, Szcześniak's designs combined with Paweł Mykietyn's evocative acoustic scenography encapsulated the director's staging of social spaces that have been described by Grzegorz Niziołek, a prominent theorist on the director, as 'a place of scars, of painful and repressed experiences' (2015: 55).

Jacek Poniedziałek, who has appeared in every Polish production Warlikowski has directed since 1999, played the eponymous role. Reviewers consistently returned to descriptions of Poniedziałek's body, both his suppleness and flexibility as a performer and also the beauty of his musculature. This calls to mind critics' keen interest in the unconstrained athleticism of Ryszard Cieslak's physicality in Jerzy Grotowski's *Constant Prince* in 1967. Unlike the contemporaneous reviews of Grotowski's production, however, homoeroticism had begun to appear more explicitly in theatre criticism by the end of the 1990s, though frequently in pejorative terms. Poniedziałek's sexually explicit performance became a hallmark of Warlikowski's staging of embodied discourse. Janusz Kowalczyk observed that the male striptease, a recurrent device in the catalogue of Teatr Rozmaitości aesthetics, signalled a lack of inventiveness that was nothing but a 'conglomerate of perversion' (1999).[2] Not only does this claim exemplify the discomfort with male (homo)sexuality that was prevalent at the time, it also neglects the consideration of the corporeal as central to Warlikowski's directorial intentions. The exposure of the body is not merely a stage effect. In *Hamlet*, Poniedziałek's body established the production's formal unity through its sublimation, eroticisation, and denigration. Entirely emptied of pathos and sentimentality, the meekness of Hamlet's voice stood out against his raw sexuality and physical strength, forcing audiences to lean forward to catch his colourless, throwaway utterances. In contrast to louder or more impassioned Polish Hamlets who have voiced fervent proclamations of national spirit on public stages, Poniedziałek's soft voice exemplified how Warlikowski was both reframing masculinity in relation to national character and, similar to his critique of patriarchal homosocial bonding in *Taming of the Shrew* (see Adamiecka-Sitek 2006), problematic paradigms of received masculinity.

Hamlet is seen in Poland as the ultimate test of a director's intellectual capacities, and productions are judged as much for their scenographic competence as for a director's ability to reignite the text's dramatic power. A barrage of criticism of Warlikowski's production was underscored by unfavourable comparisons with Konrad Swinarski's sketched-out plans for *Hamlet* that never saw the stage due to the revered director's premature death in 1975. Warlikowski certainly privileged the relationship between actors over the aesthetic coherency that would emerge with startling force in his later work. Poniedziałek has claimed that Warlikowski's method is 'long and slow', dependent upon question marks rather than exclamation marks. This is a process that places enormous demands on the actors, in which nothing is assumed in advance of rehearsals (cited in Wyżyńska 1999a).

Jan Kott, who was evoked by both older and younger critics of the production, famously suggested that *Hamlet* is a sponge that absorbs each particular historical moment, a mirror through which any generation can recognise itself (1964: 84); and it is perhaps for this reason that there was such a striking discrepancy in critical responses. Those longing for Swinarski's abandoned production only saw a superficial rendering that was overly reliant on shock tactics rather than genuine theatrical innovation. The final blow for critics who believed in the tenets of Polish Romanticism was the choice to make Hamlet's father an actor. Rendering the ghost in a disappointing material form – a feeble father rather than a bloodthirsty ancestor demanding a settling of scores – went far to undermine the metaphysical potential that many had traditionally sought out in the theatre in Poland. Alternatively, younger audiences were largely excited by Warlikowski's feverish and apposite attempts to portray heightened sexuality and rampant disappointment in political spheres. Critic and dramaturg Roman Pawłowski described Warlikowski's target audience at the time as 'a generation deceived by their elders', who were 'deeply implicated in wrongs from the past, and forced to make decisions beyond their strength' (1999).

Warlikowski's next production for the Teatr Rozmaitości was Euripides' *Bacchae*, the first significant production of the play in Poland since 1945. With the exception of Grotowski and Włodzimierz Staniewski, very few memorable performances of Greek tragedy were produced after the Second World War, the most famous being Andrzej Wajda's *Antigone* in 1984, which placed the play's central themes in the context of communist despotism. Although there is a preoccupation with the trivialities and pettiness of family life in his work, Warlikowski rarely dwells on the domestic space, and when he does it is frequently mutilated, ruined, or corrupted. Shunning conventional realism, the performance space of *Bacchae* was composed of an eclectic clutter of opposing elements: a pool of water, a rectangle of sand, a worn carpet, a table, and shiny metal plates that suggested 'a temple, slaughterhouse or morgue' (Gruszczyński 2001). On entering the theatre, it was difficult to trace a coherent mapping of aesthetics in this assemblage that one expected to find in Staniewski's celebrated productions of Greek tragedy in Gardzienice. While Staniewski usually veers towards universalising narratives that evoke the constant or eternal in humankind through music, Warlikowski used Euripides as a means of diagnosing changing material circumstances and psychic states in contemporary society, highlighting instability and the obstacles presented by political rapprochement with the neoliberal West.

Warlikowski connected the local to the global through his adaptation of the Greek tragedy and made a productive exchange between the sacrosanct and the profane that focused a debate around atheism, a theme that had largely been eschewed in the 1990s with the forceful re-emergence of the Catholic Church. Much chided for his ruthless editing of classical texts, Warlikowski argued that 'all of my directing is a battle with conventionalised theatre' (cited in Cieślak 2001). This includes a rigorous editing process that brings out the multiple strands of a text's embedded ambiguities. As a disquisition on contemporary spirituality that did not rely on Polish Romanticism, Warlikowski successfully decoupled 'the conflation of political and national issues from religious questions' and implicitly criticised religious fervency that had developed in the country over the previous decade (Niziołek 2015: 62). The sublime status of Christian symbolism was diminished by associations with the orgiastic spectacle of paganism, favouring the corporeal over the spiritual. The Bacchants' pseudo-Catholic devotion juxtaposed the low-key spirituality of Kadmos and Tiresias, who resembled ageing hippies as they twisted their bodies into painful yoga positions on a threadbare carpet that signalled a new interest in non-Western cultures. Divorced from the promise of transcendence from the material world, ritual was opened up to parody, and the pleasures and pains of the flesh were revealed as the limits of human existence. Warlikowski created 'a ritualistic theatre that does not propose renewal' (Niziołek 2006: 38), and in which, unlike Polish Romanticism, suffering fails to transubstantiate victims into martyrs. This explains, I would argue, Warlikowski's persistent interest in European texts that are culturally transgressive, such as the plays of Koltès and Kane.

Many comparisons were drawn between Warlikowski's next production, *Burza* (*The Tempest*), and Jerzy Grzegorzewski's stage adaptation of W. H. Auden's long poem 'The Sea and the Mirror' (1944) at the Teatr Studio, both in 2003. Whereas Grzegorzewski, one of the most acclaimed Polish directors of the late twentieth century, focused on Prospero's creative potential in Auden's contemplation of *The Tempest*, Warlikowski emphasised the constructedness of Prospero's troubling moral system on the island. As with *Hamlet* and *Bacchae*, the audience surrounded the borders of the performance on three sides. Seated at the edge of the playing space, demarcated by a burnished mirrored floor, spectators were close enough to the action to allow the actors to experiment with more intimate stage signs, vocal colour, and physical gesture. In this enmeshment of the private realm of the audience and the interior world of the actor, Warlikowski challenged the conventional binary, as articulated by Marvin Carlson, between iconic and indexical space. Carlson distinguishes between the iconic playing space directly inhabited by the actors, in which every discrete object is transformed into a signifier, and offstage, indexed locations (2010: 198), such as Milan in *The Tempest*. While certain objects convey action and location, such as the table that functioned over the course of the performance as a home and a conference room, thus doubling as a tool for domestic and political reconciliation, the offstage indexical space intruded into or dislocated the onstage iconic or playing area given that there were no concrete borders, signifiers, or geographical references. Thus, the island became a mental map of the differing psychic states inhabited by the array of characters. In this sense, even 'distant' Milan was present both in the spatial parameters, playing its role in articulating power struggles, old feuds, and social hierarchies, and in temporal terms, colliding the contemporaneous with the historical. Such syncopations of psychology, space, and time have become the bedrock of Warlikowski's productions.

In the final scene of *The Tempest*, Prospero donned a tuxedo to match the affluence of Alonso's court and sits down at the long table to negotiate political reconciliation, an implicit reference to the infamous Round Table Talks in 1989 that formalised the demise of the communist government. Prospero's pardoning of former foes and his return to Milan is accompanied by embittered resignation rather than celebration. Joanna Krakowska-Narożniak (2003) noted that in postcommunist Poland, where victims often sit next to their former persecutors on advisory boards, practising forgiveness is nothing more than a convenient tool for taking power. Publicity focused on the play's confrontation between culprits and victims, which Warlikowski linked to the then raging debate around Polish anti-Semitism and collusion with the Nazis sparked by the publication of Jan T. Gross's *Neighbors: The Destruction of the Jewish Community in Jedwabne, Poland* in 2000. Though no direct reference was made to Jedwabne, Szcześniak's design included a back wall with temple windows that was intended as a memorial to the Jews who were burned in a barn by their Polish neighbours in 1941. On a thematic level, Warlikowski saw the marriage between Miranda and Ferdinand, whose father wanted to exterminate Prospero, as analogous to a generation of ethnic Poles and Jews creating a 'brave new world' through admissions of culpability and attempts at forgiveness. Miranda's naivety ('How beauteous mankind is!') was offset both by the physical maturity of the actress – Małgorzata Hajewska-Krzysztofik was then already in her mid-30s – and by Trinculo's moving and heartfelt karaoke rendition of Louis Armstrong's 'What a Wonderful World'. The audience was left to ponder whether the future facing the couple would be tolerant and benevolent or as bitter and partisan as their parents'. Warlikowski had thus diagnosed one of the paradigmatic problems facing the collision of generations in Poland at the start of the twenty-first century.

Rupturing cultural taboos

One of the first explicit signs of the rivalry developing between Warlikowski and Jarzyna concerned their contending productions of Sarah Kane. When Warlikowski staged *Oczyszczeni* (*Cleansed*) at the Teatr Rozmaitości in 2001, Jarzyna soon followed with *4.48 Psychosis* in 2002, which he then directed later the same year at the Dusseldorf Schauspielhaus. These contemporaneous premieres of Kane's plays in Poland implicitly pit the directors against one another, a competition which the media took great delight in aggravating. The significance of *Cleansed* in Polish theatre history rests at least partially in its triumvirate of producers: TR Warszawa, Wrocław's Teatr Współczesny, and Poznań's Teatr Polski, the latter of which then held exclusive rights to produce Kane's work in Poland. While such coproductions are not infrequent in the repertory systems of Western Europe, never before had three major theatres from different cosmopolitan centres come together in Poland in mutual support of a single production.³ One of the joint producers, Paweł Wodziński, who started the Towarzystwo Teatralne (Theatrical Society) with Paweł Łysak and other young directors, actors, and musicians in 1998, became artistic director of the Teatr Polski in Poznań. The stated aim of the Society was to stage premieres of contemporary plays by British writers at the Teatr Rozmaitości and the old Norblin Factory in Warsaw. Their production of Kane's *Blasted*, proceeded by Mark Ravenhill's *Shopping and Fucking*, ran afoul of the conservative Warsaw city council members, who did not think it was appropriate for taxpayers' money to support such contentious work, imprudently labelled 'new brutalism'. This led Warlikowski to argue that Kane required special protection in Poland (Dolińska 2002), and Wodziński expressed his hopes that the shared backing of the three major theatres would succeed in solidifying Kane's place in the Polish theatrical canon while finally dissociating her plays from accusations of scandal and pornography (Pawłowski 2001).

Boldly placing Kane beside Shakespeare, dramaturg Piotr Gruszczyński claimed that this was a writer who, having developed a new theatrical language, demanded equal genius from a director. The overlap between his stagings of Shakespeare and Kane can be seen in Warlikowski's ability to push the audience towards the abyss of the text, breaking through 'the holy armour of bourgeois peace' (Gruszczyński 2002a), a manipulation of diachronic time and simultaneous action, the exposure of the actor's body (as in *Hamlet*), and the reappropriation of gendered costumes, language, and behaviour. Material brutality was translated into psychic trauma: rape, murder, castration, and the severing of limbs are all in the text but couched in metaphors so that, although the audience does not directly see the violence, it is nevertheless experienced. Warlikowski successfully foreclosed violence as the dominant trope in Kane through this transposition of the actual to the figurative, thus effectively undermining conservative politicians and critics' protests that Kane's work promulgated violence as pure shock tactic.

During this period, the popularity of what critic Aleks Sierz would later coin 'in-yer-face' theatre in the UK was just making its imprint on the German and Polish stages. Łukasz Drewniak (2002) recognised an overlap between Warlikowski's aesthetics and avant-garde directors working in Berlin such as Christoph Marthaler, Thomas Ostermeier, and Johan Kresnik, though Hans-Thies Lehmann (2002) was quick to commend Warlikowski's sophisticated treatment of Kane in opposition to many German directors' eager capitulation to depictions of violence. Making an effort to maintain the rapid, specific rhythm of Kane's language, Poniedziałek, who translated *Cleansed* with Warlikowski, commented on the ability of the 'capacious' English language to express a wide breadth of emotions that was more difficult in Polish (cited in Matuszewska 2001). Adding a speech from *Crave* as a prologue spoken by German actress Renate Jett, whose physical appearance uncannily resembled Kane, Warlikowski anticipated that the use of a foreign performer would emphasise the universality of the text (Dolińska 2002). Reviewers commented on Jett's difficulty in speaking Polish, as they had when she played Ariel in Warlikowski's *Tempest*, but this time with more empathy, which could perhaps be best attributed to a lack of respect for Kane's text in opposition to the sanctity with which Shakespeare is treated in Poland. *Cleansed* imagines a world without God, where sexuality and desire are posited as the ultimate horizon of human experience, and where love is the single salvationary hope of mankind. Beyond the standard heterosexual relationship presented by the dancer and the doctor, iterations of sexuality in the play are complex, manifold, and divorced from gender, which is rendered an unstable category through sex change and non-camp forms of cross-dressing. It is generally acknowledged that the production included the first male homosexual kiss ever to be performed on a public Polish stage. Not only did the homosexual couple portrayed by Poniedziałek and Thomas Schweiberer offer alternative physical appearances to stereotyped gays that are commonly seen as effeminate, passive, flamboyant, or camp, the physical and emotional sacrifices Carl and Rod made for one another went far to combat associations between homosexuality, superficial sexual exchanges, and rampant promiscuity.

The production opened up a debate on a national scale that reflected the shifting experiences of theatre-going in Poland.

Warlikowski's theatre did not build community cohesion or garner consensus amongst members of the critical establishment, but it did activate and engage audiences. Censure poured in from major theatre reviewers, who variously accused Warlikowski of being devoid of artistic vision, rendering an obsessive, one-dimensional portrait of society, failing to engage his actors in convincing characterisation, falling short of a diagnosis of the contemporary historical moment, and resorting to kitsch, sadistic, vulgar, or shocking images. These critiques offered a treatise on the power of Warlikowski's theatre to not only combat the homogenisation of contemporary theatre practices but also to trigger critical reflection on what is culturally impermissible.

Respectively invited to Avignon, Edinburgh, London, Lille, Hong Kong, and Moscow, comparisons abounded between Warlikowski's *Cleansed* and Jarzyna's *4.48 Psychosis*, though reviewers like Tomasz Cyz and Pawłowski highlighted a productive symbiosis between the alternative stagings of Kane. This is perhaps not surprising given that they had a nearly identical production team. Szczęśniak brought back the indicators of the hospital, the gurney, the white tiles and showerheads, reflective floors and metal-plexiglass walls that were familiar to audiences of *Cleansed*, and Mykietyn's rich scores produced a similarly haunting mood. Despite some obvious resemblances, there was significant divergence between the productions. While *Cleansed* stirred up feelings of rebellion, anger, and compassion, Jarzyna's production primarily evoked a mood of grief and anguish. For Gruszczyński, the main difference lay in the confrontation with the actors' bodies: 'Warlikowski's performance led to the boundaries of intimacy, forcing everyone to overcome embarrassment, thus opening up new gates of perception. In Jarzyna, physicality gave way to the poetry of the text, making the theatrical effect weaker and less shocking' (Gruszczyński 2002b). Jacek Cieślak (2002), however, showed his appreciation of the strain between content and form in Jarzyna's production, arguing that 'this was not a drama composed in view of the theatre, but is rather a record of daily anguish and loneliness'.

One of the major themes in Warlikowski's work has been sexuality. *Cleansed* started a crucial public dialogue by offering alternative representations of homosexuality that found a more explicit outlet when Warlikowski directed Tony Kushner's *Angels in America* in 2007. This would be his final production for the TR Warszawa. It was also the last single play he would stage before moving on to adaptations of multiple texts. Warlikowski's determining production of *Angels in America*, which established a broadly identifiable historical shift in the treatment and perception of homosexuality and HIV/AIDS in Poland, was in sympathetic dialogue with, and later considered a significant component of, the rainbow revolution, a manifestation of gay Poles who protested against conservative Catholic groups and the loss of privileges granted to citizens across virtually the rest of Europe. During the 2005 Polish parliamentary election, Kaczyński's Law and Justice Party (PiS), describing the Third Republic as 'corrupt, immoral and anti-nationalist', promised a Fourth Republic that would place the Catholic Church at the heart of society and reawaken a sense of national dignity (Mark 2010: 15). Tomasz Miłkowski (2007) wrote disparagingly about the homophobia and hatred generated by the builders of Poland's Fourth Republic and the 'yoke of socially and historically embedded resentment' in Polish society. Warlikowski expertly collided black humour with irony, fantasy, and absurdism in his critique of modern sexual relationships. The production was identified as the bravest attempt to regulate the steep escalation of hatred against gays, which I would argue was rooted in a more comprehensive rejection of an enforced EU identity that suggested a wholesale adoption of cosmopolitan liberalism and a construction of historical memory framed by the Holocaust as universally paradigmatic.

Warlikowski's staging of *Angels in America* invited audiences to reflect on their ability to willingly ignore or readily reject those elements of cultural phenomena or individual identity that do not seamlessly map onto social norms. The acting style, which was universally praised, could be described as a heightened naturalism with symbolist interjections. This was reflected in Szcześniak's set. The scenic elements could be flipped at any moment to allow an actor to come forward and directly address the audience, thus generating a communal bond in the theatre previously established in Warlikowski's *Tempest* and *Dybuk* (2003). Niziołek interprets Warlikowski's theatrical spaces as ideograms, visible records of mental gestures that signal a deliberate eradication or withdrawal from local cultural contexts. This was exemplified in this production's use of lighting that blindingly reflects Szcześniak's shiny metal background, simultaneously animating and obscuring the stage and giving the impression of an unlocatable elsewhere. Overlapping Warsaw and New York both in urban tropes and visual cues, Warlikowski offered a blazing critique of the rise in right-wing politics and the ethical ambiguities of embracing neoliberal capitalism, making a broad comparison between Ronald Reagan and Lech Kaczyński, who had banned pride parades in Warsaw in 2004 and 2005 in his capacity as mayor before becoming President of Poland.

Despite many reviewers' focus on themes such as forgiveness, tolerance, and compassion, Warlikowski was adamant that the crucial problem in the play was the depiction of a healthy lover living with an AIDS patient (cited in Kijowska 2007). It is the very particularity of this situation that universalises the performance in a mode that is of equal consequence in the USA, the UK, Germany, or Poland. Warlikowski explained that he wanted to portray how we approach this disease and what we think about it. The insufficiency of an audience's critical self-awareness is revealed when a dying man is abandoned by the person closest to him. When Prior Walter appears in a stupor at the end of *Millennium Approaches* wearing a crown of thorns and a purple robe, this directly engaged the image of Christ's Passion for Polish spectators. Rafał Węgrzyniak (2009) argues that the Passion is virtually absent in the work of the younger generation of Polish directors, likely the result of widespread progressive secularisation and ongoing culture wars over the public role of the Catholic Church and its continued dominance of political and social life.[4] Disarticulating this familiar stage picture, which has appeared in the work of other major Polish playwrights and directors from the nineteenth and twentieth centuries such as Adam Mickiewicz, Leon Schiller, Grotowski, and Swinarski, from its traditional associations (Christ as an AIDS patient), Warlikowski troubles the legacy of artists as transmuters of Polish Romanticism and threatens the conjunction of national identity with Catholicism. Warlikowski finds many precursors for Polish taboo formulation as an incitement towards political mobilisation. Customarily, such taboos were associated with an occupying force or non-ethnic Polish identity. By making the disease the enemy around which Poles could rally, Warlikowski complicated a tendency that implicitly participates in the idealisation of heteronormative and nationalist exclusionary identity formation. However, in one interview Warlikowski warned that 'even if it seems to us that taboos have been broken, they are returning' (cited in Domagalik 2010).

Jewish memory

Hanna Krall observed that Warlikowski's theatre is based on four pillars: antiquity, the Bible, Shakespeare, and the Holocaust. In response to Krall's observation, Warlikowski argued that the Holocaust must at some point come to any Polish artist, given that it is the most Polish topic, and the most important part of Polish history (in Pawłowski 2009). The director further observed that 'if we [Poles] do not rethink the situation of the Jews in Poland in a different way, we will never be [at peace] with ourselves. Our words will not be sincere. Our theatre will not be sincere' (2015: 93–4).

Indeed, Warlikowski has perhaps become best known internationally for his major productions that deal with Jewish identity and spirituality, the Holocaust, anti-Semitism, and Polish/Jewish relations. Although there were allusions in former productions, it was not until his *Dybuk. Między dwoma światami* (*Dybbuk. Between Two Worlds*, TR Warszawa) in 2003 that Warlikowski very explicitly interrogated the absence of Jewish culture in post-war Poland. The production had a two-part structure that seamlessly fitted together Szymon Ansky's Yiddish-language play from 1920 and Krall's eponymous contemporary short story from her collection *Dowody na istnienie* (*Evidence for Existence*, 1995), and used the dybbuk, a wandering soul in Jewish mysticism that possess a living person and controls their conduct, as an ambivalent metaphor for cultural memory. Ansky's play, which absorbed the atmosphere and superstitions of the Jewish shtetl, was developed as part of his ethnographic studies that involved the documentation of the folkloric traditions of Jewish communities in, amongst other places, the Podolia and Volhynia regions. The plot centres around a young Yeshiva student, Chanan, who falls in love with Lea, the daughter of a wealthy merchant. When Lea is contracted by her father Hejnech to marry a man of her own social class, Chanan commits suicide. His spirit returns as a dybbuk that possesses Lea's body and prevents her from participating in the wedding. To exorcise the dybbuk, Hejnech hires a tzaddik, the 'righteous one', a leader and teacher of a generation that devote themselves to the study of the Torah and its commandments, who reminds him of the marriage arrangement contracted with Chanan's father when the children were in infancy. By forsaking this sacred agreement Hejnech has produced a dybbuk, and the play closes with the transcendental restitution of the rightful lovers in eternity (death). Set against the superstitious background of Jewish folk tales where the existence of God is indisputable, Ansky's play contrasted starkly with Krall's parable of modern spirituality in America. The dybbuk became the central metaphor in Warlikowski's search for meaning outside of accepted secularism in a world that had lost its sense of mystery. When asked what made the director identify so strongly with the topics presented in these texts, Warlikowski replied, 'an awareness of life, and then the destruction of Jews in Poland', which he claims is still the missing link in Polish identity today (in Gruszczyński 2003). Warlikowski did not play Klezmer music or use fake beards or robes, though the actors did wear yarmulkes, suggestive of contemporary religious identity and cultural belonging. Rather than try to ignore or eschew the particularities of Jewish traditions and identities, this provocative staging decision was rooted in a desire to rethink the philosophical questions within Ansky's text that were broadly inclusive of transnational contemporary European, Israeli, and American Jewish cultures and emphasised the ongoing relevance of the play instead of its historical distinctiveness or cultural alterity.

Attempting a rational and conscious discussion of traumatic themes opened up by the Holocaust required a break with earlier literary and theatrical forms. Warlikowski's intermingling of forms and genres provokes a critically self-reflective approach to the past that is not easily reliant on claims to the supremacy of either religious faith or historical accuracy. Warlikowski stages neither a hypostatised past nor a transparent historical teleology. Rather, these ethnographic, biographical, and fictional texts are all submitted to a critique of existing explanatory or interpretive moulds, which brings to light the mode in which various genres make particular claims on spectators. In this sense, Warlikowski offers a critique of safely conventionalised narrative forms, canonicity, and historiography that becomes even more pronounced in his use of diverse textual forms in his later adaptations.

By the mid-2000s, relations between Warlikowski and the TR Warszawa had deteriorated. After being awarded the prestigious Meyerhold Award in Moscow in 2006, Warlikowski made a barbed comment that was rumoured to reflect his thoughts on Jarzyna's evolution as a director. He observed, 'many star directors compromise their credibility in the sense that, with age, they become interested in nothing other than form. They simply have nothing new to say any more' (in Nyc 2007). Warlikowski was given funding by the city to start his own theatre and he was soon on the lookout for a new venue in Warsaw. Nowy Teatr (New Theatre) was founded in 2009, and Warlikowski's inaugural production was the most ambitious undertaking of his career. Co-produced by Avignon Festival and the Wiener Festwochen amongst other European partners, *(A)pollonia* returned to many of the themes and genres that had dominated Warlikowski's productions over the previous decade, such as Polish/Jewish memory, the Holocaust, and victimhood.

An original adaptation, *(A)pollonia* interrogates Poland's suppressed past, weaving together ancient (Euripides and Aeschylus) and contemporary (Krall and J. M. Coetzee) material, to critique elevated notions of victimhood and sacrifice deeply embedded in the Polish psyche.[5] Warlikowski staged three victims: Iphigenia, whose father demands the sacrifice of her life for her country; Alcestis, who lays down her life so that her husband might live; and Apolonia Machczyńska, mother of three who hid 25 Jews during the Nazi occupation. When confronted by an SS officer who offers her the choice to condemn her father for the crime or to denounce herself, Apolonia takes responsibility, although it is clear that execution will be the punishment. Apolonia's father, who allows his daughter to make this sacrifice on his behalf, is ultimately unable to bear the burden of guilt and dies four months later, thus rendering her sacrifice doubly superfluous and ineffectual. The adaptation of Greek tragedies also undermines the value of sacrifice. Iphigenia's infantile naivety was emphasised by the adult actor Magdalena Popławska, who wore a young girl's dress and pranced childishly around the stage, ingenuously celebrating a sacrifice that reveals nothing more than her own immaturity and ignorance. Cielecka was double cast as Alcestis and Apolonia. Heavily pregnant in both roles, the characters' sacrifices are multiplied by the cost of two lives. This doubling of the sacrifice pushes against familiar narratives in Polish culture that sublimate personal sacrifice and position it as a natural human reflex or national obligation (Ruda 2009). Warlikowski thus inverts the values traditionally associated with personal sacrifice, rendering selflessness as selfishness, and humility as vanity.

The title, *(A)pollonia*, has a number of overlapping significations. Most obviously, this indexes two characters within the production, the god Apollo and the victim-martyr Apolonia. Drawing parallels between divine and material sublimes, 'Polonia' also refers to Poland as an imagined (sublime) national community during partitions and periods of occupation and subjugation. Krystyna Duniec and Joanna Krakowska argued that, as a shared fantasy of national identity, 'Polonia' only gained a real body after independence in 1989. This body came at the cost of 'heartbreak, the burden of unfulfilled expectations, and the onus of settling historical accounts and identity dilemmas' (2014: xiv–xv). They contrast 'Polonia' with 'Polin', the name for Poland in Hebrew and Yiddish. According to legend, Jews forced to migrate as a result of religious intolerance from other parts of Europe read this as *po* (here) *lin* (dwell), which was interpreted as a good omen. Polin thus also has mythical resonances, representing the place where for centuries the Jews could feel at home, either by protecting their cultural distinctiveness or through assimilation practices. Jacek Kopciński suggested that the use of parentheses – (A) – at once suggests and negates the double referent of the title, and this attempt to simultaneously construct and deconstruct is the defining gesture of Warlikowski's production (2009: 8).

In a number of ways, *(A)pollonia* sits in the liminal space between the two parts of *Dybuk*, the historical lacuna separating Ansky and

Krall's texts. While *Dybuk* was constructed through metaphor, insinuation, and the haunting of the past, *(A)pollonia* directly engages the audience in a dialogic exchange over the Holocaust. Warlikowski remains careful never to fix the limits of contextualisation of history and attempts to interrogate rather than facilely undo binaries such as guilt/innocence, justice/injustice, victim/perpetrator, and hero/villain that have historical traction in Poland. As opposed to reinforcing these binaries, or simply dissolving them, Warlikowski places them against one another in an unresolved and mutually generative tension. In so doing, the director again uses multiple textual sources and genres without giving priority to a single form of literature, biography, philosophy, or historiography. Not only does this give rise to hybrid modes of thinking about Polish/Jewish histories, it further interferes with the renewal or reinforcement of national narratives that disavow culpability or seek easy or definitive solutions to questions of guilt and innocence, remembering and forgetting.

Not only are victims put on trial, perpetrators are given space to defend their actions. Agamemnon returns from war and is greeted by Clytemnestra in the Polish tradition with bread and salt. Refusing the mantel of heroism, however, Agamemnon desires punishment and wishes to be seen as a murderer despite the fact that as king he is entitled to absolve himself of past crimes and revise the historical record. Maciej Stuhr as Agamemnon confronted the audience with a direct address, suggesting that spectators are not morally superior to him simply because they were fortunate enough not to have encountered the same ethical dilemmas. Warlikowski employs this rhetorical convention not in a facile attempt to level the historical playing field by including the excluded voices of perpetrators, but rather to critique the deployment of dubious ethical relativism that underpins revisionist histories and criminal testimonies, such as Adolf Eichmann's testimony in his 1961 trial for crimes against humanity.

A key element in Warlikowski's exploration of new theatrical vocabularies was the introduction of the live-feed camera, reminiscent of the use of media in Thomas Ostermeier's *Hamlet* (2008) and Ivo van Hove's *Roman Tragedies* (2006–07). Video projections were used to normalise the tragic hero and to draw attention to the myth of sacrifice in Polish culture and the ethical paradoxes of fate. Krall's short story was intermingled with Euripides and Aeschylus, with the result that the hubris and heroism of men and gods were treated with equal scepticism. The performance also included mini-rock concerts, the use of skype, a harrowing hour-long lecture on cruelty to animals, and a critique of institutions that attempt to consecrate and lionise collective memory, such as the Righteous Among the Nations medal. Despite a similarity of themes, Marta Bryś noted in *Didaskalia* that the prologue of *Dybuk* created a unity between the actors and the audience that was not possible in *(A)pollonia*, where spectators were threatened with the brutality of mankind with a violence that mercilessly undermined the harmony of experienced reality. 'In *Dybuk* Warlikowski sustained a feeling of nostalgia and melancholy, but in *(A)pollonia* he abandons them, confronting the viewer with fundamental questions', Marta Bryś observed. The critic concluded that the change in perspective demonstrated a radical reversal in Warlikowski's theatrical and intellectual exploration (Bryś 2009).

Dybuk and *(A)pollonia* were created for and partly funded by the Avignon Festival, and their enormous success in France has confirmed Warlikowski's broader appeal outside of his home country, despite the cultural specificity of many of his themes. In 2005, he was named the symbol of new Polish theatre by the French newspaper *Le Monde*, who devoted an entire page of reviews to his production of Israeli playwright Hanoch Levin's *Krum*, which had a double premiere in Warsaw and Krakow the same year. Warlikowski was in fact the first Polish director to have been invited to mount a text of his own choosing in his preferred location at the festival, an honour not even extended to Tadeusz Kantor. Warlikowski has remained adamant in his belief that globalisation and intracultural theatre practices since the 1960s have led to a common language for theatre artists that disrupt facile East–West binaries. Avignon and other international festivals have played a crucial role in developing such a language.

Warlikowski has similarly argued that opera as a form produces a universal language, which shares and combines different national styles and aesthetic vocabularies. As a result, it is his contention that no such thing as a 'national opera' exists (in Hawryluk 2018). Correspondingly, it is not surprising that Warlikowski has become best known in Europe since the 2010s as an opera director. The last opera he staged in Poland, Alban Berg's *Wozzeck* at the Polish National Opera in Warsaw, was as long ago as 2006. Warlikowski abandoned the Polish opera scene, given that producers only allow for one or two stagings of productions that take him two years to prepare. Leaving Warsaw, Warlikowski has worked at the Paris Opera, Bavarian State Opera in Munich, Teatro Real in Madrid, the Royal Opera House in London, and La Monnaie in Brussels, as well as the Salzburg Festival. The Polish director confessed that he did not think after his first attempt at opera in 2000 that much would come from this 'flirtation' (in Hawryluk 2018). He interpreted Berg's *Wozzeck* as highly theatrical, built on Georg Büchner's dramatic text rather than as a classical opera libretto, and this allowed him an early entry point as a theatre director who would evolve as he took on operas that had radically different conventions to those in dramatic plays, such as Verdi's *Don Giovanni*. Excited by the potential of such operas, which have fewer limitations than theatre, he suggested that Richard Strauss, Hugo von Hofmannsthal, and Leoš Janáček have offered him works that are more daring than conventional plays and an opportunity to break the stronghold of national borders. In his production of Richard Wagner's *Parsifal* in Paris, for example, Warlikowski included footage from Roberto Rossellini's *Germany, Year Zero* (1949), a film that he argued was an exploration of precisely the forms of German culture to which *Parsifal* remains a cultural monument. Warlikowski contrasted Wagner's spiritual world with the establishment of a secular post-war Germany (still in ruins) that Rossellini sought to document. In a radically transnational gesture, a Polish director used an Italian film to frame a German opera staged in a French house as a critique of European culture and history, the dynamics of secularism in the wake of the Second World War in particular.

While opera may open dynamic possibilities in his approaches to directing, Warlikowski is less sanguine about the audiences it generates. He observes that well-known and well-loved classical operas engender audiences that are more likely to come to listen to the music and critique the inadequacy of the direction than to witness a new staging. Opera audiences can therefore be contrasted with those who attend his theatre productions. Warlikowski's theatre has built critical communities that more often align with his radical rethinking of the relationship between society, culture, and political allegiances.

Civic ensembles

Warlikowski's international appeal is in great part a result of his strong ensemble. Working time and again with the same creative team and actors, Warlikowski has developed trust and demands loyalty from his ensemble in an effort to move beyond routinised stagings connected to rational readings of classical texts, and traverse emotional and physical boundaries that typically inhibit performers in rehearsal, such as shame, pride, and vanity. Adam Ferency, who has performed in a number of Warlikowski's productions since 1998, spoke admiringly about the director's vulnerability in front of actors, observing that rather than impart a preconceived structure he often appeared helpless before his cast. Warlikowski famously undercuts actors' habits of interpretation and asks them not to hide out in the consolation of fictional personae but rather to interrogate their own experience and emotions in the rehearsal process (Ferency cited in Wyżyńska 2003). Allowing for long periods of uninterrupted improvisation, Magdalena Cielecka, who has performed in nearly all of Warlikowski's theatre productions since 1999, explained that Warlikowski offers the actor great freedom to explore the varied and deeply personal dimensions of character, which means that the first steps on stage can be quite painful for the actor without any prior guidelines, instructions, or prompts. As a result, he is capable of producing unique performances that include the actor's vision and sense of agency in the finished product. 'Even if we are going in the wrong direction', Cielecka observed, '[Krzysztof] reiterates that in each improvisation there is a little bit of what will lead us in the right direction' (cited in Wyżyńska 2003).

This tendency can be understood not as an attempt to restore ensemble practices established in Poland in the twentieth century, but rather as a revitalisation of the creative energies released through the formation of those ensembles. Warlikowski encourages an environment in which actors can push against margins bounded by social decorum or good behaviour, explore the body in a candid and unconstrained manner, and overcome or reject inhibitions. While such explorations are not inherently liberating or progressive, they do offer the potential to link agency to visibility, to construct volitional identities, and to evacuate conventional or hegemonic norms. The actors' bodily practices are part of what could be called a queer and discursive process, not because they exceed theatricality but rather because they bypass notions of 'character' circumscribed by narrative, diegesis, or fiction in an endeavour to assert the presence of alternative lives and experiences normally excluded from public discourse. This evolution of an ensemble can begin to explain the tremendous international success of Warlikowski's diverse and richly textured theatrical projects. Erika Fischer-Lichte contends that Warlikowski has connected Polish theatre with the rest of Europe, which has 'opened up the possibility of a dialogue with other European cultures, emphasizing what Polish culture shared with them instead of highlighting its otherness' (2014: 144).

In 2018, Warlikowski came back to Nowy Teatr for the first time in three years, having worked exclusively on operas outside of Poland. His production *Wyjeżdżamy* (*We Are Leaving*, 2018) heralded his return to Hanoch Levin (see Plate 16). In a radical inversion of his 2005 production of *Krum*, which charted an émigré's return to his home country, *Wyjeżdżamy* explores a community's desire to immigrate. Rejecting singular texts, Warlikowski and dramaturg Gruszczyński (with Poniedziałek as translator) edited together numerous works by Levin, Henryk Grynberg, and Marcin Wicha, as well as Tadeusz Kantor's final performance *I Shall Never Return* (1988). On the one hand, the development of this production was a direct response to the conservative PiS government's harsh judiciary, cultural, and historical policies and the resulting sense of alienation and fear they provoked for the company that resulted in conversations about migration (Cieślak 2018); on the other hand, staging an Israeli writer descended from Polish Jews during the 50th anniversary year of Poland's anti-Semitic purges in 1968 (which are specifically treated in Grynberg's writing) was a significant political act in itself. Co-funded by institutions in Belgium, France, Greece, and Switzerland, *Wyjeżdżamy* needed to be culturally intelligible to audiences outside of Poland and its symbolic and linguistic regimes, and the starting point of immigration through a foreign writer offers otherness as the radical point of departure ('We are leaving').

Again, rather than reinforcing Polishness as a singular identity category, Warlikowski explores the complexities of identification as fractured, unsettled, dispersed, and transnational. What's more, while *Krum* focused on the individual (and can thus be interpreted as a sequel to his staging of *Hamlet*), this production constructs community as its integral political configuration, even if the characters who make up this community are often cruel and petty to one another. I would argue from *Krum* to *Wyjeżdżamy* one can trace a crucial movement from a preoccupation with a singular subject to an engagement with shared publics. The stakes of this trajectory construct a politics of empathy that is reflected through the open-door policy of Nowy Teatr, whose public spaces are filled with local residents, including young children and even pets. In the programme notes to *Wyjeżdżamy* Warlikowski remarks, 'The more we are a community, the better'. Nowy Teatr today is as much a meeting space for neighbours as it is a cultural venue for talks, screenings, workshops, and performances. This venue then exemplifies Warlikowski's career, grounded in a mode of resistance to a conservative public sphere that is increasingly marked by insularism, nostalgia, and xenophobia. Responding to social and cultural restraints, a democracy in crisis, the formation of neoliberalist economies, and an increasingly polarised media, Warlikowski has given voice to publics that embrace radical inclusivity, progressive politics, and an enduring resistance to ethnic nationalism.

Five key productions

Hamlet. By William Shakespeare. Translated by Stanisław Barańczak. Set design by Małgorzata Szczęśniak. Music by Paweł Mykietyn. Lighting design by Piotr Pawlik. Perf. Stanisława Celińska, Magdalena Cielecka, Jolanta Fraszyńska, Marek Kalita, Cezary Kosiński, Maria Maj, Jacek Poniedziałek, Omar Sangare, Maria Seweryn, Robert Więckiewicz, Adam Woronowicz, Mirosław Zbrojewicz. Teatr Rozmaitości, Warsaw. 22 October 1999.

Oczyszczeni (*Cleansed*). By Sarah Kane. Translated by Jacek Poniedziałek and Krzysztof Warlikowski. Set design by Małgorzata Szczęśniak. Music by Paweł Mykietyn. Lighting design by Felice Ross. Perf. Mariusz Bonaszewski, Stanisława Celińska, Redbad Klynstra, Małgorzata Hajewska-Krzysztofik, Renate Jett, Jacek Poniedziałek, Thomas Schweiberer, Tomasz Tyndyk. Teatr Współczesny, Wrocław. 15 December 2001.

Dybuk. Między dwoma światami (*Dybuk. Between Two Worlds*). Texts by Szymon Ansky and Hanna Krall. Adapted by Krzysztof Warlikowski. Set design by Małgorzata Szczęśniak. Music by Paweł Mykietyn. Lighting design by Felice Ross. Perf. Stanisława Celińska, Andrzej Chyra, Magdalena Cielecka, Renate Jett, Marek Kalita, Irena Laskowska, Zygmunt Malanowicz, Jacek Poniedziałek, Orna Porat, Jerzy Senator, Maciej Tomaszewski, Tomasz Tyndyk. Teatr Rozmaitości, Warsaw. 6 October 2003.

Anioły w Ameryce (*Angels in America*). By Tony Kushner. Translated by Jacek Poniedziałek. Set design by Małgorzata Szczęśniak. Music by Paweł Mykietyn. Lighting design by Felice Ross. Perf. Stanisława Celińska, Andrzej Chyra, Magdalena Cielecka, Dorota Landowska, Rafał Maćkowiak, Zygmunt Malanowicz, Maja Ostaszewska, Jacek Poniedziałek, Bogusława Schubert, Danuta Stenka, Maciej Stuhr, Tomasz Tyndyk. Teatr Rozmaitości, Warsaw. 17 February 2007.

(A)pollonia. Adapted by Piotr Gruszczyński, Jacek Poniedziałek, and Krzysztof Warlikowski. Set and costume design by Małgorzata Szczęśniak. Music by Paweł Mykietyn, Renate Jett, Piotr Maślanka,

> and Paweł Stankiewicz. Lighting design by Felice Ross. Perf. Andrzej Chyra, Magdalena Cielecka, Ewa Dałkowska, Małgorzata Hajewska-Krzysztofik, Renate Jett, Danuta Stenka, Wojciech Kalarus, Marek Kalita, Zygmunt Malanowicz, Adam Nawojczyk, Anna Radwan-Gancarczyk, Maja Ostaszewska, Jolanta Fraszyńska, Jacek Poniedziałek, Magdalena Popławska, Monika Niemczyk, Maciej Stuhr, Tomasz Tyndyk. Nowy Teatr, Warsaw. 16 May 2009.

Notes

1 The Third Polish Republic refers to the period after the political transition that commenced with the demise of communism in 1989. The First Polish Republic was the Polish–Lithuanian Commonwealth (1569–1795), a bi-confederation of Poland and Lithuania ruled by a common monarch, which ended with the partitions of Poland between the Russian, Austro-Hungarian, and Prussian Empires. The Second Polish Republic refers to the short-lived period of political autonomy between the First and Second World Wars (1918–39).
2 All translations from Polish are my own.
3 Funding also came from Theorem, an association that bridges Europe with the specific intention of promoting the work of young East European artists, Berlin's Hebel Theatre, and the European Commission on Culture.
4 For an excellent study of Polish theatre and the role of the Catholic Church in Polish society, see Adamiecka-Sitek, Kościelniak and Niziołek 2018.
5 The full range of texts adapted for *(A)pollonia* include: Aeschylus' *Oresteia*; Hans Christian Andersen's 'The Story of a Mother'; J.M. Coetzee's *Elizabeth Costello*; Andrzej Czajkowski's 'Mamo, gdzie jesteś?'; Euripides' *Iphigenia in Aulis*, *Heracles*, and *Alcestis*; Hanna Krall's 'Pola' in *Tam już nie ma żadnej rzeki* and 'Narożny dom z wieżyczką' in *Żal*; Jonathan Littell's *The Kindly Ones*; Marcin Świetlicki's 'Pobojowisko' in *Zimne kraje. Wiersze 1980–1990*; and Rabindranath Tagore's 'The Post Office'. The production was produced by a number of European theatres and festivals, including Nowy Teatr, the Festival d'Avignon, Narodowy Stary Teatr Kraków, Comédie de Genève, Théâtre Royal de la Monnaie (Brussels), Théâtre National de Chaillot (Paris), Théâtre de Liège, and Wiener Festwochen. This international funding also has implications for the universalisation of themes on Polish/Jewish relations.

Bibliography

Adamiecka-Sitek, Agata (2006) '(De)konstrukcja kobiecości w "Poskromieniu złośnicy" Krzysztofa Warlikowskiego', *Dialog*, (October): 10.

Adamiecka-Sitek, Agata, Marcin Kościelniak and Grzegorz Niziołek (eds) (2018) *Teatr a Kościół*, Warszawa: Instytut Teatralny im. Zbigniewa Raszewskiego.

Bryś, Marta (2009) *'(D)ybuk w (A)polonii.* Między dwoma światami', *Didaskalia - Gazeta Teatralna*, 92/93.

Carlson, Marvin (2010) 'Space and Theatre History', in Charlotte M. Canning and Thomas Postlewait (eds), *Representing the Past: Essays in Performance Historiography*, Iowa City: University of Iowa Press, pp. 195–214.

Cieślak, Jacek (2001) 'Rozum tego nie pojmie, słowa nie opiszą', *Rzeczpospolita*, 7 February.

―――― (2002) 'Rozbrojony ładunek emocji', *Rzeczpospolita*, 11 February.

―――― (2018) '*Wyjeżdżamy* Warlikowskiego: Losy ludzi niedoskonałych', *Rzeczpospolita*, www.rp.pl/Teatr/306139934-Wyjezdzamy-Warlikowskiego-Losy-ludzi-niedoskonalych.html?preview=1&remainingPreview=4&grantedBy=preview&

Dolińska, Michalina (2002) 'Droga do katharsis', *Gazeta Wyborcza* (Poznań), 9 January.

Domagalik, Małgorzata (2010) 'Chcesz wiedzieć – idź do teatru Warlikowskiego', *Pani*, 7 June.

Drewniak, Łukasz (2002) 'Tratwa Meduzy', *Przekrój*, 13 January.

Duniec, Krystyna and Joanna Krakowska (2014) 'Introduction', in Krystyna Duniec, Joanna Krakowska, and Joanna Klass (eds), *(A)pollonia: Twenty-First Century Polish Drama and Texts for the Stage*, London, New York and Calcutta: Seagull Books, pp. xiv–xxxiv.

Fischer-Lichte, Erika (2014) *Dionysus Resurrected: Performances of Euripides' The Bacchae in a Globalizing World*, London: Wiley-Blackwell.

Gross, Jan T. (2001) *Neighbors: The Destruction of the Jewish Community in Jedwabne, Poland*, Princeton: Princeton University Press.

Gruszczyński, Piotr (2001) 'Obcy bóg', *Tygodnik Powszechny*, 4 March.

―――― (2002a) 'Brzytwa', *Tygodnik Powszechny*, 6 January.

―――― (2002b) 'Kasandra', *Tygodnik Powszechny*, 3 March.

―――― (2003) 'Dybuk, czyli Dziady', *Tygodnik Powszechny*, 21 September.

Hawryluk, Jacek (2018) 'Debiut Krzysztofa Warlikowskiego w Covent Garden. Opera "Z domu umarłych" Janacka to duchowa podróż przez piekło', *Polskie Radio*, 6 March.

Kijowska, Joanna (2007) 'Warlikowski rozpęta burzę', *Dziennik*, 17 February.

Kopciński, Jacek (2009) 'Melancholia cieni', *Teatr*, 7/8, 1 August.
Kott, Jan (1964) *Shakespeare Our Contemporary*, trans. Bolesław Taborski, New York: Double Day.
Kowalczyk, Janusz (1999) 'Nocą nago na strychu', *Rzeczpospolita*, 27 October.
Krakowska-Narożniak, Joanna (2003) '"Burza", czyli zdobycie władzy', *Dialog*, 4, 1 April, http://encyklopediateatru.pl/artykuly/75158/burza-czyli-zdobycie-wladzy
Lehmann, Hans–Thies (2002) 'Od sensu do sensualności: niemiecki teatr postdramatyczny', *Didaskalia - Gazeta Teatralna*, 51/52.
Mark, James (2010) *The Unfinished Revolution: Making Sense of the Communist Past in Central-Eastern Europe*, New Haven: Yale University Press.
Matuszewska, Małgorzata (2001) 'Bez miłości, czyli bez sensu', *Gazeta Wyborcza* (Wrocław), 14 December.
Miłkowski, Tomasz (2007) 'Anioły w Warszawie', *Przegląd*, 6 May.
Niziołek, Grzegorz (2006) 'Historia stołu', *Didaskalia - Gazeta Teatralna*.
——— (2015) 'Theatre for Neurotics', *Polish Theatre Perspectives*, 1(1): 52–62.
Nyc, Iga (2007) 'Pojedynek potworów', *Wprost*, 1 February.
Pawłowski, Roman (1999) 'Król jest nagi', *Gazeta Wyborcza*, 27 October.
——— (2001) 'Triumwirat teatrów', *Gazeta Wyborcza*, 14 December.
——— (2002) 'Oddział zamknięty', *Gazeta Wyborcza*, 25 February.
——— (2005) 'Haust świeżego powietrza', *Gazeta Wyborcza*, 14 March.
——— (2009) 'Rzecz, która nie lubi być zabijana', *Gazeta Wyborcza*, 16 May.
Ruda, Małgorzata (2009) 'Daremność ofiary', *Dekada Literacka*, 5/6, 16 May.
Schiller, Anna (1999) 'Hamlet bez właściwości', *Wprost*, 31 October.
Warlikowski, Krzysztof (2015) 'Life in a Cemetery, Krzysztof Warlikowski talks to Piotr Gruszczyński', *Polish Theatre Perspectives*, 1(1): 93–108.
Węgrzyniak, Rafał (2009) 'Pasja', *e-teatr.pl*, 14 April.
Wyżyńska, Dorota (1999a) 'Oszaleć i nie zwariować', *Gazeta Wyborcza*, 2 October.
——— (1999b) 'Tajemnica, łamigłówka, gąbka', *Gazeta Wyborcza*, 9 October.
——— (2003) 'Zawsze mówi o podróży', *Gazeta Wyborcza*, 2 January.

Chapter 17

CALIXTO BIEITO

Staging excess in, across, and through Europe

Maria M. Delgado

Most English-language publications on directors have inscribed a particular group of largely northern European and Russian figures as the key innovators of directorial practice through the twentieth century. Spanish directors have been significantly excluded from this pantheon and, as such, have been largely erased from the documentation and elaboration of directorial trends over the past 120 years.[1] The work of directors emerging in the latter years of the Franco era certainly played a significant role in opening up international interest in the Spanish stage. With the exception of Argentine director Víctor García's collaborations with Nuria Espert – *Las criadas* (*The Maids*, 1969), *Yerma* (1971), and *Divinas palabras* (*Divine Words*, 1975) – it was the work of the performance companies that was probably best known outside Spain during this period. Albert Boadella's gestural vocabularies with Els Joglars (formed in 1962), Joan Font's ludic spectacles with Els Comediants (formed in 1971), and subsequently the kinetic provocations of La Fura dels Baus (formed in 1980) functioned as the face of Spanish theatre outside its borders.[2] This may be because they have worked largely within performative (rather than theatrical) parameters and within the physical vocabularies of performance. Increasingly, however, over the past 30 years, directors have played a significant role in opening up international interest in the Spanish stage.

Perhaps the most prominent of these has been Calixto Bieito, a Barcelona-based director who proved a regular presence at the Edinburgh International Festival during the last decade of Brian McMaster's tenure as artistic director. Bieito's work was actually first seen outside Spain in 1995, two years before his Edinburgh debut, when his staging of

383

Shakespeare's *King John* was presented at the Dijon Festival. However, he had been a significant director within the Catalan theatre scene since the mid-1980s when he made his professional debut at Barcelona's Adrià Gual theatre with *El joc de l'amor i de l'atzar* (*The Game of Love and Chance*, 1985). At a time when Spanish, and particularly Catalan, theatre was defined through the acrobatic ingenuity and gestural stylisation of the performance companies, Bieito followed the example of Lluís Pasqual and Barcelona's Teatre Lliure (formed in 1976) in providing intelligent textual readings that evolved on sparse scenographic environments where shifts of mood, tone, and emphasis were often realised in fast, physical terms. While Bieito has never directly acknowledged the influence of the Lliure's trajectory on his own, it is worth noting that he worked as an assistant director to Pasqual (while the latter was Artistic Director of the Odéon-Théâtre de l'Europe) in 1992 on the staging of Valle-Inclán's *Tirano Banderas* (*Banderas the Tyrant*). Pasqual had invigorated the Catalan theatre scene between 1976 and 1983 with uncluttered productions of classical works where simplicity replaced elaboration and actor proximity was paramount, and he too became a significant 'export' during his time as artistic director of Madrid's Centro Dramático Nacional (1983–9) with key productions of García Lorca's 'impossible' plays *El público* (*The Public*, 1986) and *Comedia sin título* (*Play without a Title*, 1989), both also seen at the Odéon-Théâtre de l'Europe.[3] Like Pasqual, Bieito was to direct foreign-language works that had never had a discernible presence on the Catalan stage at the Teatre Lliure. With Molière's *Amphitryon* (presented as *Amfitrió*, 1995), Sondheim's *Company* (1997), and Schoenberg's *Pierrot Lunaire* (1998), he demonstrated a directorial dexterity that had already been evident from his early work with La Infidel, the small, touring company that he established in 1989. The latter productions also pointed to an ease with musical form and the dynamics of music theatre that were, in time, to ensure a relatively easy transition to opera.

Bieito and Barcelona

While his international reputation has primarily been forged around revisionist, aggressive productions of the classical canon which travel well across the festival circuit, Bieito's early career was defiantly marked by a pliant versatility, moving from Irish symbolism (Synge's *The Tinker's Wedding* and *The Shadow of the Glen*, presented as *Dues històries irlandes* in 1990) to Shakespeare (*Els dos cavallers de Verona* (*Two Gentlemen of Verona*) in 1989 and *El somni d'una nit d'estiu* (*A Midsummer Night's Dream*) in 1992) and modern dissenters who have probed the boundaries of dramatic form (Thomas Bernhard's *Ritter, Dene, Voss* in 1993). While Bieito has referred to Albert Boadella as arguably the most significant director working in Spain (Delgado 2003b: 61), Boadella's trajectory has pivoted almost exclusively within the tradition of group-devised work. In many ways, Bieito appears drawn to Boadella partly because he represents, perhaps more than any other Spanish director of the past 60 years, an approach to directing that is based on extended periods of development, with group research from an ensemble of performers and dramaturgical intervention as key modes of constructing theatrical productions.

Bieito's work in Barcelona has been grounded in a company ethos that allows for professional relationships to be built up across productions. Costume designer Mercè Paloma has worked on a number of his productions since *A Midsummer Night's Dream*; Teatre Lliure associate Xavi Clot has lit a significant proportion of Bieito's operatic and theatrical work since they first collaborated on *Amphitryon* in 1995; Alfons Flores has designed over 15 productions for Bieito since their operatic debut with *Il mondo della luna* for Maastricht's Opera Zuid in 1999; German scenographers Ariane Isabell Unfried and Rifail Ajdarpasic have provided the design environments for non-Castilian-language works or pieces that take place in environments that are not specifically Spanish or Catalan, as with *Il Trovatore* (2003), *Hamlet* (2003), *La Traviata* (2004), *El rei Lear* (*King Lear*, 2004), and *Elektra* (2007). Since 2006 Rebecca Ringst has proved his most regular set designer. Working in tandem with costume designer Ingo Krügler, Ringst's stark vertical designs include the shifting neon-lit frame for *Fidelio* (2013), the monochrome collapsing facades of *La forza del destino* (*The Force of Destiny*, 2015), and the yellow scaffolding set that houses the orchestra in *Die Soldaten* (2013). Between 1995 and 2009 Bieito regularly worked with a core group of actors (including his wife Roser Camí, Boris Ruiz, Mingo Ràfols, and Carles

Canut – Camí is Lady Macbeth and Ràfols is Macbeth in Plate 17's image from *Macbeth*). These effectively came to form a de facto company that played a decisive role in shaping Bieito's house style.

Bieito's early productions with La Infidel allowed for the cultivation of long rehearsal periods, a commitment to working with performers from diverse acting traditions (from music hall to acrobatics, incorporating both classical and musical training), and from different nationalities. Significantly, Bieito is one of the few Catalan-based directors of the post-1990s years – he left Catalonia to move abroad in 2011 – who sought to work in *both* Catalan and Castilian.[4] Born in Miranda de Ebro (Castile) in 1963, to a musical family with Galician roots who moved to Barcelona when he was 14, Bieito's career has been founded on moving against the monolingual register favoured both by Franco – who promoted Castilian at the expense of the other languages of the Spanish state – and Jordi Pujol, President of the Catalan Parliament, the Generalitat, between 1980 and 2003 – who sought to remedy the balance by prioritising Catalan as *the* official language of Catalonia. Bieito's recognition of the need to work across boundaries has thus been evident, not merely in a repertoire that moves from Shakespeare to Sondheim, but crucially in a conscious decision to work across the languages of Spain and beyond.

During his time as artistic director of Barcelona's Romea theatre (1999–2011), he redefined the role of one of the city's most emblematic venues. Situated in Barcelona's working-class Raval district, off the central Ramblas avenue, the Romea was effectively the home of Catalan-language drama between 1867 and the outbreak of the Spanish Civil War in 1936. While it suffered a more checkered history during the difficult years of the Franco regime, its symbolic associations with Catalan dramatists were to continue. Josep Maria de Sagarra (now known primarily through his 28 translations of Shakespeare) premiered his most significant works there between 1918 and 1959. Josep Maria Benet i Jornet and Sergi Belbel, arguably two of the most important Catalan dramatists of the post-Franco era, made conspicuous debuts at the theatre with *Una vella, coneguda olor* (*An Old Familiar Smell*) and *Elsa Schneider* in 1964 and 1989 respectively. With the establishment of a Catalan National Theatre (Teatre Nacional de Catalunya; TNC) in 1997, functioning with a lavish subsidy and a clear mandate to promote Catalan-language drama, Bieito reconceived a role for the Romea which juggled both its historical role and a new identity within a city balancing a healthy quota of established commercial venues, newer fringe spaces, and the performance complexes of the TNC and Montjuïc's cluster (the Mercat de les Flors, the new Lliure which opened in 2001 and the Institut del Teatre).

Bieito sought to balance a programme of Catalan dramaturgy, both classic and new, with current European drama, as with Conor McPherson's *The Weir* (1999) and Roland Schimmelpfennig's *Die Arabische Nacht* (*Arabian Night*, 2002) and Renaissance dramas – such as *Life is a Dream* (2000), *Macbeth* (2002), and *King Lear* (2004). The theatre hosts the work of directors and companies visiting with productions from elsewhere in Spain as with Animalario's *Urtain* in 2009, companies and foreign directors, as with the Argentine Daniel Veronese who brought his production of *El túnel* (*The Tunnel*) to the theatre in 2006. While Bieito has certainly opened the Romea to established local directors such as Xavier Albertí, Ferran Madico, Carme Portaceli, and Sergi Belbel, he has taken risks with ventures like young company Kràmpack's lucrative hit *Excuses* (2001), which served to bring a young audience to the Romea and firmly establish it in the first five years of the twenty-first century as a 'happening' place within Barcelona.

It is perhaps not surprising therefore that Bieito has chosen to situate himself as a theatrical Ferran Adrià (Delgado 2004: 75). Adrià, celebrated chef at El Bulli between 1987 and 2011, reinvented Catalan *nouvelle cuisine*, positioning his kitchen as a holistic laboratory of intense culinary investigation. Bieito too has served as a recognisable export with something of a brand identity with which he has become increasingly associated. While Bieito came to international prominence in 1997 when Brian McMaster brought his production of Tomás Breton's 1894 *zarzuela*, *La verbena de la paloma* (*The Festival of the Dove*) to the Edinburgh International Festival, he had already enjoyed a discernible presence at Barcelona's Grec Festival since 1989 with productions of Goldoni's *Els enamorats* (*The Lovers*, 1990), *A Midsummer Night's Dream* (1991), *Un dia* (*A Day*, 1993), *El rei Joan* (*King John*, 1995), and *The Festival of the Dove*

(1996). With subsequent productions of *La tempestat* (*The Tempest*, 1997), *La ópera de cuatro cuartos* (*The Threepenny Opera*, 2002), *King Lear* (2004), and *Peer Gynt* (2006). Bieito has become a significant emblem of a festival established in the euphoria of the country's transition to democracy and what was to become, following the 1992 Olympics, a lucrative tourist market.

Whether working in large auditoria, the more intimate stage of the Romea, or within appropriated spaces, Bieito's directorial approach has always involved meticulous textual research, economical stagecraft, and a detailed attention to character construction that relies on instinct rather than methodical and intellectual character analysis. Bieito's work with actors may evoke the volatile performativity of Complicite's theatre but his scenic landscapes demonstrate a debt to the distilled conceptualism of Fabià Puigserver and Cheek by Jowl's Nick Ormerod. While his early Shakespeares often evolved on a bare stage of reddish clay (as in *Mesura per mesura* (*Measure for Measure*, 1999)) or silver sand (as in *The Tempest*), *King Lear* marks a trend in his staging visible since *Macbeth*: a desire to contain the sprawling, epic structures of the plays within an enclosed and visibly identifiable environment. With *Macbeth*, first staged in German for the Salzburg Festival in 2001, with a set by Barbara Ehnes (refigured for the Spanish and Catalan productions by Flores), this was a mafia living room filled with easy-wipe-clean leather sofas, porcelain tigers growling ominously at visitors, and a cluttered drinks trolley piled high with alcoholic beverages to fuel the clan's partying (see Plate 17). A balcony running across the top of the stage served as a site for surveillance, clandestine reunions, ruminations, and soliloquies. For *Hamlet*, in 2003, Bieito substituted for the white leather sofas, black leather armchairs, a sleek bar, and a giant, pink fluorescent sign announcing the court at Elsinore as 'Palace'. Here a court at war played out rituals of mourning for old Hamlet while coming to terms with guilt, culpability, and tormented family relationships. This masculine environment was presided over by George Costigan's thuggish Claudius ably supported by Rupert Frazer's pusillanimous Polonius. Diane Fletcher's moll-like Gertrude, a good-time party girl, and Rachel Pickup's glamorous Ophelia operated as decorous ornaments, servicing the needs of the men who used and abused them.

These productions, like his 2004 *King Lear*, have been grounded around the abuses contained within the family as the fundamental microcosm of wider social units. For *King Lear*, veteran Catalan performer Josep Maria Pou, taking his first Shakespearian role, provided a larger-than-life patriarch, master of a kingdom governed through fear and intimidation. The location of the action on a bare stage defined by raked seating upstage and drab brown plastic chairs moved away from the overtly kitsch setting of *Macbeth*'s gaudy living room and *Hamlet*'s private nightclub. This was what Bieito termed a more anonymous environment, a stadium of death in an undefined country in the midst of a dictatorship, serving to create a climate of ominous surveillance where marginalised characters prowled around the raked seating at the back of the stage, watching over the proceedings developing below them (Subirana 2004: 43). The cut of the costumes suggested the late 1980s as East European dictatorships fell in quick succession, but other elements combined to draw parallels with the political present as with Pou's bearded appearance evoking something of the image of Saddam Hussein captured by US troops and Dani Klamburg's cloying Oswald recalling the conservative Spanish Prime Minister José María Aznar, a figure perceived during his second term as government leader (2000–4) to be in thrall to George W. Bush and his imperialist agenda. Pou's Lear, shown groping, slapping, and kissing his somewhat reticent daughters, pointed to a climate of possible incest and palpable fear where all jump to the King's attention or fear the consequences. Institutional abuse was inextricably linked to familial cruelty. Bieito never attempted to polarise the court into 'heroes' and 'villains'. Pep Ferrer's Albany was no moralist but a pusillanimous drunk, hovering on the fringes of the court, who fell almost by default into Lear's camp. His frustration at Goneril's defiance and her infatuation with Francesc Garrido's seductive Edmund led him both towards a fumbled attempted seduction of Regan and domestic violence towards his wife. In the extended household unit of the court, all relations were shown as tarred by the abusive brush of the father as represented by Gloucester and Lear. The final image of semi-naked or naked corpses strewn across a stage littered with paper, seats knocked around the stage, and a general state of disarray effectively conveyed the sense of a kingdom where chaos had erupted to horrendous effect, fracturing both family and state.[5]

King Lear is indicative of a number of Bieito's stagings in that it was rehearsed and conceived to work across different languages. Premiered in Catalan it then went on to tour across Spain in 2004–5, accommodating both Castilian and Catalan performances. As with the trajectory of *Macbeth* from German to Catalan and then Castilian, such multilingual stagings have allowed Bieito to explore the subtleties of working across different languages as plays are repositioned within alternative linguistic prisms. Castilian, for example, necessitates different breathing patterns from Catalan. As a more rhetorical language than Catalan, it provides a guttural but more mellifluous sound that often relies on a greater number of syllables and hence entails a longer working text.[6]

Deconstruction or desecration? 'Made in Bieito'

Directorial intervention for Bieito takes place across the terrain of the visual, the aural, and the textual. With Fernando de Rojas's dramatic poem, *La Celestina*, Bieito and his dramaturg Pablo Ley, the translator of *Threepenny Opera*, worked with a four-hour adaptation provided by Edinburgh-based playwright and translator Jo Clifford. Fernando de Rojas's dramatic poem, first published in 1499, before public theatres existed in Spain, would take more than nine hours to read aloud. The compact two-and-a-quarter-hour playing version rendered at the end of the rehearsal period, while not what Bieito would term 'a deconstruction', shaved certain characters (Centurio, Sosia, Tristán, and Alisa) while adding a barman, appropriately named Pepe, who recited de Rojas's opening prologue.

Actors regularly testify to ongoing textual revisions during rehearsals that are both 'destabilising and exciting' (Kathryn Hunter in Brown 2004: 8). In describing work in rehearsal with Bieito, Complicite regular Kathryn Hunter, cast in the role of Celestina, spoke of Bieito's parallels with Simon McBurney in that both are inclined to 'chop and change, and go for large structure, rather than detail [...] leaving you pretty unbalanced and searching all the time' (Brown 2004: 8). This 'large structure' often involves prioritising the musicality and tonal sense of a scene so that dramaturgical decisions are made on the basis of a range of factors rather than mere narrative cohesion. Certain textual moments are reworked to accommodate an interaction with the audience that attempts to transgress the restrictions of the proscenium-arch venues in which many of his productions are now staged. In *Celestina*, Bieito chose to insert a short sequence where Celestina sells to the highest bidder the virginity of Lucrecia, an employee left to perform menial bar tasks and who appears to have cerebral palsy. Opening with a rumba, 'Soy un perro callejero' (I'm a Dog of the Streets) from the popular flamenco group Los Chunguitos rendered live by the Sinfónica de Gavá, Bieito announced a framing device for the production that underscored the musicality of the language and the thematics of the piece. Rumba provided a contemporary analogy for a text that uses elegant poetry to deal with base emotions, similarly juxtaposing lyrics on prostitution and drug addiction with cheerful music. '*La Celestina* has the rhythm of rumba and rumba is protest with merriment,' Bieito stated on the eve of the opening, justifying an employment of musical interludes to both comment on the action and provide a tonal accompaniment to narrative mood (Suñén 2004: 25). Celestina's aside to the audience as Pármeno and Aréusa were fornicating on the floor that 'I suppose you think that this is the tacky part of the show, it's a Spanish classic after all' indicates that, like Brecht's Mother Courage, Hunter/Celestina can look outside the fictional archetype to engage with the anachronisms that are present in any staging of any text from an earlier era as well as providing an ironic comment on Bieito's reputation as a purveyor of pornography for the stage.

Such 'insertions' are what the Spanish daily *La Razón* has termed surreal moments from the Bieito factory or 'Made in Bieito' (Suárez 2004: 63) and it has increasingly frustrated critics who expect their classics to be 'played straight'. With *Celestina* the focus was decisively on the character of Celestina rather than the love story of Calisto and Melibea, from which de Rojas's text takes its original title. In addition, as with *Macbeth* and *King Lear*, the modes in which characters met their demise varied from those indicated in the text: Calisto did not die trying to jump over a wall following sex with Melibea but rather perished in Melibea's imagination. His death was more metaphorical than physical. Rather than throw herself over a balcony, Melibea killed herself with a gun, horrified at the thought that Calisto just wanted to bed her.

The first of his Shakespeare productions to feature a significant textual refiguration was *Macbeth*, initially translated into German by Frank Günther with the Catalan and Castilian versions that followed in 2002–3 undertaken by Miquel Desclot (Catalan) and Bieito and his assistant director Josep Galindo (Castilian). All these translations shaved the play, dispensing with the porter, the witches, Siward, the messengers, and murderers and reallocating their lines. With *Hamlet* too, working with dramaturg Xavier Zuber, Bieito cut Fortinbras, Marcellus, Bernardo, soldiers, servants, the players, the priest, and one of the gravediggers. Again lines were reassigned and soliloquies reordered to create a snappy two-hour production. With *King Lear*, again a collaboration with Zuber, the interventions were not as marked but they did involve pruning substantial sections of the play to concentrate very firmly on the domestic unit. Many of the secondary characters were dispensed with (messengers, servants, Burgundy, Curan, the Doctor, the Old Man to attend to Gloucester, the servants to Cornwall). Certain narrative moments had to be reconfigured – as with the death of Cornwall, who here perished at Edmund's hand. The decision to shift onstage deaths located *offstage* (as with Goneril's suffocation of Regan here replacing the poison, and Goneril's subsequent suicide with a handgun) provided a strong visual charge whereby Lear's death at the feet of Cordelia's bloodied body proved a surprisingly inconspicuous affair; the final disappearance of a homeless man banished from his court.

Staging Spain

My references come from my Catalan, Hispanic and Mediterranean culture. From the Spanish Golden Age, Valle-Inclán, Buñuel, Goya. The black humour that shapes my work is part of this cultural heritage. Spain is not only about flamenco and bullfighting. It's part of my imagination. It's an approach to everything I direct.

(Bieito 2003)

While Bieito's early productions evolved largely in conceptual environments, since 2000 he has increasingly opted for illustrative landscapes that play with vertical axes that encourage the spectator to look upwards rather than the more limited cinematic panorama of left to right. For *Celestina*, while the action of de Rojas's poem takes place in Salamanca, Bieito chose to relocate it to an imagined space, inspired by both the strip of motorway that runs between his then home suburb of Castelldefels and Barcelona airport and the Raval area of the city. Bieito's attraction to de Rojas's poem is based, in part, on the fact that it has proved such a pervasive myth in Spanish cultural formation. An inspiration for both Goya and Picasso, themselves strong visual referents for Bieito, the epic tale is for Bieito a significant landmark of the country's Early Modern period 'on the same level as Don Quixote or Don Juan. I was fascinated by it at school, I studied it at college, and I wrote my thesis on it at university' (Bieito, quoted in Brown 2004: 8). His own name is that of the romantic lead Calisto, who turns Celestina into a local brothel madam, to secure the object of his lust, Melibea.

The figure of Celestina has often been conceived in folkloric fashion, always larger than life, but more matronly than wily, less a procuress than a matchmaker. Directors have habitually cast *grandes dames* in the role (Jeanne Moreau in Antoine Vitez's 1989 production, Nuria Espert in Robert Lepage's 2004 staging). The emphasis has tended to be on a homely figure with a few dodgy deals on the side who 'dabbles' in witchcraft, rather than a working-class whore selling human bodies to those who can afford her rates. Kathryn Hunter's Celestina was an androgynous mafioso; part East End gangster, mostly 'butch', sometimes 'femme' to use Sue-Ellen Case's terms (1989: 291–2), hobbling around the stage in a pinstripe suit and a lethal crutch with a machete tucked into her belt. Bieito's conception of Celestina was rooted in an observation of Hunter's body evoking that of a snake (Fisher 2004: 9), able to manoeuvre herself out of tricky situations. Hunter provided an arch manipulator, preying on the vulnerability of those around her. A gravelly voiced chain-smoking survivor, she proved not an endearing witch but rather a cold, harsh survivor, a contemporary Mother Courage who had been obliged to cultivate a tough approach to survive amongst ruthless criminals and drug dealers. Hunter embodied an adaptability that demonstrated how the character had become whatever each generation has needed in a distorted mirror image of its own excesses. Her kingdom was here a sleazy lap-dancing pick-up joint on the fringes of society, inhabited by pimps, drug-addicts, and prostitutes. Calisto and Melibea were no noble aristocrats but wealthy young things with money to burn: the former a local boy who drives a 911 Porsche and likes to get his own way, the latter a spoilt teenager hooked on drugs and alcohol.

While the set was in many ways as kitsch as that of *Macbeth* and *Threepenny Opera*, it was overtly positioned within recognisably Spanish referents. Indeed, Spain's recent past under Franco – utilising torture, clandestine prostitution, institutional abuse, and sweeping undesirable elements to silent 'invisible' corners – shaped Bieito's reading of *Celestina*. Television monitors up above the bar showed replays of bullfights. Real Madrid flags, a photo of Franco, and a makeshift poster stating 'Give Gibraltar back to the Spanish' adorned the bar. Sempronio was dressed in an Atlético Madrid football kit while the waiter Pepe opened the production wearing the head of a bull. Celebrations were marked with *paella* and *sangria*. Calisto and Pármeno toasted success with the well-known brand of anise 'El mono'. Bieito's emphasis was not on reinforcing these stereotypes but rather on deconstructing them as constructs promoted by Francoism as a means of nurturing the lucrative tourist trade.

Bieito's readings push assumptions about the range of meanings a text may accommodate as well as the politics of past readings. This is particularly significant in the case of a Spanish and Catalan repertoire that is largely unknown outside the Iberian Peninsula and Spanish America. As *Celestina* indicates, Bieito's artistic choices have focused festival interest towards a Spanish canon that is not easily exoticised or envisioned through simple stereotypes. *Tirant lo Blanc* reworked Catalan Joanot Martorell's 1490 novel as a reflection on medieval culture caught between the supposedly chivalrous ideals of the past and a present marked by colonialist aspirations and rabid individualism. With a score by Carles Santos, Bieito's epic retelling, opening at the Frankfurt Book Fair in 2007, positioned a key work of Catalonia's early modernity within a contemporary milieu where the old Catalan grated with the markedly immediate context, creating an ongoing dialogue on genealogies of performance and the ghostliness of re-enacting tales themselves reformulated in literary texts created by those (including Cervantes and Vargas Llosa) who have recycled and readjusted the narrative tropes of Martorell's tale.

Already in 1997 *The Festival of the Dove* offered a dynamic reading of a popular operetta presented as sanitised entertainment under the Franco regime. Resituating the piece in an impoverished urban wasteland outside a tram shed, Bieito provided both visual nods to the late-nineteenth-century world that had generated the *zarzuela* and a resolutely contemporary style of playing that pushes performers against a reliance on clichéd acting vocabularies towards a physical choreography that comments on musical patterns. Bieito's production was not afraid to foreground the anachronistic, and he banished the folkloric in favour of an explicit denunciation of a bourgeoisie that uses its wealth as a means towards unethical exploitation. The expeditious pacing was made possible through a stage where decor was primarily rendered across and through the human body.

His subsequent two Edinburgh International Festival productions, an English-language production of Calderón's *Life is a Dream* for the Royal Lyceum Theatre and an Abbey Theatre Dublin co-production of Ramón del Valle-Inclán's *Barbaric Comedies*, similarly provided performance registers that moved firmly away from declamatory delivery and a stage cluttered by the vestiges of pictorial realism. For *Life is a Dream*, designer Carles Pujol provided a grey, sandy, lunar set overlooked by a giant suspended mirror. The hovering mirror offered a dazzling image of an elusive world that escapes containment and effectively implicated the audience in the games of the performers. For *Barbaric Comedies* too, Flores's set was deceptively simple – an exposed stage where dark metal railings hovered ominously over the characters, a metaphor for the religious constraints that mark the central conflicts.

With *La Celestina*, while Flores provided a more concrete location, a bar inhabited by the underbelly of society, the emphasis was on visual excess: a dark cavern with a spiral staircase and skylight announcing the space beyond. The impression provided was that of descending into a nightmarish underworld, likened by Flores to the paintings of Hieronymus Bosch or Brueghel (Mansfield 2004: 5). Bieito, whilst recognising the aesthetic of Goya and Picasso, evoked film directors Álex de la Iglesia, Arturo Ripstein, and Luis Buñuel as the three most palpable influences on the visual language of the production (Bieito 2004; Suñén 2004: 26). For *The Guardian*'s theatre critic Michael Billington, reviewing the production at the Edinburgh International Festival, Bieito was judged to be no less than 'the modern theatre's equivalent of Buñuel' (2004: 16).

Buñuel's black humour grounds Bieito's stagings, and this emphasis on the grotesque – which Bieito locates also in Valle-Inclán and de Rojas – has determined the type of works he has gravitated towards. With Buñuel he shares a fierce anti-clericalism shaped by a Jesuit education. *Barbaric Comedies* had a discernible reference to the parody of the Last Supper in *Viridiana* (1961). In *Un ballo in maschera*, the opening sequence of the politicians sitting on a row of toilets while reading newspapers functioned as a homage to the family eating on the lavatory in *The Phantom of Liberty* (1974). As with Buñuel, Bieito's work betrays a strong moralist vein: many of his productions denounce a market-driven economy where the fine line between hedonism and debauchery threatens to erode our humanity.[7]

Perhaps the ease with which Bieito can be positioned as a cultural ambassador and emblem of Catalan and Spanish culture has been one reason for his conspicuous critical visibility. His revisionist work with opera, questioning assumptions around the performance and production languages of music theatre, has never attempted to mask the cultural prisms through which he is reading and staging the work. He has often located the action in an environment with evident Spanish referents. His *Un ballo in maschera* for Barcelona's Liceu in 2000 (a co-production seen at the Royal Danish Opera in 2001 and English National Opera in 2002) relocated Verdi's study of the events leading to the assassination of Gustavus III of Sweden in 1792 to mid- to late-1970s Spain, then negotiating a passage from dictatorship to democracy. Gustavus was here envisaged as a hypothetical Juan Carlos, navigating the boundaries between institutional duty and private desires. Bieito's 2001 *Don Giovanni* (for English National Opera, a co-production with the Staatsoper Hanover and the Gran Teatre del Liceu Barcelona, revived in 2004) was again set in contemporary Spain, in Barcelona's Olympic Port, a symbol of the city's prosperity in the 1990s. Here Bieito provided a reading for our secular age, eschewing the Romantic associations of the myth with the vision of a lecherous, hedonistic Don driven by obsessive lust. The strength of Bieito's staging lay in exposing all the characters as tainted by the same vices they denounce in the Don, vices grounded in an environment that prostitutes itself to the commercial, tourist imperative.[8]

His *Carmen* too, first premiered in Perelada in 1999 and then reworked for the Liceu where it opened in 2010, has now been presented by over 30 companies from Venice's La Fenice to the Opera National de Paris (see Amón 2017; Delgado 2017). Deconstructing the imagery that surrounds a Spanish icon forged through the foreign imagination, Bieito's production demonstrates an awareness of how Manuel Fraga's 'Spain is different' tourist campaign in the early 1960s appropriated the iconography of Bizet to offer an image of Spain as the land of passionate happy-go-lucky *señoritas* and swarthy bullfighters. Not insignificantly Bieito relocates the action to the 1970s – in what might be the final years of the Franco regime or the early years of the transition to democracy – in a border space: the city of Ceuta in North Africa where the Spanish and the Arabic merge and collide. As in much of Bieito's work, the concept of the border served as a powerful trope for the staging, a space of passage and transition, where both the 'legitimate' military (here the Spanish Foreign Legion) and the clandestine bandits that form part of Carmen's coterie are implicated in and feed off the corruption.

The open circular set created by Alfons Flores was part-bullring, part-beach. The Spanish flag hoisted up onto the centre stage flagpole during Act 1 reappeared at the beginning of Act 4 as a kitsch towel stretched out by a bikini-clad tourist as she prepares to apply her suncream. Travel to any of the Costa del Sol beach resorts and the Spanish flag has been appropriated to tourist ends: as a beach towel, on postcards, on T-shirts, on beer glasses, and as decor lining the walls of bars, clubs, and restaurants. Nothing is sacred when commerce becomes the imperative: the flag here becomes just another commodity marketed for sale and consumption to an undiscerning user. The raising of a parliamentary question about alleged obscenities committed against the Spanish flag by a former PP Foreign Secretary, José Manuel García-Margallo, following its Opera National de Paris opening in March 2017, led to a conspicuous degree of press attention prior to the Madrid opening (see Amón 2017). Bieito's 'ajustes' (adjustments) rather than 'cambios' (changes) led to Bieito's deletion of a brief sequence that had featured in the Paris staging: a soldier's cleaning of the floor with the Spanish flag which he then used to wipe his bottom (Mateos 2017).[9] In the aftermath of the 1 October separatist referendum, at a time of heightened political tension between Madrid and Barcelona, the Spanish flag was mobilised as the dominant site for the articulation of a vision of the nation-state that conveniently ignores the commercialisation of the Spanish flag in sport and tourism. The latter was evidenced in the flag's use to signal allegiance to *la roja*, Spain's football team, binding the nation-state in celebrating victory in the UEFA Euro 2008 and 2012 finals and the 2010 World Cup as the recession took hold. Flags are refashioned as tourist fare in towels, T-shirts, on ashtrays, lighters, and other disposable commodities. Tourism accounts for 11 per cent of Spain's GDP and 2017 saw Spain break records in tourist revenue; its 82 million visitors are second only to France as the world's most popular destination for foreign visitors (Anon 2018). Furthermore, Bieito's deployment of the flag to highlight the relationship between institutional corruption and criminality – Spain's political corruption scandals have been problematically sidelined by the media attention on Catalan separatism – serves as a potent reminder of Bieito's vision of culture as a means for articulating that which remains sidelined from public or political discourse.[10]

Dissecting contemporary Europe

Since 2003, much of Bieito's work for the major European opera houses has shifted the action to an identifiably contemporary Europe of ever-shifting borders that directly acknowledges the use of singers and an artistic team from across the continent. His 2003 Staatsoper Hanover production of *Il Trovatore*, like *Don Giovanni*, eschewed Romanticism in favour of a bleak exposure of the horrific events (murder, abduction, torture) that ground Verdi's narrative. With his 2004 staging of Mozart's *Die Entführung aus dem Serail* for Berlin's Komissar Opera, Bieito chose to dispense with the Turkish setting and instead provided a European brothel populated by girls who seemed to have been brought in from the impoverished new parts of the European Union. The parallels with Berlin's brothels was not lost on critics — a local prostitutes' association was consulted by the artistic team — or on audiences and sponsors who expressed displeasure at Bieito's harsh vision of what is commonly regarded as a 'light' opera.

With *Peer Gynt*, premiered at the Bergen Festival in 2006, Bieito firmly shook off the shackles of the folkloric from Ibsen's dramatic poem in crafting a three-hour reading that examined provincialism in its multiple manifestations. This was no idealised landscape: the latrines, metallic scaffolding, and cramped tourist stalls (complete with Norwegian flags, beer, and other tourist commodities) suggested a wasteland where Peer enacts his excesses. The production interrogated the narrowness of vision of communities or nations who consistently look inward rather than outward. While the iconography of the flag kiosk suggested a Norwegian landscape in thrall to the caveats of tourism, the linguistic register of the production — Catalan — pointed to a thinly veiled commentary on Bieito's own nation. A frantic first half saw Joel Joan's Peer rape Victòria Pagès's Ingrid and trolls imagined not as folkloric mythological figures but as incarnations of humanity's basest instincts conceived through the visual register of Fassbinder, *The Rocky Horror Show*, and David Lynch's *Blue Velvet* (1986) (Ordóñez 2006). The action spilled into the interval and beyond the 'official' stages of the Grec as a fevered discussion among a group of suited businessmen held in the gardens of the open-air theatre crystallised into the opening of the second half: a formal televised debate between a now affluent Peer and a range of European entrepreneurs. A commentary on television's pervasive influence in contemporary life, partitioning and compartmentalising the information it processes and spits out for public consumption, it also remarked on the power of English as the global language of commerce. The assembled businessmen represented facets of a European economy boosted by funds from the illicit sex trade and arms sales. The conspicuous appearance of the Barça football club hymn at the end of the sequence may have further served to align Bieito's reading of the play with the more insular aspects of nascent Catalan nationalism as well as the realities of the ethical compromises that inform trade interests for even the smallest nations in the new global economy.

Platform too, Bieito's adaptation of Michel Houllebecq's 2001 novel that opened at the 2006 Edinburgh International Festival, was similarly played out in a space between Western capitalism and a problematic utopia – here created from the industry of Thailand's sex tourism. The hard sell of commercial culture was seen to saturate even the most intimate relations. The tale of Michel's (Juan Echanove) escape from bureaucratic drudgery to a Thai resort where he finds a new purpose to his life in the pleasure gained from sex with local prostitutes, *Platform* opened with Michel in a booth watching penetrative sex. Isolated from the figures behind him, equally trapped in their individual booths, silently and voyeuristically soaking in the on-screen sex, Echanove's Michel cut a forlorn figure. This opening sequence functioned as a potent metaphor for a Western culture that advocates the pursuit of material wealth and sexual liberation but that frowns on the more extreme manifestations of these quests. Crucially, the juxtaposition of the distended onscreen genitalia with images of Thailand, selling itself as a tropical virgin paradise ready for Western penetration, pointed to the more surreptitious forms of pornography that fill a media-saturated Western society. Bieito's staging provided a social world where sex is just one mode through which the relationship of the first and developing worlds can be measured. Like Bernard-Marie Koltès, Bieito comprehends that economic structures are built on commercial imperatives that taint all human relationships. Bieito takes the deal that underpins Koltès's dramaturgy to a more extreme conclusion, maimed by the phantoms of religious extremism that pounce with horrific consequences in the production's final sequences.

Conclusion

While Bieito may have admitted in past interviews that his mentors are extensively drawn from film rather than theatre – Coppola, Fellini, Kurosawa, Baz Luhrmann, Scorsese (see Billington 2002; Delgado 2003b) – his work shares significant points of contact with other European theatrical mavericks who have worked across both media: most conspicuously Roger Planchon and Patrice Chéreau. All three have provided iconoclastic readings of classic texts marked by the formal language of cinema that have responded to contemporary social concerns, political dynamics, and a commercialism where the moral is a frighteningly expendable commodity. Like Peter Sellars, Bieito uses the stage as a platform for engaging with the moral dilemmas of the day, linking them to the commercial and economic frameworks that govern political and social structures. Both argue for a stage language that never serves to sanitise transgressive works; both bring to the fore in their readings latent concerns that preoccupy them while researching a play. Where Bieito differs from other social commentators, such as Frank Castorf and Miguel del Arco, is that he works consistently through the languages of Europe – English, Castilian, Catalan, Italian, French, and German.[11] As with Declan Donnellan, Tiago Rodrigues, and Jan Lauwers, his is an aesthetic that thrives on the differences that are made manifest when negotiating the alternative linguistic registers that operate in Europe. As director of Bilbao's Arriaga theatre since 2017 he has, as he did at Barcelona's Romea previously, promoted work in the regional language – ensuring representation for linguistic difference at a time of heightened political sensibilities. His 2017 staging of Basque novelist Bernardo Atxaga's 1988 short stories *Obabakoak* was seen both at Barcelona's Teatre Lliure and Madrid's Centro Dramático Nacional.

Bieito's questioning approach to both classic texts and the adaptation of contemporary works for the stage offers a multilingual theatre that recognises a Europe that speaks (both theatrically and politically) in languages beyond English.

Five key productions

El rei Joan (*King John*). By William Shakespeare. Set design by Eduard Bucar. Costume design by Mercè Paloma. Perf. Mingo Ràfols, Carles Canut, Roser Camí, Santi Pons. Convent dels Àngels at the Grec Festival, Barcelona. 29 June 1995.

Carmen. By Georges Bizet. Libretto by Henri Meilhac and Ludovic Halévy, based on the novel by Prosper Merimée. Set design by Alfons Flores. Costume design by Mercè Paloma. Perf. Roberto Alagna, Mireia Casas, Lucio Gallo, Angela Gheorghiu, Annie Vavrille. Festival de Perelada, 8 August 1999.

Don Giovanni. By W.A. Mozart. Set design by Alfons Flores. Costume design by Mercè Paloma. Perf. Gary Magee, Claire Rutter, Nathan Berg. English National Opera at the Coliseum Theatre, London. 31 May 2001.

Macbeth. By William Shakespeare. Set design by Alfons Flores. Costume design by Mercè Paloma. Perf. Mingo Ràfols, Roser Camí, Santi Pons. Teatre Romea, Barcelona. 25 February 2002.

El rei Lear (*King Lear*). By William Shakespeare. Set design by Ariane Isabell Unfried, Rifail Ajdarpasic. Costume design by Mercè Paloma. Perf. Josep Maria Pou, Boris Ruiz, Àngels Bassas. Teatre Romea, Barcelona. 29 June 2004.

Acknowledgements

With thanks to Calixto Bieito, Antonia Andúgar, Brian McMaster, Josep Maria Pou, Lidia Giménez, Louise Jeffreys and the BITE team at the Barbican, the Teatre Romea, Birmingham Rep, the Edinburgh International Festival, and the National Library of Scotland. An earlier draft of this chapter was published in *TheatreForum*, 26 (winter/spring 2005): 10–25.

Notes

1 See, for example, Bentley 1968; Braun 1986; Cole and Chinoy 1976; Roose-Evans 1984. This trend has continued even with more recent supposed 'reassessments' as with, for example, Schneider and Cody 2002.
2 For English-language introductions to Boadella and Font, see Boadella 2007; Erven 1988: 159–72. On La Fura dels Baus, see Feldman 1998; Ollé 2004.
3 On Pasqual, see Delgado 2003a: 182–224.
4 Castilian is often referred to as Spanish. In this chapter, 'Spanish' refers to the state, 'Castilian' to the language spoken within the Spanish state.
5 For further details on these Shakespeare productions, see Delgado 2006.
6 This is developed in further detail in Bieito et al. 2005: 117–18. Bieito's engagement with Shakespeare also includes *Forests* (2012), a piece crafted from the Bard's treatment of woodland, trees, and heaths, and operatic stagings of Verdi's *Macbeth* (2005), *Otello* (2014), and *Falstaff* (2020), and Aribert Reimann's *Lear* (2016).
7 Billington (2004: 16) judged Bieito's *Celestina* as no less than a Spanish version of Ravenhill's 1996 play, *Shopping and Fucking*. For comments on the analogies, see Delgado 2005: 23. Bieito has expressed his admiration for Ravenhill's work to me on numerous occasions and collaborated with the latter on the English-language adaptation of *Die Fledermaus* for Welsh National Opera (2002).
8 On this production of *Don Giovanni*, see Delgado 2001; Wright 2007: 157–86.
9 The production was also targeted by the right-wing Plataforma Patriótica Millán Astray who, following its Paris opening, initiated a campaign both against its portrayal of the military legionnaires as violent drunkards and its use of the Spanish flag for arse wiping (Elconfidencialautonomico 2017). The platform also protested against the use of the uniforms associated with the Spanish Foreign Legion which José Millán Astray had founded in 1920 (Anon 2017).
10 For details of Spain's (2004–18) political corruption scandals, see Preston 2020: 539–65.
11 Bieito was awarded Pro Europa's 2009 European Culture Prize for his 'innovative contribution to European culture', the first director to receive the award (see Morgades 2009; www.europaeische-kulturstiftung.de/index.php). The award recognises the 'Europeanness' of his work – a term also used in this volume by Reinelt in classifying Lauwers's work (see p. 235) – and the ways in which he 'stages' national identities that comment on wider social, political, and ethical issues that have emerged through the expansion of the Continent's geographical boundaries.

Bibliography

Amón, Rubén (2017) 'La opereta de la bandera española', *El País*, 16 October, https://elpais.com/elpais/2017/10/13/opinion/1507896300_264994.html

Anon (2017) 'La plataforma Millán Astray pide retirar los uniformes legionarios de la obra Carmen', *Eldistrito.es*, 16 October, www.eldistrito.es/latina/plataforma-millan-astray-pide-retirar-uniformes-legionarios-obra

Anon (2018) 'Récord de llegadas: Más de 82 milliones de turistas internacionales han viajado a España en 2017', *La Vanguardia*, 10 January, www.lavanguardia.com/economia/20180110/434208713049/datos-turismo-2017-record-llegadas-turistas-internacionales.html

Bentley, Eric (ed.) (1968) *The Theory of the Modern Stage*, Harmondsworth: Penguin.

Bieito, Calixto (2003) 'A private interview with Maria M. Delgado', *Edinburgh International Festival*, August.

—— (2004) 'A private interview with Maria M. Delgado', London, September.

Bieito, Calixto, Maria M. Delgado and Patricia Parker (2005) 'Resistant Readings, Multilingualism and Marginality', in Lynette Hunter and Peter Lichtenfels (eds), *Shakespeare, Language and the Stage: The Fifth Wall – Approaches to Shakespeare from Criticism, Performance and Theatre Studies*, London: The Arden Shakespeare and Thomson Learning, pp. 108–37.

Billington, Michael (2002) 'People 288: Calixto Bieito', *Opera*, 53 (10): 1179–85.

—— (2004) 'The Main Event: *Celestina*', *Guardian*, 18 August, p. 16.

Boadella, Albert (2007) 'Theatre as Alchemy: On Politics, Culture and Running a Theatre Company for over 40 Years', *Contemporary Theatre Review*, 17 (3): 301–10.

Braun, Edward (1986) *The Director and the Stage*, London: Methuen.

Brown, Mark (2004) 'Pros and Cons', *Sunday Herald*, 8 August, Festival Review section, 8–9.

Case, Sue-Ellen (1989) 'Toward a Butch-Femme Aesthetic', in Lynda Hart (ed.), *Making a Spectacle: Feminist Essays on Contemporary Women's Theater*, Ann Arbor, MI: University of Michigan Press, pp. 282–99.

Cole, Toby and Helen Kritch Chinoy (eds) (1976) *Directors on Directing: A Source Book of the Modern Theatre*, New York: Macmillan.

Delgado, Maria M. (2001) 'Calixto Bieito's *Don Giovanni* Outrages British Critics', *Western European Stages*, 13 (3): 53–8.

—— (2003a) *'Other' Spanish Theatres: Erasure and Inscription on the Twentieth-Century Spanish Stage*, Manchester: Manchester University Press.

—— (2003b) 'Calixto Bieito: "Reimagining the Text for the Age in Which It Is Being Staged"', *Contemporary Theatre Review*, 13 (3): 59–66.

—— (2004) '"A Lot of Work and a Flicker of Intuition": Calixto Bieito Stages *Hamlet*', *Western European Stages*, 16 (2): 71–8.

—— (2005) 'Calixto Bieito: A Catalan Director on the International Stage', *TheatreForum*, 26 (winter/spring): 10–24.

—— (2006) 'Journeys of Cultural Transference: Calixto Bieito's Multilingual Shakespeares', *Modern Language Review*, 101 (1): 106–50.

—— (2017) 'Carmen por Calixto Bieito: Analizando un clásico contemporáneo', *Carmen*, Teatro Real programme, 19–27.

El Confidencial Autonómico (2017) 'Los defensores de Millán Astray, contra una obra de teatro que se mofa de los legionarios', *El Confidencial Autonómico*, 18 April, www.elconfidencialautonomico.com/muy_confidencial/defensores-Millan-Astray-teatro-legionarios_0_2912708706.html

Erven, Eugène van (1988) *Radical People's Theatre*, Bloomington, IN: Indiana University Press.

Feldman, Sharon (1998) 'Scenes from the Contemporary Barcelona Stage: La Fura dels Baus's Aspiration to the Authentic', *Theatre Journal*, 50 (4): 447–72.

Fisher, Mark (2004) 'Let's Get Physical', *Scotland on Sunday*, 15 August, 9.

Mansfield, Susan (2004) 'Shocked by the Power', *Scotsman*, 12 August, 5.

Mateos, Adrián (2017) 'Calixto Bieito evita la polémica en torno al descarte de la bandera española en «Carmen»', *ABC*, 10 October, www.abc.es/cultura/teatros/abci-calixto-bieito-evita-polemica-torno-descarte-bandera-espanola-carmen-201710101729_noticia.html

Morgades, Lourdes (2009) 'Calixto Bieito, premiado por su innovación en la cultura europea', *El País*, 29 July, p. 46.

Ollé, Àlex (ed.) (2004) *La Fura dels Baus, 1979–2004*, Barcelona: Editorial Electa.

Ordóñez, Marcos (2006) 'Norwegian Wood', *El País*, 29 July, *Babelia* section, 14.

Preston, Paul (2020) *A People Betrayed: A History of Corruption, Political Incompetence and Social Division in Modern Spain 1874–2018*, London: William Collins.

Roose-Evans, James (1984) *Experimental Theatre: From Stanislavsky to Peter Brook*, London: Routledge & Kegan Paul.

Schneider, Rebecca and Gabrielle Cody (eds) (2002) *Re:direction: A Theoretical and Practical Guide*, London and New York: Routledge.

Suárez, Gonzalo (2004) 'Bieito desafía a sus detractores en una *Celestina* ambientada en un burdel', *La Razón*, 18 August, p. 63.

Subirana, Jordi (2004) 'Calixto Bieito estrena en catalán *El Rei Lear*', *El Periodico de Catalunya*, 28 June, p. 43.

Suñén, Luis (2004) 'Un Celestina a ritmo de rumba', *El País*, 16 August, pp. 25–26.

Wright, Sarah (2007) *Tales of Seduction: The Figure of Don Juan in Spanish Culture*, London and New York: Tauris Academic Studies.

Chapter 18

RODRIGO GARCÍA AND LA CARNICERÍA TEATRO/BOUCHERIE THÉÂTRE

From the collective to the director

Lourdes Orozco

Argentine director Rodrigo García (b. 1964) is still one of the few Hispanic theatre practitioners to gain an international reputation within the festival circuit. He and his company, La Carnicería Teatro, now known by its French name, Boucherie Théâtre (The Butcher's Theatre), are commissioned by prominent institutions; his texts are translated and staged across the globe. Alongside names such as Socìetas Rafaello Sanzio, Jan Lauwers/Needcompany, Jan Fabre, and Guy Cassiers, García's raw and vibrant performance style has become a valuable currency in the international festival circuit, where he is perceived as a radical, innovative, and influential *auteur*. The present chapter proposes an approach to his work in the context of contemporary directors' theatre in Europe.

The beginnings

After completing a degree in media studies and design and a period working in the family business in Buenos Aires – the butcher's shop to which the company's name pays tribute – García moved to Spain in 1986 to work as a graphic designer before entering the theatre professionally. He first set up his company in Madrid in 1989 working within the city's network of small and independent spaces (*salas alternativas*), particularly with Javier García Yagüe's La Cuarta Pared

(The Fourth Wall), and closely collaborating with other small-scale companies.

In Madrid, he belonged to a generation known as the 'generación Marqués de Bradomín', whose practice was assisted by the Bradomín prize, part of a wider project to encourage the production of new theatre in Spain's recently established democracy.[1] Having left Argentina at a time when the newly elected socialist government was struggling to overturn the climate of corruption and violence left over from La Junta's dictatorship (1976–83), García arrived in a country where another recently assembled socialist government – Felipe González's PSOE (Partido Socialista Obrero Español; Spanish Socialist and Labour Party) – was carrying out a social revolution in post-Franco Spain. One of the party's main concerns in the area of culture was the democratisation of the theatre arts that resulted in a notable increase in funding to counteract the dictatorship's theatrical legacy and general under-investment in the industry. In this way, the PSOE's cultural policy originated projects such as the Centro Nacional de Nuevas Tendencias Escénicas (CNNTE/National Centre for New Trends in Performance) and its generous system of subsidy played a crucial role in the birth and development of many of today's Spanish performance groups, institutional theatre companies, playwrights, and theatre spaces.[2]

García's first pieces, however, demonstrated very clearly the minimal connections that his work bore to that of other members of his generation, whose theatre was intrinsically rooted in a dramatic tradition dominated by the hegemony of the text.[3] Reacting to a theatrical landscape in which the paradigms established by the theatre of the absurd – especially by figures such as Beckett, Ionesco, and Arrabal – were still strongly followed, and where non-text-based devised theatre was regularly perceived as a betrayal rather than an innovation, García's early proposals aimed, on the one hand, at moving beyond and questioning traditional forms of theatre in the Hispanic context, albeit maintaining the text as a core aspect of the performance and, on the other, at creating bridges between these two modes of theatrical representation. In the 1970s, Spain had already seen a wave of companies which had successfully attempted to undermine the dominance of the written word by disposing of the text completely and drawing on alternative forms of performance such as mime (Els Joglars), circus and puppetry (Comediants, Sèmola Teatre), or physical theatre (La Fura dels Baus). Nevertheless, García has on several occasions acknowledged that his influences are better found in the visual arts and in the theatre of directors such as Tadeusz Kantor, Jan Fabre, Jan Lauwers, and Romeo Castellucci, whose pieces are informed by their work as artists and their collaboration with practitioners in other fields (information technology, media, music, opera, dance, design). Fascinated by the performances of Kantor's Cricot 2 in Buenos Aires and later Madrid, where the Polish company presented *Umarla klasa* (*The Dead Class*, 1983) and *Wielopole, Wielopole* (1984) respectively, García was clearly drawn to a theatre dependent on the intersection of other art forms. He related to the freedom that the visual arts, performance art, music, dance, and physical theatre had achieved in the second half of the twentieth century, and from which Spanish theatre had stood largely aloof.[4] Having trained as a designer, García had a special interest in the work of visual artists from the beginning of his career in the theatre, as is proven by his staging of Bruce Naumann's *The Three Piglets* (*Los tres cerditos*, 1993), the assimilation of the work of artists such as Paul McCarthy, Jenny Holzer, Bill Viola, Gary Hill, and Sol LeWitt, and his particular attention to composition, plasticity, and colour on stage.

In its beginnings, La Carnicería was a relatively flexible structure where García acted as a pivotal figure, recruiting different collaborators for each production but also counting on some regular fixtures such as lighting designer Carlos Marquerie, performers Chete Lera, Patricia Lamas, Miguel Ángel Altet, and Juan Loriente, choreographer Elena Córdoba, and sound designer Ferdy Esparza. The company was intermittently supported by grants from the Spanish Ministry of Culture and occasionally commissioned by specific public institutions such as the above-mentioned CNNTE, the Casa de América, or the state-supported arts festivals of La Alternativa and Madrid's Autumn Festival (Festival de Otoño). Given García's prominent position on the international stage today and his often conflicting relationship with the Spanish theatre system, it is easy to forget that his beginnings were facilitated by the structures that the new Spanish government had put in place in the early 1980s.

State support was never sufficient to provide the company with financial stability, and this contributed to the evident scarcity of resources that shaped the 'poor theatre' aesthetics of García's first pieces. These were mostly structured around a series of monologues performed usually on an empty stage dotted by a series of strategically placed objects. The aesthetics of this early theatre was strongly shaped by a 'retro' look achieved by the use of found objects and costumes bought in second-hand shops creating a visual context familiar to La Carnicería's then audiences. Casually dressed actors spoke directly to their audiences, challenging them with pseudo-autobiographical stories of trauma, combining seemingly conflicting modes of performance. Humour and casual violence were used to a disquieting effect, taking the audience on a frantic emotional rollercoaster ride. These monologues were frequently intercalated with musical interludes and actions in which actors carried out short but detailed rituals or generated a series of tableaux, which spoke, responded to, or clashed with the texts.

The craftsmanship and audacity that shaped this early work revealed a clear intention to question the expectations of 1980s Spanish audiences, for whom traditional forms of theatre had remained largely unchallenged due to censorship and the cultural isolation experienced by the country during Franco's dictatorship. The director's potential to divide, often enrage, and frequently disgust his audiences soon became clear, as spectators regularly walked out of La Carnicería's performances.

In addition to the play texts, which offered open critiques to the pillars of Hispanic culture (religion, the family, social norms, and expectations), La Carnicería slowly began to flesh out the politics of space and the relationship between performance and spectator by either taking theatre out of conventional spaces – as was the case with *Haberos quedado en casa, capullos* (*You Should Have Stayed at Home, Dickheads*, 2000), staged in different spaces in Madrid (a peep show, an art gallery, a night bar) – or radically transforming found spaces as in the Sitges performance of *A veces me siento tan cansado que hago estas cosas* (*Sometimes I Feel So Tired That I Do Things Like This*, 2001).[5]

In spite of the reflections on individual politics found in his early works, these were still highly self-referential and self-reflective pieces in which García seemed more interested in re-examining theatre and its conventions, seeking alternative ways in which to produce meaning onstage, than engaging in a specific socio-political discourse. During the 1990s, his theatre practice both scrutinised and exposed the mechanics of theatre, questioning at once the role of the character, the validity of narrative, the place of conflict in performance, and the logics of time and space. *Protegedme de lo que deseo* (*Protect Me from What I Want*, 1997) for instance – a title inspired via a Placebo song and an installation by the US artist Jenny Holzer – is obsessively concerned with liberating theatre from the restrictive structures of the 'well-made play' while clearly unveiling the clashes between text and action that still haunt García's theatre practice today. The piece opens with a 25-minute monologue delivered by performer Chete Lera seated at a table while smoking and drinking red wine. In the background, a wooden structure creates a semi-enclosed space that the audience can only view partially through a door and a few small holes in the wall. Immediately after his long opening speech Lera rushes into the wooden room joining a group of four performers, two of whom are dwarfs, to execute a series of manic actions while heavy metal and electronica are played loudly in the background. The actions vary from static to frantic and display failed romantic sequences, a procession of sexual tableaux, and male fights. We see: a half-naked Patricia Lamas, her face obscured by a black wig, hitting the air with a baseball bat; Chete Lera and Miguel Ángel Altet having a fight while sporting surgical gloves; and performers Víctor Contreras and Fernandito frying eggs, bacon, and sausages to which they subsequently add inedible amounts of ketchup and mayonnaise. The texts speak of human deception and generate an undoubtedly pessimistic mood. In sum, *Protect Me* presents no characters, no natural progression, no clear indication as to where the action is taking place, and no specific rationale for the material with which the audience is confronted. The performance creates a world of its own and has no connection with the place and space in which it has originated. García sets out to subvert all the aspects that have habitually been part of the spectators' theatrical experience, enabling them to embark on a much freer journey and targeting their senses and emotions rather than their psychologies.

This freedom has, however, met with the disagreement of particular sectors of society, specifically on the question of the director's use of live animals in his productions. Live animals have appeared in García's work from the beginning of his career. They are usually positioned as objects of torture representing the dynamics of power of late capitalist societies. However, the use of live animals has led to productions being cancelled or partially performed. In 2007, *Accidens* – a performance where an actor kills, cooks, and eats a lobster on stage – was cancelled in Spain, France, and Italy after complaints had been issued to the theatres that had programmed the production by animal protection agencies. More recently, in 2015, his production *4* – which included actors drowning hamsters in a fish tank – was performed after the scenes with the hamsters were removed from the production. García perceived these responses as attacks on artistic freedom and has always defended the right of artists to take responsibility for their acts.[6]

France and beyond

In spite of La Carnicería's relative success within Madrid's alternative theatre circuit during the 1990s, the company very rarely managed to travel beyond the city and was seldom invited to perform on larger and more accessible stages before the international accomplishment of *After Sun*. The progressive institutionalisation of theatre that had started in Spain in the early 1980s was dramatically reversed by the arrival of José María Aznar's conservative government in 1996. Four years later, in the year 2000, Aznar's Partido Popular (Popular Party) won Spain's general election with an absolute majority, further consolidating a cultural policy hallmarked by the trimming of arts budgets, the privatisation of cultural entities, and increased support for the creation and development of large cultural institutions.[7] The new regulations were implemented at the expense of smaller-scale cultural projects and, critically, collaboration between the private and the public sector. Its effects on the performing arts were clearly felt as small theatre companies and spaces had their subsidies reduced or cut.[8] García's response to a theatre landscape dominated by musicals, outdated stagings of the classics, and a struggling alternative scene is clear in the following words:

> In amongst this desert-like landscape there were only two options: to give up (as 60 per cent of theatre and dance practitioners did), sweeten your work (37 per cent did this) or continue with the struggle. I decided to join the 3 per cent and at least I am now free not to sell my soul.
> (Bergamín 2006)

In the 1990s, La Carnicería had already presented García's works in small European festivals: *Notas de cocina* (*Cooking Notes*, 1994), for instance, had been seen in Florence and in Toulouse in 1998; and in the light of Spain's bleak theatre context, it is not surprising that the company saw this as an opportunity to begin an international career. However, it was not until the controversy caused by *After Sun* in Greece – where members of the audience had thrown chairs at the performers – that the stages of Europe, and France in particular, welcomed La Carnicería's work.

In 2000, *After Sun* was selected by the International Theatre Festival in Delphi as part of a competition that invited theatre practitioners to create new work inspired by Greek mythology. García's entrance to the circuit was not without controversy, since his postmodern staging of the myth of Phaeton was constructed as a fable of ambition fuelled by our capitalist society in which violence, references to contemporary politics, and the objectification of the human body took centre stage. The piece featured the company's core members: performers Patricia Lamas and Juan Loriente, lighting designer Carlos Marquerie; it was written, directed, and designed by García. It had an easily transportable format: two performers, two rabbits, and some found objects – table and chairs, a sofa – and, most importantly, despite being spoken in Spanish, it was clearly located within a wider cultural context and was therefore able to appeal to wider European sensibilities and aesthetics. Dealing with the universal theme of human ambition and drawing from a well-known Greek myth, *After Sun* had a clear narrative which constructed a contemporary tragedy of desperation and corruption in a culturally specific space. Tales of ambition and deception which related to Western youth culture, corporate behaviour, and politics were interrupted by scenes of violence – the abuse of two rabbits, the repeated choreography of a car and motorcycle crash, and a performer nailing herself to a table through her Nike trainers – and unattainable happiness – as when Loriente offers Lamas a birthday cake only to later crash it against his head, or when the two performers describe the inherent disillusions of friendship in the scene 'shaking hands'. The piece was centrally concerned with the integration of high and popular culture as the mythical adventure of Phaeton leading his father's carriage – the Sun – was rehashed into a contemporary tale titled after the brand of suntan lotion. *After Sun* was, like García's previous works, an organised mess which constructed its appeal by drawing from contemporary cultural iconography such as Tom Jones's 'Sex Bomb', George Bush's and Tony Blair's caricature masks, and McDonald's. Indeed, all of García's recurrent concerns were already latent in *After Sun*, as was his theatrical vocabulary, distilled through cynicism and a clear loss of hope in humanity (see Plate 18). The fascination with popular culture (cartoons, television programmes), corporate brands (McDonald's, Ikea, Disney, Nike), and trash food (hamburgers, ketchup, mayonnaise, hot dogs, potato crisps) had already been occasionally used in previous works both as images of globalisation and corporate imperialism and as primary performance materials with which to devise the visual aspects of the piece. It was in *After Sun*, however, that the director's aesthetics finally found a theatrical language.

Furthermore, *After Sun* also signified the recognition of García as a valuable currency for the international circuit since his irreverent theatre was soon able to fill auditoria and produce a growing number of followers. This in turn gave him the opportunity to access wider audiences and bigger venues, overcoming the difficulties that his work had previously encountered in reaching beyond the fringes of the Spanish theatre system. In Spain, *After Sun* was only seen in small theatres despite the support received by critic José Monleón who published the playtext and a long article dedicated to the director's theatre practice in a special issue of the widely respected theatre journal *Primer Acto*. While Monleón might have hoped to stimulate academic interest in García's work, even today the critical attention that his work has received has predominantly been from scholars based outside Spain. In Spain, García is viewed as an uncomfortable figure whose work does not fit with the country's traditional theatre landscape.

The same year that *After Sun* stormed the stages of Western Europe, two of García's works were commissioned in France: *Ignorante* (*Ignorant*), presented at the Comédie de Caen, and *Lo bueno de los animales es que te quieren sin preguntar nada* (*The Good Thing About Animals Is That They Love You Without Asking Anything*), which was the outcome of Mettre en Scène, an annual workshop held at Rennes' National Theatre.[9] France's strong support for the arts and its network of national theatres created a productive context as García's postmodern works responded to the country's curiosity for new and radical work. Furthermore, as David Bradby and Annie Sparks demonstrate, France's assimilation of foreign theatre practitioners has been consistent through the country's cultural history (Bradby and Sparks 1997: 30–1, 218–84). In this landscape, García's adoption is far from exceptional. Cultural and geographical closeness and the role of Paris as a meeting point for artists since the historical avant-garde has meant that Hispanic practitioners in fact constitute a remarkable proportion of these. Paris has accommodated Spanish playwrights and directors (Fernando Arrabal, Armando Llamas, and Lluís Pasqual) alongside Argentine practitioners such as Copi, Jorge Lavelli, Víctor García, and Alfredo Arias.[10]

The programming of Avignon and Paris's Autumn Festival (the Festival d'Automne), as well as that of the country's national-theatres network, only further consolidates this by offering a space to directors and companies from across the world whose common denominator is the creation of innovative work. García's productions sit comfortably in this context. His work is original and daring, drawing from the tradition of the European avant-garde to which the country, and, more importantly, the elite that constitutes its theatre audience, is accustomed. Furthermore, García has wilfully fed his iconoclastic reputation and marketed himself as yet another *enfant terrible* in a cultural context in which irreverence is highly praised. Two of the director's twenty-first-century productions, *Accidens. Matar para comer*

(*Accidens. Killing to Eat*, 2006) and *Cruda. Vuelta y vuelta. Al punto. Chamuscada.* (*Very Rare. Rare. Medium Rare. Charred*, 2007), clearly reflect this attitude. In the former – presented as a short action rather than a full theatre performance – actor Juan Loriente kills, cooks, and eats a lobster onstage, crudely emulating a common restaurant practice in which diners choose their meal 'alive' before consuming it.[11] In the latter, a group of 15 homeless, drug addicts and alcoholics from the streets of Buenos Aires take to the stage, performing a traditional form of carnival, La Murga, while telling their tragic stories of failure.

France has not only offered García a space in which to create but it has also turned into the director's main producer. Thus, from the year 2000, the majority of his pieces have been partially or fully commissioned by a French institution, published in French translation by Les Solitaires Intempestifs series, and included in the country's national curriculum of secondary education.[12] Indeed, García has also become the subject of academic analysis as a number of French universities study his theatre and doctorates explore his work. While it was, arguably, *After Sun* that brought García and his company to the French stage in 2001, he has since become a regular at Avignon, presenting *Creo que no me habéis entendido bien* (*I Think You Have Misunderstood Me*) in 2002, *La historia de Ronald el payaso de McDonalds* (*The Story of Ronald the Clown from McDonald's*) in 2004, and *One Way to Approach the Idea of Mistrust* and *Very Rare. Rare. Medium Rare. Charred* in 2007. The prestige of the festival has not only generated opportunities for his work to visit other international stages but has also provided a space of artistic exchange.

Since 2008, García's presence in France has intensified. His work is regularly staged in the circuit of Scènes Nationales (National Theatres) and his texts continue to be translated into French. In 2013, García was nominated artistic director of the Théâtre a 13 Vents in Montpellier. He left the post five years later in a controversy around the lack of funding to properly develop the theatre. This participation in cultural policy debates further establishes France as the cultural context in which his theatre is produced and disseminated. The director has also fully embraced the French positioning of his theatre by changing, once again, the name of his theatre and production company from its original Spanish name, La Carnicería Teatro, to its French translation, Boucherie Théâtre.

Changing structures: from La Carnicería/Boucherie to Rodrigo García

The director's success on the international stage has left an imprint on the company's structure and, most importantly, on the director's own theatre-making. First, García's intentions to maintain La Carnicería's original ethos have been regularly challenged by the pressures that travelling, external funding, and critical expectations have had on the company's journey towards international success. This is clearly felt in García's conversations with the press on his arrival in Avignon in 2004, when it had already become apparent to him that his life and career had taken a radical turn. In response to a question about France's ability to transform foreign artists, the director offers an illuminating statement:

> Now, I find myself saying no to projects that I feel are not me. Accepting has become very easy. I have been told that after Avignon there will be an absolute avalanche of offers; I have been warned. There have been other cases; Romeo Castellucci's company, for instance, from Italy. It is important that my working conditions are kept intact. [...] And, above all, we should be allowed to maintain our private lives, because it can be very damaging; it will be damaging to us as individuals and it will also affect our personal relationships.
>
> (Caruana 2002: 42)

La Carnicería has, for instance, undergone major changes in the way in which performers are recruited. Having lost all but one of its original members – Juan Loriente – García now carries out auditions and workshops across Europe and Latin America, choosing largely Spanish or Spanish-speaking actors and dancers. This means that the company's identity as a core group of members who live, work, and socialise together in the same city has been replaced by a transient troupe which generally endures short and intensive creative processes in different cities across the world.[13]

Second, the loss of a core group of collaborators has not only transformed García into the company's primary impetus but his status has arguably shifted to that of an independent *auteur*. In fact, since 2007, the company's name has been transformed from La Carnicería Teatro to the more hierarchical La Carnicería–Rodrigo García, a rubric that clearly establishes the director's distinguished position within the collective. Currently, the company goes by Rodrigo García/Boucherie Théâtre, which further emphasises the *auteur* aesthetic and the French situatedness of his theatre. This movement has been facilitated by a theatrical culture – that of the West – which has experienced a shift towards director-led theatre at the expense of collective creative structures. This fact is substantiated by the visibility that some directors have achieved within what were originally anonymous and democratic collectives. This is the case of Albert Boadella (director of performance group Els Joglars) in Spain, Simon McBurney in England, or Ariane Mnouchkine in France. In fact, I would argue that García's present status as European *auteur* responds to France's current, and indeed historical, predisposition towards the cult of the director. The twenty-first-century programming trends of Avignon – since 2004 a different artistic director has been working in conjunction with the festival's programmers – and Paris's festivals as well as the country's network of national theatres further reinstate this fact as the names of white, male, and, frequently, Western directors have become a consistent selling point.[14]

Third, as a result of the international funding that has facilitated most of the director's works since 2000, García's time spent travelling and living away from home has dramatically increased, producing more exposure to the defining features of contemporary Western society: globalisation and the increasing formation of non-spaces (airports, hotels, shopping malls), the overwhelming mediatisation of society, the intensification of social inequality, torture, exploitation, and war. García's texts have progressively examined these issues, evidencing a shift towards a more overt political theatre and, more importantly, a theatre containing a more specific and tangible 'message'. The references to abstract and 'universal' themes (such as torture, abuse, the commodification of all aspects of the human experience, the isolation of the individual) have, in his later pieces, become specific references to current political themes such as the wars in Iraq and Afghanistan, Guantánamo Bay, the Israeli–Palestinian conflict, the exploitation of developing countries – especially in Latin America – at the hands of Europe and the USA.

The Story of Ronald the Clown from McDonald's (2002) marks a decisive turning point in the director's career, as his engagement with contemporary politics takes a more specific shape within his theatre productions. The piece is the company's most performed production to date and it presents the human struggle to stay sane in a world in which Ronald McDonald has become our children's best friend. It is structured around torture as a general theme, presenting its infinite conceptual and visual manifestations in our contemporary society and drawing in recognisable iconographies of war and human terror. The production opens with a performer's impossible endeavour to stay upright – a recurrent image in García's work – under a shower of milk and wine inflicted on him by two other performers. Scenes of subordination are presented in quick succession. At one point in the piece, a performer's face is covered by a paper hat taped to his neck which is consequently filled with food, compost bags, and various liquids that impede his breathing. Standing half-naked, he becomes a representation of the hooded prisoners of Abu Ghraib. Later on, the three performers engage in an impossible task, constantly failing to walk and stand up on a stage cluttered by food and liquids, re-enacting the movements of survivors in an environmental atrocity or war. Furthermore, paranoia and an obsessive search for scapegoats are depicted as everyday modes of interaction in a society paralysed by the media's constant messages of terror. This is clearly theatricalised in the Judas monologue where a performer shares with the audience his fear that everyone around him has been transformed into a traitor. At the end of the piece, a large shower of food and drink transforms the stage into a wasteland, reminiscent of the mountains of trash that constitute the main source of nutriment for a large part of the world's population. *The Story of Ronald*'s engagement with contemporary politics is constructed around its efficacy to create images that recall those to which the audience has already been exposed by the media, while creating a direct dialogue between the stage and the world outside. In fact, this technique will be used again by García in subsequent plays, as indeed it is in *Une façon d'aborder l'idée de méfiance* (*One Way to Approach the Idea of Mistrust*, 2006), for example, where a real picture of the Columbine high-school massacre (1999) is reconstructed in 3D.[15]

The Story of Ronald is also a constant reminder of an abused and tortured body as the physically demanding actions leave traces on the largely naked bodies of the actors, which have been progressively injured and covered in dirt. A shift towards a theatre of images in which the human body is placed centre stage can also be perceived in García's later productions. *Une façon d'aborder l'idée de méfiance* (2006) and *Arrojad mis cenizas sobre Mickey* (*Throw My Ashes over Mickey*, 2006) were largely silent pieces in which the director's texts were projected rather than read by the actors. In these works, which are constructed as visual poetry for the stage, the bodies of the performers are immersed in a landscape of fluids and elements such as honey, mud, dirt, and hair. As in *The Story of Ronald* and *Compré una pala en Ikea para cavar mi tumba* (*I Bought a Spade in Ikea to Dig My Own Grave*, 2002) fast and processed food are used to create striking images, while signalling García's connections with the American avant-garde of the 1960s and, more specifically, the work of artists such as Naumann and McCarthy. The prevalence of image over text can also be read as a result of the increasing internationalisation that García's work has experienced in the past decade. Aware of his dependence on translation and the interferences that such a process might pose to his texts, the director has opted for a theatre that speaks directly to all audiences in an attempt to overcome national and cultural boundaries.

Conclusion

García's identity as an international practitioner is merely a construct that facilitates his work's currency in the international festival circuit. The days in which a small group of friends met to create some of Spain's most daring theatre might have long gone, but García's current methods have been barely modified throughout the three decades that he has been making theatre. There is still a sense of playfulness in the way in which the director approaches the creative process. García, who currently works mainly to commission, generates his productions from a broad starting point that is then explored in rehearsal. The journey is triggered by a text, a film, a news item, and so on, and is then taken through an unsystematic improvisation process in which the performers are encouraged to create material under García's guidance. Time in the rehearsal room is usually combined with solitary confinement in the studio where the director draws the productions' storyboards, selects performance material, and finalises the pieces' structure. This process is usually informed by ongoing conversations with both the performers and the technical team, but final decisions are usually taken by García.[16]

In the past 20 years, García's rise to prominence within the international festival circuit has brought about a revaluation of his theatre in Spain and Latin America, where it is now seen more often than in the period leading up to 2003. His acceptance within the Spanish theatre system has taken place thanks to the support of institutional theatres such as the Teatre Lliure of Barcelona and festivals such as the Festival de Teatro Iberoamericano de Cádiz, the disappeared Sitges Teatre Internacional, or the Festival de las Artes de Castilla y León. His 'resurrection' within the Spanish theatre scene speaks to the assimilation and commodification that his militant theatre has undergone on the international stage. Audiences are no longer disgusted or enraged. They have become accustomed to the director's irreverence and very rarely respond to his challenges. The transformation that García and his company have undergone in the past decade is paralleled by that of their audiences, as the young and driven spectators attracted by his early pieces have now become middle-class and middle-aged professionals whose nostalgia for a social revolution is generously fed by García's radicalism.

Five key productions

Protegedme de lo que deseo (*Protect Me from What I Want*). By Rodrigo García. Design by Rodrigo García. Perf. Miguel Ángel Altet, Víctor Contreras, Fernandito, Patricia Lamas, and Chete Lera. Sala Cuarta Pared, Madrid. December 1997.

Borges. By Rodrigo García. Design by Rodrigo García. Perf. Juan Loriente. Casa de América, Madrid. December 1999.

After Sun. By Rodrigo García. Design by Rodrigo García. Perf. Patricia Lamas and Juan Loriente. International Theatre Festival of Delphi. June 2000.

La historia de Ronald el payaso de McDonalds (*The Story of Ronald the Clown from McDonald's*). By Rodrigo García. Design by Rodrigo García. Perf. Ruben Ametllé, Juan Loriente, and Juan Navarro. Citemor Festival, Montemor-O-Velho, Portugal. July 2002.

Cruda. Vuelta y Vuelta. Al punto. Chamuscada (*Very Rare. Rare. Medium Rare. Charred*). By Rodrigo García. Design by Rodrigo García. Perf. Ramiro Basilio, Guillermo Cerna, Pablo Ceresa, Rodrigo Díaz, Jorge Ferreyra, Juan Loriente, Manuel Sacco, Gastón Santamarina, Pablo Suárez, Kevork Tastzian, Oscar Truncellito, Víctor Vallejo, Juan Vallejo, Leandro Vera, and David Villalba. Festival d'Avignon. July 2007.

Notes

1 Two of his early texts were selected for this prize, *Macbeth Imágenes* (*Macbeth Images*, 1987) and *Reloj* (*Watch*, 1988), both of which had stagings in 1993 and 1999 and 1994 and 1995 respectively.
2 The role of the Socialist Party in supporting Madrid's fringe circuit is examined in Ragué-Arias 1996: 146; Orozco 2007.

3 This is the case for most of the new work produced in Spain during the 1980s and 1990s as is proven by the fact that most of the texts were published rather than staged. Sergi Belbel (2007: 412–13) offers an illuminating account of this period of Spanish theatre history in relation to new work.
4 In a personal conversation held in June 2005 the director stated: 'traditional theatre has never helped me; it has never suited me, therefore I have to find other ways. I learnt a lot from the visual arts, above all, the diversity and plurality that one finds in them. Each artist has a universe. No one does the same thing. In theatre it all seems the same, there are too many similarities.'
5 This performance opened Spain's 2001 Sitges Teatre Internacional Festival.
6 For more on Rodrigo García and animals, see Orozco 2013: 1–2, 40–6, 2014.
7 In Madrid, for instance, this meant that large cultural centres such as Madrid's opera house – the Teatro Real – or the city's modern art museum – the Centro de Artes Reina Sofía – monopolised the cultural budgets.
8 Javier García Yagüe, director and manager of Madrid's most successful alternative theatre space, La Cuarta Pared, explained in the year 2000 how the change in government had been detrimental to Spanish theatre, as the Partido Popular had clearly established a market economy in the area of arts management (Orozco 2007: 285–6).
9 The workshop had been held by Flemish director Jan Fabre the previous year and clearly helped to position García within a certain group of practitioners fashioned by the French theatre.
10 With reference to Paris as meeting place for theatre directors, see Delgado and Heritage 1996: 3; Bradby and Delgado 2002.
11 The performance, which has been seen in some European cities, was banned in Spain in 2007 on the grounds of animal cruelty.
12 For more information go to www.solitairesintempestifs.com
13 The director recognises this change in an interview in www.theatre-contemporain.net/Entretien,2480
14 Examples include Jan Fabre, Jan Lauwers, Romeo Castellucci, Thomas Ostermeier, Frank Castorf, Christoph Marthaler, Calixto Bieito, Frédéric Fisbach, and Árpád Schilling. However, I would argue that the director's predominance in contemporary European theatre reaches beyond France, as is proven by the focus of this book. For more information on the Festival d'Avignon and its programming trends, see Banu and Tackels 2005.

15 The same technique was used by Romeo Castellucci in his piece *C.#01* within the *Tragedia Endogonidia* cycle, where a picture of the killing of Carlo Giuliani – an anti-globalisation campaigner assassinated by the police in Genoa in 2001 – is reconstructed (Ridout 2006: 182), and also by American choreographer William Forsythe in *Three Atmospheric Studies* (2005).

16 An extensive description of the director's rehearsal process can be found in Orozco 2010.

Bibliography

Banu, Georges and Bruno Tackels (eds) (2005) *Le cas Avignon 2005: regards critiques*, Avignon: L'Entretemps.

Belbel, Sergi (2007) 'On Writing, Directing and the Teatre Nacional de Catalunya', *Contemporary Theatre Review*, 17 (3): 411–15.

Bergamín, Beatriz (2006) 'El corrosivo y poético teatro de Rodrigo García conquista los escenarios del mundo', *El País*, 15 January, www.elpais.com/articulo/espectaculos/corrosivo/poetico/teatro/Rodrigo/Garcia/conquista/escenarios/mundo/elpepiept/20060115elpepiesp_3/Tes

Bradby, David and Maria M. Delgado (eds) (2002) *The Paris Jigsaw: Internationalism and the City's Stages*, Manchester: Manchester University Press.

Bradby, David and Annie Sparks (1997) *Mise en Scène: French Theatre Now*, London: Methuen Drama.

Caruana, Pablo (2002) 'La Carnicería se abre al encuentro del público', *Primer Acto*, 294: 44–58.

Delgado, Maria M. and Paul Heritage (1996) 'Introduction', in Maria M. Delgado and Paul Heritage (eds), *In Contact with the Gods? Directors Talk Theatre*, Manchester: Manchester University Press, pp. 1–13.

Feldman, Sharon (2005) 'Rodrigo García's Ruins', *Estreno*, 31 (1): 16–18.

García, Rodrigo (2002) 'Algunos textos de *Compré una pala en Ikea para cavar mi tumba*', *Primer Acto*, 294: 59–62.

Hartwig, Susanne (2002) '¿La escena en busca de teatralidad? Reflexiones sobre el uso del color en el Festival alternativo del 2001', *Acotaciones*, 8: 67–85.

—— (2005) 'La esquizofrénica levedad del ser: el teatro de Rodrigo García', *Estreno*, 31 (1): 8–14.

Henderson, Carlos (2004) 'La gloria no cae del cielo: Rodrigo García en Aviñón', *Primer Acto*, 305: 72–75.

Henríquez, Jorge and Juan Mayorga (2000) 'Entrevista a dos bandas: "yo no quiero ser un animal"', *Primer Acto*, 285: 15–22.

Monleón, José (2000) '*After Sun*, un pequeño relámpago en Delfos: Rodrigo García y el mito de Faetón', *Primer Acto*, 285: 15–22.

────── (2002) 'Teatro de la profanación', *Primer Acto*, 294: 67–70.

Orozco, Lourdes (2007) *Teatro y política: Barcelona (1980–2000)*, Madrid: Asociación de Directores de Escena.

────── (2010) 'Approaching Mistrust: Rodrigo García Rehearses La Carnicería Teatro in *Une façon d'aborder l'idée de méfiance* (One Way to Approach the Idea of Mistrust)', in Jen Harvie and Andy Lavender (eds), *Making Contemporary Theatre: International Rehearsal Processes*, Manchester: Manchester University Press, pp. 121–39.

────── (2013) *Theatre & Animals*, Houndmills: Palgrave.

────── (2014) 'Manifesting the Animal: Animals in Contemporary Performance Practice', in Laura Cull and Will Daddario (eds), *Manifesto Now! Instructions for Philosophy, Performance, Politics*, Bristol: Intellect, pp. 177–94.

Ragué-Arias, María José (1996) *El teatro de fin de milenio en España (de 1975 hasta hoy)*, Barcelona: Ariel.

Ridout, Nicholas (2006) 'Make-Believe: Socìetas Raffaello Sanzio Do Theatre', in Joe Kelleher and Nicholas Ridout (eds), *Contemporary Theatres in Europe: A Critical Companion*, London and New York: Routledge, pp. 175–87.

Tackels, Bruno (2003) 'Théâtre de combat', *Mouvement*, 19 February, www.mouvement.net/html

Chapter 19

KATIE MITCHELL

Learning from Europe

Dan Rebellato

In April 2009, *The Guardian*'s website published a short article by its lead drama critic, Michael Billington, entitled 'Don't Let Auteurs Take Over in Theatre'. The focus of his concern was that certain British directors were 'in danger of acquiring auteur status'. The danger of auteurism is twofold, he explains; first, the director develops a kind of cult status, gathering acolytes about them, in whose eyes the sacred director can do no wrong; second, their star shines so bright that they begin to take 'precedence over the writer'. In case the reader is in any doubt about who these dangerous figures might be, he names Emma Rice of Kneehigh, Simon McBurney of Complicite, and the subject of this essay, Katie Mitchell (Billington 2009).

Billington cannot be accused of inconsistency. His lament against auteurism has been a regular feature of his theatre reviews for several years, nowhere more clearly than in his response to Mitchell's recent work, and, in his book-length history of post-war British theatre, he gives over several pages of his afterword to a denunciation of Mitchell for the 'increasing personal stamp' that she sets on classic texts (2007: 404). Warming to his theme, he rehearses the argument to which he would return two years later in remarking that

> Mitchell [is] the controlling figure and ultimate auteur in a continental European tradition [...] In Germany, France and Italy the dearth of living writers has inexorably turned the director into a form of superstar: someone whose conceptual reading of a classic

text has become a substitute for new drama. In Britain, with its abundance of living dramatists, there is less motive for such directorial adventurism.

(Billington 2007: 405–6)

It is unusual, to say the least, for a leading theatre critic to spoil publicly for a fight with a director whose work is so widely admired, but Katie Mitchell's work has always had its detractors. From the beginnings of her work in the very early 1990s, there has been a strain of critical response that finds it miserably bleak. Critic Robert Gore-Langton once remarked that 'she's famous for staging the gloomiest writers' (2004: 18), and certainly she is drawn to the austere vision of Beckett, Strindberg, and the comfortless cruelties of Greek tragedy, but articles with titles like Heather Neill's 'Mistress of Gloom and Doom' (1999: 33) suggest a critical mixture of embarrassment and derision before what Lyn Gardner describes as these 'austere but visually ravishing shows of almost religious intensity' (1998: 15). As Mitchell herself patiently remarks in Neill's article, 'it's joyous working on texts where people are capable of facing things for what they are' (1999: 33).

Katie Mitchell and Europe

The word 'auteur', with its sinuously Gallic vowels and suspiciously un-British parsimony with concretely empirical consonants, brings together several features of the charge. It is an intellectual term, appropriated by the critics of the *Cahiers du Cinéma* in the 1950s; in applying the term 'auteur' to film directors, they were trying to transfer some of the prestige accorded to the 'author' to those creative artists working in a decisively visual medium, and, as such, the word itself – much like analogous theatrical terms such as Roger Planchon's *écriture scénique* (Bradby and Williams 1988: 52) – represents the displacement of the playwright by the director; and finally, it is a French word, and represents a form of theatre-making on which British theatre has so often turned its back, the directorial traditions of Continental Europe. I have argued elsewhere that at the moment when British theatre rediscovered its talent for playwriting, it did so by, among other things, firmly placing the director at the service of the playwright and driving out the European influence on the theatre (Rebellato 1999: 86–9, 127–54). I would suggest that Mitchell's work has a sensibility and a set of priorities that fit awkwardly into the institutional structures or critical consensus that surround British theatrical practice. Put simply, Katie Mitchell is too European for some British tastes.

Her work has moved through a number of phases, as I shall show, but it is always marked by an intense realism of performance style, matched by a rigorous and beautiful organisation of space. Her particular approach to realism means an absence of theatrical short-cuts, an absolute avoidance of 'stagey' conventions that are not drawn from the demands of character and situation. The organisation of space could be spare and evocative, in the plain floorboards, stacked wooden chairs, and rough plastered wall of *Easter* (1995), or visually enticing in the various layered interior spaces into which the audience's eye is voyeuristically drawn in *The Seagull* (2006). In her more recent, less visually realist, productions, the division of the stage into live and mediated, theatre and video, stage and screen is always rich in emotion and analysis and beautiful in its clarity and complexity. In all of her work, there is a tremendous intensity and seriousness, even when being, as in *Waves* or *Attempts on Her Life* (2007), witty and playful. The challenge of the work is not simply to its own audiences; the authenticity and groundedness of the performances have a corrosive effect on one's tolerance of cheaper attitudes to theatre visible in other productions, sometimes in the same theatres that show her work.

Mitchell herself has always been drawn to European dramatic traditions, and specifically those from Northern and Eastern Europe. She recalls her teenage encounters with the cinema of Tarkovsky, Klimov, and Shepitko, the writings of Solzhenitsyn and Tolstoy, the ideas of Jerzy Grotowski, and later, at international theatre festivals like LIFT, she saw the work of directors Lev Dodin and Anatoli Vassiliev and companies as diverse as Gardzienice from Poland and Epigonen from Belgium. At the age of 23, she went to Paris and saw Pina Bausch's *Nelken* (*Carnations*, orig. 1982) and recalls: 'I cried silently from beginning to end. I cried because it was so very beautiful – more beautiful than any performance I had ever imagined' (Mitchell 2008b). Since the late 2000s, she has worked increasingly in German-speaking theatres (particularly the Schaubühne in Berlin) where her sensibility has found a warm reception among audiences and theatre professionals. She is the first British director to have been invited to the prestigious Theatertreffen festival, with Franz Xaver Kroetz's *Wunschkonzert* (*Request Programme*, Schauspiel Köln, 2008) and *Reise durch die Nacht* (*Night Train*, adapted from the work of Friederike Mayröcker, Schauspiel Köln, 2012). The influence of these traditions has rippled through Mitchell's work from the very beginning.

Katie Mitchell was born in 1964 and studied English at Oxford University, becoming President of the Oxford University Dramatic Society (OUDS), and after attachments at the King's Head and Paines Plough, she began two years as assistant director at the Royal Shakespeare Company (RSC). So far, so conventional. Oxford, OUDS, and the RSC are well-worn stepping stones for a young director in Britain. But a sign of Mitchell's different allegiances came in 1989 when, despite beginning to establish herself at the RSC, Mitchell left England on a grant from the Winston Churchill Memorial Trust and travelled to Poland, Russia, Georgia, and Lithuania to observe directors training. As one critic has commented, 'of all her contemporaries, Mitchell is the most internationally minded' (Whitley 1995: 17), and she herself has declared the importance of travelling to 'see other people working to keep your standards high' (Kelly 1995). She spent two and a half weeks each with Vassiliev and Dodin, and then short periods with Mikheil Tumanishvili of the Film Actors Theatre in Tblisi and Eimuntas Nekrošius of the State Youth Theatre in Vilnius. In Poland she observed training courses for directors in Krakow and Warsaw and then spent one month training with Gardzienice.

Three things principally attracted Mitchell to these theatre cultures. First, the seriousness with which they approached director training. At that time in the Soviet Union and much of the Soviet bloc a director's training took five years, and a director couldn't work without it. This derived in part from the legacy of Stanislavski, (from whom many people at that time were only a generation away) and the tradition of rigorous training that he fostered. For Mitchell this compared very favourably with the British tradition of 'glorified amateurism' (Mitchell 2008c). Second, mainstream British theatre has often been dominated by the text, and literary approaches to the text at that. What she found in Dodin and his company was an entirely different emphasis: 'they didn't see performance as being about text; they saw it as being about *behaviour*. And that emphasis was so profoundly different from the tradition from here' (Mitchell 2008c). Third, and in part an explanation of the second, what Mitchell was so struck by in the work of Dodin, Vassiliev, and others was that 'the visual metaphors were so powerful – because they couldn't rely on verbal metaphors, their visual discipline was so rigorous' (Mitchell 2008c). For all these reasons, in Eastern Europe at the end of the 1980s, a theatrical culture had become established that did not see the director's task as serving the playwright but instead creating the conditions for actors to work logically, precisely, and – to use an unfashionable word – truthfully.

By chance, at the very moment Mitchell chose to visit Eastern Europe, the region was undergoing its biggest political and social transformation for a generation. She flew into Berlin where, only three weeks before, the Wall had been brought down. Soviet authority was crumbling around her, and, as she passed through newly-opened checkpoint after checkpoint, she found herself, in her words, 'constantly banging up against these enormous events that were going on' (Mitchell 2008c). In Tblisi, the Soviet-backed military had thrown gas canisters into the Theatre School and the staff were still fumigating it. In Vilnius, the ongoing independence struggle meant that rehearsals were constantly interrupted by the need to go and attend a march or demonstration. Mitchell's career as a director was forged in the dying embers of Old Europe.

This mutual entwining of theatre and politics – 'I couldn't disentangle the life experience from the artistic experience,' she remembers (Mitchell 2008c) – has left its own stamp on her work. Her work, formally engaged as it is, always responds politically to its time. The Bosnian and Rwandan crises of the early 1990s provided a focus for revivals of *Henry VI, Part 3* (1994) and *The Phoenician Women* (1995); *Easter* and *Uncle Vanya* (1998) were parables of political transition; while the ongoing war in Iraq was addressed in two Greek tragedies, *Iphigenia in Aulis* (2003, 2004) and *Women of Troy* (2007). More recently, she has increasingly explored environmental concerns in pieces like *Ten Billion* (2012) and *2071* (2014), both at the Royal Court London. In Duncan Macmillan's *Atmen* (*Lungs*, Schaubühne, 2013), all of the power required to run the show was generated onstage by the two actors on bicycles. Her production of Beckett's *Happy Days* at the Deutsches Schauspielhaus, Hamburg (2015) replaced the rising sand of the play's original with water; the arid, somewhat abstract landscape of Beckett's text became a woman in a domestic kitchen with water rising, suggesting rising sea levels as well as a woman's unnoticed domestic suffering (see McMullan 2018: 129–30). Indeed, she has increasingly demonstrated, in her words, 'a commitment to women's experience being made a central part of everything' (Peck 2017: 235), most recently through work like *Ophelias Zimmer* (*Ophelia's Room*, 2015), which reimagined the events of *Hamlet* from Ophelia's perspective and adaptations of feminist classics like Charlotte Perkins Gilman's *The Yellow Wallpaper* (2013) and Virginia Woolf's *Orlando* (2019), both at the Schaubühne. She has also been drawn to contemporary explorations of female extremity like Sarah Kane's *Cleansed* (National Theatre, 2016) and *4.48 Psychosis* (Deutsches Schauspielhaus, Hamburg, 2017), and Elfriede Jelinek's *Schatten(Eurydike sagt)* (*Shadows (Eurydice Says)*, Schaubühne, 2016).

Decisively though, she makes little distinction between artistic form and political content; political matters are always addressed through artistic decisions and the formal complexity of the work. It has often been said that the philosophical division between the British tradition of empiricism and pragmatism and the Continental European tradition of rationalist and metaphysical speculation derives from our divergent histories: Europe's tumultuous changes over the past millennium, with its continually challenged borders, alliances, and identities have provided a continual need to ask: Who are we? Britain's relative stability has allowed a greater sense of shared perspective but has also provided less need to challenge the foundations of identity. Mitchell's mature directing work began in a context where questions of being, identity, and ethics were all open, urgent, and undeniable.

The anthropological phase

More broadly, the Russian example gave Mitchell a conviction that a director's training lasts a lifetime. Each individual rehearsal and production period has its own shape, but a director can and should pursue their artistic development across a series of different projects, learning and deepening their craft. Mitchell's sense of directing as a long game sits awkwardly with British theatre's more impecunious tradition of working project by project and its tendency towards three or four-week rehearsal periods, hence her drift increasingly towards German theatre and their more generous conditions of production.

Nonetheless, Mitchell has, by establishing relationships with the two largest national companies, the RSC and the National Theatre (NT), secured the ability to ask for extended rehearsal and workshop periods, usually eight weeks, sometimes – for, say, *A Dream Play* (2005) – twelve weeks. This has allowed Mitchell to develop a distinct journey of artistic exploration and self-education that falls into several phases. Her early apprentice years give way to a period she has referred to, slightly tongue-in-cheek, as her 'anthropological phase' (Mitchell 2008c). During this phase and outliving it, there is a series of shifts in her understanding of actors that transforms the work. A transitional period follows where Mitchell seems to bump up against the limits of classic texts for the work she wants to do, which is succeeded by a radical new direction characterised by the use of digital media and a decisive move away from conventional play texts. These phases are not discrete or mutually exclusive, and they overlap in various ways, but they are useful for giving a sense of the critical turns in Mitchell's career, as well as the periods of more persistent development along a single road.

The anthropological phase is so called because of the extremely detailed research she underwent, sometimes visiting the locations of the play she was directing, often with her main designer, Vicki Mortimer. She famously travelled to Bergen to observe the light and the landscape when preparing for *Ghosts* (1993) and to the Ukraine to listen to the local patois and stories for *The Dybbuk* (1992). Directing *Rutherford & Son* (1994), she visited Nottinghamshire's industrial remnants and followed the path of the enraged Orestes through the plains of ancient Greece in preparation for *The Oresteia* (1999). These well-known episodes are easier to capture than the subtle detail of her work:

> the science of how a live performance is put together – the minute science (like the tiny details of psychology crafted by the actor second by second, or the decision about the precise time of day a scene occurs, or the selection of the colour and texture of the location for a scene). These tiny details are woven together by the director and make up the weave the audience see, and just as it is not always possible to identify each fine thread in the weave, the untrained eye can too easily concentrate on, and discuss, the larger shapes or patterns (like cuts to the text or anachronisms or research trips) and disregard the finer details altogether.
>
> (Mitchell 2008c)

What is important, particularly for this early work, is the intimate connection between place and performance. The roots of that perhaps lie in the period of time Mitchell spent working with the Polish theatre company Gardzienice in 1989. This company, with roots in Grotowski's Theatre Laboratory, live and work together in the countryside of south-east Poland, creating performances out of physical training and through a process of 'Expeditions' and 'Gatherings' where the company will travel to a nearby community and work with them and their folk traditions to create new kinds of part-ritual performances, involving ensemble physical movement and choral singing (see Allain 1997). Mitchell worked with them in 1989 and returned a year later to work with them again, and to make a show, *Diarmuid and Graine*, with fellow theatre-maker Paul Allain, that toured eastern Poland. Gardzienice left its mark on Mitchell in her early work's sense of the relations between place and behaviour, visual motifs of folk dancing, candlelight, and choral singing, and a 'poor theatre' aesthetic of bare floorboards and natural materials.

These motifs run through the productions of her company Classics on a Shoestring, which fused some of the physical-theatre work she had developed at Gardzienice with a classic-text-based theatre practice. The company lasted only three years, from 1990 to 1993, producing five plays: *Arden of Faversham* (1990), *Vassa Zheleznova* (1990), *Women of Troy* (1991), *House of Bernarda Alba* (1992), and *Live Like Pigs* (1993). The first productions were financed by Mitchell going through the directory of the Directors' Guild and writing to all of its members asking for money – 'A to H for the first production, I to P for the second' (Mitchell 2008c) – and producing flyers and operating lights herself. She was quickly noticed, and, by the fifth and final production of Classics on a Shoestring, she had already opened three productions at the RSC and was preparing to make her NT debut.

This was not merely a career move. Already she was beginning to gather around her some key members of a 'creative family' with whom she would still be working 30 years later, notably Mortimer, whom she already knew, and who designed *Arden of Faversham* and *The House of Bernarda Alba*. Some of the actors in the early productions would be key members of Mitchell's informal repertory company, like Liz Kettle, who was in *The House of Bernarda Alba*, returning in shows such as *Henry VI, Part 3*, *The Seagull*, *Waves*, and *Attempts on Her Life*. An early collaborator with a shared interest in Gardzienice was Emma Rice, later to run Kneehigh Theatre Company, Shakespeare's Globe, and Wise Children.

The peak of the anthropological approach was perhaps Mitchell's RSC production of Euripides' *The Phoenician Women*, which opened at the Other Place in October 1995 and transferred to the Pit in London the following June. As the audience entered, a brazier of fresh thyme filled the auditorium with its pungent aroma, suggesting an offering to the gods who were themselves represented by three plaster statues, lit by candles, hanging on the wall, their arms raised in apparent supplication. The audience were seated on three sides of the action on backless benches, in vague emulation of an ancient Greek theatre. Ritualistically, we were offered a sprig of thyme.

The Phoenician Women is a play of watching and waiting, a cast of characters trapped in the crossfire of a civil conflict, and the energy of the production lay in the chorus. From their first appearance, stomping and whirling across the stage, clapping and ululating, the chorus suggested both the lamenting chorus of the Greeks but also, closer to home, the grieving Balkan tribes of the blood-soaked former Yugoslavia. That civil war was not named but gave focus and meaning to the play's military struggle between Eteocles and Polynices. Mitchell's production was widely acclaimed, and it won her the Evening Standard Award for Best Director in 1996. This success was a surprise to her:

> I thought we were involved in a very purist, private experiment where the actors were teaching me about how to direct, how to work, and we were all making the work to talk about Bosnia. And then out of the blue we got a big prize for it and suddenly everything crystallised – the political agenda, the artistic agenda, and the culture's reception of the idea.
>
> (Mitchell 2008c)

Mitchell's purism extended not just to the hard, backless seats but the production played its 145 minutes without an interval, and, perhaps to encourage the absorption of the audience in the fiction and the actors in the ensemble, did not issue a programme, distributing only a simple cast list, and then only at the end.

Working with actors

In June 1994, with *Ghosts* running at the RSC and *Rutherford & Son* opening at the NT, Mitchell told an interviewer that as a child she had always wanted to be a painter but found she had no talent for it: 'so I started painting with people instead' (Pearson 1994: 34). It's an unguarded moment but reveals an early attitude she was shortly to revise very firmly.

Ghosts was one of Mitchell's most successful early productions, admired for the lucidity of its interpretation and the 'shafts of Scandinavian light' (Sierz 2003: 13) that pitilessly illuminated the events of Ibsen's harshest play. To one of its performances came

Professor Soloviova, a doyenne of actor training that Mitchell had met in Russia, with harsh words for the fledgling director:

> She said 'look, it's great work, great visual sense, great aural sense, but *absolutely nothing* is going on between the actors; you're not even directing them. What tasks did you set them?' I said, I didn't set them any tasks. I just asked them questions. She said: 'No, your job is to set them tasks; their job is to execute them. Don't ask actors what the tasks are.'
> (Mitchell 2008c)

She recognised the truth of the remarks and for a while struggled with the recognition that her most successful piece of work now seemed to her 'awful'; 15 years later she would still judge this acclaimed production as 'the worst piece of work I've made' (Mitchell 2008c). Soloviova's criticism of *Ghosts* was a sobering and vital moment for Mitchell, and she would not begin to find a solution until near the end of the decade. It marks the beginning of a longer journey away from her rehearsal practices and also the unflattering image of actors as paint. She would later entirely rethink the comments she made in 1994: 'I wanted to be a painter but I couldn't paint and my first experiments were painting with people and they were dull' (Mitchell 2008c).

To help her rethink her approach to actors, Mitchell eventually enlisted the help of two women: Tatiana Olear and Elen Bowman. Olear had trained with Dodin and performed in his company for five and a half years. Bowman, from the School of the Science of Acting, had trained with Sam Kogan who was taught at GITIS (Russian Academy of Theatre Arts, Moscow) by Maria Knebel who was taught by Stanislavski himself. They provided Mitchell with 'links back to Dodin, Kogan and, through them, to Stanislavski. It made me feel part of a chain of practitioners, each sharpening tried-and-tested tools against their culture and time' (Mitchell 2008a: 230).

What these women, Olear in particular, taught was that a director's role is to make some fundamental decisions before the rehearsal process has begun that will provide a concrete and precise starting point, a directional logic that the actors are to follow through the rehearsal period. 'The huge difference between the early work and the later work', Mitchell says, 'is that in the early work I thought that everything happened in rehearsal, but in the later work I realised that the work happens before rehearsals even begin' (Mitchell 2008c). As her thinking developed and her training intensified, it became clearer that the major work investigating the play was not something to be done on the rehearsal-room floor but through a long period of research, scrutiny, and judgement prior to the first day of rehearsals.

Katie Mitchell's book *The Director's Craft* (2008a) gathers together systematically the ideas that she developed through the late 1990s and into the 2000s. Anyone expecting a visionary manifesto in the style of, say, *The Theatre and Its Double* or *Towards a Poor Theatre* would be surprised to find a handbook for the director that is both eminently practical and extraordinarily demanding. Of its four sections, the longest by some way deals with preparing for rehearsals and requires the director to undertake an arduously meticulous examination of the text, making decisions about all aspects of its world and its characters. It is important to be clear that this does not mean Mitchell begins rehearsals with the whole production scored and planned, in the manner of Max Reinhardt at his most controlling. The preparation is a process designed so that the director can take the play apart, list the decisions that need to be taken and take them; by fixing certain aspects of the character, the actor is freed to do their own work.

> One of the things I learned about acting is that it takes the actor a long time to evolve in a deep and precise way. If the director keeps changing the starting point during rehearsals it leads to 'thin' acting, so you have to begin with a relatively deep starting position, and then you have to accept the consequences of where you started from.
>
> (Mitchell 2008c)

Undoubtedly, some actors do not wish to work like this. It is very demanding; bad theatrical habits are dismantled, approximations and short cuts are exposed. The roles are very clear: the actor is told where to start but then 'they are free to follow the logic to the most extreme degree', as Mitchell observes, adding, 'the actors who like that find it very freeing' (2008c). Indeed, many actors return time and time again to work in this way: Kate Duchêne, Anastasia Hille, Michael Gould, Ben Whishaw, Angus Wright, Justin Salinger, Dominic Rowan, Hattie Morahan, Sean Jackson, Paul Hilton, and others form a kind of informal repertory company continually training themselves and each other as part of a larger creative process that overflows and exceeds any individual production.

In general, Katie Mitchell thrives in what she calls 'well-established marriages' (2008c); she began working with Mortimer in the 1980s, the sound designer Gareth Fry in the mid-1990s, the lighting designer Paule Constable in the late 1990s, the video designer Leo Warner in the mid-2000s, and the sound designer Melanie Wilson in the early 2010s. As she observes:

> I don't like new relationships because you have to waste a lot of energy shaping the relationship and you can't work so easily because you're learning the person. My relationship with an actor should be equivalent to my relationship with my creative team: it's another exceptional adult I'm in partnership with and we're going to make something together.
>
> (Mitchell 2008c)

It is in this sense that one might detect one aspect of *création collective*, a clear commitment to the sense that a collective activity by a group of equals – with different responsibilities, to be sure, but accorded equal creative respect – is the most appropriate way to make theatre. This isn't *création collective* in the full Mnouchkinian sense of the term; one gets little sense either from the production or from the director herself that collaborative working is in any sense an end in itself, a political or ethical rehearsal for the revolution, which is the idea that hangs around the early work of Théâtre du Soleil. Mitchell is too keenly focused on the work they are making. When she tells Allison Pearson, early in her career, that she likes collaboration because 'eleven imaginations are richer than one' (Pearson 1994: 34), one senses that the advantage is to the work and it is there that any political impulse must manifest itself, not in the formal relationships of the rehearsal room.

The limits of text

By the turn of the century, Mitchell felt that, although 'the food I'd got from the Winston Churchill grant fed me through until the end of the nineties, I had reached the end of it' (Mitchell 2008c). So she returned to a similar source, the National Endowment for Science, Technology and the Arts, and managed to secure a fellowship to go back into Europe and renew her studies of theatre processes and training, in the light of Olear and Bowman's lessons. Through the early 2000s, Mitchell looked again at Stanislavski, but widened her attention to take in, amongst other things, the latest discoveries in neuroscience, the history of painting, contemporary dance theatre, the ideas of the Dogme 95 movement in cinema, and the performance experiments of John Cage.

Some of these ideas entered the work quite quickly: her production of the contemporary Norwegian play *Nightsongs* (2002) drew on Dogme 95 and used a live, improvised sound design. Perhaps because it was a contemporary play and therefore lacked the canonical status of a Greek tragedy or the classic one of naturalism, she felt freer to incorporate these innovations. But the following year, with *Three Sisters* (2003) and *Iphigenia in Aulis* (2004), Mitchell felt confident enough to widen her theatrical palette in the performance of a classic. *Three Sisters* was in many ways a conventionally faithful production, though the pursuit of naturalism also meant allowing the action to take its own time, which brought the production into the realm of durational performance, with several sequences accurately and captivatingly glimpsing the longueurs of the Prozorovs' isolation. In addition, some moments were extended more formally, with some gliding into slow motion, capturing the subjectivity of watching a loved one turn from a window, or capturing the intensity with which someone knowingly takes a wrong turn in the forking path of their life.

Iphigenia in Aulis was even bolder: the play was relocated to the immediate post-war period, with the action taking place in a requisitioned schoolroom filled – in more than a nod to Pina Bausch's *Café Müller* (1978) – with upright wooden chairs, through which the hapless Greek generals wove and blundered. Bausch's influence – but also perhaps Beckett's – was also felt in the use of the Chorus, an array of immaculately dressed war widows, hanging around with autograph books at the ready, waiting for a glimpse of Agamemnon. Occasionally, a bell would strike and they would all face front, mortified with embarrassment, and speak the Chorus's required speeches, like a flock of Beckettian Winnies from *Happy Days* (1961) or the benighted inhabitants of the urns in *Play* (1963), required to speak by some implacable unseen force. Finally, a scratchy dance record would play, and they would all, somewhat inexpertly, foxtrot, sometimes dropping a handbag, to a collective frisson of shame and recrimination, like a genteel version of the libidinal pensioners of Bausch's remarkable *Kontakthof* (1978). The self-justifying military leaders, the malleable, confused public, and the notoriously unsatisfactory ending combined in this production to offer a shattering picture of the then-new war in Iraq.

The decisions that Mitchell makes in preparing the text for performance inevitably excludes others. The key term Mitchell uses repeatedly to describe the textual level she is trying to uncover is that she is exploring the 'idea structure' of a play. Once this idea structure is uncovered it allows for the discarding of other, less fundamental, aspects of the text. What the process does is bring the text, in some sense, into conflict with itself, a kind of theatrical deconstruction (even if the rehearsal reconstructs the text anew). In the cases of *Iphigenia* and *Three Sisters* the rigorous investigation of given circumstances and so on meant that Mitchell's innovations could be – short-sightedly – considered to some extent as decorative additions to an otherwise solid reading of the text. In her next two productions for the NT, her investigation of 'idea structure' would bring the whole enterprise of staging a classic into crisis and bring out into the open some of the limitations of working within a text-centred theatre culture.

In an interview published on the eve of *Three Sisters*, Katie Mitchell candidly admitted: 'I think I'm a closet iconoclast: part of me wants to realise *Three Sisters* as precisely as Chekhov wrote it. Another part of me wants to communicate it today, which means smashing it to smithereens' (Sierz 2003: 13). When she came to direct *The Seagull* at the National Theatre in 2006, some did indeed think Mitchell's aim was less production than destruction; Billington in *The Guardian* detected, predictably, 'mise en scène being substituted for meaning' and dismissed it as 'directors' theatre at its most indulgent' (2006). Also in *The Guardian*, Martin Kettle wrote an op-ed piece titled 'Hostages in the Hands of Overindulged Meddlers', itemising a series of departures from conventional productions (in which he invests unexplained authority), alluding darkly to a 'turgid postmodern heresy' and – meaninglessly – insisting that directors should always 'trust the playwrights' in how to direct their plays (Kettle 2006: 33).

Mitchell's *Seagull* was relocated to the period between the First and Second World Wars; Konstantin's play was reimagined as a post-Dadaist modernist provocation; characters tango mournfully through the house and the comic chains of unrequited love are made more difficult by an audience of servants and the radical disrepair of Sorin's estate. There were some cuts, mostly to the old-fashioned asides and soliloquies that Chekhov had not yet fully abandoned, and the language was modernised in places. All of these, listed in one breath, may give the impression of a petulantly subverted production, but while these directorial decisions were unmistakable they were wholly coherent. Some of the discoveries of the production – that Masha may be the product of a liaison between Dorn and Polina and that Dorn is dying of tuberculosis, for example – are genuinely enlightening and plausible. The relationship between Arkadina and Trigorin, threatened by the latter's indecisive sexual interest in Nina, is often played for laughs, but the performance of Juliet Stevenson, Mark Bazeley, and Hattie Morahan found newly adult emotions in this fatal triangle. As Mitchell has remarked:

> it is confusing that people have a picture of me smashing things up for the sake of it. That isn't the case. The first step I take is careful consideration and detailed study of the material, then I work out how to communicate it now.
>
> (Higgins 2007: 11)

Her most effective rebuke to the critics was perhaps *The Director's Craft*, which uses *The Seagull* and demonstrates the minutely exacting process of reading and re-reading, questioning, and testing of Chekhov's own play that resulted in this radically original production.[1]

That said, it is clear that at moments the pursuit of the idea structure of the play can come into conflict at times with aspects of its surface. In cutting the asides, for example, Mitchell and her adaptor, Martin Crimp, were seeking to bring out more fully the experience for which Chekhov was groping. Mitchell's production of Strindberg's *A Dream Play* (2005) went even further; encouraged by her reading in neuroscience, Mitchell thought she could find a rigorous process of investigation that would find clear theatrical counterparts for all of the text's images. In the event, finding, at root, that Strindberg's aim was to stage dreams, the workshop process encouraged Mitchell to jettison large sections of the play and replace them with new dream imagery of the production's own (see Rebellato 2014: 213–14). This would mark a moment of crisis in Mitchell's relationship with *the play*.

Live cinema

Throughout the 2000s, it began to seem as though the traditional realist frames in which her classic productions played out were unable any longer to contain the diversity of imagery that she was developing. There was a build-up of pressure through *Three Sisters*, *Iphigenia in Aulis*, and *The Seagull*, and, when it broke, it broke in *Waves*.

Waves was a devised adaptation of Virginia Woolf's experimental novel, *The Waves* (1931). Its literary texture is the interweaving of the internal voices of a group of six friends. While some of Woolf's novels have been adapted for the stage or film, *Waves* is often considered unstageable, a closet drama at best, its attempt to capture the oneiric form of mental flow unamenable to visual representation. Initially, Mitchell's plan was to stage it as a radio play, with the characters' voices amplified and supported by the usual apparatus of radio drama: gravel pits to simulate walking, spot effects and soundtracks to create aural atmospheres for the voices to inhabit. Indeed, this was the form of the first third of the production, but soon these sonic interpretations were complemented by visual representations. Two high-definition video cameras roamed the stage with temporary scenes arranged in front of them, and broadcast live on a large screen above (see Plate 19, showing Liz Kettle, Jonah Russell, and Anastasia Hille doubled above and below). A piece of Perspex with a short piece of material attached to it is placed before an actress's face, another actor squirts the Perspex with water, and, up on a screen, beautifully composed, the image is a compelling image of a young woman gazing soulfully through her curtains at the rain beyond her window.

It was a stunning departure for Mitchell. It was also a fairly remarkable production for the NT; this kind of mixed-media performance and fragmented, reflexive, narrative structure one expects to see in a venue associated with performance art, not so much England's national theatre company. The technology involved was innovative, allowing for instantaneous projection of high-definition images so that, live and projected, sight and sound remained constantly in sync, creating a new hybrid that has come to be known as 'live cinema'. The mixed-media style allowed Mitchell to separate two aspects of her work into two quite different forms: the business of the actors' work, their live immediacy in the performance space, was manifested at stage level; the intense scrutiny, looking to the deep structure of a scene or text, was resolved immaterially in the play of light on a projection screen. The work of the audience became, in part, the movement of the eye, the performance structured in many ways by the ocular movement between screen and stage. One observed the beautifully realised images above but also the elaborately chaotic choreography of the actor-technicians' work below. At one beautiful moment, a pair of actors who have encircled an action many times perform an elegant slow dance that untwines their cables so that the performance may continue.

This mixed-media device has been a staple aspect of Mitchell's work ever since, being a crucial component of *Attempts on Her Life*, *... some trace of her*, *Wunschkonzert*, and *Fräulein Julie* (Schaubühne, 2010). It has proved a remarkably supple and flexible device, both as a theatrical means and a conveyor of tone and emotion. In *Waves*, the images on the screen appeared warmly to represent the unreliability of memories, all-too-elegant in their composition compared to the chaos we see below it; in *Attempts on Her Life*, by contrast, the tone was cold and brutal, the images suggesting the continuous and instant mediation of experience that immediately becomes captured in digital form, processed and able to circulate around the world. In … *some trace of her*, based on Dostoevsky's *The Idiot*, the contrast between stage and screen seemed to reflect the gap between Prince Myshkin's simple warm-hearted idealism and the brutally materialist self-interest of the world into which he unwittingly steps. In *Wunschkonzert*, the roving cameras emphasised the brutal masculine intrusion into and enjoyment of a woman's private suffering; meanwhile in *Fräulein Julie*, a radical adaptation of Strindberg's *Miss Julie*, the camera allowed access to performances of extraordinary subtlety, fulfilling and subverting the play's Naturalist ambitions (see Birringer 2014).[2]

Waves was a remarkable success for the National Theatre, bringing one of the youngest audiences to the theatre for decades, and returning the following year after a sold-out run. Mitchell continued to make a mixture of live cinema and more 'anthropological' work for the National Theatre, but the artistic director, Nicholas Hytner, by his own account (2017: 198), lost interest in supporting these experiments and, after *A Woman Killed with Kindness* in 2011, she did not direct there until a triumphant return in 2016 with *Cleansed*, a ferocious against-the-grain reimagining of Sarah Kane's play that took the surreal imagery as seriously as the extreme violence, creating a brutally compelling and wholly persuasive world in which to explore gender and sexuality, authoritarianism and pain.

Mitchell's growing interest in placing women's experience at the heart of her work, as well as her wish to see where the use of digital technology would take her, has led to a series of powerful productions, mostly in Germany. *Fräulein Julie* subverts Strindberg's notorious misogyny, seeing the action of the play entirely from the perspective of its most marginal character, the cook Kristin, played luminously by Jule Böwe. This decision also displaced Miss Julie's suicide to the edges of the play, but a challenging motif of female self-destruction, as an image of extreme pain and extreme self-assertion dominates the next decade, taking in *The Forbidden Zone* (2014), *Ophelias Zimmer, Shadows (Eurydice Says), Cleansed, 4.48 Psychosis, Anatomy of a Suicide* (2017), and *Lucia di Lammermoor* (2016).[3] Meanwhile her interest in staging women's experience has led her away from traditional playtexts, which arguably embody a distinctively masculine linearity, in favour of more radically subjective, poetic, and abstract texts such as *The Yellow Wallpaper*, Inger Christensen's collection of poems *Alphabet* (which is woven into *Fräulein Julie*), and the prose poetry of Maggie Nelson's reflections on the colour blue in *Bluets*, which Mitchell staged at the Deutsches Schauspielhaus Hamburg in 2019. In many of these pieces, the live cinema gives us access to performances of extraordinary subtlety and to experiences of terrible pain; at the same time it offers opportunities to materialise immaterially the evanescent substance of personal identity, memory, and will. The fluidity of live cinema is a way of weightlessly exploring the contradictions of gender, its insistence and its fluidity, its power and vulnerability, nowhere more persuasively than in *Orlando* (Schaubühne, 2019).[4]

Conclusion

Katie Mitchell's directing was born in the revolutions of 1989, and she has carried throughout the subsequent three decades a commitment both to the long game of a directing career but also to a firm belief that the theatre's political engagement is best made in its artistic seriousness, not merely through content. Her trajectory shows a number of sharp turns when she becomes frustrated by the limits of her current materials and ways of working. At each of these moments, she has turned to Europe, which has remained an inspiration and challenge and a resource. Although Britain has at times seemed unprepared for the unflinching seriousness and intense beauty of Mitchell's work, her ideas – and certainly her embrace of European traditions – have clearly influenced a younger generation of directors, including Marianne Elliott, Carrie Cracknell, Ellen McDougall, and Lyndsey Turner. In 2016, in a long appreciative profile in *The Guardian*, Charlotte Higgins described her as 'British theatre's queen in exile', but the steady influence of her work, her politics, and her ideas suggests perhaps that British theatre may finally be ready to embrace the *auteur*.

Five key productions

The Phoenician Women. By Euripides. Set design by Vicki Mortimer and Rae Smith. Lighting design by Tina MacHugh. Perf. Lorraine Ashbourne, Darlene Johnson, Lucy Whybrow, Antony Byrne, Rachel Clarke, Siobhan Fogarty, Daniel Goode, Michael Gould, Alice Hogg, Dermot Kerrigan, Christopher Middleton, Sean Murray, Lisé Stevenson, Peter Copley. RSC, The Other Place, Stratford-Upon-Avon. 24 October 1995.

The Seagull. By Anton Chekhov. Set design by Vicki Mortimer. Lighting design by Chris Davey. Perf. Juliet Stevenson, Ben Whishaw, Gawn Grainger, Hattie Morahan, Michael Gould, Liz Kettle, Sandy McDade, Mark Bazeley, Angus Wright, Justin Salinger, Sean Jackson, James Bolt, Beth Fitzgerald, Jonah Russell. National Theatre, Lyttelton, London. 17 June 2006.

Waves. Adapted from Virginia Woolf/devised by the company. Designed by Vicki Mortimer. Lighting design by Paule Constable. Video design by Leo Warner. Perf. Kate Duchêne, Michael Gould, Anastasia Hille, Kristin Hutchinson, Sean Jackson, Liz Kettle, Paul Ready, Jonah Russell. National Theatre, Cottesloe, London. 18 November 2006.

Fräulein Julie. Adapted from August Strindberg, with additional material by Inger Christensen. Co-directed by Leo Warner. Designed by Alex Eales. Lighting design by Philip Gladwell. Sound Design by Gareth Fry and Adrienne Quartly. Music by Paul Clark. Dramaturgy by Maja Zade. Perf. Jule Böwe, Tilman Strauß, Louise Wolfram, Cathlen Gawlich, Lisa Guth. Cameras operated by Andreas Hartmann, Stefan Kessissoglou, Krzysztof Honowski. Schaubühne, Berlin, 25 September 2010.

> *Orlando*. Adapted from Virginia Woolf by Alice Birch. Bühne: Set design Alex Eales. Costume designed by Sussie Juhlin-Wallen. Lighting designed by Anthony Doran. Video director Grant Gee. Video design by Ingi Bekk. Music and sound by Melanie Wilson. Dramaturgy by Nils Haarmann. Perf. İlknur Bahadır, Philip Dechamps, Cathlen Gawlich, Carolin Haupt, Jenny König, Alessa Llinares, Isabelle Redfern, Konrad Singer. Cameras operated by Nadja Krüger, Sebastian Pircher. Schaubühne, Berlin. 5 September 2019.

Acknowledgements

I'd like to express my thanks to Katie Mitchell for her help in preparing this chapter and for granting me a long interview covering the range of her work.

Notes

1. Kim Solga and I discuss the ambivalence of this motif and the political force of Mitchell's work more generally in Rebellato and Solga (2018). Solga (2008) also addresses this question in her analysis of *Iphigenia in Aulis* (National Theatre 2004), suggesting that Mitchell's realism contains a feminist critique of realism and foregrounds the non-identity of actor and character so as to double and complicate female representation. Malague (2013) seeks to argue positively for Mitchell's feminism and her realism and Lisa Peck (2017) offers a highly sophisticated feminist analysis of Mitchell's Stanislavskian work with actors amounting to a 'method of feminist action' that builds radically on Stanislavsky's 'method of physical action' (238).
2. Several scholars have discussed the meaning and function of 'live cinema', particularly considering the uncanny doubling effect of stage and screen being simultaneously operative. For Janis Jefferies by 'drawing sensual technologies together in a non-hierarchical way' the impact is 'sensory overload, a kind of immersive bombardment' that she calls an 'irruption of the real' in its disabling of conventional forms of viewing (2011: 409); Hadjioannou and Rodosthenous argue that the co-presence of two signifying systems subtly inform and critique each other, offering a space 'where the ontology of cinema is rejuvenated by the mediating

potential of theatre's liveness and where cinema's exploration of the world informs the ontology of theatre' (2011: 57); Erica Magris (2016) argues that live cinema and its associated devices create doublings that break down conventional theatrical characterisation and allow a fuller immersion in subjectivity; Clements (2014) considers Mitchell's use of live cinema in *Attempts on Her Life* (2007) as a formal device to respond to the radically deconstructive challenges of Martin Crimp's text.

3 There have been several valuable defences of Mitchell's radical productions of classic plays. William McEvoy (2016) argues that her production decisions in *The Seagull* bring out the complexity of the play's auto-critique of theatre and theatrical convention and its deeply neurotic playing out of the relationship between theatre and literature; John Bull (2018: 294–7) offers a robust critique of the strong decisions made in Mitchell (and Simon Stephens's) version of *The Cherry Orchard* (2014); Kidnie (2013) and Malague (2013) argue persuasively for the integrity – and sharp feminist politics – of her reworked, relocated, and rewritten *A Woman Killed With Kindness* at the National Theatre in 2011. Against self-appointed purists like Martin Kettle, Emma Cole (2015), a classical theatre specialist, argues that Mitchell's use of non-original production processes and conventions in fact offer opportunities to experience the core of a play like *Women of Troy* more directly than a more reverential production might do.

4 Several recent essays have teased out the radical implications of Mitchell's contemporary productions for thinking about character. Lepage (2008) talks about her production of *Waves* as evoking 'posthumanist' ideas about character; Liz Tomlin (2014) wrestles with the apparent paradox of Mitchell's offering highly determinate psychologically naturalistic productions of Martin Crimp's highly indeterminate plays and sees the juxtaposition as providing a critique of character and identity (see also Clements 2014); Hadjioannou and Rodosthenous see the 'Live Cinema' device, in particular, as breaking down conventional character by dividing it spatially and temporally before us (2011: 50–3); Leah Sidi (2017) has written perceptively, though not uncritically, about Mitchell's production of Sarah Kane's *Cleansed*, suggesting that the production may have explored some aspects of psychological interiority at the expense of some other aspects of the play's radicalism.

Bibliography

Allain, Paul (1997) *Gardzienice: Polish Theatre in Transition*, Amsterdam: Harwood Academic.

Angelaki, Vicky (2016). 'The Space and Culture of Translation: Ferdinand Bruckner's *Pains of Youth* by Martin Crimp and Katie Mitchell', *Journal of Adaptation in Film & Performance*, 9: 67–82.

Bassett, Kate (1994) 'Great British Hopes: Rising Stars in the Arts Firmament – Katie Mitchell', *The Times*, 18 June.

Billington, Michael (2006) Review. *'The Seagull', Guardian*, 28 June.

—— (2007) *State of the Nation: British Theatre since 1945*, London: Faber & Faber.

—— (2009) 'Don't Let Auteurs Take Over in Theatre', *theguardian.com*, 14 April, www.guardian.co.uk/stage/theatreblog/2009/apr/14/auteur-theatre

Birringer, Johannes H (2014). 'The Theatre and Its Screen Double', *Theatre Journal*, 66: 207–25.

Bradby, David and David Williams (1988) *Directors' Theatre*, London: Macmillan.

Bull, John (2018). 'Add-Aptation: Simon Stephens, Carrie Cracknell and Katie Mitchell's 'Dialogues' with the Classic Canon', *Journal of Contemporary Drama in English*, 6: 280–99.

Clements, Rachel. (2014). 'Deconstructive Techniques and Spectral Technologies in Katie Mitchell's Attempts on Her Life', *Contemporary Theatre Review*, 24: 329–39.

Cole, Emma (2015). 'The Method behind the Madness: Katie Mitchell, Stanislavski, and the Classics', *Classical Receptions Journal*, 7: 400–21.

Fowler, Benjamin, ed. (2018) *The Theatre of Katie Mitchell*, Abingdon: Routledge.

Gardner, Lyn (1998) 'The Mitchell Principles', *Guardian*, 1 April: 15.

Gore-Langton, Robert (2004) 'In the Lines of Fire', *The Times*, 21 June: 18.

Hadjioannou, Markos and George Rodosthenous (2011). 'In between Stage and screen: The Intermedial in Katie Mitchell's … Some Trace of Her', *International Journal of Performance Arts and Digital Media*, 7: 43–59.

Higgins, Charlotte (2016) 'Katie Mitchell, British Theatre's Queen in Exile' theguardian.com 14 January, www.theguardian.com/stage/2016/jan/14/british-theatre-queen-exile-katie-mitchell

Higgins, Charlotte (2007) 'The Cutting Edge', *Guardian*, (24 November, Review): 11.

Hytner, Nicholas (2017) *Balancing Acts: Behind the Scenes at the National Theatre*, London: Cape.

Jefferies, Janis (2011). '"… Some Trace of Her": Katie Mitchell's *Waves* in Multimedia Performance', *Women: A Cultural Review*, 22: 400–10.

Kelly, Rachel (1995) 'What Katie Did First', *The Times*, 7 November.

Kettle, Martin (2006) 'Hostages in the Hands of Overindulged Meddlers', *Guardian*, 1 July, Comment & Debate: 33.

Kidnie, Margaret Jane (2013). '"We Really Can't be Doing 1603 Now. We Really can't": Katie Mitchell, Theatrical Adaptation, and Heywood's *A Woman Killed with Kindness*', *Shakespeare Bulletin*, 31: 647–68.

Lepage, Louise (2008) 'Posthuman Perspectives and Postdramatic Theatre: The Theory and Practice of Hybrid Ontology in Katie Mitchell's *The Waves*', *Cultura, lenguaje y representación: revista de estudios culturales de la Universitat Jaume I*, 6: 137–49.

Magris, Erica (2016). 'Entre Dissection et Empathie: le cinéma en direct de Katie Mitchell', *Revista Brasileira de Estudos da Presença*, 6: 186–205.

Malague, Rosemary (2013). 'Theatrical Realism as Feminist Intervention: Katie Mitchell's 2011 Staging of *A Woman Killed with Kindness*', *Shakespeare Bulletin*, 31: 623–45.

McEvoy, William (2016). 'Literary Criticism, Theatre Theory and the Director's Task: Katie Mitchell's Production of Chekhov's The Seagull', *Studies in Theatre and Performance*, 36: 1–12.

McMullan, Anna (2018). 'Katie Mitchell on Staging Beckett', *Contemporary Theatre Review*, 28: 127–32.

Mitchell, Katie (2008a) *The Director's Craft: A Handbook for the Theatre*, London and New York: Routledge.

—— (2008b) 'Katie Mitchell on Pina Bausch', *Café Müller/The Rite of Spring*, Theatre Programme, London: Sadler's Wells.

—— (2008c) Personal Interview with Dan Rebellato, London, June.

Neill, Heather (1999) 'Mistress of Doom and Gloom', *Evening Standard*, 7 July: 33.

Pearson, Allison (1994) 'Secret Rapture', *Vogue*, June: 34.

Peck, Lisa. (2017). 'Katie Mitchell: Feminist Director as Pedagogue', *Stanislavski Studies*, 5: 233–46.

Rebellato, Dan (1999) *1956 and All That: The Making of Modern British Drama*, London: Routledge.

—— (2014) 'Doing the Impossible: Katie Mitchell in Conversation', in Margherita Laera (ed.) *Theatre and Adaptation: Return, Rewrite, Repeat*, London: Bloomsbury, pp. 213–26.

—— and Kim Solga (2018) 'Katie Mitchell and the Politics of Naturalist Theatre' in Benjamin Fowler (ed.) *The Theatre of Katie Mitchell*, Abingdon: Routledge, pp. 39–71.

Shevtsova, Maria (2006) 'On Directing: A Conversation with Katie Mitchell', *New Theatre Quarterly*, 22 (1): 3–18.

—— and Christopher Innes (2009) *Directors/Directing: Conversations on Theatre*, Cambridge: Cambridge University Press.

Sidi, Leah (2017). 'A Director in Search of a Narrative: Reality-testing in Katie Mitchell's Cleansed', *Performance Research*, 22: 49–56.

Sierz, Aleks (2003) 'What Katie Did Next', *Independent*, 7 August, Review: 12–13.

Solga, Kim (2008). 'Body Doubles, Babel's Voices: Katie Mitchell's *Iphigenia at Aulis* and the Theatre of Sacrifice', *Contemporary Theatre Review*, 18: 146–60.

Tomlin, Liz (2014). 'Citational Theory in Practice: A Performance Analysis of Characterisation and Identity in Katie Mitchell's Staging of Martin Crimp's Texts', *Contemporary Theatre Review*, 24: 371–75.

Whitley, John (1995) 'Women on the Verge of a Breakthrough', *Daily Telegraph*, 24 January: 17.

Chapter 20

THOMAS OSTERMEIER

A 'sociological theatre' for the age of globalised precarity

Peter M. Boenisch

> I believe that one's view of the world may change after a good night at the theatre.
>
> (Ostermeier 1999: 76)[1]

Thomas Ostermeier's theatre productions continue to challenge his audience's ideas and expectations of canonical classics.[2] Rather than with the bang of the infamous door, the German director's 2002 production of Henrik Ibsen's *A Doll's House* (titled *Nora*) ended with the bang of a gun, as his Nora eventually emptied a whole magazine of bullets into Torvald Helmer's body. His 2008 *Hamlet* started with the director's regular lead actor Lars Eidinger (who had previously played Helmer) delivering the 'To be or not to be' monologue into a video camera as he filmed Claudius and Gertrude at his father's funeral. The scene culminated in a macabre overture without words, to loud, blasting rock music, as a clumsy gravedigger failed time and again to bury the coffin into the soil that covered the entire stage. In *Ein Volksfeind* (*An Enemy of the People*, 2012), Ostermeier's Doctor Stockmann, Ibsen's protagonist who discloses his findings that the city's spa waters have been contaminated with industrial waste, addressed the play's town hall meeting with the words of *The Coming Insurrection*, a controversial anti-globalisation manifesto published online in 2007 by the French anarchist group calling itself The Invisible Committee (2009). Then, instead of the vaguely comedic portrayal of an on-stage assembly as scripted by Ibsen, Ostermeier's

453

production opened the debate to the actually assembled spectators, as actor David Ruland in his role as newspaper editor Aslaksen directly questioned the audience with the air of a contemporary TV talk show host, and microphones were passed through the auditorium to those wishing to make statements about Stockmann's radical slogans.

Especially in his series of Shakespeare and Ibsen productions, which form the central pillars of Ostermeier's directorial *oeuvre* to date, the director translates the canonical plays into a conversational German idiom of the present. Meanwhile, the spaces designed by his long-term collaborator, the architect Jan Pappelbaum (b. 1966) – whether realistically portraying hip and glossy twenty-first-century living room 'doll's houses' as in *Nora*, or a more abstract black box as in *An Enemy of the People* – further reverberate the contemporary resonances. The team's reinventions of classical plays have been as celebrated as controversially received. The 2005 *Hedda Gabler* and the 2008 *Hamlet*, the director's most successful productions to date, are, at the time of writing in spring 2020, still regularly performed in the repertoire of the Berlin Schaubühne – where Ostermeier has been Artistic Director since 1999 – as well as touring around the globe, making him the most internationally recognised contemporary German theatre director. Nevertheless, some critics, such as the New York *Village Voice*'s Michael Feingold, dismiss his work as 'dumb', 'idiotic', and 'the kind of German theater that has to wallow in self-indulgence to prove to itself that it's alive' (Feingold 2004). In this chapter, I discuss Ostermeier's distinctive neo-realist approach towards a 'sociological theatre', grounded in his 'inductive' method of theatre direction, and fuelled by his explicitly political attitude. I shall argue that – rather than being self-indulgent – Ostermeier's work over the past two decades has evolved from reflecting the specific sensibility of German society around the turn of the millennium to an engagement with a now global experience of uncertainty, dispossession, precarity, and an inability to act and make one's voice heard, which has come to characterise the sentiment of the mostly middle-class, theatre-going audiences by the end of the second decade of the twenty-first century – as much in Berlin as in New York, Beijing, and São Paulo.

Beginnings at the Baracke

Ostermeier's stellar career began as he was still studying *Regie* at the Ernst Busch Hochschule, the prestigious Russian-style theatre academy of the former East Germany that has remained a leading theatre school in the reunified country since 1989. Michael Eberth, then the head dramaturg of the renowned Deutsches Theater (DT), had noted the young directing student's ambitious projects. At the time, the DT, once the GDR's theatre flagship stage and, many decades earlier, the site of an aesthetic revolution in theatre direction under Max Reinhardt and Bertolt Brecht, sought to recapture some of its past energy and reputation, wanting to draw in some fresh air and new audiences. Eberth had just secured a grant from the 'Friends of the Theatre' patrons' organisation to convert a disused construction workshop, costume store, and former canteen next door to the theatre into a space for experimental work. He offered the unknown twenty-something, who was just about to graduate, the artistic direction of this new stage. Bringing in his friends, the Bauhaus-trained architect Pappelbaum as well as his former school friend from Bavaria, Jens Hillje (b. 1968), as dramaturg, Ostermeier turned the dilapidated concrete block into an intimate, empty, and flexible performance space, which they aptly named the Baracke (the shack).[3]

Between December 1996, when they opened with *Fette Männer im Rock* (*Fat Men in Skirts*) by New York playwright Nicky Silver, and summer 1999, eight productions premiered there, seven of them directed by Ostermeier himself. Without much technical and financial support from the main DT, these early productions were quite literally handmade, Ostermeier running and stage-managing most performances himself. Still, he was able to work with actors of the DT, recognised as one of the country's finest ensembles. The atmospheric, yet awkward small space, whose stage doors opened directly onto Schumannstraße, generated a buzz amongst a young, fashionable late 1990s crowd, mainly in their 20s, who would usually be frequenting cinemas, clubs, and concerts rather than theatres. Within two years, in 1998, the Baracke outmanoeuvred all established German theatres to be voted 'Theatre of the Year' in *Theater Heute* magazine's annual critics awards, also having two of its productions nominated amongst the season's ten best shows presented each year at the Berlin Theatertreffen festival – achievements for which other venues strive, in vain, for decades. Later that year, the team was offered the reins of the prestigious Schaubühne, made famous far beyond Germany by director Peter Stein in the 1970s. Within only three years, Ostermeier had thus been catapulted from the school stage of the Ernst Busch academy, via the makeshift space in the former East that launched his career, into the impressive Bauhaus building at Lehniner Platz in the affluent (Western) district of Charlottenburg. He opened his tenure as the Schaubühne's artistic director in January 2000, coinciding with the new millennium, aged 32 – the same age as Stein when he took over the original Schaubühne in 1970.

Ostermeier was born in Northern Germany just prior to Stein's Schaubühne appointment, in 1968, but he would grow up in the provincial Bavarian town of Landshut after his father, a soldier in the German Bundeswehr, had been transferred south. He was one of only two pupils in his high school class who did not speak the local Bavarian dialect; the other was Jens Hillje, who would remain Ostermeier's key collaborator at the Baracke and Schaubühne, until he moved on in 2009 to eventually become artistic co-director, from 2013, of the smaller Maxim Gorki Theater, also in Berlin. At school in the early 1980s, the two were passionately engaged in the afternoon school drama club. For the teenage Ostermeier, these extracurricular lessons provided an escape from his home, where he increasingly clashed with his father's right-wing world view. He eventually rebelled, moved to the other end of the political spectrum, joined a Trotskyist party, and after completing school lived as a punk squatter in Hamburg and then Berlin, while further pursuing his aspirations to perform. Auditioning, in vain, for the acting programme at Ernst Busch, he reapplied for their directing class, where, Manfred Karge, one of the school's many teachers fostered by Brecht and Helene Weigel at their Berliner Ensemble, became his teacher and mentor. During his training, Ostermeier embraced the Brechtian imperative to change society, while equally devouring Meyerhold's biomechanics.

He graduated with a devised production *Recherche Faust/Artaud*, working mainly with dancers rather than actors, whom he made speak as a chorus and repeat the same movements ever faster, up to the point of their physical exhaustion. From there, he went directly to heading the Baracke. Constrained by finances and the limited availability of their actors, Ostermeier and Hillje ran the place as a casual subcultural arts centre, also hosting readings, exhibitions, club nights, political discussions, and concerts, including performances by Ostermeier's own punk band in which he played the bass. They were determined to stage 'material that is relevant' and to create 'theatre that interests us' (Ostermeier 1998: 24). The director envisioned a theatre that was open, inviting, and accessible to everyone:

> What used to annoy me massively when I went to my local theatre was its incomprehensibility. One had to bring a sound knowledge of philosophical and aesthetical debates to the theatre, in order to get anything out of the productions. [...] The whole elitism always made me feel sick. I also had the constant impression of meeting people who were so different from myself – all dressed in black, reading different books from me, listening to different music. If you got a chocolate bar out of your pocket in the foyer of Peter Stein's Schaubühne, the other spectators would look down their noses at you.
> (Ostermeier 1998: 25, 29)

German theatre, at the time, in Ostermeier's view, essentially offered 'art crap' (in Burckhardt 1998: 102). The Baracke's repertoire therefore championed new playwriting talent which Ostermeier and Hillje found abroad; the German premiere of Mark Ravenhill's *Shoppen & Ficken* (*Shopping and Fucking*) in January 1998 became the Baracke's signature piece, eventually transferring with its production team to the Schaubühne, where it remained in repertoire for another decade. Plays by Martin Crimp, Enda Walsh, and, importantly, Sarah Kane followed, as well as those by the Russian Alexej Schipenko, the Norwegian Jon Fosse, the Swede Lars Norén, and the Serbian Biljana Srbljanović, whom Ostermeier thus helped establish in the canon of contemporary plays on Germany's stages. This soon inspired like-minded home-grown playwriting talent, most notably Marius von Mayenburg (b. 1972), who soon became another close collaborator, still working at the Schaubühne at the time of writing in 2020 as dramaturg, prolific playwright, and translator/adaptor as well as a director himself.

The R(ealism)-Effect: tradition as innovation

The new plays they presented perfectly resonated with the 'structure of feeling' of their core audience. Raymond Williams's materialist term usefully points to the individuals' bodily and sensual entanglement within their socio-cultural and economic contexts, highlighting the role of actual experience in the shaping of meaning and a Marxian 'consciousness' (see Williams 1977: ch. 9). As well as neatly echoing the director's own materialist world view, this concept seems particularly apt in pointing to a defining aspect of Ostermeier's directorial work: a shared 'structure of feeling' (rather than any psychological exploration) helps his performers to unlock their characters, just as a shared 'structure of feeling' (rather than a mere zeitgeist) establishes the critical connection with the spectators, thus encompassing all three poles of play text, production, and audience. While Ostermeier, as director, shared a liberal approach to the written text and interspersed his productions with pop songs and video projections, he was keen to avoid what he referred to as 'capitalist realism', alluding to 'socialist realism', the artistic doctrine of the former Communist bloc that expected art to promote the historical realisation of socialist society. For the director, the 'capitalist realism' of seemingly radical postmodern and postdramatic work had made theatre self-referential, drained of social relevance and political impetus, while upholding the ideals of neoliberal capitalism

> [...] with its aesthetic of 'Anything Goes' – where everything is clear, where any approach and interpretation is allowed and where it is continuously made clear that the core of a self-determined, subjective individual no longer exists, and therefore

everything is up for deconstruction [...] Such an aesthetic which we refer to as Capitalist Realism is affirmative since it shows the individual as no longer self-determined nor able to act. That suits those in power very well.

(Ostermeier 1999: 76)

Where Brecht's historical situation demanded *Verfremdung* to counter dominant conventions of seeing and spectatorship, reality and alienation have become indistinguishable in the media-saturated culture of globalised simulacra, as Baudrillard would confirm (1988). Opting for a return to realist paradigms of individual characters and 'well-made' narratives was not therefore an aesthetically motivated decision for Ostermeier – but a political act in the face of a reality that seemed to defy orientation, deny straightforward biographies, and blur coherent narratives.

With his 'reinvested' realism, Ostermeier set out to offer opportunities for identification, for experiencing coherence, and comforting familiarity. Together with choreographer Sasha Waltz, who was until 2005 the Schaubühne's artistic co-director with Ostermeier, he wrote a manifesto headed 'Der Auftrag' (The Mission), which reiterated some of these neo-realist essentials with which they launched their joint tenure in January 2000:

> Theatre can be one of these places where attempts to comprehend the world in a different way intensify into a shared worldview and into an attitude. Theatre can be a place for society to gain consciousness, thus to be re-politicised.
>
> For that aim, we need a contemporary theatre [...]. We need a new realism, because realism counters a 'false consciousness', which these days is much more a lack of any consciousness. Realism is not the simple depiction of the world as it looks. It is a view on the world with an attitude that demands change.
>
> (Schaubühne 2000: 15)

Ostermeier opened the Schaubühne in January 2000 with Lars Norén's *Personenkreis 3.1* (*Human Circle 3.1*), followed by Sarah Kane's *Crave* (a production that would remain in the theatre's repertoire, with the original cast, until the end of the Schaubühne's 2019 season). The director brought his rough and unpolished, visceral, and 'in yer face' Baracke-style with him, culminating in his first production of a canonical play, Büchner's *Danton's Death*, in 2001, followed by the internationally successful production of Ibsen's *A Doll's House* in 2002 and *Woyzeck*, created in 2003.

After years of dedication to new writing alone, this turn to canonical drama came somewhat unexpectedly. Yet, it followed a logical trajectory, further substantiating his principles. Ostermeier had initially focused – with a genuinely leftist attitude – on the underprivileged, giving those who lack representation in other media, a voice on stage. From such fairly generic declarations of good intent, his neo-realism then shifted towards 'us, in fact, the thirty-somethings getting established, having money or not, and often at the peak of their careers' (in Boenisch and Ostermeier 2016: 69). As the director himself expressed it, speaking in 2006, he turned to a greater emphasis on

> the reality of people of this age, of this class, and it's maybe much more interesting than the realism of the outcast because it is a realism that directly speaks to the people in the audience. When we do *Shopping and Fucking*, we must be aware that the people described in the play don't go to the theatre because they neither have the money nor are they interested.
>
> (ibid.)

Thus, the classics of bourgeois drama became Ostermeier's vehicle to stage and scrutinise the drama of the German middle classes in the early twenty-first century. During the 1990s, a dynamic spirit had energised the newly reunified republic, as a youthful generation of entrepreneurial and creative start-ups (including Ostermeier himself in the field of theatre) scored successes, apparently without end and limits. Yet, by the turn of the millennium, this energetic post-Unification hedonism had given way to a feeling of loss, fear, and stagnation. Even before the 2008 financial crisis, Germany found itself paralysed by angst about redundancies, fixed-term contracts, the empty public purse, faltering pension plans, and a sharp drop in house prices. The infamous 'Agenda 2010' of social-democrat Chancellor Gerhard Schröder had introduced a fundamental reform of the welfare state and the social-security systems which had characterised West German society since 1945. 'Finally Germany is once again feeling so sick [...] that the conflicts put on stage reach the audience. Finally, there is once again a real reason to make theatre!', Ostermeier cheered ironically at the time (quoted in Diez 2005).

In his radical production of *Nora*, Ostermeier's contemporary reinvention, rather than distorting Ibsen's intentions, reinforced the playwright's central analysis: even while nowadays we believe we have left the taboos of the nineteenth-century bourgeoisie behind, though the matter of Nora's loan would today be efficiently sorted out by eager lawyers, and while we are all surrounded by all kinds of digital technology and other gadgets, the pressures from which modern life was supposed to liberate us have in fact multiplied, and – further aggravated through the omnipresent distraction of digital media – still no one really communicates. Even the idea of an emancipated woman taking life into her own hands and walking away from her husband has long become yet another of the roles women in contemporary society struggle to fulfil: instead of a utopia, emancipation has become an imperative, if not a cliché – a role Anne Tismer's Nora endeavoured to satisfy as desperately as those of her children's caring mother and of the flirtatious sexy modern woman entertaining her husband and guests. Nora's drama had become the drama of the ultimate flexibility and adaptability required from neoliberal, globalised 'dolls':

> The whole production talks of different images and pictures we get from the media, which are always providing us with different ideas of how we should be. [...] In the Ibsen text Nora herself says, 'you created me after these ideas of yours, so I am a creation, I have to be what you think a woman should be like, I am not myself, but I have to play different roles.'
>
> (in Boenisch and Ostermeier 2016: 69)

Blending fictional realities with recognisable resonances of the everyday present, Ostermeier showed that distinct times and spaces may resonate with each other, that the drama of Ibsen's bourgeois protagonists still takes place in living-rooms in present-day Berlin, and – elsewhere – that Shakespeare's tragedies equally may function as an 'outside eye' whose perspective may offer a distancing otherness to our everyday experience, hence contributing to our insight, recognition, and understanding of society.

German theatre history of the twentieth century had thus, in a curious way, come full circle. Just as Brecht's Berliner Ensemble was originally launched as an offshoot of the DT to then move on to the Theater am Schiffbauerdamm, it had now sponsored Ostermeier, who began to update Brecht's political realism for the twenty-first century. Ostermeier's trajectory also echoed Peter Stein's rise to fame at the Theater Bremen in the late 1960s under the artistic director Kurt Hübner. Their Bremen path was usefully summarised in the titles of book chapters as 'Rediscovering Realism', 'Attempting a New Political Theatre', 'Testing the Classics', 'Critique of Ideology', and 'Telling Stories' (Mauer and Krauss 1973). These headings very neatly sum up the characteristics of Ostermeier's work as well.

A laboratory to observe human behaviour – and learn about society

Just as in his early years the new international playwrights had supplied Ostermeier with reverberations of the sensibilities of his generation, the classics equally were not at all the ends of his productions but, again, a means to scrutinise current societal 'structures of feeling'. Ostermeier was never after a 'modern' interpretation of a classic but, first and foremost, after an interpretation of the society around him. The Schaubühne's original *Regietheater* under Peter Stein had looked, within the worlds and psychologies of the plays, for resonances of the events of their era – the Vietnam War, the 1968 revolt, the 'Deutscher Herbst' of 1977. In the 1980s and 1990s, postmodern *Regietheater* moved towards more casual pop-cultural associations to localise and visualise the plays, staging playful deconstructions, which eventually, however, lost the critical force of deconstruction envisaged by the postmodern philosophy of Jacques Derrida as much as by a politically minded director such as the young Stein. Representing a new generation of twenty-first-century European theatre directors *after* the generation of postmodernism, Ostermeier takes the reverse approach. Instead of infusing a given text with present-day material, that contemporary context for him becomes the main text and the scripted characters and narratives essentially serve as the context in which to articulate an urgent analysis of contemporary moral and mental situations.

Turning to classics was thus a crucial step further in Ostermeier's development of what he describes as his 'sociological theatre', and hence expressly not psychological theatre – a term he had used about his own work already in the early Baracke years (see also Boenisch and Ostermeier 2016: chs 2 and 4). In an interview from 2007, he explained:

> [T]heatre is first of all about people, about human beings; and then if you're clever enough, you can also talk about *one* aspect of human beings, which is politics. But it is not the only aspect. Yes, I think politically, and I try to make political statements, especially on panels or wherever I can be in the media. But I am also – and this goes back to the Baracke – pretty interested in human relationships and how they are structured and how they function; politics is only one part of that.
>
> What I'm heading for now is to try and understand more about the complexities of things going on in the world, but not only that: also the complexity of human relationships. It seems to me to be a very sociological approach to theatre. What makes people, with fear, in a society which puts so much pressure on them about their very standing in the middle class, behave in particular ways to friends and family around?
>
> (Ostermeier and Woodall 2010: 374)

For Ostermeier, the power of theatre as a political institution thus lies in its function as a particularly rich medium to reflect on and to help us better understand present-day contradictions, crises, and conflicts within our societies. It is a laboratory to observe how 'the conduct and behaviour of human beings with each other changes in accordance with societal transformations in their environment' (Boenisch and Ostermeier 2016: 22). Just as Ibsen's ploy of letters, debt, and forgery had sparked reflection on a generation that got hopelessly stuck amidst all the splendour of an affluent life, Ostermeier's *Hamlet* interrogated a more recent socio-cultural constellation, defined not least by the 2008 financial collapse and its aftermath. His production portrayed Hamlet as a 'spoiled brat', with lead actor Lars Eidinger wearing a fatsuit to underline the point that the audience should by no means empathise with this upper-class prince. Equipped with his video camera, he solipsistically fashioned the images we get of the world around him, while aggressively exposing and seeking to thwart the scripts others have prepared for him. This approach to Hamlet explored a mindset that soon would become prominently personified by political leaders in an age of 'fake news' and aggressive spin.

For more than ten years (and more than 350 productions), Eidinger has performed the Danish prince in this work originally premiered at the Hellenic Festival in Athens in the summer of 2008. With him, only five other actors perform all the roles in this metatheatrical take on Shakespeare's drama, with which Ostermeier reached beyond the almost hyper-realistic surfaces of his previous productions. Furthermore, it exemplarily demonstrates another key aspect of his work that Ostermeier shares with Brecht: the work is never done with the first night, but is instead an ongoing process. The director watches almost every single performance of his productions, and regularly calls his actors in for rehearsals, even for a long-running show such as *Hamlet*, further working on scenes and revisiting details that have become stale or 'theatrical' – the one thing Ostermeier abhors most. That way, even such long-running productions maintain their resonances with the 'feel' of the world around them, as they are allowed to develop, mature, and even change the conception of the central character. This is most evident with *Hamlet*. Comparing both memories and the ARTE television recording of the show's 2008 performance at the Avignon Festival with a performance in 2020, one notices far more than numerous changes in the cast (except for Eidinger); rather, it reveals a very different emphasis within Shakespeare's play, if not an entirely different interpretation. Initially, Hamlet and his notably feigned madness were a take on the rich kids whose mindlessness would bring the world to the brink of collapse – as effectively happened with the fall of Lehmann Brothers, two days before the production had its Berlin premiere in September 2008. Yet, over the following years of austerity and growing populism, the emphasis shifted to the relationship between the parent generation and their offspring, the way that the generation of Claudius and Polonius, alongside Laertes who seeks to blend in, sell off the future fortune of the next generation. The moment the earlier take on Hamlet, described above, had become omnipresent on the (real) world stage, it was no longer interesting for Ostermeier. At this point, his attention shifted to an exploration of whether resistance is still possible in an age of Trump and Brexit; performances of the production (in a specially adapted version) at the Freedom Theatre of Jenin by murdered theatre-maker Juliano Mer Khamis had been decisive in nuancing the approach (Ostermeier and Klotz 2017). With *Hamlet*, the political resonances of Ostermeier's sociological theatre have thus truly become global:

> London, Berlin and Moscow are all quite similar in a way; each has a younger generation's perspective on the prospect of, say, job or no job, whether or not to have a family – but without political or utopian visions. This was something which started, radically, in Britain, under Margaret Thatcher, twenty years or so ago but which has now spread around the world – and so has the search for the key to these problems: unemployment, economic crises. These create fears, and these fears and conflicts in any big city in the world are pretty much the same. [...] As globalisation globalises economic interests and markets, it also globalises problems *coming* from globalisation.
> (Ostermeier and Woodall 2010: 364)

Punctuating the pop surface

For Ostermeier, 'realism' thus never meant an aesthetic mode of representation that pretends to be reality itself. As in the works of Sarah Kane, a playwright he greatly admires, the feel of such 'authenticity' only served as a lure on the surface to accommodate audiences, only to then confront them with the extreme explosion of societal conflicts and contradictions. The director was never interested just in face value, literal realities on stage. He also shunned widespread approaches that lifted a felt psychology straight onto the stage, where

> characters are pathologically driven the whole time, they tremble and suffer, they shout over the top and yell excessively – all of these are clichés of psychology, clichés of theatre. When I'm really serious in an argument, I say very calmly 'pack your bags and fuck off, I never want to see you again.' When I play it that way, I am truthful.
>
> (Ostermeier 2003)

One of the most memorable aspects of his gripping staging of Kane's *Blasted* was, in fact, its understated (and, in a large space such as the Barbican Theatre, London, barely audible) rendition of the lines, which amplified the dense, agonising atmosphere.

Over recent years, Ostermeier had the three main spaces in his Schaubühne theatre acoustically reconfigured so that actors no longer need to project their voices, but where instead even a whisper can be heard in the rear row of seats. At the same time, he further developed his directorial technique to assist his actors in achieving a performance devoid of clichés and false theatricality. Initially, he had drawn above all on his solid grounding in Brecht's and Meyerhold's techniques to weave a rather strict and tight net of aesthetic form. This approach characterised his work from the early Baracke productions such as *Shopping and Fucking* onwards. For Ravenhill's play, designer Rufus Didwiszus put a shabby living room into a corner of the Baracke, enclosed on two sides by the audience. The worn and torn sofa, the TV set and heaps of empty ready-meal cartons, plastic bags and other rubbish, and not least the theatre's door and window leading into the real world, made it appear like a direct continuation of Berlin's realities outside the theatre. The actors were, in their jeans and trainers, indistinguishable from almost anyone else in the room; the soundtrack of well-known songs, a fast-paced aesthetics, comic juxtapositions (as when Lulu and Robbie offered telephone sex, citing verses of Shakespeare to pay dealer Brian after Robbie had given away the drugs he was meant to sell) additionally appealed to the audience by offering a cultural experience continuous with life outside the theatre.

Yet, Ostermeier slyly married humorous hilarity with outright horror. *Shopping and Fucking*, after its mirthfully trashy, *Trainspotting*-style start, climaxed in a heart-wrenching counterpoint, as Ostermeier went even further than the playwright himself in a late moment of the play where the young rent-boy Gary invites Mark to penetrate him with a knife. As the original play text cuts to the next scene, Ostermeier showed the deadly sex full on and almost in slow motion, the performers, leaning over the sofa, facing the audience in the intimate Baracke space. This endless, wordless, and visceral scene became almost unbearable to watch, to the degree that audience members broke down in tears, others fainted. 'We did indeed cross a boundary there', Ostermeier admitted, 'but it's only this very scene which gives the entire play its full weight' (in Burckhardt 1998: 101). The example demonstrates Ostermeier's tactics: After an atmospheric community was established between performers, characters, and the audience through the pervasive and recognisable neo-realist surfaces and the light-hearted banter, which invited a Barthesian *studium*, Ostermeier then struck, making the audience physically share and bear the pain with the characters in moments of a most visceral *punctum*.[4] This strategy of affective 'punctuation' of the polished 'pop' surface would return, in varying intensities, in most of Ostermeier's productions. In his stage adaptation of Édouard Louis's novel *History of Violence* (2018), he returned to a male rape scene, choreographed in full view on stage.

As a dramaturgic device, these moments of *punctum* tie into the director's desire for a theatre that calls for change and action, while avoiding being outright 'political' in the sense of identifying with a 'cause', delivering declarations from stage, or fantasising about a utopia that would heal all problems. Instead, Ostermeier's 'sociological' approach makes palpable within the frame of dramatic fiction the effects of real political decisions and economic situations on individuals and on their relations with others, and with the world. His strategy resembles Ravenhill's analysis in *Shopping and Fucking*: 'we all need stories, we make up stories so that we can get by,' says Robbie in the play (Ravenhill 1996: 64). Ostermeier likewise offers recognisable narratives, yet his work then never exhausts itself in 'consumable' affirmation. Instead, the director shares the ultimate conclusion with Ravenhill's rent-boy Gary, that only in suffering we may still feel and experience ourselves as individuals in a capitalist world: 'The individual suffers, even if the subject is said to be no more than a construct and without a core. In pain you sense yourself' (quoted in Wille 2000: 1).

Any political attitude or demand for action in Ostermeier's view only arises from an individual impetus, especially from the affective experience of tragedy, pain, and suffering. Far from any superficial shock effect or theatrical spectacle, this is the function of the hurtful *punctum* in so many of his productions to the present day. The intensity of such scenes succeeds because they leap far beyond any plain kitchen-sink naturalism. They never disavow their theatrality.[5] Already in *Shopping and Fucking*, the bloody sex was delicately constructed, precisely choreographed, and carefully paced. It thus made palpable an experience of the rage, frustration, desperation, and hunger for love that fuelled this desperate, lethal act. Similarly, the angst, pain, and other 'real' sensibilities that drive Nora or the characters in Kane's dystopically brutal *Blasted* (once more, the rape of a man as well as crude cannibalism) were never psychologically portrayed. In rehearsal, the director hardly ever discusses a character's motivation. For him, expecting performers to actualise any prescribed psychology must put them under stress and fear of failure, of 'not feeling properly'. Emotions are, for Ostermeier, a matter for the spectators. The actors, in the meantime, should concentrate on clear, concrete, and above all physical actions – thus, very literal 'structures of feeling':

> As director, my task is to make sure that this exterior sequence makes inner action transparent. That's all, that's the whole point

of directing. I tell of the inner worlds of characters by means of sounds, light, space, and the way in which they move through these spaces. To the actor, I say 'you, please, think of yellow frogs, and not about having to create an emotional state'.

(Ostermeier 2003)

Ostermeier's peculiar physical plasticity was a distinctive aspect on the German stage of the turn of the century. It was noticeable in his Baracke works, even in the debut *Fat Men in Skirts*, where Astrid Meyerfeldt's Phyllis 'moves as if she had to continuously break an imaginary corset' (Merschmeier 1997: 16), or the crouched bodies, trundling across the stage in slow motion, in *Messer in Hennen* (*Knives in Hens*): 'the highly artificial way of acting, very disciplined in its grotesque methods, extracts the play from the *milieu*, which it doesn't possess, and opens it up for the second story Harrower tells' (Wille 1997: 43). In *Shopping and Fucking*, the simple device of the stiff leg of Bernd Stempel's drug dealer Brian (otherwise presented as a smart family man who covers up his dark side beneath a meticulous suit), along with his big gestures, conveyed his uncanny threat far more intensely than any aggressive shouting of spoken text would have done, as he entered Lulu and Robbie's living room. Meanwhile, the hysterical couple did not just sit on their realistic sofa but also climbed the walls of their run-down apartment (see Plate 20).

This particular attention to physical work and the performers' bodies dates back to Ostermeier's student fascination with Meyerhold. Right away, in the first Baracke season, he brought in Gennadij Bogdanov, one of the second-generation heirs of the Russian school of biomechanics, to work with his actors and to co-direct Brecht's *Mann ist Mann* (*Man Is Man*). Taking over the Schaubühne jointly with Sasha Waltz was equally no arranged marriage; his actors and her dancers underwent movement training together. Since 2006, Ostermeier has been appointed professor at his own former alma mater, the Ernst Busch academy, where he since has continued to develop his practical research into directing methodology with his students. What he today describes as his 'inductive method' of *Regie* thus articulates the insights of two decades of active research into the practice of theatre direction. In this approach to theatre direction, the director 'inductively' communicates with the text, as opposed to a deductive approach that would impose the director's creative vision and aesthetic signature onto the play text, onto any play text (see Boenisch and Ostermeier 2016, ch. 6).

Based on his careful exploration of a play together with his actors in rehearsal – using his techniques of the family portrait, of storytelling, and of Meisner-based repetition exercises (ibid.) – Ostermeier's *mises en scène* are predicated on a strict formal orchestration of rhythms, sounds, and physical action. Testing minutely in rehearsal how a sentence may be best spoken, he tunes the pitch of the actors' voices and the movement of their bodies, eventually weaving a tidal rhythm of enormous tension and cheerful release, which is generated by contrapuntal patterns and timings of speech, action, pauses, outbursts, silences, frantic pace, slowness, deafening noise, huge and tiny gestures. This carefully composed stratum of theatral presentation punctures the neo-realistic framework that forms the foundation of Ostermeier's theatre. Its intense affective force is generated precisely because the director's 'realism effect' is not predicated on blunt realistic imitation. Rather than seamlessly disappearing behind the fiction, the materiality of the bodies, the exposed theatrality (rather than theatricality) of his *mises en scène*, which had been emphasised particularly in *Hamlet* and since has become another core characteristic of his directorial approach, provides a counter-discourse that interacts with the characters' words and actions and comments on the narrative – while working directly on the perception and sensual experience of the spectators.

Over the past decade, Ostermeier has also opened up his rehearsal practice for more and more input from his actors and other collaborators:

> I've found in recent years that directing is not just about communicating verbally but about artistic communication. You have to be aware of what's going on in a rehearsal, pick up on either verbal or emotional feedback, encourage what's going on between the actors. The real art of the director is to let actors grow.
>
> (Ostermeier and Woodall 2010: 371)

Rather than being driven by grand 'deductive' interventionist directorial concepts, he believes in his actors as 'original creators'. Already back in 1998, he had emphasised that

> the prime function of the director is to describe and communicate with the actor. You discuss a dialogue, you agree on a situation in a play – and then it's up to the actor. [...] When something happens in rehearsals which I don't control, when something is liberated in the actors, then I leave the rehearsal room in bliss. I don't get that from feeling 'fine, my concept works'.
>
> (in Merschmeier and Wille 1998: 30)

To discuss Ostermeier as yet another of the European directorial *auteurs* – as frequently suggested from an Anglo-American perspective, usually with the pejorative undertones voiced in Feingold's review quoted in the introduction to this chapter – thus seriously misrepresents his directorial practice. His theatre – as indeed the work of many other German and contemporary European theatre directors – vitally relies on collective creation. This mode of production is, in Germany, certainly facilitated by the system of state subsidies that allows the entire team of actors, directors, dramaturgs, all the way down to the lighting operator, to work as a long-standing, permanently employed ensemble.[6] This permits the prioritisation of long-term artistic processes before the immediate product of a single production. In a way typical of many European directors, Ostermeier used his formative years to gather a core ensemble with whom he would go on to create further productions, often until the present day, enabled by the continuity afforded by his directorship of the Schaubühne as his institutional base.

The success of Ostermeier's applied sociological studies may be measured in reactions such as those of a friend of the director's whose response he often cites: 'after the performance, she said, "ah, you can see there are good contemporary writers." So she didn't know that it was a classical play, 130 years old. And that's the point' (in Boenisch and Ostermeier 2016: 67). This is, indeed, a vital point that those – like the American Feingold but also many German critics –

who look no further than their bookshelves to gauge the merits of Ostermeier's productions, would inevitably miss. Today, Ostermeier has established himself as Reinhardt's and Brecht's legitimate heir, while also actively contributing to the further, contemporary development of a Stanislavski-based directing methodology in the twenty-first century. His productions represent an important development in German (and European) *Regietheater* beyond the area of postmodern deconstruction, while stirring, around the world, important political as well as aesthetic debates for theatre in an age of globalisation.

Five key productions

Shoppen & Ficken (Shopping and Fucking). By Mark Ravenhill. Set design by Rufus Didwiszus. Perf. Jule Böwe, Bruno Cathomas, Bernd Stempel, André Szymanski, Thomas Bading. Baracke am Deutschen Theater Berlin. 17 January 1998.

Nora (A Doll's House). By Henrik Ibsen. Set design by Jan Pappelbaum. Costume design by Almut Eppinger. Perf. Anne Tismer, Jörg Hartmann, Lars Eidinger, Jenny Schily, Kay Bartholomäus Schulze, Agnes Lampkin. Schaubühne Berlin. 26 November 2002.

Zerbombt (Blasted). By Sarah Kane. Set design by Jan Pappelbaum. Costume design by Almut Eppinger. Perf. Katharina Schüttler, Thomas Thieme, Ulrich Mühe. Schaubühne Berlin. 16 March 2005.

Hamlet. By William Shakespeare. Set design by Jan Pappelbaum. Costume design by Nina Wetzel. Perf. (original cast) Lars Eidinger, Judith Rosmair, Robert Beyer, Sebastian Schwarz, Stefan Stern, Urs Jucker. Festival d'Avignon. 7 July 2008.

Ein Volksfeind (An Enemy of the People). By Henrik Ibsen. Set design by Jan Pappelbaum. Costume design by Nina Wetzel. Perf. (original cast) Stefan Stern, Ingo Hülsmann, Eva Meckbach, Christoph Gawenda, David Ruland, Moritz Gottwald, Thomas Bading. Festival d'Avignon. 18 July 2012.

Notes

1 All translations from the German are my own.
2 This chapter is a substantial revision of my introduction to Ostermeier's early work, 'Mission neo(n)realism and a theatre of actors and authors', published in the first edition of *Contemporary European Theatre Directors* in 2010, which I had completed around the Berlin premiere of his seminal *Hamlet* in 2008.
3 Note that the German word lacks the military association of the English 'barracks', but just signifies a run-down building.
4 Roland Barthes's astute terms describe the very personal two-way relationship between a spectator and a (photographic) image: the spectator brings their own cultural knowledge to bear on the meaning of the image (the *studium*), while the image may also have an effect on its spectator beyond its apparent cultural framework – this is the *punctum* that pierces through the observation and in a way returns the gaze (see Barthes 1982). Equally, Ostermeier makes sure that the audience of his productions are taken to a viscerally painful point beyond the empathy and pity which may drive a mere *studium* of a play, especially a well-known classic by Shakespeare or Ibsen.
5 Following the German approach of theatrality studies (*Theatralitätsforschung*) as pioneered by the late Rudolf Münz and Helmar Schramm, I maintain the terminological distinction between fake and deceptive 'theatricality', and the 'theatrality' generated by the dynamics of movement, meaning, and spectatorial affective perception (see Boenisch 2015, ch. 2).
6 The Schaubühne is, in fact, not a state-owned theatre, but a private cooperative of four shareholders (one of them now Ostermeier himself), which receives funding from the city of Berlin. The funding pays for the building and the wages of the theatre's more than 230 employees, yet (in contrast to 'full' state theatres) does not provide means towards production costs, which the company raises at the box office and by touring.

Bibliography

Barthes, Roland (1982) *Camera Lucida: Reflections On Photography*, London: Jonathan Cape.
Baudrillard, Jean (1988) 'Simulacra and Simulations', in Mark Poster (ed.) *Selected Writings*, Stanford, CA: Stanford University Press, pp. 166–84.
Boenisch, Peter M. (2015) *Directing Scenes and Senses: The Thinking of Regie*, Manchester: Manchester University Press.

────── and Thomas Ostermeier (2016) *The Theatre of Thomas Ostermeier*, Abingdon and New York: Routledge.

Burckhardt, Barbara (1998) 'Der Bassist als erste Geige: ein Meister-Musterschüler will zurück zu den Wurzeln und ganz nach oben – Thomas Ostermeier, Nachwuchsregisseur des Jahres', *Theater Heute*, Yearbook: 96–102.

Diez, Georg (2005) 'Das Gift in den Hirnen', *Die Zeit*, 47, 17 November, www.zeit.de/2005/47/Schaub_9fhne

Feingold, Michael (2004) 'Nora Gets Her Gun: did Ibsen's A Doll's House Need Updating? Berlin's Thomas Ostermeier Gave It a Shot', *Village Voice*, 17 November, p. 71.

Invisible Committee (2009) *The Coming Insurrection*, Los Angeles: Semiotext(e).

Mauer, Burkhard and Barbara Krauss (eds) (1973) *Spielräume – Arbeitsergebnisse: Theater Bremen 1962–73*, Bremen: Theater Bremen.

Merschmeier, Michael (1997) 'Dandies, Diven, Menschenfresser: Banale Broadway-Hits oder grelle Komödien: Wieviel Witz verträgt das deutsche Schauspiel?', *Theater Heute*, 3: 12–17.

────── and Franz Wille (1998) '"Ich muss es einfach versuchen": Ein Theater Heute-Gespräch mit Thomas Ostermeier', *Theater Heute*, 5: 26–30.

Ostermeier, Thomas (1998) 'Auf der Suche nach dem Trojanischen Pferd: Ein Theater Heute-Gespräch', *Theater Heute*, Yearbook: 24–38.

────── (1999) 'Ob es so oder so oder anders geht! Ein Gespräch', *Theater Heute*, Yearbook: 66–76.

────── (2003) 'Formal das Alltägliche betonen: Thomas Ostermeier gegen Theater als Angstveranstaltung', *Freitag*, 45, 31 October, www.freitag.de/2003/45/03451301.php

────── and Nicolas Klotz (2017) *Hamlet en Palestine*, documentary film, 93 mins.

────── and James Woodall (2010) 'Thomas Ostermeier on Europe, Theatre, Communication and Exchange', in Maria M. Delgado and Dan Rebellato (eds), *Contemporary European Stage Directors*, 1st ed. Abingdon and New York: Routledge, pp. 363–76.

Ravenhill, Mark (1996) *Shopping and Fucking*, London: Methuen Drama.

Schaubühne am Lehniner Platz (2000) 'Der Auftrag', originally published in the inaugural programme brochure for the spring season 2000, reprinted as 'Wir müssen von vorn anfangen' in *Die Tageszeitung*, 20 January, p. 15.

Wille, Franz (1997) 'All About Eva: David Harrowers *Messer in Hennen* in der Baracke des Deutschen Theaters', *Theater Heute*, 5: 42–50.

────── (2000) 'Startdeutsch: Über die abgründige Lust zu programmatischen Texten und Äußerungen unter jüngeren Theaterleitern', *Theater Heute*, 1: 1–2.

Williams, Raymond (1977) *Marxism and Literature*, Oxford: Oxford University Press.

Chapter 21

PETER SELLARS

Identity, culture, and the politics of theatre in Europe

Maria M. Delgado

There is a long tradition of American artists working 'in exile' in Europe. From the Living Theatre's presence in Paris through the 1960s, to Richard Foreman's work in the same city in the 1970s and Wilson's productions across the stages of French and German cities from the late 1960s to the present, to the Wooster Group's regular forays into Belgium since the mid-1990s, North American artists have often looked to Europe for inspiration and renewal. In turn, though, they have enjoyed a currency that has had a powerful influence on directors' theatre. Vilar's invitation to the Living Theatre to perform at the 1968 Avignon Festival was an important moment in the politicisation of French theatre and a move away from the literary stage; the influence of Wilson on Patrice Chéreau, Roger Planchon, Claude Régy, and Georges Lavaudant has been charted elsewhere (see Maurin 2002: 237–47); meanwhile, the chapter on Bieito in this anthology demonstrates a palpable debt to the work of Peter Sellars (p. 401).

Sellars was born in Pittsburgh, Pennsylvania in 1957, serving an apprenticeship as a puppeteer with Pittsburgh's Lovelace Marionettes while still a teenager. After leaving school he spent a year in Paris in the mid-1970s before entering Harvard University where he directed over 60 productions in both conventional and unconventional spaces – swimming pools, parks, on the back of pick-up trucks, in department-store windows – and in conventional and unconventional styles – one of his student productions was a puppet version of Wagner's *Ring Cycle*.

Sellars's formative year in Paris is the starting point for this interview, conducted in London in October 2007. Here he reflects on how his practice has been shaped by European political realities since 1968 and what the wider implications of the social, economic, and cultural shifts in the Continent might involve for modes of making theatre. While he has directed for a range of leading opera houses and theatre festivals in Europe – conspicuous highlights include Handel's *Theodora* for Glyndebourne (1996, 1997, 2003), Wagner's *Tristan and Isolde* for the Opéra Bastille (2005), John Adams's *Nixon in China* for English National Opera (2006), Kaija Saariaho's *L'Amour de loin* for the Salzburg Festival (2000), John Adams's *A Flowering Tree* for the New Crowned Hope Festival, which he also curated, in Vienna (2006), and Osvaldo Golijov's *Ainadamar* for Madrid's Teatro Real (2012) – here he discusses not his own work as a director but the wider social and political fabric in which he works, arguing for theatre's importance as a social and regenerative force, promoting interdisciplinarity and interculturalism, and offering structures for directors able to go beyond imperialist assumptions towards new modes of cultural discourse and production. Sellars remains a director committed to ensuring theatre and opera remain a space for discussion of pressing socio-political, cultural, and environmental issues. For *Idomeneo*, which opened the Salzburg Festival in 2019, he crafted a staging where George Tsypin's set provided footage of

> the plastic that is destroying the ocean right now and is in every one of our bloodstreams at this moment. Basically, where we are with global warming is exactly where Mozart was with this opera: an older generation still not getting it, and a younger generation already on the case in very exciting ways […]. It's not that climate change will happen: it is already deeply, deeply happening. We presented Mozart's opera *Idomeneo* as the opera that describes the angry oceans, what it means to negotiate with the oceans for the future of the next generation.
>
> (Sellars, cited in Lobec 2019)

Serge Dorny, artistic director of the Opéra de Lyon, refers to Sellars as 'a politician, in the primary sense of the word' (cited in Battle

2014), and it is the importance of the stage as a public arena for discussion of dissent and debate that continues to mark his work. Whether reflecting on the legacy of colonialism in a production of Purcell's *The Indian Queen* featuring new text from Nicaraguan author Rosario Aguilar's *The Lost Chronicles of Terra Firma* in 2015, or slavery, migrant workers, and censorship in John Adams's *The Gospel According to the Other Mary* (2014) – both seen at English National Opera – Sellars crafts a stage practice that seeks 'to put forward things that are challenging, to not let any one argument dominate, [and] to give a platform to voices society doesn't want to hear' (Sellars 2014).

MARIA M. DELGADO: Do you see your work as having close contact with the European tradition of directors' theatre?

PETER SELLARS: I first arrived in Europe on the cusp of what became known as directors' theatre, although it wasn't known as that back then. Subsequent developments I'm not so very proud of. It got a little warped and out of proportion. So much directors' theatre is obviously so decorative; it's like the fashion in restaurants of vertical food stacked up in funny shapes on a plate. I call it 'playing with your food' when in fact people are hungry and you need to have something that is nutritious.

Of course, there are marvellous directors that I have been influenced by, but I would almost say it's more in film than in theatre. A lot of what reaches me is through film because film is highly portable and able to travel now. With theatre you have to be there. Now, in the twenty-first century, more and more theatre is happening in such localised spaces that you hear about it but you don't see it. What this means is that it is no longer the same ten grand names. Theatre works in a very different mode; it has diversified, and you can't possibly keep track over everything that's going on.

MARIA M. DELGADO: You spent time in Paris in your late teens before attending Harvard University and saw work by Peter Stein, Peter Brook, Patrice Chéreau, and Ariane Mnouchkine. How were you shaped by the work you saw at this time?

PETER SELLARS: When I came to Paris at 18 for a year it was so formative. In Paris there was a tradition where artists existed and were supported. It was an amazing thing to go and see what was possible on a certain scale; the work in Paris had a scope that you could never dream of as an American director. Theatres in Paris existed truly to support a vision; productions were awe-inspiring because space and time were deeply transformed. No American director then had the courage or the budget to come close to that.

At La Mama things were going on but even there it was European, as with Andrei Şerban, for example.[1] The main American artists of that generation, Meredith Monk, Bob Wilson, Trisha Brown, Lucinda Childs, they all existed because of Europe. They worked intimately in their lofts and then dreamt big in Europe. I was really lucky because when I was in high school, in the mid-1970s, one of the teachers had spent just one year in Paris and Berlin and came back with tales of Peter Handke and of the *théâtre panique*. We did Peter Handke's *Self-Accusation* in an American high school, and my imagination was set alight.

One of the things about growing up working in a puppet theatre in Pittsburgh, Pennsylvania, the Lovelace Marionettes, is that they were doing plays by Beckett, Michel de Ghelderode, Robert Pinget, and Jean Cocteau, and experiments with Javanese shadow puppets and Japanese *bunraku*. Because of puppetry, I was a member of UNIMA – the Union Internationale de la Marionnette – and I was stunned by the avant-garde work from Czechoslovakia, Poland, and Romania that I saw in Moscow. This is what I thought of as theatre, and it was Continental. So there was some way in which a certain type of art in America was European. That's why you'd see 'Masterpiece Theater' on American television. It's why the first Los Angeles Festival featured the work of Brook and Mnouchkine. You couldn't match it in America.

When I was in Paris the great American avant-garde theatres came through the city. This is when I met John Cage and the Bread and Puppet Theatre. Europe was always this place of the possible. It made you set your sights much higher than anything in America, so it was very inspiring for that reason.

Once I started working in Europe, I felt I could make a contribution to the European discussion. I never think that theatre is a destination point; it's always the route towards something else. The European discussion seemed to me to be very top-down, and I've never been that interested in the guy in charge. The interesting question seemed to be about democratising and radicalising all of that, trying to diversify so that you're not having everything focused through one voice and one vision but rather offering a shared space that is polycentric. I admired the supreme control that Peter Stein had over everything, but also, as an American, I really objected to it. I wanted to feel the collaborators more as equals, rather than the collaborative energy just in the hands of one individual. I was, of course, one generation younger than all those people, so that was my challenge.

Politically – right down to the present and Nicolas Sarkozy – everything horrifying about America that Europe thinks will never happen here does eventually show up as the new European policy. As an American, bringing my shows over to Europe I can say: 'Advance warning: look at these things, please.' I can actually make a contribution to the European discussion so that it can move critically in both directions and isn't just about Europe soaking up a particular US influence.

MARIA M. DELGADO: Did you see practices in Europe during this time that influenced how you came to work?

PETER SELLARS: In Europe I saw Europeans taking care of their culture – Mozart, Verdi, etc. I also recognised the importance of different registers. It was very important for me to handle Mozart, which is not my culture. I could find all kinds of things in it that the Europeans perhaps couldn't see. As an outsider, coming from a lack of qualification rather than extreme qualification, I was able to say: 'We need this, we really do need what this is saying and doing and we just have to take it and we make it in our own image.' In Europe I saw these works treated as masterpieces; I tried to treat them as friends. I could joke with them and be deliberately perverse; I could engage with them in unexpected ways. The relationship was very different from that of people who were 'part of the family' and had therefore inherited the baggage that goes with that.

MARIA M. DELGADO: Were there staging traditions that you reacted against?

PETER SELLARS: Yes, but these were not exclusively European. I've always wondered why some serious French play from seventeenth-century France involves people wearing feathers on their head and fancy buckles on their shoes (indigenous cultures in the heart of the Port Royale!). I've never had a sense that plays were mere artefacts: I've never treated anything as an object because I think theatre is about everything being alive. Theatre is not about objects; it's about living beings. You treat the text as a living being not as an object. Theatre is against object culture.

MARIA M. DELGADO: For some directors, like Calixto Bieito and Thomas Ostermeier, who similarly question object culture in their work, this involves presenting radically abridged versions of classical plays.

PETER SELLARS: While I try to be very free when I'm staging the work, I'm also very scrupulous. I do uncut texts because, for me, theatre is about authenticity; it's about some type of honesty. It's about looking something in the eye and having a mature enough relationship to agree to disagree. You can't meet the play at certain points, and so you don't. But equally, you don't cover them up. I find it important to be as honest as possible about the terms of the exchange, about showing that work that's been done. As with any relationship, if you only cherish the moments where you agreed on everything, that's a sad kind of relationship. You've got also to share your total disagreements.

I grew up with Jean-Luc Godard as the *auteur* par excellence. I took very seriously on board the dislocation of sound and image that was basic to his editing structures. In its early days cinema borrowed from theatre. Now, in my generation, we're borrowing back. I'm always imagining that I'm making a film or a radio play when I'm doing theatre. You want all those layers to be present; you want the visible and the invisible; you want the imagined and the present. A lot of this was connected to the

Wooster Group and the willingness to endure confusion rather than clean it up. It should not be about ever simplifying what we're going through but rather putting it out there in its density. Shakespeare is so dense that half the time you wonder what the characters are talking about. This was Godard's position when he did *King Lear* (1987). He said he didn't understand one word of it and the film was a process of trying to understand it. It makes me think about how little we understand of the things that we claim to admire.

MARIA M. DELGADO: I want to return to Europe and to the period spent in Europe between school and university. You also visited Moscow during this time. Moscow and Paris must have seemed parts of two very different Europes during these years.

PETER SELLARS: Yes, and it was incredibly powerful to encounter Heiner Müller and a theatre that was so *enfermé*, absolutely locked in on itself and happening within a such closed circuit in order to survive. I grew up making my offerings on the altar of Brecht and then saw what Brecht had become through a very really different generation that had no interest in political indoctrination and was in fact using Brecht against Brecht. This was the time that the EU was being formed but Europe struck me as being made up of very different worlds. What was marvellous at that time was that you could taste something that could only have been made in Poland or Spain. The difference was sharp and it mattered. Theatre was the place where people could claim their identity. In the Soviet era, all the state theatres had to be in Russian but puppet theatres could still be in the national languages so the ethnic energy and commitment to speaking your own language, which only the puppets could do, was a thrilling dynamic.

Europe, of course, played host to Asian theatre in a way that America never did. My first sight of Cambodian theatre was in Paris; my first vision of Kathakali was in Paris. Mnouchkine was working with Asian traditions at this time. Certainly, there was something for me of 'shopping at the big colonial bazaars', but nonetheless it was startling to encounter that cultural range that came to Paris on a regular basis.

Maria M. Delgado: I have a sense that Paris is no longer that meeting place for different cultures. As the shape of Europe has shifted so Paris's position as a central place for encounters has waned. It doesn't enjoy the role it did in the late 1970s, '80s, and early '90s.

Peter Sellars: I think that's right. For one thing the avant-garde is well and truly over. During the early Jack Lang years, with the Festival at Nancy, there was a sense of Latin America coming to France. France became a home for all these exiled artists. Jorge Lavelli, Víctor García, and others all came in those years and were welcomed. This was a very exciting moment and it is now over. In the aftermath of '68 (I was there in '76), Paris was then playing a role in world history; you really felt this was the place where people were storming the barricades and where there could be change. During those years there was change happening in literature, in critical writing and film as well as theatre. The politics were so welcoming, I think that's why that convergence happened: people who were truly looking for change showed up in Paris.

What I saw in Paris was how theatre was part of the society and funded as such. The heart of the identity of Europe was cultural. The French knew they were French because of culture. Identity was cultural. It was a source of pride to the French to have the largest Ministry of Culture in Europe. These days are over.

Maria M. Delgado: How have things changed since you first started working in Europe?

Peter Sellars: The strange perversity of Chirac's follow-through of Mitterrand's cultural legacy is Le Musée du Quai Branly which emphasises that the arts of Africa and Asia are elsewhere, and not practised by active communities ten miles down from the Élysée Palace. It's just incredible we can deal with Africans under glass in a museum, but not in the open air in our cities. To me that is a deep problematic in European culture.

We have to remember, and this is evident to me when working in the UK, that colonialist attitudes die hard; the implied cultural superiority is, to this day, insisted upon. Everything else is treated as some kind of strange orphaned culture that has no history and comes from nowhere, that's backward, primitive, and savage or something to be encountered once a year, you do the big cultural exhibit and then go home and forget about it. This kind of non-engagement through a delicious and permanently exotic consumerist paradise I find deeply problematic. So I do try and force the issue with integrated casting, with productions where people are speaking their own language and are treated with dignity rather than as second class. It's about testing the limits and possibilities of the actual quality of interaction. For me that's what theatre was invented to do. This remains, to this day, a very complicated blind spot in Europe – the 'these Africans are not European' mentality. When Europe looks in the mirror it doesn't see very far; it doesn't see very far into the past, and it doesn't see very far into the future, and that means that it can absolutely fail to see the present.

So the make-up of all the national theatre companies in every one of these European countries has yet to reflect the actual demographics of walking down the street in Barcelona, Paris, or Stockholm.

Maria M. Delgado: Your comments have reminded me of the furore that broke out in France when Declan Donnellan cast a black actor in the title role in his production of *Le Cid* for the Avignon Festival in 1998.

Peter Sellars: For us this is basic but in Europe it is still an issue. The idea that Europe represents civilisation is very problematic. Immigrants have changed Europe, they've shaped it in ways that are just not recognised. So much of European tradition has been shaped by Africa, the Arab world, and South-East Asia and yet it's still a blind spot. I really feel compelled to do work that calls attention to the missing links.

Maria M. Delgado: Do you think things have changed over the past 30 years? That we've become more acutely aware of issues of exile and migration?

Peter Sellars: Growing up in the 1960s or 1970s everything seemed possible. But now watching the famous peace dividends at the end of the Cold War vanishing to nothingness and then seeing the Cold War be perpetuated with redoubled ferocity, it's as if we're watching history going backwards in ways I never thought possible. The Soviet Union ended with no violence but look at what's happening now. We're seeing the devastation of command capitalism given free rein in Europe. Europe is going towards this market-driven economic model that used to be an American thing, where every single thing that isn't making money is on the cutting block. Europe, for me, stood for a commitment to social welfare; it stood for people recognising and understanding that life is about intangibles. We're now watching the idealism that was underneath the European project, especially the EU, erode. It's been replaced by a hard-headed business model and cultural intolerance.

MARIA M. DELGADO: What role do you think nationalism is playing in this process?

PETER SELLARS: Culture is barely mentioned in the Maastricht Treaty precisely because it's perceived to be divisive. Nobody's willing to understand that it's the only thing that does bring people together. By deciding that culture has to be largely off the agenda, the EU actually missed what made Europe Europe. Europe has never cohered economically, and it's never cohered politically. What it does have is an amazing thing called European culture that speaks all these languages and has all these facets but at the same time is unmistakably European. The bizarre thing was that this was just thrown overboard when they made the EU. This conservative backlash is only possible because the cultural field is in such a weakened state. I think Europe is learning what we demonstrated in America: that if you eliminate culture from people's diet, the society becomes intolerant, brittle, and selfish. Culture is the one thing that invites people to imagine things otherwise. And yet increasingly culture has been put on a market 'pay-as-you-go' model. So culture is playing less and less of a role in society as a whole; it's not a central role; it's not a defining role; it's not a mediating role. It's worth mentioning here Martin Luther King's definition of leadership, which is not about acting as a thermometer, but a thermostat. You're setting the temperature not responding to it.

Maria M. Delgado: Both the Edinburgh Festival and the Avignon Festival were set up in the aftermath of the Second World War as a way of fostering a sense of community and examining how culture might find ways to bring people together.

Peter Sellars: Avignon was not just French, and Edinburgh was not just British. The jewels came from elsewhere. It was about examining what we share and how and what we exchange, about reaching outwards as well as supporting and strengthening the sense of what we're doing and accomplishing.

Maria M. Delgado: Do you think there are still great differences between Eastern and Western Europe?

Peter Sellars: There has been a very complicated set of transitions for Russian artists. Many Russian artists shaped their voices in opposition, in a kind of underground. Then in the Gorbachev transition, handed the microphone, they didn't know how to support anything; they only knew how to undermine it. It really meant a huge shift of artistic practice and I think it lost a lot of people of a certain generation. Some of the strongest forces became, in some way, irrelevant. In many cases artists were unprepared for the consequences of these huge historical transitions.

The other side of it is that *samizdat* is back and not just in Russia but all over the world (and in the increasingly Sovietised United States of America). Because this globalised picture just doesn't include so many people's stories, they turn to the underground to meet their needs. There are so many places where what comes through to us is so limited or has been heavily pasteurised by the powers that be who have made it into something that is smooth and supposedly healthy. You can no longer taste that this came from a cow. I think we're in that amazing moment where people are starting to ask for unpasteurised milk again; where we are starting to realise that maybe not everything should have been filtered and edited out. People are looking for something where you can taste a few more degrees of where it came from, who drew it, and how it is made.

Maria M. Delgado: Food is culture.

PETER SELLARS: Mad cow disease made it clear that food can become the enemy. Europe has to look at its farmers again. Really basic things have to be reconsidered.

Culture gets really hot when history is being made, and when no history is being made, culture really cools down. I feel an end-of-history exhaustion in both my country and in Europe. The large debates are being increasingly trivialised and made into administrative details. What made Europe? Europe was the Enlightenment and that sense of cultivation, of standing for something, that sense of a vision. Europe can't eat bureaucratic structures. In countries of the new Eastern European contingent or on the fringes of Europe – as with Uzbekistan and Tajikistan, for example – where institutional structures and infrastructures don't work, what does work is culture. In many parts of the world right now culture is the only thing functioning.

The hardest part of high capitalism is that it shifts everybody's perspective into just looking for a more comfortable life. I'm not judging that, but it means that people's energies are pointed in a different direction – hence the flood of Poles into England. The inability of a country to realise the hopes of its people means that they go elsewhere. That's very intense and very different from the kind of hope kept alive during the Solidarity movement. The underground pockets offered hope for positive change, now there's just wholesale abandonment and the sense that a significant sector of the population will just find their hopes and dreams elsewhere.

Nobody could have imagined that almost 20 years after Gorbachev, Russia would be in such a state of economic and environmental degradation and have the worst of rampant capitalism generating excess wealth. It's as if the tsars never shifted: serfs next to agglomerations of opulence and extravagance. I don't think anyone could have imagined that so-called 'democracy' would actually take Russia back to the era of serfdom where people were starving on the land and where the continued extermination of the Chechen people was applauded. To watch a certain type of regression which was unimaginable 20 years ago means that we are all in a strange place where artists are made mindful of the brief to be much more entertaining than ever and, at the same time, the issues are so much more serious, but are being airbrushed by a media that has difficulty focusing and that itself is desperately treading water. So it's a media that is desperate to please, and to soothe, and to entertain (and to survive).

MARIA M. DELGADO: Do you think this social, political, and economic situation is manifest in the theatre that's being made in Europe at present?

PETER SELLARS: I think that, in a way that was unthinkable 20 years ago, directors are in search of an audience. Who is going to fill the seats in the official institutional theatres? There are some really exciting younger theatres, like the KVS – the Royal Flemish Theatre in Brussels – that are taking on all these issues (dealing with Belgium's troubled history with the Congo, the right-wing racism of Flemish nationalists, dialogue with the Arab community in Brussels), and are packing the theatre with young people. Perhaps this audience knows they are not being lied to and that somebody, finally, is dealing with the real issues that matter in Europe now. There's this new younger generation running a number of European theatres in a way that is dealing with issues of migration and justice and social responsibility.

MARIA M. DELGADO: A lot of your recent work has dealt with issues of migration and journeying, of exile and identity. I'm thinking particularly of *Children of Herakles* (2003) and of your curation of the New Crowned Hope Festival in Vienna in 2006.

PETER SELLARS: I come from a country that's defined by immigrants, and so, for me, immigration is what made America great. It is actually the source of creativity and of the extraordinary accomplishment of my country. I find it shocking to watch people turn away immigrants when history has proven their roles. Albert Einstein was not born in New York; the miracle of American science was made possible by émigrés: people looking for change, rebuilding their lives, reimagining themselves and creating completely new identities, new fields of knowledge, and new fields of achievements. This is because the thirst for newness, that quest for something beyond what they have known previously, that need *not* to return to that little town in Poland, is so powerful. My country is the result of that movement. That is why I'm really shocked by the anti-immigrant mood that's swept the USA and Western Europe. So, of course, I'm trying to do work about it. It's really interesting trying to do that work in Europe, where cultural memory of complex lineages is so short and where there are so many issues that have still not been addressed by the culture at large.

The sense of integrated societies is really at risk. In every European city you see massive segregation. When I'm in Europe I'm especially committed to making a special point of these topics. It's not done, however, with any sense of superiority about being an American, for the USA is sadly at a moment of hideous schizophrenia with all these children of immigrants turning against immigrants.

MARIA M. DELGADO: Do you see differences between working in Europe and working in North America?

PETER SELLARS: I wouldn't work in North America if it weren't for Europe. Most of my productions are only made possible because of working conditions in Europe. No American theatre can match what is available in Europe. I'm dependent on Europe for most of my American work to exist. Theatre, like any other form of communication, is based on reciprocity. So I'm trying to think through the conditions of the reciprocity and what I might offer. Europe and America always had very intense reciprocal relationships. They've both needed each other at crucial crisis points in their own trajectories and I think that's ongoing.

MARIA M. DELGADO: Do you see patterns in the present that might allow for some prediction of the future direction of Europe?

PETER SELLARS: Only in the sense that I think that the virtual world creates a hunger for people to be together – but intimately. I do think that intimacy is an important thing in the future of theatre; not so much mass spectacle as the sense of an intensely shared experience amongst a small group of people, who can confirm each other's actual existence in the world. I do think that part of what people will be looking for and are looking for in theatre is touch: a tactile sense of human presence.

The best part of this new age of television, of 100 channels and the Internet, is strange pockets of difference. We don't know what anybody was watching last night. In spite of everybody's efforts to create monoculture, human beings are highly resistant to that. The Internet has given us this incredible interpenetration of worlds. You're getting difference in a way that is a few steps ahead of the people who are trying to calculate what we're all seeing.

It's very difficult to get a mass movement now, after that extraordinary day just before the Iraq War, when more people all over the world came together to protest than at any other time in human history but the democratic governments that became the 'coalition of the willing' ignored them. So after all those governments headed to war, people have been genuinely demoralised about the effectiveness of public mass demonstrations. Then everybody went home and took it back into small little groups; these small little zones of pleasure, exchange, and commitment.

MARIA M. DELGADO: You work primarily in English but it's an English that intersects with other languages: your Spanish–English version of Genet's *Les Paravents* (*The Screens*) (1998); your collaboration with John Adams on *El Niño* (2000); your production of the Chinese sixteenth-century epic, *Peony Pavilion* (1998). Do you think that the dominance of the English language threatens the 'pockets of difference' you've been talking about?

PETER SELLARS: These productions are all about making a portrait of complexity and diversity about the city where I live. Theatre mitigates against the kind of grid culture that I see in business all the time, imposing something uniform which leads to the same hamburger being available in any city on the globe. I do make theatre in resistance to that. And at the same time I actually do value English as a chance for more people to communicate with each other. English, through whatever set of historical accidents, became a language that could mitigate violence in India, offering a way for people who couldn't otherwise have a conversation to find a way of conversing. So I'm also in two minds about the dominance of English. Yes, it is dominating and controlling but in another way it's opening a path to a place where people might meet on a certain basis.

English, by its very nature – and this is also one of the reasons why it was able to prevail at this moment in history – goes with this reductionism of the whole world to economics. English is very good at turning everything into objects; it's good at quantifying and the tangibles. Other languages that focused more on intangibles are less in fashion. English is an excellent language to reduce things. It's an effort to turn the English into poetry, whereas other languages are just poetry because of the way their language is wired. With English you have to really subvert it. Shakespeare's English was more malleable than the English we're working with now and way more influenced by all these other languages.

MARIA M. DELGADO: Is opera rather than English the theatrical language of Europe?

PETER SELLARS: Music gives everybody a place to buy in that is beyond words. Within that different languages exist, but they exist with their musicalities; they exist with their emotional resonances and not necessarily with what is signified. Language actually gets to be released from a certain type of load-bearing functionality in opera. I think of opera as a real kind of real liberation for language, where words are not just denotative and don't have such sharp edges but are part of another kind of flow. Also, opera does invite people from many different cultures to converge, to listen (often to something not in their own language), and to participate.

MARIA M. DELGADO: Do you think you've contributed anything unique or particular to European theatre?

PETER SELLARS: I was shocked when I was given the Erasmus prize in Holland for a contribution to European culture because I think of myself as very American! It's not unique or particular but what I've probably been able to do was come from a long-standing commitment and interest in European culture and at the same time bring a new set of global inflections in to challenge stereotypes that I didn't share because I didn't grow up with them.

In Europe it is often thought that I'm anti-American. Nothing could be further from the truth, it's just that I'm holding America to very high standards and Europe is helpful to me in that regard. At the same time, I can return the favour and hold Europe to certain standards that my American training just takes for granted and insists upon. Hopefully it's fertile in both directions and hopefully it remains challenging in both directions. It's about using *elsewhere* as a way to shift what *here* means.

Five key productions

Saint Françoise d'Assise. By Olivier Messiaen. Conducted by Esa-Pekka Salonen. Set design by George Tsypin. Lighting design by James F. Ingalls. Costume design by Dunya Ramicova. Perf. Dawn Upshaw, José Van Dam, Thomas Young. Salzburg Festival. 17 August 1992.

The Persians. By Aeschylus. Translated by Robert Auletta. Lighting design by James F. Ingalls. Costume design by Dunya Ramicova. Perf. Cordelia González, Joseph Haj, Martinus Miroto, John Ortiz, Howie Seago. Salzburg Festival. 20 July 1993.

Theodora. By Georg Friedrich Handel. Libretto by Thomas Morell. Conducted by William Christie. Set design by George Tsypin. Lighting design by James F. Ingalls. Costume design by Dunya Ramicova. Perf. Dawn Upshaw, Lorraine Hunt. Glyndebourne Opera. 17 May 1996.

Tristan and Isolde. By Richard Wagner. Conducted by Esa-Pekka Salonen. Video by Bill Viola. Lighting design by James F. Ingalls. Costume design by Martín Pakledinaz. Perf. Waltraud Meier, Ben Hepner, Yvonne Naef. Bastille Opéra Paris. 16 April 2005.

La Passion de Simone. By Kaija Saariaho. Text by Amin Maalouf. Conducted by Susana Mälkki. Lighting design by James F. Ingalls. Costume design by Martín Pakledinaz. Perf. Dawn Upshaw, Michael Schumacher. Jugendstiltheater, Vienna. 26 November 2006.

Note

1 The Romanian director Andrei Şerban made his US debut at La Mama in 1974 with the revisionist *Fragments of a Trilogy*, formed from textual adaptations of *Medea, Electra*, and *The Trojan Women*.

Bibliography

Battle, Laura (2014) 'Peter Sellars Talks about His Spiritual Side', *Financial Times*, 7 November, www.ft.com/content/5374df38-6377-11e4-8a63-00144feabdc0

Cole, Susan Letzler (1992) *Directors in Rehearsal: A Hidden World*, London and New York: Routledge.

Delgado, Maria M. (1999) '"Making Theatre, Making a Society": An Introduction to the Work of Peter Sellars', *New Theatre Quarterly*, 15 (3): 204–17.

Green, Amy S. (1994) *The Revisionist Stage: American Directors Re-invent the Classics*, Cambridge: Cambridge University Press.

Lobec, Marijan (2019) 'Peter Sellars Talks about His New Staging of Mozart's Idomeneo', MarijanLopez, 3 January, https://marijanzlobec wordpress.com/2019/01/06/peter-sellars-talks-about-his-new-staging-of-mozarts-idomeneo/

Maurin, Frédéric (2002) 'Did Paris Steal the Show for American Postmodern Directors?', in David Bradby and Maria M. Delgado (eds), *The Paris Jigsaw: Internationalism and the City's Stages*, Manchester: Manchester University Press, pp. 232–47.

McClary, Susan (2019) *The Passions of Peter Sellars: Staging the Music*, Ann Arbor: University of Michigan Press.

Sellars, Peter (2014) 'The United States is Coming Close to Censorship', *Guardian*, 20 November, www.theguardian.com/music/2014/nov/20/peter-sellars-john-adams-the-gospel-according-to-the-other-mary

Shevtsova, Maria and Christopher Innes (2009) *Directors/Directing: Conversations on Theatre*, Cambridge: Cambridge University Press.

Thompson, Ayanna (2018) *Shakespeare in the Theatre: Peter Sellars*, London: Bloomsbury Arden Shakespeare.

Chapter 22

THE DIRECTOR'S NEW TASKS

Patrice Pavis
Translated by Joel Anderson

La mise en cause of la mise en scène

We often hear of the death of the director, after the so-called death of the author in the 1960s. Now is she dead or merely transformed, and in a state of crisis? Is the crisis faced by the director a sign of imminent demise? Nothing could be less certain. For a long time now the 'director of the stage' (to borrow the Spanish term) has ceased to be the uncontested master of her domain. She has become a limited company, a discontinuous postmodern subject whose powers are lost and dispersed (while she still receives the dividends).

Mise en scène as a semiological sign system, overseen by a single pair of eyes, has died out. The classical ambition of figures like Copeau, Craig, or even Strehler, who dreamed of replacing the *auteur*-dramatist with the *auteur*-stage director, and who would remain faithful to this end, has, since the turning point of the 1970s, shattered upon impact with the postmodern reality of the stage and the world. This was the moment of deconstruction, which, inspired by Derrida, 'dismantled' semiology as well as *mise en scène*, accusing it – rightly – of being a closed system that masked the dynamics of acting and representation; it is in that same moment that Barthes moves from 'the fashion system' to 'the pleasure of the text'.[1]

To his credit, it was Bernard Dort (1988) who warned against the risks of a closed theory and a closed performance.[2] His critique concerns the conception of the show as a *Gesamtkunstwerk* (Wagner) or as stage writing (Craig):

493

> A critique of Wagner and of Craig becomes necessary. And with it a new definition of theatrical representation which sees it, not as a static piecing-together of signs or a meta-text, but rather as a dynamic process that takes place in time and is effectively produced by the actor.
>
> (Dort 1988: 177–8)

He could not be clearer. In the manner of Vitez, he describes *mise en scène* as an autonomous production of meaning and not as a translation or an illustration of the pre-existing text:

> Today, we can observe a progressive emancipation of the elements of representation and see in this a shift in structure: the rejection of an organic unity prescribed *a priori* and the recognition of the theatrical event as a signifying polyphony, involving the spectator.
>
> (Dort 1988: 178)

Twenty years after this evaluation, it is clear that Dort's diagnosis was correct. The director, as new postmodern neo-subject, can no longer look down from a position on high.

But this loss is not so much a personal failure as a sign of the times. The failure — if this notion has any relevance in art — instead concerns a few theatrical attempts to create a school and be the founder of a system. No director would risk founding his entire work on a *Gesamtkunstwerk*. Nonetheless, the fad for total audiovisual spectacle is far from over. Thus the shows of Romeo and Claudia Castellucci appear to be animated images from which sounds, or even shreds of sentences, can emerge. Hence their obvious organicity and the equality of the signs and the materials, all of which constitutes the very opposite of theatre staging a text or even of a proposition for action or event. In his *Tragedia Endogonidia, C01–C11* (2002–4), Castellucci is not aiming to produce images that leave the spectator voiceless but, on the contrary, to offer images that will then be torn down from the inside, by way of the irruption of voice or a reality effect or the irruption of the irrational or the unconscious. The Castelluccis' creations refer to the painting of Raphael, to the opposition, conflict between the eurhythmic order, the perfection of forms, the geometric beauty of the canvases on the one hand, and on the other the rupture of this order by the dazzling evidence that calls vision into question by propelling it towards dark and unexpected places.

(Castellucci 2002: 176)

Brook's research to find a universal language of theatre, an art for everybody, does not lead to a universal production and reading of signs, but, at best, and as Vitez notes (1995: 428), to a 'translinguistic', sonar, visual, and gestural Esperanto that creates the illusion of general understanding beyond specific languages and cultures. This illusion manifests itself either as a universalising idealisation of cultures (this is the essentialism with which Brook has frequently, and sometimes unjustly, been charged), or, on the contrary, as an undifferentiated eulogy to difference, leading sometimes to sectarian communitarianism. The crisis of the intercultural, its incapacity to situate cultures both in their local specificity and in their universal humanity, does not make the task of multicultural artists any easier.

The postmodern neo-subject does not fare much better in the domain of political theatre, as no audience wants to be lectured. Brechtian epic theatre, with its sharp edge, is supposed to touch the audience at the heart of its interests, to highlight contradictions and nail down the *gestus* of the characters. But for fear of being too direct or too painful, the neo-director softens the dramaturgical analysis, staying in the realm of the general or the ambiguous.

There are hardly any 'Brechtian' directors left, nor much overtly political theatre. This does not mean, however, that the social preoccupations of theatre have gone. Thus, Mnouchkine, after the 1980s (a series of Shakespeare plays) and 1990s (a series of Greek tragedies), has returned to a theatre that is more anchored in the everyday with productions of *Le Dernier Caravansérail* (*Odyssées*) (2003) and *Les Éphémères* (2006). The collective creation of short texts by the actors – fragments of life which are literally carried onstage on a wheeled platform – as well as the way in which the realities of immigration or of collective and individual histories are evoked no longer owes much to Brecht's immense socio-critical frescoes. The words, like the gestures, are always allusive, the political discourse is implicit, almost subjective. It would seem that Mnouchkine's former vision as creator and director has given way to a thousand impressions that are ephemeral but precise, coming from the actors, who embody the nobodies of history – *sans papiers*, immigrants torn from their origins – who are also the witnesses of these fugitive Cartier-Bresson-like instants. Thus Mnouchkine's staging loses its external, overseeing, centralising eyes in favour of little notes on the ephemeral and the loss of origin. Thus, the stage work must be compared to a mosaic, and no director can stick the fragments together. In this profusion of materials, the director is the person with the courage to cut and to clarify.

This critique of the powers of theatre leaves performance without any clear perspective, reflecting the world in which we live. Finding itself in a damaged landscape, performance has trouble finding its way, there is much to be repaired and also prepared for in a future that, at least socially, is not looking too rosy.

The main thing that needs *repair* is in fact not broken, but actually works too well: it is communication; the communication of *mass media* and of ready-made messages. Theatre precisely questions the pretension of communicating everything, the tyranny of information and of surveillance. As we understand it today, *mise en scène* need not be clear, readable, or self-explanatory. Its role is not to mediate transmitter and receiver, author and audience, to 'smooth things out'. Instead of simplifying and explicating, it remains deliberately opaque. After the clarity of Brechtianism, it instead favours ambiguity and vagueness. This has been apparent in very unorthodox and rather 'aestheticising' (as one would say during the militant post-'68 years) productions.

Brecht's *La Mère* (*The Mother*), produced in 1995 by Jacques Delcuvellerie, gave the eponymous figure a sensitivity and brought ambiguity to the motivations of the play's characters. In his *Cercle de craie caucasien* (*The Caucasian Chalk Circle*, 2001), Benno Besson, as in all of his Brechtian productions, emphasised the rough, poetic, and sexual nature of the objects and costumes, humanity and the irresistible goodness of the principal character. In *L'Exception et la règle* (*The Exception and the Rule*), directed by Alain Ollivier (2002),

Les Fusils de la Mère Carrar (*Senora Carrar's Rifles*), staged by Antoine Caubet (2006), and in *Homme=homme* (*Man Equals Man*), revisited by Emmanuel Demarcy-Mota (2007), we see an identical tendency: not the reduction of the play to slogans but the reintroduction of a poetic dimension, if only by way of the short-circuiting or unsettling of grand political messages, to produce a stage materiality that does not translate into univocal signifieds.

Every *mise en scène* oscillates between construction and deconstruction. When the structure of the plays – which was once closed, coherent, and narrative – breaks down, opens up, and becomes what we – since the 1970s – have called a 'text' (in the semiotic sense, and as opposed to a 'work'[3]), it becomes difficult to read and to perform this text 'in one piece', in a univocal manner. *Mise en scène* has the specific mission of finding a compromise between this opening of the semiotic 'text' and its own natural tendency to explain, justify, and interpret the work performed in a univocal and conclusive manner. Conversely, for a coherent play with a predictable structure, that uses classical language, with an explicit story, the actor and the director reintroduce some 'text', that is some 'play', into the structures. They create a semantic ambiguity and recover the pleasure of the enigma and of complexity: Barthes's 'pleasure of the text'. When dramatic *works* become open *texts* without a clear story or when directors 'never [give] the impression of seeing the story for what it is in their shows' (Tackels 1994: 90), the *mise en scène* often sets itself the task of 'repairing' this story or at least of substituting another organising structure.

The repairs also consist of compensating for the absence of cultural references through the staging. This is one of the principal functions of *mise en scène*, in particular when the play belongs to another cultural area from that of the audience and when one must provide, as discreetly as possible, missing references, keys that are indispensable to the reading. This aid to the spectator is given without her always being aware of it, and sometimes against her will. This spectator is thus consciously manipulated. Such a manipulation is the work of ideology and of the unconscious. *Mise en scène* is always unconscious, ideological, filling-in.

The director and her doubles

Contemporary *mise en scène*, as we can see, is very much in need of repair. What was already its original function has become more and more necessary as humans have become distanced from a well-ordered world and as the disorganisation of the senses has itself come up for repair. But is repairing perhaps too normative an activity? And do things still get repaired? Do we not just discard anything that does not meet our norms?

There is a tendency, and doubtless a real necessity, to believe that *mise en scène* only pertains to the classics, or maybe text-based theatre, repertory theatre, art theatre, and that 'one is only a director when directing classics' (Planchon 1977: 53). This is why we should complement (and not replace) the notion of *mise en scène* with the Anglo-American notion of *performance*. The notion of performance, or even that of *production*, considers theatrical performance as the accomplishment of an action, and not as a 'stage writing' (Planchon's *écriture scénique*) to transpose, illustrate, and double the text.

Once *mise en scène* sees itself as performance (suggesting live and ephemeral activities and tasks), it becomes diversified and enriched. It must resolve its inherent contradiction: on the one hand, it was born of and feeds on the division of labour, which necessitates new collaborators; on the other hand, it only makes sense if it succeeds in globally seizing the spirit of the performance with some degree of coherence. The director is host to an uncomfortable tension: she must divide herself into various roles while remaining very much herself. Her collaborators (or just herself if she works alone) acquire new functions. This can be seen in the examples chosen for this volume and I shall attempt to create a profile of the real and virtual doubles of the director.

The actor

In a contemporary *mise en scène* or performance, none of the director's doubles demonstrates such duplicity as the actor. The actor, who should often instead be called a *performer*, is present in all these practices. She is not only a mimetic double of the realistic or naturalist character, but also frequently an open and empty figure, non-psychological and therefore non-mimetical, a 'face carrier' (as Marivaux would have said), which, in contemporary writing, serves as a support for the discourse without necessarily representing a real being. When the actor is her own dramaturg, she obviously is one body with what she says or shows, she becomes organically present to her words and to her actions, and to her director if the director persists in wanting to guide and control her. When the actor deconstructs a means of representation (like Claude Régy) or an imposed identity (like Marina Abramović),[4] they find a certain distance and are further distanced from their fate as a character. The director, then, is in position to decentre the actor, to 'work with the actor on not being pre-occupied' (Cantarella 2002: 63). The director's relationship with the text has changed: she no longer needs to be 'pre-occupied with knowing what is underneath' (Cantarella 2002: 65). That is, she doesn't have to worry about a hidden meaning 'under the text', but she must show 'where', in the whole disposition of the text and on its surface, the actor stands, as an element within the overall structure, as a pawn on the 'chessboard' of the stage.

In all of these configurations, the actor has become a full partner of the director: a double who is 'pre-occupied' no longer with herself, but rather with the place that she occupies in the show and in the overall functioning of the *mise en scène*. The best example would be that of Daniel Mesguich, whose actors are not psychological entities, but rather figures that take positions and oppositions on the stage (see Carmody's chapter, pp. 143–63). In Mesguich's productions of Marivaux or Racine, the effects of doubling (mistress and servant, queen and handmaid) reinforce this mirror impression: we are confronted with two interchangeable personae: one refers to the other and they are reversible. As such, Mesguich wants to show that a character is always a construction and that classical dramaturgy often operates with doubles, dialogism, and a split personality. Mesguich's use of doubles comes from his teacher Antoine Vitez, who, in the 1960s and 1970s, introduced the notion of a character who can be split into several *personae* and be embodied by different actors. Thus in his productions of Racine or Molière, Vitez would unfold a kind of actantial model, thus illustrating the different forces at play in a given situation. The fiction of a given, unified subject was then clearly questioned and the spectator was given a concrete view of this system of forces.

The author

The relationship between the director and the author has often been one of conflict, the latter feeling exploited by the former. But, after the 1980s, after the 'money years' or the 'society of spectacle' (as defined by Debord), and with the renewal of dramatic writing in the 1990s, the author now needs the director even more than she needs the actor, not so much in order to be performed but rather to recruit her in order to test and unfold the possible meanings of the text. The relationship 'profits' both parties. Thus the author no longer feels the need to stage her own play (running the risk of staying too timorous and too much a prisoner of her own text) in order to avoid betrayal, or to state the 'correct' point of view. She gladly hands the text over to an actor who will be capable of unfurling it, unfolding it, as if to better reveal it to the author and the spectator.

The dramaturg

The dramaturg, in the German sense of *Dramaturg* (literary adviser), is hardly ever used by French directors. Although it remains an essential piece of the theatrical machine in Germany and in Scandinavia, it has never taken hold in France or the Iberian peninsula. Perhaps this is because its essential and indispensable function has been absorbed by *mise en scène*. After years of re-reading the classics, dramaturgy has become too heavy a science, preventing a direct relationship with the text, masking the delicate nervous system of the text with the ballast of cultural references and political analysis, crushing the subtle and fragile work of the contemporary theatre actor. After the Brechtian wave in Western Europe, the French theatre establishment did not retain the dramaturgy that was central to this wave, as it no longer saw the necessity or the relevance of Brechtian and Marxist critical analysis. 'What would I do with a dramaturg?' Antoine Vitez once provocatively asked. Many contemporary artists, from Braunschweig to Cantarella, avoid excessive table work and any analysis that decides *a priori* the staging choices of the future *mise en scène*.

On the other hand, dramatic analysis, whether or not it is done by the dramaturg, is something from which the performance might well benefit, not just in terms of clarifying the ideological stakes, but also in order that the story be well told and its conflicts clearly outlined. This is what happened with Alain Ollivier's production of Brecht's pedagogical play *L'Exception et la règle* (*The Exception and the Rule*) at the Théâtre Gérard Philipe, Saint-Denis, in 2002. How can we transpose this classic about man's exploitation of man, the violence of the merchant towards the 'coolie', to our times? In not taking sufficiently into account the contemporary spectator and new forms of exploitation, which are less direct and more effective, and by not attempting more visible and original formal work, Ollivier missed the opportunity to 'actualise' the play, to extract its current relevance. In the absence of dramaturgical analysis, of the kind offered by a professional named the dramaturg or by a director dotting all the i's, the *mise en scène* seemed to stop short of a political and historical interpretation of the work. The task was not easy for Vitez's former actor, since it is hard to get away from the didactic heaviness of Brechtianism without falling into an 'invisible' dramaturgy, which quickly becomes insipid and anaemic. How can one transform a story that is itself a transposition of a theoretical schema that badly renders the complexity of the world?

In a German context, one that cannot escape the influence of Brecht and which remains marked by the national institution of the *Dramaturg*, it is worthwhile examining how this figure is used in various different ways in contemporary practice. One need only study the dramaturg as it is conceived by Thomas Ostermeier and Frank Castorf. Whether in directing *Woyzeck* (2004, Avignon) or *Nora* (2002) Ostermeier calls on a dramaturg who is also a recognised author, associated with the Schaubühne: Marius von Mayenburg. The latter does a conscientious and precise work of analysis and of transposition, although the pertinence of his choices is far from obvious. Thus *Woyzeck* is transposed into our contemporary world, taking place on the margins of a huge metropolis in Eastern Europe, in a sewer, where all the trafficking takes place. In a certain sense, the production is too faithful to Büchner's play, it never stops reiterating the same ideas: the violence of the world, the degradation of man, the suffering of the poor. But what was revolutionary in Büchner's era – the emergence of a sub-proletariat in a world that seeks to crush it – seems banal today. It is precisely *mise en scène* that should comment on and explain this state of affairs.

In another context, that of British theatre, it seems that the function of dramaturgical analysis is taken care of in devised work. An example is the working method of Simon McBurney, who does not mount a text that is fixed and decided in advance, but rather works with the actors and designers, and elaborates a score step by step, seeking textual material according to the needs of the story and the acting (see Knapper's chapter, pp. 259–74 for further details). The Continental notion of *mise en scène* does not correspond to the reality of this practice of devised theatre, even if the director obviously takes the final decisions. The role of McBurney remains crucial due to his capacity 'for creating images that defamiliarise and redirect the geometry of conventional, received attention to reality, and etch themselves into our imagination' (Williams 2005: 250). Thus there is an opposition between the rigidity and precision of dramaturgical analysis and the flexibility of a new kind of stage writing. Many other examples could be located in Europe of this type of practice as with the work of Els Joglars or Comediants in Spain.

The director of actors

The distilled nature of new dramatic writing, the mistrust of the lavishness of scenography and spectacle, the intimidation caused by the technical aspect of stage machinery, all of these things reinforce a desire for simplicity and a move back to basics for the director, as well as a move towards the work of the actor. This reduction of *mise en scène* to the direction of actors[5] stems from a very poor mode of production. To make a virtue of necessity, the director of actors is now only interested in acting, with the basic idea that she must give birth to the actor, in the rehearsals, who is then provoked, trapped, mistreated, and martyred. Hence actors and directors often drift into a pathological relationship. Most of the time, fortunately, everything goes in the right direction: the direction of the actors, in rehearsals or within the performance, establishes itself through a contrast and a difference within the *mise en scène*. *Mise en scène* is therefore conceived as the visible, the visual, the superfluous, the blocking, the choice of costumes and objects. The direction of actors is supposed to be the foundation of the theatrical relationship, to reproduce the human link between the actor and the organiser, the creature and God the father. We are reminded of Cocteau's statement about directors as midwives who think they are the father!

Criticism sometimes (rarely) distinguishes the two functions: the direction of actors and *mise en scène*. Sometimes we reproach a director for creating a stage set that imprisons the actor in the stage machinery, preventing her from 'breathing'. Scenographers-turned-directors or directors with a background in visual arts are often accused of this.[6]

The particular attention that we rightly place today on the direction of actors should nonetheless not eliminate the function of *mise en scène* and all that it implies or has implied historically or currently. The director certainly plays a fundamental role in the discovery and interpretation of the text and of the stage actions, but she does not eliminate the more global function of *mise en scène*, for the simple reason that direction is part of the final production. If the direction of actors animates, irrigates, and illuminates the *mise en scène*, the acting, however subtle and central it may be, only takes its meaning in the overall stage production. Therefore the *metteur en scène* cannot be reduced to the role of director of actors, and even less to that of the casting director, marketing director, or communications director.

Many contemporary directors have nonetheless chosen to concentrate first and foremost on the direction of actors, giving scenography and stage representation a secondary role, or one that is merged into the acting. The space and the world of the stage are recreated by the blocking and the rhythmic management of time. In his stagings of *Twelfth Night* (2003), *Cymbeline* (2007), or *Andromaque* (2007), Declan Donnellan places the actor in the centre of the process, in order to avoid basing the work on a preconceived conception of the staging: 'One of the aims of Cheek by Jowl is to reexamine the classic texts of world theatre and to investigate them in a fresh and unsentimental way, eschewing directorial concepts to focus on the actor and on the actor's art' (Donnellan, quoted in Giannachi and Luckhurst 1999: 19; see also Sierz's interview with Donnellan in this volume, pp. 165–84).

The aesthete of theatrical forms

Fearing that their art is drifting towards casting and management, fearing the loss of all aesthetic, dramaturgical, ideological, and political control, certain directors call on 'art theatre' and the heritage of Vitez. They reinforce the elements that give a show its aesthetic, artistic, and artificial character: theatricality, and a respect for conventions and forms. Their actors describe beautiful and clear choreographic figures with honed and precise movements; their way of speaking is deliberately rhetorical, musical, stylised, and formalised (think of artists such as Jean-Marie Villégier, Daniel Mesguich, and Robert Cantarella). The 'overacting' that results from this is not necessarily ham acting, but rather marks the movement from simple acting to choreographic, heightened acting.

Many directors seek a choreographic, heightened, theatricalised acting. This emphasis on form does not necessarily seek to make the performance seem false. Often, in fact, the theatricality goes hand in hand with a search for authenticity and for psychological precision. Patrice Chéreau, from the start of his career, under the influence in particular of Giorgio Strehler, is a good example of this aesthetic vision of the real (see Fancy's chapter, pp. 61–84). In Chéreau's shows, taking place against the often monumental scenography of his regular designer, Richard Peduzzi, he seeks the image, the attitude, the lighting effect, or the recorded sound that, thanks to their formal perfection, will aestheticise even the most sordid reality (as is the case in the plays of Koltès), and will provide a shiny surface, a perfect form, an uncanny atmosphere, a refined and sombre atmosphere. In his staging of *Phèdre* (2004), Chéreau brings together highly psychological acting and a formal declamation of the Alexandrine verse. Avoiding rhetorical and melodic tirades, the actors encourage identification with their characters. According to the training and vocal habits of the actors, a very wide palette of ways of speaking and identifying with a role is obtained. All have in common an unusual mixture of authenticity and artificiality.

The silent musician

The word and the notion of *mise en scène* (in the modern sense, from the end of the nineteenth century) were invented for theatrical practice based on the text, and in particular on the literary text that pre-existed the performance. Is *mise en scène* still a legitimate notion for a theatre that works with things other than a text, in particular images without text, with 'huge spaces of silence, so in fact virtual images?' (Corman, quoted in Corvin 1994: 126). Should we not find another word, and thus another theory, for a *mise en scène* that does not represent an already written text but which works with silence and non-verbal signs (be they visual or musical)? Can we, or should we, continue to speak of *mise en scène* in general, as if its principles had not been systematised in the nineteenth century? The notion of *mise en scène* is elastic, but also irreplaceable, if conceived as a mechanism of tuning and auto-regulation, not only for the stage, but especially for the world and the relationship between the stage and the world.

The director is sometimes comparable with a conductor, but also with a composer, since she establishes and enforces a rhythm for an entire score. From Meyerhold to Marthaler, many artists have seen their role as like that of a musician. Whatever the theme or the argument, Marthaler treats the words of the actors like polyphonic voices or instruments in an orchestration. In *Die Stunde Null* (1996) or in *Seemannslieder* (2004), the actor-orator-singers have unexpected encounters where they suddenly sing in chorus, which they do rather well, with a dry sense of humour. What results is a singing chorus, seeking not to give a verbal or visual message, but to have a nice time together, as if music, however parodic it may be, might offer an opportunity (or an illusion?) of togetherness, unison in the same universe, involvement in the same absurd and moving quest (see Barnett's chapter, pp. 207–27). Music plays the unexpected role of social cement, it gives the audience another vision of *mise en scène*, that of audio-vision. It tunes human relations as much as it tunes the performance.

The choreographer of silence

It is the choreographer, be she real or metaphorical, who is best placed to execute this tuning. Theatre becomes dance when a game is established between elements of the performance without any need to go via language. This shows that the choreographer is always present, especially when forgotten about. The music set to rhythm begins to dance, at least in the poetic sense that Corvin (1994: 125) gives it:

> Theatre disintegrates or rather is metamorphosed: it becomes dance [...] Dance does not mean choreography but specific time that, no longer depending on the necessity of exchange and dialogue, introduces play into dreams. Play, that is to say a rhythmical pulsation by which the director-author [...] makes her text breathe.

As it becomes dance and rhythmical play, *mise en scène*, such as the work of Wilson, Marthaler, or Kantor, evacuates the too-obvious signified, in order to concentrate on mute and silent images, that is, on the signifier which, for as long as possible, refuses to be interpreted and turned into a sign. This *mise en scène* understood as pure dance brings us back to silence and to the spectator. It becomes the art of teasing out the unsaid, or even the unspeakable, as one of the voices of silence. It is not (or no longer), then, the art of expressing something, of perceiving the message and the noise, when one goes from the textual to the visual. It is the art, rather, of bringing out the silence for a spectator waiting for meaning. *Mise en scène* is the *mise en vue* of silence.

All of the director's doubles – actor, author, dramaturg, director of actors, choreographer, and musician – far from relativising the importance of *mise en scène*, actually reinforce it, making it an essential concept in theatrical organisation. We should not give up on this notion and on this method, even if, in some respects, the conception of theatre work as performance and as production might be better equipped to illuminate the unpredictable relationship of art to the real, the effect produced on the spectator, the importance at times of detuning rather than tuning the performance, and the possibility of theatre encroaching on the world. Tuning and detuning, discipline and dissolution, regulation and deregulation, our heart wavers between two possibilities, as does the heart of *mise en scène*. Identities change so fast that it makes us dizzy.

Thus, *mise en scène* might be in a state of constant crisis; it might even be the art of creating and solving problems at the same time. It is therefore not disappearing, only looking for new forms and strategies. *Mise en scène* is not only a matter of fine-tuning: it is a survival kit not only for texts but also for new ways of looking at art and reality. The debate about *mise en scène/performance* has been very useful in going beyond the sterile opposition of *mise en scène* as mimesis and/or performance as performative action.

Most theatrical adaptations of films (a very common practice since the 2000s) use the film as a source of narrative, theme, and major scenes that the theatre then seeks to dramatise. With a few exceptions (Ostermeier's *The Marriage of Maria Braun*, for example[7]), stage adaptations do not duplicate filmic techniques on stage. Ivo van Hove's *The Damned*[8] is inspired by great moments in the film, but Visconti's style and cinematographic technique are not carried over into theatrical technique. Ivo van Hove relies more on his memories as a film buff and on a cultural and historical memory of Nazism (a few images of the era, preceded by a brief written commentary, setting out some of the historical events: the Reichstag fire, book burnings, the factories operating at capacity, a speech by Hitler, the concentration camps).

The fluidity of the shots and of the filmic (and subsequently theatrical) sequences are the heart beat of the production, with its irresistible drive and sudden crises. Unlike Brecht's *The Resistible Ascent of Arturo Ui*, no direct suggestions on how to resist fascism are given, which is consistent with the 'degenerate', hysterical, and perverse vision of fascism offered by both Visconti and van Hove.

The filmic images derive their meaning only in relation to the entire *mise en scène*, in other words in relation to the organisation and interaction of all these signifying systems. In this example of filmic performance, it would be of little use to compare, oppose, and radically distinguish theatrical and cinematic *mise en scène*.

Europe has for the past 60 years been a field of these eternal and pointless struggles, but it is no longer the space where all contradictions are resolved. *Mise en scène* happens elsewhere. *Mise en scène* seems like a good idea, but it has still to be reinvented and it must be immediately globalised and relativised. In Asia, the Americas, and Africa, *mise en scène* is submitted to a necessary revision. It thus is both challenged and renewed by a new type of 'performance': a mixture of 'performance' and '*mise en scène*': *performise*. It is therefore both a performance in the English sense of the word and a *mise en scène*, in the 'Continental' sense of a production of a text or of a semiotic system. Thus Europe might still be a mailbox for the world's theatrical practices, but it has become an empty mailbox for these theatrical and cultural practices – a drum, resounding with all the sounds and images of a new whole world, which keeps inventing itself. Thus the task of the director again becomes a completely new one; it has to be reinvented again, if the director wants to listen to the sounds of fury and to the images of hope of a new world order where Europe no longer has the cultural and political might it once enjoyed.

Notes

1   To use the title of two of his books, from 1967 (*Le Système de la mode*) and 1973 (*Le Plaisir du texte*) respectively.

2 In one passage from his *La Représentation émancipée*, Bernard Dort (1988: 177) quotes my 1976 book, *Problèmes de sémiologie théâtrale*. With time, it has become clear that he was quite right.
3 According to Roland Barthes's famous distinction in his 1971 essay, 'De l'oeuvre au texte' ('From Work to Text') reprinted in Barthes 1993: 1211–17.
4 Interestingly Régy is best known as a director and Abramović is performer and director of her own pieces.
5 On this question, see Proust 2006. For a study of the work of the director with young actors playing in a foreign language, see Essif 2006.
6 See the interviews with Stéphane Braunschweig in Féral 1997; Proust 2006.
7 Ostermeier's production (a reworking of his earlier production at the Munich Kammerspiele) premiered at the Schaubühne in 2009 and is an adaptation by dramaturgs Julia Lochte and Florian Borchmeye of the 1979 film by Rainer Werner Fassbinder, which was scripted by Peter Märthesheimer and Pea Frohlich.
8 *Les Damnés* opened at the Avignon Festival in 2016 and is adapted from Luchino Visconti's *La Caduta degli dei* (literally *The Twilight of the Gods*, but usually translated as *The Damned*).

Bibliography

Barthes, Roland (1993) 'De l'œuvre au texte', *Œuvres complètes*, Vol. II, Paris, Seuil, pp. 1211–17. First published in 1971.
Cantarella, Robert (2002) *L'Assemblée théâtrale*, Paris: Les Éditions de l'Amandier.
Castellucci, Romeo (2002) 'Interview', *Europe*, 873–74 (January–February).
Corvin, Michel (1994) 'Mise en scène et silence', *Revue d'esthétique*, 26: 123–28.
Dort, Bernard (1988) *La Représentation émancipée*, Arles: Actes Sud.
Essif, Les (2006) *The French Play: Exploring Theatre 'Re-creatively' with Foreign Language Students*, Calgary: University of Calgary Press.
Féral, Josette (1997) *Mise en scène et jeu de l'acteur: entretiens*, vol. II, Montreal: Éditions Jeu/Éditions Lansman.
Giannachi, Gabriella and Mary Luckhurst (1999) 'Declan Donnellan', in Gabriella Giannachi and Mary Luckhurst (eds), *On Directing*, London: Faber and Faber, pp. 19–23.
Pavis, Patrice (1976) *Problèmes de sémiologie théâtrale*, Montreal: Presses de l'Université du Québec.

Planchon, Roger (1977) 'Lecture des classiques', *Pratiques*, 15–16 (July): 34–61.

Proust, Sophie (2006) *La Direction d'acteurs dans la mise en scène contemporaine*, Paris: L'Entretemps.

Tackels, Bruno (1994) 'Le "Jeune Théâtre" de demain', *Revue d'esthétique*, 26: 89–94.

Vitez, Antoine (1995) *Écrits sur le théâtre*, vol. II, Paris: P.O.L.

Williams, David (2005) 'Simon McBurney', in Shomit Mitter and Maria Shevtsova (eds), *Fifty Key Theatre Directors*, London: Routledge, pp. 247–52.

INDEX

9/11 terrorist attacks 168–169

abduction 399
abortion 198
Abramov, Fyodor 85–86, 99–100
Abramović, Marina 16
acting 18, 21, 30, 41–42, 43, 44–48, 49–51, 53, 68, 72, 77, 78, 80, 87, 91, 92, 110, 112–115, 146, 153, 166, 167, 170–180, 189–193, 195, 207, 212–214, 223, 249–250, 267, 299, 304–5, 308, 349–51, 376–7, 435, 438–439, 468–469, 471
activism 8, 39, 42–47, 52
adaptation 103, 115–116, 290, 294, 361, 402, 507
Adjani, Isabelle 72, 74
Aeschylus 105–106; *Agamemnon* 50–51; *(A)pollonia* 371–373, 374; *Les Atrides* 50–51; *Les Danaïdes (The Suppliants)* 103; *Oresteia* 106, 115–116, 118, 129; *The Persians* 491
Afghanistan 90
Africa: Belgian colonialism 229–231, 235–236, 238, 241–244; French colonialism 70–72; Rwandan crises of the 1990s 431–432; *see also* colonialism
AIDS 166–169, 182, 280–282, 285–286, 288, 366–369, 379
Albertí, Xavier 387
Alexander, Catherine 301
Algeria 40, 71

alienation 220, 459
Allain, Paul 21, 434
allegorisation 71, 73–74, 75
Andropov, Yuri 11
animals 412, 415–416
anti-Semitism 196, 363, 369, 378
Antoine, André 6–7
Antonioni, Michaelangelo 282, 287
archaeology 51, 331
architecture 115, 293
Arden, Annabel 260–261
Argentina 14, 16, 383, 407–408
aristocracy 74–75; *see also* bourgeoisie
Arrabal, Fernando 341, 353
Artaud, Antonin 1, 48
Association Internationale de Défense des Artistes (AIDA) 57
Association Théâtrale des Étudiants de Paris (ATEP) 40
asylum seekers 52–53
Auden, W. H. 361–362
audience(s) 32–33, 34, 40–41, 43, 49–50, 87, 88–89, 105, 126, 127–128, 147, 165, 177, 196, 210, 223, 238–239, 243, 251, 264, 270, 283–285, 303, 318, 357, 360, 366, 367, 368, 375–376, 410, 445, 467, 487
Australia 53–54
Austro-Hungarian empire 55
auteur theory 2, 20, 80–81, 272, 447, 493; Declan Donnellan 169, 170; Jan Lauwers 233; Katie Mitchell 427–429;

511

INDEX

Rodrigo García 407, 418; Silviu Purcărete 104; Thomas Ostermeier 471
authoritarianism 445
avant-garde theatre 16, 40–41, 42, 192–193, 252, 356, 365, 415–416, 478, 482
awards: *Chevalier de l'Ordre des Arts et des Lettres* 275, 301; Director of the Year Award 137–138; Faust Award 222–223; Friedrich Luft Prize 128; Fritz Kortner Prize 132; Golden Lion Lifetime Achievement Award 31, 253; knighthoods 342; Kortner Prize 137–138; Laurence Olivier Awards 275, 302; Meyerhold Award 371; Nobel Peace Prize 29; Obie awards 275; Obie awards 275; *L'Officier de l'Ordre des Arts et des Lettres* 301; *Theater Heute* awards 130, 132, 138, 139, 455
Aznar, José María 389, 412–413

Balkan conflict 18–19, 31–32
ballet 169, 234; *see also* dance
Barba, Eugenio 314
Barcelona 15, 384–390
Barkey, Grace Ellen 233–234, 239, 252–253
Barrault, Jean-Louis 154
Barthes, Roland 63, 103, 288, 294, 467, 473n4, 493, 497
St Bartholomew's Day Massacre 13, 65–66, 72–76
Baudrillard, Jean 237, 459
Bausch, Pina 1–2, 16, 264, 429–430, 440–441; *Café Müller* 440–441; *Kontakthof* 441; *Nelken* (*Carnations*) 429–430
Beauvoir, Simone de 40
Bechtler, Hildegard 312, 313–314
Beckett, Samuel 217, 307–308, 311,312, 315, 432, 441; *Endgame* 217; *Footfalls* 307–308, 315; *Happy Days* 307–308, 311–312, 432, 441; *Play* 441
behaviouralist experiments 66–67, 462–465
Beijing Opera 50

Belbel, Sergi 386–387
Belgium 229–255, 487
Bellamy, Richard 12, 65, 75–76
Benet i Jornet, Josep Maria 386–387
Ben-Itzak, Paul 239, 241
Benjamin, Walter 32
Benvenuto, Gianna 190
Berg, Alban 222–223, 375
Bergamín, Beatriz 412–413
Berger, John 260
Bergman, Ingmar 16, 20, 282–285, 295
Berlin 15, 121, 123–126, 127, 130, 132, 140, 213, 399, 431, 462, 465, 467; Berlin Wall 10, 13, 123, 169, 209; East Berlin 125, 128–129
Biagini, Mario 187–188
Bieito, Calixto 2, 4–5, 11, 15, 16, 19, 20–21, 383–405; *Amfitrió* (*Amphitryon*) 384, 385; *Carmen* 397, 402; *Dues històries irlandes* 384–385; *El rei Joan* (*King John*) 387–388, 402; *El rei Lear* (*King Lear*) 385, 387–388, 389–390, 391–392, 402; *Els dos cavallers de Verona* (*Two Gentlemen of Verona*) 384–385; *Fidelio* 385; *La forza del destino* (*The Force of Destiny*) 385; *Hamlet* 385, 389; *Macbeth* 385–388, 391–392, 394, 402; *Mesura per mesura* (*Measure for Measure*) 388; *Il mondo della luna* 385; *Obabakoak* 401–402; *Peer Gynt* 13; *Platform* 400–401; *La ópera de cuatro cuartos* (*The Threepenny Opera*) 387–388, 394; *Die Soldaten* (*The Soldiers*) 33, 385; *El somni d'una nit d'estiu* (*A Midsummer Night's Dream*) 384–385, 387–388; *Un día* (*A Day*) 387–388; *La tempestat* (*The Tempest*) 387–388, *La Traviata* 385; *Il Trovatore* 385, 399; *La verbena de la paloma* (*The Festival of the Dove*) 387, 395
Bilal, Enki 22
Bilefsky, Dan 30
Billing, Christopher 280
Billington, Michael 396, 427–428, 441–442
biomechanics 456, 469

512

INDEX

Bizet, Georges 397, 402
Blair, Tony 414
Blanc, Dominique 78, 308
Boadella, Albert 383, 385, 408–409
body-subjects 305–306, 310–311, 358–359, 377; *see also* physical theatre
Boenisch, Peter 13–14, 301
Bogdanov, Gennadij 469
Bonnema, Anneke 233–234
Borowski, Piotr 4–5, 11, 15–16, 21, 185–205; *Człowiek* (*The Man/Human*) 195, 196, 202–203; *Dziady* (*Forefathers' Eve*) 192–195, 197, 198; *Henryk Hamlet Hospital H.H.H.* 188–189, 192, 196, 203; *Koniec Pieśni* (*The Song is Over*) 201–202; *Król Kier Znów na Wylocie* (*Chasing the King of Hearts*) 193, 196, 203; *Miasto* (*The City*) 191–192, 195, 196, 197–198, 202; *Parsifal* 193–194; *Party; take (a)part* 199, 203; *Północ* (*Midnight/The North*) 189, 193–194, 195, 198
Bosnian War 11, 431–432
bourgeoisie 8, 43, 45–46, 69, 70, 124, 364, 395, 461–462
Bowie, David 275–277, 281, 296
Bowman, Elen 437–438
Bradby, David 1, 6, 8, 10, 40–41, 45, 104, 415
branding 18–22, 414, 419–420, 422
Brecht, Bertolt 1, 7–8, 16, 48, 63, 68, 127–128, 214, 220, 336, 455, 456, 459, 462, 481, 495, 500–501; *Baal* 139–140; *The Caucasian Chalk Circle* 336, 496; *The Good Person of Szechwan* 302; *The Mother* 496; *Mother Courage and Her Children* 308; *The Resistible Rise of Arturo Ui* 259
Bregović, Goran 74
Breth, Andrea 138
Breton, Tomás 387–388, 395
Brexit 29–30, 32, 35, 198
Brezhnev, Leonid 11
Britain xviii, 29, 30, 32, 35, 106–107, 110, 113, 165–172, 198, 260–272, 299–319, 427–447, 465
British empire 48

Bronnen, Arnold 128, 129
Brook, Peter 15, 16, 170, 187, 300–303
Brûlé, Tyler 212
Bryant-Bertail, Sarah 50–51
Bryś, Marta 374
Buber, Martin 195
Buenos Aires 407, 416
Bulgakov, Mikhail 136
bunraku plays 51–52
Buñuel, Luis 347, 392, 396
bureaucracy 260–261
Burgess, Anthony 128
Bush, George W. 129, 259, 389, 414

Cafruny, Alan 65
Calderón de la Barca, Pedro 387, 395
Callegari, Danielle 342
Cambodia 52
Cambridge University 165, 261, 266
Camí, Roser 385–386
Camus, Albert 133, 233
Canning, Charlotte 64
Canut, Carles 385–386
capitalism 8, 12–13, 15, 53–55, 57, 124, 131, 135, 188, 212, 261, 263, 356, 368, 400, 413, 484, 486–487; 'capitalist realism' 458–459
caricatures 168, 211–212, 215–216, 414
Carlson, Marvin 10, 145, 146, 148–149, 235, 362
Carné, Marcel 154, 159
carnival 416
Carp, Stefanie 209–210, 217, 219
Caruana, Pablo 417
Cassavetes, John 265, 287
Castellucci, Romeo 2, 4–5, 11, 325–339, 494–495; *Genesi* 325; *Giulio Cesare* 325; *Inferno* 325–331, 332, 335; *Paradiso* 334–337; *Purgatorio* 328–334; *Tragedia Endogonidia* 494
Castiglione, Dario 12, 65, 75–76
Castorf, Frank 2–3, 4, 11, 13, 18, 121–141, 208; *100 Jahre CDU: Spiel ohne Grenzen* (*100 Years of the CDU: Games without Borders*) 130; *Ajax* 123–124; *Alcestis* 128; *Der Auftrag* (*The Mission*)

513

INDEX

122; *Der Bau* (*The Construction Site*) 123; *Brothers Karamazov* 139; *Caligula* 133; *A Clockwork Orange* 128; *Demons* 133–134; *Dirty Hands* 133; *Enemy of the People* 123; *Greed* 137; *Hamlet* 123–124; *The Idiot* 136; *Insulted and Injured* 134–135; *John Gabriel Borkman* 125; *King Lear* 125, 128; *Macbeth* 131; *The Master and Margarita* 136; *Miss Sara Simpson* 123–124; *Nora* (*A Doll's House*) 122–123; *Othello* 121–122; *Die Räuber* (*The Robbers*) 125; *Reise ans Ender der Nacht* (*Journey to the End of the Night*) 139; *Woyzeck* 129, 501–502
Catalan theatre 21, 384–401
Catalonia 11
Catholicism 303, 361, 368–369
Cathomas, Bruno 21
cave paintings 260
Cavendish, Dominic 87, 166, 289–292, 294
Ceauşescu, Nicolae 11, 33–34, 105
celebrity 278–282
Céline, Louis-Ferdinand 139
Celtic myths 193–194, 195
censorship 34, 365–366
Centre of Contemporary Art, Poland 199
Centrum Sztuki Współczesnej Zamek Ujazdowski 188
Chaber, Marek 194
Chekhov, Anton 15, 90, 96–97, 98, 169–170, 182, 224, 429, 431–432, 435, 441–443, 447; *Platonov/Play Without a Title* 87; *The Seagull* 429, 435, 441–443, 447; 'The Student' 97; *Three Sisters* 87, 169–170, 182, 224; *Uncle Vanya* 87, 89, 98, 431–432
Chéreau, Patrice 3–4, 8–9, 14, 15, 19, 22, 61–84, 341–342, 504–505; *Combat des nègre et de chiens* (*Black Battles with Dogs*) 70–72; *Dans la solitude des champs de coton* (*In the Solitude of the Cottonfields*) 77, 79; *La Dispute* 66, 68–69, 70, 72; *Dom Juan* 68; *Hamlet* 341–342; *I am the Wind* 79–80; *Les Paravents* (*The Screens*) 71; *Phèdre* 76–80; *La Reine Margot* 13, 65–66, 72–76; *Richard II* 66; *Ring Cycle* 3; *Les Soldats* (*The Soldiers*) 62
child abuse 33–34, 247, 332–333
Chinoy, Helen Krich 64
choreography 506–507; *see also* physical theatre
chorus 50–51, 208, 218, 231, 242–243, 436, 441, 457, 506–507
Christie, William 234
Churchill, Winston 213–214, 430
Cielecka, Magdalena 372, 376–377
Cieslak, Ryszard 358–359, 377–378
cinema 55, 65–66, 72–76, 170, 187–188, 265, 279, 280–281, 282, 286, 287, 289–292, 296, 347, 392, 396, 429–430, 443–446; live cinema 443–446
circus 408–409
civil war 31–32, 386, 435–436
Cixous, Hélène 51–53, 145
Claudel, Paul 48
Coetzee, J. M. 371–372
Cohen, Lynne 219–220
Cold War 103–104
Cole, Toby 64
collective creation 39, 42–47, 52–53, 56–58, 439
colonialism 14–15, 70–72, 229–231, 235–236, 238, 241–244
Comediants 408–409
Comédie Française 280–281, 286, 289–292, 296
comedy 48, 67, 136; caricatures 72–73, 168, 211–212, 215–216, 414; musicals 48; *see also* humour
commedia dell'arte 42, 44, 47, 49, 50, 151–154
communism 11, 18, 33–34, 105, 360, 362, 456; *see also* Soviet Union
Congo, Belgian 229–231, 235–236, 238, 241–244
Conservative government of John Major 168
Copeau, Jacques 7–8, 41
Les Copiaus 41
Coppermann, Annie 77
Corneille, Pierre 16–17, 167–168, 182
cosmopolitanism 39, 52–58, 367

514

Costigan, George 388
counterculture *see* revolution
Cracknell, Carrie 35
Cramesnil, Joël 43–44
création collective 39, 42–47, 52–53, 56–58, 439
criminality 33–34, 364, 399
Crimp, Martin 429, 435, 443, 444–445
critics 87, 106–107, 123–124, 130, 137–138, 140, 239, 252, 253, 271, 309, 311, 358–360, 391, 427–429, 455–456; *see also* awards; festivals
Cuesta, Jairo 190–191

Dahl, Hans Petter 233–234
dance 20, 50–51, 123, 131, 172, 175, 188, 190–191, 192, 231, 232–233, 239, 242, 249, 252, 264, 269, 332, 334, 338–339n6, 346, 352, 409, 440, 444, 457, 469, 506
Dante, Alighieri 325–339
Dardenne, Jean-Pierre & Luc 13
decentralisation 62
Declaration of the Rights of Man 74
deconstruction 127, 129, 131, 390–392
Delgado, Maria M. 165, 166, 167
democracy 31–35, 74–75; deficity 65
demonstrations 57, 63, 193, 303, 462–463
Denić, Aleksander 139, 140
deportation 52, 57, 260
Déprats, Jean- Michel 49
Dercon, Chris 140
Derrida, Jacques 5, 53, 61–62, 145, 462–463; 'L'Autre Cap' ('The Other Heading') 5
Desclot, Miquel 392
Descôteaux, Nicolas 342
design, theatre 22, 35, 63, 67–8, 104, 114, 115, 122, 134, 136–137, 139, 167, 173, 174, 175–176, 218, 232, 281–282, 312–315, 317–318, 336, 341, 358, 363, 385, 395, 454, 466–467, 504–505
detention centres 53
Detje, Robin 121–122, 130–131
developmental reviews 64
D'Huys, An 281

Dickson, Andrew 16, 20, 22–23, 280
Didwiszus, Rufus 466–467
direct address 49, 192, 367, 373, 410
Disney 414
distortions 19–20
Dodin, Lev 3–5, 7–8, 11, 16, 18, 19, 85–101 181, 431, 437; *Brothers and Sisters* 85–86, 89, 92, 97, 98; *Gaudeamus* 86, 87; *The House* 98; *King Lear* 98–99; *Life and Fate* 94–95, 97, 98; *Platonov/Play Without a Title* 87; *The Possessed* 88, 89; *Stars in the Morning Sky* 85; *Three Sisters* 87; *Uncle Vanya* 87, 89, 98
Dolińska, Michalina 364, 365
domination 65, 66
Donnellan, Declan 2–3, 4–5, 16–17, 18, 21, 31, 165–184, 309, 312, 504; *The Actor and the Target* 170; *Andromaque* 174, 175–176, 504; *Angels in America* 166–167, 168, 174; *As You Like It* 167, 168, 175; *Bel Ami* 170; *Boris Godunov* 168, 174–175; *The Changeling* 169; *Le Cid* 167, 181, 483; *The Country Wife* 171; *Cymbeline* 167, 175, 176–177, 504; *The Duchess of Malfi* 175, 181; *Falstaff* 168; *A Family Affair* 168; *Fuente Ovejuna* 166, 168; *Homebody/Kabul* 168–169; *Lady Betty* 167–168; *Macbeth* 168; *Measure for Measure* 167, 168; *Much Ado About Nothing* 168; *Othello* 168; *Sweeney Todd* 168; *The Tempest* 169–170; *Troilus and Cressida* 169; *Twelfth Night* 169, 177–178, 504; *Vanity Fair* 167; *The Winter's Tale* 169, 181
Dorny, Serge 476–477
Dort, Bernard 63, 66, 67–68, 71, 493–494; *lieu piège* 69
Dostoevsky, Fyodor 88, 90, 91, 133–136, 141, 445
dramaturgy 19, 22–23, 144, 145, 212–213
dreams 210–211
Drewniak, Łukasz 364–365
Duggan, Lisa 291–292, 294
Dumas, Alexandre 72
Dürrenmatt, Friedrich 260–261
Dusigne, Jean-François 47–49

INDEX

Dutroux, Marc 33–34
Ebner, Martin 212
economic recession 398
écriture scénique (scenic writing) 2, 104, 428–429
ECSC (European Coal and Steel Community) 9
EEC *see* European Economic Community
Église des Célestins, Paris 325–337
Ehnes, Barbara 388
Eidinger, Lars 453
El Bulli (restaurant) 387
Eliot, T. S. 315–316, 319
emotional infidelity 66–67
English language, globalisation 15
Enlightenment 66–70
ensemble company ideals 20–21
ensemble practices 376–378
Eötvos, Peter 106
epic theatre 50–51, 56; *see also* ancient Greek tradition
eroticism 239, 243–244; *see also* body-subjects
Erschöpfung (exhaustion) 217
escapism 44
Espert, Nuria 383
ethnic hate crimes 30
Euripides 11, 50–51, 128, 360, 371, 374, 447
Europe xix, 1–25, 29–36, 39–40, 48, 52, 54, 61–62, 63–66, 70–71, 73–77, 80–81, 87, 89, 90–91, 104–107, 109–110, 117, 133, 165, 169–170, 181, 212, 234–236, 241, 243, 259, 260, 261–262, 265, 268, 286, 291, 317, 329, 330–331, 375, 377, 399–400, 401–402, 413, 415, 427, 428–430, 431, 432, 446, 475–476, 477–480, 481–491, 508; *see also* European Union
European Coal and Steel Community (ECSC) 9
European Commission (EC) 64–65
European Common Market 64–65
European Continental philosophy 22–23
European Economic Community (EEC) 9–10
European Union (EU) 17, 31, 367, 399

Eurotrash 22–23
excess in theatre 383–405
exile 11, 34, 348–349, 475–492
Eyre, Richard 18–19, 260

Fabre, Jan 16, 407, 409
The Fall (band) 221
far right 31–35, 196, 367, 377–378, 412–413; *see also* nationalism
Farage, Nigel 32
fascism 31–35, 196, 367, 377–378, 412–413; *see also* nationalism
Fassbinder, Rainer Werner 399–400
fast food 14–15, 419–420, 422
Fayard, Nicole 145, 146
Féral, Josette 47–50, 49
Ferreri, Marco 347
festivals 17, 30–31; Aix-en-Provence festival 79; Autumn Festival, Madrid 409, 415–416; Avignon Festival 10, 30–31, 79–80, 143, 325–337, 341–342, 371, 415–418; Bath Shakespeare International Festival 106; Belgrade [BITEF] Festival 30; Bergen Festival 399; Chichester Festival Theatre 106; Dijon Festival 383–384; Dublin Festival 30; Edinburgh Festival 10, 103; Edinburgh International Festival 105, 106, 383–384, 387–388, 400; Festival d'Automne 61; Festival for New International Drama (FIND) 22–23; Glyndebourne Festival 106; Grec Festival 387–388; International Theatre Festival, Delphi 413; LIFT 106, 429–430; Madrid Festival 30–31, 409; Manchester International Festival 286; Paris Autumn Festival 415–416; Poznań Festival 30–31; Roma Europa Festival 314; Salzburg Festival 168, 388, 476; Sarajevo Festival 30–31; Sibiu Festival 30–31; Spoleto Festival 66; Taormina Festival 30–31; Theatertreffen Festival 125, 129, 135, 137–138, 140, 430; Theatre of Nations Festival 186; UTE 105–106; Wiener Festwochen 371; Zurich Festival 30–31

516

film-making *see* cinema
First World War 55, 95
Fischer-Lichte, Erika 303, 304–305, 310, 312–313, 316, 377
Fisher, Mark 393–394
Fletcher, Diane 388
Flores, Alfons 385, 395–396, 397–398
Font, Joan 383
football 398
Ford, John 169–170
formalism 39, 47–52, 57
Forsythe, William 234
Fortuyn, Pim 32
Fosse, Jon 14, 79, 79–80
Foucault, Michel 66, 80–81
France 1–2, 5, 7, 8, 13, 15–16, 30, 39–58, 61–82, 90, 91, 108–109, 110–111, 133, 143–161, 265, 266–267, 280–281, 301, 311, 341–353, 374, 415–417, 418, 427–428, 480, 482, 483, 500; Nazi occupation of 12–13
Franco, Francisco 11, 386–387, 394, 410
fraternité concepts 74
Frazer, Rupert 388
Frears, Stephen 13
Frédric, Kristian 4, 20, 22, 23, 341–354; *Andromaque 10–43*, 347–348; *Big Shoot* 344, 345, 347, 351; *Camille* 346; *Cavalleria Rusticana* 345; *Dans la solitude des champs de coton* (*In the Solitude of the Cotton Fields*) 343, 348; *Hamlet* 341–342; *Jaz* 349; *La Nuit juste avant les forêts* (*Night Just Before the Forests*) 347; *Orphée et Eurydice* 344; *Pagliacci* 345; *Quai Ouest* 344–345
Freedom Party (far right party) 32
Freeman, Elizabeth 284
French empire 48, 56–57
Frljić, Oliver 36
Freud, Sigmund 145, 170

Galin, Alexander 85, 99
García, Rodrigo 4, 5, 14–15, 16, 17, 19, 20, 21, 23, 407–425; *Accidens. Matar para comer* (*Accident. Killing to eat*) 412, 415–416; *After Sun* 412, 413–415, 416; *Arrojad mis cenizas sobre Mickey* (*Throw my Ashes over Mickey*) 420; *A veces me siento tan cansado que hago estas cosas* (*Sometimes I Feel So Tired That I Do Things Like This*) 410; *Borges* 14, 422; *Lo bueno de los animals es que te quieren sin preguntar nada* (*The Good Thing About Animals is They Love You Without Asking Anything*) 415; *Compré una pala en Ikea para cavar mi tumba* (*I Bought a Spade in Ikea to Dig My Grave*) 420; *Cruda. Vuelta y Vuelta. Al punto. Chamuscada* (*Very Rare. Rare. Medium Rare. Charred*) 415–416, 422; *Une façon d'aborder l'idée de méfiance* (*One Way to Approach the Idea of Mistrust*) 416, 420; *Goya* 14; *Haberos quedado en casa, capullos* (*You Should Have Stayed at Home, Dickheads*) 410; *La historia de Ronald el payaso de McDonalds* (*The Story of Ronald the Clown from McDonald's*) 14–15, 419–420, 422; *Protegedme de lo que deseo* (*Protect Me from What I Want*) 411, 422; *Reloj* (*Watch*) 422n1
García, Victor 1–2, 383
García Lorca, Federico 384
García Marquéz, Gabriel 90, 106, 231, 254
Gatti, Armand 63–64
Gémier, Firmin 7–8, 61
gender politics 57, 73, 216–217, 239, 241, 243, 304, 309–311, 318, 356, 365, 448n1, 449n3; *see also* masculinity
Genet, Jean 14, 71; *The Maids*
genocide 31–32
Germany 13–14, 16, 20, 30, 42, 62, 90, 110, 115, 121–141, 208–209, 223, 243, 356, 365, 375, 427–428, 430, 433, 445–446, 453–473, 500–502; East Germany 11, 18, 121–127, 129, 132–133, 221, 455; German unification 11, 13, 25n11, 124–127, 129, 221, 460; Nazi Germany 290
Gesamtkunstwerk 6

INDEX

Giannachi, Gabriella 165, 170, 299–300, 302, 303, 311, 312, 315
Gibbons, Scott 331–337
Gilman, Charlotte Perkins 432, 446
globalisation 3, 13–15, 23, 32, 53–58, 61, 75–76, 140, 208, 215, 243, 261, 330, 374, 400, 414, 418–419, 453–454, 459, 461, 465, 472, 508; *see also* nationalism
Gluck, Christoph Willibald 337, 341
Goethe, Johann Wolfgang von 106, 140
Golden Dawn (far right party) 32
Goldoni, Carlo 387–388
Goold, Rupert 35
Gorbachev, Mikhail 11, 259
Gordon, Fiona 261
Gosch, Jürgen 138–139
Gourvil, Yves 341
Gray, Ramin 35
Greece 32, 413
Greek fascist governments 31–32
Greek tragedy 237, 250, 360–361, 372, 432; *see also* tragedy
Gregory, Mercedes 187–188
Grigolli, Olivia 212–213
Gross, Jan T. 362–363
Grossman, Vasily 86, 94–95, 97, 98, 100
Grotowski, Jerzy 15, 185–192; *Constant Prince* 358–359
Gruszczyński, Piotr 364, 366, 370, 377, 379–380
Grynberg, Henryk 377–378
Grzegorzewski, Jerzy 361–362
Guantánamo Bay 419
The Guardian newspaper 396, 427–428, 441–442, 446–447

Hall, Lee 170
Hall, Michael C. 281
hanamichi 48–51
Handke, Peter 478
Handel, Georg Friedrich 476, 491
Haneke, Michael 282
Harneit, Johannes 222–223
hate crimes 30, 33–34, 196, 367; *see also* murder
Hauptmann, Gerhart 6–7
Hauthal, Janine 235
Hawryluk, Jacek 374–375
Hecq, Christian 150
hedonism 460–461
Héliot, Armelle 144–145
heritage films 74–75
Heritage, Paul 165, 166, 167
Hermanis, Alvis 336
Heywood, Thomas 445
Hillje, Jens 22
Hindu theatre 56
Hodge, Alison 192
Holocaust 74, 196, 367, 369–373; *see also* Jewish memory
Holzer, Jenny 411
homoeroticism 358–359
homophobia 33–34, 196, 367
homosexuality 365, 366–367
Honecker, Erich 11, 128
Houben, Jos 261
Houllebecq, Michel 400–401
Hübchen, Henry 123
Hübner, Kurt 462
Huelsenbeck, Richard 210
Hugo, Victor 34, 140
human rights 31, 74; *see also* democracy
Humbert, Brigitte 73, 74–75
Humboldt University, Berlin 122
humour 214, 367, 466–467; *see also* comedy
Hunter, Kathryn 260–261, 390–391, 393–394
Hussein, Saddam 389
Huxley, Julian 31
hyperminimalism 357–358
Hytner, Nicholas 445

Ibsen, Henrik 32–33, 122–123, 332, 399, 436–437, 453–454, 461–462, 464; *An Enemy of the People* 32–33, 123, 453, 454, 472; *A Doll's House* 13–14, 122–123, 453, 459–460, 461, 472; *Ghosts* 6–7, 433–434, 436–437; *John Gabriel Borkman* 125; *Peer Gynt* 13, 387–388, 399
Icke, Robert 35

518

iconoclasm 123–124, 131, 143, 401, 415, 441
Ifans, Rhys 303, 306
Iglesia, Álex de la 396
Ikea 14–15, 414
immigrants 57, 134–135, 247–248, 260, 377–378; *see also* xenophobia
improvisation 41–44, 45, 46, 49–50, 52–53, 54, 111, 114, 266, 376–377, 421, 440
India 52
individualism 8, 19, 21,22, 63, 64, 80–81, 112, 211–212, 215–216, 293, 301, 330, 378, 395, 458–459
infidelity 66–67
intellectualism 143, 144–145, 161n1
International Theatre Institute (ITI) 31
internationalism 12, 22–23, 259
intertextuality 145–147, 148–149, 316, 317
in-yer-face theatre 364–365
Ionesco, Eugene 103–104, 112–113
Islamic State of Iraq and Syria (ISIS) 56
Israeli-Palestinian conflict 419
Italy 8, 15, 30, 88, 187–188, 325–339, 417, 427–428
Italian theatre 325–339

Jackson, Glenda 303, 304–306
Jans, Erwin 237
Jansen, Tom 233
Japan 51, 259, 265
Jarfi, Ihsane 33–34
Jarry, Alfred 105, 117, 169–170
Jarzyna, Grzegorz 356–357, 363, 366
Jett, Renate 365
Jewish memory 369–376; anti-Semitism 193–196, 362–363; *see also* Holocaust
Jones, Tom 414
jouer frontal (playing out front) 49–50
Jouvet, Louis 147–148
Joyce, James 234
junk food 14–15, 419–420, 422

Kabuki 50
Kaczyński, Lech 32, 196, 367, 368, 377–378

Kafka, Franz 53, 143
Kaladin, Sergei 86
Kalman, Jean 312, 314–315
Kane, Sarah 14, 109, 192, 356, 363–366, 432, 445, 466; *Blasted* 364, 466, 468, 472; *Cleansed* 363–367, 445; *Crave* 192, 459–460
Kantor, Tadeusz 1–2, 377–378
Keaton, Buster 129
Keene, Daniel 341
Kellaway, Kate 316
Kelleher, Joe 20
Kettle, Martin 442, 449
Kennedy, Susanne 36
Khmer Rouge 52
Kiernander, Adrian 52
Kimmig, Stephan 138
Klaic, Dragan 17
Klamburg, Dani 389
Kleist, Heinrich von 160
Klett, Elizabeth 300, 302, 306, 309, 310, 311
Knapper, Stephen 20
knighthoods 342
Knowles, Ric 8–9
Kohl, Helmut 130
Koltès, Bernard-Marie 14, 64, 70–72, 77, 195, 343, 344, 348, 350, 356, 400–401; *Combat de nègre et de chiens* (*Black Battles with Dogs*) 65–66, 70–72, 82; *Dans la solitude des champs de coton* (*In the Solitude of the Cotton Fields*) 77, 79, 341, 353; *La nuit juste avant les forêts* (*Night Just Before the Forest*) 341, 353; *Quai Ouest* 341; *Roberto Zucco* 195
Kornaś, Tadeusz 186–187, 193–194
Kott, Jan 42–43, 359–360
Kowalczyk, Janusz 358–359
Kraaj, Peter van 293
Krall, Hanna 193, 196, 203, 369–370, 371–374
Kresnik, Johan 131–132
Kriegenburg, Andreas 129, 131, 138
Kritzman, Lawrence 74, 75
Kruger, Steven F. 61, 166–167
Krügler, Ingo 385

Krukowski, Wojciech 199
Kuhlmann, Annelis 314
Kümmel, Peter 220
Kunitzsch, Michael 217–218
Kushner, Tony 168–169, 170, 285–286, 288, 366–369, 379; *Angels in America* 166–167, 168–169, 182, 280–282, 285–286, 288; *Homebody/Kabul* 168–169
Kwahulé, Koffi 341, 353

labour demonstrations of May 1968 63
Lacan, Jacques 145
Landolt, Patrick 220
Lang, Jack 74–75
Langhoff, Thomas 138
language 11, 14, 15, 34, 77, 80, 88, 107, 109, 171–172, 211, 213–214, 221, 223, 234–235, 264, 330, 348, 350–351, 364–365, 374–375, 390, 401–402, 489–490, 495
Laurent, Anne 62–63
Lauwers, Jan 4–5, 11, 13, 19, 229–257, 409; *Already Hurt and Not Yet War* 233; *Antony and Cleopatra* 249; *The Blind Poet: on the lies of history* 234, 252, 253; *The Deer House* 11, 246–247, 249–253, 254; *Images of Affection* 246; *Isabella's Room* 229, 231–253, 254; *Julius Caesar* 233, 237; *Kindermord (Child Killings)* 247; *King Lear* 233, 234–235, 239, 253; *The Lobster Shop* 13, 234–236, 237, 246–248, 252–253, 254; *Macbeth* 239; *No Comment* 234; *Snakesong Trilogy* 239
Lavelli, Jorge 1–2, 415, 482
Law and Justice Party (PiS), Poland 32, 196, 367, 377–378
Lawton, Tijen 233, 234
Le Pen, Marine 32
Le Roy, Frederik 246, 253
Lecoq, Jacques 260, 261; training 41–42, 50
Lega Nord (far right party) 32
Lehmann, Hans-Thies 207, 209, 210, 219, 244, 365
Lemêtre, Jean-Jacques 49

Lenz, Jakob 62
Léoncavallo, Ruggero 341
Lessing, Gotthold 123–124, 141
Levin, Hanoch 374, 377–378
liberalism 367; *see also* globalisation
Lilienthal, Matthias 212–213
Littlewood, Joan 1
Lobec, Marijan 476
Longhurst, Michael 35
Lorca, Federico García *see* García Lorca, Federico
Loriente, Juan 417–418
Los Angeles Philharmonic 22–23, 259
loss 241–242, 249–253; *see also* tragedy
Louis, Édouard 467
Lubchenko, Anoton 106
Luckhurst, Mary 165, 170, 299–300, 302, 303, 311, 312, 315
Lupa, Krystian 355
Luxemburg, Rosa 130
Lycée Louis Le Grand, Paris 62
Lynch, David 333, 399–400
Łysak, Paweł 364
Lyubimov, Yuri 15, 86

Maastricht Opera Zuid 385
Machiavelli, Nicolò 72–73
Macmillan, Duncan 432
Madico, Ferran 387
Magni, Marcello 260–261
The Mahabharata 56
Major, John 168
manada (wolf pack) 33
Mann, Thomas 291
Marcus, Sharon 278–279
marginalised people 44, 126; hate crimes 30, 33–34, 196, 367; immigrants 57, 134–135, 247–248, 260, 377–378
Marivaux, Pierre de 65–70, 81, 499
Marlowe Christopher 66
Marthaler, Christoph 4, 11, 13, 15, 16, 17, 22, 129–130, 207–227, 505; *20th Century Blues* 216; *Drei Schwestern (Three Sisters)* 212; *Geschichten aus dem Wiener Wald (Tales from the Vienna Woods)* 212; *Groundings* 13, 209–210,

211–216, 219–221, 223, 224; *Murx den Europäer...* (*Kill the European*) 22, 129–130, 208–209, 217, 223; *Stunde Null oder die Kunst des Servierens* (*Zero Hour, or, The Art of Serving*) 217–218, 221, 223, 505–506
Martorell, Joanot 394–395
Marxism 2–3, 456
Mascagni, Pietro 341, 353
masculinity 33, 64, 239, 388
Masuch, Bettina 218–219
Mateos, Adrián 398
McBurney, Simon 4, 8–9, 16, 20, 21, 22, 23, 259–274, 301, 390–91, 502; *Anything for a Quiet Life* 260–261, 272; *A Disappearing Number* 259; *The Elephant Vanishes* 259; *The Encounter* 259, 273; *Genoa 01* 261–272; *Measure for Measure* 261; *A Minute Too Late* 261; *Mnemonic* 260, 261, 273; *More Bigger Snacks Now* 261; *Put It on Your Head* 261; *Shun-Kin* 259; *The Street of Crocodiles* 260, 272; *The Three Lives of Lucie Cabrol* 260, 261, 272; *Vanishing Points* 260; *The Vertical Line* 260
McCormick, John 40–41
McDonald's 14–15, 414, 419–420
McDougall, Ellen 35
McEvoy, William 300, 316, 317
McIntyre, Blanche 35
McIntyre, Loren 259, 273
McMaster, Brian 383–384, 387–388
McPherson, Conor 387
Mee, Charles 234
Mei Lan Fang 48
Melillo, Joseph V. 232, 281
melodrama 48
Melrose, Susan 52–53
memory 34, 229, 244–249, 369–376
Menut, Benoit 341
Mercat de les Flors 386–387
Merschmeier, Michael 124, 469, 471
Mesguich, Daniel 4, 18, 19, 22, 143–163, 499–500; *Antony and Cleopatra* 160; *Boulevard du boulevard du boulevard* 144–145, 160; *Dom Juan* 147–160; *The Dybbuk* 161n9; *Esther* 161n9; *Hamlet* 143, 146–147, 148; *King Lear* 143; *Miroir et Métaphore* 143–144; *Phasmes* 145, 160; *Le Prince de Hombourg* 160
Messiaen, Olivier 491
metaphor 8, 87, 364
metteur en scène 8, 42, 503
Meyerhold, Vsevelod 1, 7–8, 15, 16, 90–91, 469
Mickiewicz, Adam 189, 193–194
migrant workers 44, 54–55
migrants 52–53
military junta of Argentina 14, 408
military surveillance 33
Miłkowski, Tomasz 367
Miller, Arthur 259
Miller, Jonathan 8
Milton, John 316, 325–339
mime 401, 408–409
mise en scène 19, 23, 104, 144, 146–147, 151–152, 158–160, 175–176, 180–181, 190, 233, 238, 341, 442, 493–510
misogyny 444–446, 447
Mitchell, Katie 4–5, 11, 16, 21, 22, 307, 427–452; *Anatomy of a Suicide* 446; *Arden of Faversham* 435; *Atmen* (*Lungs*) 432; *Attempts on Her Life* 429, 435, 444–445; *Bluets* 446; *Cleansed* 445; *Diarmuid and Graine* 434; *The Director's Craft* 438, 442–443; *A Dream Play* 433, 443; *The Dybbuk* 433; *Easter* 429, 431–432; *The Forbidden Zone* 445–446; *Fraulein Julie* (*Miss Julie*) 444–446, 447; *Ghosts* 433, 436–437; *Happy Days* 432, 441; *Henry VI, Part 3* 431; *The House of Bernarda Alba* 435; *Iphigenia in Aulis* 432, 440–441, 443; *Live Like Pigs* 435; *Lucia di Lammermoor* 445–446; *Nightsongs* 440; *Ophelias Zimmer* (*Ophelia's Room*) 432, 445–446; *The Oresteia* 433–434; *Orlando* 432, 446, 448; *The Phoenician Women* 11, 431–432, 435, 447; *Reise durch die Nacht* (*Night Train*) 430; *Rutherford & Son* 433, 436; *Schatten (Eurydike sagt)* (*Shadows (Eurydice Says)*) 432; *The Seagull* 429,

435, 441–443, 447; *... some trace of her* 445; *Ten Billion* 432; *Three Sisters* 440, 441; *Uncle Vanya* 431; *Vassa Zheleznova* 435; *Waves* 429, 435, 443–445, 447; *A Woman Killed with Kindness* 445; *Women of Troy* 432, 435, 449n3; *Wunschkonzert (Request Programme)* 430, 444–445; *The Yellow Wallpaper* 432, 446
Mitterand, François 5, 74–75
Mnouchkine, Ariane 3, 4, 12–13, 14, 20, 21, 39–60, 266, 481, 495–496; *1789* 12–13, 44–46, 53–54, 56–57, 58; *1793* 12–13, 44; *L'Âge d'Or (The Golden Era)* 13, 44, 47, 48–49, 54–55, 56–57; *Les Atrides (The House of Atrius)* 50–51; *Une Chambre en Inde* 56, 58; *Les Clowns* 44, 47; *Le Dernier Caravansérail (The Last Halting Site)* 13, 52–53, 54–55, 57, 58; *Les Éphémères (Ephemera)* 57; *Macbeth* 55; *Les Naufragés du Fol Espoir* 55; *Richard II* 49; *Tambours sur la digne (Drums on the Dam)* 51, 54; *Twelfth Night* 49
Molière 62, 106, 147–160, 499–500; *Amphitryon* 384, 385; *Dom Juan* 62, 68, 81, 147–150, 160; *Le malade imaginaire (The Imaginary Invalid)* 106
Molina, Tirso de 148
Le Monde (French newspaper) 374
Monleón, José 414–415
Monteverdi, Claudio 233, 234
Montjuïc cluster 386–387
Morgenpost 128
Mortimer, Vicki 22
Mouchel, Luce 149
Mozart, Wolfgang Amadeus 149–150, 337, 375, 397, 399, 402; *Don Giovanni* 149–150, 375, 397, 402; *Die Entführung aus dem Serail* 399; *The Magic Flute* 337
Mrożek, Sławomir 356
Müller, Heiner 122, 123, 208, 209, 459; *Der Auftrag (The Mission)* 122, 459; *Der Bau (The Construction Site)* 123
Müller, Ida 36
murder 33–34, 364, 399
La Murga carnival 416

Murnau, F.W. 347
music 74, 77–78, 115, 139, 146, 148, 151, 153, 186, 188, 190, 192, 195, 198, 208, 214, 218, 222–223, 232–234, 246, 268–269, 293–294, 336–337, 345, 350, 352, 384, 386, 391, 490, 505–506; rock music 122–125, 221, 453
musical comedies 48
Muynck, Viviane De 233, 239–240
Mykietyn, Paweł 358, 366

Nagano, Kent 222–223
Nagel, Ivan 125–126, 132
narrative 19
National Front/National Assembly (far right party) 32
National Geographic 259, 273
national heritage 76–77
nationalism(s) 6, 10–13, 53–54, 55, 61–62, 74–76, 196, 367, 368–369, 372–374, 378, 397–398, 400, 484; in France 74–75; in Poland 196, 357–358, 359, 367, 368–369, 372–374, 378; in Spain 397–398, 400
national-states 12, 64–65
nation-building 10
nation-state sovereignty 65
naturalism 170–171, 333; *see also* realism
Nazi Germany 12–13, 289–291, 362–363; *see also* Holocaust
neoliberalism 3, 6, 53, 57, 346, 349, 356, 368, 378, 461
Netherlands 234, 275–296, 490
Neuenfels, Hans 138
Neumann, Bert 134–135, 136, 139
New Europe 61–62, 65–66
New York 22–23, 168–169, 280
Nietzsche, Friedrich 68–69
Nijinsky, Vaslav 192
Nike 414
Niziołek, Grzegorz 358, 367–368
Nobel, Peter 212, 215–216
Nocher, François 341
Noh 50
Norén, Lars 459–460
Norris, Frank 137

522

INDEX

nouvelle cuisine 387
Nübling, Sebastian 138
nymphomania 72–73

Obama, Barack 259
Olear, Tatiania 437–438
Ollivier, Alain 496–497
Olympics 315–316
O'Neill, Eugene 90, 136
opera 50, 63, 79, 106, 114, 139, 222–223, 234, 301, 337, 342, 344–348, 352, 374–376, 384, 385, 396–399, 476–477, 490; and Calixto Bieito 33, 387–388, 394, 396–399; and Christopher Marthaler 222–223; and Deborah Warner 301; and Frank Castrof 139; and Jan Lauwers 233, 234; and Kristian Frédric 341, 344–348, 352; and Krzysztof Warlikowski 374–376; and Patrice Chéreau 63, 79; and Sylviu Purcărete 106, 114
Orbán, Viktor 32
Ordóñez, Marcos 399
orientalism 14, 39, 47–52
Ormerod, Nick 22, 165–166, 168, 169, 312
Ostermeier, Thomas 2–3, 4–5, 8–9, 10, 11, 13–14, 18, 21, 22, 23, 32–33, 453–474, 501–502; *Blasted* 466; *Danton's Death* 460; *Ein Volksfeind (An Enemy of the People)* 32–33, 453, 453; *Fette Männer im Rock (Fat Men in Skirts)* 455–456, 469; *Hamlet* 453, 454, 464–465, 470, 472; *Hedda Gabler* 13–14; *Nora (A Doll's House)* 453–454, 461–462; *Recherche Faust/Artaud* 457; *Shoppen & Ficken (Shopping and Fucking)* 364, 457, 466–468, 469, 472; *Woyzeck* 501–502
Ostrovsky, Alexander 167–168
otherness 13–14, 50–51, 56–57, 71, 377
Oxford University 40, 430

Pacino, Al 259
pain (concept) 68–69, 445
Palais des Papes, Chateaublanc, Église des Célestins 325–337

Paloma, Mercè 385
pantomime 48
Pappelbaum, Jan 22, 454
Paravidino, Fausto 261–272
Paris 7, 8, 16, 45, 56, 57, 66, 67, 110, 261, 264–266, 346, 415, 418, 475–476, 477–479, 481–482
parody 396; *see also* caricatures; satire
Pärt, Arvo 333
Partido Popular/Popular Party 412–413
Partido Socialista Obrero Español (PSOE) 408
Pasolini, Pier Paolo 279, 289, 347
Pasqual, Lluís 384
patriarchy xx 57; homosocial bonding 358–359; *see also* masculinity
Pattinson, Robert 170
Paul, Arno 210
Pauw, Josse De 234
Pawłowski, Roman 360, 364, 366
Peace Camp (Cultural Olympics) 315–316
Pearson, Allison 439
Pearson, Mike 316
peasantry 54–55, 260
Peduzzi, Richard 3, 63, 77, 80, 81–82, 504–505
Peel, John 221
People's Party (far right party) Denmark 32
Perceval, Luk 138
performance theory 143
performative space 312–314
Peymann, Claus 137–138, 140
phantasmatic qualities of theatre 249
philharmonic orchestras 22–23, 259
physical theatre 305–306, 310–311, 358–359, 377, 408–409, 469–470
Piscator, Erwin 125
Planchon, Roger 1, 3–4, 8, 41, 63, 67, 104, 428–429; *La Dispute* 66; *La Seconde Surprise de l'Amour (The Second Surprise of Love)* 67
poetry 189, 259, 315–316, 361–362, 391, 393–396
Poland 95, 106, 185–202, 355, 379, 430, 434–435

523

politics: American artists working in exile 475–492; Berlin Wall 121–142; censorship 34, 365–366; far right 31–35, 196, 367, 377–378, 403, 412–413; ideals 12–13; legitimacy 11; religion 53–56, 303, 361, 368–369

Pollesch, René 135, 136, 137, 208; *Insourcing des Zuhause: Menschen in Scheiss-Hotels* (*Insourcing at Home: People in Shit-Hotels*) 136; *The Prater Trilogy* 135, 136, 137; *Das Revolutionäre Unternehmen* (*The Revolutionary Enterprise*) 137; *Der Stadt als Beute* (*The City as Booty*) 136

Poniedziałek, Jacek 358, 365, 377

popular culture 14–15, 414, 419–420, 422, 462–463, 466–472

populism 31, 32–33, 34, 75–76

Portaceli, Carme 387

Portugal 31–32

postcolonialism 14, 238, 477

postdramatic theatre 207–227

Pou, Josep Maria 389–390

Prawo i Sprawiedliwość/Law and Justice (PiS) 32, 196, 367, 377–378

pride parades 368

Priestley, J. B. 31

Probenleiter (leading rehearsals) 20, 42

Profokiev, Sergei 169

Protestantism 72–73

protest *see* demonstrations

PSOE (Partido Socialista Obrero Español) 408

Puigserver, Fabià 388

Pujol, Carles 395

puppeteering 51, 408–409

Purcărete, Silviu 3–5, 11, 16, 17, 18, 19, 20, 103–119; *Les Danaïdes* (*The Suppliants*) 103; *Decameron* 106; *Macbett* 103–104, 112–113; *Measure for Measure* 106, 111, 112, 115; *Of Love and Other Demons* 106; *Pantaguel's Cousin* 118; *Phaedra* 106; *A Romanian Oresteia* 115–116; *Titus Andronicus* 106; *Twelfth Night* 106; *Ubu Rex with Scenes from Macbeth* 108, 115

Pushkin, Alexander 16–17, 168, 169–170

Putin, Vladimir 168

Pye, Tom 312

querelle des images (battle over images) 63

Quillet, Françoise 51

race 30, 71–72, 229–231, 235–236, 238–244

Racine, Jean 16–17, 65–66, 143, 167–168; *Andromaque 10-43* 143, 167–168

radicalism 19, 126; far right 31–35, 196, 367, 377–378, 403, 412–413; terrorism 56, 168–169

Ràfols, Mingo 385–386

Ramanujan, Srinivasa 259

Rand, Ayn 286, 291–294, 295

rape 238–239, 364, 399–400, 467–468

Rau, Milo 33–34

Ravenhill, Mark 14, 364, 457, 466–468, 469, 472, 476

realism 41, 87, 132, 169, 171, 248, 360, 395, 429, 448n1, 458–460, 462, 466, 470; 'capitalist realism' 458–459; magical realism 231; neo-realism 45, 460; socialist realism 123, 458; *see also* naturalism; reality theatre

reality theatre 129

Rebellato, Dan 16, 20

Reese, Oliver 140

refugees 13, 52–53, 53, 57, 149

Regietheater 137–138, 291, 356

rehearsals 20, 35, 42, 72, 87, 93, 111–115, 173–180, 185, 187, 191, 193–194, 199 212–214, 267–268, 299, 300, 301, 304, 305–308, 312, 318, 352, 376, 386, 390–391, 421, 431, 433, 437–439, 468, 470–471, 503

Reinelt, Janelle 65, 236–237

Reinhardt, Max 7–8, 48, 125, 438, 471–472

Reiter, Wolfgang 217–218

religion 53–56, 303, 361, 368–369; *see also* secularism; St Bartholomew's Day Massacre

Remshardt, Ralf 135
revolution 12, 32, 34, 44–46, 57, 140, 208, 357, 408, 422, 439, 446; French Revolution 12–13, 44–45; rainbow revolution 367
Ricci, Christina 170
Richards, Thomas 187–191, 200
Ricoeur, Paul 229, 244–245
Ridout, Nicholas 20
Rieger, Silvia 122–123
right-wing politics 31–35, 196, 367–368, 377–378, 403, 412–413
Rigola, Àlex 170
Ringst, Rebecca 33, 385
riots *see* protest
Ripstein, Arturo 396
Rodowicz, Tomasz 186
Rodrigues, Tiago 34
Rojas, Fernando de 391, 393–396
Rollende Road Show 137
Roloff-Momin, Ulrich 125–126
Romania 11, 18, 29, 103–118
Romans, Pierre 341
Romanticism 397, 399; Polish Romanticism 16, 189, 194, 197, 356, 360, 361, 368
Ronconi, Luca 8, 15, 46
Rossellini, Roberto 375
Rouse, John 80–81
Roverato, Juri 334
Rowley, William 169
Różewicz, Tadeusz 356
Rudolf (Crown Prince of Austria) 55
Rudolph, Sebastian 211–212
Ruiz, Boris 385–386
Ruland, David 453–454
Rumsfeld, Donald 129
Rundle, Erika 233, 237
Russell-Beale, Simon 305
Russia 15, 16, 85–100, 134–135, 168, 169, 173–175, 179, 181, 351, 437, 469, 485, 486; *see also* Soviet Union
Rutter, Carol Chillington 300–302, 304, 307–309, 313–314
Rwanda 431–432
Ryner, Magnus 65

Saariaho, Kaija 491
sadism 68–69
Sagarra, Josep Maria de 386
St Bartholomew's Day Massacre 13, 65–66, 72–76
Salino, Brigette 239–240
Salter, Christoph 137
Salvini, Matteo 32
samizdat 485
Santos, Carles 395
Sartre, Jean-Paul 40, 133
satire 259, 260–261; *see also* caricatures
Savorani, Davide 334–337
Scènes Nationales (National Theatres) 416
scenic writing *see* écriture scènique
Schiller, Friedrich 124–125, 141
Schimmelpfennig, Roland 387
Schipenko, Alexej 14
Schleef, Einar 208
Schlingensief, Christoph 131–132, 133, 135, 138, 139
Schmitter, Philippe 65
Schneider, Rebecca 301
Schoenberg, Arnold 384
Schönberg, Claude-Michel 168
Schwerfel, Heinz Peter 209
Schwitters, Kurt 213–214
Scott-Smith, Giles 64–65
Second World War 10, 12–13, 85–86, 97, 263, 360, 375
secularism 53–54
Seghers, Maarten 233–234
segregation 14–15; *see also* otherness
Sellars, Peter 6, 15, 18, 19, 23–24 475–492; *The Gospel According to the Other Mary* 477; *Idomeneo* 476; *The Indian Queen* 477
Sennett, Richard 289
separatism 398
sex 467–468; infidelity 66–67; scandals 168
sexual abuse 33, 238–239, 364, 399–400, 467–468
sexuality 72–76, 239, 358–359, 365, 366–367, 455

INDEX

Shakespeare, William: *Antony and Cleopatra* 160, 279–280; *As You Like It* 168, 181; *Coriolanus* 279–280; *Cymbeline* 167, 169; *Hamlet* 123–124, 143, 146–147, 148, 188–189, 192–193, 341–342, 357–358, 359–360, 373–374, 378, 379, 385, 389, 453, 454, 464–465, 470, 472; *Henry IV*, Part 1 49; *Julius Caesar* 279–280, 301, 305; *King John* 302, 313, 383–384, 385, 387–388; *King Lear* 125, 128, 143, 233, 234–235, 239, 253, 302, 303, 304, 305, 311, 312, 314–315, 318, 385, 387–388, 389–390, 391–392, 402; *Macbeth* 55, 103–104, 131, 168, 239, 385–388, 391–392, 394, 402; *Measure for Measure* 106, 167, 168, 261, 388; *A Midsummer Night's Dream* 42–43, 166, 384,385, 387–388; *Much Ado About Nothing* 168; *Othello* 12–13, 50–51, 56–57, 71, 121–122, 168, 377; *Périclès, Prince de Tyr* 169–170; *Richard II* 49, 58, 66, 302, 309, 311, 312, 313, 319; *Roman Tragedies* 278–279, 285, 295, 373–374; *Richard II* 49, 286, 306, 309–314; *Richard III* 330; *Romeo and Juliet* 169; *Taming of the Shrew* 359; *The Tempest* 169–170, 361–363, 365, 367–368, 387–388; *Titus Andronicus* 106, 117–118, 300–301, 302; *Troilus and Cressida* 169–170; *Twelfth Night* 106, 169; *Two Gentlemen of Verona* 384–385; *The Winter's Tale* 169
Shaw, Fiona 299, 303, 307, 308, 310, 311–312, 315–316
Shevtsova, Maria 166, 168, 169
Shrödinger, Erwin 35
Sieg, Katrin 243
Sierz, Aleks 21, 165–166, 364–365
Sihanouk (King) 52
Silverstone, Catherine 300, 309
Siméon, Jean-Pierre 341
Sissay, Lemn 286
site-referenced theatre 315–317
Sleichim, Erich 281, 293–294
Slowiak, Jim 190–191
Sluhovsky, Moshe 72–73

socialism 2–3, 122, 123, 131, 408, 458–459
Societas Raffaello Sanzio (SRS) 325–339
Société Coopérative Ovrière de Production (SCOOP) 40
sociological theatre 453–474
Sondheim, Stephen 168, 384
Sophocles 277, 285, 360
sorcery 72–73
sovereignty of the nation state 65
Soviet Union 3, 5, 11, 12, 85–86, 87, 89, 90, 94, 122, 181, 187, 259, 430–431, 481, 484
Spain 16, 32, 33, 383–402, 407–422, 502; fascist governments 31–32; far right 32, 33, 403
Spanish Civil War 386
Sparks, Annie 45, 415
spatiality of theatre 303, 314–315
Speckenbach, Jan 136
Srbljanovic, Biljana 457
Stalpaert, Christel 253
Staniewski, Włodzimierz 186, 192, 360–361
Stanislavski, Konstantin 7–8, 15, 16, 18, 90, 92–93, 170, 351, 430–431, 437, 440, 448n1, 472
Stasi 121–122
Stein, Jeff 326
Stein, Peter 1, 7–9, 137–138, 356, 456, 462
Stephens, Simon 35, 282
Stevenson, Juliet 286
Strauss, Richard 79, 192, 385
Strehler, Giorgio xix, 3, 7–8, 15, 16, 20, 23, 31, 61–63, 107, 267, 493, 504
Strindberg, August 6–7; *A Dream Play* 443; *Fraulein Julie* (*Miss Julie*) 6–7, 444–446, 447
structure of feeling 458–459, 468–469
Studium Teatralne 11, 21
Sturm und Drang 62
Suárez, Gonzalo 391
subsidy 17, 39, 40, 371, 387–388, 408, 473n6
surveillance 33

INDEX

Swift, Jonathan 103, 106
Switzerland 13, 208–224
symbolism: 361, 385; *see also* metaphor
symbolism of dreams 210–211
Synge, John Millington 384–385
Szcześniak, Małgorzata 357–358, 366, 367

taboos 363–369; *see also* gender; sexuality
Tanztheater 131; *see also* Bausch, Pina; Waltz, Sasha
Tarantino, Quentin 347
Taylor, Paul 301, 309, 318
technology 245–247
terrorism 56, 168–169
text, attitudes to 2, 13–15, 17,19–20, 22, 42, 49–50, 67, 76–78, 104, 109–112, 115, 116–117, 144–149, 160, 171, 193, 207, 210, 214, 232–233, 281–282, 284, 287–289, 291, 299, 302, 305–309, 316–318, 330, 352, 361, 365, 394, 408, 42-, 431, 433, 441, 463, 470, 480, 494, 497, 499–500, 505, 508; *see also* intertextuality; textuality
textuality 292; Borowski/Studium Teatralne 192–195; branding 19; Calixto Bieito 388, 390–391; Daniel Mesguich/*mises en scène* 145–146, 148–149; Deborah Warner 316; epic theatre 50–51; French classicism 76–77; Katie Mitchell 440–443; Krzysztof Warlikowski 370–371; Ostermeier/anti-globalisation 469–470; Patrice Chéreau 63
Thalheimer, Michael 138
Thamin, Jean-Louis 341
Thatcher, Margaret 261
Theater Heute 124, 130–132, 137–138, 139, 455
theatres and theatre companies: Abbey Theatre Dublin 395; Adrià Gual Theatre 384; Almeida Theatre 35, 312; Animalario theatre company 387; Anklam Theatre 121–122; Athénée Théâtre Louis-Jouvet 147–148; Baracke Theatre 455–458; Barbican 106; Bavarian State Opera 375; Berliner Ensemble 138–139; Boucherie Théâtre 407–425; Bulandra Theatre 105; La Carnicería Teatro 8–9, 407–425; Centre Dramatique National de Limoges 105–106; Centro Dramático Nacional 384; Centro Nacional de Nuevas Tendencias Escénicas (CNNTE) 408, 409; Cheek by Jowl 8–9, 16, 21, 165–184, 312; Classics on a Shoestring 434–435; Compagnie Jérôme Deschamps 261; Complicite 8–9, 166, 168, 259–261, 301–302, 304, 307–308, 310–312, 314, 317, 433, 435, 436–437, 441–445; Deutsches Schauspielhaus 13, 208–209, 363, 432; Deutsches Theater 125; English Touring Company 261; Epigonentheater zlv 233; Kràmpack theatre company 387; La Fura dels Baus 383, 408–409; Garrick Theatre 315; Gardzienice 15–16, 185–188, 192, 201, 360–361, 429–430, 434–435; International Theatre Amsterdam (ITA) 8–9, 20–21, 277, 278; Kick Theatre Company 302, 304; Kleines Theater 7–8; Komissar Opera 399; Kràmpack theatre company 387; Lézards Qui Bougent 342–343; Lliure Theatre 386–387; Lyric Hammersmith 106; Maly Drama Theatre 8–9, 18, 85–86, 87–88, 169; Maxim Gorki Theater 456; Meingen Theatre 30; Moscow Arts Theatre 7–8; National Actors' Theatre, New York 22–23, 259; National Opera, Warsaw 374–375; National Theatre *see* Royal National Theatre; National Theatre, Craiova 105, 106; Needcompany 11, 229–253; Neues Theater am Schiffbauerdamm 7–8; Nottingham Playhouse 106; Nowy Teatr 371, 377; NTGent 33–34; Odéon-Théâtre de l'Europe 66, 77, 384; Old Vic 303; Opéra de Lyon 476–477; Opéra National de Lorraine 106; Paris Opera 375; Piccolo Teatro 46, 63, 66; Prince Edward Theatre 168; Radu Stanca National Theatre 106;

527

INDEX

Residenztheater 139; Romea Theatre 11, 20–21, 386–387; Royal Court Theatre xix, 172, 261, 432; Royal Lyceum Theatre 395; Royal National Theatre (NT) 166, 168, 259, 260–261, 301–302, 304, 307–308, 310–312, 313, 314, 317, 433, 435, 436–437, 441–445; Royal Opera House, London 375; Royal Shakespeare Company (RSC) 103–104, 300–301, 302, 312, 313, 430, 433, 435, 436–437; Schaubühne 8–9, 13, 14, 21, 432, 446, 448, 456, 457–458, 459–460, 462–463; Schauspielhaus 13, 208–209, 363, 432; Schiller Theater 126; Setagaya Public Theatre of Japan 22–23, 259; Staatsoper Hamburg 222, 399; Stadium Teatralne 5, 11, 21, 185–205; Teatr Dramatyczny 356; Teatre Lliure 384, 385; Teatre Nacional de Catalunya (TNC) 386–387; Teatre Romea 11, 20–21, 386–387; Teatr Nowy 356; Teatr Polski 364; Teatr Rozmaitości 356–357, 358–364; Teatro Fabbricone 337; Teatro Real 375; Theater am Turm 135; Theater Regensberg 106; Théâtre a 13; Vents 416; Théâtre de Chaillot 314; Théâtre de la Cité 63, 66; Théâtre de l'Athénée 147–148; Théâtre de la Métaphore 148; Théâtre de l'Union 105–106; Théâtre de Sartrouville 62; Théâtre des Bouffes du Nord 300–301; Théâtre des Nations 61; Théâtre du Miroir 143–144; Théâtre du Soleil 8–9, 12–13, 20–21, 39–60, 439; Théâtre du Vieux-Colombier 7–8, 41; Théâtre Gérard Philipe 143–144; Théâtre Libre 6–7; Théâtre Nanterre-Amandiers 64, 70; Théâtre National de Lille 143–144; Théâtre National Populaire (TNP) 8–9, 41, 61, 66; Theatre-Studio 7–8; Towarzystwo Teatralne 364; Tramway Theatre 106; Vakhtangov Theatre 106; Volksbühne 13, 121–142
theatre training institutions: Akademia Ruchu 199; Central School of Speech and Drama 302; Conservatoire National Supérieur d'Art Dramatique 18; Conservatoire Supérieur d'Art Dramatique 143; Cours Mesguich 144; Ernst Busch Hochschule 18, 455, 456, 469; École Jacques Lecoq 41–42; Institut del Teatre 386–387; Jacques Lecoq School 261; National Academy of Theatre Arts (PWST) 355–356; Shanghai Academy of the Performing Arts 146–147: Union Theatre Academy 105–106
theatricality of form 47–48
Theurich, Werner 222
Thielemans, Johan 313
Thompson, Danièle 73
Threlfall, David 306
Thurman, Uma 170
Tierra del Fuego 55
Till, Nicholas 208, 214
T'Jonk, Pieter 230, 239, 243
Todorov, Tzvetan 237
Tóibín, Colm 34, 299, 303, 308, 312
tolerance 31
Tolstoy, Leo 6–7
torture 399
totalitarianism 53–54
tourism 398
tragedy 78, 133, 237, 240–242, 248, 278–279, 285, 295, 315, 325–339, 413–414; *see also* Greek tragedy
translation 15, 56–57, 146, 276, 365, 392, 420
Trussler, Simon 166–167
Tsypin, George 476

Ubenauf, Malte 222–223
UKIP (far right party) 32; *see also* Brexit
Unfried, Ariane Isabell 385
Union des Théâtres de l'Europe (UTE) 23, 31, 105–106
United Kingdom *see* Britain

Valentine, Graham F. 213–214
Valle-Inclán, Ramón del 384, 395, 396
van Hove, Ivo 5, 10, 16, 17, 20, 21, 22–23, 34, 275–296, 307, 313, 315,

507–508; *All About Eve* 281; *Angels in America* 280, 281, 285–286, 288; *Antigone* 277, 285; *The Antonioni Project* 282 *Les Damnés (The Damned)* 280–281, 286, 289–290, 291, 507–508 *Death in Venice* 291 *The Fountainhead* 286, 292–294; *Lazarus* 275, 276–277, 296n1; *A Little Life* 287; *Romeinse tragedies (Roman Tragedies)* 279–280, 285; *Re:Creating Europe* 286; *Scènes uit een huwelijk (Scenes from a Marriage)* 282–285; *Song from Far Away* 282
Vanity Fair 167–168
Vega, Lope de 166, 168, 181
Veraart, Karin 278, 287–289
Verdi, Giuseppe 168, 375, 396–397, 399; *Un ballo in maschera* 396–397; *Falstaff* 168
Verfremdung see alienation
Verne, Jules 55
Veronese, Daniel 387
Verswyveld, Jan 22, 281–282, 292–293
verticality 190
Viala, Alain 144
Viebrock, Anna 209, 218–220
Vietnam War 139, 462–463
Vilar, Jean 7–8, 41, 61, 67, 148, 475; *Le Triomphe de l'Amour (The Triumph of Love)* 67
Villeurbanne 41
Vinaver, Michel 64
Vincent, Jean-Pierre 62
Vinci, Leonardo 106
Vinge, Vegard 36
violence 56, 75, 103, 128, 216, 247–248, 278, 290, 341, 346, 348–349, 364–365, 374, 408, 410, 413–414, 445, 467, 502; domestic violence 389–390
Visconti, Luchino 280–281, 286, 289–292, 296
visual arts 20, 103, 104, 114, 116, 172, 198, 232, 329, 396, 409, 503
Vitez, Antoine 146
Vlaams Blok/Vlams Belang (far right party) 32
von Becker, Peter 124
von Mayenburg, Marius 22, 457–458

VOX (far right party) 32, 33
voyeurism 239

Wagner, Richard 6, 62; *Parsifal* 139, 193–194, 375; *The Ring Cycle* 81, 139, 475; *Tristan and Isolde* 476, 491
Wajda, Andrzej 360
Wälchli, Tan 220
Walsh, Enda 275, 276–277
Waltz, Sasha 459
war 11,13, 18–19, 31–32, 55, 65–66, 72–76, 139, 217–218, 221, 223, 386, 389, 414, 419, 431–432, 435–436, 462–463, 505–506; *see also* First World War; Second World War
Warlikowski, Krzysztof 4, 16, 34, 355–382; *Anioły w Ameryce (Angels in America)* 366–369, 379; *(A)pollonia* 371–373, 374, 379–380; *Bacchae* 361–362; *Crave* 365; *Don Giovanni* 375; *Dybuk. Między dwoma światami (Dybbuk. Between Two Worlds)* 367–368, 369, 372–373, 374, 379; *Hamlet* 357–358, 359–360, 378, 379; *Oczyszczeni (Cleansed)* 363–364, 365, 366–367, 379; *Parsifal* 375; *The Tempest* 361–363, 365, 367–368; *Winter's Tale* 356; *Wyjeżdżamy (We Are Leaving)* 34, 377–378; *Wozzeck* 375
Warner, Deborah 4, 5, 15, 20, 34, 35 299–323; *The Angel Project* 315, 316; *Footfalls* 308, 315; *The Good Person of Szechwan* 302; *Happy Days* 307–308; *Julius Caesar* 301, 305; *King John* 302, 313; *King Lear* 302, 303, 304, 305, 311, 312, 314–315, 318; *Mother Courage* 308, 310; *Peace Camp* 315–316; *The Power Book* 307, 310, 314; *Richard II* 302, 309, 311, 312, 313, 319; *The St Pancras Project* 315, 316, 318; *The Testament of Mary* 299, 303, 308; *Titus Andronicus* 300–301, 302; *The Tower Project* 315, 316; *The Wasteland* 315, 316, 317
Warner, Leo 22, 439
Waś, Arek 195

Weber, Carl 336
Webster, John 168
Wedekind, Frank 62, 66, 106, 222, 224
Weller, Jeremy 129
Wengeriek, Reinhard 123
Wesker, Arnold 42–43
West, Mae 136
Whitton, David 143, 148, 158
Wicha, Marcin 377–378
Wiener Festwochen 371
Wilkins, George 169–170
Wille, Franz 132, 469, 471
Williams, David 1, 6, 8, 42, 104
Williams, Raymond 458
Williams, Tennessee 134–135, 141
Wilson, Melanie 439, 448
Wilson, Robert 3–4, 68, 208, 287, 475
Winterson, Jeanette 307, 314
Wodziński, Paweł 364
wolf pack (*la manada*) case 33
women 44; butchness 393–394;
vilification 72–76; *see also* gender
Woodall, James 14, 21, 463, 465, 470
Woolf, Virginia 448; *Orlando* 432, 446; *Waves* 429, 435, 443–445, 447
Wyspiański, Stanisław 357–358

xenophobia 30, 32–35, 196, 367

Yagüe, Javier Garcia 407–408
Yanagihara, Hanya 287
Yarden, Tal 281
Yeung, Peter 30
Yugoslavia 10, 74, 436

Zadek, Peter 137–138, 138
Żakowski, David 194, 198
Zehelein, Klaus 218–219
Zimmerman, Pier Paolo 332
Zimmermann, Alois 33
Zuber, Xavier 392
Zweifel, Stefan 212